The **Rough Gu**

D1110458

Provence &
the Côte d'Azur

written and researched by

Neville Walker and Greg Ward

with additional contributions from
Kate Baillie

ROUGH
GUIDES

www.roughguides.com

Contents

A taste of Provence
colour section
following p.176

◄◄ Spring in the Luberon ◄ Nice

Introduction to

Provence & the Côte d'Azur

The ancient Provençal version of Genesis maintains that prior to introducing Adam, the Creator realized he had several materials left over; large expanses of celestial blue, all kinds of rocks, arable soil filled with seeds for a sumptuous flora, and still-unused tastes and smells ranging from the most subtle to the most powerful. "Well," He thinks, "why don't I make a beautiful résumé of my world, my own special paradise?" And so Provence came into being.

This paradise encompasses the snow-peaked lower Alps and their foothills, which in the east descend to the sea and in the west almost to the Rhône. In central Provence, the high plateaux are cut by the deepest gorge in Europe – the Grand Canyon du Verdon. The coastal hinterland consists of range after range of hills; rocky in places, but elsewhere thickly forested, while the shore is an ever-changing series of geometric headlands alternating with deep, narrow inlets, like miniature fjords – the *calanques* – and with beaches of sand or shingle. In the marshlands of the Camargue, the shoreline itself becomes an abstraction as land and sea merge in infinite horizons.

Fact file

• The Provence-Alpes-Côte d'Azur (PACA) *région* is one of 22 in France, divided into six départements, each governed by a local *préfecture*. The Hautes-Alpes *département*, though part of the region, is not covered by this book. Once notorious as a stronghold of the extreme-right *Front National*, Provence has edged back towards the political mainstream in recent years.

• Bordered by the Rhône River to the west, the Alps to the north and the east, and the Mediterranean to the south, PACA covers 31,400 square kilometres. It contains some of the most diverse terrain in France, from rocks and scrub to pine forests and alpine peaks, wetlands and canyons.

• Provence is the third-largest *région* in France in terms of population, with around 4,800,000 residents. Some ninety percent live in urban areas, while the rural Haute-Provence has one of the lowest population densities in France. Catholicism is the dominant religion, although in Marseille around a quarter of the residents are Muslim. Small Jewish and Protestant communities also exist.

• The region is France's third most important economically and attracts more visitors than any other; a staggering 35 million annually.

But all these elements would be nothing without the Mediterranean light. At its best in spring and autumn, it is both soft and brightly theatrical, as if each landscape had lighting rigged by an expert for maximum colour and definition. It is no surprise that of all the arts, painting should be the one that owes so much of its European history over the last hundred years to the beauty of Provence. Most of the great artists of the Modern period came here to work – among them Matisse, Renoir, Signac, Léger, Dufy, Bonnard, Chagall, Cocteau and Picasso – and their works are exhibited across the region.

Food and wine are the other great pleasures of Provence, with local produce – olives and garlic, grapes and honey, *cêpe* and *morille* mushrooms, almonds and sweet

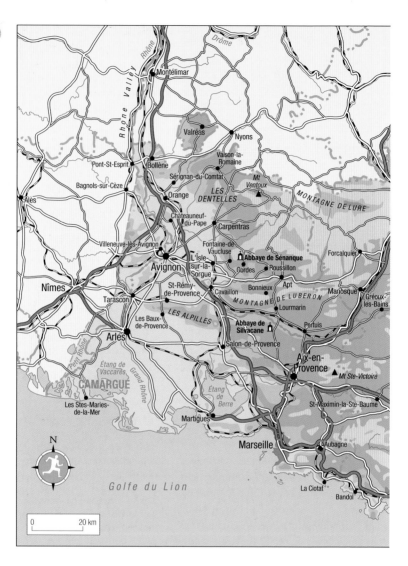

chestnuts, basil and wild thyme – forming an integral part of the hot, sensual environment. The wines, too, from the dry, light rosés of the Côtes de Provence to the deep and delicate reds of the Côtes du Rhône and Châteauneuf-du-Pape, both complement and owe their brilliance to the intense sunshine.

Such earthly pleasures, however, have been both a blessing and a curse. Successive waves of invaders and visitors have found the paradise they sought in Provence, and at the height of summer on the Riviera an unoccupied strip of beach can seem a fanciful idea.

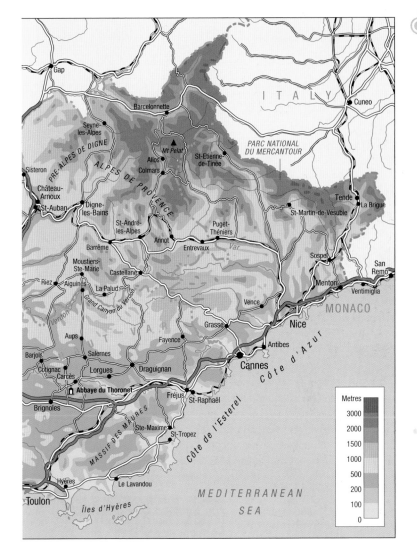

Where to go

This is a large and diverse region, whose contrasting landscapes encompass the mountains of Haute-Provence, the pastoral paradise of the Var or Vaucluse and the rocky natural beauty of the coast. The Riviera's capital, **Nice** – an intriguing blend of Italianate influence, *belle époque* splendour and high art – makes a perfect base, with wonderful food, affordable accommodation and lively nightlife. North of

the city, densely wooded alpine foothills are home to exquisite **perched villages**, while to the east, the lower Corniche links the picturesque coastal towns of **Villefranche**, **St-Jean-Cap-Ferrat** and **Beaulieu**; the higher roads offer spectacular coastal driving en route to the perched village of **Èze** and the tiny principality of **Monaco**. Beyond here lie the resort and castle of **Roquebrune-Cap Martin**, and the charming border town of **Menton**, with its lemon groves and atmospheric old quarter. The Riviera's western half claims its best beaches – at jazzy **Juan-les-Pins** and at **Cannes**, a glitzy centre of designer shopping and film. The coastal resorts also boast some heavyweight cultural attractions, including the Picasso museum in **Antibes** and Renoir's house at **Cagnes-sur-Mer**, while further gems nestle in the hills above, such as the superb **Fondation Maeght** near the attractive perched village of **St-Paul-de-Vence**, and Matisse's magnificent chapel just outside the ancient town of **Vence**.

West of the ancient Massif of the **Esterel**, beyond the Roman towns of **Fréjus** and **St Raphaël**, lie the dark wooded hills of the **Massif des Maures**. Here, the shoreline is home to the beach resort of **Ste-Maxime**, to infamous **St-Tropez** – still a byword for glamour and excess – and to the

8

contrasting delights of the unspoiled **Corniche des Maures**, with its pristine sandy beaches. Beyond lies the original Côte d'Azur resort of **Hyères** with its elegant villas, fascinating old town, and offshore **Îles d'Hyères**, popular with nature lovers, naturists and divers.

Further west, past the great natural harbour of **Toulon** and the superb wine country of the **Bandol** AOC, lies the buzzing port of **Marseille**, the region's largest city. For all its rough reputation it's a lively place, cosmopolitan and very likeable. On its eastern edge lie the

▲ Vieille Ville, Aix-en-Provence

calanques, beautiful rocky coves accessible to walkers and boaters, with the picture-postcard harbour of **Cassis** and the port of **La Ciotat** beyond, linked by the spectacular **Corniche des Crêtes**. North of Marseille is the elegant city of **Aix**, with its handsome stone houses, café-lined boulevards and wonderful markets. Cézanne lived and painted here, taking his inspiration from the countryside around the **Montagne Ste-Victoire**.

Beyond Aix, the Lower Rhône Valley is home to some of Provence's most ancient cities. **Arles** and **Orange** still boast spectacular Roman structures, while **Avignon**, city of the popes and for centuries one of the great artistic centres of France, has an immaculately preserved medieval core and, of course, its famous bridge. The Rhône runs by the vineyards of **Châteauneuf-du-Pape** and the impressive fortifications of **Villeneuve-lès-Avignon**, before meeting the sea amid the **Camargue**'s lagoon-studded marshland.

Inland from Marseille is the **Luberon**, a fertile rural hinterland whose attractive villages are now dominated by second-home owners. Nearby are the medieval monasteries of **Silvacane** and **Sénanque**. Beyond the **plateau de Vaucluse** rise the imposing **Mont Ventoux** and the jagged pinnacles of the **Dentelles de Montmirail**, where celebrated wine-producing villages include **Beaumes de Venise**, known for its sweet dessert wines. East of the Luberon is the Provençal heartland, whose archetypal landscape of lavender fields dotted with old stone villages stretches north towards the dramatic **Grand Canyon du Verdon**.

The art of Provence

Describing the south of France in a letter to Pissarro, Cézanne once wrote, "the silhouettes you see here are not only black and white, but also blue, red, brown and violet." His words go some way towards explaining the region's attraction for **painters**, and indeed over the last hundred years or so, Provence and the Côte d'Azur have been home and inspiration to some of the greatest names of modern art – **Van Gogh**, **Renoir**, **Matisse** and **Picasso** among them. The brilliant **southern light** was one of the most influential factors in their work here, with Matisse remarking that, had he gone on painting in the north, "there would have been cloudiness, greys, colours shading off into the distance…". Instead, during his time in Nice he produced some of his most famous, colourful works, such as *Interior with Egyptian Curtains* (*Le Rideau égyptien*) and *Icarus* (*Icare*). It was in Provence that Van Gogh fully developed his distinct style of bright, contrasting colours. His landscapes of olive trees, cypresses and harvest scenes, such as *La Sieste* and *Champ de Blé et Cyprès* (*Wheat Field With Cypresses*), all pay tribute to the intensity of the **Provençal sun**.

The painters in turn had a major impact on the region. Hand in hand with the writers and socialites who flocked to the Côte d'Azur during the interwar years, their artistic, and touristic, legacy helped to shape the region that exists today.

Beyond the canyon but within easy reach of the Riviera, narrow **clues**, or gorges, open onto a secret landscape perfect for cycling and horseriding, with the fortified towns of **Entrevaux** and **Colmars** defining the old frontier between France and Savoy. A third fortress town, **Sisteron**, on the Durance, marks the gateway to the **Alps** proper, where **Barçelonnette** provides skiing and snowboarding in winter and kayaking and hiking in the summer. Stretching south from here towards the **Roya valley** and the Italian border

▼ Hikers in Parc National du Mercantour

is the **Parc National du Mercantour**, a genuine wilderness, whose only permanent inhabitants are its wildlife: ibex, chamois, wolves and golden eagles.

When to go

Beware **the coast** in high summer, when the heat, humidity, crowds and expense can be overwhelming. In some respects the coast is more pleasant – and certainly more affordable – at almost any other time, with fewer crowds, less traffic, and spells of fine (if not particularly warm) weather even in the depths of winter. **February** is a great month on the Côte d'Azur – museums, hotels and restaurants are mostly open, the mimosa is in blossom, and the contrast with the northern European winter is delicious. May and September are excellent for **sightseeing**, with more comfortable temperatures than the summer peak, while the best months for **swimming** are June to mid-October. The worst month is **November**, when almost everything is shut and the weather turns wet.

The same applies to inland Provence. The lower Alps are usually under snow from late November to early April; October can erupt in storms that quickly clear, and in May, too, weather can be erratic. In **summer**, vegetation is at its most barren save for high up in the mountains. Wild bilberries and raspberries, purple gentians and leaves turning red or gold are the rewards of **autumn** walks. **Springtime** brings a profusion of wild flowers, and in March, a thousand almond orchards blossom.

Movie mania

The Côte d'Azur may not be as synonymous with film making as Hollywood, but its role in the evolution of cinema is nevertheless important. It was at La Ciotat (see p.82) that the movie camera was invented by the Lumière brothers who, in 1895, filmed the first ever moving picture – a less than glamorous shot of local workers leaving the family-owned car factory at closing time. In the 1920s Nice's Victorine studios produced many of France's most innovative films, and local writers Marcel Pagnol and Jean Cocteau were among the many who set their movies in the area. But it was **Brigitte Bardot**, and **French New Wave cinema**, that truly put the Riviera on the map, with Roger Vadim's *Et Dieu Créa la Femme* (1956) being the first in a long series of classic postwar films that included Hitchcock's *To Catch a Thief* (1956), and *Masque de Fer* (1962), both shot along the coast. Nice's studios no longer make movies, but the world's top stars are still drawn to the Riviera for the annual Cannes Film Festival (see p.312) whose Palme d'Or awards remain among the film industry's most prestigious prizes.

The only drawback with the off seasons is the **Mistral wind**. This is a violent, cold, northern airstream that is sucked down the Rhône Valley whenever there's a depression over the sea. It can last for days, wrecking every fantasy of carefree Mediterranean climes. Winter is its worst season but it rarely blows east of Toulon.

Average daytime temperatures (°C)

	Jan	Feb	Mar	Apr	May	Jun	Jul	Aug	Sep	Oct	Nov	Dec
Central Provence												
	12.2	11.9	14.2	18.5	20.8	26.6	28.1	28.4	25.2	22.1	16.8	14.1
Rhône Valley												
	7.4	6.7	10.8	15.8	17.3	25.6	27.6	27.6	23.5	16.5	10.4	7.8
Riviera/Côte d'Azur												
	12.2	11.9	14.2	18.5	20.8	26.6	28.1	28.4	25.2	22.2	16.8	14.1

Average sea temperatures (°C)

	May	Jun	Jul	Aug	Sep	Oct
Montpellier to Toulon						
	15	19	19	20	20	17
Île du Levant to Menton						
	17	19	20	22	22	19

12

For a recorded **weather forecast** phone ☏32.50 (€0.34 per min), or check ⊛www.meteo.fr.

things not to miss

It's not possible to see everything that Provence has to offer in one trip – and we don't suggest you try. What follows is a selective taste of the region's highlights: outstanding beaches and ancient sites, natural wonders and colourful festivals. They're arranged in five colour-coded categories, so you can browse through to find the very best things to see and experience. All highlights have a page reference to take you straight into the guide, where you can find out more.

01 **Les Calanques** Page **80** • Take a boat trip to these hidden inlets east of Marseille, where the shimmering white rock shelters crystal-clear waters.

02 **Scenic thrills on the Riviera's Corniches** Page **366** • Soak up the grand coastal views along one of the world's most memorable drives.

03 **Théâtre Antique, Orange** Page **137** • Beautifully preserved, Orange's Roman theatre is still used for performances in the summer.

04 **Musée Chagall, Nice** Page **359** • Spirituality and colour combine to memorable effect in Chagall's biblical canvases.

05 **The vineyards of Châteauneuf-du-Pape** Page **134** • Sample a glass of Provence's world-famous wine at the *domaine* where it was made.

06 **Les Baux** Page **97** • The eleventh-century citadel and picture-perfect *village perché* of Les Baux offer incredible views south over La Grande Crau to the sea.

07 **The Camargue** Page **108** • Saddle up one of the white Camargue horses and explore this watery marshland on horseback.

08 **Abbaye de Sénanque** Page **195** • The twelfth-century Cistercian abbey of Sénanque is enhanced by its beautiful position, surrounded by lavender fields.

09 **The gypsy pilgrimage, Stes-Maries-de-la-Mer** Page **112** • An annual spectacle of music, dancing and religious ritual dating from the sixteenth century.

10 **The perched village of Peillon** Page **363** • Built for defence, the region's *villages perchés* are much admired for their maze of streets, mellow stone houses and spectacular settings.

11 **Dining alfresco in Vieux Nice** Page **360** • Sit outside a Vieux Nice café watching the vibrant street life, and tuck into salade Niçoise, *pissaladière* or a slice of *socca* straight from the pan.

12 **Marseille** Pages **51** • Don't let its former reputation put you off visiting this earthy, multiethnic Mediterranean metropolis with good food, great bars, excellent football and bags of culture.

I ACTIVITIES I CONSUME I EVENTS I NATURE I SIGHTS I

www.roughguides.com

13 Breaking the bank at Monte Carlo Page 378 •

If you're going to lose your shirt, there's no finer place to do so than amid the *belle époque* elegance of Monaco's opulent casino.

14 Grand Canyon du Verdon Page 220 •

Europe's largest canyon offers stunning scenery and plenty of scope for activities, from cycling to bungee-jumping.

15 Avignon's Palais des Papes Page 123 •

The vast medieval building was home to a succession of popes during Avignon's fourteenth-century heyday.

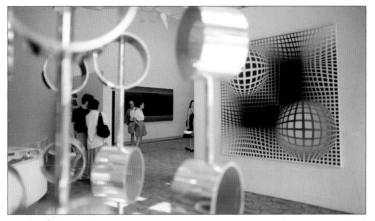

16 **Fondation Maeght** Page **343** • Don't miss this highly original art museum, whose building and setting are as impressive as the modern works of art inside.

17 **Mont Ste-Victoire by Paul Cézanne** Page **171** • Walk up to the top of the mountain that inspired so much of Cézanne's work.

18 **Relaxing on the Riviera** Page **326** • Waiters will serve chilled wine and lobster mayonnaise by the water's edge – if your wallet can stand the strain.

19 **Parc National du Mercantour** Page **243** • Ride, hike, canoe or ski in this alpine wilderness that is home to the Vallée des Merveilles and its four-thousand-year-old rock carvings.

20 **Festival d'Avignon** Page **121** • July and early August is the time to visit Avignon, when its ancient monuments provide the backdrop to a riot of theatre, music and dance.

Basics

Basics

Getting there

The quickest and cheapest way to get to Provence from the UK or Ireland is usually to fly. The region holds two of France's largest provincial airports, at Nice and Marseille, as well as lesser airports at Toulon-Hyères and Avignon. There are few direct intercontinental flights, though, so travellers from outside Europe are more likely to fly into Paris or London, then transfer flights or complete the journey by train. Eurostar rail services through the Channel Tunnel link to the fast TGV system, making rail a viable alternative, although you'll normally need to change at Paris or Lille. It's possible to reach Marseille or Nice by bus and car from the UK, too, though the journey can take up to 24 hours.

Flights from the UK and Ireland

Several **budget airlines** fly between the UK, Ireland and southern France. **Tickets** are priced for each specific flight, and vary from moment to moment. Book as early as possible for the cheapest seats, which if you're lucky can cost nothing, although airport taxes and assorted surcharges – including fees to check in, to take anything more than hand baggage, or simply to pay with a credit card – can easily add £30 or more each way.

Routes change all the time, so it's always worth checking the airline websites listed on p.26. Assuming things haven't changed since this book went to press, **Ryanair** flies to Marseille from Stansted, Edinburgh and Dublin; to Toulon from Stansted and Bristol; and to Nice from Dublin. **EasyJet** connects Nice with Belfast, Bristol, Edinburgh, East Midlands, Liverpool, Newcastle and several London airports; and Marseille with Bristol and Gatwick. **Flybe** links both Avignon and Nice with Southampton; **bmibaby** flies from Nice to Birmingham, East Midlands and Stansted; and **Jet2** operates between Nice and Leeds or Manchester; and Avignon and Leeds. Various airlines also serve Nîmes and

Montpellier, a short way west of the area covered in this book.

It's also worth checking out the **major national airlines**, like Air France, British Airways and Aer Lingus, which have been forced to cut their fares to match the budget carriers. Note however that as they're more orientated towards business travellers, it's not always cheaper to fly midweek. **British Airways** flies daily from London Heathrow and London City to **Nice**, and from Gatwick to **Marseille**; low-season return can cost less than £100 including taxes. **Aer Lingus** fly from Dublin and Cork to Nice year-round, with round-trip fares dropping below €100 in low season and rising to more like €150 in summer; and to Marseille between May and September only, at similar prices.

Flights from the US and Canada

Very few **direct flights** connect the US and Canada with southern France. **Delta Airlines** flies year-round from JFK airport in **New York** to Nice from around $650 in the winter low season, with prices rising to around $1200 at the summer peak. Additionally, Canadian charter carrier **Air Transat** links **Montréal** with Nice and

Marseille in summer (approximately May–Oct), with a greater frequency in July and August. **Fares** start at around Can$777 return in May, rising to Can$1277 in July and August.

These direct flights aside, most journeys to Provence from North America will involve a **transfer**, either using an internal North American flight to hook up with the Delta or Air Transat flights or flying direct to Paris or some other major European hub, with onward connections by air or train.

Several major airlines have **scheduled flights to Paris** from the US and Canada. A return midweek flight to Paris typically costs around $850 from Los Angeles, $750 from Houston and $650 from New York. From Canada, prices to Paris are in the region of Can$850 from Montréal and Toronto, and Can$1100 from Vancouver. **Air France** operates frequent flights from around fifteen north American cities and has a dense network of internal flights in France, including frequent services to Nice, Marseille, Toulon-Hyères and Avignon. Many internal Air France flights depart from Paris Orly airport, which requires a cross-town transfer from Charles de Gaulle, but there are also internal flights to Marseille and Nice from Charles de Gaulle, which is the main portal for intercontinental flights.

Although **flying to London** is usually the cheapest way to reach Europe, price differences are so minimal that there's no point travelling to France via London unless you've specifically chosen to visit the UK as well.

Flights from Australia, New Zealand and South Africa

There are **no direct flights** to Provence from Australia, New Zealand or South Africa. Most travellers from **Australia** or **New Zealand** choose to fly to France via London;

Six steps to a better kind of travel

At Rough Guides we are passionately committed to travel. We feel strongly that only through travelling do we truly come to understand the world we live in and the people we share it with – plus tourism has brought a great deal of **benefit** to developing economies around the world over the last few decades. But the extraordinary growth in tourism has also damaged some places irreparably, and of course **climate change** is exacerbated by most forms of transport, especially flying. This means that now more than ever it's important to **travel thoughtfully** and **responsibly**, with respect for the cultures you're visiting – not only to derive the most benefit from your trip but also to preserve the best bits of the planet for everyone to enjoy. At Rough Guides we feel there are six main areas in which you can make a difference:

- Consider what you're contributing to the **local economy**, and how much the services you use do the same, whether it's through employing local workers and guides or sourcing locally grown produce and local services.
- Consider the **environment** on holiday as well as at home. Water is scarce in many developing destinations, and the biodiversity of local flora and fauna can be adversely affected by tourism. Try to patronize businesses that take account of this.
- Travel with a purpose, not just to tick off experiences. Consider **spending longer** in a place, and getting to know it and its people.
- Give thought to how often you **fly**. Try to avoid short hops by air and more harmful night flights.
- Consider **alternatives to flying**, travelling instead by bus, train, boat and even by bike or on foot where possible.
- Make your trips "**climate neutral**" via a reputable carbon offset scheme. All Rough Guide flights are offset, and every year we donate money to a variety of charities devoted to combating the effects of climate change.

the majority of airlines can add a Paris leg to an Australia/New Zealand–Europe ticket. Flights via Asia or the Middle East, with a transfer or overnight stop in the airlines' home ports, are generally the cheapest option; those routed through the US tend to be slightly pricier. The cheapest return fares start at around Aus$2000 from Sydney, Perth and Darwin and NZ$2000 from Auckland.

From **South Africa**, Johannesburg is the best place to start, with Air France flying direct to Paris from around R8000 return; from Cape Town, they fly via Amsterdam and cost from around R11,000. BA, flying via London, comes in slightly more expensive, at upwards from R11,000 from Johannesburg and R12,000 from Cape Town.

By train

For visitors arriving by air in Paris, fast TGV trains link Charles de Gaulle airport with Marseille in a little under four hours, with one-way fares from around €58; direct trains from Charles de Gaulle to Nice take around six and a half hours, with one-way fares from around €67.

The **channel tunnel** provides a direct train link from England. **Eurostar** trains from London St Pancras International, which carry foot passengers only, take two hours twenty minutes to reach **Paris** Gare du Nord. On Saturdays in summer only (mid-July to mid-Sept), one **direct train** in each direction connects London and Avignon in just six hours. All year, travellers heading for **Avignon** and other stations on the TGV line to **Marseille** can change at **Lille**, one hour twenty minutes out from London; the entire journey to Marseille takes around seven hours, with non-flexible fares starting at around £109 return. **Nice**-bound travellers have to change at Paris, transferring from the Gare du Nord to the Gare du Lyon; the journey time is around ten hours and fares start at around £119. **Tickets** can be bought directly from Eurostar, or from all main train stations in Britain.

Eurostar offers **concessionary fares** to young people (under 26), over-60s, and holders of international rail passes. Bicycles can be carried free of charge in the carriage provided that they can fold; if not, they

should be declared as "Re[g...] Baggage" a day in advance (£20 per [...] per journey).

By bus

Eurolines (☎08717/818 181, ⊛www.euro lines.co.uk), offers **bus** services from London Victoria to Lyon with onward connections to **Marseille, Hyères, Toulon, Cannes** and **Nice**; journey time to Marseille is 21 hours and 45 minutes and to Nice approximately 24 hours, and involves a change at Lyon. Buses are air-conditioned and fitted with toilets. **Fares** are cheaper than the equivalent train journeys but are likely to be undercut by budget airlines for much of the year, making the gruelling journey worth considering only if avoiding tight airline baggage restrictions is a consideration.

By car

Getting to Provence **by car from the UK** is relatively straightforward, with ferries from England operating to seven French ports. The easiest way to access the French autoroute network is to take either a ferry from Dover or Folkestone, or the Channel Tunnel, to **Calais**. From there, the best driving route follows the E17 to the east of Paris via Troyes and Dijon – avoiding the capital's congestion – linking with the E15, which continues via Lyon south to Provence. For much of the journey, **traffic** is light; as a rule, congestion is only a problem south of Lyon.

The entrance to the **Channel Tunnel** is less than two hours' drive from London, off the M20 at Junction 11A, just outside Folkestone. Once there, you drive your car onto a two-tier train, which takes 25–35 minutes to reach Coquelles, just outside Calais. The sole operator, **Eurotunnel** (☎0870/535 3535, ⊛eurotunnel.com), offers a continuous service with up to four departures per hour (1 per hr midnight–6am).

Fares are calculated per car, regardless of the number of passengers. Rates depend on time of year, time of day and length of stay. In low season, travelling at antisocial hours, you can make the round trip for around £100; a return fare in July or August, with weekend departures, can reach £400. **Bikes** are carried on a specially adapted carriage that makes the crossing twice a day – it costs £32 for bike and person if you are staying more than five days, £16 if it's just a short break (all bike reservations on ℡01303/282 201).

If you're travelling by **ferry**, which route you take will obviously depend on where you're starting from. The very cheapest fares, which start at less than £100, are on the sailings from Dover to Calais (operated by SeaFrance and P&O), and Dunkerque (NorfolkLine).

From Ireland, Brittany Ferries links Cork with Roscoff in Brittany; Irish Ferries links Rosslare with Roscoff and with Cherbourg; and LD Lines also connects Rosslare and Cherbourg. Off-season return fares start from around €340 for a car, two adults and two children.

Airlines, agents and operators

Airlines

Aer Lingus 🖥aerlingus.com
Air Canada 🖥aircanada.com
Air France 🖥airfrance.com
Air Transat 🖥airtransat.com
American Airlines 🖥aa.com
bmi 🖥flybmi.com
bmibaby 🖥bmibaby.com
British Airways 🖥ba.com
British European 🖥flybe.com
Continental Airlines 🖥continental.com
Delta 🖥delta.com
easyJet 🖥easyjet.com
Flybe 🖥flybe.com
Jet2 🖥jet2.com
Northwest/KLM 🖥nwa.com
South African Airways 🖥www.flysaa.com
United Airlines 🖥united.com
US Airways 🖥usair.com

Travel agents

North South Travel 🖥northsouthtravel.co.uk
STA Travel 🖥statravel.com
Trailfinders 🖥trailfinders.com
Travel.com 🖥travel.com.au

Agents and operators

Abercrombie & Kent US ℡1-800/554 7016, 🖥abercrombiekent.com. Deluxe canal and river cruises, and train tours.

Adventure Center US ℡1-800/228 8747, 🖥adventurecenter.com. Small-group hiking or cycling tours. Eight-day "Cycling in Provence" from $1080.

The Alternative Travel Group UK ℡01865/315 678, 🖥atg-oxford.co.uk. Five- and eight-day walking tours in the Luberon from £495.

Austin Lehman Adventures US & Canada ℡1-800/575-1540, 🖥austinlehman.com. Biking and hiking tours; seven-day "Taste of Provence" cycle trip costs $3598.

Backroads US ℡1-800/462-2848, 🖥backroads .com. Trendy bike tour company offering six-day Provence cycling or hiking trips from $2998.

Belle France UK ℡01580/214 010, 🖥bellefrance .co.uk. Cycling, walking, painting and motoring holidays in and around St Rémy and the Camargue.

Butterfield & Robinson US & Canada ℡1-866/551-9090, 🖥butterfield.com. Seven-day Provençal biking or walking tours from Can$5795.

Canvas Holidays UK ℡0845/268 8027, 🖥canvasholidays.co.uk. Camping holidays on the Côte d'Azur.

CIT Holidays ℡1300/361 500, 🖥www.cittravel .com.au. Australian operator offering mid-priced hotels in major resorts on the Riviera, and in Aix, Avignon and Marseille.

Club Cantabrica UK ℡01727/866 177, 🖥cantabrica.co.uk. Specializing in the upper end of the mobile home, caravan and campsite market, with a site in Port Grimaud.

Contiki Tours UK ℡0845/075 0990, 🖥contiki .co.uk. Holidays in Provence for travellers aged 18–35.

Dominique's Villas UK ℡020/7738 8772, 🖥dominiquesvillas.co.uk. Upmarket agency with a diverse range of tempting properties, mostly for larger groups.

EC Tours ℡1-800/388-0877, 🖥ectours.com. Ten-day tours of Provence and the Riviera from Paris, for $1825.

Eurocamp UK ℡0844/406 0402, 🖥eurocamp .co.uk. Camping at or near the coast and at Castellane.

Explore Holidays Aus ℡02/9423 8080, 🖥www .exploreholidays.com.au. Two- to five-star hotel packages, predominantly in Nice.

France Vacations ℡1-800/539 7098, 🖥francevacations.net. Flight/hotel and fly-drive packages, including ten-day trips to Provence and the Riviera for $1500 and up, and five-day cooking courses.

The French Experience ℡1-800/283 7262, 🖥frenchexperience.com. Flexible escorted and self-drive tours, air-fare arrangements, plus day-trips from Avignon, and châteaux, apartment and cottage rentals.

French Travel Connection ☎02/9966 1177, ⓦwww.frenchtravel.com.au. Australian company offering everything to do with travel to and around France: accommodation, car hire, tours and even cooking classes.

Holiday in France ☎01225/310 822, ⓦholidayinfrance.co.uk. Upmarket villas and houses to rent, including some very large properties.

Gîtes de France ⓦgites-de-france.fr. Comprehensive list of houses, cottages and chalets throughout France that can be booked online, or through Brittany Ferries (☎0871/244 0744) in the UK.

Infohub ⓦinfohub.com. Web portal with a huge range of escorted and self-guided cultural, gastronomy and activity holidays in France.

Inntravel ☎01653/617 910, ⓦwww.inntravel.co.uk. Award-winning operator offering walking, riding and cycling holidays. Three-night "Scented Hills of the South" walking tour from £198.

Keycamp ☎0844/406 0200, ⓦkeycamp.co.uk. Camping and mobile home holidays on the Côte d'Azur.

Lagrange Holidays ☎020/7371 6111, ⓦlagrange-vacances.com. Self-catering and hotel-based holidays on the Côte d'Azur.

Martin Randall Travel ☎020/8742 3355, ⓦmartinrandall.com. Cultural tours on specialist themes including art, archeology and gastronomy. Seven-day "Roman and Medieval Provence" tour £1950.

Mountain Travel Sobek US & Canada ☎1-888/831-7526, ⓦwww.mtsobek.com. Hiking trips in Provence; eight-day walking tour from Avignon $2795.

Peregrine Adventures UK ☎0844/736 0170, Australia ☎1300/854 444; ⓦperegrine.net.au. Small-group adventure and cultural tours. Seven-day "Secrets of Provence" cycling tour £1375.

Susie Madron's Cycling for Softies UK ☎0161/248 8282, ⓦcycling-for-softies.com. Upmarket cycling holidays starting and finishing at St Rémy.

Viatour Australia ☎02/8219 5400, ⓦviator.com. Bookings for hundreds of travel suppliers worldwide, covering all regions of France.

Viking River Cruises US ☎1-800/304-9616, ⓦvikingrivercruises.com. French river cruises,

including a week-long trip to Avignon along the Saône and the Rhône, starting at $1356 in low season.

Walkabout Gourmet Adventures Aus ☎02/9980 2928, ⓦwalkaboutgourmet.com. Walking tours with an emphasis on cooking and good food. "A Week in Provence", starting from Aix, costs Aus$3645.

Wilderness Travel US & Canada ☎1-800/368-2794, ⓦwildernesstravel.com. Seven-day "Toujours Provence" trips from $4395.

World Expeditions US ☎1-800/567-2216, ⓦworldexpeditions.com. Self-guided and escorted cycling and trekking holidays, including seven- to ten-day cycling trips in Provence.

Rail contacts

CIT World Travel Australia ☎1300 361 500, ⓦwww.cittravel.com.au

Eurail ⓦeurail.com

European Rail UK ☎020/7619 1083, ⓦeuropeanrail.com

Europrail International Canada ☎1-888/667-9734, ⓦeuroprail.net

Eurostar ☎0870/518 6186, ⓦeurostar.com

Inter Rail ⓦinterrailnet.com

Rail Europe US ☎1-800/622-8600, Canada ☎1-800/361-7245, UK ☎0844/848 4064, Australia ☎03/9642 8644, South Africa ☎11/628 2319; ⓦraileurope.com

Rail Plus Australia ☎613/9642 8644, New Zealand ☎649/377 5415; ⓦrailplus.co.nz

Ferry contacts

Brittany Ferries ☎0871 244 0744, ⓦbrittanyferries.com

Condor Ferries ☎0845 609 1024, ⓦcondorferries.co.uk

Irish Ferries ☎0818/300 400, ⓦirishferries.com

LD Lines ☎0844 576 8836, ⓦldlines.co.uk

NorfolkLine ☎0844 847 5042, ⓦnorfolkline.com

P&O Ferries ☎0871 664 5645, ⓦpoferries.com

Sea France ☎0871 423 7119, ⓦseafrance.com

Transmanche Ferries ☎0800 917 1201, ⓦtransmancheferries.com

Getting around

Travelling by train is the most reliable and economical means of visiting Provence's main cities. Once you reach your destination you can use the local bus networks to get around, both in the town and out into the surrounding areas. Away from the major towns, however, it's best to have your own transport: the rail network is sparse, and bus services infrequent and often extremely slow.

By train

SNCF (☎08.05.90.36.35, ⓦwww.voyages-sncf.com) is the national rail network, responsible for the vast majority of rail services in Provence. Pride of the network is the high-speed **TGV** (*train à grande vitesse*), capable of speeds of over 300kph and which links the region with Paris and the rest of France, with stations at Orange, Avignon, Aix and Marseille, before continuing via Toulon, Hyères and Les Arcs-Draguignan to serve major Riviera resorts, including St-Raphaël, Cannes, Nice and Monaco.

Once in Provence you'll find **TER** (Transport Express Régional) services more useful. These trains are often still impressively modern and comfortable, and stop at more intermediate stations. Outside peak hours (7–9am & 4.30–6.30pm) you can carry a **bicycle** free of charge on these trains, stowing it either in the baggage car or in the bicycle spaces provided. In addition to the principle lines along the Rhône valley and the coast, a second major line heads north from Marseille through Aix and along the Durance to Manosque, Sisteron and beyond, towards Gap and Grenoble; another line heads north from Nice towards the Italian border at Tende, linking many of the communities of the *pays-arrière niçois* with the coast.

Tickets can be bought through the website ⓦwww.voyages-sncf.com, which has an English-language option, by phone or at stations, and must be validated in the bright yellow *compostage de billets* machines prior to boarding the train.

Timetables are divided into cheaper blue (off-peak) and white (peak) periods. From June to September you can buy a €12 **Carte Isabelle**, which gives one day's unlimited travel on the Côte d'Azur from Fréjus to the Italian border and inland as far as Grasse and Tende; it's not valid on TGV trains. The similar but cheaper **Carte Bermuda** (€5) gives one day's unlimited travel on the Marseille–Miramas line, but only on weekends, from June to September. If you're planning a longer stay in the region it may be worth considering one of the TER annual regional travel cards, which are cheaper and potentially more useful than the national ones offered by SNCF. The €30 **Carte Tout Public PACA** entitles adults to 50 percent reductions at weekends and 25 percent on weekdays for a year from date of issue. The **Carte Jeune Région PACA** (€15) gives even better discounts but is only available to travellers aged 12–26.

Provence's other rail network is the narrow-gauge **Chemin de Fer de Provence** (ⓦwww.trainprovence.com), a wonderfully scenic (if slow), meandering ride from Nice to Digne.

By bus

Along the coast and between the major towns, Provence is well served by **buses**, with the best and most frequent routes being the fast Aix–Marseille and Marseille–Aubagne shuttles, and the services that link Nice with the other principal resorts along the Riviera. Elsewhere bus services are much less satisfactory, being geared to the needs of schoolchildren and shoppers visiting local markets, and usually both slow and infrequent – even more so in school holidays.

SNCF buses are useful for getting to places on the rail network no longer served by passenger trains, such as intermediate stops on the Manosque–Sisteron line and the entire Château Arnoux–Digne line. **Inter-urban buses** are otherwise coordinated on a departmental basis, with **timetables** and other information often available online: ⓦwww.lepilote.com for Marseille and surroundings; ⓦwww.transports.var.fr for the Var, ⓦwww.vaucluse.fr for Avignon, the Vaucluse and around; ⓦwww.cg06.fr for Nice and the Riviera, and for the Alpes de Haute-Provence. Most towns have a central **gare-** (or **halte-**) **routière** (bus station), frequently – though not invariably – close to the gare SNCF.

By car

Away from the big cities, Provence is a superb, scenic place to get behind the wheel. Driving allows you to explore the more remote villages and the most dramatic landscapes, which are otherwise inaccessible; roads such as the Route Napoléon, the Grande Corniche and the roads around the Grand Canyon du Verdon were built expressly to give breathtaking views. In the **cities**, driving is much less enjoyable – the old historic parts of many towns are all but inaccessible, car crime is a problem and traffic and parking can be nightmarish, particularly in Nice and Marseille.

Unleaded (95 and 98 octane), diesel (*gazole*) and LPG **fuel** are all readily available. In common with other European countries, fuel **costs** are higher than North American drivers will be used to. Most places accept credit cards, though note that in the Marseille region some filling stations insist on prepayment before you fill up, and that in rural areas, filling stations are scarce, pumps are often automated out of hours and foreign credit cards are not invariably accepted. It's therefore a good idea to keep your tank topped up, especially if touring in remote parts of Provence. Outside the travel-to-work area of Marseille, **tolls** apply on the autoroutes: you pick up a ticket at the entrance to a toll section and pay in cash or by credit card when you leave the toll area. In contrast to the rest of France, autoroutes in Provence are often congested.

Car rental agencies cluster around the airports and at major rail stations, with most well-known international operators represented; addresses are listed throughout the guide. Prepaying via a website usually produces the best deals. **Rates** for the smallest cars (Citroën C1 or similar) start at around €220 for a week, though it's worth shopping around.

The French **drive on the right**. Most people used to driving on the left find it easy to adjust; the biggest problem in a right-hand-drive car tends to be visibility when you want to overtake. Although the law of *priorité à droite* – which means you have to give way to traffic coming from your right, even when it's coming from a minor road – has largely been phased out, it still applies on some roads in built-up areas, so be vigilant at junctions. A sign showing a yellow diamond on a white background indicates that you have **right of way**, while the same sign with an oblique black slash warns you that vehicles emerging from the right have priority. **Stop signs** mean stop completely; *Cédez le passage* means "Give way". Other signs warning of potential dangers include *déviation* (diversion), *gravillons* (loose chippings) and *chaussée déformée* (uneven surface).

Speed limits are 50kph in towns (with 30kph quite common in villages and historic towns), 90kph outside built-up areas and 110kph on dual carriageways, with a limit of 130kph on autoroutes in fine weather, reduced to 110kph in the rain. Speed limits are also lower on autoroutes that pass through urban areas, including the stretch of the A8 that runs along the Riviera. Radar detectors are illegal and EU drivers exceeding the speed limit by more than 40kph can have their licence seized immediately; on-the-spot **fines** for motoring offences are severe – though along the Riviera in particular you wouldn't know it, as people drive fast and erratically, with lack of attention often a problem at junctions and lights.

Car rental agencies

Alamo ⓦwww.alamo.com
Auto Europe ⓦwww.autoeurope.com
Avis ⓦwww.avis.com
Budget ⓦwww.budget.com
Europcar ⓦwww.europcar.com
Europe by Car ⓦwww.europebycar.com
Hertz ⓦwww.hertz.com

Holiday Autos Ⓦ www.holidayautos.com
National Ⓦ www.nationalcar.com
SIXT Ⓦ www.sixt.com
Thrifty Ⓦ www.thrifty.com

By bike

As the proliferation of specialist biking tours demonstrates, **cycling** on backroads of rural Provence can be delightful, if strenuous due to the often rugged terrain. Cycles can easily

be **hired**, particularly down on the coast where many towns have a branch of the Holiday Bikes chain (Ⓦ www.holiday-bikes .com), which also rents out motorcycles and scooters. Marseille and Nice also have Paris-style credit card-operated public bike rental stations. You can even take your bike free of charge on the regional TER **trains**.

Information on cycling **tours** can be found on p.26.

Accommodation

Finding accommodation on the spot in the larger towns and cities of Provence is only likely to prove difficult during high season, July and August. On the Riviera, however, things get booked up earlier in the year: in May, the Cannes Film Festival makes it extremely difficult to find reasonably priced accommodation on the western Riviera, while the Monaco Grand Prix creates the same problem along the coast east of Nice. In any case, booking a couple of nights in advance is reassuring at any time of year.

Hotels

Hotels in Provence, as in the rest of France, are **graded** zero to five **stars**. The price more or less corresponds to the number of stars, though the system is a little haphazard, having more to do with ratios of bathrooms per guest than genuine quality; ungraded and single-star hotels are often very good. North American visitors accustomed to staying in rooms equipped with coffee-makers, safes and refrigerators should not automatically expect the same facilities in French hotels, even the more expensive ones. Lifts are also the exception rather than the rule. Genuine **single rooms** are rare; lone travellers normally end up in an ordinary double let at a slightly reduced rate. On the other hand, most hotels willingly equip rooms with extra beds, for three or more people, at a good discount.

Prices in the swankier **resorts** such as Cannes or St-Tropez tend to be higher than in the rest of the region – though Nice has a good supply of cheap accommodation throughout most of the year – and in high

season (July–Aug), rates soar in the Côte d'Azur resorts.

One of the great pleasures of travelling in rural Provence is the sheer quality of **village hotels**. The fixtures and fittings may not always date from the twentieth century, let alone the twenty-first, but the standards of service are consistently high, and most take pride in maintaining a good-value restaurant serving local food.

In addition, outlets of several French **budget motel chains** have proliferated in recent years, usually alongside motorway exits and major through-routes on the outskirts of larger towns. While characterless, these are generally inexpensive, and can make a good alternative option for motorists, especially late at night. They have in turn prompted their traditional rivals to sharpen themselves up, with more en-suite rooms, brighter decor, and cable or satellite TV. **Wi-fi** is very widely available in hotels and motels alike.

Note that many **family-run hotels close** for two or three weeks a year in low season. In smaller towns and villages they may also

Accommodation price codes

All **hotel prices** in this book have been coded using the symbols below. The price shown is for the **least expensive double room in high season**. For categories ① and ②, this may well mean a room without private bath, shower or toilet, though there's usually a washbasin; it's also common to have a shower but not a toilet. In the ③ category and above, all rooms tend to be equipped with private facilities, but how much comfort you get also depends on geography – you'll get more for your money outside the most popular resorts, in small towns and in cities such as Toulon or Marseille.

Although many hotels offer rooms at differing prices, ranges (such as ②–⑦) are only indicated when the spectrum is especially broad, or where there are relatively few rooms in the lowest category.

① €40 and under	④ €66–80	⑦ €121–150
② €41–50	⑤ €81–100	⑧ €151–200
③ €51–65	⑥ €101–120	⑨ €201 and over

shut up shop for one or two nights a week, usually Sunday or Monday. Details are given where relevant in the Guide, but as dates change from year to year and some places may decide to close for a few days in low season if they have no bookings, it's always wise to call ahead to check.

Breakfast, which is not normally included in the quoted price, can add €7–15 per person, though there is no obligation to take it. The cost of eating **dinner** in a hotel's restaurant can be a more important factor to bear in mind when picking a place to stay. Officially hotels are not supposed to insist that you take meals, but they often do, and in busy resorts you may not find a room unless you agree to **demi-pension** (half-board). If you are unsure, ask to see the menu before checking in; cheap rooms aren't so cheap if you have to eat a €30 meal.

The largest and most useful of the French **hotel federations** is **Logis de France** (⊛logis-de-france.fr), an association of over 3500 independent hotels, promoted together for their consistently good food and reasonably priced rooms; they're recognizable on the spot by a green-and-yellow logo of a hearth. They produce a free annual guide, available from French tourist offices (see p.45), Logis de France itself, or from member hotels. Two other (more upmarket) federations worth mentioning are **Châteaux & Hôtels de France** (⊛chateauxhotels.com) and the **Relais du Silence** (⊛relaisdusilence .com).

Chambres d'hôtes, rented accommodation and gîtes

In country areas, in addition to standard hotels, you will come across **chambres d'hôtes**, **bed-and-breakfast** accommodation in someone's house or farm. These vary in standard, but are rarely an especially cheap option; they usually cost the equivalent of a two-star hotel. However, if you strike lucky, they can be good sources of traditional home cooking. Average prices range between €60 and €100 for two people including breakfast; payment is almost always expected in cash. Some offer meals on request (*tables d'hôtes*), usually evenings only.

It's also worth considering renting **self-catering** accommodation. This will generally consist of self-contained country cottages known as **gîtes** or **gîtes ruraux**. Many *gîtes* are in converted barns or farm outbuildings, though some can be quite grand.

Lists of both *gîtes* and *chambres d'hôtes* are available from **Gîtes de France** (☎01.49.70.75.75, ⊛gites-de-france.fr); you can search their website for accommodation by type or theme as well as area, for example choosing a *gîte* near fishing or riding opportunities. Tourist offices maintain lists of places in their area that are not affiliated to Gîtes de France, and you can also find self-catering accommodation, often foreign-owned, advertised online, including through the outlets listed on pp.26–27.

Budget chain motels

The following motel chains are listed in approximately ascending order of price and comfort.

Formule 1 ℡ 08.92.68.56.85, ⊛ hotelformule1.com
B&B ℡ 01.72.36.51.06, ⊛ hotel-bb.com
Première Classe ℡ 01.73.21.98.99, ⊛ premiereclasse.fr
Etap Hôtel ℡ 08.92.68.89.00, ⊛ etaphotel.com
Ibis ℡ 08.92.68.66.86, ⊛ ibishotel.com
Campanile ℡ 01.73.21.98.99, ⊛ campanile.fr

Hostels, gîtes d'étape and refuges

Auberges de Jeunesse – **youth hostels** – are invaluable for single travellers on a budget, costing anything from €12 to €25 per night for a dormitory bed. For couples, however, and certainly for groups of three or more people, they won't necessarily work out less than the cheaper hotels – particularly if you've had to pay a bus fare out to the edge of town to reach them. However, many are beautifully situated, and they do allow you to cut costs by preparing your own food in their kitchens, or eating in cheap canteens.

To stay at hostels run by the two rival **French hostelling associations** – the Fédération Unie des Auberges de Jeunesse (FUAJ; ⊛ fuaj.org), and the much smaller Ligue Française pour les Auberges de Jeunesse (LFAJ; ⊛ auberges-de-jeunesse .com) – you will be expected to show a current **Hostelling International** (**HI**) **membership card**. Visit ⊛ hihostels.com for details of your national youth hostel association and membership prices, as well as for worldwide booking facilities.

In addition, alone among Provençal cities, **Nice** has a sizeable **independent hostel** sector. Most of the **backpacker** places are clustered south of the *gare SNCF*; standards vary widely, but the best are at least as good as the traditional youth hostels and they generally have a less institutional feel, though their prices tend to be a little higher.

A further hostel-type alternative exists in the countryside, especially in hiking or cycling areas, in the form of the **gîtes d'étape**. Less formal than hostels, these are often run by the local village or municipality, and provide basic hospital-style beds and simple kitchen facilities from around €10. They are marked on the large-scale IGN walkers' maps and listed in individual GR *Topoguides*.

In the mountains there are **refuge huts** on the main GR routes; these are extremely basic and not always very friendly places, and must be booked three weeks in advance in high summer. **Costs** per night are usually around €15 depending on facilities. The refuges in the Mercantour are run by the Club Alpin Français des Alpes-Maritimes (⊛ cafnice.org), whose website lists the refuges under its care and the contact details for reservations, which can be made online as well as by phone.

For more information on both *gîtes* and refuges, visit ⊛ www.gites-refuges.com.

Camping

Most villages and towns in Provence have at least one **campsite** (notable exceptions being Marseille, which has none, and Nice, which has only one, a long way out). Camping is extremely popular with the French and, especially for those from the north, Provence is a favourite destination. The cheapest sites – from around €12 – are often the **camping municipaux** run by the local authority in small communes in rural Provence. Another countryside option – usually with minimal facilities – is camping **à la ferme** – on private **farmland**. Local tourist offices will usually have lists of such sites.

On the Côte d'Azur, **commercial sites** can be monstrously large, with hundreds of *emplacements* and elaborate facilities including swimming pools and restaurants; reckon on paying anything up to €35 per night for a car, tent and two people in high season on the coast.

Lists of sites are available from the Camping France website (@www.camping france.com), Gîtes de France (@gites-de -france.fr), or at local tourist boards. The *Camping Qualité* designation (@www .campingqualite.com) indicates campsites with particularly high standards of hygiene, service and privacy, while the *Clef Verte* (@laclefverte.org) label is awarded to sites run along environmentally friendly lines.

If you plan to camp a lot, an **international camping carnet** is a good investment. The carnet gives discounts at member sites and serves as useful identification. Many campsites will take it instead of making you surrender your passport during your stay,

and it covers you for third-party insurance when camping. In Britain, it costs £4.95 from the **Camping and Caravanning Club** (T0845/130 7701, @campingand caravanningclub.co.uk).

Camping rough (*camping sauvage*) is strongly discouraged in summer due to the high risk of forest fires; in any case, you should never camp rough without first asking the landowner's permission, as farmers have been known to shoot first and ask questions later. Camping on the **beach** is not permitted in major resorts and is not terribly desirable either, since promenades are generally too brightly lit to allow a decent night's sleep.

Food and drink

Food is as good a reason as any for going to Provence. The region boasts one of the most distinctive and exceptional regional cuisines, as well as some very fine wines in the Vaucluse, on the coast and at Châteauneuf-du-Pape.

Provence has a considerable number of top gourmet **restaurants**, particularly in the cities and along the Côte d'Azur where – if your budget can stretch to perhaps €100 or more – you can enjoy the creations of some of France's most celebrated kitchens. Unfortunately, the risk of a mediocre or even bad meal in the heavily touristed areas is ever greater, but if you take your time – treating the business of choosing a place as an appetizer in itself – you should be able to eat well without spending a fortune.

The **markets** of Provence are a sensual treat as well as a lively social event; the best ones are listed in the Guide. The region is also the homeland of **pastis**, the aniseed-flavoured spirit traditionally served with a bowl of olives before meals.

For a **glossary** of food and drink terms, see pp.419–427; for more on the region's food, see *A taste of Provence* colour section.

Breakfast

Depending on the class of hotel or hostel, **breakfast** may be a simple affair of coffee and freshly baked baguette with jam and butter, or a much more elaborate spread involving croissants or a hot and cold buffet – though the splendour of the breakfast buffet will be reflected in the **bill**: a breakfast buffet in even a mid-range hotel might set you back €12 per day, whereas a simpler bread-and-coffee affair in a cheaper hotel might be half that. If you're sure that you're going to be staying in town it can be cheaper and just as convenient to opt out and go instead to a local café for a croissant, *pain au chocolat* (a chocolate-filled croissant) or a sandwich, washed down with coffee or hot chocolate – though if you decide to do this, be sure your hotel understands you do not require breakfast so it is not added to your bill.

Lunch and dinner

At lunchtime, and sometimes in the evening, you'll find many restaurants and cafés offer good-value **plats du jour** (chef's specials) at prices below the **à la carte** menu prices. You'll also come across lunchtime **formules** – a menu of limited or no choice, including perhaps a main course and a drink. Most restaurants also have one or more elaborate **prix-fixe** (set-price) menus, which usually offer a limited selection of the dishes available on the full à la carte menu at a reduced price. The usual accompaniment to a full meal is wine; stick to the house wine – often served in 25 or 50cl *pichets* – if you want to keep the bill down.

If you want to experience the full glory of **Provençal cooking** you really need to eat in a **restaurant**. It's still possible to eat well for €30 or less in a small, family-run place where you'll enjoy hearty, home-cooked dishes such as *daube de boeuf* or *pieds et paquets*, though the restaurant business is a highly competitive one, particularly in the resorts, and the real gems are not as easy to find as they were.

One very appealing and affordable alternative to Provençal cuisine – particularly in Marseille – is **North African** food; other inexpensive ethnic options include the numerous **Asian** fast-food buffets, though the quality of Asian cooking in Provence is very variable, even in the more upmarket restaurants, and some visitors may find the food rather bland, as spicing tends to be toned down to suit less adventurous French palates.

For vegetarians in particular, the numerous **pizzerias** can be a godsend, usually advertising pizza cooked *au feu de bois* – in a wood-fired oven – and served with a drizzle of oil. Pizza tends to be one of the cheapest options, though quality and price vary enormously. Fresh **pasta**, a speciality of Nice, is affordable and often very good – and another safe option for veggies.

Brasseries and **cafés** vary widely in price and style, from those that are merely large bars serving a restricted food menu to very grand (and expensive) affairs resembling the celebrated Parisian eateries of the Left Bank; generally speaking, brasseries serve **quick meals** at any time of the day, including salads and lighter options. **Crêperies and salons de thé** are also a good bet for light meals.

Snacks and street food

Provence – and especially Nice – is a wonderful place to eat on the hoof. Colourful **markets** are an excellent source of fresh produce, meats and cheeses, while **patisseries** often sell the delicious savoury *pain fougasse*, a finger-shaped bread that may contain olives, anchovies, sausage, cheese or bacon. Along the Riviera the **sandwich** of choice is the *pan bagnat*, a delicious mix of tuna, hard-boiled egg and bitter *mesclun* salad leaves drizzled with oil, usually available for less than €5; **Niçois street food** includes the simple onion tart *pissaladière*, *farcis* (vegetables stuffed with a meat mixture) and hot wedges of *socca* – a pancake made with chickpea flour. In **Marseille** in particular, other options include Tunisian snacks such as *brik à l'oeuf* (a delicious filo pastry snack stuffed with soft-set egg), spicy Merguez sausages and falafel.

Drinks

Coffee is the beverage of choice, served long and milky as a *café au lait* at breakfast time and drunk short and strong as an *express* (espresso) later in the day – ask for *une crème* or *une grande crème* if you want a coffee with milk in a café. Ordinary **tea** is usually Lipton's, served in the cup with a tea bag; ask for *un peu de lait frais* if you want it with milk, English style. Herb or fruit teas – known as infusions or *tisanes* – are also widely available.

Draught **beer** – usually Kronenbourg – is one of the cheaper alcoholic drinks you can buy; you'll also see French and Belgian bottled beers and, in larger towns and cities, a big international selection in Dutch- or Irish-style pubs. Provençal **wines** include the very grand vintages of Châteauneuf-du-Pape, the renowned wines of Vacqueyras, Gigondas and Bandol, and the famous dessert wines of Beaumes de Venise; prices for these nobler wines can be high, but there's plenty of inexpensive Côtes de Luberon or Côtes de Provence to enjoy too. Red, white and rosé varieties are available in all price ranges, and in the summer heat the allure of a crisp, pale Provençal rosé can be irresistible.

For those in search of something stronger, **pastis** is the ubiquitous *aperitif*, and there's also an abundance of cognac, armagnac and various flavours of *eaux de vie*, of which the most delicious is Poire Williams; *marc* is a spirit distilled from grape pulp. Cocktails are served at most late-night bars and discos.

The media

For anyone who can read French, or understand it when spoken, the print and electronic media in France match any in the world. Otherwise, English-language newspapers are usually available, many hotels offer English-language TV, and BBC radio can easily be picked up.

Newspapers and magazines

Getting hold of **international editions** of British and north American **newspapers** and magazines in Provence is relatively easy. Newsstands at airports and railway stations, and at branches of Virgin in the major cities invariably stock the major publications, though such is the influx of English-speaking expatriates that these days you may just as easily find the latest edition of the **Wall Street Journal** or **Financial Times** on sale in some idyllic village in the Luberon.

As for the **French press**, *Le Monde* (Ⓦlemonde.fr) is the most intellectual and respected of the national dailies, though it can be a bit tedious; *Libération* (Ⓦliberation.com; *Libé* for short), which has its own Marseille edition, is moderately left-wing, independent and more colloquial, *L'Humanité* (Ⓦhumanite.fr) is communist and *Le Figaro* (Ⓦlefigaro.fr) is the most respected of the right-leaning newspapers. That said, you're more likely as a visitor to find the major regional newspapers such as Marseille's *La Provence* (Ⓦlaprovence.com) or Nice's down-market *Nice Matin* (Ⓦnicematin.com) useful, more for their listings than their indifferent news coverage.

Weekly publications, on the *Newsweek/Time* model, include the wide-ranging left-leaning *Le Nouvel Observateur* (Ⓦnouvelobs.com), its right-wing counterpoint *L'Express* (Ⓦlexpress.fr), and *Marianne* (Ⓦmarianne2.fr), the centrist with bite. The best, and funniest, investigative journalism is in the satirical *Canard Enchaîné* (Ⓦlecanardenchaine.fr), unfortunately almost incomprehensible to non-native speakers.

Although it's aimed more at expats than visitors, the **English-language magazine** *Riviera Reporter* (Ⓦwww.riviera-reporter.com), which you can pick up at English bookshops and occasionally at tourist offices, and can also be downloaded in its entirety, often contains articles of interest.

Radio

Riviera Radio (106.5FM in France, 106.3FM in Monaco, Ⓦrivieraradio.mc) broadcasts out of Monaco and faithfully reflects its British expat audience with a down-home local-radio mix of suburban chat and middle-of-the-road hits; it's also worth listening to if you're on the Côte d'Azur, thanks to its news and events coverage. Useful for drivers on the southern French autoroutes, **Radio Trafic** (107.7FM) broadcasts a mix of French and international hits interspersed with French and English-language traffic bulletins. **English-language** broadcasts can also be heard on the **BBC** (Ⓦbbc.co.uk/worldservice), **Radio Canada** (Ⓦrcinet.ca), and **Voice of America** (Ⓦvoa.gov). See their websites for local frequencies.

Television

French **terrestrial TV** has six channels: three public (France 2, France 3 and Arte/France 5); one subscription (Canal Plus – with some unencrypted programmes); and two commercial open broadcasts (TF1 and M6). Of these, TF1 and France 2 are the most popular, showing a broad mix of programmes.

Arte/France 5 (also known as La Cinquième) is a joint Franco-German cultural venture that transmits simultaneously in French and German; offerings include documentaries, art criticism, French and German movies and complete operas. During the day (7am–7pm), its frequency broadcasts educational programmes. **Canal Plus** is the main movie channel, with repeats of foreign films usually shown at least once in the original language. **France 3** is strong on regional news and more heavyweight movies, including undubbed foreign films. The main **French news broadcasts** are at 8pm on France 2 and TF1.

Cable and **satellite** channels you may find available in hotels include CNN, BBC World and BBC Prime, Eurosport, MTV, Planète, which specializes in documentaries, Ciné Première and Canal Jimmy. The main French-run music channel is MCM.

Festivals

Provence is home to some of France's most celebrated festivals. The real cultural heavyweights are the Avignon (ⓦwww.festival-avignon.com) and Aix (ⓦwww.festival-aix.com) events, which use the historic settings of the two cities to stunning effect as a backdrop for high culture in the early summer.

Also internationally known are Juan-les-Pins' Jazz à Juan (ⓦwww.jazzjuan.com), the region's most prestigious **jazz festival**, and its equivalent in Nice (ⓦwww.nicejazzfestival.fr), and the Chorégies d'Orange **opera festival** (ⓦwww.choregies.asso.fr) at the Roman theatre in Orange in July. Most famous of all Provence's festivals is the **Cannes Film Festival** (ⓦwww.festival-cannes.fr), held every year in May, but this is a trade-only event and, other than the occasional glimpse of a Hollywood star surrounded by paparazzi, you're unlikely to feel a part of it.

Much more accessible are Nice's pre-Lent **carnival** (ⓦwww.nicecarnaval.com) with its celebrated Bataille de Fleurs, Menton's annual **Fête du Citron** (lemon festival) in February and the **gathering of the gypsies** in Les-Stes-Maries-de-la-Mer in May.

Arles and Les-Stes-Maries-de-la-Mer still have Spanish-style *férias* or **bullfights**, while Marseille's *Fiesta des Suds* world **music and arts festival** (ⓦwww.dock-des-suds.org) strikes a more contemporary and cosmopolitan note in the industrial setting of the city's docklands each October.

The principality of Monaco makes up for its modest size with a packed programme of events of its own, from the **Monte Carlo Rally** in January (ⓦwww.acm.mc) to the **Printemps des Arts** (ⓦwww.printempsdesarts.com) arts festival in March and April and the **Grand Prix** (ⓦwww.acm.mc) in May.

On a less spectacular scale, many small towns and villages in Provence have more traditional and authentic **fêtes** of their own, a contrast to the hype and glitz of the coast and well worth checking out if you happen to be in the region at the right time. Details of the most popular festivals, as well as many smaller-scale events, are listed throughout the Guide.

Sports and outdoor activities

Spectator sports

Football is the most popular spectator sport in Provence, especially in Marseille, home of Olympique de Marseille (Ⓦwww.om.net), one of the top French teams. Motor racing takes precedence in Monaco, while enthusiasm for **cycle racing** is as great as anywhere in France, and the annual **Tour de France** generally has a stage in Provence, most notoriously on Mont Ventoux. In and around the Camargue, the number one spectator sport is **bullfighting**; though not to everyone's taste, it is, at least, less gruesome than the variety practised in Spain. The world-famous **Formula One Grand Prix** takes place in Monaco in May, while some of Provence's remote inland routes make perfect terrain for **rallying**. Monaco also hosts an international **Tennis Open** championship.

The characteristic Provençal sporting pastime is **pétanque**, the region's version of *boules*, which you'll see played in practically every town or village square, in parks and sometimes in purpose-built arenas. The principle is the same as in bowls, but the terrain is rough, never grass, and the area of play much smaller.

Sailing and watersports

There can scarcely be a coast anywhere in the world with as many **yachting facilities** as the Côte d'Azur, and most coastal resorts have at least one marina, often more. Of the **regattas**, Hyères hosts the Semaine Olympic des Voiles in the spring, a major sailing event that national teams often use to select their Olympic teams. In September, the attraction of St-Tropez's Les Voiles is as much glamour as sport, while Marseille's Septembre en Mer offers all manner of nautical activities, from sunset sea-kayak trips along the coast to voyages on a historic barque.

The chief problem for **watersports** enthusiasts on the Côte d'Azur is simple congestion,

with the thousands of yachts dodging jetskis, motorboats and windsurfers and adding up to a traffic headache. Nonetheless, the sea is warm and placid and there are plenty of opportunities to hire equipment.

Elsewhere, there are opportunities for **diving** in the clear waters around Cassis, Bandol and Sanary, along the Corniche des Maures and at Fréjus. **Swimming** is most enjoyable in the *calanques* of Marseille or around the quieter and more remote beaches away from the big cities; purpose-built **water parks** on the coast offer extensive facilities in exchange for their rather steep entry prices.

Sailing operators

Absolute Boat ☎06.11.73.30.56, Ⓦwww .absoluteboat.com. The place in Cannes to charter that drop-dead speedboat or motor yacht for film festival posing, if money is no object.
Bateau École Olivier Lacourtablaise ☎04.94.83.11.21, Ⓦwww.permisbateau83 .com. Sailing school based at Port Santa Lucia in St Raphaël.
Bormes Plongée ☎04.94.64.91.28, Ⓦwww .bormesplongee.fr. Diving tuition for adults and children, off Port Cros and Porquerolles.
École de Croisière Sillages ☎04.94.40.83.80, Ⓦpagesperso-orange.fr/sillages. Learn to sail as a group, with family or friends, on a yacht based at the old harbour in St Raphaël.

Outdoor and adventure activities

Provence makes a superb venue for **outdoor sports** and **adventure pursuits**. The beautiful alpine scenery is wonderful for walking, particularly around the Grand Canyon du Verdon (see p.220) and in the Parc National du Mercantour (see p.243). The former is also popular for **hiking**, **rafting**, **canyoning**, **kayaking**, **rock climbing**, **hang-gliding**, **mountain biking** and **horse-riding**: Castellane and La Palud Sur Verdon are the two main centres for active sports in the gorge; nearby St-André-les-Alpes is popular for **paragliding** and hang-gliding, and Fayence is a centre for **gliding**. Gentler airborne pursuits include **hot-air ballooning** in the Pays de Forcalquier. Closer to the coast, the Gorge du Loup is another centre for canyoning.

The Camargue is Provence's most famous centre for **horseriding**; information on holidays on horseback is included in "Agents and operators" p.26.

Cycling is popular almost everywhere, with public bike hire schemes in Marseille and Nice and bicycle rental available in most other towns, and there are numerous organized cycling **tours** available (see p.26). **Bike rental** information is given throughout the Guide. Cycle tourism is particularly well supported in the Luberon and Pays de Forcalquier, where you can even arrange to have your luggage transported ahead of you to your next hotel. Bikes are by no means confined to paved roads: in the alpine districts of the Alpes Maritime and Parc du Mercantour there are signposted and mapped VTT (*vélo tout terrain*) trails for mountain-biking enthusiasts.

Outdoor and adventure operators

Club Alpin Français des Alpes-Maritimes ☎04.93.62.59.99, ⊛www.cafnice.org. Nice-based branch of the national mountaineering union, which manages refuges in the Parc National du Mercantour.

Envol de Provence ☎04.94.90.86.13, ⊛www.envolprovence.com. Paragliding school at Signes, near St-Maximin de la Sainte-Baume.

Holiday Bikes ⊛www.holiday-bikes.com. Leading rental agency for bikes and scooters in the region, with outlets in many coastal resorts.

Luclimb Adventure ☎04.88.84.12.17, ⊛www.luclimb.com. Rock-climbing in the Dentelles, plus canyoning, Via Ferrata, hiking.

Montgolfière Vol-Terre ☎06.03.54.10.92, ⊛www.montgolfiere-luberon.com. Balloon flights over the Luberon.

La Palud Sur Verdon ⊛www.lapaludsurverdon.com. Website of the Maison des Gorges du Verdon, with masses of links for climbing guides, canyoning, walking, horseriding and mountain biking in and around the Grand Canyon du Verdon.

Parc National du Mercantour ⊛www.mercantour.eu. Web portal (in French) for the

national park that straddles the French-Italian border.

Les Poneys de Sophie ☎06.70.75.28.91, ⊛www.lesponeysdesophie.com. Riding instruction at all levels, plus trekking from stables at St Aygulf, near Fréjus.

Relais Équestre de la Mène ☎06.11.81.11.32, ⊛www.rem83.com. Horseriding in the Massif des Maures.

Rustr'aille Colorado ☎04.90.04.96.53, ⊛www.parapente.biz. Tandem paragliding jumps above the Colorado Provençal.

Velo Loisir en Luberon ☎04.90.76.48.05, ⊛www.veloloisirluberon.com. Network of mapped cycle routes in the Luberon, with affiliated accommodation, cycle hire and repair.

Verdon Passion ☎04.92.74.69.77, ⊛www.verdon-passion.com. Moustiers-Ste-Marie-based activity outfit organizing canyoning, climbing, paragliding, etc.

Skiing and snowboarding

Thanks to the unique topography of the region, it's possible to **ski** remarkably close to the coast – the closest resort to the Côte d'Azur being Gréolières-les-Neiges, a short distance from Grasse. More reliable snow and more extensive facilities are, however, found inland: at Valberg, Isola 2000, La Foux d'Allos, Auron and in the resorts around Barçelonette.

Ski resorts

Auron ⊛www.auron.com. Resort with ski and snowboarding schools and 135km of pistes.

La Foux d'Allos ☎04.92.83.02.81, ⊛www.valdallos.com. Purpose-built, high-altitude ski resort in the Val d'Allos, which has 230km of pistes – the most extensive network in the southern Alps.

Isola 2000 ☎04.93.23.15.15, ⊛www.isola2000.com. At an altitude of 2000m on the fringe of the Parc National du Mercantour, with 120km of pistes.

Valberg ☎04.93.23.24.25, ⊛www.valberg.com. Resort claiming the best snow record in the region, with 90km of downhill pistes and a preponderance of red runs.

La Vallée de l'Ubaye ⊛www.ubaye.com. The region around Barçelonette harbours several skiing resorts, including Le Sauze Super Sauze, Sainte Anne la Condamine and Pra Loup, whose pistes link up with those of La Foux d'Allos.

Shopping

Provence offers a rich variety of local **crafts** and **produce** to buy as souvenirs, with everything from *santons* in Aubagne or Marseille to high-quality glassware in Biot and fine (and sometimes not so fine) art and handicrafts in every chic village along the Côte d'Azur.

Food can be a particular joy, from soft nougat and farmhouse honey to olive oil and fine wine, *marrons glacés* from Collobrières and *calissons* from Aix. One of the pleasures of shopping in Provence is the opportunity to taste oils and wines as you go; another is the sheer colour and choice in the region's many excellent markets.

Most larger towns have considerable shopping facilities in the centre, including perhaps a **department store** as well as the usual range of **fashion** and **footwear** chains; most Provençal towns of any size also have sizeable edge-of-town **retail parks** which include not only mammoth supermarkets but also discount shoe and clothing retailers. Some of the Côte d'Azur resorts – in particular St-Tropez, Cannes, Nice and Monte Carlo – also have a considerable selection of luxury stores, with all the usual international **designer** names.

Travel essentials

Costs

Provence is one of the most **expensive** French regions to visit: prices in some of the chic hotspots on the Côte d'Azur can rival those in the more prestigious *arrondissements* of Paris, and costs for accommodation on the coast soar during the July and August peak season when foreign visitors have to compete with the French for scarce hotel rooms.

For a reasonably comfortable stay, including a hotel room for two, a light restaurant lunch and a proper restaurant dinner, plus moving around, café stops and museum visits, you need to allow a **budget** of around €100 a day per person. By counting the pennies, staying at hostels (€15–30 for bed and breakfast) or camping (€15–35 for two people), and being strong-willed about extra cups of coffee and doses of culture, you could manage on €60 a day.

Costs vary a great deal within the region, with the Riviera more expensive than the rest of the Provence – St-Tropez and Monaco in particular considerably so.

As in other European Union countries, you'll routinely find that Value Added Tax (*TVA*) makes up part of your hotel, restaurant or shopping bill – but prices are usually quoted inclusive of the **tax**. At restaurants you only need to leave an additional cash **tip** if you feel you have received service out of the ordinary, since restaurant prices almost always include a service charge.

Crime and personal safety

Though certain sections of **Marseille**, **Toulon** and **Nice** have a distinctly dodgy feel, violent crime against tourists is pretty rare. **Petty theft**, however, is endemic along the Côte d'Azur and also a problem in the

Emergency numbers and helpline contacts

Police ☎17.
Medical emergencies/ambulance ☎15.
Fire brigade/paramedics (*pompiers*) ☎18.
Rape crisis (*SOS Viol*) ☎04.91.33.16.60.
Homophobia (SOS Homophobie) ☎08.10.10.81.35.

more crowded parts of the big cities, while occasional serious crimes contribute to the region's somewhat lurid reputation. In response, the authorities have ramped up security and policing measures, including the issuing of taser stun-guns to local police and the increased use of closed circuit television (CCTV) cameras. Note that although there are two main types of **police** in France – the Police Nationale and the Gendarmerie Nationale – for all practical purposes they are indistinguishable.

Visitors to the region should take the normal **precautions**: don't wave money or travellers' cheques around, never let valuables out of your sight and carry wallets and bags securely, particularly in crowded places. **Drivers** face perhaps the greatest problems, particularly with regard to break-ins: never leave valuables in an unattended car. Drivers on the Riviera in particular are susceptible to robbery by thieves on motor-bikes while stuck in heavy traffic.

Pedestrians should take great care when crossing roads – inattentiveness is still a great problem among French drivers and many pay little heed to pedestrian crossings or lights. Do not step onto a crossing assuming traffic will stop for you.

Drug use is just as prevalent in Provence as anywhere else in Europe – and just as risky; the authorities make no distinction between soft or hard drugs. People caught smuggling or possessing drugs, even just a few grams of marijuana, are liable to find themselves in jail.

As a long-standing stronghold of the extreme right, Provence has a regrettable reputation for **racism**, directed mainly against the Arab community. As a result,

particularly Arab, but also black and Asian visitors, may encounter an unwelcome degree of curiosity or suspicion from shopkeepers, hoteliers and the like. If you suffer a **racial assault**, contact the police, your consulate or one of the local anti-racism organizations (though they may not have English-speakers): SOS Racism (🌐www.sos-racisme.org) and Ligue Internationale Contre le Racisme et l'Antisémitisme (LICRA; 🌐www.licra.org) – the latter has contacts in most major towns in the region. One other general resource for travellers is the Paris-based, **English-speaking helpline** SOS Help (☎01.46.21.46.46, daily 3–11pm; 🌐www.soshelpline.org). The service is manned by trained volunteers who not only provide a confidential listening service, but also offer practical information for foreigners facing problems in France.

Electricity

The French electricity supply runs at 220V, using plugs with two round pins. If you need a transformer, it's best to buy one before leaving home, though you can find them in large department stores in France.

Entry requirements

EU citizens can travel freely in Provence and can stay for an unlimited amount of time, while those from **Australia**, **Canada**, **New Zealand** and the **United States**, among other countries, do not need a visa for a stay of up to ninety days. **South African** citizens require a short-stay visa for up to ninety days, which costs €60. You'll need to have a return ticket, and provide evidence that you have accommodation in France, and sufficient funds for your stay.

Non-EU citizens who wish to remain longer than ninety days must apply to the local *mairie* or town hall for a **residence permit** (a *titre de séjour*, also known as a *carte de séjour*), for which you will have to show proof of – among other things – a regular income or sufficient funds to support yourself, evidence of medical insurance and the appropriate visa (if required).

For further information about visa regulations consult the Ministry of Foreign Affairs website: 🌐www.diplomatie.gouv.fr.

Visa requirements for **Monaco** (an independent principality) are identical to those of France; there are no border controls between the two.

Gay and lesbian travellers

The prevalence of conservative attitudes traditionally meant **lesbian and gay** life in Provence was rather discreet, but in the cities at least that has changed: both Nice and Marseille have annual gay pride celebrations and **Nice** in particular has quite a respectable range of lesbian and gay-friendly accommodation, cafés, bars and clubs.

Perhaps the most relaxed attitudes can be found in the smaller, chic resorts such as **Cannes** and **St-Tropez**, where the gay presence is both long-established and relatively integrated into the mainstream. Away from the coast, both **Aix** and **Avignon** have small-scale but lively bar scenes.

The national gay magazine *Têtu* is widely available, but more useful listings are found in the free bar **magazines** such as *Link Xtra*; ⓦwww.gaymapmarseille.com and ⓦwww .nicegay.fr are also worth a look, though not everything on them may be up to date.

Health

There are no compulsory vaccinations for visiting Provence, tap water is safe to drink and most travellers will encounter little in the way of **health problems**: sunburn, heat exhaustion and insect bites (including bed bugs) are the most usual complaints. If you do need to access healthcare, standards of treatment in France are among the best in the world.

Under the French **health system**, all services, including doctor's consultations, prescribed medicines, hospital stays and ambulance call-outs, incur a charge which you have to pay upfront. **EU citizens** are entitled to a refund (usually between 70 and 100 percent) of medical and dental expenses, providing the doctor is government-registered (*un médecin conventionné*) and provided you have the correct documentation (the **European Health Insurance Card** – EHIC; application forms available from main post offices in the UK). This can still leave a hefty shortfall, however,

especially after a stay in hospital, so you might want to take out some additional insurance. All **non-EU visitors** should ensure they have adequate medical insurance cover.

For **minor complaints** go to a *pharmacie*, signalled by an illuminated green cross. You'll find at least one in every small town and even some villages. They keep normal shop hours (roughly 9am–noon & 3–6pm), though some stay open late and in larger towns at least one (known as the *pharmacie de garde*) is open 24 hours according to a rota; details are displayed in all pharmacy windows.

For anything more serious you can get the name of a **doctor** from a pharmacy, local police station, tourist office or your hotel. Alternatively, look under "Médecins" in the *Yellow Pages*.

In **emergencies**, you will always be admitted to the nearest general hospital (*centre hospitalier*). Phone numbers and addresses of hospitals in all the main cities are given in the Guide. The national number for the **ambulance** service is ☎15.

Insurance

Even though **EU citizens** are entitled to healthcare privileges in France, it's worth having insurance against theft, loss, illness or injury. Before paying for a new policy, however, check whether you are already covered: some all-risks home insurance policies cover your possessions when overseas, and many private medical schemes include cover when abroad. In Canada, provincial health plans usually provide partial cover for medical mishaps overseas, while holders of official student/ teacher/youth cards in Canada and the US are entitled to meagre accident coverage and hospital in-patient benefits. **Students** will often find that their student health coverage extends during the vacations and for one term beyond the date of last enrolment.

A typical **travel insurance policy** usually provides cover for the loss of baggage, tickets and – up to a certain limit – cash or cheques, as well as cancellation or curtailment of your journey. Most exclude so-called dangerous sports unless an extra

Rough Guides travel insurance

Rough Guides has teamed up with WorldNomads.com to offer great **travel insurance** deals. Policies are available to residents of over 150 countries, with cover for a wide range of **adventure sports**, 24-hour emergency assistance, high levels of medical and evacuation cover and a stream of **travel safety information**. Roughguides.com users can take advantage of their policies online 24/7, from anywhere in the world – even if you're already travelling. And since plans often change when you're on the road, you can extend your policy and even claim online. Roughguides.com users who buy travel insurance with WorldNomads.com can also leave a positive footprint and donate to a community development project. For more information go to ⓦ**www.roughguides.com/shop**.

premium is paid, and many policies can be chopped and changed to exclude coverage you don't need – for example, sickness and accident benefits can often be excluded or included at will.

If you do take medical coverage, ascertain whether benefits will be paid as treatment proceeds or only after you return home, and if there is a 24-hour medical emergency number. When securing baggage cover, make sure that the per-article limit will cover your most valuable possession. If you need to make a claim, you should keep receipts for medicines and medical treatment. In the event you have anything stolen, you must obtain an official statement from the police (called a *constat de vol*).

Internet

Most hotels in Provence offer **internet access** of some sort, and even in quite modest hotels free wi-fi is frequently available; it's often provided by cafés and bars too. Shops offering cheap international phone calls and internet access are easy enough to find in bigger towns, particularly in Nice where they cluster in the streets south and east of the *gare SNCF*; in smaller towns, it's often worth enquiring at the local library or *médiathèque*. Most larger post offices also offer internet access. Some places advertise English-language format **keyboards**; if not, expect terminals to have French format (non-QWERTY) keyboards, which may take some getting used to.

Laundry

Inexpensive self-service laundries or *laveries automatiques* are commonplace in Provençal

towns, and are listed in the guide for larger destinations such as Nice. They are often unattended, so come armed with small change. The alternative *blanchisserie* or pressing services are more expensive, as are hotel laundry services. Most hotels forbid doing laundry in your room, though you should get away with just one or two items.

Living in Provence

EU citizens are free to work in France on the same basis as a French citizen. This means you no longer have to apply for a residence or work permit except in very rare cases – contact your nearest French consulate for further information. **Non-EU citizens**, however, will need both a work permit – of which there are various kinds, depending on your circumstances – and a residence permit; again, contact your nearest French consulate or, if already in France, the local *mairie* or *préfecture* to check what rules apply in your particular situation.

Most **non-EU citizens** who manage to survive for long periods of time in France do it on luck, brazenness and willingness to live in pretty basic conditions. Bar or club work, busking, teaching English, translating or working as an au pair are some of the ways people scrape by; there may also be seasonal work in ski resorts or crewing yachts. Remember that unemployment is high: the current rate stands at around eight percent and is on the rise, and without a good working knowledge of French your options (and your earning power) will be limited.

Finding a job **teaching English** is best done in advance, in late summer. Courses and jobs are listed on ⓦwww.elgazette.com

and www.tefl.com, while the **British Council** (Ⓦwww.britishcouncil.org) recruits and helps train TEFL teachers for work abroad. **Au pair work** is usually arranged through an agency, who should sort out any necessary paperwork; you'll find agencies listed on Ⓦwww.iapa.org.

The Riviera has a large expat Anglophone community, and there is consequently demand for **English-language services** of various kinds, from domestic staff to *immobiliers* and experienced crew members on yachts. Riviera Radio (see p.35) often carries job ads, though even these usually require fluent French as well as English. It may also be worth checking the business section of the *Riviera Times* (Ⓦwww.riviera times.com) or the classified sections of *Anglo Info* (Ⓦriviera.angloinfo.com; provence .angloinfo.com).

Study and work programmes

AFS Intercultural Programs Ⓦwww.afs.org. Intercultural exchange organization with programmes in over fifty countries.

American Institute for Foreign Study Ⓦwww .aifs.com. Language and culture courses in Cannes over a summer, a semester or a year.

Mail

As a rule, **post offices** (*bureaux de poste* or PTTs) are open from around 8.30am to 6/7pm Monday to Friday, and from 8.30am to noon on Saturday; look for bright yellow *La Poste* signs. However, main offices in larger towns remain open throughout the day (8am–7pm), while lunch hours and closing times in the villages can vary enormously.

Sending **letters**, the quickest international service is by *aérogramme*, sold at all post offices. You can buy ordinary **stamps** (*timbres*) at any *tabac* (tobacconist). When this book went to press, the rates for standard letters (*lettres*, weighing 20g or less) and postcards (*cartes postales*) were €0.65 for the UK and Europe, and €0.85 for North America, Australia and New Zealand. For further information, log on to Ⓦlaposte.fr.

Maps

In addition to the maps in this guide and the various free town plans and regional **maps** you'll be offered along the way, you'll probably also want a good, up-to-date **road map** of the region. The *Michelin* 1:200,000 area maps of Provence–Alpes–Côte d'Azur (527) is reliable for driving and other purposes; virtually every road it shows is passable by any car, and those that are tinged in green are usually "scenic routes". Both Michelin (Ⓦviamichelin.fr) and the Institut Géographique National (IGN; Ⓦign.fr) also produce excellent **larger-scale maps** of specific regions, and spiral-bound road atlases, while **Rough Guides** publishes its own hard-wearing map of France.

If **walking**, it's worth investing in the more detailed (1:25,000) IGN maps (see above). **Free town maps** handed out by tourist offices are often surprisingly good; the quality of those covering rural areas is more variable and they tend to be geared more towards inspiring you than providing practical information.

Money

France's currency, the **euro**, is divided into 100 cents (often still referred to as *centimes*). There are seven **notes** – in denominations of 5, 10, 20, 50, 100, 200 and 500 euros – and eight different **coins** – 1, 2, 5, 10, 20 and 50 cents, and 1 and 2 euros. At the time of writing, the **exchange rate** for the euro was around €1.10 to the pound sterling (or £0.91 to one euro) and €1.50 to the dollar (or $0.67 to one euro). See Ⓦxe.com for current rates.

By far the easiest way to access your money in France is to use your credit or debit card to withdraw cash from an **ATM** (known as a *distributeur* or *point argent*); machines are every bit as ubiquitous as in Britain or north America, and most give instructions in several languages. Check with your bank before you leave home if you're in any doubt, and note that there is often a transaction fee, so it's more efficient to take out a sizeable sum each time rather than making lots of small withdrawals.

Similarly, all major **credit cards** are almost always accepted in hotels, restaurants and shops, although some smaller establishments don't accept cards, or only for sums above a certain threshold. Visa – called Carte Bleue in France – is almost universally recognized, followed by MasterCard (also known as EuroCard). American Express ranks a bit lower.

Usual **banking hours** are Monday to Friday 9am to noon and 2 to 4.30pm. Some branches, especially those in rural areas, close on Monday, while those in big cities may remain open at midday and may also open on Saturday morning. All are closed on Sunday and public holidays.

Opening hours and public holidays

Basic **hours of business** are Monday to Saturday 9am until noon, and 2pm to 6pm. In big city centres, shops and other businesses stay open throughout the day, while in July and August most tourist offices and museums are open without interruption. Otherwise almost everything – shops, museums, tourist offices, most banks – closes for a couple of hours at midday.

If you're looking to buy a picnic lunch, you'll need to get into the habit of buying it before you're ready to eat. Small food shops often don't reopen until halfway through the afternoon, closing around 7.30pm or 8pm just before the evening meal.

The standard **closing days** are Sunday and Monday. Food shops tend to close on Monday rather than Sunday, but in smaller towns you may well find everything except

Public holidays

January 1 New Year's Day
Easter Sunday
Easter Monday
Ascension Day (forty days after Easter)
Pentecost or Whitsun (seventh Sunday after Easter, plus the Monday)
May 1 May Day/Labour Day
May 8 Victory in Europe Day
July 14 Bastille Day
August 15 Assumption of the Virgin Mary
November 1 All Saints' Day
November 11 Armistice Day 1918
December 25 Christmas Day

the odd *boulangerie* (bakery) shut on both days.

Museums are not very generous with their hours, tending to open at around 10am, close for lunch at noon until 2pm (sometimes 3pm) and then run through until only 5 or 6pm. Summer opening times, usually applicable between mid-May or early June and mid-September (but sometimes only during July and August) often differ from winter times; variations are indicated throughout this book. The closing days are usually Monday or Tuesday, sometimes both.

Phones

To **call to France** from your home country, dial ☎00 33 from the UK or Ireland, ☎011 33 from the US, Canada or Australia, or ☎00 44 33 from New Zealand, and then the last nine digits of the ten-digit French number (thus omitting the initial 0).

To **make a phone call within France** – local or long-distance – simply dial all ten digits of the number. Numbers beginning with ☎08.00 up to ☎08.05 are free; those beginning ☎08.10 and ☎08.11 are charged as a local call; anything else beginning ☎08 is premium-rated (typically €0.34 per minute). None of these ☎08 numbers can be accessed from abroad. Calls to mobile phones (numbers starting with ☎06) are also charged at premium rates.

To speak to the **operator** dial ☎13; **directory enquiries**, both national and international, are on ☎12; **medical emergencies**, ☎15; the **police**, ☎17; **fire**, ☎18.

Mobile phones

If you want to use your **mobile (cell) phone**, contact your phone provider to check whether it will work in France and what the call charges are – they tend to be pretty exorbitant, and remember you're likely to be charged extra for receiving calls. French mobile phones operate on the European GSM standard, so US cellphones won't work in France unless you have a tri-band phone.

If you are going to be in France for any length of time and will be making and receiving a lot of local calls, it may be worth buying a **French SIM card** (which will give

Calling home from France

Note that the initial zero is omitted from the area code when dialling the UK, Ireland, Australia and New Zealand from abroad.

US & Canada international access code + 1 + area code
Australia international access code + 61 + city code
New Zealand international access code + 64 + city code
UK international access code + 44 + city code
Ireland international access code + 353 + city code
South Africa international access code + 27 + city code

you a local phone number) and pre-paid recharge cards (*mobicartes*). You can buy a SIM card from any of the big mobile providers (Orange, SFR and Boygues Telecom), all of which have high-street outlets. They cost from around €30, and you'll need to have an address in France to register – that of your hotel or a friend will usually suffice.

Calling home from France

You can make international calls using either a standard **télécarte**, as sold at *tabacs*, newsagents and post offices, which will work with almost all payphones (coin-operated payphones are becoming rare), or a pre-paid **phone card**, also sold in *tabacs*, which can be used from both payphones and private phones.

Smoking

Smoking is banned in all public places, including public transport, museums, cafés and restaurants.

Time

France is in the **Central European Time Zone** (GMT+1). This means it is one hour ahead of the UK, six hours ahead of Eastern Standard Time and nine hours ahead of Pacific Standard Time. **Daylight Saving Time** (GMT+2) in France lasts from the last Sunday of March to the last Sunday of October. Between March and October France is one hour behind South Africa, eight hours behind eastern Australia and ten hours behind New Zealand; from October to March it is the same time as South Africa, ten hours behind southeastern Australia and twelve hours behind New Zealand.

Tourist information

The **French Government Tourist Office** (Maison de la France) has offices throughout the world, each with its own website holding general country-wide information. For practical details on a specific location, such as hotels, campsites, activities and festivals, contact the relevant regional or departmental tourist offices; contact details are listed below and can also be found online at Ⓦfncrt.com and www.fncdt.net respectively.

In France itself, practically every town and many villages have a **tourist office** – usually an **Office du Tourisme** (OT) but sometimes a **Syndicat d'Initiative** (SI). These provide local information, including hotel and restaurant listings, leisure activities, car and bike rental, bus times, laundries and countless other things; many can also book accommodation for you. Most can provide a town plan, and sell maps and local walking guides.

Local tourist **websites** are listed throughout the Guide; in addition, good regional sites include: Ⓦalpes-haute-provence.com, which carries information on the alpine regions of Provence; Ⓦcotedazur-tourisme.com, the official site for tourism on the Côte d'Azur; Ⓦwww.provenceguide.com, which covers the Vaucluse, including Avignon, Orange, the Dentelles and the Luberon; and Ⓦvisit provence.com, a portal for the Bouches du Rhône *département*, which includes Marseille and Aix-en-Provence.

French Government tourist offices abroad

Australia and New Zealand Ⓦau.franceguide .com
Britain Ⓦuk.franceguide.com

Canada ⓦ canada.franceguide.com
Ireland ⓦ ie.franceguide.com
South Africa ⓦ za.franceguide.com
US ⓦ us.franceguide.com

Travellers with disabilities

Travellers with **disabilities**, and particularly those using wheelchairs, will find haphazard parking habits, stepped village streets and cobbled paving among the challenges of a visit to Provence – with the proliferation of dog mess on many pavements an additional and unwelcome hazard. Some **hotels** have lifts, but it's worth checking that your wheelchair will fit before booking – smaller hotels may have the diminutive older-style lift shaft with the staircase wrapped around it. Museums, stations and other sites are gradually being adapted with **ramps** or other forms of access, though provision varies and is rarely comprehensive. The **public transport** situation is improving as transport networks are modernized: Nice's new Tramway, for instance, has been designed to be fully accessible.

The national association APF (Association des Paralysées de France) is a useful source of information and has representatives in each *département*.

APF – Association des Paralysées de France
ⓦ www.apf.asso.fr (in French).
Avignon ☎ 04.90.16.47.40
La Garde (Var) ☎ 04.98.01.30.50
Manosque ☎ 04.92.71.74.50
Marseille ☎ 04.91.79.99.99
Nice ☎ 04.92.07.98.00

Travelling with children

Children and babies are generally welcome everywhere, including most bars and restaurants. Hotels charge by the room, and many either hold a few large **family rooms**, or charge a small supplement for an additional bed or cot. Family-run places will often **babysit** or offer a listening service while you eat or go out. Especially in seaside towns, most restaurants have **children's menus** or cook simpler food on request. SNCF charge nothing on trains and buses for under-4s, and half-fare for 4–11s. If you're renting a car, however, baby seats will normally cost extra.

Most tourist offices have details of specific **activities for children** – in particular, many resorts supervise "clubs" for kids on the beach, while plentiful attractions along the coast in particular range from funfairs to water parks to zoos. Something to be aware of – not that you can do much about it – is the difficulty of negotiating a child's buggy on the steep and cobbled streets of the typical Provençal *village perché*.

Travelling with pets from the UK

If you wish to take your dog or cat to France from the UK, the **Pet Travel Scheme** (PETS) enables you, so long as certain conditions are met, to avoid putting your pet in quarantine when you re-enter the UK. Current regulations are available on the Department for Environment, Food and Rural Affairs (DEFRA) website ⓦ www.defra.gov.uk, or through the PETS Helpline (☎ 0870/241 1710).

Guide

Guide

www.roughguides.com

1

Marseille and around

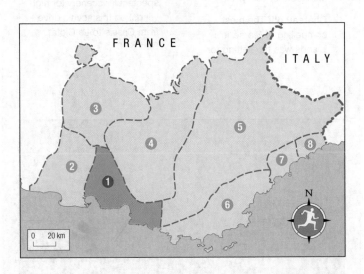

CHAPTER 1   # Highlights

* **The Vieux Port, Marseille**
An intoxicating blend of
food, history, water and
sunlight at the very heart of
France's great Mediterranean
metropolis. **See p.56**

* **L'Unité d'Habitation,
Marseille** Le Corbusier's
masterpiece is a truly ground-
breaking piece of modernist
architecture. **See p.64**

* **Château d'If** The most
compelling of Marseille's
islands was the setting for
Dumas' *The Count of Monte
Cristo.* **See p.65**

* **Calanques** Whether you
walk, swim or simply take a
boat trip, don't miss the clear
waters and fjord-like inlets
of the coastline between
Marseille and Cassis. **See p.71**

* **Corniche des Crêtes** Don't
get blown away by the
spectacular scenery (or high
winds) on this scenic drive
from Cassis to La Ciotat.
See p.80

▲ Viewpoint along the Corniche des Crêtes

Marseille and around

T he **Marseille** conurbation is by far the most populated and industrialized part of Provence, and indeed of southern France. After Lyon and Paris it is France's third-largest urban region, an area where tourism takes a back seat to other industries: to shipping in Marseille city; and petrochemicals around the Étang de Berre. Yet the area also has vast tracts of deserted mountainous countryside and a shoreline of high cliffs, jagged inlets and sand beaches with stretches still untouched by the holiday industry.

For visitors, the great attraction is Marseille itself, a vital commercial port for more than two millennia. France's second city is, for all its notorious reputation, a wonderful place with a distinctive, unconventional character that never ceases to surprise. The first foreigners to settle in Provence, the ancient **Greeks** from Phocaea and their less amiable successors from **Rome**, left evidence of their presence in Marseille, where museums guard reminders of the indigenous peoples whose civilization they destroyed.

The wider region has strong military connections. **Salon-de-Provence** holds a training school for French air-force pilots but also preserves reminders of Nostradamus; **Aubagne** is home to the French Foreign Legion but also to the characters of **Pagnol**. There are great seaside attractions here too: the pine-covered rocks of the **Estaque**; the *calanques* (rocky inlets) between Marseille and **Cassis**; the sand beaches of **La Ciotat** bay; and the heights from which to view the coast, most notably on the **route des Crêtes**. The area also has great **wines** at Cassis, and great **seafood**, particularly in Marseille, home of the famous fish stew, *bouillabaisse*.

Marseille

Like the French capital, **MARSEILLE** has both prospered and been ransacked over the centuries. It has lost its privileges to sundry French kings and foreign armies, refound its fortunes, suffered plagues, religious bigotry, republican and royalist terror and had its own Commune and Bastille-storming. It was the presence of so many Revolutionaries from Marseille marching their way from the Rhine to Paris in 1792 which gave the name to the Hymn of the Army of the Rhine that became the national anthem, *La Marseillaise*.

Marseille has been a **trading city** for over two and a half thousand years, ever since ancient Greeks from Ionia discovered shelter in the Lacydon inlet, today the Vieux Port, and came to an agreement with the local Ligurian tribe. The story goes that the locals, noticing the exotic cargo of the strangers' boats, sent them off to the king's castle where the princess's wedding preparations were in full swing.

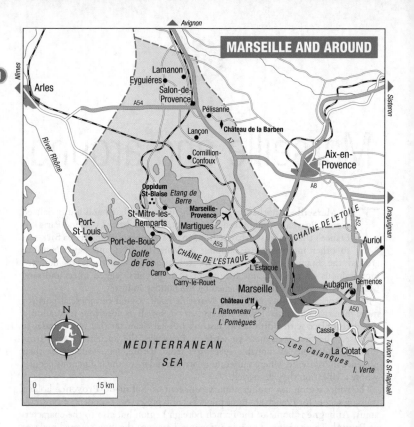

The Ligurian royal custom at the time was that the king's daughter could choose her husband from among her father's guests. As the leader of the Greek party walked through the castle gate, he was handed a drink by a woman and discovered that she was the princess and that he was the bridegroom. The king gave the couple the hill on the north side of the Lacydon and Massalia came into being. And there ends, more or less, Marseille's association with romance.

Which is not to say Marseille cannot be romantic. It has a powerful magnetism as a true Mediterranean city, surrounded by mountains and graced with hidden corners that have the unexpected air of fishing villages. Built (for the most part handsomely) of warm stone, it has its triumphal architecture; it has, too, the cosmopolitan atmosphere of a major port. Perhaps the most appealing quality is the down-to-earth nature of its gregarious, talkative inhabitants.

In recent years the city has undergone a marked **renaissance**, shaking off much of its old reputation for sleaze to attract a wider range of visitors. The TGV has made it accessible to northerners, the rejuvenated docks have become a magnet for cruise ships and the shops in the streets south of La Canebière are increasingly trendy or elegant. In 2008, a Marseille restaurant was awarded three Michelin stars for the first time; in 2009, the city was selected to be European Capital of Culture 2013, at the head of a consortium of Provençal towns. The forward march of progress is not, however, relentless. All too often, last year's prestige civic project becomes this year's broken, bottle-strewn fountain, while Marseille's easy tolerance of graffiti means it sometimes *looks* like the toughest city in France. In short, it's a rough diamond. See past the grit, and chances are you'll warm to this down-to-earth, vital metropolis.

Arrival and information

Arriving by **car**, you'll descend into Marseille from the surrounding heights of one of three mountain ranges. From any direction the views encompass the vast roadstead with docks stretching north from the central **Vieux Port** and Marseille's classic landmark, the **Basilique de Notre-Dame-de-la-Garde**, perched on a high rock to the south. Follow signs for the Vieux Port to reach the city centre.

The city's **airport**, the Aéroport de Marseille-Provence (℡04.42.14.14.14, Ⓦwww.mrsairport.com), is 20km northwest of the city centre at Marignane; a shuttle bus runs to the **gare SNCF St-Charles** (5.10am–12.10am; every 20min; €8.50), on the northern edge of 1er arrondissement on esplanade St-Charles. The modern **gare routière** is integrated into the station complex, though buses to Aix depart from the Porte d'Aix. From esplanade St-Charles, a monumental staircase leads down to boulevard d'Athènes, which becomes boulevard Dugommier before reaching **La Canebière**, Marseille's main street. La Canebière runs to the head of the **Vieux Port**, a fifteen-minute walk to the right of the intersection. Marseille's main **tourist office** is at 4 La Canebière (Mon–Sat 9am–7pm, Sun & public hols 10am–5pm; ℡04.91.13.89.00, Ⓦwww.marseille-tourisme.com).

City transport

Marseille has an efficient **bus** and **métro** network, supplemented by two modern **tram** lines running from Blancarde to Euroméditerranée and from Noailles to Les Caillols. You can get a plan of the **transport system** from RTM at 6 rue des Fabres (Mon–Fri 8.30am–6pm, Sat 9am–12.30pm & 2–5.30pm; Ⓦwww.rtm.fr), one street north of La Canebière near the Bourse, the city's stock exchange. **Tickets** are flat rate for buses, trams and the métro and can be used for journeys combining all three as long as they take less than one hour. You can buy individual **tickets** (€1.50) from bus and tram drivers, and from métro ticket offices, or **multi-journey** *Cartes Libertés* (in increments of €6.30 and €12.60), which are valid for five and ten journeys respectively; these can be bought from métro stations, RTM kiosks and shops displaying the RTM sign. If you're likely to be hopping on and off public transport frequently, you might consider the good-value one-day *Carte Journée* (€5) or three-day *Carte 3 Jours* (€10.50). Tickets need to be punched in the machines on the bus, on tramway platforms or at métro gates. The métro runs Monday to Thursday 5am to 10.30pm, and until 12.30am at weekends. **Night buses** run out from the centre from 9.30pm to 12.30am, from rue des Fabres: pick up a timetable from the RTM office or métro sales points or check them online. Marseille also has a public **bike rental** scheme, *Le Vélo* (Ⓦwww.levelo-mpm.fr), with self-service cash card-operated hire points approximately every 300m throughout the city; you pay €1 for a one-week subscription, after which the first half hour is free, with each subsequent half hour costing €1.

Accommodation

Demand for accommodation in Marseille isn't as tied to the tourist season as in the coastal resorts, and finding a room in August is no more difficult than in November. **Hotels** are plentiful, with lots of reasonable two- and three-star options around the Vieux Port and on the streets running south from it; real

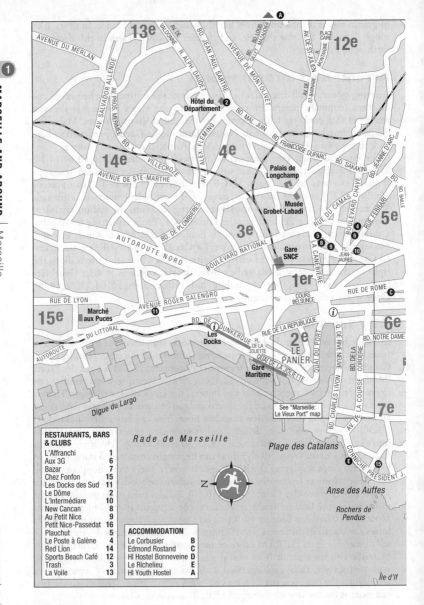

RESTAURANTS, BARS & CLUBS

L'Affranchi	1
Aux 3G	6
Bazar	7
Chez Fonfon	15
Les Docks des Sud	11
Le Dôme	2
L'Intermédiare	10
New Cancan	8
Au Petit Nice	9
Petit Nice-Passedat	16
Plauchut	5
Le Poste à Galène	4
Red Lion	14
Sports Beach Café	12
Trash	3
La Voile	13

ACCOMMODATION

Le Corbusier	B
Edmond Rostand	C
HI Hostel Bonneveine	D
Le Richelieu	E
HI Youth Hostel	A

budget bargains are rarer, while of late the number of more luxurious options has risen considerably. The simplest way to **reserve a room** is through the tourist office website. The cheapest options are the city's **youth hostels**, both quite a way from the centre.

Hotels are marked on the Vieux Port map (see pp.58–59) unless otherwise specified.

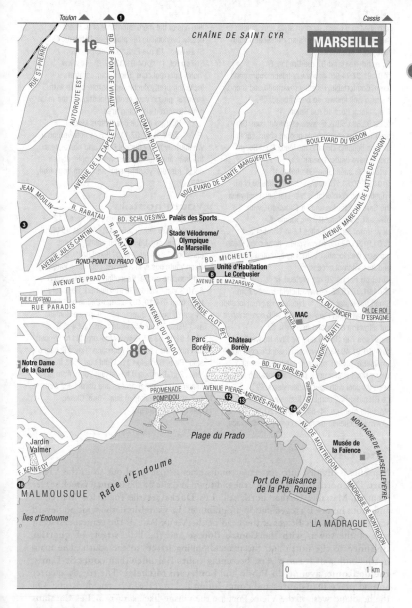

Hotels

Alizé 35 quai des Belges, 1er ☎04.91.33.66.97,
ⓦwww.alize-hotel.com. Comfortable, soundproofed
rooms with attractive modern decor and free wi-fi; the
more expensive ones look out onto the Vieux Port. ④

Bellevue 34 quai du Port, 2e ☎04.96.17.05.40,
ⓦwww.hotelbellevuemarseille.com. Boutique-style

hotel on the port with chic modern decor, a/c and
wi-fi, but no lift. ⑤

Le Corbusier Unité d'Habitation, 280 bd
Michelet, 8e (see Marseille map above)
☎04.91.16.78.00, ⓦwww.hotellecorbusier.com.
Stylish hotel on the third floor of the renowned
architect's iconic high-rise (see p.64). Rooms are

furnished in a clean, modern style sympathetic to the architecture and there's an excellent restaurant. Book in advance. ❸

Edmond-Rostand 31 rue Dragon, 6ᵉ ☎04.91.37.74.95, ⓦwww.hoteledmondrostand .com. Comfortable, recently revamped and friendly; it's also well known, so book ahead. ❹

Etap Vieux Port 46 rue Sainte, 1ᵉʳ ☎08.92.68.05.82, ⓦwww.etaphotel.com. Big branch of the comfortable budget chain, set in a historic building close to the Vieux Port. Some rooms have timber beams. ❸

Lutétia 38 allée Léon-Gambetta, 1ᵉʳ ☎04.91.50.81.78, ⓦwww.hotelmarseille.com. Friendly and comfortable two-star hotel between the Gare St Charles and La Canebière, with pleasant, soundproofed a/c rooms. ❹

New Hôtel Select 4 allée Léon-Gambetta, 1ᵉʳ ☎04.91.95.09.09, ⓦwww.new-hotel.com. Clean, modern, well located, with soundproofed a/c rooms and free internet access. ❹

Hôtel du Palais 26 rue Breteuil, 6ᵉ ☎04.91.37.78.86, ⓦwww.hotelmarseille.com. Smart three-star sister to *Lutétia*, in a great location a short walk from the Vieux Port, with conservative but attractive decor and free wi-fi. ❺

Radisson Blu 38–40 quai de Rive Neuve, 7ᵉ ☎04.91.91.49.93, ⓦwww.radissonblu.com/hotel -marseille. Stylish, primarily business-oriented luxury hotel with a great port-side location and an open-air pool with spectacular views. ❾

Le Richelieu 52 corniche Kennedy, 7ᵉ (see Marseille map, pp.54–55) ☎04.91.31.01.92, ⓦwww.lerichelieu-marseille.com. Friendly place,

and one of the more affordable of the corniche hotels, overlooking the plage des Catalans. ❹

St Ferréol 19 rue Pisançon, corner rue St-Ferréol, 1ᵉʳ ☎04.91.33.12.21, ⓦwww .hotel-stferreol.com. Three-star comforts including pretty decor and marble baths with jacuzzis, plus a very central location in the main pedestrianized shopping area. ❻

🏃 **Vertigo** 42 rue des Petites Maries, 1ᵉʳ ☎04.91.91.07.11, ⓦwww.hotelvertigo.fr. Wonderfully funky budget hotel and hostel near the train and bus stations, with simple, stylish decor, friendly, youthful staff and dorm beds from €25. ❸

Youth hostels

HI youth hostel 76 allée des Primevères, 12ᵉ (see Marseille map, pp.54–55) ☎04.91.49.06.18, ⓦwww.fuaj.org. Bus #8 from Centre Bourse (direction "St-Julien", stop "Bois Luzy"). Cheap, clean youth hostel in a former château a long way out from the centre. Reception 7.30am–noon & 5–10.30pm (until 11.30 in summer). Dormitory beds from €12.10. Closed mid-Dec to early Jan.

HI youth hostel Bonneveine impasse Bonfils, av J-Vidal, 8ᵉ (see Marseille map, pp.54–55) ☎04.91.17.63.30, ⓦwww.fuaj.org. Mᵒ rond-point du Prado, then bus #44 (direction "Roy d'Espagne", stop "Place Bonnefon") or night bus #583 from Vieux Port. Renovated hostel just 200m from the beach, with internet access and dorm beds from €17.40. Reception open 6am–1am. Closed mid-Dec to mid-Jan.

The City

Marseille is divided into sixteen arrondissements that spiral out from the **Vieux Port**. Due north lies **Le Panier**, the old town and site of the original Greek settlement of Massalia; further north still **Les Docks** are the focus for Marseille's ambitious inner-city regeneration programmes. **La Canebière**, the wide boulevard starting at quai des Belges at the head of the Vieux Port, is the central east-west axis of the town, with the **Centre Bourse** and the little streets of **quartier Belsunce** to the north and the main shopping streets to the south. The main north-south axis is **rue d'Aix**, becoming **cours Belsunce** then **cours St-Louis**, **rue de Rome**, **avenue du Prado** and **boulevard Michelet**. The trendy quarter around **place Jean-Jaurès** and **cours Julien** lies to the east of rue de Rome. On the headland west of the Vieux Port are the village-like *quartiers* of **Les Catalans** and **Malmousque** from where the **Corniche** heads south past the city's most favoured residential districts towards the beaches, bars and restaurants of the **Plage du Prado**.

The Vieux Port

The **Vieux Port** is, more or less, the ancient harbour basin, and the original inlet that the ancient Greeks sailed into, though nowadays its historic resonances are

▲ Vieux Port

drowned by traffic noise, which the sunglass-wearing idlers on the port-side café terraces affect to ignore. The morning **fish market** on the quai des Belges provides some natural Marseillais theatre; and the seafood restaurants on the **pedestrianized streets** between the southern quay and cours Estienne d'Orves ensure that the Vieux Port stays busy well into the evening.

Two fortresses guard the harbour entrance. St-Jean, on the northern side, dates from the Middle Ages when Marseille was an independent republic, and its imposing Tour Carré du Roy René is open for temporary exhibitions (Fri–Sun 1–7pm; free) pending completion of the new national **Musée des Civilisations d'Europe et de la Méditerranée**, which is scheduled to be open in time for 2013. The enlargement of the Fort St-Jean in 1660, and the construction of St-Nicolas fort on the south side of the port, represented the city's final defeat as a separate entity. Louis XIV ordered the new fort to keep an eye on Marseille after he had sent in an army, suppressed the city's council, fined it, arrested all opposition and, in an early example of rate-capping, set ludicrously low limits on Marseille's subsequent expenditure and borrowing. The Fort St-Nicolas is still a military installation today.

The best view of the Vieux Port is from the **Palais du Pharo**, built on the headland beyond Fort St-Nicolas by Emperor Napoléon III for his wife and now used as a conference centre. Its surrounding park (8am–9pm) hides an underground *mediathèque* and exhibition space. For a wider-angle view, head up to the city's highest point, **Notre-Dame-de-la-Garde**, on boulevard André-Aune (daily: summer 7am–8pm; winter 7am–7pm; bus #60), which tops the hill south of the harbour. Crowned by a monumental gold Madonna and Child and dating from the Second Empire, it's a monstrous riot of neo-Byzantine design and the most distinctive of Marseille's landmarks. Inside, model ships hang from the rafters while the paintings and drawings displayed are by turns kitsch, unintentionally comic and deeply moving, as they depict the shipwrecks, house fires and car crashes from which the virgin has supposedly rescued grateful believers. A World War I soldier's helmet pierced by a bullet hole is a prominent exhibit.

There are two small museums on the south side of the port which are worth checking out. The **Musée du Santon**, 47 rue Neuve Ste-Catherine (Tues–Sat

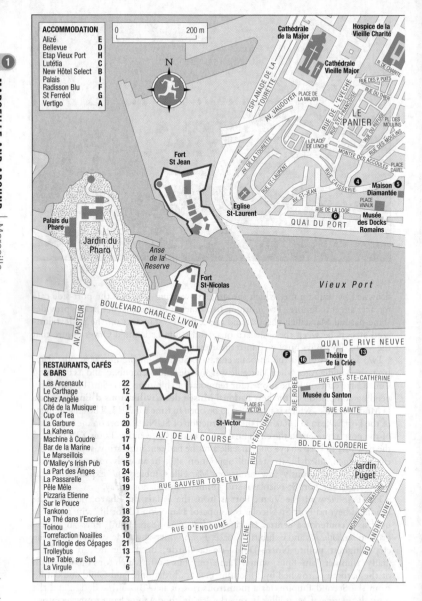

ACCOMMODATION

Alizé	E
Bellevue	D
Etap Vieux Port	H
Lutétia	C
New Hôtel Select	B
Palais	I
Radisson Blu	F
St Ferréol	G
Vertigo	A

0   200 m

N

Cathédrale de la Major

Hospice de la Vieille Charité

R. DE CHARITE

ESPLANADE DE LA TOURETTE

AV. VAUDOYER

RUE DES P. PUITS

Cathédrale Vieille Major

RUE DE L'EVECHE

PLACE DE LA MAJOR

RUE STE-FRANÇOISE

RUE DU THIER

LE PANIER

RUE DU REFUGE

PL. DES MOULINS

AV. DE LA TOURETTE

L.PLACE DE LENCHE

RUE DES MOULINS

MONTÉE DES ACCOULES

PLACE DAVIEL

Fort St Jean

RUE ST-LAURENT

RUE CAISSERIE

Maison Diamantée

Eglise St-Laurent

AV. ST-JEAN

PLACE VIVAULX

Palais du Pharo

RUE DE LA LOGE

QUAI DU PORT

Musée des Docks Romains

Jardin du Pharo

Anse de la Reserve

Fort St-Nicolas

Vieux Port

BOULEVARD CHARLES LIVON

AV. PASTEUR

QUAI DE RIVE NEUVE

Théâtre de la Criée

RUE NVE. STE-CATHERINE

Musée du Santon

RUE SAINTE

RUE ROBE

PLACE ST-VICTOR

St-Victor

AV. DE LA COURSE

BD. DE LA CORDERIE

Jardin Puget

RUE D'ENDOUME

RUE SAUVEUR TOBELEM

MONTÉE DE L'ORATOIRE

BD. ANDRE AUNE

BD. TELLENE

RUE D'ENDOUME

RESTAURANTS, CAFÉS & BARS

Les Arcenaulx	22
Le Carthage	12
Chez Angèle	4
Cité de la Musique	1
Cup of Tea	5
La Garbure	20
La Kahena	8
Machine à Coudre	17
Bar de la Marine	14
Le Marseillois	9
O'Malley's Irish Pub	15
La Part des Anges	24
La Passarelle	16
Pêle Mêle	19
Pizzaria Etienne	2
Sur le Pouce	3
Tankono	18
Le Thé dans l'Encrier	23
Toinou	11
Torrefaction Noailles	10
La Trilogie des Cépages	21
Trolleybus	13
Une Table, au Sud	7
La Virgule	6

10am–12.30pm & 2–6.30pm, also open Mon during Dec; free), is part of the Carbonel workshop, one of the most renowned producers of the crib figures for which Provence is famous. The **Maison de l'Artisanat et des Métiers d'Art**, 21 cours Estienne d'Orves (Tues–Fri 10am–noon & 1–6pm, Sat 1–6pm; free), hosts excellent temporary exhibitions of applied arts and crafts. Two doors away is the intellectual haunt of *Les Arcenaulx* (see p.66): a restaurant, *salon de thé* and bookshop.

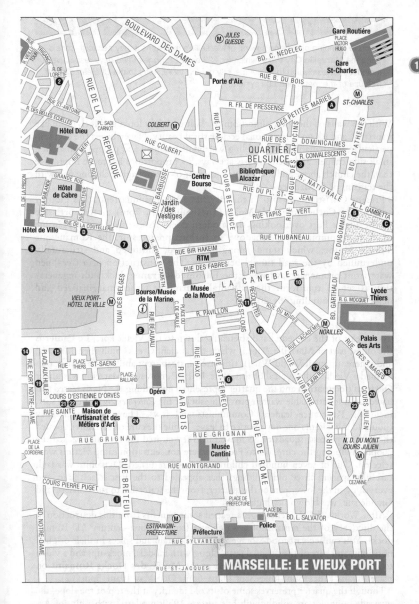

A short way inland from the Fort St-Nicolas, above the Bassin de Carénage and the slip road for the Vieux Port's tunnel, is Marseille's oldest church, the **Abbaye St-Victor** (daily 9am–7pm; €2 entry to crypt). Originally part of a monastery founded in the fifth century on the burial site of various martyrs, the church was built, enlarged and fortified – a vital requirement given its position outside the city walls – over a period of two hundred years from the middle of the tenth century.

> ## The Marseille City Pass
>
> If you're planning on visiting several of Marseille's museums it may be worth consid-
> ering the **Marseille City Pass**, which for €20 or €27 for one or two days respectively
> includes free admission to museums, city guided tours, entry to the Château d'If and
> free use of the métro and bus system.

With the walls of the choir almost 3m thick, it certainly looks and feels more like
a fortress, and it's no conventional ecclesiastical beauty. Nevertheless the crypt, in
particular, is fascinating: a crumbling warren of rounded and propped-up arches,
small side chapels and secretive passageways, its proportions are more impressive
than the church above and it contains a number of sarcophagi, including one with
the remains of St Maurice.

Present Christian worship in the city has as its headquarters a less gloomy
edifice. The **Cathédrale de la Major** (Tues–Sun 10am–7pm), on the north side
of the Vieux Port overlooking the modern docks, is a striped neo-Byzantine
block that completely overshadows its forlorn predecessor, the Romanesque
Vieille Major, which stands alongside, closed, shuttered and structurally
undermined by the road tunnel beneath it. The construction of a tree-lined
waterfront promenade as part of the **Euroméditerranée** docklands regeneration is set to transform the cathedral's currently rather marginalized and
neglected surroundings by 2011.

Le Panier
To the east of the cathedral and stretching down to the Vieux Port, **Le Panier** is
the oldest part of Marseille. This is where the ancient Greeks built their Massalia,
and where, up until World War II, tiny streets, steep steps and a jumble of houses
formed a Vieille Ville typical of this coast. In 1943, however, Marseille was under
German occupation and the quarter represented everything the Nazis feared and
hated, an uncontrollable warren providing shelter for *Untermenschen* of every sort,
including Resistance leaders, Communists and Jews. They gave the twenty
thousand inhabitants one day's notice to leave. While the curé of St-Laurent pealed
the bells in protest, squads of SS moved in; they cleared the area and packed the
people, including the curé, off to Fréjus, where concentration camp victims were
selected. Out of seven hundred children, only 68 returned. Dynamite was laid,
carefully sparing three old buildings that appealed to the Fascist aesthetic, and
everything in the lower part of the quarter, from the waterside to rue Caisserie and
Grande rue, was blown sky high.

After World War II, archeologists reaped some benefits from this destruction in
the discovery of the remains of a warehouse from the first-century AD Roman
docks. You can see vast food-storage jars for oil, grain and spices in their original
positions, and part of the original jetty, along with models, mock-ups and a video
to complete the picture, can be viewed at the **Musée des Docks Romains** on
place Vivaux (Tues–Sun: June–Sept 11am–6pm; Oct–May 10am–5pm; €2).

Though the quarter preserves some of its old identity at the top of the slope, the
quayside buildings are solidly built but austere 1950s modern, with a hint of Art
Deco in places. Amongst all this are the landmark structures that the Nazis spared:
the seventeenth-century **Hôtel de Ville** on the quay; the half-Gothic, half-
Renaissance **Hôtel de Cabre** on the corner of rue Bonneterie and Grande rue; and
the **Maison Diamantée** of 1620, so-called for the pointed shape of its facade
stonework, on rue de la Prison. This exceptionally beautiful building houses the
information bureau for Marseille's stint as European Capital of Culture 2013.

Overlooking the small **place Daviel** nearby is an impressive eighteenth-century bell tower, all that remains of the Église des Accoules, destroyed in 1794 as it had served as a meeting place for counter-revolutionaries after the French Revolution. To the north of here, above the place Daviel, is the vast nineteenth-century **Hôtel Dieu**, now a nursing college. At the junction of rue de la Prison and rue Caisserie, the steps of montée des Accoules lead up and across to **place de Lenche**, site of the Greek agora, a few blocks south of the cathedrals and a good café stop.

What's left of old Le Panier is above here, though the fifteen windmills of place des Moulins disappeared in the nineteenth century. If you climb rue du Réfuge you'll find yourself in a modern piazza, with new buildings in traditional styles, and an uninterrupted view of the refined **Hospice de la Vieille Charité** at the far end. This seventeenth-century workhouse, with a gorgeous Baroque chapel surrounded by handsome columned arcades in pink stone, is now a cultural centre, hosting some excellent temporary exhibitions and two museums, a café and a bookshop. The **Musée d'Archéologie Méditerranéenne** (Tues–Sun: June–Sept 11am–6pm; Oct–May 10am–5pm; €2, combined ticket for entire complex €4.50) contains some very beautiful fourth- and fifth-century BC pottery and glass, an Egyptian collection with mummies and their accompanying boxes for internal organs plus a mummified crocodile. It also displays fascinating finds from a Celto-Légurian settlement at Roquepertuse, between Marseille and Aix, including a double-headed statue. The other permanent collection is the **Musée des Arts Africains, Océaniens et Amérindiens** (same hours and prices as Musée d'Archéologie), which in addition to its sculptures and masks has a collection of dried heads.

Euroméditerranée and Les Docks

From the Vieille Charité it's a short walk along rue de Lorette and down a steep flight of steps to rue de la République, the formerly run-down nineteenth-century boulevard that leads north from the Vieux Port. The walk is a graphic illustration of the ambitious nature of the regeneration scheme known as **Euroméditerranée**, for the buildings along the entire length of the rue de la République are having their facades cleaned and the commercial premises on their lower floors refurbished and re-let, with many now housing stylish and upmarket boutiques. The avenue ends at place de la Joliette, from which the magnificently restored warehouses of **Les Docks** stretch towards a cluster of new tower blocks by star architects, including Zaha Hadid's sleek 33-storey **Tour French Line**. The sheer scale of the warehouses makes their conversion into an office complex impressive, with one long central corridor lined with restaurants and shops linking atria between the original buildings. Most animated at its southern end close to place de la Joliette, the complex is – unusually for Marseille – a little sterile in its further reaches; nevertheless, it's worth continuing as far as the **Centre d'Informations** (Mon–Fri 11.30am–6.30pm) to see what else is planned for this part of the city: among the most exciting projects is the conversion of a dockside grain silo into a new concert hall, due to open in 2011. One block to the south on boulevard des Dames, the delightful 1928 Art Deco building that once belonged to the **Compagnie Générale Transatlantique** – the celebrated French Line – is a reminder of the glamour that was once attached to sea travel, with murals depicting the old company's routes to North Africa, North and South America in the vestibule. The building is still occupied by shipping lines today.

La Canebière and around

La Canebière, the grandiose (if dilapidated) boulevard that runs for about 1 km east from the port, is Marseille's main street. Named after the hemp (*canabé*) that once grew here and provided the raw materials for the town's thriving rope-making

Marseille's Commune

Within the space of four years from its completion in 1867, the Marseille **Préfecture** had flown the imperial flag, the red flag and the tricolour. The red flag was flying in 1871, during Marseille's Commune. The counter-revolutionary forces advanced from Aubagne, encountering little resistance, and took the heights of Notre-Dame-de-la-Garde from where they directed their cannons down onto the Préfecture. The defeat was swifter but no less bloody than the fate of the Parisian Communards. One of the Marseillaise leaders, Gaston Crémieux, a young idealistic bourgeois with great charisma, escaped the initial carnage but was subsequently caught. Despite clemency pleas from all quarters of the city, Thiers, president of the newly formed Third Republic and a native of Marseille, would not relent and Crémieux was shot by a firing squad near the Palais du Pharo in November 1871.

trade, it was originally modelled on the Champs Elysées, though it's no pavement-café hotspot and its shops are – with one or two exceptions – fairly lacklustre nowadays. It is also home, at the port end, to two museums. The **Musée de la Marine et de l'Economie** (daily 10am–6pm; €2), on the ground floor of the Neoclassical stock exchange, contains a superb collection of model ships, including the legendary 1930s transatlantic liner *Normandie* and Marseille's very own prewar queen of the seas, the *Providence*. A bit further up at no. 11, the **Musée de la Mode** (Tues–Sun: June–Sept 11am–6pm; Oct–May 10am–5pm; €4) hosts temporary exhibitions on fashion-related themes.

Behind the stock exchange is the ugly **Centre Bourse** shopping centre and the **Jardin des Vestiges**, where the ancient port extended, curving northwards from the present quai des Belges. Excavations have revealed a stretch of the Greek port and bits of the city wall with the base of three square towers and a gateway, dated to the second or third century BC. The beautifully lit and spaced **Musée d'Histoire de Marseille**, inside the Centre Bourse (Mon–Sat noon–7pm; €2), shows the main finds of Marseillaise excavations, of which the most dramatic is a third-century AD wreck of a Roman trading vessel. There are models of the city, reconstructed boats, everyday items such as shoes and baskets, and a beautiful Roman mosaic of a dolphin, plus a great deal of information on text panels and a video about the Roman, Greek and pre-Greek settlements. Laws that were posted up in Greek Massalia are cited, forbidding women to drink wine and allowing would-be suicides to take hemlock if the 600-strong parliament agreed.

The **Bibliothèque Alcazar** on cours Belsunce is another of the regeneration projects gradually supplanting the dilapidated tenements north of La Canebière, its slick modernity softened by a Beaux-Arts portal that recalls the old Alcazar music hall where the likes of Tino Rossi and Yves Montand once performed. The continuation of cours Belsunce, rue d'Aix, stretches to **Porte d'Aix**, Marseille's Arc de Triomphe, modelled on the ancient Roman arch at Orange. This was part of the city's grandiose mid-nineteenth-century expansion which included the Cathédrale de la Major and the Joliette docks, paid for with the profits of military enterprise, most significantly the conquest of Algeria in 1830. Today it's a popular meeting place for north African men, as is the **quartier Belsunce** to the east. Bordered by cours Belsunce/rue d'Aix, boulevard d'Athènes and St-Charles, this dynamic district is home to hundreds of tiny shops selling north African food, music, household goods and cheap sportswear. There's a smaller north African market (Mon–Sat 8am–7pm) around the lively **Marché des Capucins** by the Noailles métro and tram station, with spectacular displays of fresh fruit, vegetables, meat and fish. The streets around here are pretty seedy, with plenty of insalubrious hotels and, come nightfall, prostitutes on every corner, particularly along the handsome rue Sénac de Meilhan.

The prime shopping quarter of Marseille centres around three streets running south from La Canebière: rue de Rome, rue Paradis and rue St-Ferréol, which terminates at the pseudo-Renaissance **Préfecture**, where demonstrations in the city traditionally converge. The streets are lined with chic designer boutiques, and there's a scattering of cafés and patisseries.

Between rue St-Ferréol and rue Paradis, on rue Grignan, is the city's most important art museum, the **Musée Cantini** (Tues–Sun: June–Sept 11am–6pm; Oct–May 10am–5pm; €3, more during temporary exhibitions), housing paintings and sculptures dating from the end of the nineteenth century up to the 1950s. The Fauvists and Surrealists are well represented along with works by Matisse, Léger, Picasso, Ernst, Le Corbusier, Miró and Giacometti. Only a proportion of the permanent collection is displayed at any one time, and it may not be visible at all during some of the excellent temporary exhibitions.

East of rue de Rome, the streets around **cours Julien** are full of bars and music shops, and the *cours* itself, with its pools, fountains, restaurant tables and enticing boutiques, is populated by Marseille's bohemian crowd and its diverse immigrant community. By day this is one of the most pleasant places to idle in the city, though almost every surface is buried under graffiti; the atmosphere at night can be a little edgy, particularly around the métro station. Madame Zaza of Marseille, an original and affordable Marseillaise couturier, is one of a number that has a shop here (at no. 73); there are also bookshops and art galleries to browse in, plus stamp and secondhand book markets, with antiques and junk every second Sunday (see p.69). The **daily market**, known as **La Plaine**, on place Jean-Jaurès, supplements its food stalls with cheap shoes and clothes on Saturdays and with flowers on Wednesdays. Between cours Julien and place Jean-Jaurès at 1 place Carli, the **Fondation Regards de Provence** (daily 10am–6pm; €4.50) mounts excellent temporary exhibitions of painting and sculpture on themes related to Marseille and Provence in the grandiose setting of the Palais des Arts.

Palais de Longchamp and around

The **Palais de Longchamp**, 2km inland from the port (bus #8 from La Canebière, or métro Longchamp-Cinq-Avenues), was completed in 1869, the year the Suez Canal opened, bringing a new boom for Marseillaise trade. It was built as the grandiose conclusion of an aqueduct at Roquefavour (no longer in use) bringing water from the Durance to the city. Water is still pumped into the centre of the colonnade connecting the two palatial wings of the building. Below, an enormous statue looks as if it's honouring some great feminist victory: three well-muscled women stand above four bulls wallowing in a pool from which a cascade drops the four or five storeys to ground level.

The palace's north wing houses the **Musée des Beaux-Arts**, whose collection embraces Italian, French and Flemish old masters, including works by Rubens and Jordaens, and nineteenth-century French art, with works by Corot and Signac. It's currently closed for refurbishment, and is scheduled to reopen in 2012. The palace's other wing is taken up with the **Musée d'Histoire Naturelle** (Tues–Sun 10am–5pm; €4) and its collection of mouldy stuffed animals and lots of fossils. Opposite the palace, at 140 boulevard Longchamp, is the **Musée Grobet-Labadi** (Tues–Sun: June–Sept 11am–6pm; Oct–May 10am–5pm; €2), an elegant late nineteenth-century bourgeois town house filled with exquisite tapestries, paintings and *objets d'art*.

About 1km northeast of the palace, at the end of boulevard Mal-Juin, stands the futuristic **Hôtel du Département** (métro St-Just; guided visits by appointment, Mon–Fri 9.30am & 2.30pm; ☏04.91.21.29.77). Deliberately sited in the run-down St-Just-Chartreux *quartier*, the new seat of government for the Bouches-du-Rhône *département* was the biggest public building to be built in the French provinces in the twentieth century, designed by English architect Will Alsop in characteristically expressive style. In front of the Hôtel stands the **Dôme**, a venue for shows and exhibitions.

South of the centre: Parc Chanot, Unité d'Habitation, MAC and Parc Borély

Avenue du Prado, the continuation of rue de Rome, is an eight-lane highway, with impressive fountains and one of the city's biggest **daily markets** between métros Castellane and Périer. At the rond-point du Prado, the avenue turns west to meet the corniche road.

The city's north-south axis continues as boulevard Michelet past **Parc Chanot**, home to Olympique de Marseille's ground. OM's reputation for occasional brilliance means that home matches are almost always sold out, but tickets may be available online from the team's website (Ⓦ www.om.net). At the far side of the stadium on rue Raymond-Teisseire, the vast **Palais des Sports** hosts boxing matches, tennis, showjumping and other spectacles.

Beyond Parc Chanot, set back from the west side of the boulevard, is a mould-breaking piece of architecture, Le Corbusier's **Unité d'Habitation**, designed in 1946 and completed in 1952. A seventeen-storey housing complex on stilts, the Unité was the prototype for thousands of apartment buildings the world over, though close up the difference in quality between this – the *couture* original – and the industrially produced imitations becomes apparent. Confounding expectations, this concrete modernist structure is extremely complex, with 23 different apartment layouts, to suit single people and varying sized families: the larger apartments are split across two floors with balconies on both sides of the building, giving unhindered views of mountains and sea. It's a remarkably happy place; many of the original tenants are still in residence, and people chat and smile in the lobby. At ground level the building is decorated with Corbusier's famous human figure, the Modulor, while on the third floor is a small café-bar with a terrace and superlative Mediterranean views, and a hotel (see p.55). The iconic, sculptural rooftop recreational area is probably the highlight, and it's here that Le Corbusier's infatuation with ocean liners seems most obvious. Some parts of the roof are not open to visitors, but a stroll around the running track is essential. To reach the Unité take the métro to rond-point du Prado, then bus #21 (direction "Luminy").

Further south, at 69 avenue d'Haïfa (bus #23 or #45 from métro rond-point du Prado; stop "Haïfa" or "Marie-Louise"), is the contemporary art museum, **MAC** (Tues–Sun: June–Sept 11am–6pm; Oct–May 10am–5pm; €4). The permanent collection, displayed in perfect, pure-white surroundings, is the continuation of the Cantini collection, with works from the 1960s to the present. The artists include the Marseillais César and Ben, along with Buren, Christo, Klein, Niki de St-Phalle, Tinguely and Warhol. Between avenue d'Haïfa and the sea, just off avenue Prado, is **Parc Borély** (daily 6am–9pm; free), with ponds, palm trees, a rose garden, botanical gardens (Tues–Sun 10am–5pm, 6pm in summer; €3) and no restrictions about walking or picnicking on the grass. It was originally the grounds of the Château Borély, an eighteenth-century mansion that once hosted temporary art exhibitions and is now slated for conversion into a museum of decorative arts.

The corniche and south to Les Goudes

The most popular stretch of sand close to the city centre is the small Plage des Catalans, a few blocks south of the Palais du Pharo. This marks the beginning of

Marseille's **corniche Président J.F. Kennedy**, initiated and partly built after the 1848 revolution, and currently being doubled in width by extending it out over the sea. Despite its inland bypass of the Malmousque peninsula, it's a corniche as good as any on the Riviera, with *belle époque* villas on the slopes above, the Îles d'Endoume and the Château d'If in the distance, cliffs below and high bridge piers for the road to cross the inlets of La Fausse-Monnaie and Les Auffes. Here, the Monument aux Morts de l'Armée d'Orient frames its statue against the setting sun, while further along the corniche, a modernist memorial commemorates the *pieds noirs* who returned from North Africa.

Prior to 1948, Malmousque and the **Vallon des Auffes** were inaccessible from the town unless you followed the "customs men's path" over the rocks or took a boat. There was nothing on Malmousque, but the Vallon des Auffes had a freshwater source and a small community of fishermen and rope-makers. Amazingly, it is not much different today, with fishing boats pulled up around the rocks, tiny jumbled houses and restaurants serving the catch. Only one road, rue du Vallon-des-Auffes, leads out; otherwise it's the long flights of steps up to the corniche.

Malmousque is now a very desirable residential district, favoured by the champagne-socialist set, and home to Marseille's most distinguished hotel-restaurant, *Le Petit Nice-Passedat*. Behind La Fausse-Monnaie inlet, a path leads to the Théâtre Silvain, an open-air theatre set in a wilderness of trees and flowers. There's more greenery, of a formal nature, a short way further along the corniche in the **Jardin Valmer** (bus #83; stop "Corniche J-Martin"), and you can explore the tiny streets that lead up into this prime district of mansions with high-walled gardens.

The corniche J-F-Kennedy ends at the **Plage du Prado**, the city's main sand beach backed by a wide strip of lawns and overlooked by the Ecale Borély complex of bars and restaurants, best visited at night when it is one of the liveliest night spots in town. The promenade continues all the way to Montredon. Set in a huge park that extends to the foot of the Montagne de Marseilleveyre is the **Musée de la Faïence** (Tues–Sun: June–Sept 11am–6pm; Oct–May 10am–5pm; €2), in the elegant nineteenth-century Château Pastré, 157 avenue de Montredon (bus #19 from métro rond-point du Prado; stop "Montredon-Chancel"). The eighteenth- and nineteenth-century ceramics, many of them produced in Marseille, are of an exceptionally high standard (look out for the vibrant productions of Théodore Deck), but there's also a small collection of novel modern pieces.

From Montredon to Les Goudes, where the gleaming white, beautifully desolate hills finally meet the sea and the coast road ends, there are easily accessible *calanques* (rocky inlets) that face the setting sun, ideal for evening swims and supper picnics. If you prefer to walk, the GR98 to Cassis starts from the top of avenue de la Grotte-Roland, off avenue de Montredon a short way beyond the Pastré park. It splits into the 98a which follows the ridge inland and 98b which descends to the sea at Callelongue, the last outpost of Les Goudes. Here, amid the rocky wilderness, is the improbable site of *La Grotte*, 1 rue des Pébrons (☎04.91.73.17.99), nowadays a rather fancy restaurant.

The islands

Blacker than the sea, blacker than the sky, rose like a phantom the giant of granite, whose projecting crags seemed like arms extended to seize their prey.

So the **Château d'If** (Tues–Sun: May to early Oct 9.30am–6pm; early Oct–April 9.30am–5.30pm; €5) appears to Edmond Dantès, hero of Alexandre Dumas' *The*

Count of Monte Cristo, having made his watery escape after five years of incarceration as the innocent victim of treachery. In reality, most prisoners of this island fortress died before they reached the end of their sentences – unless they were nobles living in the less fetid upper-storey cells, such as one de Niozelles who was given six years for failing to take his hat off in the presence of Louis XIV; and Mirabeau, who had run up massive debts with shops in Aix. More often, the crimes were political. After the revocation of the Edict of Nantes in 1685, thousands of Marseillais Protestants, who refused to accept the new law, were sent to the galleys and their leaders entombed in the Château d'If. Revolutionaries of 1848 drew their last breath here.

Apart from the castle, there's not much else to the Île d'If; it's little more than a rock that you can swim off, with a small snack bar. Dumas fans will love it, others may raise an eyebrow at the cell marked "Dantès" in the same fashion as non-fictional inmates' names. However you find it, it's a horribly well-preserved sixteenth-century edifice and the views back towards Marseille are wonderful.

Boats leave from the quai des Belges from 9am onwards (up to two per hour in summer; seven daily in winter; €10), with the last boat back timed to coincide with the château's closing time; the journey takes twenty minutes. Alternatively, you can do a round-trip taking in the other two islands of the Frioul archipelago, **Pomègues** and **Ratonneau** (€15), which are joined by a causeway enclosing a yachting harbour. In days gone by these islands were used as a quarantine station, most ineffectually in the early 1720s when a ship carrying the plague was given the go-ahead to dock in the city, resulting in the decimation of the population.

Eating and drinking

Fish and seafood are the main ingredients of the Marseillais diet, and the superstar of dishes is the city's own invention, **bouillabaisse**, a saffron- and garlic-flavoured fish soup with croûtons and *rouille* to throw in. There are conflicting theories about which fish should be included and where and how they must be caught, though it's generally agreed that *rascasse* is essential. The other city speciality is *pieds et paquets*, mutton or lamb belly and trotters.

The best, and most expensive, **restaurants** are close to the corniche, though for international choice the trendy cours Julien is the place to head, while rue Sainte is good for smart and fashionable dining close to the opera and Vieux Port. The pedestrian precinct behind the south quay of the Vieux Port is more tourist-oriented and fishy, while Le Panier has a few tiny, inexpensive **bistros**.

Unless otherwise stated, the places listed below are marked on the Vieux Port map, pp.58–59.

Cafés

Le Carthage 8 rue d'Aubagne, 1ᵉʳ. Diminutive *salon de thé* close to the Marché des Capucins, with the best Tunisian patisseries and Turkish delight in town.
Cup of Tea 1 rue Caisserie, 2ᵉʳ. Delightful Le Panier bookshop and *salon de thé* serving pastries, quiches and salads with iced tea on a shady terrace.
Plauchut 168 La Canebière, 1ᵉʳ. Excellent *patissier-chocolatier-glacier* and *salon de thé*, established in 1820; the seating migrates to a street-front terrace in summer when the very pretty interior gets too hot.
Le Thé dans l'Encrier 52 cours Julien, 6ᵉʳ ☎09.53.51.43.43. Delightfully laid-back restaurant, *glacier* and *salon de thé* where arty photography fills the walls and plump divans spill onto the street outside. Closed Mon.
Torrefaction Noailles 56 la Canebière, 1ᵉʳ. Celebrated confectioner and café, with high stools, a wonderful aroma of fresh ground coffee and plenty of nougat, *calissons*, candied fruits and caramels to take away afterwards. Closed Sun.

Restaurants

Les Arcenaulx 25 cours d'Estienne-d'Orves, 1ᵉʳ ☎04.91.59.80.30, ⓦwww .jeanne-laffitte.com. Lovely, atmospheric intellectual haunt that's also a bookshop; the €18 lunch menu is good value, otherwise there's a *menu découverte* at €57. The adjacent *salon de thé* offers excellent lunch specials.

Chez Angèle 50 rue Caisserie, 2ᵉʳ ☎04.91.90.63.35. Packed Le Panier local, dishing up fresh pasta and pizza. Closed lunchtimes Sat & Sun.

Chez Fonfon 140 Vallon des Auffes, 7ᵉʳ (see Marseille map, pp.54–55) ☎04.91.52.14.38, ⓦ www.chez-fonfon.com. There's no debate about the quality of the *bouillabaisse* ingredients here, for this chic restaurant overlooking a small fishing harbour is one of an elite band of restaurants guarding the true recipe of the dish. Expect to pay €46. Closed Sun, Mon lunch (all day Mon in winter).

La Garbure 9 cours Julien, 6ᵉʳ ☎04.91.47.18.01, ⓦ www.la-garbure.fr. Rich specialities from southwest France, including *cassoulet* and *magret de canard*. Menus around €26. Closed Sat lunch, & Sun.

La Kahena 2 rue de la République, 2ᵉʳ ☎04.91.90.61.93. Popular Tunisian restaurant near the Vieux Port, with grills and couscous from €9. Open daily.

Le Marseillois quai du Port, 2ᵉʳ ☎04.91.90.72.52, ⓦ www.lemarseillois.com. Set on the deck of an old sailing vessel in the Vieux Port, with lots of fish and seafood on the €26 *prix-fixe* menu. Closed Sun and Mon.

La Part des Anges 33 rue Sainte, 1ᵉʳ ☎04.91.33.55.70, ⓦ www.lapartdesanges.com. Wonderful *cave de vins*, with a chalked-up menu of hearty, reasonably priced daily specials to mop up the classy alcohol. Closed Sun.

La Passarelle 52 rue du Plan Fourmiguier, 7ᵉʳ ☎06.68.62.77.87. Wonderfully rustic and informal, tucked behind La Criée theatre and with mismatched furniture and seasonal Mediterranean food. Mains around €15.

Petit Nice-Passedat Anse de Maldormé, Corniche J.F. Kennedy, 7ᵉʳ (see Marseille map, pp.54–55) ☎04.91.59.25.92, ⓦ www.passedat.fr. Gerald Passedat's gorgeous hotel-restaurant on the Corniche is the undisputed pinnacle of fine dining in Marseille, with three Michelin stars and highly inventive, seafood-based menus from €85 to €230.

Pizzaria Étienne 43 rue la Lorette, 2ᵉʳ; no phone. An old-fashioned Le Panier pizzeria; hectic, cramped and crowded. Pizzas from €8; grilled meats from €14.

Sur le Pouce 2 rue des Convalescents, 1ᵉʳ. Inexpensive Tunisian restaurant in the *quartier* Belsunce, with couscous from €5.

Une Table, au Sud 2 quai du Port, 2ᵉʳ ☎04.91.90.63.53, ⓦ www.unetableausud.com. Stylish *restaurant gastronomique* overlooking the Vieux Port; chef Lionel Lévy's contemporary take on Provençal cooking includes his famous *bouillabaisse*

milkshake. Lunch €33, otherwise menus at €47 and €74.

Toinou 3 cours St-Louis, 1ᵉʳ ☎04.91.54.08.79, ⓦ www.toinou.com. Just off La Canebière, with spectacular displays of fresh seafood including live crab and lobster; *moules-frites* from around €11. Open daily.

🍴 **La Trilogie des Cépages** 35 rue de la Paix, 1ᵉʳ ☎04.91.33.96.03. A truly vast selection of wines accompanies the *cuisine gastronomique* at this popular, classy restaurant close to the Vieux Port. Lunch menu €22, dinner menus from €27.

La Virgule 27 rue de la Loge, 2ᵉʳ ☎04.91.90.91.11, ⓦ www.lavirgule.marseille .free.fr. Lionel Lévy's funky but affordable brasserie offers the likes of octopus salad or salmon tartare with lime and ginger; set lunch €19; evening menu €25.

Bars

Aux 3G 3 rue St-Pierre, 5ᵉʳ (see Marseille map, pp.54–55). Marseille's most popular lesbian bar, regularly packed to the rafters at weekends when it's open until 2am.

O'Malley's Irish Pub 9 quai du Rive Neuve, 1ᵉʳ. A wildly popular Vieux Port boozer with the usual "Irish" trimmings plus, of course, Beamish and Guinness.

Bar de la Marine 15 quai Rive-Neuve, 1ᵉʳ. A favourite bar for Vieux Port lounging, and inspiration for Pagnol's celebrated Marseille trilogy (see p.415).

Au Petit Nice 26 place Jean-Jaurès, 1ᵉʳ (see Marseille map, pp.54–55). The place to head for on Saturday morning during the market, with an interesting selection of beers. Open Fri and Sat until 2am.

Red Lion 231 av Pierre-Mendès-France, 8ᵉʳ (see Marseille map, pp.54–55). Large, raucous British-style pub close to Plage Borély, with a big selection of beers and whiskies. Open until 4am Fri & Sat.

Sports Beach Café 138 av Pierre-Mendès-France, 8ᵉʳ (see Marseille map, pp.54–55). Open-air bar, terrace and Cuban restaurant by the sea, with a swimming pool and a soundtrack that ranges from salsa to reggae and rock. Open for lunch and dinner, but it fills up fast on weekend nights.

Trash 28 rue du Berceau, 5ᵉʳ (see Marseille map, pp.54–55). Slick, cruisy gay men's bar with DJ, live entertainment and plenty of dark corners. Open until 2am weekdays, later at weekends; closed Tues.

La Voile 148 av Pierre-Mendès-France, 8ᵉʳ (see Marseille map, pp.54–55). Spacious, stylish brasserie and cocktail bar by the sea in the Escale Borély complex, with a big terrace, DJs and a rather club-like ambience. Open daily until 2am.

Nightlife and entertainment

Marseille's **nightlife** has something for everyone, with plenty of live rock and jazz, nightclubs and discos, as well as theatre, opera and classical concerts. Theatre is particularly innovative and lively in Marseille. The Virgin Megastore at 75 rue St-Ferréol, the book and record shop FNAC on the top floor of the Centre Bourse and the tourist office's ticket bureau are the best places to go for **tickets** and **information** on gigs, concerts, theatre, free films and cultural events. Virgin also stocks a wide selection of English books and runs a café on the top floor, open, like the rest of the store, Monday to Saturday until 8.30pm and on Sundays until 8pm. There is a free weekly **listings** mag *Ventilo*, and a monthly, *César*, both of which you can pick up from FNAC, Virgin, tourist offices, museums and cultural centres.

Live music and nightclubs

Unless otherwise stated, the places listed below are marked on the Vieux Port map, pp.58–59.

L'Affranchi 212 bd de St Marcel, 11ᵉʳ ☎04.91.35.09.19, ☻www.l-affranchi.com. Venue in the eastern suburbs with a varied programme of clubs and live gigs, including rai, hip-hop and reggae. Open from 8.30pm when concerts are on (mostly Fri or Sat).

Bazar 90 bd Rabatau, 8ᵉʳ ☎04.91.79.08.88, ☻www.lebazarclub.fr. Big, expensive mainstream disco playing house and occasionally hosting big-name international DJs. Open Fri–Sun.

Cité de la Musique 4 rue Bernard du Bois, 1ᵉʳ ☎04.91.39.28.28, ☻www.citemusique-marseille .com. Live venue with a jazz cellar and an auditorium staging jazz, classical & contemporary concerts.

Les Docks des Suds 12 rue Urbain V, 3ᵉʳ (see Marseille map, pp.54–55) ☎04.91.99.00.00. Vast warehouse that serves as the venue for Marseille's annual Fiesta des Suds world music festival. Opening hours vary according to the event.

Le Dôme 48 av de St-Just, 4ᵉʳ ☎04.91.12.21.21 (see Marseille map, pp.54–55). Marseille's large-capacity live venue, hosting big-name and tame middle-of-the-road acts.

L'Intermédiaire 63 place Jean-Jaurès, 6ᵉʳ (see Marseille map, pp.54–55) ☎04.91.47.01.25. Loud, hip bar with a variety of live bands and DJ nights, from rock to hip-hop and world music. Open daily 6pm–2am.

Machine à Coudre 6 rue Jean-Roque, 1ᵉʳ ☎04.91.55.62.65, ☻www.lamachineacoudre .com. Music café hosting alternative rock, pop and reggae acts. €4–7 entry charge depending on act. Open from 9 or 10pm, depending on the event.

New Cancan 3 rue Sénac, 1ᵉʳ ☎04.91.48.59.76, ☻www.newcancan.com. Cheesy, dated and expensive, but nevertheless Marseille's best-known and longest-running gay disco. Open Thurs–Sun 11pm–dawn.

Pêle Mêle 8 place aux Huiles, 1ᵉʳ ☎04.91.54.85.26. Intimate, smart and lively jazz bistro and piano bar. Open Tues–Sat 5pm–2am.

Le Poste à Galène 103 rue Ferrari, 5ᵉʳ ☎04.91.47.57.99, ☻www.leposteagalene.com. Live pop, rock and electro plus eighties nights and a bar. Opens 8pm, 9pm or 9.30pm, depending on the event.

Tankono 9 rue des Trois Mages, 1ᵉʳ ☎06.43.21.54.29, ☻tankono.online.fr. Small performance space between cours Julien and place Jean-Jaurès, presenting world music and theatre with a strong focus on Africa and Asia. Live music events generally start at 8.30pm.

Trolleybus 24 quai de Rive-Neuve, 7ᵉʳ ☎04.91.54.30.45, ☻www.letrolley.com. Disco in a series of vaulted rooms; house, pop, electro, hip-hop and techno. Closed Sun–Tues.

Film, opera, theatre and concerts

Alhambra 2 rue du Cinéma, 16ᵉʳ ☎04.91.03.84.66. Art-house cinema occasionally showing undubbed English-language films (*v.o.*).

Ballet National de Marseille 20 bd Gabès, 8ᵉʳ ☎04.91.32.72.72. The home base of the famous dance company, founded in 1972 by Roland Petit, with occasional open studio sessions.

Creuset des Arts 21 rue Pagliano, 4ᵉʳ ☎04.91.06.57.02. Comedy and live music venue.

Espace Julien 39 cours Julien, 6ᵉʳ ☎04.91.24.34.10. A mixed-bag arts centre, with a programme that embraces comedy, hip-hop, chanson, variety and world music.

La Friche la Belle de Mai 41 rue Jobin, 3ᵉʳ ☎04.95.04.95.04. Interdisciplinary arts complex occupying a former industrial site in the north of the city, hosting theatre, dance, live music and arts exhibitions.

Odéon 162 La Canebière, 1ᵉʳ ☎04.96.12.52.70. Marseille's municipal theatre, with a repertoire that embraces both serious drama and operetta.

Opéra 2 rue Molière, 1er ℡04.91.55.11.10.
Symphony concerts and operas in a magnificent
setting, part Neoclassical, part Art Deco.
Théâtre de Lenche 4 place de Lenche, 2er
℡04.91.91.52.22. Everything from dance to
cabaret and drama is showcased at this Le Panier
theatre.
Théâtre Massalia La Friche la Belle de Mai, 3er
℡04.95.04.95.70. Lively puppet theatre with

changing programme of adult (evening) and
children's (matinee) shows.
Théâtre National la Criée 30 quai de Rive-Neuve,
7er ℡04.91.54.70.54. Home of the Théâtre
National de Marseille, and the city's best theatre.
Variétés 37 rue Vincent-Scotto, 1er
℡08.92.68.05.97. Cinema showing the odd
undubbed English-language film (*v.o.*).

Markets and shops

The city's copious **street markets** provide a feast of fruit and veg, olives, cheeses,
sausages and spit-roast chickens – everything you'd need for a picnic except for
wine, which is most economically bought at supermarkets. The markets are also
good for cheap clothes. La Plaine and avenue du Prado are the biggest; the
Capucins the oldest.

Marseille's Sunday flea market, **Marché aux Puces**, is a brilliant spectacle and
good for serious haggling. There's a relaxed atmosphere, plenty of cafés, and
everything and anything for sale, including very cheap fruit and veg.

Markets

Capucins place des Capucins, 1er; M° Noailles.
Fish, fruit and veg. Mon–Sat 8am–7pm.
Cours Julien 6er; M° N.D. du Mont Cours Julien.
Food Mon–Sat 8am–1pm; stamps Sun 8am–1pm;
antiquarian books second Sat of month 8am–1pm;

organic produce Wed 8am–1pm; flowers Wed
8am–1pm; secondhand goods second Sun of the
month 8am–7pm.

Marché aux Puces av du Cap-Pinède, 15er; bus
#35 from the Vieux Port (stop "Cap-Pinède") or
bus #36 or #70 from M° Bougainville (stop

▲ Marseille fish market

"Lyon"). Food Wed–Sun 8am–1pm; antiques Fri–Sun 9am–7pm; bric-a-brac Sat; flea market Sun 9am–7pm.

Place Carli 1er; M° Noailles. Antiquarian books and records. Mon–Sat all day.

La Plaine place Jean-Jaurès, 5er; M° N.D.du Mont Cours Julien. Food Mon–Sat 8am–1pm; bric-a-brac Tues, Thurs & Sat 8am–1pm; flowers Wed 8am–1pm.

Prado av du Prado, 6er; M° Castellane and Périer. Fruit, veg, fish and general food produce daily 8am–1pm; flowers Thurs 8am–1pm.

Quai des Belges Vieux Port, 1er; M° Vieux Port. Fish sold straight off the boats. Daily 8am–1pm.

Shops

La Compagnie de Provence 18 rue Francis Davso, 1er, and 1 rue Caisserie, 2er. Authentic Marseille soaps and upmarket toiletries.

Four des Navettes 136 rue Sainte, 7er. Marseille's oldest bakery is famous for its delicious, subtly orange-scented *navette* biscuits.

La Maison du Pastis 108 quai du Port, 2er. There are 95 varieties of *pastis* and absinthe on sale in this store, right on the Vieux Port.

Place aux Huiles 2 place Daviel, 2er. Taste the oils before you buy them at this Le Panier shop, which is an Aladdin's cave for lovers of olive oil, tapenade, *anchoïade* and other edible treats. Open daily.

Listings

Airlines Air France 14 La Canebière, 1er ☎04.91.39.39.90; Cathay Pacific 41 La Canebière, 1er ☎04.91.91.14.69.

Bike hire Cycles Ulysse, 3 av du Parc Borély ☎04.91.77.14.51; Tandem, 16 av du Parc Borély ☎04.91.22.64.80.

Bookshops Virgin, 75 rue St-Ferréol, 1er, and FNAC in the Centre Bourse have English books sections.

Bus, tram and métro information ☎04.91.91.92.10.

Car parks cours Estienne-d'Orves, 1er; rue Breteuil, 6e; Centre Bourse, 1er; place Géneral-de-Gaulle, 1er; place Jean-Jaurès 5er.

Car rental Avis, Gare St-Charles ☎08.20.61.16.36; National Citer, Square Narvik, 1er ☎04.91.05.90.86; Europcar, Square Narvik, 1er ☎04.91.64.13.22; Hertz, Square Narvik, 1er ☎04.91.05.51.20. All also have head offices at the airport.

Consulates Britain, 24 av du Prado, 6er ☎04.91.15.72.10; US, place Varian-Fry/12 bd Paul-Peytral, 6er ☎04.91.54.92.00.

Emergencies Ambulance ☎15; SOS Médecins ☎04.91.52.91.52; SOS Voyageurs, Gare St-Charles, 3er ☎04.91.62.12.80.

Ferries SNCM, 61 bd des Dames ☎03260, ⓦwww.sncm.fr. Runs ferries to Corsica, Tunisia and Algeria.

Internet *Info-Café* 1 quai du Rive Neuve, 1er ☎04.91.33.74.98.

Lost property 41 bd de Briançon, 3er ☎04.91.14.68.97 (Mon–Fri 8am–2pm).

Pharmacy 7 rue de la République, 2er ☎04.91.90.32.27 (English speaking); 7 quai du Port, 2er ☎04.91.91.63.10 (open daily).

Police Commissariat Centrale, 2 rue Antoine-Becker, 2er (24 hr; ☎04.91.39.80.00).

Post office 1 place de l'Hôtel-des-Postes, 1er.

Taxis Taxi Radio Marseille ☎04.91.02.20.20; Taxi Blanc Bleu ☎04.91.51.50.00; Taxi Plus ☎04.91.03.60.03; Taxi Radio Tupp ☎04.91.05.80.80.

Train information ☎3635.

L'Estaque and Carry-le-Rouet

Marseille's docks finally end at **L'ESTAQUE**, an erstwhile fishing village much loved by painters in the nineteenth century, and easy to get to by train (13min on Miramas train). It was no rural paradise even in 1867, as a gouache by Cézanne of the factory chimneys of L'Estaque shows (originally given to Madame Zola and now exhibited in his studio in Aix). Yet it still has fishing boats moored alongside yachts, lovely old villas and a short but engrossing walk along an art-themed trail marked with bilingual plaques – pick up a free map from the tourist office at 122 place de l'Estaque (July–Sept Wed–Sun 10am–5pm; ☎04.91.13.89.00). The very pleasant artificial beaches to the west ensure that L'Estaque remains a popular escape from the city. The simple terrace restaurant *L'Hippocampe* on the coast road a little west of the village

(☎04.91.03.83.78; closed Sun eve) is the place to go for a fish **dinner**, or if you simply want a **snack**, the local *chichis* (hot, doughnut-like confections) from the kiosks alongside the main road are delicious.

Between L'Estaque and Carry-le-Rouet, the hills of the **Chaîne de l'Estaque** come right down to the coast, a gorgeous wilderness of white rock, pines and brilliant yellow scented broom. The shore is studded with picturesque little *calanques* where the real estate is exceptionally desirable and the water exceptionally clean; you can look across the roadstead of Marseille to the islands and the entrance of the Vieux Port. At weekends in summer, road access to these *calanques* is strictly limited and you may have to park some distance from the sea. The train tunnels its way above the shore while the main road, the D568, then D5, takes an inland route through **La Rove** and **Ensues-la-Redonne**, with smaller roads looping down to the fishing villages and summer holiday homes of **Niolon**, **Méjean** and **La Redonne**. At Méjean simple meals of grilled fish and *petites fritures* are served overlooking the tiny port at *Le Mange Tout* (☎04.42.45.91.68; closed Dec–Feb).

The peace and intimate scale of this coast end at the small but bustling resort of **CARRY-LE-ROUET**, its harbour encircled by popular restaurants and overshadowed by a rather unfortunate 1960s tower block. Nonetheless, Carry is modestly swanky and even boasts a casino. It was the home of the jazz singer Nina Simone towards the end of her life, and it was here that she died in 2003. The **tourist office** in the Espace Fernandel (July & Aug Mon–Sat 10am–noon & 2–6pm; Sept–June Tues–Sat 10am–noon & 2–5pm; ☎04.42.13.20.36, ⒲www .carry-lerouet.com) has a list of hotels and private rooms, but there's no real reason to stop other than to visit the wonderful **restaurant**, *L'Escale* (☎04.42.45.00.47, ⒲www.escalecarry.fr; lunch menu €18; closed Mon), on a terrace above the right-hand side of the port, where the fish-heavy *carte* includes the likes of *bouillabaisse* and *marmite du pêcheur*. If you're **camping**, head further west to the tiny, relatively peaceful Calanque de Tamaris, where the sites include *Lou Cigalon* (☎04.42.49.61.71, ⒲www.loucigalon.com; €20 per tent; closed Oct–March), and the neighbouring *Les Tamaris* (☎04.42.80.72.11, ⒲www .camping-lestamaris.com; €21 per tent; closed Oct–March). Both are located right on the pleasant, sandy cove.

Carry merges into its western neighbour Sausset-les-Pins, where the beaches are stony and artificial, without any break in the seaside houses and apartment buildings. For **beaches** it's best to head beyond Tamaris where there are long, sandy beaches around the pleasantly downmarket family resorts of **CARRO** and **LA COURONNE**, though you may be put off by the proximity of the petrochemical plants on the southern shore of the Étang de Berre.

The south shore of the Étang de Berre

The shores of the 22-kilometre-long and 15-kilometre-wide **Étang de Berre**, northwest of L'Estaque, are not the most obvious holiday destination. The lagoon's southern edges are heavily polluted, and the sources are only too visible: oil refineries, petrochemical plants and tankers heading in and out of the Caronte Canal linking the lagoon with the vast industrial complex and port on the Golfe de Fos.

There are, however, some unexpected pockets worth exploring: the ancient remains at **St-Blaise**, the perched village of **St-Mître-les-Remparts** and, despite its close proximity to Europe's largest oil refinery, the town of **Martigues**.

Martigues

MARTIGUES straddles both sides of the Caronte Canal and the island in the middle, at the southwest corner of the Étang de Berre. In the sixteenth century when the union of three separate villages, Jonquières to the south, Ferrières to the north and the island, known simply as l'Île, created Martigues, there were many more canals than the three that remain today. But Martigues has joined the long list of places with waterways to be dubbed the "Venice" of the region, and it deserves the compliment, however fatuous the comparison.

In the centre of l'Île, in front of the sumptuous facade of the airy Église de la Madeleine, a low bridge spans the Canal St-Sébastien where fishing boats moor and houses in ochre, pink and blue look straight down onto the water. This appealing spot is known as the **Miroir aux Oiseaux** and was painted by Corot, Ziem and others at the turn of the twentieth century. Some of these artists' works, including Ziem's *Vieux Port de Marseille*, can be seen in the wonderful **Musée Ziem** on boulevard du Juillet in Ferrières (July–Aug Mon & Wed–Sun 10am–noon & 2.30–6.30pm; Sept–June Wed–Sun 2.30–6.30pm; free). The collection includes works by the likes of Dérain, Dufy and Signac, while François Picabia's 1905 *Étang de Berre* shows the lagoon to be every bit as choppy as it is today. Upstairs is a well-presented local history display, as well as some more contemporary art exhibits.

Practicalities

Buses from Marseille stop at place des Aires in Ferrières, close to the bridge. From the **gare SNCF** take bus #3 (direction "Ferrières") to the centre. The plush modern **tourist office** (June Mon–Fri 9am–6pm, Sat 9am–12.30pm & 2.30–5.45pm, Sun 9.30am–12.30pm; July until 7pm weekdays, Aug until 6.30pm; Oct–Nov Mon–Sat 9am–noon & 1.45–5.30pm, Sun 10am–12.30pm; Dec–May Mon–Fri 9am–12.30pm & 1.30–5.45pm, Sun 10am–12.30pm; ☎04.42.42.31.10, ⓦwww.martigues-tourisme.com) is in Ferrières, on the Rond Point, close to the police station and the *mairie*.

The best of the **hotels** is the *St-Roch*, avenue Georges-Braque, Ferrières (☎04.42.42.36.36, ⓦwww.hotelsaintroch.com; ⓞ), while the pleasant *Le Cigalon*, 37 boulevard du 14 Juillet, Ferrières (☎04.42.80.49.16, ⓦwww.lecigalon.fr; ❸), is in a noisy spot but is soundproofed and a lot cheaper.

July and August see the spectacle of the *Sardinades*, when thousands of plates of grilled sardines are sold cheaply each evening along the quays near the *mediathèque* in the Quartier de L'Île. Aside from these, the **food** to look out for is *poutargue*, a paste made from salted mullet, and *melets*, seasoned fish-fry fermented in olive oil. **Restaurants** to try on l'Île include *Quei Dou Traou Dou Mast*, 15 quai Toulmond (☎04.42.80.63.92; menus from €22), and the scenically situated *Le Miroir*, quai Brescon (☎04.42.80.50.45; menus from €25); there is a scattering of bars and cafés on place de la Libération on l'Île.

St-Mître-les-Remparts and St-Blaise

About 6km beyond Martigues, on the road to Istres, lies the walled village of **ST-MÎTRE-LES-REMPARTS**, where original gateways allow entrance to its minuscule, cramped heart. Some of the houses are built into the medieval defences, while others have a surprising architectural grandeur. From the unusual church at the culmination of the corkscrew of streets you can see westwards over the Étang du Pourra and Étang d'Engenier towards the Fos complex.

From the main road the D51 leads away from St-Mître village up to a hill between two more lagoons, the Étang de Citis and Étang de Lavalduc. On the hill stands the twelfth-century Chapelle St-Blaise beside a thirteenth-century wall and the **Oppidum St-Blaise** archeological site (Mon–Fri 8.45am–12.30pm & 1.30–5.30pm; free). The ancient inhabitants of this well-defended site left their mark throughout eight distinct periods, from 7 BC to the fourteenth century. If the site is closed you can still walk around it, see the extraordinary surviving Greek ramparts through the fence, and generally enjoy the woods and water, which can sometimes appear pink because of the algae encouraged by a high salt content.

Salon-de-Provence and around

The northern exit from the Autoroute du Soleil to **SALON-DE-PROVENCE** takes you past a memorial to **Jean Moulin**, the Resistance leader who was parachuted into the nearby Alpilles range in order to coordinate the different *maquis* groupings in Vichy France. He was caught on June 21, 1943, tortured, deported and murdered by the Nazis. The bronze sculpture, by Marcel Courbier, is of a lithe figure landing from the sky like some latter-day Greek god, very beautiful though somewhat perplexing if you're not aware of the invisible parachute.

Today, one of Salon's principal activities is teaching air-force pilots to fly – indeed, legendary 1930s singer Charles Trenet was just one of thousands to undertake their military service here – and at times the planes scream overhead day and night. In medieval times, Salon's economy was dependent on its tanneries, a saffron crop and flocks of sheep reputed for the quality of their mutton. True prosperity arrived in the shape of the small black **olives** that produced an oil, *olivo selourenco*, of great gastronomic renown. By the end of the nineteenth century the Salonais were making soap from their oil, a highly profitable commodity manufactured in appalling conditions in subterranean mills. Those to whom the dividends accrued built opulent *belle époque* villas, the grandest of which are in the streets between the town centre and the *gare SNCF* to the west, and though most have long since been given over to other uses or divided into apartments, they give the town a quiet, surprising grace.

The famous predictions of **Nostradamus** were composed in Salon, though the museum dedicated to him is less appealing than the mementoes of **Napoléon** in Salon's castle, the Château de l'Empéri. A good time to visit Salon is mid-July when the **jazz festival** takes place, or in July and August for the annual **classical music festival** (ⓌWwww.festival-salon.fr) in the château.

The countryside **around Salon** affords glimpses of the traditional agriculture of the arid Crau region, as well as a remarkable cave-village at Lamanon and a child-friendly castle and zoo at La Barben.

Nostradamus and the Canal de Craponne

Salon lies at the eastern edge of Provence's most arid region, La Crau, and suffered perennial droughts until the mid-sixteenth century, when the town's most famous resident, Michel de Nostradamus, financed the building of a canal. Engineered by Adam de Craponne, the waterway ran from the River Durance through a gap in the hills at Lamanon and across La Crau to the Étang de Berre, and today the area west of Salon is criss-crossed with similar canals. A contemporary account describes the people of Salon greeting the arrival of the waters with "applause, astonishment and joyful incredulity".

Arrival, information and accommodation

From the **gare SNCF** on avenue Émile-Zola, the long straight boulevard Maréchal-Foch leads you past the **gare routière** on place Jules-Morgan to cours Pelletan on the western edge of the Vieille Ville. The **tourist office** (July–Aug Mon–Sat 9.30am–6.30pm, Sun 9.30am–12.30pm; Sept–June Mon–Sat 9.30am–12.30pm & 2–6pm; ☎04.90.56.27.60, ⓦwww.visitsalondeprovence .com) is on the other side of the ring road around the Vieille Ville, at 56 cours Gimon. From here, you can buy a seven-day **Pass Avantages Séjour** for €12, which provides numerous discounts with local businesses plus free entry to local museums.

Finding **accommodation** should not be difficult at any time of year, with plenty of inexpensive small hotels in the centre and the usual chains on the outskirts. There's also a three-star **campsite**, *Camping Nostradamus* (☎04.90.56.08.36, ⓦwww.camping-nostradamus.com; closed Nov–Feb; €20 per tent), just off the D17 towards Eyguières, which also has some **mobile homes**.

Hotels

Hôtel d'Angleterre 1 rue des Frères John et Robert Kennedy ☎04.90.56.01.10, ⓦwww .hotel-dangleterre.biz. Soundproofed and very central, though no lift; the cheapest rooms make do with a fan and shower while more expensive ones are a/c. ❷

Grand Hôtel de la Poste 98 cours Carnot ☎04.90.56.01.94, ⓦwww.ghpsalon.com. Handsome, comfortable and renovated old hotel in a central location, with parking. ❸

Hostellerie de l'Abbaye de Sainte Croix Route du Val de Cuech ☎04.90.56.24.55, ⓦwww.hotels -provence.com. Luxury in the atmospheric surroundings of an ancient abbey, 3km from Salon on the D16. Doubles from €215 in high season. Open weekends only in winter. ❾

Le Mas du Soleil 38 chemin Saint-Côme ☎04.90.56.06.53, ⓦwww.lemasdusoleil.com. In a quiet location a short distance from the town centre, with ten comfortable and individually styled rooms, a pool and a renowned restaurant. ❽

The Town

In the mid-1960s, the Salon town council initiated a programme of demolition and rebuilding in the **Vieille Ville**, which was completed in the late 1980s and which, for many years, seemed to have failed in its objective of rejuvenating the quarter. Of late, however, boutiques and restaurants have colonized the old town, lending it the pleasingly animated air it shares with the rest of the town centre – particularly on market days, when Salon bustles.

Dominating everything is the **Château de l'Empéri**, the centrepiece of the Vieille Ville. This massive structure is a proper medieval fortress, built to suit the worldliness of its former proprietors, the archbishops of Arles. It now houses the **Musée de l'Empéri** (Mon & Wed–Sun 10am–noon & 2–6pm; €4.50, or this plus any two municipal museums for €7.50), whose collections of military uniforms cover the period from Louis XIV to World War I; the sections devoted to the Revolution and Napoleon are particularly fascinating. The castle also houses the **Éspace Théodore Jourdan** (same hours; free) whose exhibition of paintings and drawings by the eponymous local artist is a precursor to a planned new museum of Salon and La Crau.

Flights of steps run down the castle rock to place des Centuries, a wide-open space fringed by café terraces and the **Musée Grévin de la Provence** (Mon–Fri 9am–noon & 2–6pm; Sat & Sun 2–6pm; €4.50), a series of waxwork scenes illustrating episodes from the legends and history of Provence, with taped commentaries available in several different languages. Opposite, the thirteenth-century **Église St-Michel**, with two belfries, adds a touch of old-world charm, as does **rue Moulin-d'Isnard**, leading off the place de L'ancienne Halle to the north of the square.

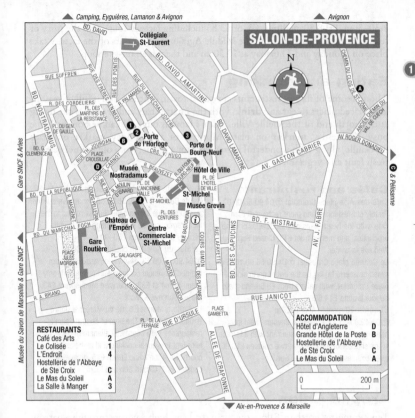

RESTAURANTS
Café des Arts	2
Le Colisée	1
L'Endroit	4
Hostellerie de l'Abbaye	
de Ste Croix	C
Le Mas du Soleil	A
La Salle à Manger	3

ACCOMMODATION
Hôtel d'Angleterre	D
Grande Hôtel de la Poste	B
Hostellerie de l'Abbaye	
de Ste Croix	C
Le Mas du Soleil	A

Just east of the place de L'ancienne Halle stands the **Museé Nostradamus** (same hours and price as Musée Grévin), on the street now named after the soothsayer. Nostradamus (see p.73) arrived in Salon in 1547, already famous for his aromatic plague cure, administered in Aix and Lyon, and married a rich widow. After some fairly long Italian travels, he returned to Salon and settled down to study the stars, the weather, cosmetics and the future of the world. Translations in numerous languages of his *Centuries*, the famous predictions, are displayed in the house along with pictures of events supposedly confirming them. There are waxwork tableaux and visuals meant to fill you with wonder, but nothing particularly earth-shattering – the most interesting exhibit is the 1979 sculpture by François Bouché in the courtyard. Nostradamus died in Salon in 1566 and his tomb is in the Gothic Collégiale St-Laurent, at the top of rue du Maréchal-Joffre, north of the Vieille Ville.

To reach Collégiale St-Laurent from the museum, you'll pass through **Porte de l'Horloge**, the principal gateway to the Vieille Ville. This is a serious bit of seventeenth-century construction, with its Grecian columns, coats of arms, gargoyles and wrought-iron campanile. Through the arch is place Crousillat, which centres on a vast mushroom of moss concealing a three-statued fountain; a wonderful spot for a café break.

To the west of the Vieille Ville and located within a working *savonnerie*, the **Musée du Savon de Marseille**, 148 avenue Paul-Bourret (Mon–Thurs 8.30am–noon &

1.30–5pm, Fri 8.30am–4pm; €3, or €3.85 including factory tour), tells the story of soap-making in Provence from the Middle Ages onwards. Tours of the factory take place on Monday and Thursday at 10.30am and there is an on-site shop.

Eating and drinking

Though some of its best restaurants are out of town, central Salon is full of reasonably priced places to **eat** and **drink**, with the smarter bars and brasseries clustering at the north end of the Vieille Ville. Salon's famous olive oil can be bought at the busy Wednesday **market** on place Morgan, or the Sunday market on place de-Gaulle, along with wonderful ingredients for a picnic, from olives or cheeses to fresh fruit and vegetables.

Cafés and restaurants

Café des Arts place Crousillat ☎04.90.56.00.07. Prettily old-fashioned and more restaurant than café, with the hearty likes of *andouillettes* or lamb brochettes, and menus from €13. Closed Sun, & Wed eve in winter.

Le Colisée place Crousillat ☎04.90.56.00.10. Big, swish brasserie taking up the entire north side of place Crousillat, with salads from €8.50 and *plats du jour* around €14.50.

L'Endroit 20 montée André Viallat ☎04.42.85.85.32. Provençal flavours meet international influences at this restaurant with a terrace in the shadow of the château; two courses €13.90, three courses €18.90. Closed Sun.

Hostellerie de l'Abbaye de Sainte Croix rte du Val de Cuech ☎04.90.56.24.55. Innovative *cuisine gastronomique* that is nevertheless rooted in the local *terroir*, served in the setting of a twelfth-century abbey. Menus €60–90.

Le Mas du Soleil 38 chemin Saint-Côme ☎04.90.56.06.53, ⓦwww.lemasdusoleil.com. Refined Provençal cooking with a weekday-only menu *terroir* at €33; otherwise menus from €43. Closed Sun eve & Mon.

La Salle à Manger 6 rue du Maréchal-Joffre ☎04.90.56.28.01. The best of central Salon's restaurants, with beautiful Italianate decor, excellent Provençal cooking and a sheltered courtyard at the back. Lunch €15, otherwise two courses €27. Closed Sun and Mon.

Around Salon

Ten kilometres north of Salon, the main road and highway pass through a narrow gap in the hills by **LAMANON**, a village which was never much more than a stopover on the transhumance routes (used for the moving of flocks, and still followed by the Crau shepherds every June), though it does have a château. Above the village, hidden amongst rocks and trees, is a remarkable troglodyte village, the **Grottes de Cales**, which was inhabited from Neolithic times until the nineteenth century. Stairs lead down into grottoes, part natural, part constructed, with hooks and gutters carved into the rock; at the centre is a sacrificial temple. Access is free, though some parts of the complex are fenced off for safety reasons: follow the Montée de Cales which ascends from opposite the tourist office, where there's a small **museum** (Sun 2.30–5pm; free); the circuit of the *grottes* itself is on the GR6 footpath. The countryside west of Lamanon is typical of the dry Crau region: around **EYGUIÈRES** you may see llamas grazing along with goats and horses. Llamas are excellent at keeping forest firebreaks trim – so, too, are goats, but the latter are forbidden from running loose in the forests, thanks to an unrevoked Napoleonic law.

Bears, elephants, big cats, hippos and a host of other non-native mammals and birds are kept for more conventional purposes at the **Château de la Barben** (château: tours April–Nov daily 11am–5pm; Feb to early March & weekends during March hourly 2–5pm; €8, or €13 including dungeons; zoo: Sept–June daily 10am–6pm; July & Aug 9.30am–7pm; €13.50), 12km east of Salon, just beyond Pélissanne. This is very much a place to take young children, with plenty of entertainment such as miniature train rides, as well as the standard zoo delights. The château was lived in for a while by Napoleon's sister, Pauline Borghese, and her apartments are still decorated in imperial style, while the rest retains a feeling of seventeenth-century luxury.

Aubagne

Marseille's suburbs extend relentlessly east along the autoroute and D8N corridor to **AUBAGNE**, set between rugged mountain ranges. With a triangle of autoroutes around it and dismal postwar developments encroaching on its historic core, the town is easy to pass by. Yet Aubagne is not without interest, as the headquarters of the French Foreign Legion and a major centre for the production of *santons*, the traditional Provençal Christmas figures. Its main claim to fame, however, is as the birthplace of writer and film-maker **Marcel Pagnol** (1895–1974) and the now much-altered setting for his tales. The international success in the 1980s of Claude Berri's films of Pagnol's *Jean de Florette* and *Manon des Sources*, starring Gérard Depardieu and Emmanuelle Béart, has widened Pagnol's appeal. In *Jean de Florette*, an outsider inherits a property on the arid slopes of the Garlaban mountain, whose rocky crest rears north of Aubagne like a stegosaurus's back. The local peasants who have blocked its spring watch him die from the struggle of fetching water, delighted that his new scientific methods won't upset their market share. You can visit Pagnol's birthplace, the **Maison Natale**, at 16 cours Barthelémy (April–June daily 9am–12.30pm & 2.30–6pm; July–Aug daily 9am–6pm; Sept–March Tues–Sun 9am–12.30pm & 2.30–5.30pm; €3), where in addition to the displays there's a fascinating fifteen-minute film (in French only). Enquire at the tourist office (see p.78) about **walks** into the surrounding country-side to visit the locations of Pagnol's films, though these don't take place from July until the second weekend of September due to the fire risk.

The fertile soil around Aubagne makes excellent pottery, hence the town's renown for *santons* and ceramics. From mid-July to the end of August and in December, a huge daily **market of ceramics** and **santons** takes place on the central street of cours Maréchal-Foch, and in December a giant crèche is set up, featuring 120 figures. At any time of the year you can visit the potters' workshops that are dotted all over town – pick up a leaflet from the tourist office. Other interesting displays can be found at the top of the Vieille Ville in the **Ateliers Thérèse Neveu** (open daily during exhibitions only; free), in the cour de Clastre behind St-Saveur church. The most impressive display of *santons* is to be found at **Le Petit Monde de Marcel Pagnol** (mid-Feb to mid-Nov daily 9am–12.30pm & 2.30–6pm; free) in a diorama on esplanade de-Gaulle. The finely detailed figures of Pagnol characters (including Pagnol himself) play out their parts on a model of the district, complete with farms and villages.

Aubagne's other claim to fame is commemorated by the **Musée de la Légion Étrangère** (Tues, Wed & Fri–Sun 10am–noon & 3–6pm; free), inside the barracks in the *quartier* Vienot on the far side of the A50 autoroute from the town. The tradition of foreigners serving in France's armies dates back to 1346, but the Legion as it exists today was created by King Louis Philippe in 1831. It received its baptism of fire in Algeria in 1832, and was closely associated with North Africa for much of its history, founding the garrison at Sidi Bel Abbès in 1843. The town grew to be a city of 100,000 and remained the Legion's home until France withdrew from Algeria in 1962. How sudden that withdrawal was is demonstrated by the fact that just one year previously the Legion had opened a new Salle d'Honneur in Sidi Bel Abbès to commemorate its fallen. Today, the Salle d'Honneur is on the ground floor of the museum, and with its soundtrack of martial music it's a suitably sombre place. The displays upstairs catalogue the Legion's campaigns and include the white *képis* familiar from cinematic depictions of Beau Geste.

Practicalities

Buses from Marseille arrive at the *pôle d'échanges* alongside the **gare SNCF**, from where it is a five-minute walk along avenue Jeanne d'Arc to cours Foch and on to cours Barthelémy, where the **tourist information office** is at no. 8 (July & Aug Mon–Sat 9am–1pm & 2–7pm, Sun 10am–12.30pm; Sept–June Mon–Sat 9am–noon & 2–6pm; ☏04.42.03.49.98, ⓦwww.oti-paysdaubagne.com). It can provide information on Pagnol itineraries and local potteries and *santon* makers. There's little reason to **stay** in Aubagne, though the village of Gémenos (bus #7 from Aubagne; see p.202) to the east makes an enticing overnight stop en route to the Chaine de la Sainte Baume. Cours Voltaire and cours Foch are Aubagne's prime spots for **café** lounging.

Cassis

It's hard to imagine the little fishing port of **CASSIS**, on the main coast road south from Marseille, as a busy industrial harbour in the mid-nineteenth century, trading with Spain, Italy and Algeria. Its fortunes had declined by the time Dérain, Dufy and other Fauvist artists started visiting at the turn of the twentieth century. In the 1920s Virginia Woolf stayed while working on *To the Lighthouse*, and later Winston Churchill came here to paint. These days it's scarcely an undiscovered secret, as one glance at the local property prices or the crowds in the port-side restaurants will tell you. The place bustles with activity: stalls sell artisans' handicrafts, guitarists busk round the port and day-trippers endlessly circle the one-way system trying to find a parking space. But many people still rate Cassis the best resort this side of St-Tropez, its residents most of all.

Arrival, information and accommodation

Vehicle access to the central port area of Cassis is restricted, so **buses** drop their passengers at the *Gendarmerie* a little above the town, from where it's a short walk downhill to the port. The **gare SNCF** is 3km out of town, and connected to the centre by a shuttle bus (roughly hourly on weekdays, less frequent at weekends) which takes around fifteen minutes to reach Cassis. The **tourist office** is on the port at quai des Moulins (March–June & Sept–Oct Mon–Fri 9am–12.30pm & 2–6pm, Sat 9.30am–12.30pm & 2–5.30pm, Sun 10am–12.30pm; July–Aug Mon–Fri 9am–7pm, Sat & Sun 9.30am–12.30pm & 3–6pm; Nov–Feb Mon–Fri 9.30am–12.30pm & 2–5.30pm, Sat 10am–12.30pm & 2–5pm, Sun 10am–12.30pm; ☏08.92.25.98.92, ⓦwww.ot-cassis.com).

Hotels

Le Clos de Arômes 10 rue Abbé Paul-Mouton ☏04.42.01.71.84, ⓦwww.le-clos-des-aromes .com. Charming, quiet hotel a short way inland from the bustle of the port, with a lovely garden restaurant. Closed Jan & Feb. ❹

Le Golfe 3 place du Grand Carnot ☏04.42.01.00.21, ⓦwww.legolfe-cassis.fr. In the

middle of all the action, overlooking the port, and with a lunchtime brasserie. Closed Nov–March. ❺

Joli Bois rte de la Gineste ☏04.42.01.02.68, ⓦwww.hotel-du-joli-bois.com. Just off the main road to Marseille, 3km from Cassis. A bargain, but as it has only ten rooms, best book ahead. It's in a pretty remote spot but there's plenty of parking space. ❷

Laurence 8 rue de l'Arène ℡04.42.01.88.78, ⓦwww.cassis-hotel-laurence.com. A short way inland from the port and market, modernized and with a/c. Some rooms have views of the harbour or château. Closed Nov–Jan. ❸

Les Roches Blanches av des Calanques ℡04.42.01.09.30, ⓦwww.roches-blanches -cassis.com. Handsome old hotel in a perfect position overlooking the bay, with smart rooms, terraces and a pine wood leading down to the water. Closed Nov to mid-March. ❼

Hostel, chambre d'hôte and campsite

Château de Cassis Traverse du Château ℡04.42.01.63.20, ⓦwww.chateaudecassis.com. Luxurious suites and double rooms in the spectacular setting of Cassis' clifftop castle. Doubles from €220. ❾

Les Cigales ℡04.42.01.07.34, ⓦwww .campingcassis.com. Campsite on the corner of the rte de Marseille and av de la Marne, 1km from the port. €19.10 per tent. Closed mid-Nov to mid-March.

HI youth hostel La Fontasse ℡04.42.01.02.72, ⓦwww.fuaj.org. In the hills above the calanques west of Cassis. By car from Cassis, take the D559 for 4km then turn left. The Cassis–Marseille bus stops on the D559 (bus stop "Les Calanques"). It's a 3km walk from the Calanque de Port Miou on the edge of Cassis; take av des Calanques from the port. The facilities are basic (there are no showers, and power and water are rationed), but if you want to explore this wild, uninhabited stretch of limestone heights, the people running it will advise you enthusiastically. €11.20 per night. Reception 8–10.30am & 5–9pm. Closed Jan to mid-March.

The Town

The cliffs hemming it in and the value of its vineyards on the slopes above have prevented Cassis becoming a relentless sprawl, and the little modern development that exists is small-scale. Port-side posing, eating *oursins* (sea urchins) and drinking aside, there's not much to do except sunbathe and look up at the town's medieval **castle**. It was built in 1381 by the counts of Les Baux and refurbished last century by Monsieur Michelin, the authoritarian boss of the family tyres and guides firm, and it remains in private hands.

▲ Port-side dining, Cassis

Cassis has a small **museum** (April–Sept Wed–Sat 10.30am–12.30pm & 3.30–6.30pm; Oct–March Wed–Sat 10.30am–12.30pm & 2.30–5.30pm; free), in the seventeenth-century presbytery on rue Xavier-d'Authier just behind the tourist office. It has a bit of everything: nineteenth-century paintings and photographs of Cassis and Marseille, old furniture, costumes and Roman amphorae.

One of the most popular tourist activities is to take a **boat trip to the calanques** (from around €13), the narrow, deep, fjord-like inlets that cut into the limestone cliffs. Several companies operate from the port, but check if they let you off or just tour in and out, and be prepared for rough seas. If you're feeling energetic, you can **walk** along the GR98 footpath from the avenue des Calanques behind the western beach; it's about a ninety-minute walk to the furthest and best inlet, **En Vau**, where you can climb down rocks to the shore. Intrepid pine trees find root-holds, and sunbathers find ledges on the chaotic white cliffs. The water is deep blue and swimming between the vertical cliffs is an experience not to be missed. Note that smoking, "wild" camping and lighting fires is prohibited in the *massif*, and that from June until the end of September access is subject to restrictions at times of high fire risk.

Eating and drinking

Sea urchins accompanied by the delicious, crisp Cassis **white wine** are the speciality here. **Restaurant** tables are abundant along the port side on quai des Baux, quai Calandal and quai Barthélemy; prices vary but the best bet is to follow your nose, and seek out the most enticing fish smells.

Cassis **wines**, from grapes grown on the slopes above the D559, are very special. Mistral described the white as "shining like a limpid diamond, tasting of the rosemary, heather and myrtle that covers our hills". It's best to call ahead before visiting local **vineyards**; the tourist office can supply a list. Alternatively, there's the **Maison des Vins** (℡04.42.01.15.61) on the D559 route de Marseille. For **picnic food** to go with the wine, head for the **market**, held around place Baragnon east of the port on Wednesday and Friday mornings.

Restaurants and cafés

Chez Gilbert 19 quai des Baux ℡04.42.01.71.36, Ⓦwww.restaurant-chez-gilbert.fr. Renowned port-side restaurant where the attractions are the authentic *bouillabaisse* (€38), and freshly grilled fish priced according to weight. Closed Wed lunch, all of Jan and Tues eve out of season.

Le Clos des Arômes 10 rue Abbé Paul-Mouton ℡04.42.01.71.84. Pleasant restaurant a few streets back from the port, with a pretty garden and the likes of *daube de boeuf*, salad of *rascasse* marinated in lemon and *bouillabaisse* on its *carte*. Menus €26 or €38. Closed Mon & Tues lunch, & Wed.

Bar de la Marine 5 quai des Baux. The most animated of the port-side café terraces, great for people-watching or merely soaking up the sun over a glass of wine.

Nino 1 quai Barthélemy ℡04.42.01.74.32, Ⓦwww .nino-cassis.com. *Soupe de poisson* and fillet of *rascasse* with basil are among the fishy attractions at this smart port-side restaurant. Menu €32.

La Presqu'Île presqu'île de Cassis ℡04.42.01.03.77, Ⓦwww.restaurant-la-presquile .fr. Beautifully situated by the sea to the west of the port, with a heavy emphasis on fish and seafood to the accomplished cooking. Menus €30 or €49. Booking essential. Closed Sun eve and Mon.

The Corniche des Crêtes

If you have a car or motorbike, the spectacular **Corniche des Crêtes** road south from Cassis to La Ciotat (the D141) is definitely a ride not to be missed. From Cassis the chemin St-Joseph turns off avenue de Provence, climbs at a maximum gradient to the Pas de la Colle, then follows the inland slopes of the Mont de la Canaille. Much of the landscape is often blackened by fire, but once in a while the

The Cosquer cave

In 1991, Henri Cosquer, a diver from Cassis, discovered paintings and engravings of animals, painted handprints and finger tracings in a cave between Marseille and Cassis, whose sole entrance is a long, sloping tunnel that starts 37m under the sea. The cave would have been accessible from dry land no later than the end of the last ice age, and carbon dating has shown that the oldest work of art here was created around 27,000 years ago. Over a hundred animals have been identified, including seals, auks, horses, ibex, bisons, chamois, red deer and a giant deer known only from fossils. Fish are also featured along with sea creatures that might be jellyfish. Most of the finger tracings are done in charcoal and have fingertips missing, possibly to convey a sign language by bending fingers. For safety reasons it's not possible to visit the cave, though diving schools in Cassis organize dives in the bay and the *calanques*.

road loops round a break in the chain to give you dramatic views over the sea. You can **walk** it as well, in about three and a half hours: the path, beginning from Pas de la Colle, takes a precipitous straighter line passing the road at each outer loop. The Corniche is closed in high winds.

La Ciotat and around

Cranes still loom incongruously over the old shipbuilding town of **LA CIOTAT**, where 300,000-tonne oil and gas tankers were built as recently as 1989. Today, the town's economy relies on property development, tourism and mooring and repairing yachts, yet it remains a pleasantly unpretentious place, with a golden Vieille Ville above the bustling quayside, affordable hotels and restaurants, and an attractive beach stretching northeast from the port.

In 1895 **Auguste** and **Louis Lumière** filmed the first ever moving pictures in La Ciotat and in 1904 went on to develop the first colour photographs. The town celebrates its relatively unknown status as the cradle of cinema with an annual **film festival** in June.

Arrival, information and accommodation

The **gare SNCF** is 3km from the town centre, but bus #40 is frequent at peak times and gets you to the Vieux Port in around twenty minutes. The Vieille Ville and port look out across the Baie de la Ciotat, whose inner curve provides the beaches and resort-style life of La Ciotat's beach-side extension, **La Ciotat Plage**. The **gare routière** is next to the **tourist office** (July–Sept Mon–Sat 9am–8pm, Sun 10am–1pm; Oct–June Mon–Sat 9am–noon & 2–6pm; ℡04.42.08.61.32, ⓦwww.tourisme-laciotat.com), at the end of boulevard Anatole-France by the Vieux Port. **Bikes** can be hired from Holiday Bikes/ADA at 12 avenue Camugli (℡04.42.32.13.21).

Hotels

Beaurivage 1 bd Beaurivage ℡04.42.83.26.61, ⓔfbenameur@laposte.net. Two-star hotel with parking, restaurant and a terrace. The more expensive rooms have sea views. ❹

La Marine 1 av F-Gassion ℡04.42.08.35.11, ⓕ06.03.29.45.23. The best budget option in town, just above the Vieille Ville: a pleasant, very clean place with decent-sized rooms. Popular with divers. Cheaper rooms lack bath or shower. ❷

Miramar 3 bd Beaurivage ℡04.42.83.33.79, ⓦwww.miramarlaciotat.com. Possibly the best hotel in the town, set amid pines on the seafront. ❻

81

Hôtel la Rotonde 44 bd de la République
℡04.42.08.67.50, ⒲www.hotel-larotonde-ciotat.fr.
Modern hotel near La Marine and close to the old
town, with wireless internet and some rooms with
balconies. ❷

Campsite

Le Soleil 751 av Emile Bodin ℡04.42.71.55.32,
⒲www.camping-dusoleil.com. La Ciotat has five
campsites; this two-star site is about the most
central. €19 per tent. Closed mid-Nov to mid-April.

The Town

The dignified nineteenth-century former *mairie* at the end of quai Ganteaume now
houses the **Musée du Vieux Ciotat** (July–Aug Wed–Mon 4–7pm; Sept–June
3–6pm; €3.20), charting the history of the town back to its foundation by the
ancient Greeks of Marseille, when local shipbuilding began. Further down the
quay is the seventeenth-century church, **Notre-Dame-de l'Assomption** (Mon–
Fri 10am–noon & 4–6pm, Sat 10am–noon & 9–11pm) with its Baroque facade and
a striking early seventeenth-century painting by André Gaudion of the *Descent of
the Cross* alongside modern works of art. The streets of the Vieille Ville behind the
church are uneventful and still a bit run-down, though the proliferation of estate
agents in the town suggests that is set to change.

To the east along the seafront, on the corner of boulevard A-France and
boulevard Jean-Jaurès, is the crumbly **Eden Theatre**, the world's oldest movie
house, where there's a small exhibition of photographs (Mon–Sat 10am–6pm;
free) and a glass panel through which you can peer into the original auditorium.
Further on, at plage Lumière, is a solid 1950s **monument** to Auguste and Louis
Lumière, who shot their seminal films in the garden of the family **château** at the
top of allée Lumière. The house survives, but is private property and not open to
the public. The brothers appear again in a mural on the covered market halls which
house the modern **cinema** on place Evariste-Gras, visible as you walk up rue
Réynier from boulevard Guérin north of the port.

Boat trips depart from the Vieux Port for the ten-minute trip to the tiny
offshore **Île Verte**, topped by a fort and with a small restaurant, *Chez Louisette*,
which serves seafood. The ferry *Aquilade* (℡06.63.59.16.35) makes the crossing to
Île Verte daily (€9 return), while the catamarans *Le Citharista*, *Le Ciotaden* and *Le
Mistral* (℡06.09.33.54.98) run trips to the *calanques* of Cassis and Marseille
(€16–25) from quai Ganteaume.

Film in La Ciotat

La Ciotat's train station has a commemorative plaque to the film **L'Arrivée d'un train
en gare de La Ciotat**, which was one of a dozen or so films, including **Le déjeuner
de bébé** and the comedy **L'Arroseur arrosé**, shown in the **Château Lumière** in
September 1895. The audience jumped out of their seats as the image of the steam
train hurtled towards them. Three months later the reels were taken to Paris for the
capital's citizens to witness cinema for the first time.

La Ciotat marks its association with the artform with a couple of festivals. The
Cinestival is an affordable event which takes place in mid-June, usually revolving
around a particular theme or genre and offering screenings at very low prices. Venues
include the Lumière cinema and the Chapelle des Pénitents Bleus. A rather more
glamorous event, the Berceau du Cinema, takes place in late May at the Théatre du
Golfe, screening a limited selection of films before an invited jury, which awards the
Lumières d'Honneur prize. Tickets for these screenings can be obtained free in
advance by writing to the Association Le Berceau du Cinéma, Hôtel Grimaldi-
Régusse, 18 rue Adolphe-Abeille, 1300 La Ciotat (℡04.42.71.61.70, ⒲www.berceau
-cinema.com).

Alternatively, you could explore the remarkable contorted cliff beyond the shipyards that the city's founders named "the eagle's beak" and which is now protected as the **Parc du Mugel** (daily: April–Sept 8am–8pm; Oct–March 9am–6pm). A path leads up from the entrance through overgrown vegetation and past scooped vertical hollows to a narrow terrace overlooking the sea. The cliff face looks like the habitat of some gravity-defying, burrowing beast rather than the result of erosion by wind and sea. To get there, take bus #30 (direction "La Garde"; stop "Mugel").

If you continue on bus #30 to Figuerolles you can reach the **Anse de Figuerolles** *calanque* down the avenue of the same name, and its neighbour, the **Gameau**. Both have pebbly beaches and a completely different dominant colour from the *calanques* of Cassis.

Eating, drinking and entertainment

La Ciotat's **restaurants** are not gastronomically renowned, though there is plenty of choice, with **café** and **brasserie** terraces lining the quays around the Vieux Port. There's a Sunday **market** on the quays, though the main shopping street is rue des Poilus, a little inland from the church of Notre Dame de l'Assomption. For a takeaway lunch, *Lou Pescadou*, a fishmonger's at no. 20, sells paella and other fish dishes from huge iron pans, and there are several boulangeries and an oriental patisserie nearby.

La Ciotat has a surprisingly animated **cultural** scene, including several gallery/exhibition spaces and the smart modern *Théâtre du Golfe* on the seafront at boulevard Anatole-France (℡04.42.08.92.87). Away from the port on place E-Gras, the *Atelier Convergences* is a live **jazz** venue.

Restaurants and cafés

Bar Continental 7 quai Général de Gaulle. Cocktails and ice creams in a plum port-side position, with a broad terrace for alfresco imbibing.

Coquillages Franquin 13 bd Anatole France ℡04.42.83.59.50. Close to the tourist office, with reasonably priced fish and seafood on menus from €18.50.

Le Gourman'dînent 18 rue des Combattants ℡04.42.08.00.60. Just up from the port, with a pretty terrace and the likes of marinated slices of beef fillet with brie, fig and artichoke on its creative *carte*. Menus from €29. Closed Wed, Sun eve, and Mon–Wed lunch in July & Aug.

La Mamma 3 quai François Mitterand ℡04.42.08.30.08. Bustling port-side pizzeria, with pizzas from €9, plus pasta, fish and meat dishes. Menu €25.

O'Kylian's 1 quai François Mitterand. The inevitable Irish pub also dishes up ice creams and cocktails; the Guinness helps distinguish it from its port-side competitors.

Sud 18 bd Anatole France ℡04.42.70.99.61. Informal, stylish modern restaurant, with salads from €12, as well as pasta, meat and fish from around €13. Closed Wed, & Sun & Mon eve.

Travel details

Trains

Aubagne to: Bandol (every 30min–1hr; 26min); Cassis (every 30min–1hr; 8min); La Ciotat (every 30min–1hr; 15min); Marseille (every 30min–1hr; 15–20min); Toulon (every 30min–1hr; 42min).
Marseille to: Aix (every 20min–1hr; 45min); Arles (2–3 per hr at peak times; 45min–1hr); Aubagne (every 30min–1hr; 15–20min); Avignon (every 30min at peak times; 1hr 15min); Bandol (every 30min–1hr; 40min); Cannes (hourly; 2hr); Carry-le-Rouet (every 1–2hr; 30min); Cassis (every 30min–1hr; 22min); Cavaillon (6 daily; 1hr 10min–1hr 20min); Hyères (3 daily; 1hr 20min); La Ciotat (every 30min–1hr; 30min); La Seyne-Six-Fours (every 30min–1hr; 50min); Les Arcs-Draguignan (up to 13 daily; 1hr

13min–1hr 35min); Lyon (TGV: 5 daily; 1hr 50min); Martigues (every 1–2hr; 45min); Nice (hourly; 1hr 30min–2hr 30min); Ollioules-Sanary (every 30min–1hr; 50min); Paris (TGV: hourly at peak times; 3hr 15min); Pertuis (up to 6 daily; 1hr 13min); St Cyr/Les Lecques (every 30min–1hr; 35min); St-Raphaël (hourly; 1hr 30min); Salon (6 daily; 50min–1hr); Tarascon (6 daily; 1hr 10min); Toulon (every 10–15min at peak times; 35–55min).

Salon-de-Provence to: Avignon (up to 11 daily; 55min); Marseille (5 daily; 50min).

Buses (Sundays and holidays reduced services)

Aubagne to: Aix (18 daily; 50min); Gémenos (hourly Mon–Sat; 15min); La Ciotat (hourly; 40min); Marseille (every 5min at peak times; 15–30min).

La Ciotat to: Aix (14 daily; 1hr 20min); Bandol (hourly; 45 min).

Marseille to: Aix (every 5min at peak times; 30–50min); Aubagne (every 5min at peak times; 15min); Barçelonnette (via Gap: 1–2 daily; 5hr 40min–6hr); Cassis (8 daily; 40min); Forcalquier (2–3 daily; 2hr 5min); Grenoble (1 daily; 4hr 35min); La Ciotat (every 20–45min; 35–50min); Manosque (up to 12 daily; 1hr 20min–1hr 30min); Martigues (every 30–40min; 40–45min); Nice (5 daily; 2hr 50min–4hr 5min); Sisteron (2 daily; 2hr 45min).

Martigues to: Aix (6 daily; 1hr 45min); Carry-le-Rouet (3 daily; 45min); Marseille (every 20–55min; 50min); Salon (every 2hr; 1hr).

Salon-de-Provence to: Aix TGV (every 1–2hr, 1hr 15min); Aix (hourly; 45min); Eyguières (7 daily; 15min); Marignane Airport (10 daily; 1hr); Martigues (every 1–2hr; 1hr 5min–1hr 20min).

2

Arles and the Camargue

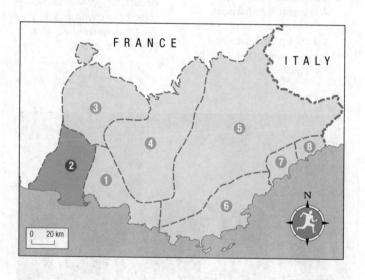

CHAPTER 2 # Highlights

✻ **Les Arènes** For its sheer size, Arles' ancient Roman amphitheatre is one of Provence's most impressive Roman remains. See p.91

✻ **Les Baux-de-Provence** Scramble over the hillsides to explore this extraordinary citadel, carved into the bleached rocks atop the Alpilles range. See p.97

✻ **Cathédrale des Images** A fascinating audiovisual extravaganza, projected into the cavernous interior of a former quarry in the Valley of Hell. See p.98

✻ **St-Paul-de-Mausole** Home for a year to Vincent van Gogh, this psychiatric hospital in picturesque St-Rémy offers an emotive insight into the artist's suffering. See p.101

✻ **The Camargue** The expansive marshland of the Rhône delta is home to pink flamingos, white horses and unearthly, watery landscapes, as well as the colourful gypsy festival in Les Stes-Maries-de-la-Mer. See pp.108–115

▲ Les Arènes, Arles

2

Arles and the Camargue

lowing south from Avignon to the sea, the River Rhône has always been a vital trading route, bringing wealth and fame to the towns that line its banks. The great riverside castles at **Tarascon** and **Beaucaire** are testament to the Rhône's strategic importance, while further south, at the point where the river divides into separate channels as the Petit and Grand Rhône, **Arles** was once the centre of Roman Provincia – which stretched from the Pyrenees to the Alps – before becoming the capital of Gaul towards the end of the Roman era. Arles' great amphitheatre still seats thousands for summer entertainments, while further evidence of Roman occupation is apparent at **Glanum**, outside **St-Rémy-de-Provence**, where you can see the overlaid remains of Greek and Roman towns; and between Arles and St-Rémy, where the ancient **Barbegal mill** demonstrates the Romans' brilliant use of water power.

South of Arles, spreading across the Rhône delta, the strange watery land of the **Camargue** has its own unique natural history and way of life. The wet expanses sustain flocks of flamingos and other birds, while black bulls and wild white horses graze along the edges of the marshes and lagoons. The Camargue also provides a sanctuary for unique social traditions – it is here, to the seaside resort of **Les Stes-Maries-de-la-Mer**, that **gypsies** come every May from all over the Mediterranean to celebrate their patron saint's day.

The modest plains to the north and east of Arles, enclosed by the River Durance and the Rhône and separated by the abrupt ridge of the **Alpilles**, are known as **La Petite Crau** and **La Grande Crau**. The villages and small towns here have retained a nineteenth-century charm, living out the customs and traditions revived by the great Provençal poet **Frédéric Mistral**. This is the countryside that **Van Gogh** painted when he spent a year at Arles and then sought refuge in St-Rémy. Both towns celebrate his tragic brilliance.

Arles

With its sun-kissed golden stone, small-town feel and splendid setting on the east bank of the Rhône, **ARLES** is one of the loveliest cities in southern France. It's also one of the oldest; the extraordinarily well-preserved Roman amphitheatre at its heart, **Les Arènes**, is simply the most famous of several magnificent monuments. Originally a Celtic settlement – the name Ar-larh meant "moist

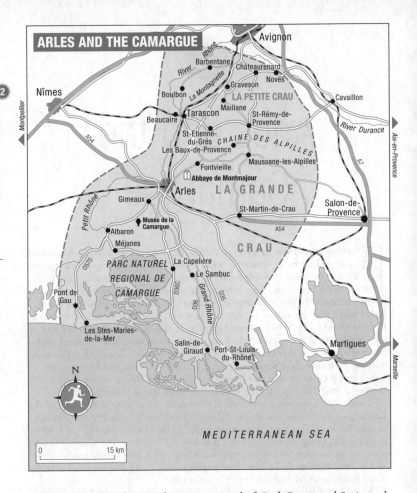

ARLES AND THE CAMARGUE

habitation" – it later became the Roman capital of Gaul, Britain and Spain, and survived the collapse of the Roman Empire as a base for the counts of Provence before unification with France.

For centuries, the port of Arles prospered by way of the inland trade route up the Rhône, profiting especially whenever France's enemies blockaded its eternal rival, Marseille. Decline set in with the arrival of the railways, however, and the town where **Van Gogh** spent a lonely and miserable – but highly prolific – period in the late nineteenth century was itself inward-looking and depressed.

Today's Arles is a pleasantly laid-back place, springing to life for the **Saturday market** that brings in throngs of farmers from the Camargue and La Crau, and during the busy **bull-fighting** season between Easter and All Saints. It also fills the year with a crowded calendar of **festivals**, of which the best known is the **Rencontres Internationales de la Photographie** (Ⓦwww.rencontres-arles .com), based around the National School of Photography, from July to mid-September.

Arrival and information

Arles' **gare SNCF** is a few blocks north of the Arènes. Most buses arrive at the unstaffed *gare routière* alongside, though some (including all local services) stop on the north side of boulevard Georges-Clemenceau, just east of rue Gambetta. In summer, drivers are better off **parking** on the periphery, such as in the **Centre** car park on boulevard des Lices, rather than venturing into the central maze of narrow, largely one-way streets. There's free parking a little further out, for example on place Lamartine and near Les Alyscamps. **Bikes** can be rented from Europbike, 1 rue Philippe-Lebon (T06.85.55.44.71), or the hostel.

The main **tourist office** is on bd des Lices directly opposite the junction with rue Jean-Jaurès (Easter–Sept daily 9am–6.45pm; Oct–Easter Mon–Sat 9am–4.45pm, Sun 10am–1pm; T04.90.18.41.20, Wwww.arlestourisme.com); there's a summer annexe in the *gare SNCF* (Easter–Sept Mon–Fri 9am–1.30pm & 2.30–5pm). For **internet access**, go to Cyber-Saladelle, 17 rue de la République (Tues–Sat 10am–7pm).

Accommodation

There's little shortage of **hotel** rooms at either end of the scale; it's nicer to stay in the historic centre, but cheap places are concentrated around Porte de la Cavalerie near the station. If you get stuck, the tourist office will find you accommodation for a €1 fee.

Hotels

Acacias 2 rue de la Cavalerie T04.90.96.37.88, Wwww.hotel-acacias.com. Modern, simple but cheerfully decorated – rooms and soundproofed – rooms in a friendly hotel, conveniently poised between the train station and town centre. Closed late Oct to March. ➍

Amphithéâtre 5–7 rue Diderot T04.90.96.10.30, Whotelamphitheatre.fr. Very central hotel, where the spacious and beautifully decorated rooms feature lots of warm colours, tiles and wrought ironwork, and large well-equipped bathrooms; rates are especially good for the four-person rooms. ➍

Arlatan 26 rue du Sauvage T04.90.93.56.66, Wwww.hotel-arlatan.fr. Set in a beautiful old fifteenth-century mansion and decorated with antiques, this distinguished hotel has plenty of character, although some rooms are rather small. Closed Jan. ➎

Calendal 5 rue Porte de Laure T04.90.96.11.89, Wwww.lecalendal.com. This welcoming hotel, facing the Théâtre Antique and glowing at sunset, offers bright a/c rooms overlooking a pleasant shaded garden. Closed Jan. ➏

Grand Hôtel Nord Pinus 14 place du Forum T04.90.93.44.44, Wnord-pinus.com. Chic, luxurious rooms in a grand mansion at the head of a pretty, lively square in the heart of the old town. Much favoured by the *vedettes* of the bullring, it's decorated with assorted trophies and evocative photos. ➑

Discount passes

Several **passes** grant free admission to differing combinations of Arles' Roman monuments, plus the cathedral cloisters, the Musée Départemental Arles Antique and the Musée Réattu. Sold at the tourist offices and the sites themselves, their precise details change each year, and are sufficiently intricate that even the sites often lose track of what you're entitled to. If you plan to visit even a couple of sites, however, a pass will almost certainly save you money. At the time of writing, the following passes were on sale:

The €9 **Arelate** pass is valid for one month and covers everything in the "Roman Arles" section.

The €9 **Liberté** pass, also valid for one month, gets you into any four Roman monuments, plus one museum only.

The €13.50 **Avantage** pass, valid for one year, covers every site.

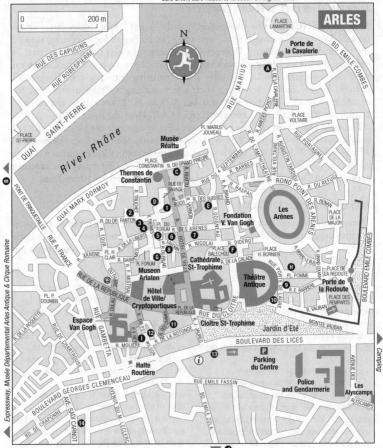

ACCOMMODATION				RESTAURANTS, CAFÉS & BARS			
Acacias	A	Grand Hôtel Nord Pinus	G	L'Apostrophe	5	L'Escaladou	9
Amphithéâtre	F	Muette	E	Café de la Nuit	8	La Gueule de Loup	7
Arlatan	D	Musée	C	Cargo de Nuit	14	Lou Marquès	13
Auberge de Jeunesse	J	Porte de Camargue	B	La Charcuterie	6	La Mule Blanche	12
Calendal	H	de Poste	I	Chez Arianne	1	La Paillote	2
				Le Cilantro	10	Pâtisserie du Forum	4
				A Coté	11	Soleileïs	3

Muette 15 rue des Suisses
☏ 04.90.96.15.39, ⓦ hotel-muette.com.
Charming old stone hotel, close to Les Arènes,
where the bright, tranquil rooms decked out in
beiges and creams look out over a sleepy little
square. Copious buffet breakfast, and friendly
management. Closed Jan & Feb. ❸

Musée 11 rue du Grand-Prieuré ☏ 04.90.93.88.88,
ⓦ www.hoteldumusee.com. Small, good-value,
family-run place, in a quiet location opposite

Musée Réattu, with a pretty, flower-filled terrace.
Closed Jan & first fortnights of March & Dec. ❸
Porte de Camargue 15 rue Noguier
☏ 04.90.96.17.32, ⓦ www.portecamargue.com.
Attractive, very peaceful hotel, with light, simple
rooms, and a rooftop terrace, just across the Pont du
Trinquetaille from the centre – parking is much easier
this side of the river. Closed late Oct to early April. ❸
De Poste 2 rue Molière ☏ 04.90.52.05.76,
ⓦ hotelrelaisdeposte.fr. Simple but comfortable

rooms in a fine eighteenth-century town house, on a surprisingly quiet square near the tourist office; the restaurant on its front terrace is open for lunch only, with menus at €12 and €15. ❸

Hostel and campsites

Auberge de Jeunesse 20 av Maréchal-Foch ☎04.90.96.18.25, ⓦfuaj.org/arles. Old-style hostel, 500m south of the centre (bus #3, stop "Clemenceau"), with rock-hard beds in large dorms (€16.10, including breakfast), and spartan facilities. Bike hire available. Reception 7–10am and 5–11pm (midnight in summer). Closed mid-Dec to mid-Feb.

La Bienheureuse on the N453 at Raphèle-lès-Arles ☎04.90.98.48.06, ⓦlabienheureuse.com. This well-shaded three-star site is the best of Arles' half-dozen campsites, 7km southeast of the city on the Arles–Aix bus route. Its restaurant is furnished in Provençal style, and decorated with pictures of popular Arlesian traditions. €15.20 per night. Open all year.

City 67 rte de Crau ☎04.90.93.08.86, ⓦcamping -city.com. Two-star campsite that's the closest to town 1.5km southeast on the Crau bus route. It's not a very attractive spot, but there's shade and a pool. €17 per night. Closed Oct–March.

The City

Although Arles is blessed with an abundance of monuments and museums, it's a delightful city simply to stroll around at random. Its compact central core, nestled against a ninety-degree curve in the river, is small enough to cross on foot in a few minutes, and holds all the major sights except the **Musée Départemental Arles Antique** to the southwest, and **Les Alyscamps** necropolis to the southeast. The main square, with the cathedral and town hall, is **place de la République**, while the hub of popular life is **place du Forum**.

Roman Arles

To this day, Arles remains recognizable as the **Roman** city that was first thrust to greatness when Julius Caesar built an entire fleet here in less than a month. After using the ships to win control of Rome, he devastated Marseille for its support of his enemy Pompey, and Arles became a major port. The Mediterranean was a little closer to the city at that time, while the extensive wheat fields of the Camargue were known as the "granary of Rome".

Having reached its height as a world trading centre during the fifth century, Arles' relative isolation after the empire crumbled allowed its heritage to be preserved. The site of its Roman forum, the **place du Forum**, still holds the pillars of an ancient archway and the first two steps of a monumental stairway, now embedded in the corner of the *Nord-Pinus* hotel.

Les Arènes

Arles' most dramatic monument, the amphitheatre known as **Les Arènes** (daily: March, April & Oct 9am–6pm; May–Sept 9am–7pm; Nov–Feb 10am–5pm; €6 with Théâtre Antique; ⓦwww.arenes-arles.com), was constructed at the end of the first century AD, and was the largest Roman building in all Gaul. Looming above the city centre, it measures 136m long by 107m wide; its two tiers of sixty arches each (the lower Doric, the upper Corinthian) were originally topped by a third, and thirty thousand spectators would cram beneath its canvas roof to watch gladiator battles and other spectacles. During the Middle Ages, it became a fortress (and effectively a miniature town), sheltering over two hundred dwellings and three churches. Since this medieval quarter was cleared away in 1830, the Arènes has once more been used for entertainment. While it's impressive from the outside, it's only worth paying for admission when a performance is taking place, like a bullfight (see p.92) or concert; it makes an absolutely stunning venue.

The bullfight

Bullfighting, or more properly *tauromachie* (roughly, "the art of the bull"), comes in two styles in Arles and the Camargue. In the local *courses camarguaises*, held at fêtes from late spring to early autumn (the most prestigious is **Arles' Cocarde d'Or** on the first Monday in July), *razeteurs* run at the bulls in an effort to pluck ribbons and cockades tied to their horns, cutting them free with special barbed gloves. The drama and grace of the spectacle is in the stylish way the men leap over the barrier away from the bull, and in the competition for prize money between the *razeteurs*. In this gentler bullfight, people are rarely injured and the bulls are not killed.

More popular, however, are the brutal Spanish-style **corridas** (late April, early July & Sept, at Arles), consisting of a strict ritual leading to the all-but-inevitable death of the bull. After its entry into the ring, the bull is subjected to the *bandilleros* who stick decorated barbs in its back; the *picadors*, who lance it from horseback; and finally, the *torero*, who endeavours to lead the bull through a graceful series of movements before killing it with a single sword stroke to the heart. In one *corrida*, six bulls are killed by three *toreros*, among whom injuries (sometimes fatal) are not uncommon.

Whether you approve or not, *tauromachie* has a long history here, and offers a rare opportunity to join in local life. It's also a great way to experience Arles' **Roman arena** in use. Assorted bullfighting events are staged at Les Arènes between Easter and October each year, including non-fatal *courses camarguaises* fights at 5pm each Wednesday between June and August; ticket prices typically range from €10–33 (Ⓦwww.arenes-arles.com).

Théâtre Antique

The **Théâtre Antique**, just south of Les Arènes (daily: March, April & Oct 9am–noon & 2–6pm; May–Sept 9am–7pm; Nov–Feb 10am–noon & 2–5pm; €6 with Arènes; Ⓦtheatre-arles.com), is nowhere near as well preserved as the amphitheatre. Only one pair of columns is still standing, all the statuary has been removed, and the sides of the stage are littered with broken chunks of stone. Built a hundred years before Les Arènes, it was quarried to build churches not long after the Roman Empire collapsed, and later became part of the city's fortifications – one wing was turned into the **Tour Roland**, whose height gives an idea where the top seats would have been. Once again, there's little to see on an ordinary day, but it's an atmospheric venue for performances and festivals year-round. Below the theatre, the pleasant **Jardin d'Été** leads down to boulevard des Lices.

Thermes de Constantin

At the river end of rue Hôtel-de-Ville, the ruins of the **Thermes de Constantin** (daily: March, April & Oct 9am–noon & 2–6pm; May–Sept 9am–noon & 2–7pm; Nov–Feb 10am–noon & 1–5pm; €3), which may well have been the biggest Roman baths in Provence, are all that remain of the emperor's palace that extended along the waterfront. You can see the heating system below a thick Roman concrete floor and the divisions between the different areas, but there's nothing to help you imagine the original. The most striking feature, the high and rather elegant wall of an apse that sheltered one of the baths, in alternating stripes of orange brick and grey masonry, is best viewed from outside on place Constantin.

Cryptoportiques

Arles' most unusual – and spookiest – Roman remains, the **Cryptoportiques** (daily: March, April & Oct 9am–noon & 2–6pm; May–Sept 9am–noon & 2–7pm; Nov–Feb 10am–noon & 2–5pm; €3.50), are reached via stairs that lead down from inside the Hôtel de Ville (see p.95). No one knows quite what these huge, dark and dank underground galleries were for, but they may have been built simply to prop up one side of the town's level open forum, which stood above, and then used as a food store, or a barracks for public slaves. They're empty now, but gloriously atmospheric for a fifteen-minute subterranean stroll.

Musée Départemental Arles Antique

The superb modern **Musée Départemental Arles Antique** (daily: April–Oct 9am–7pm; Nov–March 10am–5pm; €5.50; Ⓦ www.arles-antique.cg13.fr), the best place to get an overall sense of Roman Arles, stands immediately southwest of the city centre on a spit of land between the Rhône and the Canal de l'Ecluse. Open-plan, flooded with natural light and immensely spacious, it starts with regional prehistory, then leads through the Roman era. The story of Arles is traced from Julius Caesar's legionnaire base and its development under Augustus, via its fourth-century status as the Christian emperor Constantine's capital of Gaul, to the height of its importance as a trading centre during the fifth century. At that time, Emperor Honorius could say "the town's position, its communications and its crowd of visitors is such that there is no place in the world better suited to spreading, in every sense, the products of the earth". Excellent models show the changing layout of the city and the sheer size of its monuments, while thematic displays explore such topics as medicine, industry and agriculture, and the use of water power. Overhead walkways enable visitors to admire some fabulous mosaics, while sculptures on the sarcophagi salvaged from Les Alyscamps (see below) depict everything from music and lovers to gladiators and Christian miracles.

The museum is positioned on the axis of the second-century **Cirque Romaine**, an enormous chariot racetrack that stretched back 450m and seated twenty thousand spectators. Little is now discernible on the ground, however.

Les Alyscamps

The Roman necropolis of Arles, known as **Les Alyscamps** (daily: March, April & Oct 9am–noon & 2–6pm; May–Sept 9am–7pm; Nov–Feb 10am–noon & 2–5pm; €3.50), lies a few minutes' walk south of boulevard des Lices. Originally much larger, it was regarded as the most hallowed Christian burial ground in all Europe long after the Roman era had ended; until the twelfth century, mourners far upstream would launch sumptuous coffins to float down the Rhône, for collection at Arles. Only one of its many alleyways now survives, and even that is foreshortened by a rail line, while the finest of its sarcophagi and statues have long since disappeared. Nonetheless, ancient tombs still line the shaded walk, as painted by Van Gogh (who rendered the tree trunks azure blue), and the tranquil stroll ends at the twelfth-century Romanesque church of **St-Honorat**, wonderfully simple and cool on a hot day.

The rest of the city

Medieval Arles came to centre around what's now the place de la République, site of both the **Cathédrale St-Trophime**, with its breathtaking **cloisters**, and the Hôtel de Ville. The one area where the city's former **walls**, built over the Roman ramparts, have survived lies to the east, in a quiet and attractive little corner. Sadly, the **riverfront**, once teeming with bars and bistros where weary workers would drink and dance away their woes, was heavily damaged during World War II, though a lovely priory spared by the bombs now houses a high-quality art museum, the **Musée Réattu**.

Place de la République

Superb twelfth-century Provençal stone carving around the doorway of the **Cathédrale St-Trophime** on the central **place de la République** depicts the Last

Judgement, trumpeted by angels playing with the enthusiasm of jazz musicians. As the damned are led naked and chained down to hell, the blessed, all female and draped in long robes, process upwards. Work on the cathedral itself started in the ninth century, on the spot where, in 597 AD, Saint Augustine was consecrated as the first bishop of the English. The high nave is now decorated with d'Aubusson tapestries, while there's more Romanesque and Gothic stone carving, including an image of Saint Martha leading away the tamed Tarasque (see p.107), in the extraordinarily beautiful **cloisters** (same hours as Les Arènes; €3.50), reached by a separate entrance to the right.

The obelisk of Egyptian granite in front of the cathedral, which may once have stood in the middle of the Cirque Romaine (see p.93), was placed there by Louis XIV, who fancied himself as a latter-day Augustus. Also on place de la

Van Gogh in Arles

On February 21, 1888, **Vincent van Gogh** arrived in Arles from Paris, to be greeted by snow and a bitter Mistral wind. He started painting immediately, and within the year produced such celebrated canvases as *The Sunflowers*, *Van Gogh's Chair*, *The Red Vines* and *The Sower*. He always lived near the station, staying first at the *Hotel Carrel*, 30 rue de la Cavalarie, and then the *Café de la Gare*, until the so-called "Yellow House", at 2 place Lamartine, had been rendered fit for use as a home as well as a studio.

From the daily letters he wrote to his brother Théo, it's clear that Van Gogh found few kindred souls in Arles. He finally managed to persuade **Paul Gauguin** to join him in late October. Although the two were to influence each other substantially in the following weeks, their relationship quickly soured as the increasingly bad November weather forced them to spend more time together indoors.

Precisely what transpired on the night of December 23, 1888, will probably never be known. According to Gauguin, Van Gogh, feeling threatened by his friend's possible departure, finally succumbed to a fit of psychosis and attacked first Gauguin and then himself. He cut off the lower part of his **left ear**, wrapped it in newspaper, and handed it to a prostitute. An alternative version of the story emerged in 2009, with allegations that it was in fact an infuriated Gauguin who'd lopped off the offending lobe with a sword, and that the two artists had concocted a cover story to protect Gauguin from the law.

In any event, Gauguin left Arles, and although Vincent's wound soon healed, his mental health swiftly deteriorated. In response to a petition from thirty of his alarmed neighbours, he was packed off to the **Hôtel-Dieu** hospital, where he had the good fortune to be treated by a young and sympathetic doctor, Félix Rey. Van Gogh painted Rey's portrait while in the hospital, as well as the hospital itself, whose inmates are clearly suffering not from violent frenzy, but from an unhappiness only Van Gogh could express. Upon leaving hospital, Van Gogh also left Arles, moving voluntarily to St-Rémy (see p.99).

None of Van Gogh's paintings remains in Arles, and the Yellow House was destroyed by bombing during World War II. Vestiges of the city that he knew still survive, however. Behind the Réattu museum, lanterns line the river wall where he used to wander, wearing candles on his hat, watching the night-time light: *The Starry Night* is the Rhône at Arles. The café he painted in *Café de Nuit* is still open for business in place du Forum, while the distinctive Pont Langlois drawbridge, which he painted in March 1888, survives on the southern edge of town. The Hôtel-Dieu hospital itself, on rue du Président-Wilson, has become the **Espace Van Gogh**, housing a *mediathèque* and university departments, with a bookshop and a *salon de thé* in the arcades, and flowerbeds in the courtyard that re-create the garden that Van Gogh both painted and described.

▲ Pont Langlois

République, the palatial seventeenth-century **Hôtel de Ville** was inspired by the Palace of Versailles. A staircase inside leads down to the Roman **Cryptoportiques** (see p.92); in fact, the flattened vaulted roof of its entrance hall was expressly designed to minimize stress on the galleries below.

Musée Réattu

The must-see **Musée Réattu** (Tues–Sun: March–June & mid-Sept to Oct 10am–12.30pm & 2–6.30pm; July to mid-Sept 10am–7pm; Nov–Feb 1–6pm; €7, free on 1st Sun of month; ⑩museereattu.arles.fr) stands beside the river and opposite the Roman baths, in a beautiful fifteenth-century priory. It centres on 57 ink and crayon sketches, made between December 1970 and February 1971, donated by Pablo Picasso in appreciation of the many bullfights he'd seen in Arles. Among the split faces, clowns and hilarious Tarasque, there's a beautifully simple portrait of Picasso's mother. Other twentieth-century pieces dotted about the landings, corridors and courtyard niches include *Odalisque*, Zadkine's bronze sculpture of a woman playing a violin; Mario Prassinos' black and white studies of the Alpilles; and César's *Compression 1973*. The museum also hosts very good temporary exhibitions.

Fondation Vincent van Gogh

Housed in the Palais de Luppé, at 26 Rond-Point des Arènes on the west side of the amphitheatre, the **Fondation Vincent van Gogh** (April–June daily 10am–6pm; July–Sept daily 10am–7pm; Oct–March Tues–Sun 11am–5pm; €7; ⑩fondationvan gogh-arles.org) exhibits contemporary works inspired by Van Gogh. Francis Bacon was the first to contribute, with a painting based on Van Gogh's *The Painter on the Road to Tarascon*, destroyed during World War II. Roy Lichtenstein repaints *The Sower*; and Hockney, César and Jasper Johns also pay homage.

Eating and drinking

Arles holds a good number of **restaurants**, whether excellent-quality, cheap, or both at once. Place du Forum is the centre of **café** life, particularly at the young and noisy *Bistrot Arlésien*. Nevertheless, don't be surprised to discover that most of the city packs up for the night around 10.30pm.

Saturday's **market** extends the length of boulevard Georges-Clemenceau, boulevard des Lices and boulevard Émile-Combes and many of the adjoining streets. A smaller food market is held every Wednesday in place Lamartine, with bric-a-brac stalls spreading down boulevard Émile-Combes.

Restaurants

La Charcuterie 51 rue des Arènes
℡04.90.96.56.96, ⊛www.lacharcuterie .camargue.fr. Lyonnaise-style deli turned cramped, lively, in-the-know local bistro, with a tiny terrace. Meat-heavy menus from €16 lunch, €26 dinner. Closed Sun & Mon.

Chez Arianne 2 rue du Dr-Fanton ℡04.90.52.00.65. The eccentric Arianne rules the roost at this self-styled *bistrôt de vins*, serving a small, appealingly unpretentious menu of home-cooked rabbit and chicken dishes for around €14, washed down with fabulous organic wines. Closed Mon & Tues.

Le Cilantro 31 rue Porte de Laure
℡04.90.18.25.05, ⊛www.restaurantcilantro.com. A serene and highly expensive restaurant serving beautifully executed, imaginative dishes. The meticulous young chef prepares excellent *plats*, such as pikeperch in a truffle crust, for around €30. Lunch menus from €25, dinner from €65. Closed Sat lunch & Sun, plus Mon lunch July & Aug, all Mon Sept–June.

A Coté 21 rue des Carmes
℡04.90.47.61.13, ⊛bistro-acote.com. The cheaper sister to the much more expensive, Michelin-starred *L'Atelier de Jean Luc Rabanel*, at no. 7 on the same little alleyway, this is just as gastronomically satisfying, and has some pleasant outdoor seating. Mouthwatering tapas including aubergine caviar (€6.50), plus breakfast and fancy take-out sandwiches. Daily 9am–midnight.

L'Escaladou 23 Porte de Laure
℡04.90.96.70.43. Behind its deceptively simple facade, above the Théâtre Antique, this local favourite holds three substantial dining rooms, all often sufficiently packed for some to dismiss it as a tourist trap. It may be noisy and not exactly romantic, and the service sometimes perfunctory, but the food is delicious, with menus from €18 and some magnificently garlicky fish specials, including a sumptuous €24 Arlesian *bouillabaisse*. Closed Wed.

La Gueule de Loup 39 rue des Arènes
℡04.90.96.96.69. Cosy restaurant, squeezed into a venerable town house, and serving substantial traditional dishes such as bull *filet*

with anchovy sauce. Menus from €12 lunch, €22 dinner; reservations recommended. Closed Sun & Mon lunch, plus Mon eve Nov–Easter.

Lou Marquès *Hôtel Jules César*, 9 bd des Lices
℡04.90.52.52.52, ⊛hotel-julescesar.fr. A real gourmet delight where the specialities include langoustine risotto with Camargue rice and lobster cooked in Chateauneuf-du-Pape wine, all served with the utmost decorum; menus at €28 with no choice, €40 (four-course), and €60 (five-course). Closed Sat lunch, Sun eve & all Mon.

La Mule Blanche 9 rue du Président Wilson
℡04.90.93.98.54, ⊛restaurant-mule-blanche .com. The great appeal of dining at this laid-back brasserie/restaurant is its enormous outdoor patio on a quiet square; the food itself is rich and fruity, with salads at €10, *plats* around €15, and a €25 dinner menu offering duck with honey. Occasional jazz. Closed Sun & first half of Jan.

La Paillote 28 rue du Dr-Fanton ℡04.90.96.33.15. Very friendly place, with a good €20 menu full of Provençal starters and main courses such as *papillote de taureau* (bull), and a €28 one featuring *soufflé de foie gras*. Closed Tues lunch & Wed eve.

Cafés, bars and ice cream

L'Apostrophe 7 place du Forum
℡04.90.96.34.17. The youngest of the place du Forum bars, with modern decor and tables full of laptop-users taking advantage of the free wi-fi.

Café de la Nuit 11 place du Forum
℡04.90.96.44.56. If you sit on the terrace you'll find yourself in quite a few holiday snaps, as this is the setting of Van Gogh's *Café La Nuit*.

Cargo de Nuit 7 av Sadi-Carnot ℡04.90.49.55.99, ⊛cargodenuit.com. Café-bar with an excellent line-up of live jazz, electronic and world music concerts, mainly on Fri & Sat evenings.

Pâtisserie du Forum 4 rue de la Liberté
℡04.90.96.03.72. *Salon de thé* with a whole patisserie full of goodies to go with the Earl Grey, plus ice cream and hot chocolate. Closed Sun.

Soleileïs 9 rue du Dr-Fanton ℡04.90.93.30.76. Delicious home-made ice cream with all-natural ingredients.

La Grande Crau

East from Arles and the Rhône delta, the region known as **La Grande Crau** (or just La Crau) stretches for around 30km, as far as Salon. This was once, a very long time ago, the bed of the Rhône and the Durance. Its name derives from a Greek word meaning "stony", and even though several areas are now irrigated and planted with fruit trees, protected by windbreaks of cypresses and poplars, much of it is still **rock-strewn** desert, unbearably hot and shadeless in summer.

Only as the Grande Crau approaches the western end of the **Alpilles**, the chain of hills that defines its north edge – its peaks resemble the crest of a wave about to engulf the plain – does the countryside become more amenable, offering potentially interesting stopoffs at the **Abbaye de Montmajour** and the village of **Fontvieille**.

Abbaye de Montmajour

Just 3km north of Arles, beside the D17 as it sets off towards Les Baux, the Romanesque ruins of the **Abbaye de Montmajour** (April–June daily 9.30am–6pm; July–Sept daily 10am–6.30pm; Oct–March Tues–Sun 10am–5pm; €7; Ⓦ montmajour.monuments-nationaux.fr) climb the side of a small hill. Take heed when you climb the 124 steps of the fortified watchtower, as your arrival will undoubtedly startle dozens of pigeons; the view from the top, of La Grande Crau, the Rhône and the Alpilles, is stunning. Below, in the **cloisters**, a menacing stone menagerie of beasts and devils enlivens the bases of the vaulting. Throughout the year, the abbey hosts photographic exhibitions, in association with the Rencontres d'Arles (see p.88).

The eleventh-century funerary chapel of **Ste-Croix**, with its perfect proportions and frieze of palm fronds, is set in a farmyard 200m east, amid tombs cut out of the rock.

Fontvieille

Little **FONTVIEILLE**, 5km northeast of Montmajour, is a site of literary pilgrimage for the French, as the setting for Alphonse Daudet's nineteenth-century *Lettres de Mon Moulin*. Daudet never lived in the eponymous windmill, just south of town, but now, as the **Moulin de Daudet**, it's a small museum (daily: Feb & March 10am–noon & 2–6pm; April–Sept 9am–7pm; Oct–Dec 10am–noon & 2–6pm; €2.50).

A couple of kilometres south of the windmill, the crossroads where the D33 meets the D82 is dominated by the remains of two Roman **aqueducts** that formerly served Arles. Slightly further south still, a left turning, signposted Meunerie Romain, leads to the dramatic excavation of the sixteen-wheel **Barbegal mill**. Powered by water from one of the aqueducts, it's thought to have produced up to three tonnes of flour a day.

Les Baux-de-Provence

At the top of the Alpilles ridge, 15km northeast of Arles, perches the distinctly unreal fortified village of **LES BAUX-DE-PROVENCE**. Unreal partly because the ruins of its eleventh-century **castle** merge almost imperceptibly into the plateau, whose rock is both foundation and part of the structure. And unreal, too, because this Ville Morte (Dead City) and a vast area of the plateau around it are accessible only via a turnstile from the living village below, which remains a too-perfect collection of sixteenth- and seventeenth-century churches, chapels and mansions.

When the medieval lords of Les Baux, who owed allegiance to none, died out at the end of the fourteenth century, the town passed to the counts of Provence and then to the kings of France who, in 1632, razed the feudal citadel to the ground and fined the population into penury. For the next two hundred years, both citadel and village were inhabited almost exclusively by bats and crows. The subsequent discovery of the mineral bauxite (whose name derives from "Les Baux") in the neighbouring hills brought back some life, and tourism has more recently transformed the place. Today the population stays steady at around 400, augmented by more than 1.5 million visitors each year. Even the former bauxite quarries, cut from the jagged rocks of the **Val d'Enfer**, are now tourist attractions, as home to the imaginative gallery known as the **Cathédrale des Images**.

The great majority of Les Baux's visitors are day-trippers, who tend to be thinning out by 5pm or so. To avoid the crowds, especially in summer, it's well worth turning up later in the day.

The castle and the village

While Les Baux is undoubtedly a pretty village, the prime reason to come here is to see its enormous and extraordinary **castle** (daily: March–June 9am–6.30pm; July & Aug 9am–8.30pm; Sept–Nov 9.30am–6pm; Dec–Feb 9.30am–5pm; €7.70; audioguide in English available; ⓦwww.chateau-baux-provence.com), which though universally known as a château is in truth more of a large citadel. The only gate to the complex is at the far end of the main village street. That leads first to open ground below the walls, scattered with replica siege engines and catapults, and then to a network of footpaths over and through assorted buildings which include the ruins of the feudal castle demolished on Richelieu's orders, the partially restored **Chapelle Castrale** and the **Tour Sarrasine**. The higher you climb, the more spectacular the views become.

Down in the village itself, several beautiful buildings are given over to museums. The **Musée Yves Brayer** in the Hôtel des Porcelets (mid-Feb to March & Oct– Dec daily except Tues 10am–12.30pm & 2–5.30pm; April–Sept daily 10am–12.30pm & 2–6.30pm; €4) shows the paintings (and hats) of the twentieth-century figurative artist whose work also adorns the seventeenth-century **Chapelle des Pénitents Blancs** on place de l'Église. Changing exhibitions by contemporary Provençal artists are displayed in the **Hôtel de Manville** (hours vary; free), while the **Musée des Santons** in the old Hôtel de Ville (daily 9am–7pm; free) displays traditional Provençal nativity figures.

The Cathédrale des Images

It's said that Dante took his inspiration for the nine circles of the *Inferno* from a trip he made to the valley known as the **Val d'Enfer** (Valley of Hell), immediately north of Les Baux, while staying at Arles. Jean Cocteau in his 1959 film, *Le Testament d'Orphée* used its contorted rocks and bauxite quarries.

More recently, those same quarries have been turned into an audiovisual experience called the **Cathédrale des Images**, reached by walking or driving a few hundred metres north of the village along the D27 (daily: April–Sept 10am–6pm; Oct–March 10am–5pm; €7.50; ⓦwww.cathedrale-images.com). Projection is continuous, so you don't have to wait to go in. The effect is similar to entering an Egyptian temple carved from the rock, but here you're surrounded by images projected over the floor, ceilings and walls of the vast rectangular caverns, and by music that resonates strangely in the captured space. The precise content changes yearly, though it's often devoted to a particular artist or school of painting. Really, though, it makes little difference; the sensation is just mind-blowing, as you wander on and through the changing shapes and colours.

Practicalities

Les Baux village is pedestrianized. **Parking** costs €5 close to the gate, €3 a little lower down, and nothing at the Cathédrale des Images, so if you plan to walk there and back anyway you might as well park there. There's a **tourist office** in the Maison du Roy on rue Porte Mage (daily: July & Aug 9am–7pm; Sept–June 9am–6pm; ☎04.90.54.34.39, Ⓦlesbauxdeprovence.com).

The only moderately priced **hotel**, the *Hostellerie de la Reine Jeanne* by the entrance to the village (☎04.90.54.32.06, Ⓦla-reinejeanne.com; ❸; closed mid-Jan to mid-Feb), has very friendly staff, simple rooms with views of the citadel, and good **menus** starting at €25. There's also *Le Prince Noir*, an eccentric **B&B** in the uppermost house in the village, on rue de l'Orme (☎04.90.54.39.57, Ⓦleprincenoir.com; ❺; 2-night minimum stay). Luxurious options in the surrounding countryside include the beautiful *Oustau de Baumanière* (☎04.90.54.33.07, Ⓦoustaudebaumaniere.com; ❾; closed Nov–Feb), spectacularly situated just west of Les Baux en route to the Val d'Enfer.

Crêperies, pizza places and snack bars, few of them inexpensive, are dotted throughout the village; *Les Variétés*, 29 rue du Trencat (☎04.90.54.55.88; closed Oct–Feb), has a lovely interior courtyard and sells good salads and pasta dishes for around €10.

St-Rémy-de-Provence

The dreamy, little-changed community of **ST-RÉMY-DE-PROVENCE**, where Van Gogh sought psychiatric help and painted some of his most lyrical works, nestles against the northern base of the Alpilles, 30km from either Arles or Avignon. St-Rémy is a beautiful spot, centring on a charmingly low-key old town – the **Vieille Ville** – that's barely 500m across, and encircled by leafy boulevards. South of the old town, several exceptional sites and attractions lie within walking distance: Van Gogh's hospital of **St-Paul-de-Mausole**, a **Roman arch**, and the ruins of the ancient city of **Glanum**.

The festivals of St-Rémy

The ideal time to visit St-Rémy is for one of Provence's most vibrant traditional festivals, the **Fête de Transhumance** on Whit Monday, when a flock of four thousand sheep, accompanied by goats, rams and donkeys, makes a tour of the town before being packed off to the Alps for the summer. Other events in the busy local calendar include the **Carreto Ramado** on August 15, a harvest thanksgiving procession in which the religious or secular symbolism of the floats reveals the political colour of the various village councils; and a pagan rather than workers' **Mayday** celebration, with donkey-drawn floral floats on which people play fifes and tambourines. On July 14, August 15 and the fourth Sunday in September, the intrepid local youth attempt to set loose six **bulls** that are herded round the town by their mounted chaperones.

Arrival and information

St-Rémy's **tourist office** is just south of the old town on place Jean-Jaurès (June–Sept Mon–Sat 9am–12.30pm & 2–6pm, Sun 10am–noon; Oct–May Mon–Sat 9am–noon & 2–6pm; ℡04.90.92.05.22, ⓦsaintremy-de-provence.com). They have excellent free guides to **cycling and walking routes** in and around the Alpilles, though note that the hills are closed to walkers all summer due to the risk of fire.

No **trains** serve St-Rémy; **buses** from Avignon, Aix and Arles drop passengers in place de la République, on the eastern edge of the old town. **Bikes** can be rented from Telecycles, who deliver anywhere in the area (℡04.90.92.83.15, ⓦtelecycles-location.com).

Accommodation

Although no **accommodation** is available within the old town itself, St-Rémy has a fine selection of **hotels**, most within easy walking distance of the centre, and several **campsites** close by.

Hotels

Canto Cigalo chemin de Canto Cigalo ℡04.90.92.14.28, ⓦcantocigalo.com. Very nice, peaceful hotel, beside the canal twenty minutes' walk southeast of the old town, with good-sized rooms and cricket-themed decor (as in the insect, not the sport), plus a pool and plenty of outdoor space on the terrace and in the large gardens. ❹

Le Castelet des Alpilles 6 place Mireille ℡04.90.92.07.21, ⓦcastelet-alpilles.com. Pleasant, traditional rooms, south of the centre on the road towards Glanum; those with south-facing balconies have great views. Closed early Nov to late March. ❹

Cheval Blanc 6 av Fauconnet ℡04.90.92.09.28, ℡06.61.51.47.98 when closed, ⓦhotelducheval blanc.com. Inexpensive hotel, just outside the old town on its western edge. The cheapest rooms are not en-suite, but the four-person ones are especially good value. Closed Nov to mid-March. ❸

Gounod 18 place de la République ℡04.90.92.06.14, ⓦhotel-gounod.com. Luxurious central hotel, where the ornately decorated rooms have flat-screen TVs; there's also a swimming pool and garden. Rates include breakfast. Closed Feb & March. ❼

Le Soleil 35 av Pasteur ℡04.90.92.00.63, ⓦwww.hotelsoleil.com. Very welcoming hotel, set back from the main road a short walk south of the centre, with a pool and private parking. Nice, simple rooms but no restaurant. Closed early Nov to late March. ❸

Sous les Figuiers 3 av Taillandier ℡04.32.60.15.40, ⓦhotel-charme-provence.com. Gorgeous place just north of the old town, run by a creative team of photographer and painter. Thirteen well-appointed rooms, some with their own private garden terraces, plus swimming pool and an on-site artist's studio (art classes available). Closed mid-Jan to mid-March. ❺

Campsites

Le Mas de Nicolas av Plaisance du Touch ℡04.90.92.27.05, ⓦmasdenicolas.celeonet.fr. A four-star municipal site with its own pool, 800m from the centre on a turning off the route de Mollèges. Closed mid-Oct to mid-March. €20.50 per night.

Monplaisir chemin Monplaisir ℡04.90.92.22.70, ⓦwww.camping-monplaisir.fr. Family-run, five-acre, two-star campsite, 1km northwest of town along the rte de Maillane, with a pool and snack facilities. Closed Nov–Feb. €23 per night.

Pegomas av Jean-Moulin ℡04.90.92.01.21, ⓦwww.campingpegomas.com. Three-star site, with a pool, 1km east towards Cavaillon. Closed Nov–Feb. €20 per night.

The Town

St-Rémy's compact **Vieille Ville** is an enchanting tangle of narrow lanes and ancient alleyways, lined with stately residences and interspersed with peaceful little squares. While it only takes a few minutes to walk from one side to the other along its main east–west axis, **rue Carnot**, it's worth exploring every nook and cranny. Although it holds a couple of interesting museums, and plenty of stylish boutiques and restaurants, it's all surprisingly sleepy. There's not even a café where you can sit and watch the world go by; instead virtually all the town's commercial life takes place on the four busy boulevards that ring the entire ensemble.

To get a thorough overview of the region, start by visiting the **Musée des Alpilles**, in the Renaissance Hôtel Mistral de Mondragon, on place Favier halfway along rue Carnot (daily except Mon, plus 1st Sun of month: July & Aug 10am–12.30pm & 2–7pm; March–June & Sept–Oct 10am–noon & 2–6pm; Nov–Feb 2–5pm; €3). Interesting sections on folklore, festivities and traditional crafts include an exhibit on cicadas, a symbol of Provence associated with author Frédéric Mistral.

Another fine mansion, the eighteenth-century Hôtel d'Estrine at 8 rue Estrine, houses the **Centre d'Art Présence Van Gogh** (mid-March to April & Oct–Nov Tues–Sun 10.30am–12.30pm & 2–6pm; May–Sept Tues & Thurs–Sun 10am–12.30pm & 2–7pm, Wed 10am–7pm; €3.20), which hosts contemporary art exhibitions plus permanent displays on the painter, and has a well-stocked gift shop.

Just south of the old town, a short way beyond the tourist office, the art of the twentieth-century Greek painter, Mario Prassinos, who settled in the nearby village of Eygalières, adorns the beautiful Romanesque **chapel of Notre-Dame-de-Pitié** (Wed–Sun: mid-March to June & Sept–Dec 2–6pm; July & Aug 11am–1pm & 3–7pm; free). Tree forms, his favourite motif, become a powerful graphic language in the oil paintings he created for the chapel, *Les Peintures du Supplice* (*Paintings of the Suffering*), provoked by his horror of torture.

St-Paul-de-Mausole

The former monastery of **St-Paul-de-Mausole**, where **Vincent van Gogh** was a voluntary psychiatric patient between May 8, 1889 and May 16, 1890, stands just under 2km south of St-Rémy's old town. It's only 100m east of the main road south, now known as av Vincent-van-Gogh, across from Les Antiques (see p.102), though for a more peaceful walk you may prefer to follow avenues Pierre-Barbier and Marie-Gasquet. Placards along this route, marked out as the "Promenade dans l'Univers de Van Gogh", show where he painted some of the 150 canvases he produced during the year, including *La Route aux Cyprès* and *Les Blés Verts*, though sadly it's characterized by suburban villas rather than sweeping vistas these days.

Visiting St-Paul-de-Mausole itself (daily: April–Oct 9.30am–7pm; Oct–March 10.15am–5pm; €4) is a profoundly moving experience. Amazingly enough, it's still a psychiatric hospital, and although tourists are kept well clear of the active

Nostradamus

The house where **Michel de Nostradamus** was born on December 14, 1503, still stands on rue Hoche in St-Rémy, though it's not open to visitors. Educated as a physician, Nostradamus first received recognition for his innovative treatment of plague victims. Only in the latter part of his life did his interest in astrology and the occult lead to the publication of **The Prophecies of Michel Nostradamus**, a collection of 942 prophetic quatrains. Fearing persecution should the authorities fully understand his predictions, he deliberately wrote in an obscure and cryptic style. The end result was some extremely ambiguous French verse, which has since been the subject of numerous forgeries, urban legends and off-the-wall interpretations. Events he's been credited as predicting include the rise of Napoleon and Hitler, the Great Fire of London, and the 9/11 attacks. While Nostradamus may or may not have been able to accurately foresee the future, his success as a writer remains undisputed: the collection of prophecies, now known as *Centuries*, has been in print continuously since its first publication in 1551. Neither was Nostradamus himself persecuted; by the time he died in 1566, he had become Physician-in-Ordinary to King Henry II.

area – be sure to follow the "Zone Touristique" signs – you get a real sense of its ongoing work. Displays in the church and cloisters contrast Van Gogh's diagnosis and treatment with modern-day practices, and you can see a mock-up of his former room and walk in the glorious gardens, planted with lavender and poppies. Far from being kept under lock and key, Vincent was allowed to wander around the town and Alpilles. Art therapy forms a major component of current treatment at the hospital, and patients' work is on sale in the on-site shop.

Les Antiques and Glanum

Also around 2km south of town, but this time immediately west of avenue Vincent-van-Gogh, an open batch of ground holds two Roman monuments, jointly known as **Les Antiques**; access is always free, around the clock. One is a triumphal arch celebrating the Roman conquest of Marseille, the other a well-preserved mausoleum thought to commemorate two grandsons of Augustus. Both display intricate patterning and a typically Roman sense of proportion.

Sharing the same car park (€2.50), back across the road very slightly south, the impressive ancient settlement of **GLANUM** (April–Aug daily 9.30am–6.30pm; Sept Tues–Sun 9.30am–6.30pm; Oct–March Tues–Sun 10am–5pm; €7; ⓦ glanum.monuments-nationaux.fr) was dug from the alluvial deposits at the foot of the Alpilles. This site originally held a Neolithic homestead, before the Gallo-Greeks, probably from Massalia (Marseille), built a city here between the second and first centuries BC. Then the Gallo-Romans constructed yet another town, which lasted until the third century AD.

A footpath drops from the site entrance to run through the centre of the ruins, with plenty of maps and captions along the way, but getting to grips with Glanum is far from easy. Not only were the later buildings moulded on to the earlier ones, but there was also a fashion at the time of Christ for a Hellenistic style. Greek levels can be most readily distinguished from the Roman by the stones: the earlier civilization used massive hewn rocks, while the Romans preferred smaller, more accurately shaped, stones.

Where the site narrows into a ravine at its southern end, a Greek edifice stands around the **spring** that made this location so desirable. Steps lead down to a pool, with a slab above for the libations of those too sick to descend. An inscription records that Agrippa restored it in 27 BC, and dedicated it to Valetudo, the Roman goddess of health. **Altars** to Hercules remain in evidence, however, while traces of a prehistoric settlement that also depended on this spring survive up the hill to the west. The Gallo-Romans directed the water through canals to heat houses and, of course, to the **baths** that lie near the site entrance. There are superb sculptures on the Roman **Temples Geminées** (twin temples), as well as fragments of mosaics, fountains of both periods, and first-storey walls and columns.

Eating and drinking

Brasseries and **restaurants** abound in St-Rémy, both within the Vieille Ville (along rue Carnot in particular), and along the surrounding boulevards. It's also a great place to shop for picnic food and deli items, with **markets** on Wednesday morning in the old town, and on Saturday in place de la Mairie. The liveliest **bars** are on the peripheral boulevards: try *Devin* and *Café du Lezard*, side by side at 12 boulevard Gambetta.

L'Aile ou la Cuisse 5 rue de la Commune ⓣ 04.32.62.00.25. Very romantic, upscale restaurant in the old town, with a pricey *à la carte* menu of main dishes at €26–35, as well as a deli selling posh picnic items and delectable jams and olive oils. Closed Sun & Mon.

Bistrot Decouverte 19 bd Victor-Hugo ☎04.90.92.34.49, ⊛www.bistrotdecouverte.com. Straightforward, high-quality Provençal bistro, with a fabulous wine list, on the edge of the old town. There's a two-course menu for €16, and a full dinner menu at €30. Closed Sun pm & Mon, plus mid-Nov to mid-March.

La Cassolette 53 rue Carnot ☎04.90.92.40.50. Inexpensive but high-quality little French restaurant in the old town. The prize seats are out on the pavement of this tiny street; inside things are a bit more formal. The €17 menu features *taureau*, the €22 menu is a definite step up. No credit cards.

Chez Xa 24 bd Mirabeau ☎04.90.92.41.23. Surprisingly good Asian-inspired food, such as beef curry and shrimp with coriander and coconut milk. Set menu €27. Closed Wed & Nov–March.

La Gousse d'Ail 6 bd Marceau ☎04.90.92.16.87, ⊛la-goussedail.com. Charming bistro on the western edge of the old town, with a €16 lunch menu and dinner for €27 or €34, its own vintage merry-go-round, and live jazz on Wednesday nights. Closed Thurs & Fri lunch.

La Maison Jaune 15 rue Carnot ☎04.90.92.56.14, ⊛lamaisonjaune.info. This Michelin-starred restaurant, in a seventeenth-century house with a garden terrace in the old town, serves tempting *à la carte* offerings such as polenta and pigeon roasted in Baux wines, alongside menus for €36, €56 (the lovely *Dégustation Provençal*) and €66. Closed Mon, plus Sun eve in winter, Tues lunch in summer, and all Jan & Feb.

Taberna Romana site of Glanum, av van-Gogh ☎04.90.92.65.97, ⊛taberna-romana.com. This so-called Roman restaurant, serving what it claims are authentic Roman dishes, makes a very nice open-air lunch spot, overlooking the ruins of Glanum from a well-shaded terrace; you don't have to pay to go in, in fact you can see the ruins pretty well from here for free. The food itself is fun, zestful and a bit different, with a large mixed plate of, say, *samsa* (spicy olives), *cicerona* (chick peas) and goat's cheese for €17, or a matza, which closely resembles a chicken wrap, for €8. They also serve "Roman beer". Tues–Sun 10am–6.30pm, closed Oct–March.

La Petite Crau

The plain known as **La Petite Crau**, stretching north from the Alpilles to the confluence of the Rhône and the Durance, is today richly cultivated, with cherries and peaches as its main crops. Once, however, it was a swampy wasteland, the only extensive bit of solid ground being the rocky outcrop of **La Montagnette**, which runs parallel to the Rhône for 10km. Villages are few and far between, built on the scattered bases of rock and often retaining their medieval elements of fortified walls and churches and tangled narrow streets. This is the Provence that inspired **Frédéric Mistral** and Vincent van Gogh. Note, however, that although La Montagnette is lovely **walking** country, fire risk again precludes access between July and mid-September.

Châteaurenard

Halfway between St-Rémy and Avignon, the main town in La Petite Crau, **CHÂTEAURENARD**, is dominated by the two remaining towers of its

Markets

If you're in La Petite Crau on a Friday, the **Marché Paysan** in **Graveson**, place du Marché (early May to Oct 4–8pm; ⊛lemarchepaysan.com), is not to be missed, with *paysans* from La Grande and La Petite Crau, the Camargue and from across the Durance selling their goat's cheeses, olives, flowers, and fruit and vegetables picked the same morning.

The ordinary morning markets here are on Friday in **Graveson**, Thursday in **Maillane** and **Noves**, Sunday in **Châteaurenard**, Wednesday in **Barbentane**, and Tuesday in **Rognonas**, the village just across the Durance from Avignon.

Romanesque and Gothic medieval **castle** (May–Sept Tues–Sat 10am–noon & 2.30–6.30pm, Sun 2.30–6.30pm; Oct–April daily except Fri 3–5pm; €4), described by Frédéric Mistral as "twin horns on the forehead of a hill". The castle's **Tour du Griffon** offers fabulous views across La Petite Crau to the Alpilles and La Montagnette.

Châteaurenard's **tourist office** is at 11 cours Carnot (Mon–Sat 9am–noon & 2–5.45pm, plus Sun 10am–noon in July & Aug; ℡04.90.24.25.50, ⓦot .chateaurenard.com). Two inexpensive **hotels** stand nearby, *Le Central*, 27 cours Carnot (℡04.90.94.10.90, ⓦhotel-lecentral.com; ❷; restaurant closed Sun), and *Les Glycines*, 14 avenue Victor-Hugo (℡04.90.94.10.66, ⓦresthotelesglycines .com; ❷; restaurant closed Sun pm & Mon), both with decent **restaurants**. The town is packed out every Sunday, when it hosts a massive wholesale fruit and vegetable **market**.

Noves

Five kilometres east of Châteaurenard, the typical Petit Crau village of **NOVES** boasts a fourteenth-century gateway, and is renowned as the home of Laura, the subject of Petrarch's besotted sonnets. Set in huge gardens just outside Noves on the Châteaurenard road, the *Auberge de Noves* (℡04.90.24.28.28, ⓦaubergedenoves .com; ❽; closed Mon & Tues Oct–March) is a seriously expensive **hotel** in a beautiful farmhouse, with exquisite furnishings and impeccable service. Its **restaurant** (closed Sun & Mon) serves such delicacies as *foie gras*, snails, truffles and lobster, coupled with fine wines (weekday lunch menu €45; dinner menu from €68). For more basic comforts, Noves' **campsite** *Le Pilon d'Agel*, on the route de Mollégès (℡04.90.95.16.23, ⓦpilondagel.com; €16.50 per night; closed Oct–April), offers a pool and access for people with disabilities.

Maillane

The poet **Frédéric Mistral** was born in **MAILLANE**, 7km northwest of St-Rémy, in 1830 and buried there in 1914. Primarily responsible for the early twentieth-century revival of all things Provençal, he won the Nobel Prize for Literature in 1904, a feat no other writer of a minority language has ever achieved. The house where he lived from 1876 onwards has been preserved intact as the **Museon Mistral**, 11 rue Lamartine (Tues–Sun: April–Sept 9.30–11.30am & 2.30–6.30pm; Oct–March 10–11.30am & 2–4.30pm; €3.50).

La Petite Crau was Mistral's "sacred triangle", and its customs and legends were a great source of inspiration. In his memoirs, Mistral describes the procession of St Anthime from **Graveson**, just north of Maillane, to La Montagnette, where on reaching the abbey church of **St-Michel-de-Frigolet**, the people spread out a feast on the perfumed grass and knocked back bottles of local wine for the rest of the day. If it hadn't rained by the time they reached home, they punished the saint by dipping him three times in a ditch.

Boulbon and Barbentane

A footpath west from St-Michel-de-Frigolet leads over the Montagnette ridge and, after 5km, down to **BOULBON**. A strategic site overlooking the Rhône, Boulbon was heavily fortified in the Middle Ages, and today the ruins of its enormous fortress, built half within and half above a rocky escarpment, look like some picture-book crusader castle. Celebrated on the last Sunday of August, Boulbon's **Fête de Saint-Éloi** involves chariots drawn by teams of horses in Saracen harness doing the rounds of the village, and much drinking by all the villagers.

Eight kilometres northeast of Boulbon, at the northern edge of La Montagnette in **BARBENTANE**, the fourteenth-century **Tour Anglica** keeps watch on the confluence of the Rhône and Durance. The town has two medieval gateways and a beautifully arcaded Renaissance building, the **Maison des Chevaliers**, plus a much more recent **château** (Easter–June & Oct daily except Wed 10am–noon & 2–6pm; July–Sept daily 10am–noon & 2–6pm; €7), designed for grandeur rather than defence. Accessible on guided tours only, this seventeenth-century ducal residence has gorgeous grey and white Tuscan marble floors, and all the vases, painted ceilings, chandeliers and antique furniture that you'd expect of a house still owned by the same aristocratic family. The Italianate gardens are the highlight.

Hotels in Barbentane include the comfortable *Castel Mouisson*, *quartier* Castel Mouisson (☏04.90.95.51.17, ⊕hotel-castelmouisson.com; ❸; closed mid-Oct to mid-March), with good facilities and a pleasant garden and pool, and the more basic *St-Jean*, in the heart of town at 1 le Cours (☏04.90.15.45.22; ❶).

Tarascon and Beaucaire

Roughly halfway along the Rhône between Arles and Avignon, **Tarascon** and **Beaucaire** face each other across the river, the former in Provence on the east bank, the latter in Languedoc on the west. Each has its own majestic **castle**; though Tarascon's is the more interesting to visit, Beaucaire is a more pleasant town simply to stroll around.

Tarascon

Dozing gently beside the river, the two-thousand-year-old city of **TARASCON** feels far removed from the tourist mainstream of Provence. Despite its imposing castle, the old town centre is, apart from the arcaded rue des Halles and a couple of busy commercial alleyways running off it, not only largely residential but also quite faded and run-down. That makes Tarascon a relaxing, atmospheric place to spend a day or two. Just don't expect much drama or excitement, unless you're here for one of its annual festivals, such as June's spectacular carnival in honour of the city's namesake, the amphibious monster known as the *Tarasque*.

Arrival, information and accommodation

Tarascon's **gare SNCF** is immediately south of the centre on boulevard Gustave-Desplaces (☏08.36.35.35.35). The **tourist office** (June–Sept Mon–Sat 9am–12.30pm & 2–6pm, Sun 9.30am–12.30pm; Oct–May Mon–Sat 9am–12.30pm & 2–5.30pm; ☏04.90.91.03.52, ⊕tarascon.org) faces the château and the road bridge across to Beaucaire.

Tarascon holds a reasonable assortment of **hotels**, with no real standouts, plus a good hostel and some nice central B&Bs.

Hotels and B&Bs

Échevins 26 bd Itam ☏04.90.91.01.70, ⊕www .hotel-echevins.com. Handsome old town house, where the large but ageing bedrooms don't quite live up to the promise of the public spaces. Attractive terrace restaurant. Closed Nov–Easter. ❹

Provençal 12 cours A-Briand ☏04.90.91.11.41, ⊕leprovencal-tarascon.com. Family-run hotel near the station, offering twenty en-suite rooms with paper-thin walls. ❷

Rue du Chateau 24 rue du Château ☏04.90.91.09.99, ⊕chambres-hotes.com. This delightful red-ochre house near the castle, with a lovely interior courtyard, offers five crisp, simple but very comfortable B&B rooms. Two-night minimum stay in summer. Closed mid-Nov to Easter. ❹

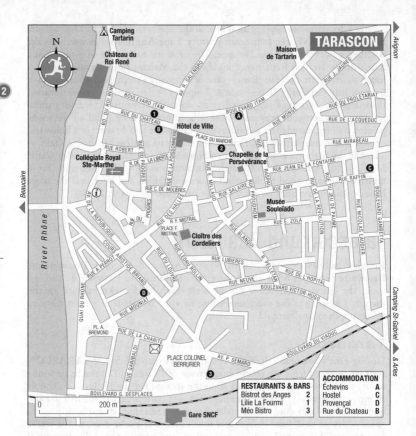

Hostels and campsites

Hostel 31 bd Gambetta ☎04.90.91.04.08, ⓦfuaj
.org/tarascon. Well-maintained town house, 850m
northeast of the *gare SNCF*, offering 65 beds in 4-
to twelve-bed dorms; 11pm curfew. €12.10 per
person (breakfast €3.60). Reception 8–10am &
5–10pm. Closed Oct to mid-March.
Camping St-Gabriel Mas Ginoux, rte de Fontvieille
☎04.90.91.19.83, ⓦcampingsaintgabriel.com.

Verdant two-star site with a pool, focused
around an old coaching inn 5km southeast of
town off the Arles road. €16 per night. Closed
Dec–Feb.
Camping Tartarin rte de Vallabrègues
☎04.90.91.01.46, ⓦcampingtartarin.fr. Well-
shaded two-star site right beside the river, just
north of the castle. €14.50 per night. Closed
Nov–March.

The Town

A vast and impregnable mass of stone, Tarascon's riverfront **Château du Roi
René** (June–Sept daily 9.30am–6.30pm; Oct–May Tues–Sun 10.30am–5pm;
€6.50; ⓦtarascon.org) has been beautifully restored to its defensive fifteenth-
century pose. Those of its towers that face the enemy across the Rhône are square,
while those at the back are round. Nowhere on the exterior is there any hint of
softness. Inside, however, is another matter. Work on the castle began in 1400, and
from 1447 onwards it was remodelled as a residence for King René of Provence,
with all the luxury that the period permitted. The mullioned windows and
vaulted ceilings of the royal apartments and the spiral staircase that overlook the

cour d'honneur all have graceful Gothic lines, and assorted wooden ceilings are painted with monsters and similar medieval motifs. Graffiti in several rooms, like the carvings of boats in the **Salles des Gallères**, testify to the castle's long use as a prison. Visits end with a climb up to the **roof**, from which revolutionaries and counter-revolutionaries alike were thrown in the 1790s.

Across the street from the castle, the crypt of the **Collégiale Royale Sainte-Marthe** (daily: 8am–6pm; free) contains the tomb of Martha, the saint who saved the town from the Tarasque monster. St Martha also appears in the paintings by Nicolas Mignard and Vien that decorate its Gothic interior, along with works by Pierre Parrocel and Van Loo.

In the central place Frédéric-Mistral, the sixteenth-century **Cloître des Cordeliers** (Mon–Sat 10am–noon & 2–6.30pm; free) has had its three aisles of light cream stone beautifully restored. It's used for exhibitions, sometimes of contemporary paintings, and often by young artists.

The **Musée Souleïado** (Tues–Sat 10am–5pm; ℡04.90.91.50.51; €6.10; Ⓦwww.souleiado.com), on a quiet backstreet at 39 rue Proudhom, pays tribute to the family business that revived Tarascon's 200-year-old **textile** tradition of making brightly coloured, patterned, printed fabrics, now sold all over Provence. As well as eighteenth-century wood blocks from which many of the patterns are still made, it tastefully displays such products as a table setting dedicated to the bulls of the Camargue.

Eating and drinking

Tarascon's best **restaurant**, the *Bistrot des Anges* on place du Marché (℡04.90.91.05.11), serves alluring Provençal dishes such as *carpaccio de taureau* and seafood tart, with an €18 set menu. For a cheaper lunch, drop in at the attractive *Lilie La Fourmi*, at 14 boulevard Itam but best entered on rue du Château (℡06.62.25.55.93; Mon–Fri, lunch only), which prepares good daily *plats*, and has a €15.50 menu. By far the best place for a **drink** is the trendy lounge-style *Méo Bistro*, on place Colonel Berrurier by the *gare SNCF* (℡04.90.91.47.74; closed Mon). There's a Tuesday **market** along rue des Halles.

The Tarasque and Tartarin

On the last full weekend of June, the **Tarasque**, a mythical 6m-long creature with glaring eyes and shark-sized teeth, storms the streets of Tarascon in the fashion of a Chinese dragon, its tail swishing back and forth to the screaming delight of children. The monster is said to have been tamed by Saint Martha after a long history of clambering out of the Rhône, gobbling people and destroying the ditches and dams of the Camargue with its long crocodile-like tail. It serves as a reminder of natural catastrophe, in particular floods, kept at bay here by the sometimes unreliable drainage ditches and walls. The weekend-long festivities involve public balls, bull and equestrian events, and a firework and music finale.

Another larger-than-life character – **Tartarin**, the mid-nineteenth-century literary creation of Alphonse Daudet – is celebrated at the same time, even though his antics have left Tarascon synonymous with foolishness in French eyes. Making himself out to be a great adventurer, Tartarin scales Mont Blanc, hunts leopards in Algeria, and brings back exotic trees for his garden at 55 bis boulevard Itam. The address is real, and serves as a museum to the fictional antihero: **Maison de Tartarin** (currently closed for restoration; check with tourist office for new opening hours). During the Tarasque procession, a local man, chosen for his fat-bellied figure, strolls through the town as Tartarin.

Beaucaire

On the opposite side of the Rhône, over in Languedoc – just 1km away but reached via a busy road bridge few would want to cross on foot in summer – Tarascon's historic rival **BEAUCAIRE** boasts a better-preserved maze of medieval streets, but even fewer specific attractions or facilities.

To reach the **Château Royale de Beaucaire**, thread your way north through the old town to the hill at the far end, atop which its one surviving tower far surmounts those of Tarascon across the river. Though you can no longer ramble freely around the ruins, they make a great setting for an hourly **falconry display**, with medieval costumes and music (daily except Wed: second half of March & Sept–Nov 2.30pm, 3.30pm & 4.30pm; April–June 2pm, 3pm & 4.30pm; July & Aug 3pm, 4pm & 5.30pm; €10; ⓦwww.aigles-de-beaucaire.com).

The castle **gardens**, however, are open to visitors (April–Oct daily except Tues 10am–6pm; free). A modern building here houses the **Musée Auguste-Jacquet** (April–Oct 10am–12.30pm & 2.15–6.15pm; Nov–March 10am–noon & 2–5.15pm; €4.70), which has a small but interesting collection of Roman remains, and displays documents relating to Beaucaire's medieval fair, once one of the largest in Europe.

The old town's most characterful square, the **place de la République** immediately below the castle, holds a sculpture of Drac, a protective dragon that's Beaucaire's equivalent of the Tarasque.

Practicalities

Beaucaire's **tourist office** is 300m straight on from the bridge, beside a canal at 24 cours Gambetta (April–June, Aug & Sept Mon–Fri 8.45am–12.15pm & 2–6pm, Sat 9.30am–12.30pm & 3–6pm; July Mon–Fri 8.45am–12.15pm & 2–6pm, Sat 9.30am–12.30pm & 3–6pm, Sun 9.30am–12.30pm; Oct–March Mon–Fri 8.45am–12.15pm & 2–6pm; ⓉT04.66.59.26.57, ⓦot-beaucaire.fr). The town doesn't have its own *gare SNCF*.

The pretty, pastel-yellow *Napoléon*, beside the river in the old town at 4 place Frédéric-Mistral (ⓉT04.66.59.05.17; ❷), is a nice budget **hotel** with some very cheap single rooms, and a restaurant serving menus from €17. Place de la République holds a few cheap snack places, but most of the **restaurants** lie along quai Générale-de-Gaulle, next to the canal; *Le Soleil*, at no. 30 (ⓉT04.66.59.28.52), featuring *tellines* from the Camargue on its €17 menu, while *Nord au Sud*, at no. 27 ter (ⓉT04.66.59.02.55), specializes in mussels for €12.

The Camargue

Spreading across the Rhône delta and bounded by the Petit Rhône to the west, the Grand Rhône to the east, and the Mediterranean to the south, the drained, ditched and now protected land known as the **CAMARGUE** is distinct in every sense from the rest of Provence. With land, lagoon and sea sharing the same horizontal plain, its shimmering horizons appear infinite, its boundaries not apparent until you come upon them.

The whole of the Camargue is a Parc Naturel Régional, making great efforts to maintain an equilibrium between tourism, agriculture, industry and hunting on the one hand, and the indigenous ecosystems on the other. When the Romans arrived, the northern part of the Camargue was a forest; they felled the trees to build ships, then grew wheat. These days, especially since the northern marshes

▲ Camargue flamingos

were drained and re-irrigated with fresh water after World War II, the main crop is **rice**. There's still some wheat, though, along with **vines** – which because their stems were underwater survived the nineteenth-century phylloxera infestation that devastated every other wine-producing region in France – as well as fruit orchards and the ubiquitous rapeseed. To the east, along the final stretch of the Grand Rhône, the chief business is the production of **salt**. Evaporation was originally undertaken by the Romans in the first century AD, and the Camargue now holds one of the biggest saltworks in the world. Saltpans and pyramids add an extra-terrestrial feel to the landscape.

The Camargue is effectively split into two separate sections by the large **Étang du Vaccarès** at its heart, a lagoon that, along with its various islands, is out of bounds to visitors. The **western** side is much busier with tourists, who flock down its main artery, the D570, to the Provençal Camargue's only sizeable town, **Stes-Maries-de-la-Mer**. Really just an overgrown village turned summer resort, Stes-Maries is a nice enough place, with a fascinating ongoing **gypsy** connection, but for a true sense of what makes the Camargue special, you're much better off spending your time exploring its marshes and dunes, or following its waterfront nature trails.

If you're driving, it's also possible to venture along the Camargue's **eastern** side as well in a single day-trip, reaching as far as the quiet little village of **Salin-de-Giraud**, alongside the Grand Rhône near its southern end. Although less agricultural and more industrial, this area holds its own share of wildlife reserves and tranquil refuges.

There's no **ideal season** to visit the Camargue. Its notorious **mosquitoes** can make the months from March to November unbearable; they're less prevalent beside the sea, but elsewhere you'll need serious chemical weaponry. Biting flies are also a problem, as are the strong autumn and winter **winds**, which make cycling hard despite the flat terrain. And finally, in summer the weather can be so hot and humid that the slightest movement is an effort.

Bulls, birds and beavers: Camarguais wildlife

The Camargue is a treasure trove of bird and animal species, both wild and domestic, with its most famous denizens being the **bulls** and the **white horses** that the region's **gardians** (herdsmen) ride. Neither beast is truly wild, though both run in semi-liberty. A distinct breed of unknown origin, the Camargue horse is born dark brown or black, and turns white around its fourth year. It is never stabled, surviving the humid heat of summer and the wind-racked winter cold outdoors.

The *gardians,* likewise, are a hardy community. Still conforming, to some extent, to the popular cowboy myth, they play a major role in guarding Camarguais traditions. Their traditional homes, or *cabanes*, are thatched and windowless one-storey struc-tures, with bulls' horns over the door to ward off evil spirits. Throughout the summer, the *gardians* are kept busy, with spectacles involving bulls and horses in every village arena; winter is a good deal harder. Although ever fewer Camarguais property owners can afford the extravagant use of land required to rear bulls, an estimated 2500 *gardians* are still active, of whom around ten percent are women.

Camargue **wildlife** ranges from wild boars, beavers and badgers; tree frogs, water snakes and pond turtles; to marsh and sea birds, waterfowl and birds of prey. The best time for **birdwatching** is the mating season, from April to June. Of the region's fifty thousand or so **flamingos**, ten thousand remain during the winter (Oct–March) when the rest migrate to north Africa. They're born grey, incidentally, then turn pink aged between four and seven. Their tendency to trample young rice shoots in the paddy fields is an ongoing problem for park managers.

The rich **flora** of the park includes reeds, wild irises, tamarisk, wild rosemary and juniper trees. Growing to a height of 6m, the junipers form the Bois des Rièges on the islands between the Étang du Vaccarès and the sea, part of the central **National Reserve** to which access is restricted to those with professional research credentials.

The western Camargue: the road to Stes-Maries

The main **information centre** for the Camargue lies in a working farm alongside the D570, 10km southwest of Arles towards Stes-Maries. It's part of the **Musée de la Camargue** (April–Sept daily 9am–6pm; Oct–March daily except Tues 10am–5pm; €4.50; T 04.90.97.10.82, W www.parc-camargue.fr), which documents the history, traditions and livelihoods of the Camarguais people, with particular emphasis on rice, wine and bulls. Overall, the displays are excellent, thought not very accessible if you don't read French, and include an audiovisual presentation on the museum building's former life as a sheep barn. A 3.5-kilometre trail loops through the adjacent farmland.

Another 23km further on, at Pont de Gau, 4km short of Stes-Maries, hiking trails across a thirty-acre marsh, circling three separate lagoons, make birdwatching easy at the engrossing **Parc Ornithologique** (daily: April–Sept 9am–sunset; Oct–March 10am–sunset; €7; W parcornithologique.com). Signs and information are plentiful, and some of the less easily spotted species are kept in aviaries.

The best **hiking trail** in the western Camargue follows a drover's path, the Draille de Cacharel, between Cacharel, 4km north of Ste-Maries, and the D37 just north of Méjanes. Running initially along the narrow strip that separates two lesser lagoons, the Étang de Consecanière and the Étang de l'Impérial, it then skirts the western shoreline of the Étang du Vaccarès.

THE CAMARGUE

Salon-de-Provence & Aix-en-Provence

Martigues

Montpellier

Tarascon & Avignon

Nîmes & Montpellier

Arles

Salon-de-Provence & Aix-en-Provence

St-Martin-de-Crau

A54

N113/E80

D35

D35

D36

D36

Villeneuve

La Capelière

Le Sambuc

Musée du Riz

Saltworks

Port-St-Louis-du-Rhône

Plage Napoléon

Domaine de la Palissade

They de la Gracieuse

Etg. de Grand Palun

Salin-de-Giraud

Ferry

Saltworks

Plage de Piemanson

Vieux Rhône

Étang de Faraman

Beauduc Lighthouse

Étang du Fangassier

Étang du Galabert

Étang de Rascaillon

Étang du Vaisseau

Gimeaux

Saliers

Gageron

Musée de la Camargue

PARC NATUREL

Albaron

Méjanes

St-Gilles

Petit Rhône

Sylvéreal

PONT DE SYLVÉREAL

Aigues-Mortes

Pin Fourcat

Pont de Gau

Parc Ornithologique

Ploch-Badet

Hostel

PETITE CAMARGUE

RÉGIONAL DE CAMARGUE

Étang du Vaccarès

RESERVE NATIONALE DE CAMARGUE

BOIS DES RIEGES

Étang du Fournelet

Étang du Lion

RESERVE DES IMPERIAUX

DIGUE DE CACHAREL

Cacharel

Étang de Malagroy

Étang de Consecanière

Étang de Ginès

Étang dit L'Impérial

DIGUE À LA MER

Stes-Maries-de-la-Mer

MEDITERRANEAN SEA

Footpaths
Dykes
Border of Parc Naturel Régional de Camargue

0   5 km

Les Stes-Maries-de-la-Mer

Although most visitors to the Camargue head straight to **LES STES-MARIES-DE-LA-MER**, 37km southwest of Arles, they find a built-up, commercialized seaside town that has much more in common with France's other Mediterranean beach resorts than with the wild and empty land that surrounds it.

Most famous for its annual **gypsy festival** on May 24–25, when Romanies celebrate **Sarah**, their patron saint, Stes-Maries is an attractive little town nonetheless. A line of **beaches**, sculpted into successive little crescents by stone breakwaters and busy with bathers and windsurfers throughout the summer, stretches away west from its central core of white-painted, orange-tiled houses, while the pleasure **port** to the east offers boat trips to the lagoons and fishing expeditions. With its *arènes* staging bullfights, cavalcades and other entertainment (events are posted on a board outside), and musicians playing in the street, a stay of a night or two can all be very good fun.

Arrival and information

The **tourist office** is on the seafront at 5 avenue Van-Gogh (daily: Jan, Feb, Nov & Dec 9am–5pm; March & Oct 9am–6pm; April–June & Sept 9am–7pm; July & Aug 9am–8pm; ☎04.90.97.82.55, ⊛www.saintesmaries.com), with abundant car **parking** nearby. **Buses** from Arles arrive at the north end of place Mireille, 150m north of the church and 400m short of the sea.

Accommodation

At any time between April and October, and especially during the Romany festival, it's necessary to book **accommodation** in Stes-Maries well in advance. Don't worry too much if you can't find a room in the town itself; several very appealing options are scattered through the marshlands nearby. Hotel rates rise considerably in summer, and those outlying *mas* (farmhouses) that rent out rooms are seldom any cheaper.

Tours and activities

Around thirty Camargue farms offer **horseriding**, with typical rates ranging from €14 for an hour up to €80 per day. Recommended options include the Domaine Paul Ricard in Méjanes (☎04.90.97.10.62, ⊛www.mejanes.camargue.fr); you can find full lists at ⊛www.saintesmaries.com and www.camargue.fr.

Bikes can be rented in Stes-Maries from Le Vélociste, back from the sea on place Mireille (☎04.90.97.83.26, ⊛www.levelociste.fr), and Le Vélo Saintois, 19 av de la République (☎04.90.97.74.56, ⊛www.levelosaintois.camargue.fr). In Salin-de-Giraud, try Mas St Bertrand (☎04.42.48.80.69, ⊛www.mas-saint-bertrand.fr).

Canoes and **kayaks** are available from Kayak Vert in Sylvéréal, beside the Petit-Rhône on the D38C 17km northwest of Stes-Maries (☎04.66.73.57.17, ⊛www.kayakvert-camargue.fr).

Ninety-minute **river trips** on the Petit Rhône, costing €10, are offered by the **paddle steamer** *Le Tiki III*, which sets off from the river mouth, 2.5km west of Stes-Maries (mid-March to mid-Nov, 1–5 trips daily; ☎04.90.97.81.68, ⊛tiki3.fr). The *Camargue* (mid-March to Oct, 1–5 trips daily; ☎04.90.97.84.72, ⊛bateau-camargue.com), and the *Quatres Maries* (April–Sept, 3–4 trips daily; ☎04.90.97.70.10, ⊛www.bateaux-4maries.camargue.fr) both leave from the port in Stes-Maries.

Finally, *Camargue Safaris Gallon* (☎04.90.97.86.93, ⊛www.safari-4x4-gallon.camargue.fr) offer **jeep safaris**, starting from Arles or Stes-Maries, which can be combined with horseriding or cycling.

The legend of Sarah and the gypsy festivals

According to legend, Mary Jacobé, the aunt of Jesus, and Mary Salomé, mother of two of the Apostles, along with Mary Magdalene and various other New Testament characters, were driven out of Palestine by the Jews and put on a boat without sails and oars.

The boat subsequently drifted effortlessly to an island in the mouth of the Rhône where the Egyptian god Ra was worshipped. Here Mary Jacobé, Mary Salomé and **Sarah**, their servant, who was herself Egyptian, set about spreading the Gospel, while the rest headed off for other parts of Provence. In 1448 their relics were "discovered" in the fortress **church** of Stes-Maries on the former island, around the time that the Romanies were migrating into the area from the Balkans and from Spain. It's thought the two strands may have been reunited in Provence.

The gypsies adopted Sarah as their patron saint, and have been making their **pilgrimage** to Stes-Maries since the sixteenth century. It's a time for weddings and baptisms as well as music, dancing and fervent religious activities. On May 24, after Mass, the shrines of the saints are lowered from the high chapel to an altar where the faithful stretch out their arms to touch them. Then the statue of Sarah is carried by the gypsies to the sea. On the following day the statues of Mary Jacobé and Mary Salomé, sitting in a wooden boat, follow the same route, accompanied by mounted *gardians* in full Camargue dress, Arlesians in traditional costume, and all and sundry present. The sea, the Camargue, the pilgrims and the gypsies are blessed by the bishop from a fishing boat, before the procession returns to the church with much bell-ringing, guitar-playing, tambourine-bashing and singing. Another ceremony in the afternoon sees the shrines lifted back up to their chapel.

A separate pilgrimage takes place on the Sunday closest to October 22, dedicated solely to Mary Jacobé and Mary Salomé and without the participation of the gypsies.

Hotels in Stes-Maries

Bleu Marine 15 av du Dr-Cambon ☏04.90.97.77.00. Friendly, peaceful retreat at the western end of town, with simple but immaculate rooms, a nice pool and easy parking. ❹

Le Dauphin Bleu/La Brise de Mer 31 av G-Leroy ☏04.90.97.80.21, ⓦwww.hotel-dauphin-bleu.camargue.fr. Good-value white-painted hotel-restaurant, on the seafront a few hundred metres from the centre at the east end of the beach road. The nicest of the rather austere rooms have balconies overlooking the sea. ❹

Mangio Fango rte d'Arles ☏04.90.97.80.56, ⓦwww.hotel-mangiofango.com. Tranquil farmhouse, overlooking the Étang des Launes 600m north of central Stes-Maries, with a Mediterranean twist. Stylish, comfortable rooms, pricey restaurant, and a pool surrounded by lush green foliage. Closed all Jan, open weekends only in Dec. ❻

Mediterranée 4 av F-Mistral ☏04.90.97.82.09, ⓦmediterraneehotel.com. Decked out in jolly flowers, this welcoming hotel has pretty Provençal-style rooms – sleeping up to four guests – and is in the heart of the town, seconds from the sea. ❷

Other accommodation in the western Camargue

Cacharel rte de Cacharel ☏04.90.97.95.44, ⓦwww.hotel-cacharel.com. Luxurious rooms in one of the Camargue's oldest farms, 4km north of Stes-Maries on the D85A, with open fires to warm you in winter, a pool to cool off in summer, and horseriding available year-round, but no restaurant. ❼

Flamant Rose Albaron ☏04.90.97.10.18, ⓦwww.leflamantrose.camargue.fr. Pleasant, inexpensive roadside hotel-restaurant, 23km north of Stes-Maries and 14km southwest of Arles, where some of the brightly decorated rooms are more tasteful than others. ❷

Hostel Pioch-Badet ☏04.90.97.51.72, ⓦwww.auberge-de-jeunesse.camargue.fr. Dorm rooms in this former school, beside the D570 10km north of Stes-Maries, hold three to ten beds (€29.70, half board obligatory). Bike rental, horse rides and other excursions available. Reception 7–10.30am &

5–11pm (midnight in July & Aug). Open all year, but you must make reservations.

Lou Mas Doù Juge rte du Bac-du-Sauvage, Pin Fourcat ☎04.66.73.51.45, ⊛loumasdoujuge.com. Lovely B&B on a working farm out in the countryside beside the Petit Rhône, 10km northwest of Stes-Maries; evening meal and horseriding available if requested in advance. ❺

Mas de Pioch Pioch-Badet ☎04.90.97.50.06, ⊛www.masdepioch.com. Great-value B&B, in a converted nineteenth-century hunting inn just off the main road 10km north of Stes-Maries. Large rooms and a pool. Book well in advance. ❷

Hostellerie du Pont de Gau rte d'Arles, Pont de Gau ☎04.90.97.81.53, ⊛www.pontdegau .camargue.fr. Old-fashioned Camarguais decor and

a good restaurant, 4km north of Stes-Maries near the Parc Ornithologique. Closed Jan to mid-Feb. ❸

Campsites

Camping La Brise rue Marcel-Carrière ☎04.90.97.84.67, ⊛camping-labrise.fr. Three-star site, near the sea on the east side of Stes-Maries, with a pool and laundry facilities. Tents, mobile homes or bungalows available for rent. Closed mid-Nov to mid-Dec. €21 per night.

Camping Le Clos du Rhône rte d'Aigues-Mortes ☎04.90.97.85.99, ⊛camping-leclos.fr. Busy four-star site at the mouth of the Petit Rhône, 800m west of central Stes-Maries along an easy seaside path, with a pool, laundry and shop. Closed early Nov to early April. €24 per night.

The Town

The spiders-web tangle of streets and alleyways at the heart of old Stes-Maries, filled with everything from supermarkets and delis to bucket-and-spade shops and art galleries, opens out into a sequence of spacious squares on all sides of its grey-gold Romanesque **church**. Fortified in the fourteenth century in response to frequent attacks by pirates, the church has beautifully pure lines and fabulous acoustics. During the era of Saracen raids, it provided shelter for all the villagers, and even holds its own freshwater well. Downstairs, in the crypt below the altar, the tinselled and sequined statue of Sarah (see p.113) is surrounded by candles, abandoned crutches and calipers, and naïve ex-voto paintings dedicated in thanks for blessings and cures. Although you can't climb to the top of the tower, paying €2 allows you to scramble onto and over the church roof (daily: July & Aug 10am–sunset; March–June & Sept to mid-Nov 10am–12.30pm & 2pm–sunset), for great views over the town.

The **Musée Baroncelli**, on rue Victor-Hugo (April to mid-Oct daily except Tues 10am–noon & 2–5.30pm; €1.50), is named after the man who, in 1935, was responsible (along with various *gardians*) for initiating the gypsies' procession down to the sea with Sarah. This was motivated by a desire to give a special place in the pilgrimage to the Romanies. Displays cover this event, as well as other Camarguais traditions and local fauna and flora.

Eating and drinking

Of a summer evening, Stes-Maries gets very lively indeed, with the *terrasses* of its **restaurants** and bars sprawling out across the streets and squares, and flamenco guitarists and buskers everywhere. Camarguais **specialities** include *tellines*, tiny shiny shellfish served with garlic mayonnaise; *gardianne de taureau*, bull's meat cooked in wine, vegetables and Provençal herbs; eels from the Vaccarès; rice, asparagus and wild duck; and *poutargue des Stes-Maries*, a mullet roe dish. The town **market** takes place on place des Gitans every Monday and Friday.

La Bouvine av F-Mistral ☎04.90.97.87.09. Very large restaurant on Stes-Maries' main dining street, with lots of outdoor seating and a choice of pretty much any French or Spanish dish you care to mention, from paella (€12) to *marmite de pêcheur* (€13.50), plus a €15 set menu.

Brûleur de Loups av Léon Gambetta ☎04.90.97.83.31. Smart, all-round Provençal restaurant with a terrace that's among the very few places in Stes-Maries where you get a sea view while you eat. Menus €17–40. Closed Tues pm, Wed, & mid-Nov to mid-Dec.

Le Delta 1 place Mireille ☎04.90.97.81.12.
Mostly seafood, with regional specialities such as
bourride de baudroie and *aïoli de morue*, and

tellines on the €19.50 menu. Menus €11–27.
Closed Mon & Jan.

The eastern Camargue

Although the D35 and D36, respectively paralleling the east and west banks of the
Grand Rhône all the way from Arles, are the principal access routes into the
eastern half of the Camargue, the **D36b** along the eastern edge of the Étang du
Vaccarès allows you to enjoy the best of the scenery.

An information centre at **La Capelière** (April–Sept daily 9am–1pm & 2–6pm,
Oct–March daily except Tues 9am–1pm & 2–5pm; ☎04.90.97.00.97, ⓦreserve
-camargue.org; €3), 23km out of Arles and 19km northwest of Salin-de-Giraud,
holds rather faded displays on Camargue wildlife and how to see it. Outside, a
short but excellent 1.5-kilometre initiation trail circles a small lagoon, with
superb **birdwatching** opportunities along the way from camouflaged hides
equipped with telescopes (strict silence is observed). Another good hiking trail,
which is also a prime observation point for **flamingos**, starts 5km west of
Salin-de-Giraud, and follows the dyke between the Étangs du Fangassier and
Galabert.

Further south, 7km beyond Salin-de-Giraud just off the D36d beside the
Grand Rhône, the **Domaine de la Palissade** (March to mid-June & mid-Sept
to mid-Nov daily 9am–6pm; mid-June to mid-Sept daily 9am–6pm; mid-Nov
to Feb Wed–Sun 9am–5pm; €3; ⓦconservatoire-du-littoral.fr) concentrates on
the fauna and flora of its neighbouring lagoons. It has a small and rather dull
exhibition, but a good nine-kilometre trail past duck and flamingo nesting
grounds, as well as a shorter 1.5-kilometre path. In summer, one- or two-hour
guided **horseback** tours cost €15 and €25 per person respectively.

Salin-de-Giraud

In total contrast to Stes-Maries, **SALIN-DE-GIRAUD**, just west of the Grand
Rhône in the southeastern corner of the Camargue, is an industrial village,
based on the saltworks company and its related chemical factory, with tall,
terraced workers' houses built on a strict grid pattern during the Second
Empire.

There's nothing really to see in Salin, nor even a town centre for that matter.
If you'd like a look at the lunar landscape of the **salt piles** – the saltworks here
cover 110 square kilometres and produce a million tonnes a year for domestic
use and export – there's a viewing point with information panels a short way
south, just off the D36d. A regular **ferry**, the *bac de Barcarin*, crosses the Grand
Rhône from Salin (every 15min; €4.50); at **Port-St-Louis-du-Rhône**, just
downstream, the rice and salt of the Camargue are loaded onto ships, and a small
fishing fleet is still active.

Salin holds two reasonable **hotels**: the nice little family-run *Saladelles*, 4 rue des
Arènes (☎04.42.86.83.87; ❶), with a popular restaurant on its shaded terrace
serving menus from €13; and the *Camargue*, further west at 58 boulevard de la
Camargue (☎04.42.86.88.52; ❷; closed Jan), which offers larger rooms and a
pricier restaurant. More luxurious accommodation is available at the *Mas de Peint*,
13km north on the D36 (☎04.90.97.20.62; ⓦmasdepeint.com; ❾), a rural resort
with opulent rooms and a gourmet restaurant.

Travel details

Trains

Arles to: Avignon (17 daily; 20min); Avignon TGV (2 daily; 20min); Marseille (23 daily; 45min–1hr); Nîmes (7 daily; 30min); Tarascon (4 daily; 10min).

Buses

Arles to: Aix (4 daily; 1hr 30min); Albaron (7 daily; 30min); Avignon (8 daily; 1hr); Avignon TGV (8 daily; 55min); Les Baux (2 daily; 1hr); Salin (Mon–Sat 5 daily, Sun 2 daily; 1hr); Salon (6 daily; 1hr 15min); Stes-Maries (4–7 daily; 55min); St-Rémy (3 daily; 50min); Tarascon (8 daily; 20min).

St-Rémy to: Arles (3 daily; 40min); Avignon (8 daily; 40min); Les Baux (4 daily; 15min); Cavaillon (3 daily; 35min).

Tarascon to: Arles (10 daily; 20min); Barbentane (5 daily; 25min); Boulbon (5 daily; 10min).

3

Avignon and the Vaucluse

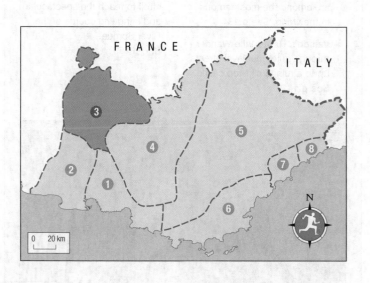

CHAPTER 3 # Highlights

❋ Palais des Papes Avignon's most spectacular monument makes a superb backdrop for the Festival d'Avignon, held each July. See p.123

❋ Villeneuve-lès-Avignon More laid-back than its bigger cousin across the river, Villeneuve has no shortage of impressive sights. See p.131

❋ Châteauneuf-du-Pape Châteauneuf's rich red wines are among the most famous in the world. See p.134

❋ Vaison's Haute Ville Wander through quiet medieval streets up to a ruined cliff-top castle. See p.141

❋ Les Dentelles This region of jagged limestone pinnacles is home to some exceptional and varied wines, as well as plenty of good hiking trails. See p.143

❋ Mont Ventoux Western Provence's highest summit offers unrivalled panoramas. See p.146

❋ Fontaine-de-Vaucluse Enjoy a ravishing riverside stroll to reach the spectacular and intriguing source of the River Sorgue. See p.153

▲ Palais des Papes, Avignon

Avignon and the Vaucluse

As an area with a distinct identity, the **Vaucluse département** dates back only as far as the Revolution. It was created to tidy up assorted bits and pieces: the **Papal Enclave** of the Comtat Venaisson that became part of France in 1791, the principality of Orange won by Louis XIV in 1713, plus parts of Provence that didn't fit happily into the initial three *départements* drawn up in 1791. While still somewhat messy, with the papal territory wholly enclosed within the Drôme *département*, its boundaries are basically natural – the **River Rhône** to the west, **Mont Ventoux** to the east, the northern boundary of the huge **Vaucluse plateau to the north**, and the **River Durance** to the south.

Above its confluence with the Durance, the Rhône was formerly the frontier between Provence and France. **Avignon** on the Provençal side, the great city of the popes from medieval times until the Revolution, squared off against the heavily fortified town of **Villeneuve-lès-Avignon** across the river on the French side. Today, Avignon is a major tourist destination, thanks not only to its rich history but also to its role as an artistic centre, epitomized by its summer festival. Otherwise, the region's best-known attractions are the smaller towns of **Orange** and **Vaison-la-Romaine**, with their remarkable Roman remains, but away from the monuments, museums and ruins, the **villages** and countryside of this part of Provence also hold great appeal. Just north of Avignon, the vineyards of **Châteauneuf-du-Pape** are the most famous in a rich green sweep of wine-producing country that stretches from the banks of the Rhône northeast past the jagged hills of the **Dentelles** to the bare, imposing slopes of Mont Ventoux. Gorgeous little hill towns and rural communities that make wonderful overnight stops include **Séguret**, **Pernes-les-Fontaines**, and the mysterious source of the **River Sorgue** to the south at **Fontaine-de-Vaucluse**.

Avignon

AVIGNON, capital of the Catholic Church during the early Middle Ages and for centuries one of the major artistic centres of France, can be dauntingly crowded in summer and stiflingly hot. Away from the main tourist drag, the old town is often remarkably unkempt and somewhat intimidating, with a laissez-faire approach to

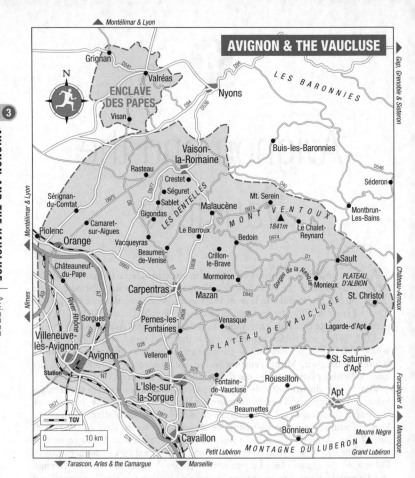

Montélimar & Lyon

Gap, Grenoble & Sisteron

AVIGNON & THE VAUCLUSE

N

Grignan

Valréas

ENCLAVE DES PAPES

Nyons

LES BARONNIES

Visan

Buis-les-Baronnies

Séderon

Vaison-la-Romaine

Montélimar & Lyon

Rasteau

Crestet

Séguret

Sablet

Sérignan-du-Comtat

Gigondas

Malaucène

Mt. Serein

Montbrun-Les-Bains

Camaret-sur-Aigues

Le Barroux

MONT VENTOUX

1841m

Le Chalet-Reynard

Piolenc

Orange

Vacqueyras

Beaumes-de-Venise

Bedoin

Château-Arnoux

Châteauneuf-du-Pape

Crillon-le-Brave

Gorges de la Nesque

Sault

PLATEAU D'ALBION

Nîmes

Carpentras

Mormoiron

Monieux

St. Christol

Mazan

Sorgues

Pernes-les-Fontaines

Venasque

Lagarde-d'Apt

PLATEAU DE VAUCLUSE

Forcalquier & Manosque

Villeneuve-lès-Avignon

Avignon

Velleron

St. Saturnin-d'Apt

Station

L'Isle-sur-la-Sorgue

Fontaine-de-Vaucluse

Roussillon

Apt

TGV

Beaumettes

Bonnieux

Mourre Nègre

0   10 km

Cavaillon

Petit Lubéron

MONTAGNE DU LUBERON

Grand Lubéron

Tarascon, Arles & the Camargue   Marseille

rubbish collection and an intrusive graffiti problem that leaves even the prettiest facades disfigured. But it's worth persevering for its spectacular monuments and museums, countless impressively decorated buildings, ancient churches, chapels and convents. During the **Festival d'Avignon** in July and the beginning of August, it is *the* place to be.

Central Avignon is still enclosed by its medieval **walls**, built in 1403 by the antipope Benedict XIII, the last of nine **popes** who based themselves here during the fourteenth century. The first pope to come to Avignon, **Clement V**, was invited over by the astute King Philippe le Bel ("the Good") in 1309, ostensibly to protect him from impending anarchy in Rome. In reality, Philip saw a chance to extend his power by keeping the pope in Provence, during what came to be known as the Church's "Babylonian captivity". Clement's successor, **Jean XXII**, had previously been bishop of Avignon, so he re-installed himself quite happily in the episcopal palace. The next Supreme Pontiff, **Benedict XII**, acceded in 1335; accepting the impossibility of returning to Rome, he demolished the bishop's palace to replace it with an austere fortress, now known as the **Vieux Palais**.

Though Gregory XI finally moved the Holy See back to Rome in 1378, this didn't mark the end of the papacy here. After Gregory's death in Rome, dissident local cardinals elected their own pope in Avignon, provoking the Western Schism, a ruthless struggle for the control of the Church's wealth, which lasted until the pious Benedict fled Avignon for self-exile near Valencia in 1409. Avignon remained papal property right up to the Revolution.

As home to one of the richest courts in Europe, fourteenth-century Avignon attracted princes, dignitaries, poets and raiders, who arrived to beg from, rob, extort and entertain the popes. According to Petrarch, the overcrowded, plague-ridden papal entourage was "a sewer where all the filth of the universe has gathered".

Arrival and information

Driving into Avignon involves negotiating a nightmare of junctions and one-way roads. The cheapest and easiest **parking** options for day-trippers are two free, guarded car parks, connected with the town centre by free shuttle buses: **Île Piot** (Mon–Fri 7.30am–8.30pm, Sat 1.30–8.30pm), which is actually part of the Île de la Barthelasse between Avignon and Villeneuve, and **Parking Des Italiens** (Mon–Sat 7.30am–8.30pm), beside the river immediately northeast of the old town. Both are primarily intended for commuters; neither stays open late, and only Île Piot is ever open on Sundays or public holidays, and even then only in high summer. Otherwise, the oversubscribed parking spaces inside the city walls are expensive, starting at €1.50 per hour; check to see whether your hotel offers free or discounted parking.

Both Avignon's **gare SNCF** and the adjacent **gare routière** are just outside the walls on the south side of the old city. The **TGV station**, 2km south, is connected to the centre by regular shuttle buses, which stop on cours President Kennedy next to the post office (daily, 2–4 services per hr; departures from station

---

The Festival d'Avignon

Starting in the second week in July, the annual, three-week **Festival d'Avignon** focuses especially on **theatre**, though it also features classical music, dance, lectures and exhibitions. The city's great buildings make a spectacular backdrop to the performances. Everything stays open late, and the huge number of visitors means getting around or doing anything normal becomes virtually impossible.

Founded in 1947 by actor-director **Jean Vilar**, the festival has included, over the years, theatrical interpretations as diverse as Euripides, Molière and Chekhov, performed by companies from across Europe. While big-name directors draw the largest crowds to the main venue, the Cour d'Honneur in the Palais des Papes, lesser-known troupes and directors also stage new works, and the festival spotlights a different culture each year.

The main **festival programme** is available from the second week in May from the Bureau du Festival d'Avignon, 20 rue du Portail Boquier (Ⓦ festival-avignon.com), or from the tourist office. Tickets (€13–50) go on sale on June 15 – via the festival's own website, the FNAC website (Ⓦ fnac.com), FNAC shops all over France, or by phone (Ⓣ 04.90.14.14.14) – and remain available until three hours before each performance.

The fringe contingent known as the **Festival Off** (5 rue Ninon Vallin; Ⓣ 04.90.85.13.08, Ⓦ www.avignonleoff.com) adds an additional element of craziness and magic, with a programme of innovative, obscure and bizarre performances taking place in more than a hundred venues as well as in the streets. Ticket prices range from €10 to €20 and a *Carte Public Adhérent* for €13 gives you thirty percent off all shows.

6.18am–11.05pm, from town 5.44am–11.20pm; €2.80; Ⓦwww.tcra.fr); a **taxi** into town (call Ⓣ04.90.82.20.20) can cost €15 or more. Avignon-Caumont **airport** (Ⓣ04.90.81.51.51, Ⓦwww.avignon.aeroport.fr), connected with Southampton and Exeter on Flybe (Ⓦflybe.com), and Leeds on Jet2 (Ⓦjet2.com), is 8km southeast of the centre.

The principal stops on the extensive TCRA **local bus** network (Ⓦwww.tcra.fr), for example if you're heading for Villeneuve, are on cours President Kennedy and outside Porte de l'Oulle facing the river (tickets €1.20 each; book of ten €9.60; one-day pass €3.60).

A free **boat** service crosses the river from just east of Pont St-Bénézet to the Île de la Barthelasse, an island in the middle of the Rhône where the city's campsites are located (July & Aug daily 11am–9pm; April–June & Sept daily 10am–12.30pm & 2–6.30pm; Oct–Dec Wed 2–5.30pm, Sat & Sun 10am–noon & 2–5.30pm).

Avignon's main **tourist office** is at the southern end of the old city, at 41 Cours Jean-Jaurès (Easter–Oct Mon–Sat 9am–6pm, 9am–7pm in July, Sun 9.45am–5pm; Nov–Easter Mon–Fri 9am–6pm, Sat 9am–5pm, Sun 10am–noon; Ⓣ04.32.74.32.74, Ⓦwww.avignon-tourisme.com). There's another smaller branch by the Pont St-Bénézet (daily: July & Aug 10am–1pm & 2–7pm; April–June, Sept & Oct 10am–1pm & 2–6pm).

Accommodation

Even outside festival time, finding a **room** in Avignon can be a problem: cheap **hotels** fill fast, so book in advance. Remember, too, that Villeneuve-lès-Avignon is only just across the river and may have rooms when its larger neighbour is full. Between the two, the Île de la Barthelasse is an idyllic spot for **camping**.

Hotels and B&Bs

Angleterre 29 bd Raspail Ⓣ04.90.86.34.31, Ⓦhoteldangleterre.fr. Located in a quiet neighbourhood in the southwest corner of the old city, well away from night-time noise, this is a traditional hotel with very small, plain but low-priced rooms. ❹

🏃 **Boquier** 6 rue du Portail Boquier Ⓣ04.90.82.34.43, Ⓦhotel-boquier.com. Extremely welcoming little hotel near the tourist office, with funkily decorated, widely differing, and consistently inexpensive rooms, some very small and some sleeping three or four guests. ❸

Cloître St-Louis 20 rue de Portail Boquier Ⓣ04.90.27.55.55, Ⓦcloitre-saint-louis.com. A large but personable and good-value hotel, with elegant modern decor in the seventeenth-century setting of a former Jesuit school. Some of the a/c rooms have attractive wood-beamed ceilings, and there's a rooftop pool. ❽

🏃 **Le Clos du Rempart** 33–37 rue Cremade Ⓣ04.90.86.39.14, Ⓦclosdurempart.com. Delightful B&B in a pretty nineteenth-century house behind the Palais des Papes, with two large, luxurious and very peaceful en-suite rooms; there's a wonderful wisteria-covered breakfast terrace and a hammock to doze in on sunny afternoons. ❼

Colbert 7 rue Agricol Perdiguier Ⓣ04.90.86.20.20, Ⓦavignon-hotel-colbert.com. At the south end of

town and handy for local trains and buses, this hotel has somewhat brisk management, but warmly and imaginatively decorated rooms, mostly large, plus a pleasant central courtyard complete with fountain. Rates drop significantly in low season. Closed Nov–Feb. ❻

Europe 12 place Crillon Ⓣ04.90.14.76.76, Ⓦwww.heurope.com. A sixteenth-century town house, unpretentiously classy and set back in a shaded courtyard, with bright, modern, sound-proofed rooms, home-made breakfasts and an excellent restaurant. ❾

Médiéval 15 rue Petite Saunerie Ⓣ04.90.86.11.06, Ⓦhotelmedieval.com. Very central hotel in a fine seventeenth-century town-house, with very reasonable rates and a lovely garden courtyard but rather plain, dated rooms of widely varying sizes. Closed Jan. ❹

Mignon 12 rue Joseph Vernet Ⓣ04.90.82.17.30, Ⓦhotel-mignon.com. The decor may be a little too fussy, but this small hotel is great value for money considering its fantastic location on a chic street. Closed Jan. ❹

Splendid 17 rue Agricol Perdiguier Ⓣ04.90.86.14.46, Ⓦwww.avignon-splendid -hotel.com. Very decent one-star in a great location just off the main drag; there's a steep narrow staircase to reach the upper floors. Fresh

Avignon Passion passports

The tourist offices in Avignon and Villeneuve-lès-Avignon distribute free **Avignon Passion passports**. After paying the full admission price for the first museum you visit – so for the greatest savings, make that a cheap one – you and your family receive discounts of 10–50 percent on the entrance fees of all subsequent museums in Avignon. The pass also gives discounts on tourist transport (such as riverboats and bus tours), and is valid for fifteen days after its first use.

bathrooms and friendly management. Closed mid-Nov to mid-Dec. **3**

Villa Agapè 13 rue St Agricol ☎04.90.85.21.92, ⓦvilla-agape.com. Secreted away above a pharmacy, this beautiful B&B has three rooms and a rooftop pool. It's also possible to rent out the whole house (four rooms), self-catered. Book well in advance. Minimum two-night stay. **6**

Hostel and campsites

Auberge des Jeunes Bagatelle *Camping Bagatelle*, Île de la Barthelasse ☎04.90.86.30.39, ⓦcampingbagatelle.com. Rather basic hostel facilities in the grounds of the *Camping Bagatelle* site. Beds in eight-person dorms for €17.50 per person, plus private rooms sleeping from two to four, with and without en-suite facilities; all rates include breakfast. **1**–**5**

Camping Bagatelle Île de la Barthelasse ☎04.90.86.30.39, ⓦcampingbagatelle.com. Three-star campsite, with laundry facilities, a shop and café. It's the closest to the city centre, visible

as you cross the Daladier bridge from Avignon; bus #20 from the post office to "Bagatelle" stop, or a 15min walk from place de l'Horloge. €22 for two people with a tent. Open all year.

Camping du Pont d'Avignon Île de la Barthelasse ☎04.90.80.63.50, ⓦcamping-avignon.com. Well shaded four-star site, with a lovely pool, on the island directly facing Pont St-Bénézet across the river, a fair walk from the centre on bus route #20. €23.50 for two people and a tent. Closed Nov to mid-March.

Les Deux Rhônes chemin de Bellegarde, Île de la Barthelasse ☎04.90.85.49.70, ⓦcamping2rhone .com. Avignon's smallest campsite, around 3km from the city on the north side of the island, with pool and restaurant; bus #20 ("Gravière" stop). €13.66 for two with tent. Open all year.

Parc des Libertés 4682 rte de l'Islon la Barthelasse ☎04.90.85.17.73, ⓦparcdeslibertes .fr. The cheapest of Avignon's four campsites, 5km from the centre; no laundry. €11.10 per tent. Closed mid-Sept to Easter.

The City

Avignon's low **walls** still form a complete loop around the city. Despite their menacing crenellations, they were never a formidable defence, even when sections were girded by a now-vanished moat. Nevertheless with the gates and towers all restored, the old ramparts still give a sense of cohesion and unity to the old town, dramatically marking it off from the formless sprawl of the modern city beyond.

The city's major monuments occupy a compact quarter inside the northern loop of the walls, just beyond its main square the **place de l'Horloge**, itself at the northern end of rue de la République, the old town's principal axis. Besides the colossal **Palais des Papes**, home to the medieval popes, other palaces are scattered around the centre, as well – of course – as several churches.

The Palais des Papes

The vast **Palais des Papes** (daily: first half of March 9am–6.30pm; mid-March to June & mid-Sept to Oct 9am–7pm; July & first half of Sept 9am–8pm; Aug 9am–9pm; Nov–Feb 9.30am–5.45pm; last ticket 1hr before closing; €10.50, €13.50 with Pont St-Bénézet, €8.50/10 with Avignon Passion pass; ⓦwww .palais-des-papes.com) soars above the east side of the cobbled place du Palais. With its massive stone vaults, battlements and sluices for pouring hot oil on attackers, the palace was built primarily as a fortress, though the two pointed

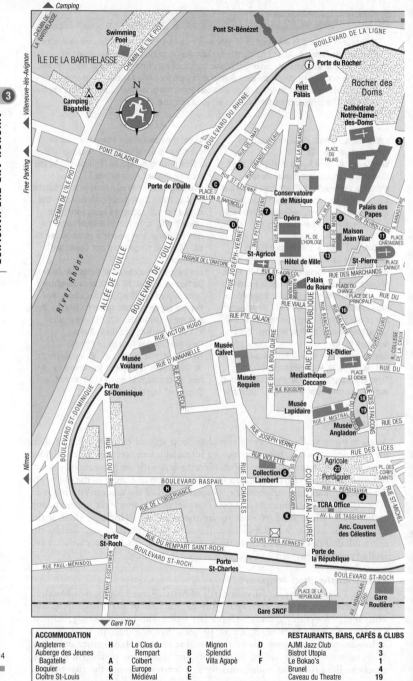

ACCOMMODATION				RESTAURANTS, BARS, CAFÉS & CLUBS	
Angleterre	**H**	Le Clos du		AJMI Jazz Club	**3**
Auberge des Jeunes		Rempart	**B**	Bistrot Utopia	**3**
Bagatelle	**A**	Colbert	**J**	Le Bokao's	**1**
Boquier	**G**	Europe	**C**	Brunel	**4**
Cloître St-Louis	**K**	Médiéval	**E**	Caveau du Theatre	**19**
		Mignon	**D**		
		Splendid	**I**		
		Villa Agapè	**F**		

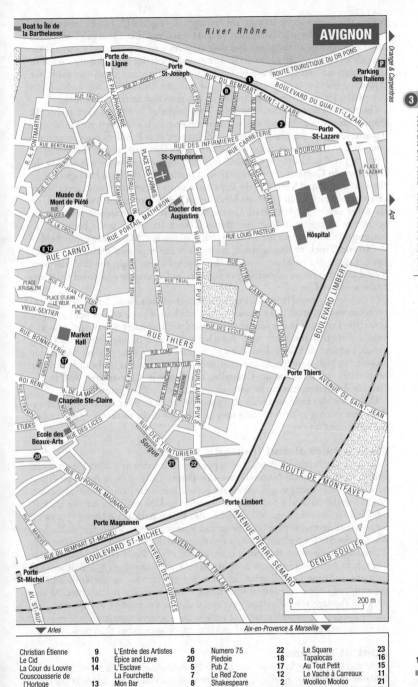

Christian Étienne	9	L'Entrée des Artistes	6	Numero 75	22	Le Square	23
Le Cid	10	Épice and Love	20	Piedoie	18	Tapalocas	16
La Cour du Louvre	14	L'Esclave	5	Pub Z	17	Au Tout Petit	15
Couscousserie de l'Horloge	13	La Fourchette	7	Le Red Zone	12	Le Vache à Carreaux	11
		Mon Bar	8	Shakespeare	2	Woolloo Mooloo	21

towers that hover above its gate are incongruously graceful. Inside, however, so little remains of the original decoration and furnishings that it's easy to be deceived into thinking that all the popes and their retinues were as pious and austere as the last official occupant, Benedict XIII. The denuded interior leaves hardly a whiff of the corruption and decadence of fat, feuding cardinals and their mistresses, the thronging purveyors of jewels, velvet and furs, the musicians, chefs and painters competing for patronage, and the riotous banquets and corridor schemings.

The first building on the audioguide tour (included in the entrance fee) is the **Pope's Tower**, also known as the Tower of Angels; it's accessed via the vaulted **Treasury**, where the Church's deeds and finances were handled. Four large holes concealed in the floor of the smaller downstairs room (now visible through glass) held the papal gold and jewels. The same cunning storage device was used in the **Chambre du Camérier** or Chamberlain's Quarters, off the Jesus Hall upstairs. In the adjoining **Papal Vestiary**, the Pope had a small library and would dress before receiving sovereigns and ambassadors in the **Consistoire** of the Vieux Palais, on the other side of the Jesus Hall. On the floor above, the **kitchen** offers powerful testimony to the scale of papal gluttony, with its square walls becoming an octagonal chimney piece for a vast central cooking fire. Major feasts were held in the **Grand Tinel**, or dining room, where only the pope was allowed to wield a knife. During the conclave in which they elected a new pope, the cardinals were locked into this room, adjourning to conspire and scheme in additional chambers to the south and west.

Once you've crossed from the Vieux Palais to the **Palais Neuf**, both Clement VI's bedroom and his study, the Chambre du Cerf, bear witness to this pope's secular concerns. The walls in the former are adorned with wonderful entwined oak- and vine-leaf motifs, the latter with superb hunting and fishing scenes. Providing almost the first dash of colour during the tour, these rooms can get unbearably crowded in high summer. As you continue, austerity resumes in the cathedral-like proportions of the **Grande Chapelle**, or **Chapelle Clementine**, and in the **Grande Audience**, its twin in terms of volume on the floor below.

The circuit also includes a walk along the roof terraces, which offer such tremendous views that it's worth heading up a little higher to the rooftop café even when the signs insist it's closed.

The cathedral and the Petit Palais

Alongside the Palais des Papes, and topped by an enormous gilded Virgin on its belfry, the **Cathédrale Notre-Dame-des-Doms** (daily: July & Aug 7am–7pm; Sept–June 8am–6pm) might once have been a luminous Romanesque structure, but its interior has had a bad attack of Baroque, and the result is a stifling clutter.

Behind the cathedral, the hilly **Rocher des Doms park** is a relaxing spot, with lovely views down the pont St-Bénézet and across the river to Villeneuve. The best place in the city for a picnic, with its fountains and ducks, it also holds a little café.

Immediately west of the park's main entrance, the **Petit Palais** (daily except Tues: June–Sept 10am–1pm & 2–6pm; Oct–May 9.30am–1pm & 2–5.30pm; €6) contains a daunting collection of first-rate thirteenth- to fifteenth-century painting and sculpture, most of it by masters from northern Italian cities. As you progress through the collection, you can watch as the masters wrestle with and finally conquer the representation of perspective – a revolution from medieval art, where the size of figures depended on their importance rather than position.

Pont St-Bénézet

Now merely jutting half-way out to the Île de Barthelasse, the twelfth-century **Pont St-Bénézet** originally reached right over to Villeneuve, and was the only

▲ Typical facade, Avignon

bridge to cross the Rhône between Lyon and the Mediterranean. A picturesque ruin since a flood in 1668, with only four of its 22 arches surviving, the bridge is famous not for its truncated state, but because it's the **Pont d'Avignon** immortalized in the famous song *Sur le pont d'Avignon* ("… *l'on y danse, l'on y danse* …"). The song has existed in various forms for five centuries, but both words and tune as we know them today come from popular nineteenth-century French operettas. It's generally agreed that the lyrics should really say "*Sous le pont*" (under the bridge) rather than "*Sur le pont*" (on the bridge), and referred to goings-on on the Île de Barthelasse of the general populace, who would dance on the island on feast days, or of the thief and trickster clientele of a tavern there, who were dancing with glee at the arrival of more potential victims.

The narrow bridge itself is open for visitors (same hours as Palais des Papes; €4.50, €13.50 with Palais des Papes). Displays beneath its landward end explain the history of both bridge – which may have been erected on the site of a larger Roman bridge by the eponymous Bénézet, who later became the patron saint of architects – and song, with assorted celebrity recordings. After that, you're free to walk to the end and back, and dance upon it too for that matter.

Place de l'Horloge and around

Frenetically busy throughout the year, the café-lined **place de l'Horloge** holds the city's imposing **Hôtel de Ville** and **clock tower**, as well as the **Opéra**. Around the square, on rues de Mons, Molière and Corneille, famous faces appear in windows painted on the buildings. Many of these figures depict historical visitors to Avignon, who described the powerful impact of hearing over a hundred bells ring at once. On Sunday mornings – traffic lulls permitting – you can still hear myriad different peals from churches, convents and chapels in close proximity.

To the south, on rue Collège du Roure, the gateway and courtyard of the beautiful fifteenth-century **Palais du Roure** are well worth a look. A centre for Provençal culture, the palace often hosts temporary art exhibitions; for a rambling tour through the attics to see Provençal costumes, publications and presses, photographs of the Camargue in the 1900s and an old stagecoach, turn up at 3pm on Tuesday (€4.60).

On rue de Mons, east of the square, the seventeenth-century Hôtel de Crochans is home to the **Maison Jean Vilar** (July daily 10.30am–6.30pm; Sept–June Tues–Fri 9am–noon & 1.30–5.30pm, Sat 10am–5pm; free; Ⓦmaisonjeanvilar.org), named after the great theatre director who set up the "Week of Dramatic Art" in 1947, which was to become the Festival d'Avignon. The building houses festival memorabilia, an excellent library dedicated to the performing arts, and recordings of everything from Stanislavski to last year's street theatre.

The rest of the old city

The **quartier de la Banasterie**, immediately east of the Palais des Papes and north of place Pie, dates almost entirely from the seventeenth and eighteenth centuries. With tourism largely kept in check, this remains an atmospheric and beautiful district, particularly at night. Its heavy wooden doors, with their highly sculptured lintels, today bear the nameplates of lawyers, psychiatrists and doctors. Between Banasterie and **place des Carmes** lies a tangle of tiny streets where you're almost certain to get lost. Pedestrians have priority over cars on many of them, and there are plenty of tempting café or restaurant stops.

Avignon's main **pedestrianized area**, however, lies a little further south, stretching between the chainstore blandness of rue de la République and the jaw-dropping (some might say, hideous) modern **market hall** on **place Pie** (mornings Tues–Sun). **Rue des Marchands** and **rue du Vieux-Sextier** have their complement of chapels and late medieval mansions, in particular the **Hôtel des Rascas** on the corner of rue des Marchands and rue Fourbisseurs; and the **Hôtel de Belli** on the corner of rue Fourbisseurs and rue du Vieux-Sextier. The Renaissance **church of St-Pierre** on place St-Pierre (Mon–Wed & Sun 10am–1pm; Thurs–Sat 10am–1pm & 2–6pm) has superb doors sculpted in 1551, and a retable dating from the same period. To the south on place St-Didier, more Renaissance art is on show in the fourteenth-century **church of St-Didier** (daily 8am–6.30pm), chiefly *The Carrying of the Cross* by Francesco Laurana, commissioned by King René of Provence in 1478. There are also fourteenth-century frescoes in the left-hand chapel.

South of place Pie, the **Chapelle Ste-Clare** is where the poet Petrarch first saw and fell in love with Laura, during the Good Friday service in 1327, as recorded in a note on the pages of his copy of Virgil. A little way east, the atmospheric **rue des Teinturiers** was a centre for calico printing during the eighteenth and nineteenth centuries. The cloth was washed in the Sorgue canal, which still runs alongside, though the four of its mighty watermills that survive no longer turn.

Musée Angladon

The **Musée Angladon**, 5 rue Labourer (April–Nov Tues–Sun 1–6pm, Dec–March Wed–Sun 1–6pm; €6; Ⓦangladon.com), displays what remains of the private collection of *couturier* Jacques Doucet. Apart from Antonio Forbera's extraordinary *Le Chavalet du Peintre*, a trompe l'oeil painting from 1686 depicting the artist's easel, complete with sketches and palette as well as work in progress, the older works are largely unexceptional, but Doucet's contemporary collection alone is worth the admission price. It includes Modigliani's *The Pink Blouse*, various Picassos, including a self-portrait from 1904, and Van Gogh's *The Railroad Cars*, his only Provençal painting on permanent display in the region.

Musée Calvet and Musée Lapidaire

The excellent, airy **Musée Calvet** is housed in a lovely eighteenth-century palace at 65 rue Joseph-Vernet (daily except Tues 10am–1pm & 2–6pm; €6, or €7 with

Musée Lapidaire; W musee-calvet.org). Highlights include a wonderful gallery of languorous nineteenth-century marble sculptures, including Bosio's *Young Indian*; the Puech collection of silverware and Italian and Dutch paintings; and works by Soutine, Manet and Joseph Vernet, as well as Jacques-Louis David's subtle, moving *Death of Joseph Barra*. It also holds some much more ancient artefacts, like enigmatic *stelae* from the fourth-century BC, carved with half-discernible faces, and Bronze Age axes.

Larger pieces from the Musée Calvet's archeological collection are displayed in the separate **Musée Lapidaire**, in a Baroque chapel at 27 rue de la République (daily except Tues 10am–1pm & 2–6pm; €2, or €7 with Musée Calvet; W musee-calvet .org). Besides Egyptian statues and Etruscan urns, this abounds in Roman and Gallo-Roman sarcophagi, and early renditions of the mythical Tarasque (see p.107).

Musée Vouland

At the **Musée Vouland** (Tues–Sun: July–Sept noon–6pm; Oct–June 2–6pm; €6; W vouland.com), at the end of rue Victor-Hugo near Porte St-Dominique, you can feast your eyes on the fittings, fixtures and furnishings enjoyed by French aristocrats both before and after the Revolution.

Collection Lambert

Avignon's one contemporary art gallery, the thoughtfully curated and splendidly displayed **Collection Lambert** (July & Aug daily 11am–7pm; Sept–June Tues–Sun 11am–6pm; €5.50; W collectionlambert.com), at 5 rue Violette just west of the tourist office, shows off works by the likes of Cy Twombly, Jasper Johns and Roni Horn. It also stages three stimulating temporary exhibitions each year, one of which is usually devoted to a specific contemporary artist.

Eating and drinking

Avignon has an enormous number of **restaurants**, ranging from expensive gastronomic rendezvous to cheap snack places and takeaways. The large **café-brasseries** on the terraces of place de l'Horloge and rue de la République all serve quick, if not necessarily memorable, meals, while the old pedestrian lanes are packed with atmospheric possibilities.

Restaurants

Brunel 46 rue de la Balance ☎04.90.85.24.83. Superb regional dishes, including *bourride*, plus *plat du jour* for €11 and dinner menus from €32.50. Closed Sun, plus Mon except in July.

Caveau du Theatre 16 rue des Trois Faucons ☎04.90.82.60.91, W caveaudutheatre.com. Cheerful bistro, with pretty painted walls, jolly red tables and occasional live jazz, serving delicious dishes like market-fresh fish with an artichoke and champagne reduction (€15). Lunch *formule* €12, dinner menus €18 and €22. Closed Sat lunch, Sun, and 2nd half of Aug.

Christian Étienne 10 rue de Mons ☎04.90.86.16.50, W christian-etienne.fr. Avignon's best-known gourmet restaurant, housed in a twelfth-century mansion and offering such mouthwatering Provençal delights as a whole menu devoted to tomatoes, or autumn vegetables – with meat and fish, naturally – or lobster with ginger, asparagus and sesame seeds followed by orange and carrot macaroons with almond sorbet. Dinner menus range €65–125, but you can sample the delights for €31 at lunchtime. Closed Sun & Mon.

La Cour du Louvre 23 rue St-Agricol ☎04.90.27.12.66. Hidden peacefully away from the old-town bustle in a delightful interior courtyard at the end of a *cour*, with a romantic atmosphere and good Mediterranean cooking; menus from €32 for lunch, €29 for dinner. Closed Sun & Mon.

Couscousserie de l'Horloge 2 rue de Mons ☎04.90.85.84.86. Popular Algerian-run restaurant, upstairs overlooking the place de l'Horloge, with a jovial atmosphere and excellent North African food. Try the delicious tagine *aux prunes* at €14.50.

L'Entrée des Artistes 1 place des Carmes ☎04.90.82.46.90. Cool, small bistro on a nice little square, serving traditional French dishes on menus at €21 and €26. No bank cards. Closed Sun & Mon.

Épice and Love 20 rue des Lices ℗ 04.90.82.45.96. Dining in this friendly, funky and hugely popular little local restaurant feels like sharing hearty home cooking in someone's living room, stuffed with random gewgaws, many of them butterfly related. Priced at €17 for three courses or €15 for two, the menu changes every night, with staples like lasagne or tagine alongside subtler dishes like roasted squid or fish. Come early or you may well have to wait for a table.

La Fourchette 17 rue Racine ℗ 04.90.85.20.93. Bright, busy yet refined restaurant serving up classic and sophisticated fish and meat dishes – try the tasty sardines marinated in coriander – on €33 and €42 dinner menus. Closed Sat, Sun & first three weeks in Aug.

Numero 75 rue Guillaume Puy ℗ 04.90.27.16.00, ⓦ numero75.com. Housed in a beautiful mansion, with indoor and garden seating, this smart haute-cuisine restaurant serves dinner menus from €32.50, but offers a €10 lunchtime *plat du jour*. Closed Sun, except in July.

Piedoie 26 rue des Trois Faucons ℗ 04.06.21.86.51.53. Romantic little restaurant specializing in fresh, zestful Provençal cuisine; the salads are particularly recommended. Lunch sees a €19 market menu, while dinner menus start at €32. Closed Tues & Wed, plus two weeks in Feb and two weeks in Aug.

Au Tout Petit 4 rue d'Amphoux ℗ 04.90.82.38.86. This tiny, unpretentious place, tucked away down a side alley near Les Halles, may not look like much, but the food is imaginative, fresh and unbeatable, and the owner extremely friendly. Two-course lunch *formule* for €11, dinner menus from €15. Closed Wed & Sun.

Woolloo Mooloo 16 bis rue des Teinturiers ℗ 04.90.85.28.44, ⓦ woolloo.com. Set in a former printshop, this hip canalside hangout serves dishes from around the world – tagines, *mafé* from West Africa, lasagne – and a good selection of teas. Lunch menus from €15, dinner menus from €23.

Cafés, bars and salons de thé

Bistrot Utopia 4 rue Escaliers Ste-Anne ℗ 06.37.57.52.31. In the shadow of the Palais des Papes, this café has changing exhibitions adorning the walls, live jazz some nights, and adjoins a good cinema. Daily noon–midnight.

Le Cid 11 place de l'Horloge ℗ 04.90.82.30.38, ⓦ lecidcafe.com. Trendy mixed gay/straight bar and terrace that opens up at 6.30am daily, and keeps going until 1am, long after the rest of place de l'Horloge has closed for the night.

Mon Bar 17 rue Portail Matheron. Pleasantly old-fashioned café with a laid-back atmosphere. Open daily 7am–10pm.

Shakespeare 155 rue Carreterie ℗ 04.90.27.38.50. Welcoming English bookshop and *salon de thé*. Closed evenings and all Sun & Mon.

Le Square Agricole Perdiguier ℗ 06.21.86.71.94. There's nothing fancy or even particularly exceptional about this outdoor café/brasserie, but its setting, sprawling outdoors in a spacious pedestrianized park behind the tourist office, makes it a great spot for a summer-morning coffee, or a simple lunchtime salad or *plat* for under €10. Closed after sunset.

Tapalocas 15 rue Galante ℗ 04.90.82.56.84. Tapas and Spanish music, sometimes live, in a large, atmospheric bar. Daily noon–1am.

Le Vache à Carreaux 14 rue Peyrollerie ℗ 04.90.80.09.05. Intimate, homely wine bar that serves food and stays open until 1am.

Nightlife and entertainment

Though the city saves a lot of its energy for the festival, Avignon sees a fair amount of **nightlife** and **cultural events** all year round, particularly café-theatre. For more information, drop in at the tourist office.

Live music and clubs

AJMI Jazz Club c/o La Manutention, 4 rue Escalier Ste-Anne ℗ 04.90.86.08.61, ⓦ www .jazzalajmi.com. Hosts major acts and some adventurous new groups. Check the website for a programme of what's on.

Le Bokao's 9 bis bd du Quai St-Lazare ℗ 04.90.82.47.95, ⓦ bokaos.fr. Popular

mainstream club, in a converted barn across from the river just outside the walls, playing an eclectic mix of music styles including house and techno at the weekends. Wed–Sat 10pm–5am.

L'Esclave 12 rue du Limas ℗ 04.90.85.14.91. Avignon's gay and lesbian bar, with regular DJs, drag shows and karaoke nights. Tues–Sun from 11pm.

Pub Z 58 rue Bonneterie ☏ 04.90.85.42.84. Student-oriented rock bar, decorated in black and white in honour of the zebra, with DJs at the weekend. Daily except Sun until 1.30am.

Le Red Zone 25 rue Carnot ☏ 04.90.27.02.44, ☻ redzonebar.com. Sweaty, crimson club where DJs play anything from salsa to electro according to the night. Nightly 9pm–3am.

Theatre and cinema

Théâtre du Balcon 38 rue Guillaume-Puy ☏ 04.90.85.00.80, ☻ theatredubalcon.org. A venue staging everything from African music and twentieth-century classics to contemporary theatre.

Théâtre des Carmes 6 place des Carmes ☏ 04.90.82.20.47, ☻ theatredescarmes.com. Run by one of the founders of Festival Off, this theatre specializes in avant-garde performances.

Théâtre du Chêne Noir 8 bis rue Ste-Catherine ☏ 04.90.86.58.11, ☻ chenenoir.fr. May have mime, a musical or Molière on offer.

Opéra place de l'Horloge ☏ 04.90.82.81.40, ☻ www.operatheatredavignon.fr. Classical opera and ballet. Oct–June.

Cinéma Utopia 4 rue Escalier Ste-Anne ☏ 04.90.82.65.36, ☻ www.cinemas-utopia.org. Cinema showing art-house, obscure or old-time favourites, always in the original language.

Listings

Bike rental Provence Bike, 52 bd St-Roch ☏ 04.90.27.92.61, ☻ provence-bike.com; also scooters and motorbikes.

Boat trips Grands Bateaux de Provence, allée de l'Oulle ☏ 04.90.85.62.25, ☻ mireio.net. Dinner cruises upstream towards Châteauneuf-du-Pape and downstream to Arles €48–65, meal included. Shorter cruises from €8.50. April–Sept.

Bookshops Shakespeare, 155 rue Carreterie ☏ 04.90.27.38.50, ☻ shakespeare.bookshop .free.fr (closed Sun & Mon); FNAC, 19 rue de la République, ☻ fnac.com (closed Sun).

Emergencies Doctor/ambulance ☏ 15; hospital, Centre Hospitalier H. Duffaut, 305 rue Raoul-Follereau ☏ 04.32.75.33.33; night chemist, call police ☏ 04.90.85.13.13 for addresses.

Laundry 9 rue du Chapeau-Rouge; 27 rue Portail-Magnanen; 113 av St-Ruf.

Markets Flea market: place des Carmes (Sun morning). Flowers: place des Carmes (Sat morning). Food: in the covered halls on place Pie (Tues–Fri until 1.30pm; Sat & Sun until 2pm).

Police Municipale 13 ter bd du Quai St-Lazare ☏ 08.00.00.84.00 or 04.90.85.13.13.

Post office cours Président Kennedy (Mon–Fri 8.30am–6.30pm, Sat 8.30am–noon).

Swimming pool Piscine Jean Clement, Chemin de la Martelle ☏ 04.90.31.38.73.

Taxis place Pie ☏ 04.90.82.20.20. Velocité (bicycle taxis €1 per km) ☏ 06.37.36.48.89.

Villeneuve-lès-Avignon

Pretty and prosperous, though little more than a village at its core, **VILLE-NEUVE-LÈS-AVIGNON** (also spelled Villeneuve-lez-Avignon) rises up a rocky escarpment above the west bank of the Rhône, looking down upon its older and larger neighbour from behind far more convincing fortifications. Despite ongoing rivalry, Villeneuve has effectively been a suburb of Avignon for most of its history, with palatial residences constructed by the cardinals and a great monastery founded by Pope Innocent VI.

To this day, Villeneuve is technically a part of Languedoc and not Provence, and might well be better known were it further from Avignon, whose monuments it can almost match for colossal scale. It is, however, a very different – and really rather sleepy – kind of place, and as such retains a repose and a sense of timelessness that bustling Avignon inevitably lacks. In summer it provides venues for the Avignon Festival as well as alternatives for accommodation overspill, but it's certainly worth a day spent exploring, whatever time of year you visit.

Arrival, information and accommodation

The half-hourly #11 **bus** takes ten minutes to reach Villeneuve from cours Président-Kennedy in Avignon, or just five minutes from Porte de l'Oulle. The unprepossessing place Charles-David, where the bus stops, is home to the **tourist office** (April–June, Sept & Oct Mon–Sat 9am–12.30pm & 2–6pm; July Mon–Fri 10am–7pm, Sat & Sun 10am–1pm & 2.30–7pm; Aug daily 9am–12.30pm & 2–6pm; Nov–March 9.30am–12.30pm & 2–5pm; ☎04.90.25.61.33, ⓦvilleneuvelezavignon.fr/tourisme), as well as **markets** devoted to food on Thursday morning and bric-a-brac on Saturday morning. The **Avignon Passion** pass detailed on p.123 is also valid in Villeneuve.

In terms of **accommodation**, Villeneuve is more a boutique destination than a mere alternative to Avignon, with a handful of charming, good-value **hotels** and **B&Bs**.

Hotels

L'Atelier 5 rue de la Foire ☎04.90.25.01.84, ⓦhoteldelatelier.com. Very tasteful rooms in a sixteenth-century house with a central stone staircase bathed in light, plus huge open fireplaces and a shady walled garden. Closed Jan. ❹

Les Écuries des Chartreux 66 rue de la République ☎04.90.25.79.93, ⓦecuries-des-chartreux.com. B&B in a light and airy rustic house with exposed stone walls and antique furniture. ❺

Jardin de la Livrée 4 bis rue Camp de Bataille ☎04.90.26.05.05, ⓦla-livree.oxatis.com. Clean, comfortable B&B rooms in an old house in the centre of the village, with a swimming pool, and a restaurant, closed Sun pm and Mon, that serves an €18 lunch menu and a €26 dinner menu. The one drawback is the noise of passing trains. ❺

Prieuré 7 place du Chapitre ☎04.90.15.90.15, ⓦleprieure.com. If you fancy being surrounded by tapestries, finely carved doors, old oak ceilings and other baronial trappings, this old priory surrounded by a peaceful flower-filled garden is indisputably the first choice. The restaurant serves Provençal cuisine with a gourmet twist. Closed Nov–March. ❽

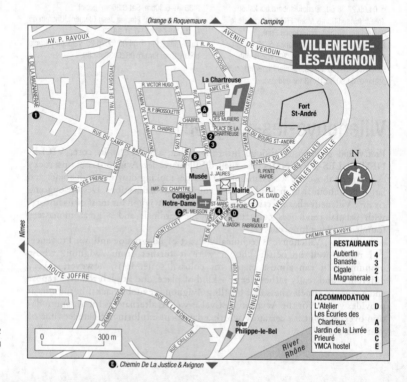

Orange & Roquemaure ▲ ▲ Camping

VILLENEUVE-LÈS-AVIGNON

Fort St-André

La Chartreuse

Musée

Mairie

Collègial Notre-Dame

Tour Philippe-le-Bel

River Rhône

RESTAURANTS
Aubertin 4
Banaste 3
Cigale 2
Magnaneraie 1

ACCOMMODATION
L'Atelier D
Les Écuries des Chartreux A
Jardin de la Livrée B
Prieuré C
YMCA hostel E

0 — 300 m

ⓔ, Chemin De La Justice & Avignon ▼

Hostel and campsite

Camping Municipal de la Laune chemin St-Honoré ☎04.90.25.76.06, ⊛camping -villeneuvelezavignon.com. A three-star site off the D980, near the sports stadium and swimming pools. €15 for two people with a tent. Closed mid-Oct to mid-March.

YMCA hostel 7bis chemin de la Justice ☎04.90.25.46.20, ⊛ymca-avignon.com.

Beautifully situated overlooking the river by Pont du Royaume (the extension of Pont Daladier), with balconied rooms for one to four people (from €25 for dorm bed, or available as private rooms), with and without en-suite facilities, and an open-air swimming pool (stop "Pont d'Avignon" on Avignon–Villeneuve bus or "Gabriel Péri" on the Villeneuve–Avignon bus). ❶

The Town

Villeneuve today has a lazy small-town feel, its daily activity centred around the lovely little place Jean-Jaurès. Originally, however, the town was enclosed within the walls of its mighty castle, the enormous **Fort St-André**, on a rise to the east. Then, in 1770, the Rhône shifted its course roughly 1km to the south, and the fort lost its strategic importance. Now basically a hollow shell, it can be reached by climbing either the montée du Fort from place Jean-Jaurès, or the "rapid slope" of rue Pente Rapide, a cobbled street of tiny houses that leads off rue des Recollets on the north side of place Charles-David.

Once inside the bulbous, double-towered gateway that penetrates the fort's vast white walls, you find yourself on what used to be the narrow main street of the town. Buying a ticket for the fort itself (daily: April to mid-May & mid-Sept to Oct 10am–1pm & 2–5.30pm; mid-May to mid-Sept 10am–1pm & 2–6pm; Oct– March 10am–1pm & 2–5pm; €5) allows you to continue up the street, passing assorted tumbledown ruins, and then walk along the parapets, where a cliff-face terrace offers tremendous views of both modern Villeneuve and Avignon across the river. You can also pay separately to visit its former **abbey**, now privately owned (Tues–Sun: April–Sept 10am–12.30pm & 2–6pm; Oct–March 10am–12.30pm & 2–5pm; €4), which as well as more magnificent views holds gardens of olive trees, ruined chapels, lily ponds and dovecotes.

Below the fort, **La Chartreuse du Val du Bénédiction** (April–Sept daily 9am–6.30pm; Oct–March Mon–Fri 9.30am–5pm, Sat & Sun 10am–5pm; €6.50) is one of the largest Carthusian monasteries in France, founded by the sixth of the Avignon popes, Innocent VI. Sold off after the Revolution and gradually restored last century, the buildings are totally unembellished, and except for the Giovanetti frescoes in the chapel beside the refectory, all the paintings and treasures have been dispersed. You're free to wander around unguided, through the three cloisters, the church, chapels, cells and communal spaces, which have little to see but plenty of atmosphere to absorb. It's one of the best venues of the Festival of Avignon.

Another festival venue, the fourteenth-century **Église Collègiale Notre-Dame** (daily: April–Sept 10am–12.30pm & 2–6.30pm; Oct–March 10am–noon & 2–5pm; free) and its cloister, stand on place St-Marc close to the *mairie*. Notre-Dame's most important treasure is a rare fourteenth-century smiling Madonna and Child made from a single tusk of ivory. It's now housed in the **Musée Pierre-de-Luxembourg**, just to the north along rue de la République (Tues–Sun: Jan, March & Oct–Dec 10am–noon & 2–5pm; April–Sept 10am–12.30pm & 2–6.30pm; €3), along with many of the paintings from the Chartreuse, including the stunning *Coronation of the Virgin*, painted in 1453 by Enguerrand Quarton.

South of the centre, beside the main road from Avignon, the stout **Tour Philippe-le-Bel** (Tues–Sun: March, Oct & Nov 10am–noon & 2–5.30pm; April–Sept 10am–12.30pm & 2–6.30pm; €2.10) was built to guard the western end of Avignon's Pont St-Bénézet. The rather tricky climb to the top is rewarded with one last overview of Villeneuve and Avignon.

Eating and drinking

Most of Villeneuve's **restaurants** are special-treat places for day-trippers from Avignon, though there a handful of pleasant little cafés on place Jean-Jaurès where you can enjoy a simple snack with your drink.

Aubertin 1 rue de l'Hôpital
℡04.90.25.94.84. Set in the shade of the old arcades by the Collègiale Notre-Dame, serving simple local dishes followed by fabulous desserts: try the chocolate and raspberry tart. €40 menu. Closed Sun & Mon.
Banaste 28 rue de la République
℡04.90.25.64.20. Bountiful Provençal and Languedocian *terroir* meals. More pleasant indoors than on the cramped roadside terrace. Menus €26–43. Closed Thurs low season & last three weeks of Jan.

Cigale 38 rue de la République ℡04.32.70.22.34. Inexpensive restaurant specializing in fish dishes. *Plats* around €10, menus from €18. Closed Wed.
Magnaneraie 37 rue du Camp de Bataille ℡04.90.25.11.11, ⊛www.hostellerie-la -magnaneraie.com. Excellent, upmarket restaurant 5min walk west of the centre, serving delicacies such as foie gras marinated in peach wine. There's an evening menu at €35; going à la carte will cost more. Closed Wed & Sun eve, plus Sat lunch Nov–April.

Châteauneuf-du-Pape

Roughly halfway along the back road between Avignon and Orange, the large village of **CHÂTEAUNEUF-DU-PAPE** takes its name from the summer palace of the Avignon popes. However, neither the views down the Rhône valley from its ruined fourteenth-century **château** (freely accessible) nor its medieval streets give Châteauneuf its special appeal. It is, of course, the local **vineyards** that produce the magic, with the grapes warmed at night by large pebbles that cover the ground and soak up the sun's heat by day. Their rich ruby-red wine is one of the most renowned in France, though the lesser-known white, too, is exquisite.

As in so many Provençal villages, commercial activity in Châteauneuf is largely confined to the main road that loops around the base of its small central hill. Climb

▲ Vines at Châteauneuf-du-Pape

towards the castle from the busy little **place du Portail**, and you're soon in a delightful tangle of sleepy, verdant alleyways.

During the first full weekend of August, the **Fête de la Véraison** celebrates the ripening of the grapes, with free *dégustation* (tasting) stalls throughout the village, as well as parades, dances, equestrian contests, folklore floats and so forth. As well as wine, a good deal of grape liqueur (*marc*) is imbibed. At other times, several places throughout the village offer free **tastings**, including the **Musée du Vin** on avenue Pierre-de-Luxembourg (daily: May to mid-Oct 9am–1pm & 2–7pm; mid-Oct to April 9am–noon & 2–6pm; free). Before you tackle the multitude of *caves* in and around town, pick up a list of producers at the tourist office (see below). No single outlet sells all the Châteauneuf-du-Pape wines; the best selection under one roof is at **La Maison des Vins**, 8 rue du Maréchal Foch (daily: mid-June to mid-Sept 10am–7pm; mid-Sept to mid-June 10.30am–noon & 2–6.30pm; Ⓦwww.vinadea.com).

Practicalities

Châteauneuf's **tourist office** is on place du Portail (June–Sept Mon–Sat 9am–6pm; Oct–May Mon, Tues & Thurs–Sat 9.30am–12.30pm & 2–6pm; ℡04.90.83.71.08, Ⓦwww.ccpro.fr/tourisme).

Of the handful of pleasant small **hotel-restaurants** nearby, the lively *Mère Germaine*, on avenue Cdt-Lemaître (℡04.90.83.54.37, Ⓦlameregermaine.com; ❸), has eight welcoming rooms and serves well-crafted Provençal cuisine on menus from €21, while the cosy *Garbure*, 3 rue Joseph-Ducos (℡04.90.83.75.08, Ⓦwww .la-garbure.com; ❹; closed three weeks in Nov), also holds eight cheerful rooms. The charming *Sommellerie*, a renovated country house 3km north on route de Roquemaure (℡04.90.83.50.00, Ⓦla-sommellerie.fr; ❻; closed Jan), has modern pastel-painted rooms, a pool, and a restaurant (closed Sat lunch & Mon lunch) producing superb dishes such as grilled lamb with garlic, rosemary and tapenade, on menus starting at €30 for lunch, €46 for dinner. There's also a two-star **campsite**, *Islon St-Luc*, about 2km down chemin de la Calade, south from place Portail (℡04.90.39.13.46, Ⓔla.goutte.bleue@orange.fr; €15 per tent).

Away from the hotels, you can eat well for around €15 at the **brasserie** *La Mule du Pape*, 2 rue de la République (℡04.90.83.79.22). *Le Verger des Papes*, at 4 montée du Château at the top of the hill (℡04.90.83.50.40, Ⓦwww.vergerdespapes.com; closed Sun eve), serves traditional food on a peaceful terrace, with menus at €19 (lunch) & €29 (dinner).

Orange

Thanks to its spectacular **Roman theatre**, the small town of **ORANGE**, well west of the Rhône 20km north of Avignon, is famous out of all proportion to its size. Now home to fewer than thirty thousand citizens, it was founded as Aurisio in 35 BC; only much later did its name become conflated with the fruit and colour. In the eight century, Charlemagne made it the seat of the counts of Orange, a title that passed to the Dutch crown in the sixteenth century. The family's best-known member was Prince William, who ascended the English throne with his consort Mary in the 1688 "Glorious Revolution", and whose supporters in Ireland established the Protestant Orange Order. More recently, Orange became notorious for electing a Front National mayor in both 1995 and 2001; he's still in office, although now as a member of the right-wing Mouvement Pour La France.

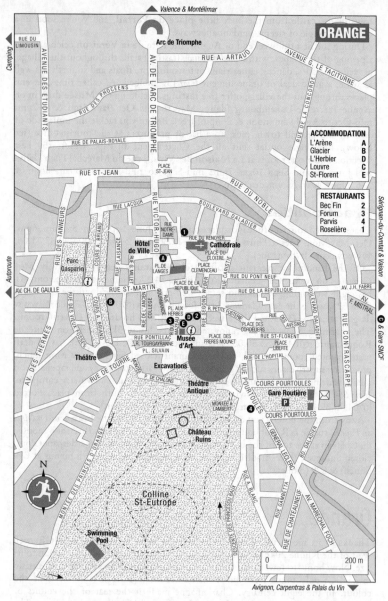

Valence & Montélimar

ORANGE

Arc de Triomphe

RUE DU LIMOUSIN

Camping

AVENUE DES ETUDIANTS

RUE DES PHOCEENS

AV. DE L'ARC DE TRIOMPHE

RUE A. ARTAUD

AVENUE G. LE TACITURNE

RUE DE PALAIS-ROYALE

RUE DE LA CONCORDE

PLACE ST-JEAN

RUE ST-JEAN

RUE DU NOBLE

Seignan-du-Comtat & Vaison

ACCOMMODATION
L'Arène · · · · · · **A**
Glacier · · · · · · **B**
L'Herbier · · · · · **D**
Louvre · · · · · · **E**
St-Florent · · · · · **C**

RESTAURANTS
Bec Fin · · · · · **2**
Forum · · · · · · **3**
Parvis · · · · · · **4**
Roselière · · · · **1**

RUE DES TANNEURS

RUE LACOUR

COURS A. BRIAND

RUE VICTOR-HUGO

BOULEVARD DALADIER

RUE NOTRE-DAME

RUE DU RENOYER

Hôtel de Ville

Cathédrale

PLACE DU CLOÎTRE

PLACE CLEMENCEAU

RUE CARISTIE

RUE DU PONT NEUF

RUE PLAISANCE

Parc Gasparin

PL. DE LANGES

PLACE DE LA REPUBLIQUE

WEBER

RUE DE LA REPUBLIQUE

AV. J.H. FABRE

AV. CH. DE GAULLE

RUE ST-MARTIN

COURS A. BRIAND

RUE DE L'ANCIEN COLLEGE

GOURMANDE

PL. AUX HERBES

RUE SEGOND

R. PETITE FUSTERIE

AV. F. MISTRAL

C & Gare SNCF

RUE DES VIEILLES FOSSES

AV. DES THERMES

MAZEAU

Musée d'Art

RUE PONTILLAC

R. TOURGAYRANNE

PL. SILVAIN

RUE DES CORDELIERS

PLACE DES AVESNES

RUE ST-FLORENT

PLACE DES FRERES MOUNET

PLACE LIBERTE

BOULEVARD DALADIER

RUE CONTRASCARPE

Théâtre

RUE DE TOURRE

Excavations

P. DE CHALONS

Théâtre Antique

RUE DE L'HOPITAL

COURS POURTOULES

Gare Routière

AV. DES PRINCES D'ORANGE

MONTEE A LAMBERT

MONTEE DES PRINCES D'ORANGE

Château Ruins

COURS POURTOULES

AV. GENERAL LECLERC

BD DALADIER

N

Colline St-Eutrope

DESCENTE DES PRINCESSU BAUX

RUE A. BLANC

RUE GAMBETTA

RUE DE CHATEAUNEUF

AV. MARECHAL FOCH

Swimming Pool

0   200 m

Avignon, Carpentras & Palais du Vin

Now known as the Théâtre Antique, the Roman theatre is the city's one must-see attraction, at its best and busiest during the Chorégies **opera festival** in July (see p.138). Otherwise, with its medieval street plan, fountained squares, houses with ancient porticoes and courtyards, and Thursday market, Orange is an attractive enough place to stroll around, but the only reason to stay more than a day or two is to use it as a quiet base for exploring the region.

Arrival, information and accommodation

There's very limited **parking** in the city centre; for short stays; use the metered parking along cours Aristide Briand, or stay overnight in the underground car park east of the theatre, entered from boulevard Edouard-Daladier near the *gare routière*. The *gare SNCF* is 1.5km east of the centre, at the end of avenue Frédéric-Mistral.

The main **tourist office** is at 5 cours Aristide Briand (April–June & Sept Mon–Sat 9am–6.30pm, Sun 10am–1pm & 2–6.30pm; July–Aug Mon–Sat 9am–7.30pm, Sun 10am–1pm & 2–7pm; Oct–March Mon–Sat 10am–1pm & 2–5pm; ☏04.90.34.70.88, ⓦotorange.fr), with a subsidiary, summer-only office facing the Théâtre Antique (July–Aug Mon–Sat 9am–7.30pm).

To get a real sense of the old town, it's best to pick a hotel in the centre. **Accommodation** only becomes hard to find during the Chorégies festival in July.

Hotels

L'Arène place de Langes ☏04.90.11.40.40, ⓦhotel-arene.fr. Very presentable hotel, with spacious rooms, on a quiet, pedestrianized (though not especially attractive) square. ❺

Glacier 46 cours Aristide-Briand ☏04.90.34.02.01, ⓦwww.le-glacier.com. Comfortable, cosy Provençal-style rooms – think yellows and blues with pretty quilts and floral curtains. All are en-suite and a/c, but they vary widely in size and amenities. Closed Fri–Sun, Nov–Feb only. ❸–❻

L'Herbier 8 place aux Herbes ☏04.90.34.09.23, ⓦlherbierdorange.com. A good budget option, set in a seventeenth-century house overlooking a pretty square near the Théâtre Antique. Rooms are simple and clean, but the cheapest aren't en-suite, but there are some good-value family rooms. Note that the parking they offer is a public car park 500m away. ❷

Louvre 89 av Frédéric-Mistral ☏04.90.34.10.08, ⓦwww.hotel-louvre-orange.com. A pleasant three-star hotel, close to the train station, with somewhat anonymous modern a/c rooms, a garden and a small pool. ❹

St-Florent 4 rue du Mazeau ☏04.90.34.18.53, ⓦhotelsaintflorent.com. Very central, inexpensive hotel, with appealingly kitsch decor and a wide assortment of rooms; some have four-poster beds, not all are en-suite, and there are some extremely cheap singles. ❷

Campsite

Le Jonquier rue Alexis-Carrel ☏04.90.34.49.48, ⓦcampinglejonquier.com. Popular campsite, 1.5km northwest of the centre, equipped with tennis courts, mini-golf and a pool. €25.50 for two people and a tent. Closed mid-Sept to March.

The Town

Orange is small enough to cover easily on foot. Everything is dominated by the enormous wall of the **Théâtre Antique**, at the southern end of the medieval centre, with the hill of St-Eutrope rising behind. Said to be the world's best-preserved Roman theatre, it's the only one with its stage wall still standing. Around 55 AD, audiences of ten thousand could spend their days off watching farce, clownish improvisations, song and dance and, perhaps, for the sake of a visiting dignitary, a bit of Greek tragedy in Latin. Having survived periods as a fortification, slum and prison before its careful reconstruction in the nineteenth century, the Théâtre still hosts musical performances in summer, and is also open to visitors as an archeological site (daily: March & Oct 9.30am–5.30pm; April, May & Sept 9am–6pm; June–Aug 9am–7pm; Nov–Feb 9.30am–4.30pm; €7.90 including **Musée d'Art et Histoire**; ⓦwww.theatre-antique.com).

Spreading a colossal 36m high by 103m wide, the Théâtre's outer face resembles a monstrous prison wall, despite the ground-level archways leading into the backstage areas. Once inside, an excellent audioguide paints an evocative picture of its history and architecture. Its enormous **stage**, originally sheltered by a mighty awning, could accommodate vast numbers of performers, while the

Orange Chorégies

When Orange's **Chorégies** (☏04.90.34.24.24, ⓦwww.choregies.asso.fr), or **choral festival**, began in 1879, it marked the first performance at the Théâtre Antique in 350 years. The festival now commences in mid-July each year and lasts for three weeks, with a varied programme of opera, oratorios and orchestral concerts. Tickets cost from €14 to €240, and go on sale in October of the preceding year. Check the Théâtre's own website, ⓦwww.theatre-antique.com, for details of other concerts, performances and film shows throughout the year.

acoustics allowed a full audience to hear every word. Once you've seen the theatre itself, you're free to follow in their footsteps. Spectators who grew bored during the day-long performances could slip out of the west door to a semicircle complex cut into the rock. Some archeologists suggest the complex contained baths, a stage for combats and a gymnasium equipped with three 180-metre running tracks; others say it was the forum, or even a circus.

Though missing most of its original decoration, the inner side of the wall above the stage is extremely impressive. Below columned niches, now empty of their statues, a larger-than-life-size statue of Augustus, raising his arm in imperious fashion, looks down centre stage. Seating was allocated strictly by rank; an inscription "EQ Gradus III" (third row for knights) remains visible near the orchestra pit. Arches along the uppermost internal passageway now hold audiovisual displays, including footage of rock festivals held here during the 1970s.

The best **viewpoint** over the entire theatre, on St-Eutrope hill, can be accessed without paying from both east and west. As you look down towards the stage, the ruins at your feet are those of the short-lived seventeenth-century castle of the princes of Orange. Louis XIV had it destroyed in 1673 and the principality of Orange was officially annexed to France forty years later.

The Musée d'Art et Histoire and Arc de Triomphe

Across from the Théâtre, Orange's **Musée d'Art et Histoire** (daily: March & Oct 9.45am–12.30pm & 1.30–5.30pm; April, May & Sept 9.15am–6pm; June–Aug 9.15am–7pm; Nov–Feb 9.45am–12.30pm & 1.30–4.30pm; €4.50, or €7.90 with theatre) covers local history from the Romans onwards, and also hosts temporary exhibitions. Artefacts taken from the Théâtre complex include the largest known Roman land-survey maps, carved on marble (though these were badly damaged when the museum itself collapsed in 1962), along with a couple of sphinxes and a mosaic floor. The two upper levels are dedicated to the Gasparin family, who promoted the safeguarding of Roman Orange, and are filled with family portraits, mementoes and a reconstructed *salon*.

Don't miss the town's second major Roman monument, the triple-bayed **Arc de Triomphe**, on the main road north of the centre. Built around 20 BC, its intricate friezes and reliefs celebrate the victories of the Roman Second Legion against the Gauls.

Eating and drinking

Orange is the kind of place where you can walk round and round main squares like place de la République and place Clemenceau, passing plenty of pleasant open-air bars and brasseries that are ideal for an evening **drink**, without ever finding a dinner menu that leaps out from the rest. Some good little **restaurants** lie tucked away along the side streets, however, and prices are generally reasonable.

Bec Fin rue Segond Weber ℡04.90.34.05.10, Ⓦrestaurant-le-bec-fin.com. Large restaurant, with tables both indoors and sprawled along a narrow alley with equally narrow views of the Théâtre Antique, this place serves hearty salads and tasty pizzas for around €10, plus a really good €21 dinner menu, featuring gazpacho, whole roast monkfish and a delicious dessert.

Forum 3 rue du Mazeau ℡04.90.34.01.09. Small, intimate restaurant near the Théâtre. Menus (from €22) revolve around seasonal ingredients; in January, truffles feature heavily, while in May, it's asparagus. Often booked up, so reserve ahead. Closed Mon, Sat lunch & Sun eve.

Parvis 55 cours Pourtoules ℡04.90.34.82.00. The best Provençal food in Orange. Straight from the market, ingredients are whipped up into tempting, good-value dishes such as pike-perch with asparagus *millefeuille*. Lunch menus €12 two-course, €17 three-course, dinner €22.50 and €26 respectively. Closed Sun & Mon, plus last 3 weeks in Nov & last 3 weeks in Jan.

Roselière 4 rue du Renoyer ℡04.90.34.50.42. Lovely little restaurant by the Hôtel de Ville, where you can sample tasty veal and duck dishes on menus priced at €15–23. Closed Sun & Mon, plus all Aug.

Sérignan-du-Comtat

The most celebrated resident of **SÉRIGNAN-DU-COMTAT**, a pretty eight kilometre drive northeast of Orange, was **Jean-Henri Fabre** (1823–1915), who spent the last 36 years of his life here. A remarkable self-taught scientist, Fabre is famous primarily for his insect studies; he also composed poetry, wrote songs and painted his specimens with artistic brilliance. In his forties, with seven children to support, he was forced to resign from his teaching post at Avignon because parents and priests considered his lectures on the fertilization of flowering plants licentious, if not downright pornographic. His friend John Stuart Mill eventually bailed him out with a loan, allowing him to settle in Orange. Although he was too religious to be an evolutionist, Fabre also had lengthy correspondence with Darwin.

A **statue of Fabre** stands beside the red-shuttered *mairie*, while his actual house, which he named the **Harmas** (Latin for fallow land), is on the edge of the village on the N976 from Orange (April–June & Sept–Oct Mon, Tues, Thurs & Fri 10am–12.30pm & 2.30–6pm, Sun 2.30–6pm; July & Aug Mon, Tues, Thurs & Fri 10am–12.30pm & 3.30–7pm, Sun 3.30–7pm; €6). Inside, you can look round Fabre's study, with its various specimens of insects and other invertebrates and his complete classification of the herbs of France and Corsica. The room gives a strong sense of a person in love with the world he researched, an impression echoed in Fabre's extraordinary **watercolours** of the fungi of the Vaucluse, displayed on the ground floor. The stunning colours and almost hallucinogenic detail make these pictures seem more like holograms. After visiting the house you're free to wander round the **garden**, where over a thousand species grow in wild disorder, exactly as the scientist wanted it.

The Enclave des Papes

Heading north from Orange, the **Enclave des Papes**, centred on the town of **Valréas**, is not part of the Drôme *département* that surrounds it, but part of Vaucluse, an anomaly dating back to 1317 when the land was bought by Pope Jean XXII as part of his policy of expanding the papal states around his Holy See at Avignon. When the Vaucluse *département* was drawn up, the enclave was allowed to keep its old links and hence remains part of Provence.

Grignan, just outside the western edge of the enclave, and Valréas both have luxurious **châteaux**, and there are many **vineyards**, most edged with roses as an attractive early-warning system of aphid attack. East of the enclave, the pretty, undulating landscape comes to an abrupt end with the arc of mountains around **Nyons**, a reasonably pleasant little town, famous for its olives, which lies outside Provence and is therefore beyond the scope of this book.

Valréas

VALRÉAS, at the heart of the enclave, lies 35km northeast of Orange. The former Château de Simiane, a mainly eighteenth-century mansion whose arcades, windows and balustrades would look more at home in Paris, now serves as the **Hôtel de Ville** (July & Aug daily except Tues 10.30am–noon & 3–6pm; Sept–June Mon, Tues, Thurs–Sat 3–5pm; free). A few rooms can be visited, including the *salon de mariage* and the library, and it hosts contemporary art shows in summer.

Valréas' role as a centre for cardboard production is honoured in the surprisingly intriguing **Musée du Cartonnage et de l'Imprimerie**, in a warehouse just outside town on the road west to Orange (April–Oct Mon & Wed–Sat 10am–noon & 3–6pm, Sun 3–6pm; Nov–March Mon & Wed–Sat 10am–noon & 2–5pm, Sun 2–5pm; €3.50).

The main local **festivals** are the **Nuit de Petit St-Jean** on June 23 and 24, when there's a night-time procession and show, and the **Fête des Vins de l'Enclave** on the first Sunday in August. At other times, most visitors are here to buy local **wines**. As well as the Côtes du Rhône *appellation*, there's also Valréas Villages and Visan Villages, distinctive enclave wines, with flavours of violet, red fruits and pepper; such wines were supposedly what persuaded Pope Jean XXII to buy this area in the first place. The **Cave Coopérative** is at the Caveau St-Jean, avenue de l'Enclave des Papes (☎04.90.35.00.66); the tourist office has full lists of private cellars.

Practicalities

Valréas' **tourist office** is north of town on avenue Maréchal Leclerc (July & Aug Mon–Sat 9.15am–12.30pm & 2.30–6.30pm, Sun 9am–12.30pm; Sept, Oct & March–June Mon–Sat 9.15am–12.15pm & 2–6pm; Nov–Feb Mon–Fri 9.15am–12.15pm & 2–5pm, Sat 9.15am–12.15pm; ☎04.90.35.04.71, ⓦot-valreas.fr). Good places **to stay** include the *Grand Hôtel*, near the cardboard museum on the outskirts of town at 28 avenue Général-de-Gaulle (☎04.90.35.00.26; ❸; closed late Dec to Jan), a *logis* with pleasant gardens, a pool and menus from €21; and the nice little blue-fronted *Camargue*, 49 cours Jean-Jaurès (☎04.90.35.01.51, ⓦlacamargue84.com; ❶), where you can dine cheaply on the pavement terrace outside. The beautiful *Café de la Paix*, opposite the *Grand Hôtel* at 26 rue de l'Hôtel de Ville (☎04.90.28.14.32; ❷), makes a great spot to sample the **local wines**, serves menus at €18 and €22, and also has some inexpensive rooms. There's a two-star **campsite**, *Camping de la Couronne*, by the river on route du Pègue (☎04.90.35.03.78, ⓦlacoronne.new.fr; €18 per tent; closed Oct to mid-March).

The **market** is held on Wednesday on place Cardinal-Maury and cours du Berteuil on the eastern side of town, with local truffles figuring prominently between November and March.

Grignan

GRIGNAN, on the main route west from Valréas, is dominated by its **château** (daily 9.30–11.30am & 2.30–5.30pm, closed Tues Nov–March; €5.50). The enormous building takes up all the high ground of the town, rising above the heavy towers and walls of St-Saveur's church and the medieval houses below the southern facade. Though eleventh-century in origin, the château was transformed in the sixteenth century into a Renaissance palace, with tiers of huge windows facing the south and statues lining the roof; the older parts lie to the north. It hosts a **jazz festival** in November.

The château's most famous resident, the writer **Madame de Sévigné**, came here for long periods to visit her daughter, the countess of Grignan. You can see the comforts and craftsmanship of the contemporary furnishings, plus eighteenth-century additions, in the tour of the *salons*, galleries and grand stairways, Mme de Sévigné's bedroom and the count's apartments.

Four kilometres east of Grignan, just outside the village of Grillon, the three-room **hotel-restaurant** *Auberge des Papes* (T 04.90.37.43.67, W aubergedespapes.free.fr; half board obligatory July & Aug; ❺; closed Sept), offers quiet, comfortable rooms and meals in which truffles feature heavily (menus from €18; restaurant closed Wed out of season).

Vaison-la-Romaine

The charming old town of **VAISON-LA-ROMAINE**, 27km northeast of Orange, is divided into two very distinct halves, either side of the deep gorge cut by the River Ouvèze and connected by a single-arched Roman bridge. Throughout its history, the town centre has shifted from one side to the other, depending on whether its inhabitants needed the defensive position offered by the steep, forbidding hill south of the river. Now known as the **Haute Ville**, and topped by a ruined twelfth-century castle, this was the site of the original Celtic settlement. The **Romans**, however, built their homes on the flatter land north of the river, and that's where all the activity of the modern town is centred; the medieval lanes on the Haute Ville side attract throngs of day-trippers, but are largely residential.

Arrival, information and accommodation

Vaison's **tourist office** (April–June & Sept to mid-Oct Mon–Sat 9am–noon & 2–5.45pm, Sun 9am–noon; July–Aug 9am–12.30pm & 2–6.45pm; mid-Oct to March Mon–Sat 9am–noon & 2–5.45pm; T 04.90.36.02.11, W vaison-la -romaine.com) is on place du Chanoine-Sautel, between the two Roman sites. If there's no room to **park** on the central place Montfort, there should be spaces on quai Pasteur down by the river. The *gare routière* is on avenue des Choralies, east of the centre.

Vaison makes a lovely base for exploring the surrounding area, mostly because of its wonderful **hotels**. Be sure to book well in advance.

Hotels and B&Bs

Le Beffroi rue de l'Evêché T 04.90.36.04.71, W le-beffroi.com. Beautiful, luxurious rooms in a sixteenth-century residence in the Haute Ville with a pool, a great restaurant and unsurpassable views over the valley. Hotel closed Feb–March; restaurant closed Nov–March. ❺

Burrhus 2 place Montfort T 04.90.36.00.11, W burrhus.com. Large, modern if somewhat characterless bedrooms in the heart of town, with tiled floors and very comfortable beds. As it's overlooking the main square, it can be noisy at weekends, but the sunny breakfast balcony is a real plus. ❸

L'Evêché rue de l'Evêché T 04.90.36.13.46, W eveche-vaison.com. Lovely B&B in the Haute Ville, with comfortable modern rooms and a homely atmosphere. Enjoy coffee and croissants on the little terrace at the back. ❺

La Fête en Provence place du Vieux Marché T 04.90.36.36.43, W www.hotellafete-provence .com. Gorgeous, comfortable rooms and apartments surrounding a pool and flower-decked patio in the Haute Ville. ④

Campsite

Camping du Théâtre Romain Chemin du Brusquet, off av des Choralies, quartier des Arts ⊕04.90.28.78.66, ⊚camping-theatre.com. Small, four-star campsite 500m northeast of the centre, with good facilities. Reserve well ahead in summer. Closed early Nov to mid-March. €20.40 per tent.

The Town

Vaison's two excavated **Roman** residential districts lie to either side of avenue Général-de-Gaulle. You can get an overview by simply peeking through the railings, but you'll get a much better sense of the style and luxury of the era if you pay for admission (€8 for both sites, plus cathedral cloisters), which includes a brief but succinct audio tour, as well as the excellent **museum**.

The **Vestiges de Puymin** (daily: March 10am–12.30pm & 2–5pm; April & May 9.30am–6pm; June–Sept 9.30am–6.30pm; Oct–Feb 10am–noon & 2–5pm) stretch up a gentle hillside to the east. The ground plans of several mansions and houses are discernible in the foreground, along with a colonnade known as the *portique de Pompée*, while slightly higher up the museum holds all sorts of detail and decoration unearthed from the ruins. Everyday artefacts include mirrors of silvered bronze, lead water pipes, weights and measures, taps shaped as griffins' feet and dolphin doorknobs, and there are also some impressive statues and stelae. A rather thrilling tunnel through the hillside leads to an ancient Roman **theatre**, which still seats seven thousand people during the July **dance festival** (⊚vaison -danses.com)

To the west, the **Vestiges de la Villasse** (daily except Tues morning: March 10am–12.30pm & 2–6pm; April & May 10am–noon & 2.30–6pm; June–Sept 10am–noon & 2.30–6.30pm; Oct–Feb 10am–noon & 2–5pm) are less substantial, but reveal a clearer picture of the layout of a comfortable, well-serviced town of the Roman ruling class. As well as a row of arcaded shops, there are more patrician houses (some with mosaics still intact), a basilica and the baths.

The former **Cathédrale Notre-Dame** lies a little further west. Its apse is a confusing overlay of sixth-, tenth- and thirteenth-century construction, some of it using pieces quarried from the Roman ruins, while the **cloisters** (same hours as Roman sites, but closes 15min earlier) are fairly typical of early medieval workmanship, pretty enough but not wildly exciting.

It says a great deal for Roman engineering that the **Pont Romain** survived relatively unscathed when the River Ouvèze burst its banks in 1992, killing thirty people and causing a great deal of material damage – unlike the modern road bridge to the west, which was completely destroyed. From its south side, Rue du Pont Romain climbs upwards towards place du Poids and the fourteenth-century gateway to the medieval **Haute Ville**. More steep zigzags take you past the Gothic gate and overhanging portcullis of the belfry and into the heart of this sedately quiet, uncommercialized and rich *quartier*. There are fountains and flowers in all the squares, and right at the top, from the twelfth- to sixteenth-century **castle**, you'll have a great view of Mont Ventoux. In summer, the Haute Ville livens up every Tuesday when Vaison's **market** spreads up here.

Eating and drinking

Vaison holds a large number of good **restaurants**, on both sides of the river. For a more local feel, stick to the modern town, particularly around place de Montfort and cours Taulignan, though the places in the Haute Ville cannot be beaten for their lovely views. The **cafés** on place Montfort are the best place to head for

drinks, while for buying **wine** to take home, the Maison des Vins, in the same building as the tourist office (Tues–Sat 9.30am–12.30pm & 2.30–6.30pm), has several wines from the vineyards of the Dentelles and Ventoux.

3

L'Auberge de Bartavelle 12 place Sus-Auze ☎04.90.36.02.6. A lively place in the modern town, immediately south of place Montfort, with decent and affordable specialities from southwest France – rabbit ravioli, *confit de canard* and the like – on menus from €16 lunch, €22 dinner. Fun black and white photos on the wall honour the playwright and filmmaker Marcel Pagnol. Closed Mon, Fri lunch & Jan.

Le Brin d'Olivier 4 rue de Ventoux ☎04.90.28.74.79, 🌐restaurant-lebrindolivier.com. Welcoming Provençal restaurant, serving lunch menus from €18 and dinner from €28 on a nice little terrace down by the river, albeit with no great views. Closed Wed lunch & Sat lunch July–Sept, all Wed Oct–June.

La Lyriste 45 cours Taulignan ☎04.90.36.04.67. Of several restaurants spreading across the broad pavements of this quiet boulevard, just north of place Montfort, the *Lyriste* stands out for its changing, high-quality menus, based around themes like cheese, exotic fruits or scallops. The simple €18 menu *découverte* is great value.

The Dentelles

Running northeast to southwest between Vaison and Carpentras, the jagged hilly backdrop of the **DENTELLES DE MONTMIRAIL** is best appreciated from the contrasting landscape of level fields, orchards and vineyards lying to their south and west. The range is named after lace (*dentelles*), its pinnacles slanting, converging, standing parallel or veering away from each other, like the contorted pins on a lace-making board – though the alternative connection with "teeth" (*dents*) is equally appropriate. For geologists, the Dentelles are Jurassic limestone folds, forced upright and then eroded by the wind and rain.

On the western and southern slopes lie the **wine-producing villages** of **Gigondas**, **Beaumes-de-Venise**, **Séguret**, **Vacqueyras** and, across the River Ouzère, **Rasteau**. Several boast their own individual *appellation contrôlée*, within the Côtes du Rhône or Côtes du Rhône Villages areas, meaning their wines are exceptional.

Besides wine-tasting and bottle-buying, the Dentelles are good for long **walks**, happening upon mysterious ruins or photogenic panoramas of Mont Ventoux and the Rhône Valley. The jagged hills are also favourite destinations for **rock-climbers**: the Col de Cayron pinnacle is prized by serious climbers, while the Dent du Turc needs only decent shoes and a head for heights to give a thrill.

For **walking and climbing information**, go to the *Gîte d'Etape des Dentelles* in Gigondas (see p.144), whose owner is a serious mountain climber, or the tourist office in Gigondas (see p.144).

Rasteau

For a good introduction to the art and science of wine-making and the whole business of wine-tasting, head for the **Musée du Vigneron** (daily except Tues & Sun: July & Aug 10am–6pm; April–June & Sept 2–6pm; €2; 🌐beaurenard.fr), on the D975 just east of the tiny, ivy-covered village of **RASTEAU**. For the serious wine enthusiast, the collection of old bottles, nineteenth-century agricultural implements, pickers' baskets and root injectors for fighting phylloxera is less interesting than the instructive displays on geology, soil, vine types, parasites and wine-growing throughout the world. Visits end with a free tasting (no obligation to buy).

Near the River Ouvèze south of Rasteau, the *Belle Rive* on route Violes (☎04.90.46.10.20, 🌐hotel-bellerive.fr; ❻; closed Oct–March) is a quiet **hotel** with a pool and fine view from its terrace; its restaurant serves good food, including *crème brûlées* flavoured with rosemary, chestnut and the like. For walkers, *CLAEP* on route du Stade (☎04.90.46.15.48, ⓦclaep-rasteau.net) offers dormitory accommodation, either half-board (€32.50) or full-board (€39). It's often reserved for large groups, so always call in advance.

Séguret

The star Dentelles village, **SÉGURET**, is an alluring spot that blends into the side of a rocky cliff, with a ruined castle soaring high above. With its steep cobbled streets, vine-covered houses and medieval structures, including an old stone laundry and a belfry with a one-handed clock, the village embodies many of Provence's charms. The **Fête des Vins et Festival Provençal Bravade** in the last two weeks of August, a relatively recent festival, incorporates processions for the Virgin Mary and the patron saint of wine-growers.

Perched near the top of the village, behind the Église St-Denis and commanding fabulous views south to the village of Sablet, there's a gorgeous **hotel**, ⚜ *La Table du Comtat* (☎04.90.46.91.49, ⓦtable-comtat.fr; ❺; closed 2nd half of Nov & mid-Feb to mid-March), with comfortable rooms and a small pool. The rooms are comfortable and quiet, and there's a small deck pool, but the real reason to come is to enjoy zestful Provençal **food** (restaurant closed Tues evening & Wed except in July & Aug) upon its delightful shaded terrace, with good-value lunch menus from €20, dinner from €34, and inexpensive organic wines. Dining alternatives in the village include *Le Mesclun*, rue des Poternes (☎04.90.46.93.43, ⓦlemesclun.com; closed Mon, Tues & Jan–Feb), which also has a nice terrace, and the cheaper *Café des Poternes* (☎04.90.46.93.74).

Additional attractive accommodation is available down on the plain nearby, at the *Domaine de Cabasse*, route de Sablet (☎04.90.46.91.12, ⓦdomaine-de-cabasse .fr; ❼; closed Nov–March; half-board obligatory in July & Aug), and the more rustic *Bastide Bleue*, route de Sablet (☎04.90.46.83.43, ⓦpagesperso-orange.fr /labastidebleue; ❹; restaurant closed Tues & Wed in low season), both of which also have good restaurants.

Gigondas

Known as "Jocunditas" (light-hearted joy) in Roman times, the village of **GIGONDAS** sits at the base of a hill, spreading upwards to the **église Ste-Catherine**. From the church, you get one of the region's best views of limestone pinnacles emerging from the vineyards below. A separate eminence in the upper reaches of the village holds the vestiges of the old fortifications and château, which now serve as a *Cheminement de Sculptures* (always open; free), a collection of contemporary sculptures and installations.

Gigondas' wine has the highest reputation of all the Dentelles *appellations*. Almost always red, quite strong, it has a back taste of spice or nuts and is best aged at least four or five years. Sampling the varieties could not be easier; the **Syndicat des Vins** runs a *caveau des vignerons* (daily 10am–noon & 2–6pm) in place de la Mairie where you can taste and ask advice about the produce from forty different *domaines*. Bottles cost exactly the same here as at the vineyards.

Gigondas' **tourist office**, on place du Portail (April–June & Sept–Oct Mon–Sat 10am–12.30pm & 2.30–6pm; July & Aug Mon–Sat 10am–12.30pm & 2.30–6.30pm, Sun 10am–1pm; Nov–March Mon–Sat 10am–noon & 2–5pm; ☎04.90.65.85.46, ⓦwww.gigondas-dm.fr), supplies lists of particular *domaines* or *caves* grouping several *vignerons* for the other villages.

At the entrance to Gigondas, the *Gîte d'Etape des Dentelles* (☎04.90.65.80.85, ⓦgite-dentelles.com; ❶; closed Jan & Feb) offers cheap double **rooms**, and dorm beds (€13 per person). There's also a charming **hotel**, *Les Florets*, 2km from the village towards the Dentelles (℡ 04.90.65.85.01, Ⓦ hotel-lesflorets.com; ❻; closed Jan & Feb), with an excellent **restaurant** (menus from €21; closed Wed) serving wines from its own vineyard. The best dining in the village centre is at *L'Oustalet*, on place du Portail in the village (℡ 04.90.65.85.30; Nov–April closed Mon), with a pleasant shaded terrace and dinner menus from €27.

Vacqueyras

Three kilometres south of Gigondas, the village of **VACQUEYRAS** is best known as the birthplace of a troubadour poet **Raimbaud**, who wrote love poems to Beatrice in Provençal and died in the Crusades in 1207. Another Dentelles village with its own *appellation*, Vacqueyras is home to an annual **wine festival** (on July 13 & 14) and a wine-tasting competition on the first weekend of June.

The upmarket **hotel** *Montmirail*, in spacious grounds just south of the centre (℡ 04.90.65.84.01, Ⓦ hotelmontmirail.com; ❺; closed Nov to mid-March), has a good Provençal restaurant, serving lunch menus from €22, dinner from €33.

Beaumes-de-Venise

The most distinctive wine of the region, and elixir for those who like it sweet, is Beaumes-de-Venise muscat. Pale amber in colour and with a hint of roses and lemon following the muscat flavour, it can usually convince the driest palates of its virtue. The place to buy it is at **BEAUMES-DE-VENISE**, at the Cave des Vignerons, in a huge low building on the D7 overlooked by the Romanesque bell tower of **Notre-Dame-d'Aubune** (Mon–Sat 8.30am–12.30pm & 2–7pm, Sun 9am–12.30pm & 2.30–7pm). The *cave* also sells red, rosé and white Côtes du Rhône Villages, and the light Côtes du Ventoux. The **church** in Beaumes reflects the key local concern in the trailing vines and classical wine containers sculpted over the door. Nearby, the **tourist office** (Mon–Sat: June–Sept 9am–noon & 2–6.30pm; Oct–May 9am–noon & 2–6pm; ℡ 04.90.62.94.39, Ⓦ ot-beaumesdevenise.com) has lists of *domaines* and *caves*.

Both the village's two quiet, old-fashioned **hotels** are a short walk away on the other side of the river, and have good restaurants. The *Auberge St-Roch* is on avenue Jules-Ferry (℡ 04.90.65.08.21, Ⓔ aubergestroch@orange.fr; ❸; closed mid-June to early July & mid-Nov to mid-Dec); the *Le Relais des Dentelles* (℡ 04.90.62.95.27, Ⓦ lerelaisdesdentelles.com; ❹; closed Jan to mid-Feb) is across the street. On route de Lafare, 2km north towards Malaucène, there's also a **campsite**, the *Roquefiquier* (℡ 04.90.62.95.07, Ⓔ camping.roquefiquier@orange.fr; €7 per tent; closed Nov–Feb).

Le Barroux

To the east of the Dentelles, on the Vaison–Malaucène road, the largely untouristy **LE BARROUX** is a perfect *village perché*, with narrow, twisting streets leading up to its château at the top. Dating from the twelfth to the eighteenth century, the **château** (daily: June–Sept 10am–7pm; April–May & Oct 2–6pm; €4) was restored just before World War II, set on fire by the Nazis in 1944 – the blaze burned for ten days – then restored again from 1960 to 1990, and is now open to the public.

In the heart of the village, on place de la Croix, *Les Géraniums* (℡ 04.90.62.41.08, Ⓦ hotel-lesgeraniums.com; ❹; closed Nov–Jan & first two weeks in March) is a very peaceful, comfortable and unpretentious *logis* **hotel** with views of the Dentelles. Its popular *terrasse* restaurant serves decent food with lunch and dinner menus for €18 and €28 respectively.

Mont Ventoux and around

From the Rhône, Luberon and Durance, the summit of **MONT VENTOUX**, east of the Dentelles, repeatedly appears on the horizon. White with snow, black with storm-cloud shadow or reflecting myriad shades of blue, the barren pebbles of the final 300m are like a coloured weather vane for all of western Provence. From a distance the mountain looks distinctly alluring. Indeed, the fourteenth-century Italian poet Petrarch climbed the heights simply for the experience; the local guides he chartered for the two-and-a-half-day hike considered him completely crazy.

▲ Mont Ventoux

Meteorological information is gathered, along with TV transmissions and Mirage fighter jet movements, from masts and dishes at the top. The tower directing the conglomeration of receptors is in consequence no beauty, its essential design characteristic being to withstand winds from every direction, including the northern Mistral that can accelerate across Ventoux to 250km per hour. Wind, rain, snow and fearsome sub-zero temperatures are the dominant natural accompaniments to this tarmacked mountain top.

The deforestation of Mont Ventoux dates from Roman times, and by the nineteenth century it had got so bad that the entire mountain appeared shaved. Oaks, pines, boxwood, fir and beech have since been replanted and the owls and eagles have returned, but the greenery is unlikely ever to reach the summit again. The road that zigzags up the 1900m and down again with such consummate, if convoluted, ease was built to test prototype cars, an activity that continued until the mid-1970s. Mont Ventoux is also a sporadic highlight of the Tour de France, hence its appeal in summer for passionately committed cyclists. Around the tree line is a memorial to the great British cyclist **Tommy Simpson**, who died here from heart failure in 1967 on one of the hottest days ever recorded in the race; legend has it that his last words were: "Put me back on the bloody bike."

Despite the unpromising environment, rest assured that from the summit you have one of the most wonderful **panoramas**, not just in France, but in all Europe. Between **November and May** the road is covered by snow, with only the tops of the black and yellow poles beside the road still visible; then, people ascending Mont Ventoux will be on **skis**, leaving base either at Mont Serein on the north face or from the smaller southern station of Chalet-Reynard.

Bedoin and around

If you want to ascend Mont Ventoux **on foot**, the best path to take is from Les Colombets or Les Fébriers, hamlets off the D974 east of **BEDOIN** whose **tourist office**, on Espace M.L.-Gravier (mid–June to Aug Mon–Fri 9am–12.30pm & 2–6pm, Sat 9.30am–12.30pm & 2–6pm, Sun 9.30am–12.30pm; Sept to mid-June Mon–Fri 9am–12.30pm & 2–6pm, Sat 9.30am–12.30pm; ☎04.90.65.63.95, Ⓦwww.bedoin.org), can provide details. It also organizes a weekly **night-time ascent**, in July and August, leaving at 11.30pm on Wednesdays and Fridays to camp near the summit and await the sunrise. Bedoin Location on chemin de la Feraille (☎04.90.65.94.53, Ⓦbedoin-location.fr) rents out **bikes** if you want to join the superfit cyclists in braving the gusts and horribly long steep inclines. It also organizes trips in which you are transported to the summit, and can cycle back down. In **Mont Serein** the Chalet d'Accueil Mt-Serein (☎04.90.63.42.02, Ⓦstationdumontserein.com) can provide info on **ski-rental**, runs and lifts.

Bedoin has several **campsites**, including the two-star *Camping Pastory*, 1km from the village on the Malaucène road (☎04.90.12.85.83, Ⓦcamping-pastory.com; €9 per tent; closed Oct–March), and more than a dozen **gîtes ruraux** for anyone considering spending a week or more in the area. In **Crillon-le-Brave** just west of Bedoin, the *Hostellerie de Crillon le Brave*, place de l'Église (☎04.90.65.61.61, Ⓦcrillonlebrave.com; ❾; closed Dec to early March), offers luxurious rooms in seven restored village houses, along with a swimming pool.

Gorges de la Nesque

The **GORGES DE LA NESQUE** lie south of Ventoux, on the D942 between Carpentras and Sault. The River Nesque is dry most of the year and invisible from most of the road that clings to the rocks above the river – itself a feat of engineering even more impressive than the geological fault itself. This barren area has just one landmark, the 200-metre-high **Rocher du Cire** on the southern side 5km southwest of the village of Monieux. Coated in wax from numerous hives made by wild bees, the rock supposedly provided the men of the nearby village with the reputation-enhancing exploit of abseiling down it to gather honey. This may well be a macho myth; certainly no one does it now.

A little **restaurant** in **MONIEUX**, *Les Lavandes* (☎04.90.64.05.08; menus €25 & €32; closed Jan & Feb), serves local specialities such as stag terrine and foie gras in Beaumes-de-Venise muscat.

Sault

At **SAULT**, 6km northeast of Monieux, the steep forested rocks give way to fields of lavender, cereals and grazing sheep. Wild products of the woods – *lactaire* and *grisel* mushrooms, truffles and game, as well as honey and lavender products – are bought and sold at its Wednesday **market**; autumn is the best time for these local specialities. If you miss the market, La Maison des Producteurs on rue de la République can sell you all the goodies. Sault also has **fairs** on the Wednesday before Palm Sunday, St John's feast day (June 23), August 16 and the end of November.

Le Signoret, avenue de la Résistance (☎04.90.64.11.44; ❷; restaurant closed Fri eve and all Sun in low season), is a pleasant little **hotel-restaurant** in the heart of town.

Carpentras and around

With a population of around 30,000, **CARPENTRAS** is a substantial city for this part of the world. It's also a very old one, its known history commencing in 5 BC as the capital of a Celtic tribe. The Greeks who founded Marseille came to Carpentras to buy honey, wheat, goats and skins, and the Romans had a base here. For a brief period in the fourteenth century, it became the papal headquarters and gave protection to Jews expelled from France. Today, the town is in the throes of gradual refurbishment, so that immaculately restored squares and fountains alternate with gently decayed streets of seventeenth- and eighteenth-century houses, some forming arcades over the pavement.

To experience Carpentras at its liveliest, come during the last fortnight in July for the **Estivales**, a series of music, theatre and dance performances staged in front of the cathedral.

Although Carpentras is very much the largest town hereabouts, a high proportion of visitors who pass this way are in fact heading for two smaller but more attractive communities nearby, **Pernes-les-Fontaines** to the south and **Venasque** to the southeast.

3

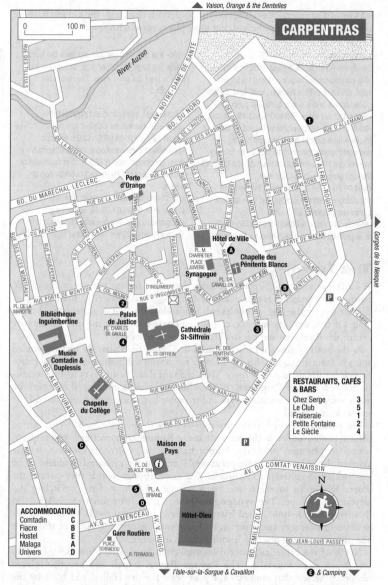

Vaison, Orange & the Dentelles

CARPENTRAS

0   100 m

River Auzon

Gorges de la Nesque

Porte d'Orange

Hôtel de Ville

PL. M. CHARRETIER
PLACE JUIVERIE

Chapelle des Pénitents Blancs

Synagogue

PL. D'INGUIMBERT

Bibliothèque Inguimbertine

Palais de Justice
PL. CHARLES DE GAULLE

Cathédrale St-Siffrein

PL. ST-SIFFREIN

Musée Comtadin & Duplessis

PL. DE LA MAROTTE

Chapelle du Collège

Maison de Pays

PL. DU 25 AOUT 1944

RESTAURANTS, CAFÉS & BARS	
Chez Serge	3
Le Club	5
Fraiseraie	1
Petite Fontaine	2
Le Siècle	4

PL. A. BRIAND

Hôtel-Dieu

N

AV. DU COMTAT VENAISSIN

ACCOMMODATION	
Comtadin	C
Fiacre	B
Hostel	E A
Malaga	A
Univers	D

Gare Routière
PLACE TERRADOU

l'Isle-sur-la-Sorgue & Cavaillon   E & Camping

Arrival, information and accommodation

Carpentras' **tourist office** is in the Maison de Pays (July & Aug Mon–Sat 9am–1pm & 2–7pm, Sun 9.30am–1pm; Sept–June Mon–Sat 9.30am–12.30pm & 2–6pm; ☎04.90.63.00.78, ⓦcarpentras-ventoux.com). **Buses** arrive nearby, either on avenue Victor-Hugo (from Marseille, Aix and Cavaillon) or at the **gare routière** on place Terradou (from Avignon, Vaison, and other points north and west).

Most of Carpentras' **hotels** are on the boulevards that circle the old town; there are plenty of bargains to be had, but most places come with few frills.

Hotels

Comtadin 65 bd Albin-Durand ☎04.90.67.75.00, ⓦle-comtadin.com. Nicely restored traditional hotel, affiliated to Best Western, with light, double-glazed rooms and a sunny breakfast patio. ❺

Fiacre 153 rue Vigne ☎04.90.63.03.15, ⓦhotel-du-fiacre.com. Grand eighteenth-century town house, with a central courtyard and nicely decorated rooms, two with terraces. The friendly owners can help plan walking and cycling tours. ❹

Malaga place Maurice-Charretier ☎04.90.60.57.96. Rather kitsch but perfectly satisfactory, centrally located and with its own pavement brasserie. ❷

Univers 110 place A-Briand ☎04.90.63.00.05, ⓦwww.hotel-univers.com. The actual bedrooms inside this imposing old building, near the tourist office, are large but rather drab, though the four-person ones are good value. The restaurant is good. ❷

Hostel and campsite

Logis des Jeunes du Comtat Venaissin 200 rue Robert-Lacoste ☎04.90.67.13.95, ⓦetape-gitecouvert-carpentras.com. Hostel offering simple dorm accommodation (€12.50), 2km southeast of the centre near the Pierre de Coubertin sports centre.

Lou Comtadou route St-Didier, av Pierre-de-Coubertin ☎04.90.67.03.16, ⓦcamping loucomtadou.com. Shaded rural campsite, 1km south of town. €22 per tent; closed Nov–Jan.

The Town

A bird's-eye view of Carpentras clearly shows the ancient perimeter line of the town (rues Vigne, des Halles, Raspail, du Collège and Moricelly), itself encircled further out by the ring of boulevards that follow the line of the medieval town wall. Of this, only the massive, crenellated **Porte d'Orange** and the odd rampart on rue des Ramparts and rue des Lices-Monteux remain.

At the heart of town on place Charles-de-Gaulle, the **Palais de Justice** (guided tours in summer; check with tourist office for details) was built as an episcopal palace to indulge the dreams – or more likely the unrealized desires – of a seventeenth-century cardinal of Carpentras. Nicolas Mignard was commissioned to fresco the walls with sexual scenes of satyrs and nymphs, but a later incumbent had all the erotic details effaced.

The palais is attached to the fifteenth-century **Cathédrale St-Siffrein**, behind which, almost hidden in the corner, stands a **Roman arch** inscribed with imperial scenes of prisoners in chains. Fifteen hundred years after its erection, Jews – coerced, bribed or otherwise persuaded – entered the cathedral in chains to be unshackled as converted Christians. The door through which they passed, the **Porte Juif** on its southern side, bears strange symbolism of rats encircling and devouring a globe. The **synagogue** (Mon–Thurs 10am–noon & 3–5pm, Fri 10am–noon & 3–4pm; closed Jewish feast days; free), near the Hôtel de Ville, is a seventeenth-century construction on fourteenth-century foundations, making it the oldest surviving place of Jewish worship in France.

North of the cathedral, place d'Inguimbert is lined with plane trees, lanterns and black swan fountains. The **Passage Boyer**, a high and beautiful glazed shopping arcade that connects the *place* with rue des Halles, was built by the unemployed in a short-lived scheme to generate jobs after the 1848 revolution.

West of the centre, the **Musée Comtadin** and **Musée Duplessis** occupy separate floors of the same building on boulevard Albin-Durand (April–Sept only, daily except Tues 10am–noon & 2–6pm; €2 combined ticket). Both were closed for restoration as this book went to press; assuming they re-open with the same contents, the Comtadin contains an unimaginative collection of keys, guns, *santons*, seals, ex-votos, papal bulls, bells and bonnets, as well as some more interesting French paintings from the eighteenth and nineteenth centuries, while the Duplessis upstairs holds assorted Roman artefacts and some wonderful Renaissance miniatures.

The huge **Hôtel Dieu**, just south of place Aristide-Briand, still functions as a hospital. Its opulent original **pharmacy** (guided tours in summer; check with tourist office for details) still holds gorgeously decorated vials and boxes containing cat's foot extract, Saturn salt, deer antler shavings and dragon blood; the painted lower cupboards tell a very "Age of Reason" moral tale of wild and happy monkeys ending up as tame and dutiful labourers.

Eating and drinking

The winding streets of Carpentras' ancient core hold plenty of small **restaurants**, while brasseries spread across the larger squares to the south. As for **drinking**, *Le Siècle* on place Charles-de-Gaulle offers a shady spot right in front of the cathedral, but virtually the only place to stay open late is *Le Club*, a piano bar in front of the *Hôtel l'Univers* at 106 place Aristide-Briand.

Carpentras is very proud of its sweet speciality of **berlingots**: small, striped *bonbons* made from fruit syrup that you'll see on signs, in shops, and at the end of your meal as an accompaniment to your bill – the mint flavour is the most famous, but the coffee one is absolutely delicious.

Chez Serge 90 rue Cottier ℡04.90.63.21.24, ⊛chez-serge.com. Sleek bistro serving changing daily *plats* on its tree-shaded terrace. The lunch menu is €15, dinner menus start at €32, and there's a wide selection of pizzas for around €10. Closed Mon lunch.
Fraiseraie 125 bd Alfred-Rogier ℡04.90.67.06.39. Appealing restaurant, draped in lush foliage and featuring its own wine bar, which cooks up tasty

Provençal dishes like beef grilled in thyme (€15), and has truffles in season. Dinner menus €16–46. Closed Wed.
Petite Fontaine 13/17 place du Colonel Mouret ℡04.90.60.77.83. Cheery restaurant, situated as the name suggests beside a little fountain, and serving delicious fresh food, with menus from €25. Closed Wed & Sun.

Pernes-les-Fontaines

The delightful small town of **PERNES-LES-FONTAINES** lies 6km south of Carpentras. Everything in Pernes, from the 36 fountains for which it's named to the ramparts, gateways, towers, covered market hall, Renaissance streets and half a dozen chapels – seems to blend into a single complex structure, and the passages between its squares feel more like corridors between rooms.

Of Pernes' fourteenth-century ramparts, only three gates now remain. The Porte Villeneuve, dating from 1550 and flanked by two imposing round towers, leads along rue Gambetta from the main road, av Jean-Jaurès, to the old centre. The **Tour Ferrande** here – the massive twelfth-century keep of the castle of the counts of Toulouse – has been turned into a clocktower by the simple expedient of sticking two big clocks onto it halfway up. It contains the town's great medieval artwork, immaculately preserved fourteenth-century **frescoes** that portray scenes from the legend of William of Orange and the life of Charles of Anjou.

Head left, down rue Victor-Hugo and along rue de la Halle, to reach the sixteenth-century Porte Notre-Dame, the elegant **cormorant fountain** and the seventeenth-century market hall. From this gateway, rue Raspail heads south past the fifteenth-century **reboul fountain**, the oldest of Pernes' fountains, and onto the other remaining gate, the Porte St-Gilles.

Practicalities

The **tourist office** (April–June Mon–Fri 9am–noon & 2–6pm, Sat 9am–noon & 2–5pm; July & Aug Mon–Fri 9am–12.30pm & 2.30–7pm, Sat 9am–12.30pm &

2.30–6pm, Sun 9.30am–12.30pm; Sept & Oct Mon–Fri 9am–noon & 2–6pm, Sat 9am–12.30pm; Nov–March Mon–Fri 9am–noon & 2–5pm, Sat 9am–noon; ℡04.90.61.31.04, Ⓦville-pernes-les-fontaines.fr) is at 72 cours Frizet, just behind the site of Pernes' Saturday market, place Gabriel-Moutte.

Hotels in Pernes-les-Fontaines include *La Margelle*, place Aristide-Briand, on the boulevard ring south of the village (℡04.90.61.25.83; ❷), which has a rambling back garden and serves menus at €18 and €26. Immediately behind that in the old town, *Au Fil de Temps*, 73 place L-Giraud (℡04.90.30.09.48; closed Sun & Mon), is a delightful **restaurant** where the €16 and €25 menus feature exquisite delights like a *filet mignon* of rabbit. The municipal **campsite** is in the *quartier* Coucourelles (℡04.90.66.45.55; €12 per tent; closed Oct–March).

Venasque

VENASQUE, 9km east of Pernes just before the road starts to wind over the Plateau de Vaucluse towards Apt (see Chapter 4), is a perfectly contained village on a spur of rock. At its highest end are three round towers and a curtain wall; at its lowest end is a sixth-century baptistry, built on the site of a Roman temple dedicated to Venus. Like most Provençal villages it swings between a sleepy winter state and a tourist honey pot in summer. The best time to visit is in May and June, before the main season begins, and when the daily **market** concentrates exclusively on the sale of local cherries.

Practicalities

Venasque's **tourist office** is on Grande Rue (April–June & Sept–Oct Tues–Sat 10am–noon & 2–6pm, Mon & Sun 2–6pm; July & Aug Tues–Sat 10am–12.30pm & 3–7pm, Mon & Sun 3–7pm; ℡04.90.66.11.66, Ⓦtourisme-venasque.com). The finest place to both **sleep** and **eat** is the *Auberge La Fontaine* on place de la Fontaine (℡04.90.66.02.96, Ⓦauberge-lafontaine.com; ❼; restaurant closed Wed), which holds four smart split-level apartments and serves dinner by reservation only in a fancy, formal dining room, with menus at €25 and €41. The cheaper *Remparts*, at the top of the main street, rue Haute (℡04.90.66.02.79, Ⓦhotellesremparts.com; ❸; closed mid-Nov to Feb), also has an excellent restaurant, with lunch menus from €15.50, dinner menus from €24.50; the rabbit *confit* with red wine caramel is particularly good.

L'Isle-sur-la-Sorgue

Halfway between Carpentras and Cavaillon to the south, and 23km east of Avignon, **L'ISLE-SUR-LA-SORGUE** straddles five branches of the River Sorgue, with little canals and waterways running through and around the centre. Its waters were once filled with otters and beavers, eels, trout and crayfish, and turned the power wheels of a **medieval cloth industry**. Tanneries, dyeing works, and subsequently silk and paper manufacturing, all ensured considerable prosperity for "the Island".

Nowadays, the huge blackened waterwheels turn for show only, and the mills and tanneries stand empty, plants growing through the crumbling brickwork. But in summer, fishing punts continue to crowd the streams and L'Isle is a cheerful place, particularly on Sundays, when people arrive for its well-known **antiques market**, which centres on the Village des Antiquaires on avenue de l'Égalité and spills out onto the boulevards.

L'Isle-sur-la-Sorgue's claim to be the Venice of Provence may stretch a point, but it's a pleasant waterside location in which to spend an afternoon. While there are few sights to head for, the central **place de l'Église** and **place de la Liberté** do provide reminders of past prosperity, most obviously in the Baroque seventeenth-century **church** (July & Aug Tues–Sat 10am–noon & 3–6pm, Sun 3–6pm; Sept–June Tues–Sat 10am–noon & 3–5pm), by far the richest religious edifice for many kilometres around. Each column in the nave supports a sculpted Virtue: whips and turtledoves are Chastity's props, a unicorn accompanies Virginity, and medallions and inscriptions carry the adornment down to the floor.

Two museums worth popping into are the little **Musée du Jouet et de la Poupée Ancienne** (daily 10.30am–6pm; €3.50), which shows off a private collection of remarkably intact dolls dating from 1880 to 1920; and the **Maison Renē Char**, housed in the elegant Hôtel Donadei de Campredon on 20 rue Docteur Tallet (daily 10am–12.30pm & 2–5.30pm; €6.20), where the poet and part-time surrealist Renē Char was born in 1907. The ground floor of the *hôtel* holds temporary art exhibitions, while upstairs you'll find the *ecrivain's* writing desk and various documents *du jour*.

Every year the Isle's fishermen retain their medieval guild tradition of crowning a king of the Sorgue, whose job is to oversee the rights of catch and sale. The **Festival de la Sorgue** at the end of July sees them out in traditional gear, with two teams battling from boats in an ancient jousting tournament.

Practicalities

The **tourist office** is in the former granary on place de l'Église (Mon–Sat 9am–12.30pm & 2.30–6pm, Sun 9am–12.30pm; ☎04.90.38.04.78, ⓦwww .oti-delasorgue.fr), while the **gare SNCF** is southwest of the centre. **Buses** arrive by pont Gambetta, next to the post office.

La Prévôté, 4 rue J.J. Rousseau (☎04.90.38.57.29, ⓦla-prevote.fr; ❼), is a charming **hotel** with five rooms decked out in beautiful terracotta tiles, wooden beams and Provençal quilts; its small, superb restaurant, downstairs in the old sacristy (closed Tues, plus Wed Sept–June), serves top-quality menus from €26. A decent cheaper alternative is the *La Gueulardière*, 1 cours René Char (☎04.90.38.10.52, ⓦgueulardiere.com; ❹; restaurant closed Mon). The three-star municipal **campsite**, *La Sorguette*, 41 Les Grandes Sorgues (☎04.90.38.05.71, ⓦcamping-sorguette.com; €20.90 per tent; closed mid-Oct to mid-March), is by the river on the Apt road.

For a gastronomic feast, head for the delightful *Vivier*, 800 cours Fernande Peyre (☎04.90.38.52.80, ⓦlevivier-restaurant.com; closed lunchtime Fri & Sat, Sun eve & Mon), where menus start at €28 lunch, €43 dinner; or the lovely *L'Oustau de l'Isle*, set in a beautiful country house 1.5km out of town at 147 chemin du Bosquet (☎04.90.20.81.36, ⓦrestaurant-oustau.com; closed Tues & Wed). Lighter meals can be enjoyed at *Bistro de l'Industrie* on quai de la Charité by place E-Char (☎04.90.38.00.40), which offers decent *plats du jour* for €10, rounded off with excellent coffee.

Fontaine-de-Vaucluse

The source of the Sorgue River, and of several other diverging streams, is a mysterious tapering fissure, 7km east of L'Isle-sur-la-Sorgue at the foot of towering 230-metre cliffs. Said to rank among the most powerful natural springs in the world, and compellingly beautiful into the bargain, it's a hugely popular tourist attraction. All access is via the ancient riverside village of **FONTAINE-DE-VAUCLUSE**, downstream; from there a gentle 500-metre footpath, the chemin de la Fontaine, climbs through a narrowing gorge to the *fontaine* itself. Both the village and the full length of the path are heavily (albeit reasonably tastefully) commercialized, but it's still a gorgeous spot, with the glorious green river cascading beneath thickly wooded slopes.

The actual village of Fontaine-de-Vaucluse is no more than a tiny and very pretty little cluster of old houses, centred around the place de la Colonne. Seven centuries ago, the poet Petrarch spent sixteen unrequited years pining in this rustic backwater for his Laura. To learn a little more about the lovelorn rhymester, drop into the **Musée de Pétrarque**, just across the bridge south of the river (daily except Tues: April–May 10am–noon & 2–6pm; June–Sept 10am–12.30pm & 1.30–6pm; Oct 10am–noon & 2–5pm; €3.50, or €4.60 with **Musée d'Histoire**).

Several interesting diversions punctuate the riverside path. French-speakers keen to learn more about the spring can visit the **Ecomusée du Gouffre**, also known as La Monde Souterrain (Feb to mid-Nov daily 9.30am–12.30pm & 2–6pm; last admission 1hr before closing; hourly tours in French only; €5.50). Volunteers eager to communicate their passion for crawling about in the bowels of the earth lead forty-minute tours through mock-up caves and passages, while displays document the intriguing history of the exploration of the spring, from the first 23-metre descent in 1878 to the robotic camera that reached the bottom a few years ago, its blurry pictures showing a horizontal passage disappearing into the rock. It's thought that water seeping through a vast plateau of chalk hits an impermeable base that slopes down to Fontaine. The museum winds up with a collection of underworld concretions, ranging from huge, jewellery-like crystals to pieces resembling fibre optics.

However the water arrives, it has long been put to use in turning the wheels of manufacturing. The first paper mill was built at Fontaine in 1522, and the last, built in 1862, ceased operations in 1968. The medieval method of pulping rags to paper has been re-created in the **Moulin à Papier Vallis Clausa**, in the same half-buried complex as the Ecomusée du Gouffre (daily: July & Aug 9am–7.30pm; Sept–June hours vary enormously, but always closed 12.30–2pm; free). Here, flowers are added to the pulp and the resulting paper is printed with all manner of drawings, poems and prose, ranging from Martin Luther King's "I Have A Dream" speech to assorted cloying homilies and delightful etchings, then sold in the vast adjoining gift shop.

A little further along chemin de la Fontaine, the impressive and intense **Musée d'Histoire 1939–1945** is subtitled "l'Appel de la Liberté", and deals with life and resistance in occupied France (March Sat & Sun 10am–noon & 2–6pm; April, May & Oct daily except Tues 10am–noon & 2–6pm; June–Sept daily except Tues 10am–6pm; Nov & Dec Sat & Sun 10am–noon & 2–5pm; €3.50, or €4.60 with Musée de Pétrarque).

The path continues a few hundred metres more, with swimming spots down in the river below, and the silhouette of a ruined fourteenth-century castle atop the hill on the other side. Most visitors continue beyond the safety barriers at its far end, stepping gingerly down the rubble-strewn slopes to get close-up views of the limpid pool of azure-blue water that wells up from a cave beneath the cliffs.

Practicalities

Parking at Fontaine-de-Vaucluse is often a problem; the largest car park is a short walk south of the river. The local **tourist office** (daily 10am–1pm & 2–6pm; ℡04.90.20.32.22, Ⓦwww.oti-delasorgue.fr) is beyond the village towards the spring, alongside the **Moulin à Papier**. Despite its uninspiring exterior, the most luxurious place to **stay** is L'Hotel du Poète (℡04.90.20.34.05, Ⓦhoteldupoete.com; ❺; closed Dec–Feb), below the main D25 on the north bank of the river, just before the village, which has large, comfortable rooms and a pool. The characterful Sources on the south bank (℡04.90.20.31.84, ⓦhoteldessources.com; ❺; closed Oct to mid-Feb) offers nice old-fashioned rooms and a decent restaurant. There's also a very pretty little **B&B** in the heart of the village, *Auberge La Figuière* (℡04.90.20.37.41, ⓦla-figuiere.com; ❸; closed Oct to mid-Feb), with simple but attractive rooms, a flowery garden, and a restaurant with menus from €20 to €58; and a pleasant **hostel**, 1km south on the chemin de la Vignasse towards Gordes (℡04.90.20.31.65, ⓦfuaj .org/fontaine-de-vaucluse; €16.90 including breakfast; closed mid-Nov to Jan), which offers camping in its grounds for €6.90 per person. The *Les Prés* **campsite** is beside the river's south bank 500m downstream from the village, and has a pool (℡04.90.20.32.38; €13.90 per tent; closed Nov–Feb).

The central **place de la Colonne** is surrounded by terraced **restaurants** and cafés overhanging the river, including *Lou Fanau* (℡04.90.20.31.90; closed Wed), which has menus of solid regional food from €15.90. Slightly more expensive is *Le Château* on quai du Château Vieux (℡04.90.20.31.54; closed Sun & Mon eve out of season), where menus cost €21.50–36. **Market** day is on Tuesday.

In summer, Kayak Vert (℡04.90.20.35.44) rents **canoes** for a half-hour or hour's paddling, or for a fairly effortless eight-kilometre trip down to L'Isle-sur-la-Sorgue (where the canoes can be left).

Cavaillon

Approaches to **CAVAILLON**, directly south of L'Isle-sur-la-Sorgue and 25km southeast of Avignon, pass through fields of fruit and vegetables, watered by the Durance and Coulon rivers. Market gardening is the major business of the city and Cavaillon, its Roman origins notwithstanding, is known simply as a **melon** town. The melon in question is the Charentais, a small pale green ball with dark green stripes and brilliant orange flesh, in season from May to September. Together with asparagus and early spring vegetables, they are sold every weekday morning at one of the largest **wholesale markets** in Europe; and the fruit is honoured every year in mid-July during the town's **melon festival**. It must be said, however, that Cavaillon is not a wildly alluring place, and there's no great reason to linger long.

Although it's ringed by broad boulevards busy with traffic, the partly pedestrian-ized old town is usually pretty sleepy. All that remains of Roman Cavaillon is the **Arc de Triomphe** on place du Clos, which on Mondays is surrounded by the weekly **market**. The **Cathédrale St-Véran**, due north of place du Clos (April–Sept Mon–Sat 8.30am–noon & 2–6pm; Oct–March Mon–Sat 9am–noon & 2–5pm), is an archaic-looking building, on the south side of which God appears above a sundial looking like a winged and battered Neptune. Inside, in the St-Véran chapel above the altar, there's a painting of Saint Véran hauling off a slithery reptile known as Couloubre, who terrorized the locality in 6 AD.

For a panoramic view of the surrounding countryside, you can climb the steep path from behind the Roman arch to the **Chapelle Saint-Jacques**. Built on the site of a temple to Jupiter, it was a regular outpost for hermits, whom the peasants would pay to warn them of impending storms (or Couloubre appearances) by ringing the chapel bell.

Practicalities

Marked by a giant melon, Cavaillon's **tourist office** faces the town's main car park on place François-Tourel (Mon–Sat 9am–12.30pm & 2–6.30pm; ℡04.90.71.32.01, ⓦcavaillon-luberon.com). Both the **gare SNCF** and the **gare routière** are across town on avenue P-Semard.

The most attractive budget **hotel** is the central *Toppin*, a Logis de France at 70 cours Gambetta (☎04.90.71.30.42, ⓦhotel-toppin.com; ❸), with warmly decorated, comfortable rooms, while the pricier *Le Parc*, an elegant former *maison bourgeoise* right by the tourist office at 183 place F-Tourel (☎04.90.71.57.78, ⓦwww.hotelduparccavaillon.com; ❹), is also very agreeable: its flamboyant decor suits the building, though the rooms themselves are more subdued; breakfast is served in a pleasant courtyard. The three-star *Durance* **campsite**, southwest of the centre at 495 avenue Boscodomini (☎04.90.71.11.78, ⓦcamping-durance.com; €15.70 per tent; closed Oct–March), is always crowded in summer.

For the best local **dining**, head to *Le Prevot*, at 353 avenue de Verdon on the road out to St-Rémy (☎04.90.71.32.43, ⓦrestaurant-prevot.com; closed Mon & Sun), where lunch menus start at €25, and there's a €35 vegetarian menu for dinner, along with special menus organized around themes or ingredients such as mushrooms. Behind its lavender exterior, *Le Fin de Siècle*, at no. 46 on the dull modern place du Clos (☎04.90.71.12.27; closed Tues, Wed & Aug lunch), serves menus from €13.50 at lunch, €23 dinner, with a kitsch upstairs dining room decorated with dolls. Lively places to **drink** line up along cours Gambetta; *Celt's House Pub*, next to *Le Toppin* at no. 60, attracts a youngish crowd.

Travel details

Trains

Avignon to: Arles (hourly; 20–45min); Cavaillon (9–14 daily; 35min); Lyon (half-hourly; 2hr 30min); Marseille (14 daily; 1hr 5min); Orange (17 daily; 15min); Valence (half-hourly at peak times; 1hr 20min).

Avignon TGV to: Aix-en-Provence TGV (22 daily; 20min); Lille-Europe (5 daily; 4hr 30min); Lyon (14 daily; 1hr 10min); Marseille (half-hourly; 30min); Paris (17 daily; 2hr 40min); Paris CDG Airport (5 daily; 3hr 30min).

Orange to: Paris (2 daily; 2hr 30min).

Buses

Avignon to: Aix (6 daily; 1hr 15min); Arles (10 daily; 50min); Carpentras (half-hourly; 35–45min); Cavaillon (9 daily; 35min); Fontaine-de-Vaucluse (4 daily; 55min); L'Isle-sur-la-Sorgue (10 daily; 40min); Orange (daily every 30–45min; 50min); Vaison (3 daily; 1hr 25min).

Carpentras to: Cavaillon (2–5 daily; 45min); Gigondas (1–3 daily; 30min); L'Isle-sur-la-Sorgue (5 daily; 20min); Orange (3 daily; 40–45min); Vaison (4 daily; 45min).

Cavaillon to: L'Isle-sur-la-Sorgue (7 daily; 15min); Pernes-les-Fontaines (7 daily; 35min).

L'Isle-sur-la-Sorgue to: Fontaine-de-Vaucluse (5 daily; 15min).

Orange to: Carpentras (3 daily; 40–45min); Châteauneuf-du-Pape (1 Thurs; 30min); Séguret (2 daily; 40min); Vaison (2 daily; 40–50min).

Aix-en-Provence, the Durance and the Luberon

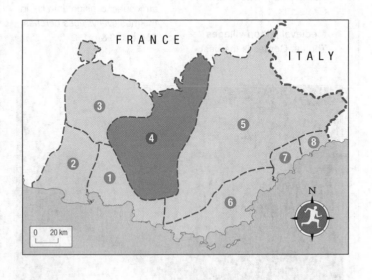

FRANCE

ITALY

3

4

5

8

2

7

1

6

N

0   20 km

CHAPTER 4

Highlights

* **Cézanne's Aix** Visit his atelier then explore a living Cézanne landscape in the country around the Mont Ste-Victoire. See p.167 & p.171

* **Forcalquier** Explore this once grand, now slumbering, historic town, and its beautiful, unspoilt *pays*. See p.185

* **Ochre in the Luberon** Brilliant colour enfolds the friendly villages of Rustrel and Roussillon, and enlivens the extraordinary mine of Bruoux. See p.193

* **Medieval hilltop villages** Though Gordes is the best known, Lacoste, Saignon and Simiane-la-Rotonde are equally picturesque and much less busy. See p.194, p.197, p.189 & p.188

* **Abbaye de Sénanque** The ancient Cistercian monastery is as much a symbol of Provence as the lavender fields surrounding it. See p.195

* **Abandoned hilltop ruins** Quiet and crumbling, Oppède-le-Vieux and the Fort de Buoux provide an atmospheric insight into life in the medieval *villages perchés*. See p.196 & p.190

▲ Abbaye de Sénanque

Aix-en-Provence, the Durance and the Luberon

A wide, rushing torrent in winter that reduces to a dribble in summer, the **Durance** is one of the great alpine rivers of France, slashing 320km southwest from its source near Briançon to its confluence with the Rhône near **Avignon**. Four *départements* converge where the Durance meets the Verdon, a few kilometres northeast of the Pont Mirabeau. Three of the four – the Alpes de Haute Provence, the Vaucluse and the Bouches du Rhône – are at their most atypical here. The portion of the Alpes de Haute Provence, west of the Durance, lacks the genuine alpine grandeur of the area to the east; the **Luberon**'s history of dissent during the Wars of Religion distinguishes it from the papal tradition of the Vaucluse as a whole; and the pastoral charms of the Coteaux d'Aix and grandeur of the Mont Ste-Victoire contrast strongly with the metropolitan feel of the Marseille conurbation. Unrepresentative of their *départements*, together these regions offer a distillation of all that, for visitors, seems most typically Provençal – of lavender and honey, crumbling hilltop villages and ancient abbeys, lively markets and excellent cuisine rooted in the *terroir*.

The charms of **Aix-en-Provence** – the region's only real city – are commonly sung. With a historic core as perfect as any in France, it glories in the medieval period of independent Provence, the riches of its seventeenth- and eighteenth-century growth and the memory of its most famous sons, Zola and Cézanne.

To the north of Aix, the transition between Mediterranean and Alpine France becomes clear along the valley of the Durance. Downstream, the fruitful country-side between sleepy **Cadenet** and bustling **Pertuis** is classically Provençal, but east of Pertuis, the landscape becomes wilder, the valley narrowing to a rocky gorge at the Défilé de Mirabeau. To the north, **Manosque** offers a rare taste of urban life, while dramatic **Sisteron** acts as a gateway to the Alps and as the northern point of departure from Provence. West of the Durance, the delights of the **Pays de Forcalquier** include the venerable town of **Forcalquier** itself and the remote and beautiful hilltop village of **Simiane-la-Rotonde**.

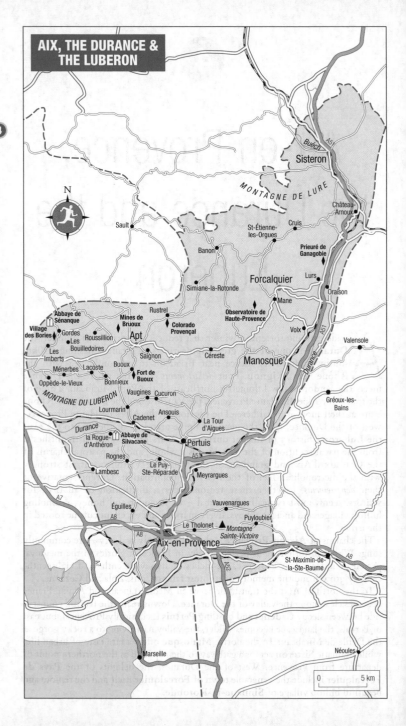

AIX, THE DURANCE &
THE LUBERON

Sweeping further to the west, the great green surge of the **Luberon** massif is as lauded as any landscape in France, not least in the books of Peter Mayle, and its beautiful villages are nowadays distinctly chic. Its principal centre, **Apt**, is a lively market town slowly evolving in the face of the influx of wealthy Parisians and foreigners that has transformed the surrounding districts. The attractions of the countryside are diverse: the multi-hued ochre mines of **Bruoux**, **Rustrel** and **Roussillon**, the abandoned villages at **Buoux** and **Oppède-le-Vieux**, the immaculate village of **Gordes** and the twelfth-century Cistercian monasteries at **Sénanque** and **Silvacane**.

Aix-en-Provence and around

With its colourful markets, splashing fountains, pavement cafés and general air of civilized ease, **AIX-EN-PROVENCE** measures up to the popular fantasies of the Provençal good life better than any city in the region. It's a stunningly beautiful place, its riches based on landowning and the liberal professions. Hundreds of foreign students, particularly Americans, study in Aix, reinforcing the city's youthful feel.

Aix began life as Aquae Sextiae, a Roman settlement based around its **hot springs** – there's still a thermal establishment on the site of the Roman baths in the northwest corner of the Vieille Ville. From the twelfth century until the Revolution Aix was the capital of Provence. In its days as an independent fiefdom, its most beloved ruler, King René of Anjou (1409–80), held a brilliant court renowned for its popular festivities and patronage of the arts. René introduced the muscat grape to the region, and today he stands in stone in picture-book medieval fashion, a bunch of grapes in his left hand, looking down the majestic seventeenth-century replacement to the old southern fortifications, the cours Mirabeau.

The humanities and arts faculties of the university Aix shares with Marseille are based here, where the original university was founded in 1409. In the nineteenth century Aix was home to two of France's greatest contributors to painting and literature, Paul Cézanne and his close friend Émile Zola. A series of brass studs set into the pavements now allows visitors to follow a Cézanne trail through the heart of the city.

Aix also makes an ideal base for **excursions** into the beautiful surrounding countryside, a landscape made famous by Cézanne.

Arrival, information and accommodation

Aix's **gare TGV** lies 8km southwest of the town, and is connected every thirty minutes by minibus (€3.70) to the **gare routière** (℡08.91.02.40.25) on avenue de l'Europe, southwest of the fountain-dominated place du Général-de-Gaulle and the city's main drag, cours Mirabeau. Local trains, including those from Marseille, arrive about 500m from here at the old **gare SNCF** on rue Gustave-Desplaces. The **tourist office** (Mon–Sat 8.30am–7pm, Sun 10am–1pm & 2–6pm; ℡04.42.16.11.61, Ⓦwww.aixenprovencetourism.com) is at 2 place du Général-de-Gaulle, between avenues des Belges and Victor-Hugo, with an information desk for the local bus network, **Aix en Bus** (Ⓦwww.aixenbus.com), and an **accommodation booking service** upstairs (℡04.42.16.11.84). At the time of writing, construction was scheduled to begin on a new tourist office next to the main post office at the top end of avenue des Belges, close to the existing one.

If you're planning to visit in the summer, particularly during the June and July festivals, it's worth reserving **accommodation** well in advance.

Hotels

Hôtel des Arts 69 bd Carnot ☎04.42.38.11.77, ✉hotelaix@yahoo.fr. The cheapest rooms in the centre of Aix – a bit noisy, but very welcoming. You can't book ahead, so turn up early. ❷

Hôtel des Augustins 3 rue de la Masse ☎04.42.27.28.59, ⓦwww.hotel-augustins.com. Atmospheric, smart hotel in a converted medieval monastery, just off the cours Mirabeau. ❺

La Caravelle 29 bd Roi-René ☎04.42.21.53.05, ⓦwww.lacaravelle-hotel.com. Well-maintained, friendly and soundproofed hotel set back slightly from the boulevards ringing Vieil Aix. The more expensive rooms overlook courtyard gardens. ❸

Hôtel Cardinal 24 rue Cardinale ☎04.42.38 .32 .30, ⓦwww.hotel-cardinal-aix.com. A clean, peaceful and welcoming hotel in the *quartier* Mazarin, with classically furnished rooms. ❹

Grand Hôtel Nègre Coste 33 cours Mirabeau ☎04.42.27.74.22, ⓦwww.hotelnegrecoste.com. Splendidly situated hotel in a handsome eighteenth-century house with a/c, refurbished bathrooms and comfortable, soundproofed, high-ceilinged rooms. ❻

🏃 **Le Manoir** 8 rue d'Entrecasteaux ☎04.42.26.27.20, ⓦwww.hotelmanoir .com. Tucked away on a pretty courtyard off a quiet but central street, with agreeable rooms furnished with antiques. Remarkably peaceful for central Aix, and you eat breakfast in the medieval former monastery cloister. Closed Jan. ❸

Hôtel Paul 10 av Pasteur ☎04.42.23.23.89, ✉hotel.paul@wanadoo.fr. Good value for Aix, and with its own leafy garden, though on a busy road. ❷

Hotel le Pigonnet 5 av du Pigonnet ☎04.42.59.02.90, ⓦwww.hotelpigonnet.com.
Four-star luxury in the beautiful setting of an eighteenth-century *bastide* surrounded by lush gardens, 10min on foot from the *quartier* Mazarin. Doubles from €320. ❾

Hôtel des Quatre Dauphins 54 rue Roux-Alphéran ☎04.42.38.16.39, ⓦwww .lesquatredauphins.fr. Warm, old-world charm in the *quartier* Mazarin, with small, prettily furnished rooms. ❹

St-Christophe 2 av Victor-Hugo ☎04.42.26.01.24, ⓦwww.hotel-saintcristophe.com. Comfortable, a/c, soundproofed rooms above a smart Art Deco brasserie close to the tourist office and cours Mirabeau. ❺

Hostel and campsites

Airotel Camping Chantecler rte de Nice, Val St-André ☎04.42.26.12.98, ⓦwww.camping chantecler.com. Four-star site 3km southeast of town; take bus #3. Expensive, but the facilities are excellent and include a pool. €20.30 per tent. Open year-round.

Camping Arc-en-Ciel Pont des Trois Sautets, av Malacrida ☎04.42.26.14.28, ⓦwww.camping arcenciel.fr. Close to Chantecler on Aix's south-eastern outskirts (take bus #3), this is another four-star site; it's not particularly cheap, but it has very good facilities. €18.40 per tent. Open April–Sept.

Youth hostel 3 av Marcel-Pagnol ☎04.42.20.15.99, ⓦwww.auberge-jeunesse-aix.fr. Two kilometres west of the centre, next to the Fondation Vasarely; take bus #4 (direction "la Mayanalle", stop "Vasarely Auberge de la Jeunesse"). Reception 7am–1.30pm & 5pm–midnight. Facilities include dining room, bar, washing facilities, TV, wireless internet and parking for cars and cycles. From €19 a night with breakfast; closed mid-Dec to early Feb.

The City

The old city, **Vieil Aix**, defined by its ring of boulevards and the majestic cours Mirabeau, is in its entirety the great monument here, far more compelling than any one single building or museum within it. With so many streets alive with people, so many tempting restaurants, cafés and shops, plus the best markets in Provence, it's easy to pass several days wandering around without any itinerary or destination. Beyond Vieil Aix, there are a few museums in the **quartier Mazarin** south of **cours Mirabeau** and, further out, the **Vaserely Foundation**, **Cézanne's studio** and the Cézanne family home, **Jas de Bouffan**. The **Cité du Livre** cultural complex is part of a major regeneration across the entire west side of Vieil Aix.

Cours Mirabeau

As a preliminary introduction to life in Aix, take a stroll beneath the gigantic plane trees of **cours Mirabeau**, stopping off along the way at one of the many cafés along its sunny north side. In contrast, the shady south side is decidedly businesslike, lined with banks and offices lodged in seventeenth- to eighteenth-century mansions. These have a uniform hue of weathered stone, with ornate wrought-iron balconies and Baroque decorations, at their heaviest in the tired old musclemen holding up the porch of the *Hôtel d'Espargnet* at no. 38.

Opposite the hotel is Aix's most famous café, *Les Deux Garçons*, with a reputation dating back to World War II of serving intellectuals, artists and their entourage; earlier still, Cézanne was a customer. The interior is all mirrors with darkening gilt panels and reading lights that might have come off the old *Orient Express*.

Vieil Aix

To explore the heart of Aix, wander north from cours Mirabeau and then anywhere within the ring of cours and boulevards. The layout of **Vieil Aix** is not designed to assist your sense of direction, but it hardly matters when there's a fountained square to rest at every 50m and a continuous architectural backdrop of treats from the sixteenth and seventeenth centuries.

Starting from the eastern end of cours Mirabeau, heading north into place de Verdun brings you to the **Palais de Justice**, a Neoclassical construction on the site of the old counts of Provence's palace. Count Mirabeau, the aristocrat turned champion of the Third Estate, who accused the États de Provence, meeting in Aix for the last time in 1789, of having no right to represent the people, is honoured here by a statue and allegorical monument.

Further west, in place de l'Hôtel de Ville at the heart of Vieil Aix, a massive (though delicate) foot hangs over the architrave of the old corn exchange, now the **post office**. It belongs to the goddess Cybele, dallying with the masculine Rhône and Durance. On the west side of the *place*, the **Hôtel de Ville** itself displays perfect classical proportions and filigreed wrought iron above the door. Alongside stands a **clock tower** which gives the season as well as the time.

Rue Gaston de Saporta takes you up from place de l'Hôtel de Ville to the **Cathédrale St-Sauveur** (daily 8am–noon & 2–6pm), a conglomerate of fifth to sixteenth-century buildings full of medieval art treasures. Its most notable painting, *The Burning Bush*, commissioned by King René in 1475, is currently undergoing restoration and is consequently not on show, though there's an English-language audiovisual lecture on it (enquire at the entrance to the cathedral). The carved pillars of the beautiful Romanesque **cloisters** (tours half-hourly: 10–11.30am & 2.30–5pm) are perhaps the best sculptures in the cathedral. The four corner pillars depict the four beasts of the Revelation: man, the lion, the eagle and the bull. Also remarkable are the cathedral's west doors, carved by Toulon carpenter Jean Guiramand in the early sixteenth century to depict four Old Testament prophets and twelve sibyls, the wise women of antiquity who supposedly prophesied Christ's birth, death and resurrection.

Close by, across place des Martyrs de la Résistance at the side of the cathedral, is the former bishop's palace, the **Ancien Archevêché**, the setting, each July, for part of Aix's grandiose music festival. It also houses the **Musée des Tapisseries** (daily except Tues: mid-April to mid-Oct 10am–6pm; mid-Oct to mid-April 1.30–5pm; €3), a collection of wonderful tapestries. Highlights include the

---

Aix for less

Offering excellent value, the Aix **Visa** (€2) gives discounted admission to the principal museums, plus half-price guided tours and reduced-rate travel on the city's buses. Alternatively, an Aix City Pass (€15) offers free entry to four attractions and a free tour of Cézanne's studio.

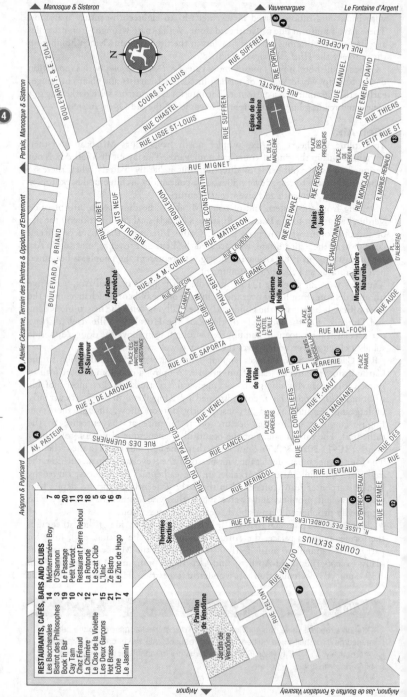

AIX-EN-PROVENCE, THE DURANCE AND THE LUBERON

RESTAURANTS, CAFÉS, BARS AND CLUBS

Les Bacchanales	14
Bistrot des Philosophes	3
Book in Bar	19
Cay Tam	2
Chez Féraud	12
La Chimère	1
Le Clos de la Violette	15
Les Deux Garçons	21
Hot Brass	17
Icône	4
Le Jasmin	
Méditerranéen Boy	7
O'Shannon	8
Le Passage	20
Petit Verdot	11
Restaurant Pierre Reboul	13
La Rotonde	18
Le Scat Club	5
L'Unic	6
Ze Bistro	16
Le Zinc de Hugo	9

Manosque & Sisteron

Vauvenargues

Le Fontaine d'Argent

RUE SUFFREN

RUE LACEPEDE

RUE PORTALIS

RUE CHASTEL

RUE MANUEL

COURS ST-LOUIS

RUE EMERIC-DAVID

RUE SUFFREN

RUE THIERS

RUE CHASTEL

Église de la Madeleine

PETIT RUE ST

RUE LISSE ST-LOUIS

PL DE LA MADELEINE

PLACE DES PRECHEURS

BOULEVARD F. & E. ZOLA

RUE MIGNET

PLACE DE VERDUN

RUE PEYRESC

RUE CONSTANTIN

R. MARIUS-RENAUD

RUE DU PUITS NEUF

RUE BOULEGON

RUE MONCLAR

RUE LOUBET

Palais de Justice

RUE MATHERON

RUE RIFLE RAFLE

RUE LOUBON

RUE CHAUDRONNIERS

Ancien Archevêché

RUE P. & M. CURIE

RUE GRANET

PL D'ALBERTAS

RUE PAUL-BERT

Ancienne Halle aux Grains

Musée d'Histoire Naturelle

BOULEVARD A. BRIAND

RUE GRIFFON

RUE GIBELIN

RUE AUDE

RUE CAMPRA

Cathédrale St-Sauveur

PLACE DE L'HÔTEL DE VILLE

PLACE RICHELME

RUE MAL-FOCH

PLACE DES MARTYRS DE LA RESISTANCE

RUE G. DE SAPORTA

Hôtel de Ville

RUE DE LA VERRERIE

PLACE RAMUS

RUE J. DE LAROQUE

RUE DES MARSEILLAIS

RUE VENEL

RUE F.-GAUT

AV. PASTEUR

RUE DES GUERRIERS

RUE CANCEL

RUE DES CORDELIERS

RUE DES MAGNANS

RUE DES

PLACE DES CARDEURS

RUE DU BON PASTEUR

RUE LIEUTAUD

RUE

RUE MERINDOL

RUE FERMEE

R. D'ENTRECASTEAUX

Thermes Sextius

RUE DE LA TREILLE

R. LISSE DES CORDELIERS

COURS SEXTIUS

RUE VAN LOO

Pavillon de Vendôme

RUE CELONY

Jardin de Vendôme

Avignon, Jas de Bouffan & Fondation Vasarely

Avignon

Atelier Cézanne, Terrain des Peintres & Oppidum d'Entremont

Avignon & Puyricard

Pertuis, Manosque & Sisteron

Manosque & Sisteron

N

▲ Place Miollis & Bd. Carnot   ▲ Cours Gambetta, Campsites, Nice & Toulon

Theatre du Jeu de Paume

RUE D'ITALIE

RUE DE L'OPÉRA

St-Jean-de-Malte

Musée Granet

RUE ROUX-ALPHERAN

RUE SALLIER

...JEAN

PLACE FORBIN

RUE TOURNEFORT

QUARTIER MAZARIN

F

RUE DE 4 SEPTEMBRE

PLACE DES 4 DAUPHINS

H

15

17

BOULEVARD DU ROI RENÉ

RUE CLEMENCEAU

VIEIL AIX

D

Musée Arbaud

RUE CABASSOL

RUE GOYRAND

RUE MAZARINE

RUE CARDINALE

AVENUE A. FRANCE

Parc Jourdan

RUE PAPASSAUDI

RUE NAZARETH

RUE ESPARIAT

R. COURTEISSADE

COURS MIRABEAU

19

AVENUE MALHERBE

R. BEDARRIDES

RUE DE LA MASSE

RUE LAROQUE

20

RUE DE VILLARS

AVENUE VICTOR-HUGO

TANNEURS

DE LA COURONNE

14

16

PLACE DES AUGUSTINS

RUE VICTOR-LEYDET

PLACE JEANNE D'ARC

18

PLACE DU GENERAL DE GAULLE

G

RUE GONTARD

i

i

RUE G. DESPLACES

RUE BRUYÈS

RUE DES BERNARDINES

VIEIL AIX

PLACE NIOLLON

AV N. BONAPARTE

AVENUE DES BELGES

Gare SNCF

BOULEVARD DE LA RÉPUBLIQUE

RUE LAPIERRE

UNDERPASS

K

ACCOMMODATION
Hôtel des Arts	B
Hôtel des Augustins	E
La Caravelle	I
Hôtel Cardinal	F
Grand Hotel Nègre Coste	D
Le Manoir	C
Hôtel Paul	A
Hôtel le Pigonnet	K
Hôtel des Quatre Dauphins	H
St-Christophe	G
Youth Hostel	J

musicians, dance...
life of Don Q...
being dive...
Russière...
tem...

▲ Gare Routière, Gare TGV, Marseille, Pavillon Noir, Grand Théâtre de Provence **21**   ▲ Cité du Livre, Gare TGV, Marseille, Pavillon Noir, Fondation Vasarely & **J** rs and animals in a 1689 series of grotesques; nine scenes from the Quixote, woven in the 1730s, including one with a club-footed cat sted of its armour by various *demoiselles*; and four superbly detailed *Jeux* (*Russian Games*) from a few decades later. A contemporary section hosts porary exhibitions, and there's also a section given over to the costumes, stage esigns and history of the music festival.

South of place de l'Hôtel de Ville is the elegant, cobbled eighteenth-century Rococo **place d'Albertas**, which hosts occasional concerts on summer evenings. The square is just off rue Espariat, which runs west to place du Général-de-Gaulle and has a distinctly Parisian style. Many of Aix's classiest couturier shops are clustered in this area. At 6 rue Espariat, the impressive seventeenth-century *Hôtel Boyer d'Eguilles* houses the **Musée de l'Histoire Naturelle** (daily 10am–noon & 1–5pm; €3), where the cherubs and garlands decorating the ceilings are slightly at odds with the stuffed birds and beetles, ammonites and dinosaur eggs below. Nonetheless, it makes for a good rainy day – or sunstroke – refuge.

Quartier Mazarin

Taking rue Clemenceau south over cours Mirabeau brings you into the heart of the **quartier Mazarin**, built in five years in the mid-seventeenth century by the archbishop brother of the cardinal who ran France when Louis XIV was a baby. It's a very dignified district, and very quiet.

Before you reach the beautiful place des Quatre Dauphins with its four-dolphin fountain, you'll pass **Musée Arbaud** (Tues–Sat 2–5pm; €3), at 2 rue du 4 Septembre, a dark, musty old house, to which you are grudgingly granted admission after ringing the bell. The museum's main collection is of Marseillais and Moustiers ceramics, but there are more interesting items tucked away in the claustrophobic rooms of leather-bound books, silk wallpaper and painted and panelled ceilings; the best is a portrait by Pierre Puget of his mother. There are also portraits of Mirabeau, and family and royalist trinkets such as nobles' rings offered as bail for Louis XVI while he was imprisoned in Paris.

A couple of blocks east of the dolphin fountain, on place St-Jean-de-Malte in the former priory of the Knights of Malta, is the most substantial of Aix's museums, the **Musée Granet** (Tues–Sun: June–Sept 11am–7pm; Oct–May noon–6pm; €10). Covering art and archeology, the museum exhibits finds from the Oppidum d'Entremont (see p.171), a Celto-Légurian township 3km north of Aix, along with the remains of the Romans who routed them in 124 BC. Its paintings are a mixed bag, from Italian, Dutch and French art of the seventeenth- to nineteenth-century to works by Cézanne, who studied on the ground floor of the building, and modernist pieces by Giacometti, Picasso and others. Rather overshadowing the permanent collection are the excellent summer exhibitions, which began in 2006 with a hugely successful show marking the centenary of Cézanne's death and followed in 2008 with a retrospective devoted to François Granet (1775–1849), the Aixois painter whose collection formed the nucleus of the museum.

West of Vieil Aix: Jas de Bouffan, Vasarely Foundation and the Cité du Livre

The man who came to be regarded as the father of modern painting cut a lonely figure for much of his life, spurned by the Parisian art establishment and happier away from the capital in his beloved Aix. **Paul Cézanne** was born in Vieil Aix at 28 rue de l'Opéra, the son of a hatter of Italian descent turned prosperous banker, but he grew up in a grand eighteenth-century house to the southwest of the city. The house, known as **Jas de Bouffan** (June–Sept tours daily every hour from 10.30am–4.30pm; April–May & Oct tours Tues, Thurs & Sat same hours; Jan–March Wed and Sat at 10am; €5.50), can be seen only on a pre-booked tour from Aix tourist information office. The house itself is currently undergoing restoration, but the tour points out the vantage points in the lovely garden from which Cézanne painted pictures including *Le Bassin du Jas de Bouffan en hiver*.

In Cézanne's day this area was still outside the city, but today Aix has spread far beyond the family home. The hill of Jas de Bouffan is now dominated by the **Fondation Vasarely**, 1 avenue Marcel-Pagnol (Tues–Sat 10am–1pm & 2–6pm; €7), a building in black and white geometric shapes created by the Hungarian-born artist in 1976. To get there take bus #4 (stop "V. Vasarely"). The seven hexagonal spaces of the ground floor are hung with Vasarely's monumental kinetic tapestries and paintings, while the rest of the museum hosts large-scale temporary exhibitions. The Fondation's messy history stands in stark contrast to Vasarely's clean, boldly geometric art. In 1995, the artist's daughter-in-law obtained a court order to remove the bulk of the exhibits donated to the Fondation, leaving just the monumental works, a decision disputed by Vasarely's grandson, who has since battled to regain control. Then, in 2005, the Fondation's erstwhile director, Charles Debbasch, was convicted of selling off works privately and pocketing the cash during his tenure from 1981 to 1993; he escaped prison by settling in Togo, though he was briefly detained in Belgium in 2007.

Calmer cultural waters are to be found a little closer to the centre of Aix at the **Cité du Livre**, a delightful arts centre in the old match-making factory at 8–10 rue des Allumettes (Tues, Thurs & Fri noon–6pm, Wed & Sat 10am–6pm; free), and at the **Pavillon Noir**, just to the north of it. The Pavillon is one of the jewels in Aix's contemporary artistic crown, home to the internationally renowned Ballet Preljocaj (Ⓦwww.preljocaj.org). The building is a startling web of black concrete columns designed by the Algerian-born Provençal architect Rudi Ricciotti. Immediately to the north is the equally impressive modern **Grand Théâtre de Provence**, designed by Italian architect Vittorio Gregotti and opened in 2007.

The Atelier Paul Cézanne and the Terrain des Peintres

Cézanne used many studios in and around Aix, but at the turn of the twentieth century, four years before his death, he had a house built for the purpose at what is now 9 avenue Paul-Cézanne, overlooking Aix from the north. By this stage in his life Cézanne had achieved both financial security and the recognition that had so long eluded him. It was here that he painted the *Grandes Baigneuses*, the *Jardinier Vallier* and some of his greatest still lifes. The **Atelier Paul Cézanne** (daily: April–June & Sept 10am–noon & 2–6pm, tour in English at 5pm; July & Aug 10am–6pm, tour in English at 5pm; Oct–March 10am–noon & 2–5pm, tour in English at 4pm; €5.50; timed admission, with film show while you wait) has been left exactly as it was at the time of his death in 1906: coat, hat, wine glass and easel, the objects he liked to paint, his pipe, a few letters and drawings – everything save the man himself, who would probably have been horrified at the thought of it being public. The guides are true enthusiasts, and provided the atelier isn't too busy a visit is a real joy. To get to the house, take bus #1 or #20 (stop "Cézanne"); otherwise it's a ten-minute walk or so uphill from the north end of the Vieille Ville.

Two kilometres further north up the hill of Les Lauves at Chemin de Marguerite (bus #20; stop "Les Peintres") is the **Terrain des Peintres** (free access), an informal

Mediterranean garden on the spot where, towards the end of his life, Cézanne painted Mont Ste-Victoire over and over again. Despite the suburban development that has covered Les Lauves since Cézanne's day, the view is intact, and this is still the highest vantage point in Aix from which to view the mountain. At the top of the garden plaques depict several of the Mont Ste-Victoire canvases, though they're scarcely necessary, as it would be impossible to imagine this now as anything other than Cézanne's landscape.

Eating

Aix is stuffed full of places to eat. Place des Cardeurs, west of the Hôtel de Ville, is nothing but restaurant, brasserie and café terraces; rue de la Couronne on the western fringe of Vieil Aix has several worthwhile options, and the elegant **café-brasseries** lining cours Mirabeau, though occasionally pricey, are tempting. That said, Aix's **restaurant** scene repays careful exploration, as some of the best places are away from these hotspots.

Les Bacchanales 10 rue de la Couronne ℡04.42.27.21.06. Inventive Provençal cooking, featuring dishes such as saddle of lamb in herb pastry with mushrooms; menu €29. Closed Sun.

Le Bistrot des Philosophes 20 place des Cardeurs ℡04.42.21.64.35. About the classiest of place des Cardeurs' offerings, with hearty *plats* and a spacious outdoor terrace.

Book in Bar 4 rue Cabassol ℡04.42.26.60.07. English café and bookshop with regular book signings, lectures and theme nights.

Cay Tam 29–31 rue de la Verrerie ℡04.42.27.28.11. Smart, well-regarded Vietnamese restaurant with menus at €12 and €15.50 and a few Chinese, Thai and Korean dishes. Closed Mon and lunch Fri–Sun.

Chez Féraud 8 rue du Puits Juif ℡04.42.63.07.27. Classy, romantic Provençal restaurant in a quiet corner near the Hôtel de Ville, with chickpea salad with tapenade, grilled sea bass with fennel and *pieds et paquets* on a superb €30 menu. Closed Sun, Mon & all Aug.

La Chimère 15 rue Bruyès ℡04.42.38.30.00. Fun, distinctive restaurant with over-the-top Baroque decor, loud colours and plenty of choice on the eclectic, inventive menu: €28 for two courses, €32 for three. Evenings only; closed Sun.

Le Clos de la Violette 10 av de la Violette ℡04.42.23.30.71, ⊛www.closdelaviolette.com. Brigitte and Jean-Marc Banzo's restaurant now has a slick, contemporary look, and remains one of Aix's most renowned gastronomic temples, offering the likes of roast duck with poached rhubarb or caramelized cherry and sea bream with stewed beets, anchovy jus and *socca galette*. Menus at €50, €90 and €130. Closed Sun, plus Mon & Wed lunchtimes.

Les Deux Garçons 53 cours Mirabeau ℡04.42.26.00.51. The erstwhile haunt of Albert Camus is done up in faded period style and still attracts a motley assortment of literati. Good brasserie food, but not especially cheap.

Le Jasmin 6 rue de la Fonderie ℡04.42.38.05.89. Iranian food on €20 and €26 menus. Closed Sun.

Le Passage 10 rue de Villars ℡04.42.37.09.00, ⊛www.le-passage.fr. More a culinary complex than a straightforward restaurant, with a pretty garden, stylish and creative Mediterranean cooking downstairs and a Thai restaurant upstairs. There's also a cookery school. Lunchtime *formule* €13, dinner menus from €28.

Petit Verdot 7 rue Entrecasteaux ℡04.42.27.30.12, ⊛www.lepetitverdot.fr. Tables made from old wine boxes set the scene at this amiable restaurant. Foie gras with coriander and nectarine chutney and sardines *escabeche* are on the menu, and Coteaux d'Aix is on the wine list. Mains €16–20.

Restaurant Pierre Reboul 11 petite rue St Jean ℡04.42.20.58.26. This stylish, Michelin-garlanded restaurant is among Aix's best, with funky, fairly minimalist decor and a plethora of gourmet nibbles like artichoke in transparent ravioli with langoustine *bouillabaisse*. Lunch menu €39, dinner from €78. Closed Sun & Mon.

Ze Bistro 7 rue de la Couronne ℡04.42.39.81.88. Inventive, informal new bistro on the western fringes of Vieil Aix, with simple decor, seasonal produce and lots of fresh fish.

Le Zinc de Hugo 22 rue Lieutaud ℡04.42.27.69.69. Funky modern bistro with big portions of beautifully presented food; the €22 three-course menu is great value. Service is friendly, but struggles a bit at peak times. Closed Sun and Mon.

Nightlife and entertainment

For its size, Aix has a remarkably heavyweight cultural scene, notably as home to the internationally renowned contemporary **dance** company, Ballet Preljocaj. There is a smattering of **live theatre**, some good **live music** venues, and **classical concerts** in the city's churches and at the imposing new **Grand Théâtre de Provence**. If you fancy a trip to the **cinema**, Le Mazarin, 6 rue Laroque (℡08.92.68.72.70), and Le Renoir, 24 cours Mirabeau (same number), show foreign films in their original language.

For what's-on information check out *Le Mois à Aix*, available free from the tourist office, where you can also book tickets for events in Aix and elsewhere. The best time for Aix nightlife is during the summer **festivals**, when much of the entertainment happens in the streets.

As for **drinking**, Aix's preferred style is to lounge on a café or brasserie terrace rather than cram into a noisy bar; there are plenty of the former and a (lively) handful of the latter.

Bars, clubs and live music venues

Hot Brass 1857 chemin d'Eguilles-Célony ℡04.42.23.13.12, ⓦwww.hotbrassaix.com. Famous jazz club that still attracts live acts including some star performers, though these days it's more of a disco for the over-25 crowd; smart dress is expected. Open Fri, Sat and nights before public holidays until 6am.

Icône 3 rue Frédéric Mistral ℡04.42.27.59.82. One of Aix's hippest late-night venues, a blend of Italian restaurant and lounge bar with electro music. Bar open until 2am. Closed Sun and Mon.

Méditerranéen Boy 6 rue de la Paix ℡04.42.27.21.47. Aix's most established gay bar is small and discreet but frequently packed. Open daily until 2am.

O'Shannon 30 rue de la Verrerie ℡04.42.23.31.63, ⓦwww.oshannon-aix.fr. Boisterous Irish pub that's just about the liveliest spot for serious beer drinking in Aix. Open until 2am, closed Sun.

La Rotonde 2a place Jeanne d'Arc. ℡04.42.91.61.70. Trendy brasserie on a prime site at the western end of cours Mirabeau, with a wide terrace, electro music and a clubby ambience. Open until 2am.

Le Scat Club 11 rue de la Verrerie ℡04.42.23.00.23. All kinds of rock, funk and R&B – the best live-music venue in Vieil Aix. Closed Sun and Mon.

L'Unic 40 rue Vauvenargues ℡04.42.96.38.28. One of the nicest of the bar/cafés facing onto lively place Richelme, with a terrace that's animated at any hour of the day. Open daily until 2am.

Theatre and dance

Cité du Livre 8–10 rue des Allumettes ℡04.42.91.98.88. Concerts, plays, cutting-edge contemporary dance, poetry readings and films.

La Fontaine d'Argent 5 rue de La Fontaine-d'Argent ℡04.42.38.43.80. Café-theatre with a diverse programme including comedy.

Grand Théâtre de Provence 380 av Max Juvénal ℡04.42.91.69.69. The international stars of classical music and dance, in suitably imposing, modern surroundings opposite the Pavillon Noir.

Le Pavillon Noir 530 av Wolfgang Amadeus Mozart ℡04.42.93.48.00, ⓦwww.preljocaj.org. Architecturally impressive performance base for the celebrated Ballet Preljocaj.

Théâtre du Jeu de Paume 17–21 rue de l'Opéra ℡08.20.00.04.02. Aix's grandest venue for mainstream theatre, in opulent and historic Rococo surroundings.

The festivals

For much of June and July, Vieil Aix is taken over by its music festivals and the accompanying street entertainers of the alternative scene – street theatre, rock concerts and impromptu gatherings turn the whole area into one long party. The main events are the **Aix en Musique** (ⓦwww.aixenmusique.fr), a rock, jazz, experimental and classical music event in June, and the **Festival International d'Art Lyrique** (ⓦwww.festival-aix.com), dedicated to opera and classical concerts in July.

Tickets for the festivals' mainstream events can cost as much as €70, but unsold tickets are available at reduced price shortly before the performances. For the Aix

▲ Market, Vieil Aix

en Musique festival, tickets are available from Espace Forbin, on place John-Rewald (☎04.42.21.69.69); for the Festival International d'Art Lyrique from place de l'Archevêché (☎08.20.92.29.23).

Markets and shopping

On Tuesdays, Thursdays and Saturdays the whole of Vieil Aix is taken up with **markets**. Fruit, vegetables and regional specialities are sold on **place des Prêcheurs**; **Place de l'Hôtel de Ville** is filled with lilies, roses and carnations, while around **Palais Monclar** and the law courts to the east and on cours Mirabeau you can buy clothes – new, mass-produced, handmade or secondhand. Beyond the Palais de Justice, **place de Verdun** hosts the flea market. A farmers' market takes place daily in **place Richelme**; an antiquarian book market is held on the first Sunday of each month in place de l'Hôtel de Ville.

While Aix's markets provide the greatest retail pleasure, there are also some very good **specialist shops**. The finest **chocolates and sweets** are sold at Puyricard, 7 rue Rifle-Rafle, though they cost around €31 for a 240g box. For Aix's speciality almond and melon sweets, **calissons**, head to Du Roy René, 10 rue Clemenceau, or Confiserie Entrecasteaux, 2 rue d'Entrecasteaux, which also sells nougat.

On the last weekend in July, the Coteaux d'Aix **wines** are celebrated with a fair on cours Mirabeau.

Listings

Bike rental Cycles Zammit, 27 rue Mignet
☎04.42.23.19.53 (electric bikes); Holiday Bikes
ADA, 27 bd de la République ☎04.42.26.72.70.

Car rental AGLC Thrifty, 34 rue Irma-Moreau
☎04.42.64.64.64; Avis, 11 bd Gambetta
☎04.42.21.64.16; Europcar, 55 bd de la République
☎08.25.89.69.76.

Emergencies SAMU ☎ 15; Centre Hospitalier,
av de Tamaris ☎ 04.42.33.90.28; SOS Médecins
☎ 04.42.26.24.00.
Laundry 60 rue Boulégon; 36 cours Sextius;
11 rue des Bernardines; 5 rue de la Fontaine.
Money exchange L'Agence, 15 cours Mirabeau
☎ 04.42.26.84.77.

Police Av de l'Europe ☎ 04.42.93.97.00;
emergency ☎ 17.
Post office 2 rue Lapierre.
Taxis Taxi Radio Aixois 24hr service
☎ 04.42.27.71.11; Taxi Mirabeau
☎ 04.42.21.61.61.

Around Aix

There is gorgeous countryside to be explored around Aix, particularly to the east, where you'll find **Cézanne**'s favourite local subject, the **Montagne Ste-Victoire**. In addition, there is the ancient site at **Oppidum d'Entremont** and Picasso's château in **Vauvenargues**. North of the city, the vineyards of the **Coteaux d'Aix** stretch towards the **Abbaye de Silvacane** and the river Durance.

Oppidum d'Entremont

On the northern outskirts of Aix behind impressive ramparts is the Celto-Ligurian archeological site of **Oppidum d'Entremont** (April–Oct Wed–Mon 9am–noon & 2–6pm; Nov–March Wed–Mon 9am–noon & 2–5pm; free; bus #21 or 24, stop "Entremont"), for a brief period the chief settlement of one of the strongest confederations of indigenous people in Provence. Built around 175 BC, it was divided into two parts: the upper town, where the warriors are thought to have lived; and the larger lower town for artisans and traders. Though much of the site remains unexcavated the distinction is still clear, with the latter the more interesting to explore, and there's a helpful explanatory signage in English. The site lay on an important trade crossroads from Marseille to the Durance Valley and from Fréjus to the Rhône. Marseille merchants finally persuaded the Romans to dispose of this irritant to their expanding business (see p.166). The elevated site ensures sweeping views across Aix towards Mont Ste-Victoire.

The Mont Ste-Victoire circuit

The sixty-kilometre circuit of Mont Ste-Victoire makes a rewarding day-trip from Aix. Leaving the city, the D10 road east to Vauvenargues passes the quarry

---

Climbing Mont Ste-Victoire

If you're interested in **climbing Mont Ste-Victoire**, you'll find the northern approaches considerably easier than the sheer 500m southern face, though the ascent still requires stamina (and at times of high fire risk or high wind may not be permitted at all). Avoid attempting the walk between about 11am and 3pm in the summer months, when you should always wear a hat, and bring suncream and a minimum of two litres of water per person. A number of routes ascend from the north to the monumental **Cross of Provence**, a pilgrimage **chapel** and the 1011m **Pic des Mouches**, which is the summit; the walk along the ridge itself is for serious hikers, with the route following some breathtakingly vertiginous cliff faces. Allow around three to four hours for the ascent. For more information and good free maps with suggested routes, visit the **Maison Sainte Victoire** (July & Aug Mon–Fri 10am–6.30pm, Sat & Sun 10.15am–7pm; April–June & Sept–Oct Mon–Fri 9.30am–6pm, Sat & Sun 10.15am–7pm; Nov–March daily 9.30am–6pm; ☎ 04.42.66.84.40), off the D17 in the hamlet of Saint Antonin sur Bayon on the south side of the mountain.

of **Bibémus**, painted by Cézanne (guided walks €6.60: book through Aix tourist office), and the lake and barrage of Bimont. At **VAUVENARGUES** itself, 14km from Aix, the weatherbeaten, red-shuttered fourteenth-century **château** bought by Picasso in 1958 stands just outside the village with nothing between it and the slopes of the mountain. **Picasso** lived there till his death in 1973, and is buried in the gardens, his grave adorned with his sculpture *Woman with a Vase*. The château is strictly private, though it opened briefly in 2009 to coincide with the Musée Granet's Picasso-Aix retrospective, and it may be worth asking at Aix tourist office if further temporary openings are scheduled. If the village appeals, you can stay at the pleasant small **hotel**, *Le Moulin de Provence*, 33 avenue des Maquisards (℡04.42.66.02.22, ⓦwww.lemoulindeprovence.com; ❶), with views over Mont Ste-Victoire and the château, and a terrace restaurant (menus from €20).

East of Vauvenargues, the D10 splits, with the right fork eventually becoming the D223, which heads south before joining the D23 to Pourrières. To the west of here, along the D57, is **PUYLOUBIER**, where you can visit the French Foreign Legion's **Pensioners' Château**, which sits in a magnificent landscape surrounded by vineyards 1.5km from the crossroads in Puyloubier at the end of the chemin de la Pallière. Its small **museum** (Tues–Sun 10am–noon & 2–5pm; free) is one for the military buffs, its extensive collection of uniforms including an intriguing series of handkerchiefs printed with instructions on everything from hygiene to boot care and how to assemble a revolver. A shop sells Legion sweatshirts, books and souvenirs.

From Puyloubier, the D17 skirts the spectacular southern side of Mont Ste-Victoire to **LE THOLONET**, with its Italianate seventeenth-century château (closed to the public). On the east side of the village, an old windmill, the **Moulin de Cézanne** (hours vary according to exhibitions), has been converted into an exhibition space for art and sculpture, with a bronze relief of Cézanne himself on a stele outside. The Le Tholonet region also has its own tiny AOC, the Vins de Palette, comprising just 57 acres and a handful of producers. At the main Le Tholonet crossroads there's a popular **restaurant**, *Chez Thome* (℡04.42.66.90.43), with tables under the trees and menus starting at €25.

The Route des Vins and the Abbaye de Silvacane

To the north and west of Aix, the vineyards of the **Coteaux d'Aix** fan out across a broad belt of countryside between the city and the river Durance. At 35 square kilometres, this is the second-largest AOC in Provence after the Côtes de Provence itself, and one which is still forging its reputation. The soil is particularly suited to the production of great red wines, with Grenache, Syrah, Cabernet Sauvignon and Vermentino the main grape varieties grown. The rosés are rich and fruity and go well with Provençal dishes like *bourride*; white wines are much less common, but are fresh and fragrant. A signposted **Route des Vins** follows a circuit through the heart of the AOC, beginning and ending in the village of **Éguilles**, 9.5km west of Aix on the D17; along the circuit the opportunities to stop and try the wines are fairly frequent. The tourist office on place Gabriel Payeur in Éguilles (Mon–Fri 10am–noon & 2–6pm; ℡04.42.92.49.15, ⓦwww.eguilles.fr) can supply a list of producers with opening times and a map of the Route des Vins. Some of the vineyards also produce *vin cuit*, a Provençal curiosity that is heated during maturation.

The D543 from Éguilles cuts through the heart of the wine-growing district to Rognes. Six kilometres further to the north, the D543 intersects with the D561; a little to the west of the junction along the D561 stands the **Abbaye de Silvacane**, built by the same order and in the same period as the abbeys of

Sénanque (see p.195) and Le Thoronet (see p.209), although the "wood of rushes" from which the name Silvacane derives had already been cleared by Benedictine monks before the Cistercians arrived in 1144. As at the other two great monasteries, the architecture of Silvacane reflects the no-nonsense rule of Saint Benedict (Benoît) in which manual work, intellectual work and worship comprised the three equal elements of the day. You can visit the stark, pale-stoned church and its surrounding buildings and cloisters (June–Sept daily 10am–6pm; Oct–May daily except Tues 10am–1pm & 2–5pm; €7, plus €2 parking if you arrive by car). The buildings look pretty much as they did seven hundred years ago, with the exception of the refectory, rebuilt in 1423 and given Gothic ornamentation that the earlier monks would never have tolerated. The windows in the church would not have had stained glass either. The only heated room would have been the *salle des monies* where the work of copying manuscripts was carried out, and the only areas where conversation would have been allowed were the *salle capitulaire*, where the daily reading of "the Rule" and the hearing of confessions took place, and the *parloir* (literally, a room for talking in).

Along the Durance

Twenty-six kilometres from Aix and just east of the Abbaye de Silvacane, the D543 reaches the broad River Durance at the **Pont de Cadenet**, an incongruously impressive structure – particularly in summer, when the mighty alpine river it crosses is often reduced to a pathetic dribble. The countryside on the river's north bank shelters below the massifs of the Grand and Petit Luberon and is Mediterranean in climate – hot and dry, fragrant with pines and wild thyme, ablaze with yellow and gold honeysuckle and immortelle, and alive with the quick movements of sun-basking lizards. The Durance Valley is highly fertile and yields the region's classic crops, including all the ingredients for ratatouille, while the lower slopes of the Luberon massifs are dotted with cherry trees and vines, grown both for wine and grapes. Because of the importance of agriculture, the villages here are still very Provençal in character, with fewer Parisians and other foreigners than in the northern Luberon.

As a touring base **Cadenet** has its charms, while the market town of **Pertuis** has the best transport links in the area. The beautiful villages of **Lourmarin**, **Vaugines** and **Cucuron** sit amidst vineyards and the unspoilt countryside of the Grand Luberon foothills, while **La Tour d'Aigues** and **Ansouis** boast elegant châteaux.

East of the dramatically narrow Défilé de Mirabeau and north of its confluence with the Verdon, the Durance has a somewhat different character. The Alps are close here, the river itself is exploited for electricity generation and the valley is busier and more urbanized. The major centres are **Manosque**, a bustling market town, and **Sisteron**, dominated by its splendid citadel. Between the two, the A51 Marseille-Grenoble autoroute speeds along the River Durance, bypassing the industrial town of **St-Auban** and its older neighbour **Château-Arnoux**, renowned for its superb restaurant, *La Bonne Étape*. The views from the fashionable little village of **Lurs** and the ancient **Prieuré de Ganagobie** have not been affected, nor has their isolation. **Volx** is the site of an impressive new museum devoted to the olive, while La Brillane is the nearest *gare SNCF* to Lurs.

Cadenet

The main road heading north to Lourmarin detours round **CADENET**, lending the place a sleepy charm with few of the chichi airs of the villages to the north. The town has a small museum, the **Musée de la Vannerie** (April–Oct daily except Wed & Sun 10am–noon & 2.30–6.30pm, Wed & Sun 2.30–6.30pm; €3.50), set in a former atelier on avenue Philippe-de-Girard and devoted to basket-weaving, which is a traditional industry in the area. The central place du Tambour d'Arcole holds a statue of a manic drummer-boy, hair and coat-tails flying as he runs. The monument commemorates André Étienne for his inspired one-man diversion that confused the Austrians and allowed Napoleon's army to cross the River Durance in 1796. Also on the square is Cadenet's **tourist office** (Mon–Sat: July & Aug 10am–12.30pm & 1.30–6pm; Sept–June 9.30am–12.30pm & 1.30–5.30pm; ℡04.90.68.38.21). There's an excellent lakeside **campsite** southwest of the village off chemin de Pile, the four-star *Val de Durance* (℡04.90.68.37.75, ⓦwww.homair.com; April–Sept), and a **restaurant**, *Le Cinq Sens*, 35 rue Gambetta (℡04.90.68.07.14; closed Sun & Tues eve, & Mon), with menus from €18. **Market** day is Monday.

Otherwise, there's not a great deal to detain you here, though a short but energetic climb from the centre of the village brings you to the remains of Cadenet's château, from which there are wonderful views over the surrounding countryside. There are various routes on foot, though chemin des Rougettes off cours Voltaire is the easiest for car users and has a small parking area.

Lourmarin

LOURMARIN stands at the bottom of a *combe* 4km north of Cadenet, its Renaissance **château** lording it over the village from a small rise to the west. A fortress once defended this strategic vantage point but the current edifice dates from the sixteenth century when comfort was beginning to outplay defence – hence the generous windows. Since 1929 the château has belonged to the University of Aix, who use it to give summer sabbaticals to artists and intellectuals. Many have left behind works of art, which you can see on a 45-minute **guided tour** (Jan Sat & Sun 2.30–4pm; Feb, Nov & Dec 10.30–11.30am & 2.30–4pm; March, April & Oct 10.30–11.30am & 2.30–4pm; May & Sept 10–11.30am & 2.30–5.30pm; June–Aug 10am–6pm; €5.50) through vast rooms with intricate wooden ceilings, massive fireplaces and beautifully tiled floors where the favoured cultural workers socialize. **Concerts** are held in the château during July, August and September, and throughout the spring, summer and

---

The wars of religion in the Luberon

During five days in April 1545 a great swathe of the Petit Luberon, between **Lourmarin** and **Mérindol**, was burnt and put to the sword; three thousand people were massacred and six hundred sent to the galleys. Their crime was having Protestant tendencies in the years leading up to the devastating Wars of Religion. Despite the complicity of King Henri II, the ensuing scandal forced him to order an enquiry which then absolved those responsible – the Catholic aristocrats from Aix.

Lourmarin (see above) itself suffered minor damage but the castle in Mérindol was violently dismantled, along with every single house. Mérindol's remains, on the hill above the current village on the south side of the Petit Luberon, are a visible monument to those events, and to this day the south face of the Petit Luberon remains sparsely populated.

autumn art **exhibitions** of all sorts are staged (visit Ⓦwww.chateau-de
-lourmarin.com for information).

The most famous literary figure associated with Lourmarin is the writer **Albert
Camus**, who spent the last years of his life here and is buried in the cemetery.
Nowadays the village is extremely chic, and often overrun with visitors in
summer.

Practicalities

Lourmarin's **tourist office**, 9 avenue Philippe-de-Girard (Mon–Sat 10am–12.30pm
& 3–6pm; Ⓣ04.90.68.10.77, Ⓦwww.lourmarin.com), organizes Camus-themed
literary walks. In the village, the *Moulin de Lourmarin* (Ⓣ04.90.68.06.69, Ⓦwww
.moulindelourmarin.com; ❺) is the luxury place **to stay**, with stylish Provençal decor
and a restaurant; the wonderfully situated *Hostellerie Le Paradou* (Ⓣ04.90.68.04.05,
Ⓦwww.hotelparadou.com; ❺), on the D943 at the start of the *combe*, *is* a more
secluded option. More affordably, back towards Lourmarin, the *gîte d'étape Le Four à
Chaux* (Ⓣ04.90.68.24.28, Ⓦwww.le-four-a-chaux.com) has dormitory beds (€13)
and a few rooms (❶); there's also a three-star **campsite**, *Les Hautes Prairies*, on route
de Vaugines (Ⓣ04.90.68.02.89, Ⓦcampinghautesprairies.com; €17.40 per night),
with a pool, food store and free wireless internet.

There are several **restaurants** around Lourmarin's fountained squares,
including *La Récréation*, 15 rue Philippe de Girard (Ⓣ04.90.68.23.73), which
serves good and reasonably priced organic dishes, with menus from €25. Further
out of town, the expensive but excellent hotel-restaurant *L'Auberge de la Fenière*
on route de Cadenet (Ⓣ04.90.68.11.79; menus from €35) uses absolutely fresh
ingredients to create seriously gourmet concoctions and has a few stylish,
individually designed **rooms** (❽).

East to Pertuis

East from Lourmarin, the first place along the minor D56 road is **VAUGINES**, a
gorgeous little village with the charming *Café de la Fontaine*, opposite the *mairie*,
and a **hotel** with great views, the *Hostellerie du Luberon* (Ⓣ04.90.77.27.19, Ⓦwww
.hostellerieduluberon.com; ❺). Vaugines is the meeting point of the GR97 trail
from the Petit Luberon and the GR9 which crosses the Grand Luberon to Buoux
in one direction and in the other loops above Cucuron and skirts the Mourre-
Nègre summit before running along the eastern end of the ridge.

The neighbouring village of **CUCURON** is larger but even more fetching, with
some of its ancient ramparts and gateways still standing and a bell tower with a
delicate campanile on the central place de l'Horloge. Cucuron had a glimpse of
fame when it was taken over by the film industry for the shooting of Rappeneau's
1995 movie *The Horseman on the Roof*, based on a Giono novel and, at the time, the
most expensive French film made; the village has been revisited by film location
crews many times since. Cucuron's main business, however, is olive oil; there's a
sixteenth-century mill in a hollow of the rock face on rue Moulin à l'Huile that is
still used to press olives. At the top of the rock a scrubby open **park** surrounds the
surviving *donjon* of the citadel; the journey up to the castle above the Tour de
l'Horloge takes you through the oldest and most beautiful parts of the village. At
the other end of Cucuron is the **Église Notre-Dame-de-Beaulieu**, which
contains a seventeenth-century altarpiece in coloured marble originally commissioned for the Chapelle de la Visitation in Aix. From the end of May to the middle
of August a huge felled poplar leans against the church, a tradition dating back to
1720 when Cucuron was spared the plague. On rue de l'Église, a short way from
the church, is a small **museum** (10.30am–noon & 2–5.30pm; closed Tues

morning; ring the bell in the hallway to gain entry; free) on local traditions and early history, with a collection of daguerreotypes.

On the north side of the village, by a reservoir bordered by plane trees, the **hotel-restaurant** *l'Étang* (℡04.90.77.21.25, Ⓦwww.hoteldeletang.com; ❹) serves very pleasant food (menus from €22); its neighbour, *La Petite Maison* (℡04.90.68.21.99, Ⓦwww.lapetitemaisondecucuron.com; menu €60), is altogether grander, with a Michelin star. **Campsites** include *Lou Badareu*, 800m from the village on route de l'Étang de la Bonde (℡04.90.77.21.46, Ⓦwww .loubadareu.com; €11.10 per tent; open April to early Oct). A Tuesday **market** is held on place de l'Étang.

Halfway between Cucuron and Pertuis, the lovely hilltop village of **ANSOUIS** has a superb **château** (Wed–Mon, guided tours only: 10.30am for groups, 2.30pm & 4pm for individuals; €7), which had been lived in since the twelfth century by the same family until it was sold at auction in 2008. In the village below, the **Musée Extraordinaire** (daily 2–6pm; €3.50) is dedicated to underwater life and has some extremely kitsch touches.

Pertuis and La Tour d'Aigues

The one sizeable place this side of the Durance is **PERTUIS**, likeable enough but of interest primarily as a transport hub and potential touring base. Like so many towns in the area, it only really comes to life on **market** day, Friday in this case. In July, the Festival de l'Enclos brings jazz, soul and world music to Pertuis and a month later there's a big-band festival.

Pertuis is served by the TER (regional train network) from Marseille and Aix. The **gare SNCF** is 1km to the south of town; buses stop at the **gare routière** on place Garcin, within easy walking distance of the centre: leave the square on the opposite side from the bus station and turn left up rue Henri-Silvy. The town centres around place Parmentier, rue Colbert, the main clothes shopping street leading up to place Jean-Jaurès, and the more historic place Mirabeau just to the north. The **tourist office** is on place Mirabeau (July & Aug Mon 10am–12.30pm & 2–6.30pm, Tues–Fri 9am–12.30pm & 2–6.30pm, Sat 9.30am–12.30pm & 2.30–6.30pm; Sept–June Mon 10am–noon & 2–6pm, Tues–Fri 9am–noon & 2–6pm, Sat 9.30am–noon & 2.30–6pm; ℡04.90.79.15.56, Ⓦwww.vivreleluberon.com) in the old keep, all that remains of Pertuis' castle.

Of the **places to stay**, the only central option is the *Hôtel du Cours*, place Jean-Jaurès (℡04.90.79.00.68, Ⓦwww.hotelducours.com; ❷), which is small and friendly, if nothing special. Alternatively, try the newish, air-conditioned *Le Village Provençal* in the Saint-Martin industrial zone south of the town (℡04.90.09.70.18, Ⓦwww.hotel-levillageprovencal.com; ❹), with an outdoor pool and a restaurant. The three-star municipal **campsite**, *Les Pinèdes*, east of town on the Manosque road (℡04.90.79.10.98, Ⓦwww.campinglespinedes.com; €16 per tent; closed mid-Oct to mid-March), has excellent facilities.

You'll find plenty of inexpensive **bars**, **cafés** and **brasseries** on the main squares and streets, but more ambitious fare using organic produce can be found at *Le Boulevard*, 50 bd Pécout (℡04.90.09.69.31; menus €19 & €30; closed evenings Sun & Tues), midway between the town centre and the *gare SNCF*. **Bikes** can be rented at Vélos Luberon (℡04.90.09.17.33), in the Saint-Martin industrial zone.

Just west of Pertuis off the D973, the gardens and winery of **Val Joanis** (April–Oct daily 10am–7pm; Nov & Jan–March weekdays 2–5.30pm; free) surrounding the sixteenth-century *bastide* of the same name are very much a work in progress. Re-established in 1978 by Cécile Chancel and awarded the title French Garden of the Year in 2008, the gardens are an attempt to re-create an eighteenth-century

A taste of Provence

Wholesome and healthy, the cooking of Provence displays all the benefits of the Mediterranean diet, with superb fish on the coast, excellent lamb from Sisteron and, everywhere, fantastic fresh fruit and vegetables – the rewards of a sunny climate. Although the region is home to some of the world's grandest restaurants, the true glory of Provençal cuisine lies in honest home cooking based on fresh, locally sourced ingredients. Small, family-run restaurants still serve up tasty prix-fixe feasts at traditional prices, while Nice is one of the best places in Europe to find cheap, delicious street food.

Feasts from the sea

Fish and **seafood** are mainstays of the diet on the Mediterranean coast. At its most sublimely simple this means **oursins** – sea urchins – eaten raw with a sprinkling of lemon juice and a glass of crisp white Cassis wine; they're also cooked to make *oursinade* – a fish soup or sauce. But the region's love of fish is best reflected in the celebrated **soups** or **stews**: **bourride**, made with monkfish, where the cooking liquor is thickened with *aïoli* afterwards and served separately as a soup, and the famous **bouillabaisse** of Marseille, originally a humble meal cooked on the beach by fishermen but now quite a grand affair, the authenticity of which is guarded by a small, elite band of restaurants. The high cost of eating *bouillabaisse* reflects the quality of the ingredients used – notably *rascasse* or scorpion fish.

Bouillabaisse ▲

Olive stall ▼

The fat of the land

The richness of the region's agriculture is on display at any good Provençal market: green or black olives marinated a dozen different ways; neat little *chèvres* (goat's cheeses) that range in intensity from creamy mild to pungent; the mysterious black Tricastin truffle. Meat and game are good, from Sisteron's lamb to Arles' salami-style *saucisson sec* or the young rabbit that has grazed on the aromatic Mediterranean herbs of the garrigue. The region's most famous meat-based dish is the slow-cooked beef stew, **daube de boeuf**. Recipes vary, but it commonly contains a curl of orange peel, a few juniper berries, chopped bacon and a great deal of red wine, in which the beef is marinated overnight before cooking, in order to develop the rich, deep flavour.

Sweet treats

With such an abundance of fresh produce, **fruit** is the obvious end to a meal in Provence, from peaches and nectarines to cherries and melons. Not that there's a lack of sugary treats: Aix-en-Provence is famous for its wonderful **calissons** – lozenge-shaped sweetmeats made from candied melon and ground almonds. Almonds also feature in the deliciously soft, honey-flavoured **nougat** that is found everywhere in the region, though the traditional centre of the industry is in the Rhône Valley town of Montélimar just outside Provence. Orange water lends a delicate scent to the **fougassettes** of Grasse, while lavender often adds an exotic flavour to *crème brûlée*. Candied fruit and flowers and the **violet-scented ice cream** of Tourrettes-sur-Loup are among the many other indulgences that Provence has to offer.

▲ *Calissons*

▼ Nougat stall

▼ Café, Vieux Nice

Nice and simple

Nice has a cuisine all its own, with the strong Italian influence reflected in excellent fresh pasta, particularly the **ravioles** that are characteristic of the city, often stuffed with spinach and cheese; or the unfortunately named *merda de can*, which are a variety of gnocchi. For all the city's glamorous reputation, there's no finer place to eat simply, cheaply and well than a Vieux Nice café, where you can bite into a generous **pan bagnat** sandwich with tuna, olives and *mesclun*, or tuck in to **farcis** (vegetables stuffed with a meat mixture) and **beignets** (vegetables in batter). Cheapest of all Nice's street food is the chickpea pancake, **socca**, cooked in front of you on huge round griddles, sliced and eaten hot.

Tapenade ▲

Pistou ▼

Aromatic extras

One of the most distinctive characteristics of Provençal cuisine is the use of strongly flavoured **condiments** derived from a variety of fresh ingredients.

Aïoli

A mayonnaise-like sauce made by pounding crushed garlic with chillis and breadcrumbs, and adding olive oil, **aïoli** derives its name from the Provençal for garlic (*ail*) and olive (*oli*). When you see *un grand aïoli* on restaurant menus, however, you're not being offered a large helping of garlic mayonnaise, but rather an elaborate dish of salt cod, boiled beef, mutton and stewed vegetables, served with *aïoli* and garnished with boiled eggs and snails.

Pistou

The cooking of eastern Provence is closely related to that of Italian Liguria, and **pistou** – the name comes from the Provençal *pestar*, to crush – is the Provençal equivalent of the celebrated Italian pesto sauce. It's made with basil, crushed garlic and olive oil, and most famously added to the vegetable-based *soupe au pistou*.

Rouille

A thick, pinky-orange, *aïoli*-like sauce, **rouille** is made with chilli, garlic and saffron, pounded with breadcrumbs or potato, to which are added olive oil and stock. Along with finely grated cheese – usually Gruyère – it's one of the classic accompaniments to a Provençal fish soup.

Tapenade

A pungent savoury spread, **tapenade** is made with capers (*tapenos* in Provençal), anchovies, finely chopped or puréed black olives, olive oil and lemon juice. As well as accompanying fish or crudités, it's often simply eaten on toast.

garden with both ornamental and productive elements, including a traditional kitchen garden and a beautiful long arbour planted with rambling roses. The vineyard produces increasingly respected Côtes du Luberon wines, and there are opportunities to taste these and the estate's olive oil.

Heading northeast from Pertuis towards Grambois brings you to **LA TOUR D'AIGUES**, where a vast shell of a **château** dominates the village centre. It was half destroyed during the Revolution but the most finely detailed Renaissance decoration, based on classical designs including Grecian helmets, angels, bows and arrows and Olympic torches, has survived on the gateway arch. You can admire most of the ruins' glories from the outside, but there's also a **Musée de Faïence** and a small exhibit on the rural habitat of the area inside (July & Aug daily 10am–1pm & 2.30–6pm; April–June, Sept & Oct Sun & Mon 2.30–6pm, Tues 10am–1pm, Wed–Sat 10am–1pm & 2.30–6pm; Nov–March Mon 2–5pm, Tues 10am–noon, Wed–Sat 10am–noon & 2–5pm, Sun 2–5pm; €4.50), covering local archeological finds, the development of traditional rural homes (*mas*) in the area, plus temporary exhibitions. The château is also a popular venue for year-round music and dance concerts (☏04.90.07.50.33, ⓦwww.chateau-latourdaigues .com). There's a fairly basic **café** on the far side of the main road from the **château**, and one **hotel**, *Le Petit Mas de Marie*, not far from the centre on the Pertuis road (☏04.90.07.48.22, ⓦwww.lepetitmasdemarie.com; ❸).

Manosque and around

MANOSQUE, 36km northeast of Pertuis, is an ancient town, strategically positioned just above the right bank of the River Durance. Its small old quarter is surrounded by nondescript blocks, and beyond them by ever-spreading industrial units and superstores. It is a major population centre in the *département* of Alpes de Haute Provence, profiting from the new corridor of affluence that follows the autoroute north.

Manosque is home of the phenomenally successful soap and oil retailer **L'Occitane en Provence**, founded in 1976 by Olivier Baussan, and thus is as responsible as anywhere for propagating the idyllic image of Provence internationally. For the French, however, it is most famous as the home town of the author **Jean Giono**, born here in 1895. As well as mementoes of the writer, the town contains an extraordinary work of art on the theme of the Apocalypse by the Armenian-born painter **Jean Carzou**.

Arrival, information and accommodation

The **gare SNCF** is 1.5km south of the centre along avenue Jean Giono and avenue Lattre de Tassigny, linked by infrequent **buses** to the **gare routière** on boulevard Charles-de-Gaulle (☏04.92.87.55.99). Turn left out of the *gare routière* and then right onto avenue Jean Giono to reach the **tourist office** (March to mid-June Mon–Sat 9am–12.15pm & 1.30–6pm; mid- to late June & mid-Sept to Oct same hours plus Sun 10am–noon; July & Aug Mon–Sat 9am–1pm & 2–7pm, Sun 10am–noon; Nov–Feb Mon–Fri 9am–12.15pm & 1.30–6pm, Sat 9am–12.15pm; ☏04.92.72.16.00, ⓦwww.manosque-tourisme.com) on place du Dr-Joubert just before you reach Porte Saunerie, the southern entrance to the Vieille Ville.

For reasonably priced **rooms** in the centre, try *François 1er*, 18 rue Guilhempierre (☏04.92.72.07.99, ⓔhotel-francois1er@wanadoo.fr; ❷). Further out of town, the charming *Le Pré St Michel* on route de Dauphin overlooks Manosque (☏04.92.72.14.27, ⓦwww.presaintmichel.com; ❺), while the most luxurious (and costly) option is the *Hostellerie de la Fuste* (☏04.92.72.05.95, ⓦwww.lafuste .com; ❻), across the Durance and 1km along the D4 towards Oraison. There's a one-star **campsite**, *Les Ubacs*, on avenue de la Repasse (℡04.92.72.28.08; €11.40 per tent; closed Oct–March).

The Town

Barely half a kilometre wide, **Vieux Manosque** is entered through two of its remaining medieval gates: Porte Saunerie in the south and Porte Soubeyran in the north, which sports a tiny bell suspended within the iron outline of an onion dome. Once through the gates it's a little dull, the streets lined with practical but unexciting country-town shops (and quite a few empty premises in the quieter streets); rue Grande is much the most enticing, with a fishmonger, a couple of *chocolatiers*, shops selling chèvre de Banon cheese and wine, and a branch of L'Occitane en Provence. Things get livelier for the weekly **market** on Saturday. Midway between the two gates, on rue Grand, a more intricate bell tower graces the **Église de St-Sauveur**. Neither this nor the **Église de Notre-Dame-de-Romigier**, further up the same street, is a particularly stunning church, though the walls of both bow outwards with the weight of the centuries, and the latter's Black Virgin (black due to the effect of gold leaf on wood) boasts a lengthy resumé of miracles. At the heart of old Manosque, the **Place de l'Hôtel de Ville** is a pleasant place to linger awhile at a pavement café, though the seventeenth-century town hall itself has suffered from bland modernization.

The attractive eighteenth-century house that is now the **Centre Jean Giono** (April–June & Sept Tues–Fri 9.30am–12.30pm & 2–6pm, Sat 9.30am–noon & 2–6pm, plus Sun 9.30am–noon & 2–6pm in July & Aug; Oct–March Tues–Sat 2–6pm; €4), on boulevard Elémir-Bourges by Porte Saunerie, was the first house built outside the town walls. As well as manuscripts, photos, letters and a library of translations of Giono's work, the centre has an extensive video collection of films based on his novels, as well as interviews and documentaries. Giono himself did not live here, but at **Le Paraïs** (guided tours on Fridays by arrangement only: call ℡04.92.87.73.03; free), off montée des Vrais Richesses, 1.5km north of the Vieille Ville.

Giono was imprisoned at the start of World War II for his pacifism, and again after liberation because the Vichy government had promoted his belief in the superiority of nature and peasant life over culture and urban civilization, as supporting the Nazi cause. In truth, far from being a fascist, Giono was a passionate ecologist, and the countryside around Manosque plays as strong a part in his novels as do the characters. World War II embittered him, and his later novels are less idealistic. Giono never left Manosque and died here in 1970.

Giono's contemporary, **Jean Carzou**, confronts the issues of war, technology, dehumanization and the environmental destruction of the planet head on in his extraordinary, monumental **L'Apocalypse**. The work is composed of painted panels and stained-glass windows in the former church of the Couvent de la Présentation, now the **Fondation Carzou** (June & Sept Tues–Sat 2.30–6.30pm; July & Aug Tues–Sun 10am–noon & 2.30–6.30pm; Oct–May Wed–Sat 2.30–6.30pm; free), on boulevard Elémir-Bourges just up from the Centre Jean Giono. Everything from the French Revolution to Pol Pot's massacres is portrayed here, in nightmarish detail.

On the far side of the A51 autoroute in the industrial quarter of Saint-Maurice is the **L'Occitane en Provence** factory, free one-hour guided tours of which can be booked through the Manosque tourist office; the tour includes a film and a workshop on the ingredients used in the products. To the northwest of Manosque on chemin de la Thomassine, the Parc Naturel Régional du Luberon runs the **Maison de la Biodiversité** (July–Sept Tues–Sat 10.30am–1pm & 3–6.30pm;

Oct–June Wed 10am–12.30pm & 2–4.30pm; €4), which explains the domestication of fruits and other crops by man, aided by a series of terraced gardens in the shade of a traditional Provençal *bastide*. There's everything from palms to roses, figs and willows, plus a section devoted to old varieties of food crops.

Eating and drinking

The **restaurants** in the Vieille Ville are generally good value. Michelin-listed *La Barbotine* on place de l'Hôtel de Ville (℡04.92.72.57.15; closed Sun) offers satisfying meals from around €26, with a veggie menu at €18, while *Restaurant le Luberon*, 21 bis place du Terreau (℡04.92.72.03.09; closed Mon & Sun eve out of season), has menus from €29. If you want a change from Provençal cuisine, there are a couple of reasonably priced Vietnamese/Chinese restaurants on the boulevards circling the Vieille Ville.

The Écomusée l'Olivier at Volx

Just over 8km north of Manosque and signposted off the busy D4096 in the village of **Volx** is the **Écomusée l'Olivier** (July & Aug Mon–Fri 10am–12.30pm & 2–6.30pm, Sat & Sun 2–6.30pm; Sept–June same hours but closed Sun; €4) which tells, with the help of attractively laid out interactive exhibits and audiovisual displays, the story of the olive – the "gift of the Mediterranean" – and the cultures that have nurtured it, from Provence to the eastern Mediterranean. You can also taste and buy Provençal oils of exceptional quality here.

Lurs and around

Perched on a narrow ridge above the west bank of the Durance some 20km north of Manosque, **LURS** is a *village de caractère*, undeniably charming yet extremely conscious of its picturesque status. Immaculately restored houses stand amid immaculately maintained ruins; there's a tiny, Roman-style theatre, but little commerce. From the top of the village, you can see across the wide, multi-branching river to the abrupt step up to the Plateau de Valensole, with the snowy peaks beyond; to the south the land drops before rising again in another high ridge along the river; while to the west and north the views are just as extensive, from the rolling hills around Forcalquier to the Montagne de Lure.

The best way to appreciate this geography is to follow the paths to the small chapel of **Notre-Dame-de-Vie** along the narrowing escarpment. The right-hand path goes through the woods and is practically overgrown; the eastern path, the **Promenade des Evêques**, is marked by fifteen small oratories.

By the late 1940s Lurs was deserted save for the odd passing bandit, but it gained international notoriety in 1952 when the British scientist Sir Jack Drummond and his family were murdered while camping alongside the Durance below the village. The case was never satisfactorily solved: the man convicted of the murder was spared execution and ultimately released from custody, and in recent years it has been suggested that Sir Jack was a victim of the Cold War, assassinated because he was a British spy.

The village has latterly become a centre for **graphic artists** and **printers**, including the author of the universal nomenclature for typefaces, and their presence has brought life back to Lurs. There's even an annual conference here, the Rencontres Internationales de Lure, which draws in practitioners of the graphic arts, from calligraphers to computer-aided-design consultants, over the last week in August. If you decide **to stay**, there's a hotel-restaurant, *Le Séminaire*, near the car park on place de la Fontaine (℡04.92.79.94.19, Ⓦwww.hotel-leseminaire.com; ❺; menu €35), housed in the old summer residence of the bishops of Sisteron.

The Prieuré de Ganagobie

About 7km north of Lurs, in the twelfth-century **Prieuré de Ganagobie** (Tues–Sun 3–5pm; free), you'll find some fine examples of complex design skills that far predate the invention of printing. The floor of the priory church is covered with mosaics composed of red, black and white tiles: they depict fabulous beasts whose tails loop through their bodies, and the four elements represented by an elephant (earth), a fish (water), a griffon (air) and a lion (fire). Interlocking and repeating patterns show a strong Byzantine influence, and there's a dragon slain by a St George in Crusader armour.

After visiting the church, you can walk through the oaks and broom, pines and lavender east along the allée des Moines to the edge of the Plateau de Ganagobie, 350m above the Durance, or west along allée de Forcalquier for views to the Montagne de Lure and beyond.

The Pénitents des Mées and Château-Arnoux

North of the priory, the impending confluence of the Durance and Bléone is announced by the **Pénitents des Mées**, a long line of pointed rocks on the east bank, said to be the remains of cowled monks, literally petrified for desiring the women slaves a local lord brought back from the Crusades. By the time you reach **CHÂTEAU-ARNOUX**, hills once more close in and the river takes on a smoother, more majestic prospect, with a barrage just east of the town creating a 7km-long artificial lake. Dominating the centre of the town – pounding traffic aside – is an imposing Renaissance **castle** (closed to the public), with five towers and multicoloured roof tiles. The main reason to stop, however, is to eat at *La Bonne Étape* (℡04.92.64.00.09; ⓦwww.bonneetap.com; menus €42–150; Oct–April closed Mon & Tues), just across the road. Renowned as one of the best **restaurants** in Provence, its cooking celebrates the produce of the region without trendy foreign influences. If your budget won't stretch to this, the simpler *Au Gout du Jour* next door is part of the same concern, with menus at €18 and €24. You can also **stay** (❸) in considerable comfort.

Sisteron and around

The last Provençal stretch of the Route Napoléon (see p.322) runs from Château-Arnoux to **SISTERON**, the first sight of which reveals its strategic significance as the major mountain gateway to Provence. The town, fortified since ancient times, was half-destroyed by the Anglo-American bombardment of 1944, but its **citadel** still stands as a fearsome sentinel over the city and the solitary bridge across the river. After heavy rains the Durance, the colour of *café au lait*, becomes a raging torrent pushing through the narrow Sisteron gap.

Sisteron gave Napoleon something of a headache. Its mayor and the majority of its population were royalist, and given the fortifications and geography of the town, it was impossible for him to pass undetected. However, luck was still with the Corsican in those days, as the military commander of the *département* was a sympathizer and removed all ammunition from Sisteron's arsenal. Contemporary accounts say Napoleon sat nonchalantly on the bridge, contemplating the citadel above and the tumultuous waters below, while his men reassembled and the town's notables, ordered to keep their pistols under wraps, looked on impotently. Eventually Napoleon entered the city, took some refreshment at a tavern and received a tricolour from a courageous peasant woman before rejoining his band and taking leave of Provence. Sisteron today is a lively place, its prosperity based as much on the extensive industrial zone that has grown up to the north along the D4075 as it is on tourism.

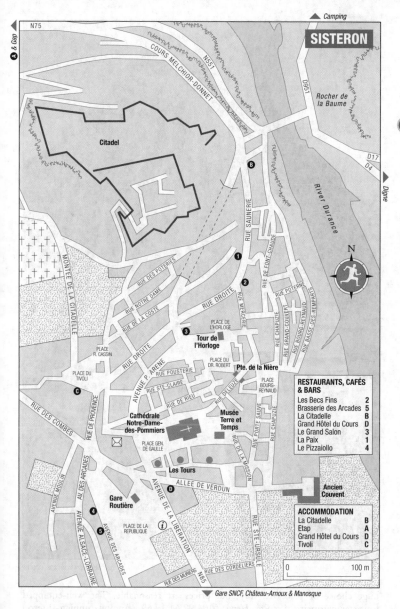

SISTERON

Camping

N75

N551

COURS MELCHIOR-DONNET

N551

D951

Rocher de la Baume

D17
D4

Citadel

& Gap

A & Gap

River Durance

Digne

RUE SAUNERIE

B

N

MONTÉE DE LA CITADELLE

RUE DES POTERIES

RUE DE FONT-CHAUDE

RUE DROITE

RUE MERCERIE

RUE POTERIE

RUE CHAPUZIE

RUE GRAND-COUVERT

RUE BOURG-REYNAUD

RUE BASSE-DES-REMPARTS

1
2

RUE NOTRE DAME

RUE DE LA COSTE

3 Tour de l'Horloge

PLACE DE L'HORLOGE

PLACE R. CASSIN

RUE DROITE

PLACE DU DR. ROBERT

Pte. de la Nière

PLACE DU TIVOLI

AVENUE P. ARÈNE

RUE POUSTERIE

PLACE BOURG-REYNAUD

C

RUE STE-CLAIRE

RUE DE RIEU

RUE DELEUZE

RUE PORTE SAUVE

RUE CHAPUZIE

RUE DES COMBES

RUE DE PROVENCE

Cathédrale Notre-Dame-des-Pommiers

Musée Terre et Temps

RESTAURANTS, CAFÉS & BARS	
Les Becs Fins	2
Brasserie des Arcades	5
La Citadelle	B
Grand Hôtel du Cours	D
Le Grand Salon	3
La Paix	1
Le Pizzaiollo	4

PLACE GEN. DE GAULLE

RUE DE LA MISSION

D

Les Tours

ALLÉE DE VERDUN

AVENUE MOULIN

AV DES ARCADES

AVENUE DE LA LIBÉRATION

Ancien Couvent

Gare Routière

4
5

AVENUE ALSACE-LORRAINE

AVENUE DES ARCADES

PLACE DE LA RÉPUBLIQUE

(i)

RUE STE-URSULE

ACCOMMODATION	
La Citadelle	B
Etap	A
Grand Hôtel du Cours	D
Tivoli	C

RUE DES MURIERS

N85

RUE DES CORDELIERS

0   100 m

Gare SNCF, Château-Arnoux & Manosque

Arrival, information and accommodation

From Sisteron's **gare SNCF** turn right and head along avenue de la Libération until you reach place de la République. Here you'll find the **gare routière**, post office and **tourist office** (Sept–June Mon–Sat 9am–noon & 2–5pm; July & Aug Mon–Sat 9am–7pm, Sun 10am–5pm; ☎04.92.61.36.50, ⓦwww.sisteron.fr), which can provide details of good walks and advise on **bike rental**. There's not a

▲ Sisteron from the citadel

huge choice of places to **stay**, but prices are reasonable. The well-equipped four-star **campsite**, *Les Prés-Hauts* (☎04.92.61.19.69, ⓦwww.camping-sisteron .com; €17 per tent; closed Nov–Feb), is 3km north of Sisteron off the D951.

Hotels

La Citadelle 126 rue Saunerie ☎04.92.61.13.51, ⓔlanouvellecitadelle@free.fr. Inexpensive option overlooking the river, with a restaurant and bar. ❷

Etap parc d'activités Sisteron-Nord ☎08.92.68.07.55, ⓦwww.etaphotel.com. Modern, well-equipped budget chain hotel, by the exit from the A51 autoroute 4km north of town. ❸

Grand Hôtel du Cours Allée de Verdun, ☎04.92.61.04.51, ⓦ www.hotel-lecours.com. Sisteron's best – and snootiest – option, right in the centre of town, with three-star comforts and a good restaurant. ❹

Tivoli 21 place du Tivoli ☎04.92.61.15.16, ⓦ www.hotel-tivoli.fr. Decent two-star hotel just off place de la République. Cheerful and good value. ❶

The Town

To do justice to the **citadel** (daily: July & Aug 9am–7.30pm; April & Oct to mid-Nov 9am–6pm; May 9am–6.30pm; June & Sept 9am–7pm; ☎92.61.27.57; €5.80), you could easily spend half a day scrambling from the highest ramparts to the lowest subterranean passage. There is a leaflet in English but no guides, just tape recordings in French attempting to re-create historic moments, such as Napoleon's march and the imprisonment in 1639 of Jan Kazimierz, the future king of Poland. Most of the extant defences were constructed after the Wars of Religion, and added to a century later by Vauban when Sisteron was a frontline fort against neighbouring Savoy. No traces remain of the first Ligurian fortification nor of its Roman successor, and the eleventh-century castle was destroyed in the mid-thirteenth century during a pogrom against the local Jewish population.

As you climb up to the fortress, there seems no end to the gateways, courtyards and other defences. The outcrop on which the fortress sits abruptly stops at the lookout post, **Guérite du Diable**, 500m above the narrow passage of the Durance, and affording the best views. On the other side of the ravine, the vertical folds of the **Rocher de la Baume** provide a favourite training ground for local mountaineers.

In the fortress grounds, a **festival** known as *Nuits de la Citadelle* takes place in late July and early August, with open-air concerts and performances of opera, drama and dance. There is also a **museum** with a room dedicated to Napoleon, and an exhibition about Vauban in the vertiginous late medieval chapel, **Notre-Dame-du-Château**, restored to its Gothic glory and given very beautiful subdued stained-glass windows in the 1970s.

Outside the citadel, perhaps the most striking features of Sisteron are the three huge **towers** which belonged to the ramparts, built around the expanding town in 1370. Though one still has its spiralling staircase, only ravens use them now. Beside them is the much older former **Cathédrale Notre-Dame-des-Pommiers**, whose strictly rectangular interior contrasts with its riot of stepped roofs and an octagonal gallery adjoining a square belfry topped by a pyramidal spire. The altarpiece incorporates a Mignard painting; other seventeenth-century works adorn the chapels.

At the rear of the cathedral, a former convent of the Visitandine order houses the **Musée Terre et Temps** (Tues–Sat 9.30am–noon & 2.30–6pm; closed mid-Nov to end Jan; €2.50), which charts the measurement of time from ancient sundials through calendars to the latest atomic clocks, in parallel with the measurement of geological time, though after the thrills of the citadel it's a bit dull. From the museum, you can follow a signposted route through the lower town, along narrow passages with steep steps that interconnect through vaulted archways, known here as **andrônes**. Houses on the downslope side of rue Saunerie, overlooking the river, often descend at the back a further three or four storeys to the lanes below. In the troubled days of 1568 (during the Wars of Religion) sixty lanterns were put in place to light the alleyways and deter conspiracies and plots; there's no such luxury today, and Old Sisteron can take on a spooky aspect at night. In the upper town, on the other side of rue Saunerie and rue Droite, the houses, like the citadel, follow the curves of the rock.

Place de l'Horloge, at the other end of rue Deleuze from the church, is the site for the Wednesday and Saturday **market**, where stalls congregate to sell sweet and savoury *fougasse*, lavender honey, nougat and almond-paste *calissons* that rival those from Aix. On the second Saturday of every month the market becomes a **fair**, and there are likely to be flocks of sheep and lambs, and cages of pigeons as well as stalls selling clothes and bric-a-brac.

Eating and drinking

Sisteron has no outstanding **restaurants**, though you can certainly have a filling meal at a reasonable price. The best nougat and *calissons* come from Canteperdrix on rue de Provence, which also runs *Le Grand Salon*, a *salon de thé* on place Paul Arène serving salads, cakes and ice creams. Sisteron is an early-to-bed, early-to-rise sort of town with little nightlife; the best bet for relaxed drinking is the *Brasserie des Arcades* on avenue des Arcades.

Restaurants

Les Becs Fins 16 rue Saunerie ℡04.92.61.12.04, Ⓦbecsfins.free.fr. Sisteron's best restaurant, with the likes of lamb with honey and rosemary or cassoulet of snails with champagne; menus €19–46. Closed Sun eve, & Mon in low season.

La Citadelle 126 rue Saunerie ℡04.92.61.13.51. Informal brasserie and bar with a €12 weekday lunchtime *formule* and a menu at €19.

Grand Hôtel du Cours Allée de Verdun ℡04.92.61.04.51. Copious meals in comfortable surroundings, including the renowned *gigot d'agneau de Sisteron*; the kitchen closes around 9.30pm.

La Paix 41 rue Saunerie ℡04.92.62.62.29. Good pizzas from €7, as well as a few more substantial dishes.

Le Pizzaiollo 2 av des Arcades ℡04.92.62.62.60. Friendly and informal, with big portions of pizza and salad plus a few local specialities including *pieds et paquets Sisteronnais*; pizzas from €8. Closed Sun lunch.

From the Durance to the Luberon

Bounded in the east by the valley of the Durance, to the north by the **Montagne de Lure** and shading to the south and west into the **Parc Naturel Régional du Luberon** (see box, p.192), the **Pays de Forcalquier** is a beguiling mix of agrarian plenty and scenic beauty, with honey, fruit aperitifs, olive oil and cheese to savour and clear skies and pure air to enjoy. It's a region far removed from urban centres, and even the venerable capital, **Forcalquier**, has a sleepy, rural feel to it. The countryside, gentle enough around Forcalquier and the neighbouring village of **Mane**, becomes progressively wilder towards the Plateau d'Albion in the west. Here, remote villages such as **Simiane-la-Rotonde** and **Banon** have a particular charm, not yet as smart as the villages of the Luberon but easily their equal for beauty and history. It's in the more northerly villages of the Pays de Forcalquier, including Banon, that you're likely to hear Provençal being spoken and see aspects of rural life that have hardly changed over centuries. It was in a tiny place, on the Lure foothills due north of Banon called Le Contadour, that Jean Giono (see p.178) set up his summer commune in the 1930s to expostulate the themes of peace, ecology and the return to nature. But it's not all bucolic and timeless, for the pristine atmospheric conditions have also attracted the attentions of astronomers, whose **Observatoire de Haute-Provence** sits in splendid isolation close to the village of **St-Michel-l'Observatoire**.

Forcalquier

Mellow **FORCALQUIER**, 11km west of the Durance on the D12, dominates the surrounding countryside, its distinctive hilly outline visible for many kilometres around. Close up, the glories of the little town's history are there for all to see, and consequently Forcalquier is as appealing as anything in the gentle, hilly countryside that surrounds it. The town is at its most animated on Mondays, when the **market** takes place.

Arrival, information and accommodation

Buses drop you off at place Martial Sicard, one block back from the main place du Bourguet, where you'll find the **tourist office** at no. 13 (mid-June to mid-Sept Mon–Sat 9am–12.30pm & 2.30–6.30pm, Sun 10am–noon; mid-Sept to mid-June Mon–Sat 9am–noon & 2–6pm; ☎04.92.75.10.02, ⓦwww.forcalquier.com). You can **rent bikes** from Forcalquier Moto Cycles on boulevard de la République (☎04.92.75.12.47).

The best place **to stay** is the attractive *Auberge Charembeau* (☎04.92.70.91.70, ⓦwww.charembeau.com; closed mid-Nov to Feb; ❹), 2km out of town at the end of a long drive signed off the road to Niozelles. *Le Colombier* (☎04.92.75.03.71, ⓦwww.lecolombier.fr; ❹) is another pleasant countryside retreat, 3km south of Forcalquier off the D16. In town, the inexpensive *Grand Hôtel*, 10 boulevard Latourette (☎04.92.75.00.35, Ⓔg.hotel@wanadoo.fr; ❷), has soundproofed rooms at the foot of the Vieille Ville. The three-star *Camping Indigo* (☎04.92.75.27.94, ⓦwww.camping-indigo.com; €19.60 per tent; closed mid-Oct to early April) is 500m out of town on the road to Sigonce, past the cemetery; it also rents out mobile homes.

The Town

Despite its slumbering air, Forcalquier was once a place of some significance, as its **public buildings** and the elaborate architectural details of its Vieille Ville betray. In the twelfth century the counts of Forcalquier rivalled those of Provence, with dominions spreading south and east to the Durance and north to the Drôme. Gap, Embrun, Sisteron, Manosque and Apt were all ruled from the **citadel** of Forcalquier, which even minted its own currency. When this separate power base came to an end, Forcalquier was still renowned as the *Cité des Quatre Reines*, since the four daughters of Raimond Béranger V, who united Forcalquier and Provence, all married kings. One of them, Eleanor, married Henry III of England, a fact commemorated by a modern plaque on the Gothic fountain of place du Bourguet.

Not much remains of the ancient citadel at the summit of the rounded, wooded hill that dominates the town, though the view is worth the steep climb from the Vieille Ville. Beside the ruins of a tower, sole vestige of the counts of Forcalquier's castle, and the half-buried walls of the original cathedral, stands a neo-Byzantine nineteenth-century chapel, **Notre-Dame-de-Provence**, visible for many kilometres from the surrounding countryside.

Looming over the central place du Bourguet, the former **Cathédrale Notre-Dame** has an asymmetric and defensive exterior, a finely wrought Gothic porch and a Romanesque nave. Behind the cathedral, the houses of the **Vieille Ville** date from the thirteenth to the eighteenth century. From place Vieille or rue Mercière you can bear right for place St-Michel and the ancient street-fronts of Grande Rue, rue Béranger, place du Palais and rue du Collège. Place St-Michel has another fountain, whose decorative figures are embroiled in activities currently banned under biblical sanction in half the states of the USA.

At the top and to the left of rue Passère, south from place Vieille, you reach montée St-Mari, which leads up to the citadel. East of place Vieille on rue des

Cordeliers, the old **synagogue** marks the site of the former Jewish quarter; just beyond it is the one remaining gateway to the Vieille Ville, the Porte des Cordeliers. The superior power of the Roman Catholic Church is represented by the **Couvent des Cordeliers** at the end of boulevard des Martyrs. Built between the twelfth and fourteenth centuries, it bears the scars of wars and revolutions but preserves a beautifully vaulted scriptorium and a library with its original wooden ceiling, though sadly the interior is not open to the public.

Eating and drinking

Place du Bourguet has a few decent places to **eat**: the *Deux Lions* (☏04.92.75.25.30; closed evenings Sun & Tues, plus Wed) offers traditional fare, with menus from €23, while *L'Estable*, in impasse Louis Andrieux at the back of *Le Commerce* (☏04.92.75.39.82), serves Provençal cuisine with menus starting at €23. In the Vieille Ville, *L'Aïgo Blanco*, 5 place Vieille (☏04.92.75.27.23), is a classy restaurant and *salon de thé* with a wonderfully shady terrace and a €17 lunch menu.

Another product of the town, based on fruits and nuts from further south, is **exotic alcohol**. The Distillerie et Domaines de Provence has its shop on avenue St-Promasse (just down from the tourist office), where you can buy cherries, pears and mixes of different fruits and nuts pickled in liqueur. For leisurely **drinking**, the *Brasserie La Fontaine* on place St-Michel is a friendly locals' watering hole, or there's the very central *Café L'Hôtel de Ville*, on place du Bourguet.

Mane

The village of **MANE**, 4km south of Forcalquier at the junction of the roads from Apt and Manosque, still has its feudal citadel – now a private residence and closed to the public – and Renaissance churches, chapels and mansions remarkably intact. The most impressive building is a former Benedictine priory, **Notre-Dame-de-Salagon** (Feb–April & Oct daily 2–5pm; May & Sept daily 10am–12.30pm & 2–6.30pm; June–Aug daily 10am–7.30pm; Nov–Dec Sun only 2–5pm; €6 with audioguide April–Oct, €4 in winter), half a kilometre out of Mane off the Apt road. The fortified twelfth-century Romanesque church shows traces of fourteenth-century frescoes and sculpted scenes of rural life. Archeological digs in the choir have revealed the remnants of an earlier, sixth-century church. In addition to the church, the complex comprises fifteenth-century monks' quarters, seventeenth-century stables and a smithy, which is used to display traditional farm tools; there's also an exhibition about lavender. The **gardens**, one of aromatic plants, another of medicinal plants, and a third cultivated as the medieval monks would have used it, have been re-created to illustrate the way in which the monks used the land; the priory is also the venue for various exhibitions, seminars and discussions.

Further along the Apt road, past a medieval bridge over the River Laye, you come to a palatial residence that has been called the Trianon of Provence. The pure eighteenth-century ease and luxury of the **Château de Sauvan** (guided tours at 3.30pm: Feb–March Sun; April–June & Sept to mid-Nov Thurs, Sat, Sun & hols; July & Aug daily except Sat; €7.50) come as a surprise in this harsh territory, leagues from any courtly city. Though there are hundreds of mansions like it around Paris and along the Loire, the residences of the rich and powerful in Haute Provence tend towards the moat and dungeon, not to French windows giving onto lawns and lake. The furnishings are grand and the hall and stairway would take some beating for light and spaciousness, but what's best is the setting: the swans and geese on the square lake, the peacocks strutting by the drive, and the views back to the aristocratic house itself.

L'Observatoire de Haute-Provence

The tourist literature promoting the pure air of Haute Provence is not just hype. Proof of the fact is the National Centre for Scientific Research **observatory** on the wooded slopes 2.5km north of the village of St-Michel-l'Observatoire, southwest of Mane, sited here because it has the fewest clouds, the least fog and the lowest industrial pollution in all France. Visible from many kilometres around, it presents a peculiar picture of domes of gleaming white mega-mushrooms pushing up between the oaks. It's open for **guided tours** (July & Aug Tues, Wed & Thurs 1.30–4.30pm; spring & autumn Wed 2–4pm; closed Nov to early April; €4.50), in which you get to see some telescopes and blank monitors, and the mechanism that opens up the domes and aims the lens. More exciting, however, are the night-time sky-watching vigils at the associated **Centre d'Astronomie**, just east of St-Michel-l'Observatoire (9pm: July & Aug Tues–Fri; Sept Tues–Thurs; Oct–May monthly; €9.75; ⓦ www.centre-astro.fr).

Banon

The houses of the tiny Haute Ville of **BANON**, 25km northwest of Forcalquier on the D950, form a guarding wall. Within the impressive fourteenth-century fortified gate, the **Portail à Machicoulis**, the bustle of the modern village below disappears and all is peaceful and immaculate; the houses of the rue des Arcades arch across the roadway and the village peters out just beyond the former chapel of the château at the top of the slope, with only a few stretches of ruined masonry beyond.

Banon is famous above all for its **cheese**. The *plateau des fromages* of any half-decent Provence restaurant will include a round goat's cheese marinated in brandy and wrapped in sweet chestnut leaves, but there's nothing like tasting different ages of the untravelled cheese, sliced off for you by the *fromager* at a market stall on place de la République. As well as ensuring that you taste the very young and the well-matured varieties, they may give you an accompaniment in the form of a sprig of *savory*, an aromatic local plant of the mint family.

Accommodation options in Banon are limited, as there's no hotel. You could enquire about *chambres d'hôtes* at the **Point d'Information** on place de la République (Mon 2.30–5pm, Tues–Wed 9.30am–12.30pm & 2–5pm, Thurs until 5.30pm, Fri & Sat until 6pm, Sun 9am–12.30pm; ☎04.92.72.19.40, ⓦ www.village-banon.fr). Otherwise there's a **campsite**, *L'Épi Bleu*, just outside the village (☎04.92.73.30.30, ⓦ www.campingepibleu.com; €16 per tent; closed Oct–March), with a pool and organized children's activities. For meals or snacks, there's the *Bar-Restaurant Les Voyageurs*, the *Café de France* on the main street, or *La Braserade* pizzeria close by.

The Montagne de Lure

Roads north of Banon peter out at the lower slopes of the **Montagne de Lure**. To reach the summit of the Lure, by road or the GR6, you have to head east to **St-Étienne-les-Orgues**, 12km north of Forcalquier. The footpath avoids the snaking road for most of the way, but you're walking through relentless pine plantation and it's a long way without a change of scenery (about 15km). Just below the summit you'll see the **ski lifts**.

When the trees stop you find yourself on sharp stones without a single softening blade of grass. The summit itself is a mass of telecommunications aerials and dishes; a grimmer high-perched desert would be hard to find. That said, the point of the climb is that the Lure has no close neighbours, giving you 360 degrees of mountainscape, as if you were airborne. The view of the distant snowy peaks to the north is the best; those with excessive stamina can keep walking towards them along the GR6 to Sisteron. If you feel like lingering in the area, you could **stay** in the appealing little village of **CRUIS**, 5km northeast of St-Étienne-les-Orgues, at the *Auberge de l'Abbaye* (℡04.92.77.01.93; ❸), with a well-regarded restaurant serving refined creations using local produce on its €45 menu.

Simiane-la-Rotonde

The spiralling cone of **SIMIANE-LA-ROTONDE**, 9.5km southwest of Banon on the D51, marks the horizon with an emphasis greater than its size would warrant. However many *villages de caractère* (Simiane's official classification) you may have seen, this is one to re-seduce you, though it is gradually acquiring the same patina of metropolitan chic as the Luberon villages to the west.

The modern village and much of the commerce – what there is of it – lies in the plain by the D51, cleanly separated from the old village's winding streets of honey-coloured stone in which each house is part of the medieval defensive system. The zigzags end at the **Rotonde** (March, April & Sept to early Nov Wed–Mon 1.30–6pm; May & Aug daily 10.30am–1pm & 1.30–7pm; €4), a large domed building that was once the chapel of the castle but looks more like a keep. Nineteenth-century restoration work added smooth limestone to its rough-hewn fortress stones, but the peculiar feature is the asymmetry between its interior and exterior, being hexagonal on the outside and irregularly dodecagonal on the inside. The set of the stones on the domes is wonderfully wonky and no one knows what once hung from or covered the hole at the top. In August the Rotonde is a venue for the annual international **festival of ancient music** (Ⓦwww.festival-simiane.com).

Beyond the Rotonde there's a path to the chapel of **Notre-Dame-de-Pieté**, which stands amongst old windmills. As you head back down through the village you pass all sorts of eye-catching architectural details: heavy carved doors with stone lintels in exact proportion, wrought-iron street lamps, the scrolling on the dark wooden shutters of the building opposite the covered hall of the **old market**, Simiane's most stunning building. With its columns framing open sky, the hall almost overhangs the hillside on the steepest section of the village; no longer used as a marketplace, it's now occupied by café tables.

Practicalities

Tourism is not Simiane's main preoccupation, but it does have a **tourist office**, housed in the Rotonde (same hours; ℡04.92.73.11.34, Ⓦwww.simiane-la-rotonde.fr). There's only one simple **hotel**, the *Auberge du Faubourg* (℡04.92.75.92.43; ❷), with just eight rooms. There are, however, several **gîtes** and **chambres d'hôtes** in and around Simiane, including *Le Chaloux*, (℡04.92.75.99.13, Ⓦwww.gite-chaloux.com; ❸), off the D51 about 3km south of the village, and right on the GR4 footpath. There's also a two-star **campsite**, *Camping de Valsaintes*, on the main road (℡04.92.75.91.46; closed late Oct to March). Simiane isn't richly endowed with places to **eat** or **drink**: there's a bar-tabac, *Le Chapeau Rouge*, and a *salon de thé*, *Aux Plaisir des Yeux*, where you can also buy honey, liqueurs and *crème de marrons*.

The Luberon

The great fold of rock of the Luberon runs for fifty-odd kilometres between the Coulon and the Durance valleys, and sits at the heart of the **Parc Naturel Régional du Luberon**. The massif is divided by the **Combe de Lourmarin**, a narrow gorge through which a lone metalled road gives access south to Cadenet and Aix. The **Grand Luberon** is the portion of the massif to the east of the Combe de Lourmarin, while the **Petit Luberon** is the section to the west. Though many forestry tracks cross the ridge, they are barred to cars (and too rough for bikes), and where the ridge isn't forested it opens into tableland pastures where sheep graze in summer. The northern slopes have Alpine rather than Mediterranean leanings: the trees are oak, beech and maple, and cowslips and buttercups announce the summer. But it is still very hot and there are plenty of vines on the lower slopes. North of the massifs, the lively market town of **Apt** is the chief urban centre of the Luberon: close to it the remnants of ochre extraction have created the extraordinary **Colorado Provençal**, the vibrant orange-red landscapes of **Roussillon** and the dramatic subterranean spaces of the **Mines de Bruoux**. The most beguiling of the Luberon's **villages** stand on high ground overlooking the vale of the Calavon: **Saignon**, **Bonnieux**, **Lacoste**, **Ménerbes** and, to the north, **Gordes**. Equally beguiling – and mysterious – are the ruined villages of **Buoux** and **Oppède-le-Vieux**.

The Colorado Provençal and the Grand Luberon

RUSTREL, 13km southwest of Simiane-la-Rotonde, is a sweet little village with a small and welcoming **hotel**, the *Auberge de Rustréou*, 3 place de la Fête (T04.90.04.90.90, F04.90.04.98.06; ❸), and a convivial **bar**, *Les Platanes* (T04.90.75.63.96), which serves good beers and has live music most Friday nights. It is also home to a series of dramatic ochre quarries, known as the **Colorado Provençal** (daily: May–June 9am–6pm; July & Aug 8am–6pm; parking and admission €4, guided tours €6), signed off the D22 towards Gignac. The track round the quarries begins at the car park entrance. Having passed the remains of old settling tanks that look like unearthed foundations and a small ruined building, take the track on the right marked with white. The full, circular, route takes about an hour and a half to walk, and the **map** they provide you with at the car park will prove useful, as the route can be quite hard to follow – particularly when the stream meanders onto the creamy ochre sand of the path. Persevere and you will end up in an amphitheatre of coffee, vanilla and strawberry ice-cream-coloured rock, whipped into pinnacles and curving walls. If you continue up above a little waterfall, you can turn left, then left again onto a wider path, which soon brings you to the gods' seats over the quarry. Continue and you'll end up on the same route leading back to the settling tanks.

Saignon

Fourteen kilometres south of Rustrel, **SAIGNON** is 4km from Apt but sits high enough to have an eagle-eye view not just of the town, but of the whole region. From below, the village rises like an immense fort with natural turrets of rock; on closer inspection it has an almost troglodyte charm, its houses – some exquisitely

The Couleur Pass Luberon

Sixteen of the Luberon's major tourist attractions can be visited at reduced rates with the Couleur Pass Luberon, which costs €5 and offers discounts of up to fifty percent on admission fees. It's sold through participating attractions and tourist information offices throughout the region.

restored, others still in a crumbly state – set among the rocky outcrops on which the village's castle once stood. The very best of the views are from the pulpit-like **Rocher de Bellevue** at the far end of the village. The panorama here is almost 360 degrees; given the exposed, windy vantage point, the experience is properly breathtaking, but bear in mind that the steps to the top are a little uneven.

There's a pleasant **hotel** in the centre of the village, the *Auberge du Presbytère*, place de la Fontaine (☎04.90.74.11.50, ⓦwww.auberge-presbytere.com; ❸–❼), with pretty and individually styled rooms, some with beams.

Fort de Buoux

From Saignon the D232 heads 5.5km west towards the D113 and the village of **Buoux**, from where a minor road leads the short distance to the fortified, abandoned hilltop village known as the **Fort de Buoux** (daily sunrise till sunset; €3). It stands on the northern flank of the Grand Luberon massif, overlooking a canyon forged by the once powerful River Aiguebrun at the start of its passage through the Luberon. To reach the fort follow the road signed off the D113 to the gateway at the end, beyond which it's a 400-metre uphill walk to the entrance.

Numerous relics of prehistoric life have been found in the Buoux Valley, and in the earliest Christian days anchorite monks survived against all odds in tiny caves and niches in the vertical cliff face. In the 1660s, Fort de Buoux was demolished by command of Richelieu for being a centre of Protestantism, but the ruins – including cisterns, storage cellars with thick stone lids, arrow-slitted ramparts, the lower half of a Romanesque chapel and a near-intact keep – give a good impression of life here over the centuries. Today, the spot is popular with **climbers**, many of whom can be seen clinging to the cliff face as you approach the fort.

Back at the junction with the D113, a left turn takes you past the slender Romanesque tower of the former Prieuré de St-Symphorien to the Lourmarin road, while a right turn leads up to the present-day village of **BUOUX** (the "x", by the way, is pronounced). Just outside it, the *Auberge de la Loube* **restaurant** (☎04.90.74.19.58; no credit cards; closed Sun eve, Mon & Thurs) has a considerable local reputation: some say it's pretentious and overpriced, others that it's *génial* and serves delicious food. Judge for yourself with the midday €23 menu. For **accommodation** try the *Auberge des Seguins* (☎04.90.74.16.37, ⓦwww.aubergedesseguins.com; *demi-pension* or full *pension* only; ❺; closed mid-Nov to March), tucked away in the spectacular canyon not far from the Fort de Buoux.

Apt and around

The main settlement in the Luberon, **APT** lies northeast of the Combe de Lourmarin, nestling beneath the northern slopes of the Grand Luberon on the banks of the River Coulon. Best known for its crystallized fruit and preserves, Apt, like so many of the surrounding villages, is gentrifying rapidly as foreigners and wealthy Parisians move in. For now, though, the balance between timeless market town and newly fashionable urban oasis is about right, and Apt is a likeable and bustling little place with one of the oldest cathedrals in Provence, excellent shops and a lively Saturday **market**. In July *Les Tréteaux de Nuit* **festival** provides a choice of shows with concerts, plays, café-theatre and exhibitions. If you have your own transport, Apt also makes a good base for visiting the ochre mine at **Bruoux** and the famous ochre village of **Roussillon**.

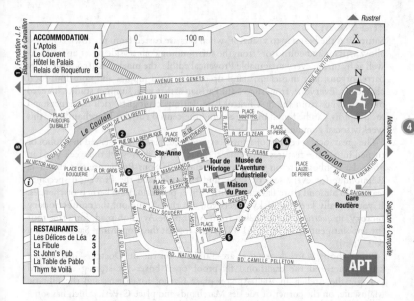

Arrival, information and accommodation

Buses drop you off either at the focal **place de la Bouquerie** or at the **gare routière** (℡04.90.74.20.21) on avenue de la Libération at the eastern end of the town. The **tourist office** is at 20 avenue Philippe-de-Girard (July & Aug Mon–Sat 9am–7pm, Sun 9.30am–12.30pm; May–June & Sept Mon–Sat 9.30am–12.30pm & 2.30–6.30pm, Sun 9.30am–12.30pm; Oct–April Mon–Sat 9.30am–12.30pm & 2.30–6.30pm; ℡04.90.74.03.18, Ⓦwww.luberon-apt.fr), just to your left as you face the river from place de la Bouquerie. Arriving by **car**, you can park either along the river or to the east of the town centre. You can **rent bikes** from Luberon Cycles, 86 quai Général-Leclerc (℡04.90.74.17.16), or Extrem Bike, 422 avenue Victor Hugo (℡04.90.74.61.66). Infotelec, at 44 quai de la Liberté, has **internet** access.

There's a reasonable choice of **accommodation** in and around Apt; hotels in the town are less likely to be booked up here than in the more scenic hilltop villages.

Hotels

L'Aptois 289 cours Lauze de Perret ℡04.90.74.02.02, Ⓦwww.aptois.fr. Overlooking place Lauze de Perret and the Saturday market, this clean, basic hotel is reasonably priced and cyclist-friendly. ❶

Le Couvent 36 rue Louis-Rousset ℡04.90.04.55.36, Ⓦwww.loucouvent.com. Stylish *maison d'hôtes* in a seventeenth-century convent in the centre of the town, with simple, spacious rooms. ❹

Hôtel le Palais 24 bis place Gabriel-Péri ℡04.90.04.89.32, Ⓔhotel-le-palais@wanadoo.fr. Inexpensive option bang in the centre of town, above a rather uninspired pizzeria. Closed mid-Nov to mid-March. ❸

Relais de Roquefure Le Chêne, 6km from Apt on the D900 towards Avignon ℡04.90.04.88.88, Ⓦwww .relaisderoquefure.com. A large, renovated country house with a pool, and ochre-tinted rooms with en-suite bathrooms. Closed late Dec to late Jan. ❺

Campsites

Camping les Cèdres av de Viton ℡04.90.74.14.61, Ⓦwww.camping-les-cedres.fr. A two-star site within easy walking distance of the town, across the bridge from place St-Pierre. €14.50 per tent. Closed mid-Nov to Feb.

Camping le Luberon rte de Saignon ℡04.90.04.85.40, Ⓦwww.camping-le-luberon .com. Three-star site, less than 2km from town, with swimming pool, restaurant and disabled facilities. €23 per tent. Closed Oct–March.

The Town

Saturday is the best day to visit Apt, when cars are barred from the town centre to allow artisans and cultivators from the surrounding countryside to set up stalls. As well as featuring every imaginable Provençal edible, the **market** is accompanied by barrel organs, jazz musicians, stand-up comics, aged hippies and notorious local characters. Everyone, from successful Parisian artists with summer studios here, to military types from the St-Christol base, serious ecologists, rich foreigners and local Aptois, can be found milling around the central **rue des Marchands** for this weekly social commerce.

The great local speciality of fruits – crystallized, pickled, preserved in alcohol or turned into jam – features at the market, but during the rest of the week you can go to La Bonbonnière on the corner of rue de la Sous-Préfecture and rue de la République for every sort of sweet and chocolate and the Provençal speciality *tourron*, an almond paste flavoured with coffee, pistachio, pine kernels or cherries. If you're really keen on sticky sweets you can ring Aptunion, the **confectionery factory**, in *quartier* Salignan, 2km from Apt on the Avignon road, for a free tour (by appointment; ℡ 04.90.76.61.43) or just to visit the shop (Mon–Sat 9am–noon & 2–7pm).

Other **shops** worth looking at are Tamisier, on rue du Docteur-Gros, selling kitchenware and the traditional fly-proof open boxes for storing cheese and sausage; the Atelier du Vieil Apt on place Carnot for *faïence*; and the Librarie Majuscule, on the corner of rue des Marchands and place G-Péri, which has some English books for sale.

While window-shopping along rue des Marchands, you'll see the **Tour de L'Horloge** (bell tower) spanning the street, and the **Cathédrale de Ste-Anne** (Mon–Fri 9am–noon & 2.30–6pm, Sun 2.30–6pm), one of the oldest cathedrals in Provence – not the most coherent architecturally, but an agreeable enough mishmash of styles. The oldest parts of the cathedral include a beautiful fourth-century carved stone ceiling in the *crypte inferieure*; elsewhere slabs dating from the eighth and ninth centuries were reused in the twelfth. The cathedral's chief relic is a veil said to have belonged to St Anne herself.

Elsewhere in town, Apt's industrial heritage is the subject of the **Musée de l'Aventure Industrielle**, 14 place du Postel (June–Sept Mon & Wed–Sat 10am–noon & 3–6.30pm, Sun 3–7pm; Oct–May Mon & Wed–Sat 10am–noon & 2–5.30pm; €4), laid out over three floors and covering the major industries of the town and surrounding area: ochre, candied fruits and the production of fine *faïence*. Exhibits include the re-creation of a potter's studio, plus works by the sculptor Alexis Poitevin, who was inspired by industrial themes. The adjacent **Atelier d'Art Fernand Bourgeois** (Mon & Wed–Sat 2–5.30pm; free) is the occasional venue for temporary art exhibitions.

The industrial district of les Bourguignons to the west of the town is the unlikely setting for the **Fondation J.P. Blachère** (Tues–Sun 2–6.30pm; free or €3

Parc Naturel Régional du Luberon

The **Parc Naturel Régional du Luberon** is administered by the Maison du Parc in Apt at 60 place Jean-Jaurès (Mon–Fri 8.30am–noon & 1.30–6pm; April–Aug also Sat 8.30am–noon; ℡ 04.90.04.42.00, ⊛ www.parcduluberon.fr). It's a centre of activity with laudable aims – nature conservation and the provision of environmentally friendly tourist facilities – though many people have misgivings about the practicalities of the project. Be that as it may, the Maison du Parc is the place to go for information about the fauna and flora of the Luberon, footpaths, cycle routes, pony-trekking, gîtes and campsites.

during summer exhibition), 384 avenue des Argiles, which stages two or three exhibitions each year devoted to contemporary African sculpture and painting.

Eating and drinking
Apt is big enough to have a reasonable choice of **restaurants**, though it's worth travelling out of town for some of the more ambitious options. The best places for a **drink** are the brasseries on place de la Bouquerie, or *St John's Pub* on place St-Pierre, a good option for leisurely drinking.

Restaurants
Les Délices de Léa 87 rue de la République ☎04.90.74.32.77. Inventive cooking in pretty, simple surroundings in Apt's Vieille Ville, with the likes of prawns flambéed with anis and lamb tagine with prunes; €16.90 lunch menu, *plats* €10.50.
La Fibule 132 rue de la République ☎04.90.04.08.82. Moroccan restaurant with decent couscous from €12.
La Table de Pablo Petits Cléments ☎04.90.75.45.18, ⊛www.latabledepablo.com. It's

worth making the trek north of Apt to this restaurant close to the village of Villars for dishes such as veal tartare with coriander and vegetable mille-feuille or confit lamb with rosemary and courgettes. Menus at €16, €28 and €39. Closed all day Wed, & lunch Thurs & Sat.
Thym te Voilà 59 place St-Martin ☎04.90.74.28.25. Hip, relaxed restaurant with a chalked-up *carte* of international dishes, from chilli con carne to lasagne with courgettes and pesto. €19 two courses, €23 for three. Closed Sun & Mon, and eves Tues & Wed.

The Mines de Bruoux
The newest of the Luberon's ochre-related sites opened to the public is the extraordinary ochre mine of **Bruoux** at Gargas, north of Apt on the route de Croagne (daily: July & Aug 10am–8pm; May, June & Sept to mid-Oct 10am–7pm; mid-March to April & mid-Oct to mid-Nov 10am–1pm & 2–6pm; €7.50).The redundant mine is entered via a bright orange cliff face into which a number of tall, arched entrances have been cut. These lead to a forty kilometre network of subterranean passageways, 15m high in places. The 45-minute guided tour takes you 650m underground, which is enough to give you a good impression of the strong colour, eerie atmosphere and strikingly beautiful, monumental form of the tunnels – altogether more reminiscent of the temple of some lost civilization than of a workaday place of mineral extraction.

Roussillon
Perched precariously atop soft-rock cliffs 10km northwest of Apt, the buildings of **ROUSSILLON** radiate all the different shades of the seventeen ochre tints once quarried here. A spiralling main street leads past potteries, antique shops and restaurants up to the top of the village, and it's worth the effort of walking up for the views over the Luberon and Ventoux. Just outside Roussillon, on the Apt road, an old **ochre factory** has been renovated as the **Conservatoire des Ocres** (daily 9am–6pm). You can look round the various washing, draining, settling and drying areas, though you probably won't get much out of a visit without joining a guided tour (daily 11am, 3pm & 4pm; English tours on request; €6). It also hosts excellent exhibitions on themes related to the use and production of ochre, with accompanying workshops for both adults and children. The **ochre quarries** themselves are close to the centre of the village and can be visited on the **Sentier des Ocres** (daily: March & Nov 9am–5pm; April–June & Sept–Oct 9am–5.30pm; July & Aug 9am–7.30pm; €2.50).

Roussillon's tourist office is on **place de la Poste** (Mon–Sat 10am–noon & 1.30–5pm, longer hours in high season; ☎04.90.05.60.25, ⊛www.roussillon -provence.com). If you need somewhere to stay, the *Rêves d'Ocres* **hotel**, on route

Ochre quarrying has been practised in the Vaucluse since prehistoric times, producing the natural dye that gives a range of colours (which don't fade in sunlight) from pale yellow to a blood red. By the nineteenth century the business had really taken off, with first donkeys and (by the 1880s) trains carrying truckloads of the dust to Marseille to be shipped round the world. At its peak in 1929, 40,000 tonnes of ochre were exported from the region. Twenty years later it was down to 11,500 tonnes, and in 1958 production at Roussillon was finally stopped, in part because the foundations of village were being undermined. Production continues at Gargas, east of Roussillon.

de Gordes (☎04.90.05.60.50, ⓦwww.hotel-revesdocres.com; ❹; closed mid-Nov to Feb), is warm, welcoming and has some rooms with good views of the Luberon. There's also a very pleasant two-star **campsite**, *Camping L'Arc en Ciel*, in pine woods 2km along the D104 to Goult (☎04.90.05.73.96, ⓔcampingarcenciel @wanadoo.fr; €13 per tent; closed Nov to mid-March). For **meals**, try *La Treille*, 1 rue du Four (☎04.90.05.64.47), which serves tagines and pasta with menus at €13 and €26, or you can get a crêpe at *La Gourmandine* on place l'Abbé-Avon.

Gordes and around

GORDES, west of Roussillon and 6km north of the main Apt–Avignon road (but only as the crow flies), tumbles to spectacular effect down a steep hillside to create one of the most photographed views in all Provence. The village is popular with film directors, media personalities, musicians and painters, many of whom have added a Gordes address to their main Paris residence. As a result, the place is full of expensive restaurants, cafés and art and craft shops.

There are good reasons for its popularity with the rich and famous. The approach at sunset is particularly memorable as the ancient stone turns gold. In addition, in the vicinity, you can see a superb array of dry-stone architecture in **Village des Bories**, as well as the **Abbaye de Sénanque**, and a couple of museums dedicated to glass and olive oil. There's also a festival, **Les Soirées d'Été de Gordes**, in the first two weeks of August when the village is awash with theatrical performances, jazz and world music.

The village

In the past, near-vertical staircases hewn into the rock gave the only access to the summit of the village, where the church and houses surround a twelfth- to sixteenth-century **castle** with few aesthetic concessions to the business of fortification. By the early twentieth century most of Gordes' villagers had abandoned the old defensive site and it was in ruins. A centre of resistance during World War II, Gordes was rediscovered by artists, including Chagall and the Hungarian scientist of art and design, Victor Vasarely.

Vasarely undertook the restoration of the castle and, in 1970, opened his Didactic Museum in the Renaissance interior. On his death in 1995, the collection was reclaimed by his family and the space devoted to the very different and less accessible **Musée Pol Mara** (daily 10am–noon & 2–6pm; €4). The career of the Belgian artist, also seduced by the beauty of Gordes, moves from Post-Expressionism to Pop Art with one dominant theme – the female body.

Practicalities

Gordes does not lie on any major public transport routes and it's likely you'll arrive under your own steam. Infrequent **buses** connecting it with Cavaillon, 16km to the west, arrive at place du Château. Gordes' helpful **tourist office**, in the Salle des Gardes of the castle (Mon–Sat 9am–noon & 2–6pm, Sun 10am–noon & 2–6pm; ℡04.90.72.02.75, Ⓦwww.gordes-village.com), has lists of accommodation and details of local events. One of the best-value **hotels** in the village is the reasonably priced *Le Provençal*, on place du Château (℡04.90.72.10.01, Ⓦwww.le-provencal .fr; ❹), with just seven rooms. Overlooking the village on the route de Sénanque, the old country house *Les Romarins* (℡04.90.72.12.13; Ⓦwww.hoteldesromarins .com; ❼) has comfortable, traditionally styled rooms and a pool. The most luxurious option in the village is *La Bastide de Gordes* (℡04.90.72.12.12, Ⓦwww .bastide-de-gordes.com; ❾), with spacious, elegant rooms and stunning views over the Luberon from its pool and terrace. Halfway between Gordes and Murs on the D15 is a very pleasant two-star **campsite**, *Camping des Sources* (℡04.90.72.12.48, Ⓦwww.campingdessources.com; €20 per night; closed Oct–March); early booking is advisable.

Five kilometres south of Gordes in Les Imberts, *Le Mas Tourteron*, chemin de St-Blaise (℡04.90.72.00.16; menu €62; closed Nov–Feb & Mon & Tues, eves only Wed–Sat, lunch only Sun), is an excellent and pretty **restaurant** where you can eat gorgeous Provençal specialities in a shaded garden. Opposite the château in Gordes itself, *L'Artégal* (℡04.90.72.02.54; closed Tues eve & Wed out of season; menu €35; closed Jan to mid-March) offers the likes of tomato & confit onion tarte with *chèvre* or roast sea bass with herbs, while *Le Jardin*, on route de Murs (℡04.90.72.12.34; closed Mon out of season), is a gay-friendly café-gallery with a pretty terrace and salads.

Village des Bories

About 4km east of Gordes, signed off the D2 to Cavaillon, is an unusual rural agglomeration, the **Village des Bories** (daily 9am–sunset; €6). This walled enclosure contains dry-stone houses, barns, bread ovens, wine stores and workshops constructed in a mix of unusual shapes: curving pyramids and cones, some rounded at the top, some truncated and the base almost rectangular or square. They are cleverly designed so that rain runs off their exteriors and the temperature inside remains constant whatever the season. To look at them, you might think they were prehistoric, and Neolithic rings and a hatchet have been found on the site, but most date from the eighteenth century and were inhabited until the early nineteenth century. Some may have been adapted from or rebuilt over earlier constructions, and there are extraordinary likenesses with huts and dwellings as far apart as the Orkneys and South Africa.

Abbaye de Sénanque

About 4km north of Gordes, **Abbaye de Sénanque** (guided tours only: Jan & mid-Nov to Dec two daily at 2.50pm & 4.20pm; Feb–March & Oct to mid-Nov four daily 10.30am–4.30pm; April, May & Sept 5 daily 10.10am–4.30pm; June seven daily 10.10am–4.30pm; July & Aug 11 daily 9.50am–4.30pm; closed Sun mornings and certain religious festivals; €7) is one of a trio of twelfth-century monasteries established by the Cistercian order in Provence, and predates both the *bories* and the castle. It stands alone, amid fields of lavender in a hollow of the hills, its weathered stone sighing with age and immutability. Though it has become one of the most familiar Provençal views, visitor numbers are tightly regulated and visitors are asked to dress modestly and to respect the silence to which the abbey is consecrated. The shop at the end of the visit sells the monks' produce, including liqueur, as well as honey and lavender essence.

From the abbey, the loop back to Gordes via the D177 and D15 reveals the northern Luberon in all its glory.

Les Bouilladoires

The area around Gordes was famous for its olive oil before severe frosts killed off many of the trees. A still-functioning Gallo-Roman press, made from a single slice of oak 2m in diameter, as well as ancient oil lamps, jars and soap-making equipment, can be seen at the **Moulin des Bouillons** (April–Oct daily except Tues 10am–noon & 2–6pm; €5) in **LES BOUILLADOIRES**, on the D148 just west of St-Pantaléon, 3.5km south of Gordes, and well signed from every junction. The ticket also gives admittance to the **Musée du Vitrail Frédérique Duran** (same hours), signalled by a huge and rather gross sculpture by Duran and housed in a semi-submerged bunker next to the Moulin. Duran's contemporary stained-glass creations are garish, but if you want to learn about the history of stained glass, you can, though perhaps the most attractive items are the strutting fowl and hedges of rosemary in the gardens outside.

Musée de la Lavande

If you've travelled through Provence in high summer you will have seen, smelled and probably tasted lavender. The **Musée de la Lavande** (daily: Feb, March, Nov & Dec 9am–12.15pm & 2–6pm; May–Sept 9am–7pm; April & Oct 9am–1pm & 2–6pm; €6), on the route de Gordes near the hamlet of Coustellet, offers a chance to learn more about lavender and its uses. Exhibits include copper stills dating back to the sixteenth century; there's a film show and free English-language audio guide, plus the inevitable shop. In July and August there are also daily demonstrations of outdoor distillation.

The Petit Luberon

The **Petit Luberon** has long been popular as a country escape for Parisians, Germans, the Dutch and the British – it was the setting for Peter Mayle's *A Year in Provence* – and *résidences secondaires* are everywhere. It remains a beguiling pastoral idyll, though these day's it's a rich man's retreat, its hilltop villages increasingly chic and its ruins, like **de Sade**'s **château** in **Lacoste** and the **Abbaye de St-Hilaire** near Bonnieux, being restored by their private owners.

Oppède-le-Vieux

OPPÈDE-LE-VIEUX, above the vines on the steeper slopes of the Petit Luberon, remains relatively free of the yuppie invasion, and ravishingly beautiful. There are a couple of cafés, the *Petit Café* on place de la Croix (T04.90.76.74.01, Wwww.petitcafe.fr; closed Wed eve & Thurs; rooms ❾) being the most pleasant, and a shop selling classy pottery. With its Renaissance gateway, the square in front of the ramparts suggests a monumental town within. But behind the line of restored sixteenth-century houses there are only the romantic, overgrown ruins that stretch up to the remains of the medieval **castle**; here and there isolated new homes have been crafted from restored fragments of the complex. Take care when exploring the ruins, as there are no fences or warning signs, steps break off above gaping holes, paths lead straight to precipitous edges and at the highest point of the castle you can sit on a 30cm-wide ledge with a drop of ten or more metres below you. The views at the very top are every bit as lovely as the castle itself.

Ménerbes

Heading east from Oppède-le-Vieux, **MÉNERBES** is the next hilltop village you come to. Shaped like a ship, its best site, on the prow as it were, is given over to the dead. From this cemetery you look down onto an odd jigsaw of fortified buildings and mansions, old and new. In the other direction houses with exquisitely tended terraces and gardens, all shuttered up outside holiday time, ascend to the mammoth wall of the citadel, now another *résidence secondaire*.

Outside Ménerbes, left off the D103 towards Beaumettes, is the wine-producing Domaine de la Citadelle's **Musée de Tire-Bouchon** (Museum of Corkscrews; April–Oct daily 10am–noon & 2–7pm; Nov–March Mon–Sat 9am–noon & 2–5pm; €4), housed in a château dating back to the seventeenth century. The intriguing collection includes a Cézar compression, a corkscrew combined with pistol and dagger, others with erotic themes and many with beautifully sculpted and engraved handles. You can also visit the wine cellars for a free tasting. Between Ménerbes and Lacoste, on the D109, is the **Abbaye de St-Hilaire** (daily: week before Easter to June 9am–7pm; July to Oct 9am–8pm; Dec 26 to New Year's Day 10am–6pm; €2), with its fine seventeenth-century cloisters, exquisite Renaissance stairway and ancient dovecotes, though it's currently undergoing restoration and parts of the abbey may be off limits.

If you're looking **to stay** in Ménerbes, there's the quiet and very agreeable *Hostellerie Le Roy Soleil* (℡04.90.72.25.61, ⓦwww.roy-soleil.com; ⑥), just outside the village on route des Baumettes, with a bistro (closed Oct–April) and a restaurant *gastronomique* (closed mid-Oct to mid-April). For cheap snacks and drinks head for the friendly *Café du Progrès*, featured in *A Year in Provence*, which has superb views over the surrounding countryside and a newsstand selling *The Financial Times*.

Lacoste

LACOSTE and its **château** can be seen from all the neighbouring villages, and are particularly enticing in moonlight, while a wind rocks the hanging lanterns on the narrow cobbled approaches to the château, and the castle itself is a floodlit beacon, visible from many kilometres around. Its most famous owner was the Marquis de Sade, who retreated here when the reaction to his writings got too hot, but in 1778, after seven years here, he was locked up in the Bastille and the castle destroyed soon after. Semi-derelict, it was bought by *couturier* Pierre Cardin in 2001 and greatly restored, and it now hosts a **festival** of music and theatre each year in July. These days you're as likely to hear American as French voices in Lacoste, since much of the village forms an outpost of the Savannah College of Art and Design.

For **accommodation**, there are eight rooms above the excellent *Café de France* (℡04.90.75.82.25; ❶), which also provides inexpensive sandwiches, quiches and pizzas; the alternative pit stop is the pretty *Café de Sade*. **Market** day is Tuesday.

Bonnieux and around

From the *terrasse* by the old church on the heights of the steep village of **BONNIEUX** you can see Gordes, Roussillon and neighbouring Lacoste, 5km away. Halfway down the village, on rue de la République, there's a museum of traditional bread-making, the **Musée de la Boulangerie** (July & Aug daily except Tues 10am–1pm & 3–6.30pm; April–June & Sept–Oct Mon & Wed–Sun 10am–12.30pm & 2.30–6pm; €3.50), while on the route de Lacoste, artworks by the American sculptor Louise Bourgeois grace the seventeenth-century Couvent d'Ô, also known as the **Église Louise Bourgeois** (July and first ten days of Sept 10am–1pm & 3–6pm; €6).

From Bonnieux the D149 joins the Apt–Avignon road just after the triple-arched **Pont Julien** over the Coulon, which dates back to the time when Apt was the Roman base of Apta Julia. Well before you reach the bridge you'll see signs for the **Château La Canorgue**, a good place to sample the light and very palatable Côtes de Luberon wines (Mon–Fri 9am–noon & 2.30–6pm; call in advance ℡04.90.75.81.01).

Livelier than its neighbours, Bonnieux makes a good base in which to **stay**. There's a very pleasant *chambre d'hôtes*, Le Clos du Buis (℡04.90.75.88.48, Ⓦwww .leclosdubuis.fr; ❺), in a former boulangerie on rue Victor Hugo close to the centre of the village, with air conditioning, a pool and views of Mont Ventoux. Failing that, the *César*, on place de la Liberté at the top of the village (℡04.90.75.96.35, Ⓦwww.hotel-cesar.com; ❹), is nice enough, with classy furnishings in the lobby and wonderful views from some of the rooms. For **eating**, try *Le Fournil*, overlooking the fountain in place Carnot (℡04.90.75.83.62; closed Mon & lunch Sat), which serves lovely Provençal dishes laced with olive oil and garlic; two-course menus are €19.60, three €25.50. Friday is **market** day.

Travel details

Trains

Aix TGV to: Paris (every 1–2hr; 3hr).
Aix to: Château-Arnoux-St Auban (up to 9 daily; 1hr 20min); Marseille (every 20–30min; 45min); Manosque/Gréoux Bains (up to 9 daily; 55min); Pertuis (up to 7 daily; 27min); Sisteron (up to 9 daily; 1hr 30min).

Buses

Aix TGV to: Aix (68 daily; 15min).
Aix to: Aix TGV (66 daily; 15min); Apt (2 daily; 1hr 45min); Arles (3 daily; 1hr 25min); Aubagne (12 daily; 50min); Cavaillon (3–5 daily Mon–Sat; 1hr 15min); La Ciotat (hourly; 1hr 35min–1hr 55min); Éguilles (every 30min–1hr; 35min); Manosque (up to 13 daily; 58min); Marseille (every 5min at peak times; 30min); Marseille-Provence Airport (40 daily; 30min); Nice (3–5 daily; 2hr 50min–4hr 5min);

Pertuis (every 30min–1hr; 40min); Puyloubier (4 daily; 45min); Salon (every 30min–1hr; 35–45min); Sisteron (1–2 daily; 2hr 45min); Vauvenargues (6 daily Mon–Sat; 30min).
Apt to: Aix (2 daily; 2hr); Avignon (up to 10 daily; 1hr 10min); Avignon TGV (4 daily; 1hr 40min); Bonnieux (3 daily; 20min); Cadenet (2 daily; 55min); Lourmarin (2 daily; 40min); Pertuis (2 daily; 1hr 10min).
Forcalquier to: Manosque (3–7 daily; 30min); Marseille (1–3 daily; 2hr 10min).
Pertuis to: Aix (every 30min–1hr; 40min); Apt (3 daily; 1hr 15min); Cadenet (up to 7 daily; 15min); Cavaillon (6 daily; 1hr 40min); La Tour d'Aigues (3–4 daily; 15min).
Sisteron to: Aix (2 daily; 2hr 15min); Château–Arnoux (up to 9 daily; 20min); Digne (up to 9 daily; 50min–1hr 10min); Manosque (1–2 daily; 55min); Marseille (2 daily; 3hr 15min).

The Haut Var and Haute Provence

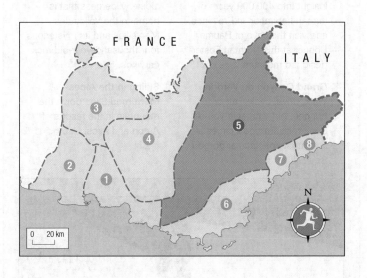

CHAPTER 5 # Highlights

* **Abbaye du Thoronet** An exquisite rose-coloured monastic complex, and the oldest of Provence's three great Cistercian monasteries. See p.209

* **Aups** With its fabulous crop of well-priced hotel-restaurants, this lovely rural town makes a perfect overnight stop. See p.211

* **Musée de Préhistoire des Gorges du Verdon** Gain an insight into 400,000 years of human habitation in Provence, and visit the cave of Baume Bonne, at this Norman Foster-designed museum. See p.213

* **Grand Canyon du Verdon** Walk, drive, cycle, raft or bungee, but whatever you do, don't miss Europe's largest and most spectacular gorge. See p.220

* **Entrevaux and Colmars** Both these picturesque towns retain beautifully preserved fortifications designed by Vauban. See p.235 & p.232

* **The Clues of Haute Provence** A hidden landscape of rocky gorges, tiny villages and rural tranquillity, a mere 40km from the Riviera. See pp.237–239

* **Parc National du Mercantour** An unspoiled alpine wilderness that is home to the Vallée des Merveilles and its mysterious four-thousand-year-old rock carvings. See p.243

* **Skiing in the Alpes-Maritimes** Slide down the mountain in the resorts of Auron and Allos. See p.241 & p.231

▲ Musée de Préhistoire facade

The Haut Var and Haute Provence

S tretching from the **Chaîne de la Ste-Baume** up to the **Alpes-de-Haute-Provence**, the unspoiled geographical heartland of Provence is characterised by deep valleys and snowcapped mountains in the north, the source of several rivers that flow down to the gentle undulating fields of vines, lavender, sunflowers and poppies in the south. Small towns and villages such as **Aups** and **Cotignac** still thrive on their traditional industries of making honey, tending sheep, digging for truffles and pressing olive oil; and in isolated areas it's hard to believe this is the same country, never mind province, as the Côte d'Azur.

True, foreigners have bought second homes in the idyllic **Haut Var villages**, but the tidal wave of new-house building barely extends north of the Autoroute Provençale (A8). Nor has the Marseille–Gap highway, which follows the **River Durance**, encouraged major industrialization. Prices here remain much lower than on the coast or in western Provence.

Landscapes are exceptional, from the gentle countryside of the Haut Var or Pays de Forcalquier to the wild emptiness of the **Plateau de Canjuers**, the untrammelled forests east of Draguignan and, most spectacularly of all, Europe's largest ravine, the **Grand Canyon du Verdon**.

Food is fundamentally Provençal: lamb from the high summer pastures, goat's cheese, honey, almonds, olives and wild herbs. The soil is poor and water scarce, but the Côtes de Provence wine *appellation* extends to the Upper Var.

The towns, like busy but workaday **Draguignan**, are not the prime appeal. First and foremost, this is an area for **walking** and **climbing**, or **canoeing** and **windsurfing** on the countless lakes that provide power and irrigation. The Grand Canyon du Verdon is a must, even if only seen from a car or bus. The best way to discover the area, however, is simply to stay in a village that takes your fancy, eating, dawdling and letting yourself drift into the rhythms of local life.

The mountainous northeastern corner of Provence, **Haute Provence**, is a different world from season to season. In **spring** the fruit trees in the narrow valleys blossom, and melting waters swell the Verdon, the Vésubie, the Var, the Tinée and the Roya, sometimes flooding villages and carrying whole streets away. In the foothills, the groves of chestnut and olive trees bear fruit in **summer** and **autumn**, while higher up the pine forests are edged with wild raspberries and bilberries, and the moors and grassy slopes with white and gold alpine flowers. Above the line where vegetation ceases there are rocks with eagles' nests and snowcaps that never melt. In **winter** the sheep and shepherds retreat to warmer pastures, leaving the snowy heights to antlered mouflons and chamois, and the perfectly camouflaged ermine. The villages, where the shepherds came to summer markets, are battened down for the long cold haul, while modern conglomerations of Swiss-style chalet houses, sports shops and discotheques come to life around the ski lifts. From November to April many of the mountain passes are closed, cutting off the dreamy northern town of **Barçelonnette** from its lower neighbours.

This is not an easy place to live. Abandoned farms and overgrown terraced slopes bear witness to the declining viability of mountain agriculture. But the **ski resorts** bring in money, while summer sees an influx of trekkers, naturalists and climbers. One area, covering 75km from east to west, protected as the **Parc National du Mercantour**, has no permanent inhabitants at all. It's crossed by numerous paths, with refuge huts providing basic food and bedding for trekkers.

For centuries the border between Provence and Savoy ran through this part of France, a political divide embodied by the impressive fortifications of **Entrevaux** and **Colmars**, the principal town of the Haut Verdon. To this day, most of the region is not considered to be part of Provence. The French refer to it by the geographical term, the **Alpes-Maritimes**, which is also the name of the *département* that stretches from between the Haut Var and Verdon valleys and just above the source of the Tinée Valley to the Italian border, and includes the Riviera. Where Provence ends and the Alps begin is debatable, with the **Tinée Valley** usually cited as definitely belonging to the latter – the mountains here are pretty serious and the Italian influence becomes noticeable.

Running along the southern limit of the Alps, the **Nice–Digne rail line**, known as the Chemin de Fer de Provence, is the only remaining segment of the region's nineteenth- and twentieth-century narrow-gauge network. One of the great train rides of France, it takes in the isolated Var towns of **Puget-Théniers** and **Entrevaux**, and ends at low-key **Digne**, the centre of the lavender industry. Away from the Nice–Digne line, public transport is a problem except in the **Roya Valley**, over in the east, where the **Nice–Turin rail line** links the Italianate towns of **Tende** and **Sospel**. Buses are infrequent and many of the best starting points for walks or the far-flung pilgrimage chapels are off the main roads. With your own transport, you'll face tough climbs and long stretches with no fuel supplies, but you'll be free to explore the most exhilaratingly beautiful corner of Provence.

The Chaîne de la Ste-Baume

East of **Aubagne**, described in Chapter One (see p.77), the urban sprawl that surrounds Marseille finally slips away in the unspoiled **Chaîne de la Ste-Baume**, a sparsely populated region of rich forests. The plateau to the north is wonderful territory for walking and cycling, its northern face holding a profusion of woods, flowers and wildlife rare in these hot latitudes. The entire area north to **St-Maximin**, south to **Signes**, west to **Gémenos** and east to **La Roquebrussanne** is protected. You are not allowed to camp in the woods or light fires, and a still-extant royal edict forbids the picking of orchids.

Gémenos

Thanks to the beautiful seventeenth-century château that serves as its Hôtel de Ville, **GÉMENOS**, 3km east of Aubagne, is a tempting place to stop. **Cafés**, **bars** and **patisseries** surround the château, and the **restaurant** *Le Fer à Cheval* on place de la Mairie (☏04.42.32.20.97) serves good menus from €17.

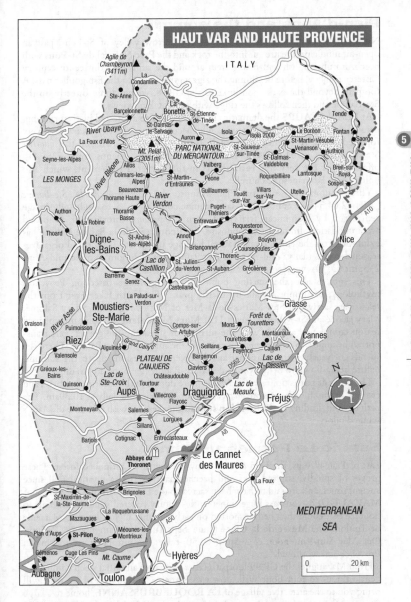

A magnificent luxury **hotel**, the *Relais de la Magdeleine* (☎04.42.32.20.16,
Ⓦwww.relais-magdeleine.com; lunch menu €35, otherwise €44 & €58; ❻;
closed mid-Nov to mid-March), stands in a lovely, vine-covered eighteenth-
century manor house in a park designed by Le Nôtre, just off the Rond Point de
la Fontaine on the N396 route d'Aix. Two minutes' walk further along the
N396, the friendly *Le Provence* (☎04.42.32.20.55, Ⓦle-provence-hotel.com; ❷)
is much cheaper, and has family rooms for up to five people.

Plan-d'Aups and the summit

Northeast of Gémenos, the D2 follows the narrow valley of St-Pons, past an open-air municipal theatre cut into the rock and the **Parc Naturel de St-Pons** with beech, hornbeam, ash and maple trees around the ruins of a thirteenth-century Cistercian abbey, before beginning the zigzagging ascent to the Espigoulier pass. A footpath beyond the park soon links to the GR98, which climbs directly up the Ste-Baume and then follows the ridge with breathtaking views.

At **PLAN-D'AUPS** the dramatic climb levels out to a forested plateau running parallel to the ridge of Ste-Baume, which cuts across the sky like a massively fortified wall. A comfortable small **hotel**, *Lou Pèbre d'Aï*, in the *quartier* Ste-Madeleine (℡04.42.04.50.42, Ⓦloupebredai.com; menus from €26; ❸), offers one of the very few **restaurants** in this scattered settlement, which also holds a tiny Romanesque church.

· Three kilometres east of Plan-d'Aups, the *Hôtellerie de la Ste-Baume* (℡04.42.04.54.84, Ⓦhotellerie-saintebaume.com; ❶) is a roadside pilgrimage centre run by Dominican friars and open for prayers, information, food and accommodation. Immediately opposite, the **Écomusée de la Sainte Baume** has exhibitions on the cultural and natural heritage of the Ste-Baume and organizes seasonal events (daily: mid-April to Oct 9am–noon & 2–6pm; Nov to mid-April 2–5pm; €3; Ⓦwww.ecomusee-saintebaume.u-3mrs.fr).

This spot is also the starting point for a **pilgrimage** based on Provençal mythology, or simply a walk up to the peaks. The myth takes over from the sea-voyage arrival in Stes-Maries-de-la-Mer of Mary Magdalene, Mary Salomé, Mary Jacobé and St-Maximin (see p.113). **Mary Magdalene**, for some unexplained reason completely at odds with the mission of spreading the gospel, gets transported by angels to a cave (*grotte*) just below the summit of Ste-Baume. There she spends 33 years, with occasional angel-powered excursions up to the summit, before being flown to St-Maximin-de-la-Ste-Baume (see opposite) to die.

The difficult **paths** up from the *Hôtellerie* are dotted with oratories, calvaries and crosses. In the suitably sombre *grotte* at the top, Mass is held daily at 10.30am. The path beyond, leading to the **St-Pilon summit**, makes you wish for some of Mary's winged pilots.

East to La Roquebrussanne

East of Plan-d'Aups, the D95 crosses many kilometres of unspoiled forest. These groves of spindly, stunted oaks and beeches have exerted a mystical pull since ancient times, and are said to have been sacred to the Druids. Around the village of **MAZAUGUES**, you pass huge, nineteenth-century covered stone wells, built to hold ice that could then be transported on early summer nights down to Marseille or Toulon. The **Musée de la Glace** (June–Sept Tues–Sun 9am–noon & 2–6pm; Oct–May Sun 9am–noon & 2–5pm; €2.50) traces the history of ice-making in Provence and worldwide.

From Mazaugues the GR99 footpath takes you, after an initial steep climb, on a gentle three- to four-hour walk down to Signes. Continuing east by road will bring you to the attractive village of **LA ROQUEBRUSSANNE**, home to a large Saturday food **market**; a pleasant **hotel**, *La Loube* (℡04.94.86.81.36; ❹; menus from €27); and a **gliding-school**, Fly Azur (℡04.94.86.97.52, Ⓦfly.azur.free.fr).

Méounes-les-Montrieux

Seven kilometres south of La Roquebrussanne, the tiny village of **MÉOUNES-LES-MONTRIEUX** holds an astonishing eleven fountains. It also has a Sunday market, a couple of **hotels**, including the small, welcoming *Hôtel de France* on place de L'Église (☎04.94.33.95.92; closed Jan–April, ❷), and two **campsites**, of which the best is the *Blue Garden* (☎04.94.48.95.34, ⓦchateau-gavaudan.com; €23), 1.5km out at the Château de Gavaudan.

Signes

Ten kilometres west of Méounes along the D2, which follows the lovely Gapeau stream back towards its source, **SIGNES** is yet another appealing little village. Palm trees and white roses grow around the war memorial, the clocktower is more than 400 years old, and the people make their living from wine, olives, cereals and market gardening or, in the case of two small enterprises, **biscuits** and **nougat**. At Lou Goustetto (Mon–Sat 10am–12.30pm & 3–6pm), just west of the centre at 15 route de Marseille, you can sample hard, unsweetened biscuits in natural flavours that include Provençal herbs and nuts, lemon, cinnamon, cocoa and honey. Nougat Fouque (Sept–Dec daily 9am–noon & 2–7pm; ⓦnougat-fouque.com), 2 rue Louis-Lumière, produces a seasonal black or white nougat which provides a honey overdose that manages not to stick to your teeth.

The village has a Thursday **market** on place Marcel-Pagnol, and a **tourist office** in the *médiathèque* on rue Frédéric-Mistral (Wed–Sat 10am–noon & 2–6.30pm; ☎04.94.98.87.80, ⓦsignes.com). The Garcia family's wonderful **chambres d'hôtes** at the *Château de Cancerilles* (☎04.94.90.81.45, ⓦwww .chateaudecancerilles.com; ❺) is an old stone farm surrounded by vines on the route de Belgentier, where rooms rent by the week in high season but by the night for the rest of year. Places to **eat** on rue Bourgade include the traditional *Marmite de Mathilde* at no. 6 (☎04.94.90.83.21), and *Pizzeria Chez Pat* at no. 1 (☎04.94.90.82.11).

St-Maximin-de-la-Ste-Baume

The handsome old town of **ST-MAXIMIN-DE-LA-STE-BAUME** is where, in 1279, the count of Provence supposedly discovered a crypt containing the relics of Mary Magdalene and Saint Maximin, which had been hidden by local people during a Saracen raid. He set about building a basilica and **monastery** on place de l'Hôtel-de-Ville, which took their present shape in the fifteenth century, and have since been extravagantly decorated in stone, wood, gold, silk and oil paint.

There is, therefore, plenty to look at in the substantial Gothic **basilica** (daily 8am–6pm), including beautiful wood panelling in the choir and paintings on the nave walls, as well as Ronzen's lovely *Retable de la Passion* (1520). Also look out for the wonderfully sculpted fourth-century sarcophagi, and the grotesque skull once venerated as that of Mary Magdalene, encased in a glass helmet framed by a gold neck and hair, in the **crypt**.

The thirteenth-century **cloisters** and chapterhouse of the monastery, reached via the *Couvent Royal* (see below; free), are much more delicate. Look down the well to see the escape route that the Dominican friars used on several occasions in the sixteenth century when the monastery was placed under siege. Today, the monastery is the setting for classical concerts (call ☎04.94.59.84.59 for details).

South of the church, a covered passageway leads into the arcaded rue Colbert, a former Jewish ghetto. All the medieval streets of St-Maximin, with their uniform tiled roofs at anything but uniform heights, have considerable charm, and there's a reasonable assortment of restaurants, as well as shops selling the work of local artisans.

Practicalities

The **tourist office** (Mon–Sat 9am–12.30pm & 2–6pm, Sun 10am–12.30pm & 2–5pm; ⓣ04.94.59.84.59, ⓦst-maximin.fr) is in the Hôtel de Ville next to the basilica. Next door, the enormous, imposing ⚜️ *Couvent Royal* on place Jean-Salusse (ⓣ04.94.86.55.66, ⓦwww.hotelfp-saintmaximin.com; ⑤) has been converted into a comfortable and highly atmospheric **hotel**, with clean, excellent-value rooms, some of which used to be monks' cells. Menus in its elegant restaurant (closed Sun eve), which adjoins the cloister, start at €39. A short walk west, the well-run, friendly *Plaisance*, at 20 place Malherbe (ⓣ04.94.78.16.74; ③), is a grand town house with spacious rooms. The local three-star **campsite**, *Provençal* (ⓣ04.94.78.16.97; €18; closed Nov–March), is 3km out along the chemin de Mazaugues, the road to Marseille.

Cafés and **brasseries** congregate on place Malherbe, the present-day hub of St-Maximin. The relaxed *Table en Provence* (ⓣ04.94.59.84.61), with its outdoor tables facing the basilica entrance on rue Général-de-Gaulle, is ideal for a coffee or a simple meal, with a pasta menu at €13 and a full lunch menu for €19.

Brignoles

BRIGNOLES, 18km east of St-Maximin, is an ordinary, reasonably well-preserved provincial centre that can make for a convenient night's stay. At its heart, beyond the usual sprawling commercial zones and busy ring roads, lies a gentrified, warren-like medieval town full of quiet, shaded squares and old facades with faded painted adverts and flowering window boxes.

A thirteenth-century summer residence of the counts of Provence, at the southern end of this old quarter, now holds the fascinating, old-style **Musée du Pays Brignolais** (April–Sept Wed–Sat 9am–noon & 2.30–6pm, Sun 9am–noon & 3–6pm; Oct–March Wed–Sat 10am–noon & 2.30–5pm, Sun 10am–noon & 3–5pm; €4; ⓦmuseebrignolais.com). Displays dip into every aspect of local life, from an ancient paleo-Christian sarcophagus to a reinforced concrete boat made by the inventor of concrete in 1840. There's a statue of a saint whose navel has been visibly deepened by the hopeful hands of infertile women, a reconstruction of a bauxite mine, a crèche of *santons*, some Impressionist Provençal landscapes by Frédéric Montenard and a chapel cluttered with religious statuary.

Rue des Lanciers, with fine old houses where the rich Brignolais used to live, leads up from place des Comtes-de-Provence to **St-Sauveur**, a twelfth-century church in which, on the left-hand side, you can see the remains of an older church. Behind St-Sauveur the stepped street of rue Saint-Esprit runs down to rue Cavaillon and place Carami, the café-lined central square of the modern town.

Practicalities

Brignoles' excellent modern **tourist office** (Mon–Fri 9.30am–noon & 2–5.30pm; ⓣ04.94.72.04.21, ⓦla-provence-verte.net) is on the north side of the River Carami by the carrefour de l'Europe roundabout. **Buses** stop at place St-Louis.

The only central **hotel** is the simple *Provence*, on place du Palais de Justice (ⓣ04.94.69.01.18, ⓔhotel-de-provence@orange.fr; ②), but there's a nice five-room **chambres d'hôtes**, *La Bastide de Messine* (ⓣ04.94.72.09.06, ⓦbastide-messine.com; ④), 2km northwest on chemin de Cante Perdrix, in a renovated old farm with a pool. The two-star municipal **campsite** is 1km down the route de Nice at no. 786 (☎04.94.69.20.10, ✆campingbrignoles@aol.com; €12.50; closed mid-Oct to mid-March).

Place Carami holds several places to **eat** and **drink**, including *L'Oustau* (☎04.94.69.11.10; closed lunch Sun & Mon), which has shaded outdoor tables and serves a €9 daily *plat*, as well as good *aioli*.

The Haut Var

Northeast of Brignoles, the rocky Haut Var holds some of Provence's most delightfully picturesque medieval villages, including **Cotignac** and **Villecroze**. Further north, the **Argens Valley** to the **Verdon Gorge** is the true heart of Provence, with soft enveloping countryside of woods, vines, lakes and waterfalls, streaked with rocky ridges before the high plateaux and mountains. To the outsider, the picturesque villages merge together; to know them properly you'd have to live here for winter after winter, limiting your world to just a few square kilometres. The region is also home to the **Abbaye du Thoronet**, the oldest of Provence's three surviving Cistercian monasteries.

Barjols

Fountains are the chief attraction of **BARJOLS**, 21km north of Brignoles. No fewer than 28 such mossy water features are dotted around the village, mostly in its older, eastern half, the **quartier du Réal**. The glum, rickety buildings of the now-defunct local tanning industry have been taken over by artists and craft workers; you can visit their studios (follow signs to Art-Artisanal) down the old road to Brignoles, east of the Vieille Ville. Looking back upwards from here at the industrial ruins is a spooky night-time experience.

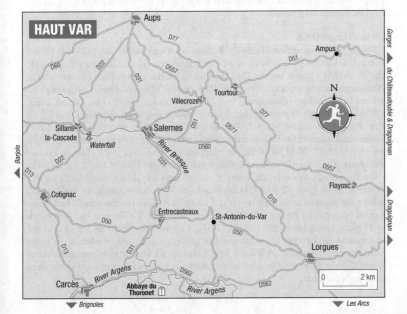

In January, a strange **festival** in honour of the town's patron saint, St-Marcel, commemorates the miraculous arrival of an ox during a famine. A cow is killed and roasted to the accompaniment of flutes and tambourines, and the refrain "Saint Marcel, Saint Marcel, the little tripe, the little tripe".

Barjols' **tourist office** (Tues 10am–noon & 2–5pm, Wed & Fri 9am–noon & 3–5pm, Thurs 10am–noon & 3–5pm, Sat 9am–1pm; ☎04.94.77.20.01, ⓦville -barjols.fr) is one block east of the broad place Rouguière on boulevard Grisolle. The **hotel-restaurant** *Le Pont d'Or* on route de St-Maximin (☎04.94.77.05.23; closed Sun eve & Mon, plus Dec to mid-Jan; ❸) serves the best **food** in town, with menus at €23–39.

Cotignac

COTIGNAC, the loveliest of all the Haut Var villages, stands 23km northeast of Brignoles. From its photogenic place de la Mairie, rue de l'Horloge heads under the clocktower and up to the church, from which a path leads to the foot of the spectacular eighty-metre cliff that forms the back wall of the village. A splendidly colourful and flower-bedecked, if at times nerve-racking, **cliffside trail** (April & early Oct Tues–Sun 2–5pm; May & June Tues–Sun 2–5.30pm; July & Aug Mon & Sun 2–6.30pm, Tues–Sat 10am–noon & 2–6.30pm; Sept Tues–Sat 10am–noon & 2–6.30pm, Sun 2–6.30pm; €2) leads past a troglodyte's dream of passageways, precarious stairways and strange little structures to the two ruined towers at the summit, relics of a long-abandoned castle. The rock between them is riddled with further caves and tunnels.

Central to the history of Cotignac are the now-defunct tanning works, once a major local industry, and the miraculous Virgin in the **Chapelle de Notre-Dame-des-Grâces**, on the summit across the valley to the south. Long venerated as a saviour from the plague, this Virgin finally hit the big time in 1638 when Louis XIII and Anne of Austria – married for 22 childless years – made their supplications to her. Nine months after the royal visit, the future Sun King let out his first demanding squall.

Practicalities

Cotignac's **tourist office** (Tues–Fri 9.15am–12.45pm & 3–5.30pm, Sat 9.15am–noon; ☎04.94.04.61.87, ⓦot-cotignac.provenceverte.fr), outside the village beside the Pont Olla Cassole on the D13, just south of the river, offers internet access. **Accommodation** options are limited to several *chambres d'hôtes*, including the atmospheric *Maison Gonzagues*, in a former tannery at 9 rue Lúon-Gúrard (☎04.94.72.85.40, ⓦwww.maison-gonzagues-cotignac.com; ❻); the *Pra de Pé*, 10 rue Pra de Pé (☎04.94.04.77.74, ⓦwww.pra-de-pe.com; ❸), which serves home-made dinners for €22; and the *Domaine de Nestuby*, amid vineyards 4km south on the D22 (☎04.94.04.60.02, ⓦsejour-en-provence.com; ❹). The municipal **campsite**, *Les Pouverels*, is 3km northeast towards Aups (☎04.94.04.71.91; €11.40).

On the cours Gambetta, the heart of the village's social life, you'll find a decent **restaurant**, *du Cours* (☎04.94.04.60.14; closed Wed, and evenings in low season), where menus start at €13 for lunch and range €17–30 in the evening. There's also a good pizzeria, *La Tarente*, and the lively *Bar de l'Union*. *Le Temps de Pose*, just north at 11 place de la Mairie (☎04.94.77.72.07), is a pretty tearoom that serves daytime snacks and sandwiches in its ramshackle garden. Cotignac's **market** is on cours Gambetta on a Tuesday. A *brocante* held four times a year attracts **antique** dealers from all over Europe; the earthier *marché paysane* takes place every Friday from June to September.

Entrecasteaux

ENTRECASTEAUX, 9km east of Cotignac along the minor D50, is scarcely more than a stone frame for its seventeenth-century **château**, which rises from box-hedged formal gardens to dominate the village. The structure owes its current condition to a Scottish painter, Ian McGarvie-Munn (1919–81), who retired in 1974 after a career that included a stint as head of the Guatemalan navy, and devoted the rest of his life to this massive restoration job.

You can visit the **château** (Easter–Nov daily except Sat, guided visits at 4pm, extra tour at 11.30am in Aug; ℡04.94.04.43.95, ⓦchateau-entrecasteaux.com; €7), and the publicly owned **Le Nôtre** gardens that separate it from the village (dawn–dusk; free). Its interior is spacious, light and charmingly rustic, typified by the terracotta tiles, a style that was all the rage when the Count and Countess of Grignan used the château as their summer residence; the opulence of the countess's bedroom, however, gives some idea of the status of the one-time inhabitants.

Practicalities

Local **chambres d'hôtes** include the terracotta *Bastide Notre Dame*, just west of the village in Adrech de Sainte Anne (℡04.94.04.45.63, ⓦbastidenotredame.free.fr; ⑤), which has four pretty rooms and a pool in the shaded garden. The welcoming **hotel-restaurant** *Lou Cigaloun*, in St-Antonin-du-Var, Entrecasteaux's even smaller neighbour to the east (℡04.94.04.42.67, ⓦwww.restaurantloucigaloun.com; closed Nov–Feb; ❹), is also a good bet; its restaurant (closed Wed; menus €19–65) offers simple but fine cooking. Decent food can also be found in Entrecasteaux at *La Forchette*, up beyond the château entrance (℡04.94.04.42.78; closed Jan & Feb, plus Mon & Tues, & Sun eve in low season), where menus range from €17 to €27. For a **snack**, head to *la Crêperie â l'Atelier* on le Collet.

The Abbaye du Thoronet

Sixteen kilometres south of Entrecasteaux, via Carcés, one of Provence's three great Cistercian monasteries, the austere, rose-coloured **Abbaye du Thoronet** (April–Sept Mon–Sat 10am–6.30pm, Sun 10am–noon & 2–6.30pm; Oct–March Mon–Sat 10am–1pm & 2–5pm, Sun 10am–noon & 2–5pm; €7; ⓦthoronet .monuments-nationaux.fr), stands deep in the forest of La Daboussière. Like Silvacane and Sénanque (see p.172 & p.195), it was founded in the first half of the twelfth century, but Thoronet is the oldest of the three and the one that was completed in the shortest time, giving it an aesthetic coherence that transcends its relatively modest size. Abandoned in 1791, it was kept intact during the Revolutionary era as an historic monument. Restoration started in the 1850s, and a more recent campaign has brought it to graceful, melancholy perfection. The *abbaye* is off the D79, between the hamlet of Le Thoronet and Cabasse.

Flayosc and Lorgues

Fifteen kilometres east of the Abbaye, across the River Argens, both **LORGUES**, and **FLAYOSC** a little further north, make excellent stops for **food**. *L'Oustaou* (℡04.94.70.42.69; menus from €28; closed all day Mon, plus Wed & Sun eve) on place Brémond, the main square of Flayosc, serves delicious local specialities in a timeless village atmosphere. *Chez Bruno*, on route de Vidauban in Lorgues (℡04.94.85.93.93, ⓦrestaurantbruno.com; mid-Sept to mid-June closed all day Mon and Sun eve), a restaurant that also has a few rooms (⑥), is considerably more expensive, but if you're prepared to pay €65 or €130 for a set menu, you can sample wonderful wild local ingredients in a chestnut and *chanterelle* soup and in the truffle and game dishes, followed by *crème brûlée* with figs in wine.

Salernes

Compared with Cotignac, **SALERNES**, 13km northeast, is quite a metropolis, with a thriving tile-making industry and enough near-level irrigated land for productive agriculture. Twenty or so studios and shops, large and small, sell a huge range of **pottery** and **tiles**, while on Sunday and Wednesday a **market** takes place beneath the ubiquitous plane trees on the *cours*.

Salernes' **tourist office** is on place Gabriel-Péri (July & Aug Mon–Sat 9.30am–7pm; Sept–June Tues–Sat 9.30am–12.30pm & 2–6pm; ☎04.94.70.69.02, Ⓦwww.ville-salernes.fr). The only **hotel** in town is the basic *Relais de la Belle Epoque*, nearby at 20 rue J.J. Rousseau (☎04.94.70.60.30, Ⓦrelais-belle-epoque-salernes.cote.azur.fr; ❸), and there's a good four-star **campsite**, *Les Arnauds*, on the Sillans road (☎04.94.67.51.95, Ⓦvillage-vacances-lesarnauds.com; €23.65; closed Oct–April).

The oldest, prettiest streets in Salernes are exclusively residential, but the commercial zone holds plenty of **restaurants**, including the good-value *Tout En Passent Chez Giles*, 20 rue Victor-Hugo (☎04.94.70.72.80; closed Mon), where lunch costs under €15 and dinner menus start at €20; and the cute little *Etcetera Café*, just below the *cours* on place Clemenceau (☎04.94.67.54.43; closed Mon), where diners sit outdoors around giant wooden reels.

Sillans-le-Cascade

Tiny **SILLANS**, 6km west of Salernes, is a nice, sleepy little village that has clung on to a brief stretch of ancient ramparts. Down below, on the Bresque River, a stunning **waterfall**, reached by a twenty-minute walk along a delightful and clearly signed path from the main road, gushes into a turquoise pool that's perfect for swimming.

An appealing **hotel-restaurant**, *Les Pins*, alongside the main road at 1 Grand Rue (☎04.94.04.63.26, Ⓦrestaurant-lespins.com; ❷), holds five simple rooms, and serves meals on a colourful patio, with dinner menus at €24–38. There's also a three-star **campsite**, *Le Relais de la Bresque* (☎04.94.04.64.89, Ⓦwww.lerelaisdelabresque.com; €22.90; closed Oct–March), 1km north on the D22 towards Aups.

Villecroze

Five kilometres northeast of Salernes, **VILLECROZE** is a charming village, though it would be easy to drive straight through and fail to realize its lovely, peaceful old quarter was even there. The inconspicuous walled medieval town lies immediately south of the main road, the D557, and is a joy to stroll around, with its lovely vaulted stone arcades.

Like Cotignac, Villecroze sits beneath a water-burrowed cliff, on its northern side. The gardens around the base are delightfully un-Gallic and informal, and intriguing grottoes in its flanks are open to visitors in summer (daily 10am–noon & 2.30–7pm; €2).

The centre of community life in Villecroze, the place du Général-de-Gaulle across the road from the old town, hosts a **market** on Thursday mornings. It also holds an absolute gem of a **hotel**, the seven-room, Norwegian-owned 🎄 *Auberge des Lavandes* (☎04.94.70.76.00; closed Jan & Feb; ❸). The airy, blue-and-white rooms in this beautiful old house are solidly furnished and fitted with large shutters, while the exceptionally friendly owners serve simple but exquisite dinners for €20 downstairs, with some outdoor tables. A neighbouring bar, the *Cercle de Avenir*, puts on music on summer evenings.

Two further **hotel-restaurants** worth recommending lie south of the village along the D557: the secluded and very comfortable *Au Bien Etre*, in *quartier* Les Cadenières,

(℡04.94.70.67.57. ⓦaubienetre.com; ❹), which has a pool and serves dinner menus from €26 (closed for lunch Mon–Wed), and *Le Colombier* on route de Draguignan (℡04.94.70.63.23, ⓦlecolombier-var.com; ❺; closed Sun eve & Mon), where menus start at €29. **Campsites** include the year-round *Cadenières*, on the D560 3km south of Villecroze (℡04.94.67.59.66, ⓦcamping-les-cadenieres.com; €22).

Tourtour

TOURTOUR, 6km north of Villecroze via the tortuous D51, sits 300m higher, atop a ridge with views extending to the massifs of Maures, Ste-Baume and Ste-Victoire. The village has a seemingly organic unity, its soft-coloured stone growing into stairways and curving streets, branching to form arches, fountains and towers. An old mill looks like it has always been in ruins, and the elephant-leg towers of the sixteenth-century bastion stand around the *mairie* as if of their own volition, while the twelfth-century **Tour du Grimaldi** might have erupted spontaneously from the ground. The two elms on the main square, planted when Anne of Austria and Louis XIII visited Cotignac, are almost as enormous as the bastion towers, though they're showing signs of decrepitude.

That said, Tourtour is all a bit unreal, full of *résidences secondaires* and *salons de thé* selling expensive fruit-juice cocktails. It also holds an upscale **hotel–restaurant**, the *Bastide de Tourtour* (℡04.98.10.54.20, ⓦverdon.net/tourtour; ❽), housed in a modern version of a traditional fortified farmhouse, equipped with jacuzzis, tennis courts and a gym, and serving classic local cuisine on menus from €28 (closed lunch Mon–Fri Sept–June).

Aups

The neat and very pleasant village of **AUPS**, 10km north of Salernes, makes an ideal base for drivers touring the Haut Var or the Grand Canyon du Verdon. While holding all the facilities visitors might need, it remains a vibrant, lived-in community, still earning its living from agriculture, and at its best on Wednesdays and Saturdays, when market stalls fill its central squares and the surrounding streets.

Though only 500m or so above sea level, this was considered by the ancients to be the beginning of the Alps; its Roman name, Alpibus, became first Alps and then Aups. The chief town of one of the Ligurian tribes, and the location for a Roman army hospital, it thrived in the Middle Ages, though it never subsequently grew any larger.

Arrival, information and accommodation

Aups' very helpful **tourist office** is on place Frédéric-Mistral (April–June & Sept Mon–Sat 8.45am–12.15pm & 2–5.30pm; July & Aug Mon–Sat 9am–12.30pm & 3–6.30pm, plus Sun 9am–12.30pm mid-July to mid-Aug; Oct–May Mon, Tues, Thurs & Fri 8.45am–12.15pm & 1.30–5pm, Wed & Sat 8.45am–12.15pm; ℡04.94.84.00.69, ⓦaups-tourisme.com).

There can hardly be another village in France with such a perfect array of good and extraordinarily well-priced **hotels**, both in the centre and in the neighbouring countryside, along with several nearby **campsites** for good measure.

Hotels and B&Bs

Auberge de la Tour rue Aloisi ℡04.94.70.00.30, ⓦaubergedelatour.net. Correct, bourgeois but appealing and great-value hotel. All the tasteful, airy, well-equipped rooms overlook a sunny, peaceful, plant-filled courtyard, and the restaurant serves good menus from €18. Closed Oct–March, restaurant also closed Tues Sept–June. ❸

Bastide de l'Estré Chemin de la Croix de Pins
℡ 04.94.84.00.45, ⓦ estre.com. B&B accommodation in an attractive rural location, off the road to Moustiers-Ste-Marie 3km north of town. There's also a *gîte* to rent, a camping barn for walkers and cyclists with dorm beds at €16, and they serve evening meals for €20. ❸

Bastide du Calalou Moissac-Bellevue
℡ 04.94.70.17.91, ⓦ bastide-du-calalou.com. Imposing country-house hotel in a small village 5km northwest of Aups on the D9. The building itself is nothing special, but it's set in grand gardens and has 32 plush rooms, a pool and a fine restaurant. ❼

Grand Hôtel place Duchâtel ℡ 04.94.70.10.82, ⓦ grand-hotel-aups.com. Traditional village hotel, just off the main square, with six plain but adequate en-suite rooms, including some that sleep up to four guests. The restaurant in front serves menus at €15.50–28.50, and there's also a nice bar. ❷

St-Marc rue Aloisi ℡ 04.94.70.06.08, ⓦ lesaintmarc.com. Rickety, earthy, but very characterful old rooms (not all en-suite) in a former olive-oil mill overlooking a tiny little square and above a good restaurant, where the €19.50 dinner menu features a deliciously garlicky fish stew; they also make pizzas over a wood fire. Closed Tues & Wed Sept–June, plus second half Nov. ❷

Campsites

Camping Les Prés route de Tourtour
℡ 04.94.70.00.93, ⓦ campinglespres.com. This well-shaded two-star site, to the right off allée Charles-Boyer just 300m southeast of the town centre, stays open all year, and has a bar, snack bar and pool. €15.50.

International Camping route du Fox-Amphoux
℡ 04.94.70.06.80, ⓦ intcamp.perso.neuf.fr. Large three-star site 500m west of town, on the D60, with pool, disco and restaurant. €19.80. Closed Oct–March.

Saint Lazare 1124 route de Moissac-Bellevue
℡ 04.94.70.12.86, ⓦ pagesperso-orange.fr /campingsaintlazare. Three-star site with a pool, 2km northwest along the Moissac road. €15.90. Closed Oct–March.

The Town

Aups centres on three ill-defined and interconnected squares, where the D557 reaches the southern end of the village: place Frédéric-Mistral, the smaller place Duchâtel slightly uphill to the left and the tree-lined gardens of place Martin-Bidouré to the right. Beyond these, the tangle of old streets, and the sixteenth-century clocktower with its campanile, make it an enjoyable place to explore.

An obelisk on **place Martin-Bidouré**, inscribed "To the memory of citizens who died in 1851 defending the Republic and its laws", commemorates a period of republican resistance all too rarely honoured in France. Peasant and artisan defiance of Louis Napoleon's coup d'état that year was at its strongest in Provence, and the defeat of the insurgents was followed by a massacre of men and women alike. At Aups, the badly wounded Martin Bidouré escaped, but was swiftly found being succoured by a peasant, and shot dead on the spot. That event may well explain the strident "République Française, Liberté, Egalité, Fraternité" sign on the **Église St-Pancrace** nearby, which was originally designed by an English architect five centuries ago.

Aups also holds a **museum of modern art** – the Musée Simon Segal, in the former convent chapel on avenue Albert-1er (mid-June to mid-Sept 10am–noon & 4–7pm; €2.50). The best works are by the Russian-born painter Simon Segal, but there are interesting local scenes in the other paintings, such as the Roman bridge at Aiguines, now drowned beneath the artificial lake of Ste-Croix.

Eating

As detailed above, several of the hotels in Aups hold excellent dining rooms, with the *St-Marc* as the pick of the crop. Otherwise, *Le Gourmet*, 5 rue Voltaire (℡ 04.94.70.14.97; closed Mon, plus Sun eve Sept–June) is the best stand-alone **restaurant**, with menus from €16.50. Along with honey, truffles are an Aups speciality, and there's a dedicated **truffle market** on Thursdays between November and the end of February. The local lamb also has a gourmet reputation, marinated and roasted with thyme.

Northwest of Aups

If you have time, two little towns northwest of Aups make potential stops before you embark on the Grand Canyon du Verdon: **Quinson**, which marks the start of the lower gorges, and workaday **Riez**, with its smattering of Roman ruins.

Quinson

QUINSON, on the attractive D13 22km northwest of Aups and 22km north of Barjols, sits at the head of the **Basses Gorges du Verdon**. If you haven't yet seen the Grand Canyon du Verdon, these 500-metre depths will strike you as quite dramatic, but, unfortunately, they're rather difficult to reach. The GR99 trail makes a short detour to the south side of the gorge a couple of kilometres downstream from Quinson, and paths off the road between Quinson and Esparron also lead to the edge of the gorge.

The chief attraction hereabouts, however, is Quinson's **Musée de Préhistoire des Gorges du Verdon**, route de Montmeyan (April–June & Sept daily except Tues 10am–7pm; July & Aug daily 10am–8pm; Oct to mid-Dec, Feb & March daily except Tues 10am–6pm; ⓦmuseeprehistoire.com; €7), designed by British architect Norman Foster in a clean and sympathetic modern style. Europe's largest museum of human prehistory, it charts a million years of human habitation in Provence, with a multimedia presentation of the cave of Baume Bonne and a 15-metre-long reconstruction of the caves of the canyon of Baudinard, with their six-thousand-year-old red sun paintings. A themed path leads from the museum past reconstructed prehistoric homes and through a Neolithic garden to the most important of the sixty or so archeological sites in and around Quinson, the cave of **Baume Bonne** itself, where human occupation has been traced back 400,000 years.

Just south of Quinson, a pleasant, old-fashioned **hotel**, the *Relais Notre-Dame* (☏04.92.74.40.01, ⓦwww.relaisnotredame-04.com; ❷; closed mid-Dec to Jan), stands close to the river before it enters the gorge.

Riez

The main business of **RIEZ**, 21km north of Quinson, is derived from the lavender fields that cover this corner of Provence – hence the hideous **lavender distillery**, 1km south across the river, which produces essence for the perfume industry. Although Riez is more village than town today, its antiquity is readily apparent. Four stately **Roman columns** stand in a field just off avenue Frédéric-Mistral at the bottom of the main allées Louis-Gardiol, while over the river on the left of the road are the disappointingly scanty remains of a sixth-century **cathedral** (open access).

For a **walk** with good views over the town, head first for the clocktower above Grande rue, then go up the steps past the cemetery where a stony curving path brings you to a cedar-shaded platform on the hilltop where the pre-Roman Riezians lived. The only building on the site today is the eighteenth-century **Chapelle St-Maxime**, with a gaudily patterned interior.

The **Maison de l'Abeille**, 1km north of the village (Mon 10am–12.30pm, Tues–Sun 10am–12.30pm & 2.30–7.30pm; closed Jan & Feb; free), is a fascinating research and visitors' centre where you can buy various **honeys** as well as hydromel, or mead – the honey alcohol of antiquity. Enthusiastic staff are very keen to share their knowledge of all aspects of a bee's life, from anthropology to sexuality and physiology; they may even show you the actual bees.

Practicalities

Riez's **tourist office** is at place de la Mairie (July & Aug Mon–Sat 9.30am–12.30pm & 3–7pm, Sun 9.30am–12.30pm; Sept–June Mon–Fri 8.30am–noon & 1.30–5pm, Sat 8.30am–noon; ℡04.92.77.99.09, Ⓦville-riez .fr). Riez is not a particularly good place to spend a night, and **hotels** are limited in any case to the modern, business-oriented *Carina*, across the river in the *quartier* St-Jean (℡04.92.77.85.43; closed Dec–Easter; ❸), with views back across to the town. The two-star *Rose de Provence* **campsite** is also across the river, on rue Edouard-Dauphin (℡04.92.77.75.45, Ⓦrose-de-provence.com; €14.50 per night; closed Nov–March).

For a long, relaxing **lunch**, head for *Le Rempart*, 17 rue du Marché (℡04.92.77.89.54), where superb Italian and Provençal *plats* cost around €16. If you're pushed for time, *L'Arts des Mets*, 26 allées Louis-Gardiol (℡04.92.77.82.60), serves great salads and pizzas for €10.

Digne-les-Bains and around

The retirement spa town of **DIGNE-LES-BAINS**, 42km north of Riez and the capital of the Alpes-de-Haute-Provence *département*, is by far the largest town in northeastern Provence. Despite the almost metropolitan swank of its main street, a handful of interesting museums, and its superb position between the Durance Valley and the start of the real mountains, it's not all that exciting, and is best seen as a convenient overnight base for trips into the surrounding mountains.

Arrival, information and accommodation

The **tourist office** is on the rond-point du 11-Novembre-1918 (June–Sept Mon–Sat 8.45am–12.30pm & 2–6.30pm, Sun 10am–noon; Oct–May Mon–Sat 8.45am–noon & 2–6pm; ℡04.92.36.62.62, Ⓦot-dignelesbains.fr), with the **gare routière** alongside. The **gare SNCF** is to the west over the river on avenue Pierre-Sémard.

As well as a fine array of **hotels** to suit all budgets, Dignes has a good crop of campsites.

Hotels and B&Bs

Central 26 bd Gassendi ℡04.92.31.31.91, Ⓦlhotel-central.com. Spacious, comfortable budget hotel, on a bustling street in the heart of town near the tourist office, with simple antique-furnished rooms. ❷

Grand Paris 19 bd Thiers ℡04.92.31.11.15, Ⓦhotel-grand-paris.com. Seventeenth-century former convent with large, tastefully decorated rooms, Digne's finest restaurant (see p.217) and a surprising menagerie in the reception. Closed Dec–Feb. ❺

Provence 17 bd Thiers ℡04.92.31.32.19, Ⓦhotel-alpes-provence.com. Behind its plain exterior, this renovated hotel is bright and friendly, with cheerful if small rooms. ❸

Vieil Aiglun Le Vieil Aiglun ℡04.92.34.67.00, Ⓦvieil-aiglun.com. Very pretty B&B, 11km west of Digne in the fifteenth-century hilltop village of Aiglun, with an inviting pool, vaulted stone ceilings and charming hosts. Closed early Nov to late March. ❻

Campsites

du Bourg rte de Barçelonnette ℡04.92.31.04.87, Ⓦcampingdigne.com. Two-star municipal campsite, with a tennis court but no pool, 1.5km northeast of the centre

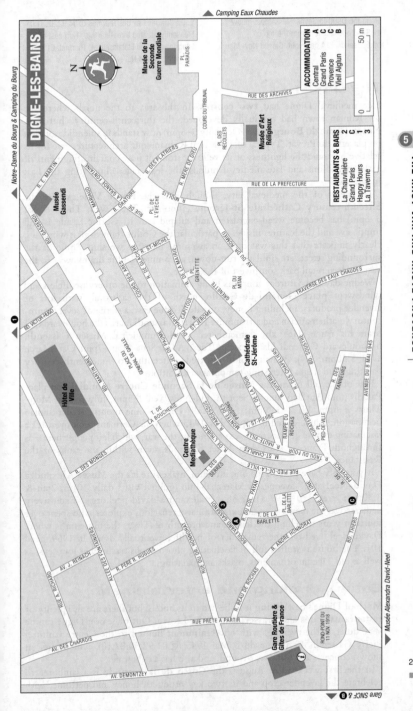

DIGNE-LES-BAINS

Camping Eaux Chaudes ▲

◀ Notre-Dame du Bourg & Camping du Bourg

Musée de la
Seconde
Guerre Mondiale

PL
PARADIS

RUE DES ARCHIVES

COURS DU TRIBUNAL

Musée d'Art
Réligieux

PL DES
RECOLLETS

RUE DE LA PREFECTURE

R. E. MARTIN

Musée Gassendi

BD GASSENDI

R. H. MARINO

R. DE LA GRANDE FONTAINE

RUE DE
L'ORATOIRE

PL. DES PLATRIERS

R. MERE DE DIEU

PL. DE
L'EVECHE

R. MIOLLIS

R. ST-MICHEL

R. DE LA MAIRIE

PL
GRENETTE

R. GRENETTE

AV. DU DR ROMIEU

PL. DU
MITAN

TRAVERSE DES EAUX CHAUDES

BD VICTOR-HUGO

COURS DES ARES

R. DE GLACIERE

R. CHAPE CAPITOU

R. ST-JEROME

PL. ST-JEROME

Cathédrale
St-Jérôme

T. DE LA TOUR

PL. DU
JUTIERE

R. DES CHAPELLES

BD SOUSTRE

R. DES
TANNEURS

AVENUE DU 8 MAI 1945

HÔTEL DE VILLE

BD MARTIN BRET

PLACE DE
GENERAL GALLE

R. DU JEU DE PAUME

R. PARASSIS

MONTEE DES
PRISONS

T. ST-PIERRE

R. HAUTE-VILLE

RAMPE DU
ROCHAS

R. CURATERIE

PL.
PIED-DE-VILLE

R. TROU DU FOUR

BD PROVENCE

R. DES MORGES

T. DE
LA BOUCHERIE

Centre
Mediathèque

R. DE L'HUBAC

T. DES
SERRES

RUE PIED-DE-LA-VILLE

M. ST-CHARLES

PL. DE LA
BARLETTE

R. DE LA LUNE

BD THIERS

BOULEVARD GASSENDI

R. DU COL PAYAN

T. DE LA
BARLETTE

R. ANDRE HONNORAT

AV. J. REINACH

R. A. RICHARD

ALLEE DES FONTAINIERS

R. PERE R. HUGUES

RUE DU DR HONNORAT

R. BEAU DE ROCHAS

RUE PRETE A PARTIR

Gare Routière &
Gîtes de France

ROND-POINT DU
11 NOV. 1918

AV. DES CHARROIS

AV. DEMONTZEY

▼ Musée Alexandra David-Neel

Gare SNCF & ⓑ ◀

ACCOMMODATION
Central	A
Grand Paris	C
Provence	C
Vieil Aiglun	B

RESTAURANTS & BARS
La Chauvinière	2
Grand Paris	C
Happy Hours	1
La Taverne	3

0 — 50 m

along the D900 to Seynes-les-Alpes; follow av Ste-Douceline left from the top of bd Gassendi. €14 per night. Closed Nov–March.

Eaux Chaudes av des Thermes ☎04.92.32.31.04. Pleasantly situated three-star site, 1km east of town towards the Établissement Thermal. €19.50 per night. Closed Nov–March.

The City

Late medieval Digne had **two centres**. In the area to the north where the pre-Roman town had originally developed, the thirteenth-century church of **Notre-Dame du Bourg** (June–Oct daily 3–6pm) now stands in splendid isolation on placette du Prévat. Typical of Provençal Romanesque architecture, save for its relative bulk and the lightness of its yellowy stone, it now contains fragments of early medallions and late medieval murals, the least faded illustrating the Last Judgement.

The heart of the medieval city, though, was the **Haute Ville**, where the fifteenth-century **Cathédrale St-Jérôme** (June–Oct Tues, Wed, Thurs & Sat 3–6pm) has become weed-encrusted and dilapidated. Its Gothic facade is still impressive and the features inside, in particular the Gothic stained-glass windows, clearly indicate that this was once an awesome place of worship. Some of the surrounding streets are similarly run-down, as commercial life drains away to the vast modern retail park southwest of the centre.

Wednesday and Saturday **markets** bring animation to the otherwise lifeless and windswept **place Général-de-Gaulle**, north of the cathedral, with lots of lavender products, including honey, on sale. To the east, a statue of seventeenth-century mathematician and astronomer **Pierre Gassendi** marks the boulevard that bears his name. He's also remembered in the municipal **Musée Gassendi**, 64 boulevard Gassendi (daily except Tues: April–Sept 11am–7pm; Oct–March 1.30–5.30pm; €4), which holds assorted sixteenth- to nineteenth-century paintings and stages interesting temporary exhibitions.

East of the old town, the **Musée de la Seconde Guerre Mondiale** on place Paradis (mid-April to June & Sept to mid-Nov Wed 2–5pm; July & Aug Mon–Thurs 2–6pm, Fri 2–5.30pm; free) recalls Digne's nine months under Italian occupation, which ended in September 1943 when the Germans took over. It's a fascinating exposé of one town's experience of the war, which left people here – as throughout France – scarred by bitter divisions, even within the ranks of the Resistance.

If you only have time to see one museum, make sure it's the **Musée Alexandra David-Neel** at 27 avenue du Maréchal-Juin (guided visits daily 10am, 2pm & 3.30pm; free; ☎04.92.31.32.38, ⓦalexandra-david-neel.org). Exclusively dedicated to the memory of an extraordinary, tenacious explorer who spent over fourteen years travelling the length and breadth of Tibet, the museum is where David-Neel lived out the remainder of her life, eventually dying in 1969, aged 101. The house is stuffed full of fascinating photographs tracing her journeys, as well as old Tibetan ornaments, masks and paintings.

Eating, drinking and entertainment

Much of Digne's best **dining** is to be had in its hotels, but there are also plenty of **restaurants**, **cafés** and **brasseries** in the old town. Out of season Digne can be very quiet in the evening, with **entertainment** limited to the Centre Culturel Pierre Gassendi, 45 avenue du 8 Mai 1945 (☎04.92.30.87.10), which puts on shows, concerts and films year-round, and also has a cybercafé.

In the first weekend in August, the **Corso de la Lavande** is a jamboree to celebrate the lavender crop and its two key products, honey and perfume, with parades of floats. In September the **Journées Tibétaines** celebrate all things Tibetan; and there are special **film** seasons in March, July and November.

Restaurants and cafés

La Chauvinière 54 rue de l'Hubac ☎04.92.31.40.03. Intimate spot in the Vieille Ville, serving traditional Provençal dishes on menus from €23; some outdoor seating. Closed Mon.

Grand Paris 19 bd Thiers ☎04.92.31.11.15, ⊛hotel-grand-paris.com. Expensive gastronomic restaurant serving good-quality Provençal dishes using local ingredients. Dinner menus €32–60. Closed Dec–Feb, plus Mon, Tues & Wed lunchtimes in low season.

Happy Hours 43 bd Victor-Hugo ☎04.92.31.23.37. Lively café with wi-fi. Closed Sun.

La Taverne 36 bd Gassendi ☎04.92.31.30.82. Modern brasserie, serving *raclette* for €16 and traditional menus from €18. Closed Sun.

The Réserve Naturelle Géologique de Haute-Provence

The largest geological reserve in Europe, the **Réserve Naturelle Géologique de Haute-Provence**, covers over 370,000 acres north and east of Dignes. To learn more about its 300-million-year-old fossils, head to the ammonite-laden **Musée-Promenade** (April–June, Sept & Oct daily 9am–noon & 2–5.30pm, closes Fri 4.30pm; July & Aug Mon–Fri 9am–1pm & 2–7pm, Sat & Sun 10.30am–12.30pm & 2–7pm; Nov–March Mon–Thurs 9am–noon & 2–5.30pm, Fri 9am–noon & 2–4.30pm; €4.60; ☎04.92.36.70.70, ⊛resgeol04.org), immediately north of the city to the left of the bridge across the river on the D900A towards Barles.

Draguignan

DRAGUIGNAN, the main settlement of the inland Var, less than 30km northwest of the coast at **Fréjus**, is a bustling place, if not particularly exciting. One of the few truly urban spots in this region, it has a couple of worthwhile **museums**, a lively **market** on Wednesdays and Saturdays around place du Marché, and a striking **theatre**. Its boulevards and compact medieval centre hold enough moderately priced hotels and restaurants to make it a potential touring base, especially out of season. It's also a military town, as evidenced by the monuments to the Resistance, the Allied war cemetery on boulevard John Kennedy and the barracks and artillery schools that use the beautiful, desolate **Plateau de Canjuers** to the north as a firing range.

The Town

Draguignan's compact old town is dominated by the distinctive seventeenth-century **Tour d'Horloge** (July & Aug guided tours only; free), which stands next to the twelfth-century Chapelle Saint-Sauveur atop a small hill just north of place du Marché. Southwest, the **Musée des Arts et Traditions Populaires de Moyenne Provence**, 15 rue Joseph-Roumanille (Tues–Sat 9am–noon & 2–6pm, plus Sun 2–6pm April–Sept; €3.50), beautifully showcases the old industries of the Var. Nineteenth-century farming techniques and the manufacturing processes for silk, honey, cork, wine, olive oil and tiles are presented within the context of daily working lives – though some scenes are spoilt by rather dire wax models.

On rue de la République, the **Musée Municipal** (Mon–Sat 9am–noon & 2–6pm; free) is housed in a former bishop's palace. Highlights include a delicate marble sculpture by Camille Claudel; Greuze's *Portrait of a Young Girl*; two paintings of Venice by Ziem; a Renoir; and upstairs in the library, a copy of the

Romance of the Rose and early Bibles and maps. Rembrandt's *Child with a Soap Bubble*, stolen from the museum on the eve of Bastille Day in 1999, remains conspicuous by its absence.

Practicalities

Draguignan's **tourist office** is at 2 boulevard Carnot (May, June & Sept Mon–Sat 9.15am–12.15pm & 1.45–6pm; July & Aug Mon–Sat 9.15am–12.15pm & 1.45–7pm, Sun 9.15am–12.45pm; Oct–April Mon–Fri 9.15am–12.15pm & 1.45–6pm, Sat 9.15am–12.45pm; ℡04.98.10.51.05, ⓦdracenie.com). The **gare routière** and the redundant **gare SNCF**, connected by shuttle buses with the main line at Les Arcs, are at the bottom of boulevard Gabriel-Péri, south of the town centre.

La Pergola (℡04.94.99.18.54; ❸) is a cheap and cheerful **hotel** with a garden, ten minutes' walk from the centre at 192 avenue du 4 Septembre, while the comfortable if rather characterless en-suite rooms at the *Hôtel du Parc*, 21 boulevard de Liberté (℡04.98.10.14.50, ⓦhotel-duparc.fr; ❹), overlook a courtyard. The grander, *belle époque Victoria*, 52 boulevard Carnot (℡04.94.47.24.12, ⓦhotelrestaurantvictoria .fr; ❹), also has a garden, though its decor is slightly staid. The two-star *La Foux* **campsite**, 2km south towards Les Arcs (℡04.94.68.18.27; €15.10), has a good pool complex.

Although the Vieille Ville and surrounding boulevards hold a wide choice of inexpensive **places to eat**, little really stands out. *Le Domino*, in a fine old mansion at 28 avenue Carnot (℡04.94.67.15.33; closed Sun & Mon), serves good menus that start at €17 for lunch, while the excellent *Mille Colonnes*, on place aux Herbes (℡04.94.68.52.58; closed Sun & Mon), has a wide-ranging brasserie menu.

North and east of Draguignan

Of the two principal routes onwards and upwards from Draguignan, the **D955** heads north towards the mighty Grand Canyon du Verdon (see p.220), with the dramatic **Gorges du Châteaudouble** as a foretaste of the scenic splendours ahead, while the **D562** sets off northeast towards Grasse, with several medieval villages as potential detours along the way.

South of the D562 lies a wonderful, almost uninhabited expanse of forest where, between January and June, you may see untended cattle with bells round their necks and sheep chewing away at the undergrowth. That these animals are once more roaming the former pasturing grounds of the transhumance routes has great ecological benefits in maintaining the diversity of the forest fauna.

Châteaudouble

Beyond the exquisitely peaceful village of **Rebouillon**, beside the River Nartuby 5km northwest of Draguignan along the D955, the scenery changes dramatically with the start of the **Gorges du Châteaudouble**. A mere scratch it may be, compared to the great Verdon gorge, but it holds some impressive sites, not least the village of **CHÂTEAUDOUBLE** hanging high above the cliffs. Nostradamus predicted that the river would grind away at the base until the village fell, but has yet to be proved right. All but deserted out of season, Châteaudouble consists of little more than a couple of churches, a handful of houses, a potter's workshop, a beekeeper and his hives, a ruined tower and ramparts, and *La Tour* restaurant on place Purgatoire (℡04.94.70.93.08; menus from €24) with a terrace overlooking the gorge.

Callas

The village of **CALLAS**, 15km northeast of Draguignan, can be reached by turning left onto the D525 12km along the road to Grasse. It's a pleasant place to stop, with a lovely square by the church at its highest point, and the tiny, inexpensive **hotel-restaurant** *de France* (☎04.94.76.61.02; menu at €16.70; ❷) further down on the shaded place Georges-Clemenceau. The *Hostellerie des Gorges de Pennafort* (☎04.94.76.66.51, ⓦhostellerie-pennafort.com; ❾; closed mid-Jan to mid-March), in the same *commune*, but overlooking the Pennafort waterfalls 7km south of the village, below the D525 on the D25, is a much grander option, with its own heliport, pool, lake and olive grove.

Bargemon

The steep, narrow D25 climbs through luscious valleys for 6km north of Callas before reaching **BARGEMON**, tucked behind fortified gates and best known these days as the site of David and Victoria Beckham's Provençal retreat. With its fountained squares shaded by towering plane trees, the village is especially picturesque in spring, when its streets are filled with orange petals and mimosa blossom. The **musée-galerie Honoré Camos**, in the little **Chapelle St-Étienne**, which forms part of the defences, hosts exhibitions of local painters (daily: May–Sept 3–6pm; Oct–April 2.30–5.30pm; free). The two angel heads on its high altar are attributed to the great Marseillais sculptor Pierre Puget.

Seillans

As you head east from Bargemon along the minor D19, the long-distance view suddenly opens out to the mountains. An ugly rash of white villas spoils the approach to the village of **SEILLANS**, 13km along, where the Vieux Village, home to the painter Max Ernst in his final years, hides behind medieval walls. A small **collection** of lesser-known lithographs by Ernst, as well as some by his companion Dorothea Tanning, is displayed on rue de l'Église (Tues–Sat: summer 3–7pm; winter 2–6pm; €2). Seillans' most spectacular piece of artistry, however, lies 1km beyond the village on the road to Fayence. A Renaissance retable, attributed to an inspired Italian monk, is housed in the Romanesque **Chapelle de Notre-Dame-de-l'Ormeau** (guided tours July & Aug Sat 9am & 11am, Sun 2pm, 3.15pm & 4.30pm). To book tours of the chapel, contact Seillans' **tourist office** (April–Sept Mon–Sat 9.30am–12.30pm & 2.30–6.30pm; Oct–March closes 6pm; ☎04.94.76.85.91, ⓦwww.seillans.fr), near the Ernst exhibition at 1 rue du Valat.

Les Deux Rocs (☎04.94.76.87.32, ⓦhoteldeuxrocs.com; closed Tues & Jan to mid-Feb; ❹), an exquisitely restored town house by the old wash house on the fountained place Font-d'Amont, is the best place to **stay** and **eat**, with beautiful antiques, warm decor, and full dinner menus that start at €40.

Fayence

Known as Favienta Loca (favourable place) by the Romans, **FAYENCE**, 6km east of Seillans, is today better known as a centre for **gliding**. Larger and livelier than most of its neighbours, it makes a good base for exploring the surrounding countryside. Fayence's charm lies in the contrast between its small-town bustle and the peaceful traffic-free side streets spilling over with flowers. Its Vieille Ville curls tightly around the steep slopes of a hill, with the imposing porchway of the *mairie* guarding its entrance; within the Vieille Ville stands a fourteenth-century gateway, the **Porte Sarrazine**. There's a **market** on place de l'Église on Tuesdays,

Thursdays and Saturdays, as well as the inevitable ateliers and souvenir shops, and great views over the countryside.

The **gliding school** is based at Fayence-Tourettes aerodrome, just south of the village (℡04.94.76.00.68, Ⓦwww.aapca.net; flights from €36 per hr).

Practicalities

Fayence's **tourist office** is on place Léon-Roux (mid-April to mid-June Mon–Sat 9am–noon & 2–6pm; mid-June to mid-Sept Mon–Sat 9am–12.30pm & 2–6.30pm, Sun 10am–noon; mid-Sept to mid-April Mon–Sat 9am–noon & 2–5.30pm; ℡04.94.76.20.08, Ⓦville-fayence.fr). The Castle bookshop, 1 rue St-Pierre (Mon 2.30–7pm; Tues–Sat 9am–12.30pm & 2.30–7pm), sells local guides and maps in English.

Accommodation options include *Les Oliviers* (℡04.94.76.13.12, Ⓦlesoliviers fayence.fr; ❺), just below the village on the D19 at 18 avenue St-Christophe, which has a pool; and the seven-room *Auberge de la Fontaine* (℡04.94.76.07.59; ❸), 3km south along the D563 towards Fréjus, beyond the junction with the D562, where Provençal cooking adds to the appeal of its isolation. For really special surroundings, however, book in at the English-owned *Moulin de la Camandoule* (℡04.94.76.00.84, Ⓦwww.camandoule.com; ❻), a converted mill 1km from town on the road out to Notre-Dame-des-Cyprès, which has a top-notch restaurant, *L'Escourtin* (Sept–June closed Wed & Thurs lunch; menus from €30 lunch, €44 dinner). Local **campsites** include three-star *Lou Cantaire*, 5km west on the D562 towards Draguignan (℡04.94.76.23.77, Ⓦsudestvacances.fr/loucantaire; €18.50; closed Dec & Jan).

Besides the hotel **restaurants**, good places to **eat** include the peaceful *Farigoulette* (℡04.94.84.10.49; closed Wed, plus Tues Sept–June), 1 place du Château, serving traditional menus from €20 in a former stable at the top of the village, and the *Patin Couffin* on placette de l'Olivier (℡04.94.76.29.96; menu at €28; closed Mon plus mid-Nov to mid-March), which is known for its large portions of good food.

The Grand Canyon du Verdon

Europe's widest and deepest gorge, the breathtaking **Grand Canyon du Verdon** – a V-shaped chasm also known as the Gorges du Verdon – cuts a 21km-long east–west swathe through the limestone foothills of the Alps. Ever-changing in its volume and energy, the River Verdon falls from **Rougon** at the eastern end of the gorge, disappearing into tunnels, decelerating for shallow languid moments, and finally exiting in full steady flow at the **Pont de Galetas** to fill the huge artificial **Lac de Ste-Croix**.

The entire circuit around the canyon, along the **Corniche Sublime** to the south and the **Route des Crêtes** to the north, is 130km long. Only preternaturally fit cyclists should attempt it, and even for drivers it's hard work, with perilous hidden bends and hairpins, and, in July and August, fearsome traffic. **Walking** is the ideal way to explore; the best trails start on the northern side, as described on p.225. Before you hike in the gorge itself, always get details of the route and advice on **weather conditions** (℡08.36.68.02.04, Ⓦmeteoconsult.fr). You'll also need water, a torch for the tunnels, and warm clothing for the cold shadows of the narrow corridors of rock. Always stick to the path and don't cross the river except at the *passerelles*; water levels change very abruptly when the dams open upstream (℡04.92.83.62.68 for recorded information), and drownings can and do occur.

Public transport is poor. You can find the latest timetables on Ⓦlapaludsurverdon .com, but broadly speaking there's one **bus** between Marseille, Aix, Moustiers,

▲ Pont de l'Artuby, Grand Canyon du Verdon

La Palud, Rougon and Castellane (July to mid-Sept Mon, Wed & Sat; mid-Sept to June Sat only); and two daily services between La Palud, Rougon and Castellane (July & Aug Mon–Sat; Easter–June & Sept Sat & Sun only, plus hols).

The south rim

The most dramatic approach to the canyon is from the southeast, taking the D955 north from Draguignan and then turning west at Comps-sur-Artuby to follow the aptly named **Corniche Sublime** along the southern rim.

Comps-sur-Artuby

The isolated settlement of **COMPS-SUR-ARTUBY** stands 20km north along the D955 from Châteaudouble (see p.218), beyond the increasingly bleak military camp of Canjuers. Though the surrounding scenery is magnificent, the village itself holds few specific sights, other than the fortified chapel of **St André**. There's a pleasant **hotel-restaurant**, the *Grand Hotel Bain*, on avenue de Fayet (Ⓣ04.94.76.90.06, Ⓦgrand-hotel-bain.fr; ❸), with menus from €17.50 and a sunny garden.

Along the Corniche Sublime

The D71 runs west from Comps through end-of-the-earth heath and hills, with each successive horizon higher than the last. When you reach the canyon, 16km along, it's as though a silent earthquake had taken place while you journeyed.

The first vantage point, of the **Balcons de la Mescla**, is a memorable *coup de théâtre*. As the view is withheld until you are almost upon it, the 250-metre drop at your feet comes as a visceral body-blow. Running west from the Balcons, the **Corniche Sublime** itself was built expressly to provide the most jaw-dropping and hair-raising views. Drivers with any fear of heights – and of course their passengers – are best advised not to come this way.

Halfway between Comps and Aiguines, perched on the very lip of the canyon, the *Grand Canyon du Verdon* (Ⓣ04.94.76.91.31, Ⓦhotel-canyon-verdon.com; ❻;

Canyon activities and information

Outfitters and guides based in the towns and villages around the gorge offer **activities** of all kinds. Most operate in summer only, between April and September. For general information, contact the **Parc Naturel Région du Verdon**, Domaine de Valx, Moustiers (℡04.92.74.68.00, ⓦparcduverdon.fr).

Multi-activity operators
UCPA La Palud (℡04.92.77.31.66, ⓦucpa-vacances.com. Climbing, walking, cycling, canoeing and nautical trekking with a trained guide.

Walking and climbing
Bureau des Guides La Palud (℡04.92.77.30.50, ⓦescalade-verdon.fr. Association of professional guides for walks, canyoning and rock-climbing.
Des Guides Pour l'Aventure La Palud (℡06.85.94.46.61, ⓦguidesaventure.com. Professional walking guides, rock-climbers and canyoneers.
Le Perroquet Vert La Palud (℡04.92.77.33.39, ⓦleperroquetvert.com. Climbing shop and *chambres d'hôtes* (see p.225).

On the water
Only attempt to **canoe** or **raft** the full length of the gorge if you are very experienced and strong; you'll have to carry your craft for long stretches. However, you can pay (in the region of €35 for 2hr, €75 for a full day) to join a group and tackle certain stretches of the river. No trips take place during hydroelectric operations, so be prepared for disappointment.
Aboard Rafting Castellane ℡04.92.83.76.11, ⓦaboard-rafting.com. Water-based activities including rafting, canoeing, canyoning, hydrospeeding and water rambling.
Base Sport et Nature Castellane and Entrevaux ℡04.93.05.41.18, ⓦbasesport nature.com. Rafting, canoeing and canyoning.

Horseriding
Ranch Les Pionniers La Palud ℡04.92.77.38.30, ⓦlespionniers.com. Horse rides with your own guide, and even cattle round-ups.
Ferme Equestre du Pesquier Castellane ℡04.92.83.63.94, ⓦchevalverdon.com. Horseriding, and day-trips combining rides with rafting.

Cycling
Le Petit Ségriès Moustiers ℡04.92.74.68.83, ⓦverdon-vtt.com. Cycle rental and guided cycling tours.

Paragliding and bungee-jumping
Verdon Passion Moustiers ℡04.92.74.69.77, ⓦverdon-passion.com. Canyoning, climbing and paragliding.
Latitude Challenge Marseille ℡04.91.09.04.10, ⓦlatitude-challenge.fr. Bungee jumps from the 182m Pont de l'Artuby.

closed Oct–Easter, plus Tues eve & Wed except in July & Aug), is a stylish Logis de France **hotel** with comfortable rooms, balconies and a dining terrace teetering above a 300-metre drop. All guests have to be on *demi-pension*.

Aiguines

AIGUINES, perched at the western end of the Corniche Sublime and 30km north of Aups, effectively consists a single long promenade high above the Lac de Ste-Croix. Its one landmark, a château of pepperpot towers that dazzle with their coloured tiles, is not open to the public. Until tourism came along, it made its living from wood-turning, and in particular crafting *boules* for *pétanque* from ancient boxwood roots.

Aiguines has a little **tourist office** on Allées de Tilleul (July & Aug Mon–Sat 9am–1pm & 2–6pm; Sept–June Mon–Fri 9am–12.30pm & 2–5.30pm; ⊤04.94.70.21.64, ⓦaiguines.com). There are two lovely Logis de France **hotels** in the heart of the village nearby: *Le Vieux Château* on place de la Fontaine (⊤04.94.70.22.95, ⓦhotelvieuxchateau.fr; ❹; closed Nov–March), which has a nice terrace bar and restaurant that serves a €23 *menu terroir*; and the fancier *Altitudes 823*, at the hairpin bend where the main road reaches the centre (⊤04.98.10.22.17, ⓦaltitude823-verdon.com; ❻; closed Nov to mid-March), which has enormous views and only accepts guests on *demi-pension*.

Opposite the *Vieux Château*, the little *Rive Gauche* **restaurant** (⊤04.94.84.23.11; closed mid-Nov to mid-March, plus Wed in low season) also has lake views, and offers a €15.50 lunch menu.

Lac de Ste-Croix

At its western end, the canyon emerges abruptly into the enormous turquoise reservoir of the **Lac de Ste-Croix**. From the Pont de Galetas, where the D957 crosses the river, you can often see river rafts rounding the final bend of the gorge. At the beach just to the north, rowing boats and pedalos are available to rent; when no floodgates are open, the waters are placid enough to set off upstream between the cliffs. **Swimming** is also good here, though when the lake levels are low, things can get a bit muddy around the edges.

A two-star **campsite**, *Le Galetas* (⊤04.94.70.20.48; ⓦaiguines.com/galetas; €14.60; closed mid-Oct to March), is located beside the D957 south of the lake, on the slopes below Aiguines.

Moustiers-Ste-Marie

The loveliest village on the fringes of the gorge, **MOUSTIERS-STE-MARIE** occupies a magnificent site near its western end, 15km east of Riez. Seven kilometres north of Lac de Ste-Croix, but set high enough to command fine views down to it, it straddles a plummeting stream that cascades between two golden cliffs. A mighty star slung between them on a chain, said to have been originally suspended by a returning Crusader, completes the perfect picture.

Not surprisingly, however, Moustiers gets very crowded in summer, when visitors throng its winding lanes and pretty bridges, and fill the many stores and galleries that sell the traditional local speciality, **glazed pottery**. To learn more about that, drop in at the small **Musée de la Faience** (Feb, March, Nov & Dec Sat & Sun 2–5pm; April–June, Sept & Oct daily except Tues 10am–12.30pm & 2–6pm; July & Aug daily 10am–12.30pm & 2–7pm; €3, free on Tues July & Aug) in the Hôtel de Ville on the east side of the stream.

Although coming to Moustiers out of season is more of an unalloyed pleasure, you can escape the commercialism year-round by puffing your way uphill to the aptly named chapel of **Notre Dame de Beauvoir**, high above the village proper.

Practicalities

The **tourist office**, which offers **internet** access, is on place de l'Église west of the stream (March & Oct daily 10am–noon & 2–5.30pm; April–June daily 10am–12.30pm & 2–6pm; July & Aug Mon–Fri 9.30am–7pm, Sat & Sun 9.30am–12.30pm & 2–7pm; Sept daily 10am–12.30pm & 2–6.30pm; Nov daily

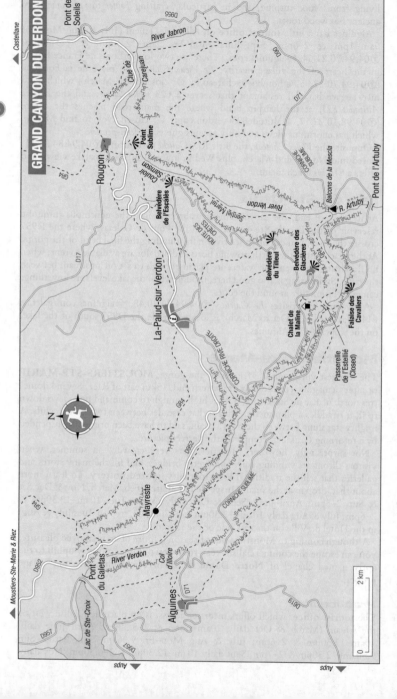

GRAND CANYON DU VERDON

Castellane

Pont de Soleils

River Jabron

D955

D90

D71

Clue de Carejuan

Point Sublime

Rougon

D17

D952

Couloir Samson

Belvédère de l'Escalès

CORNICHE SUBLIME

Sentier Martel

ROUTE DES CRÊTES

River Verdon

Balcons de la Mescla

Pont de l'Artuby

R. Artuby

Belvédère du Tilleul

Belvédère des Glacières

D71

Falaise des Cavaliers

Chalet de la Maline

Passerelle de l'Estellié (Closed)

La-Palud-sur-Verdon

CORNICHE DROITE

D952

D23

Moustiers-Ste-Marie & Riez

Aups

Aups

Mayreste

CORNICHE SUBLIME

Pont du Galetas

River Verdon

Col d'Illoire

Aiguines

D71

D19

D957

D71

D957

Lac de Ste-Croix

N

2 km

0

10am–noon & 2–5.30pm; Dec–Feb daily 10am–noon & 2–5pm; ⊕04.92.74.67.84, ⊛moustiers.fr).

Moustiers holds a considerable amount of **accommodation**. Its two most central **hotels** are very reasonably priced: the *Hotel-Café du Relais*, beside the main bridge (⊕04.92.74.66.10, ⊛lerelais-moustiers.com; ❹; closed Nov–March, plus Fri except in July & Aug), serves menus at €22 and €34 on a nice glassed-in terrace overlooking the stream, while the orange *Belvédere* on the east bank (⊕04.92.74.66.04; ❷; closed Oct–March) also has a little garden restaurant (closed Wed). Among the nicest of the many **chambres d'hôtes** is the *Clerissy*, place du Chevalier du Blacas (⊕04.92.74.62.67, ⊛clerissy.fr; ❷; closed mid-Nov to mid-March), where the four white-walled rooms are simple, clean and full of character, and the colourful pizzeria downstairs offers good-value dining. The most luxurious option of all is the *Bastide de Moustiers* (⊕04.92.70.47.47, ⊛bastide-moustiers.com; ❽; closed Jan & Feb, plus Mon), beside the main D952 just below the village, run by celebrity chef Alain Ducasse. Each room has its own theme, there's a herb garden and a helicopter pad in the grounds, and the **restaurant** offers weekday set menus at a (relatively) modest €55.

There are also several riverside **campsites** along the D957 south of the village, including the two-star *Domaine du Petit-Lac* (⊕04.92.74.67.11, ⊛lepetitlac.com; €25.80; closed early Oct to late April).

The north rim

The spectacular and tortuous D952 runs more or less parallel to the north bank of the Verdon river for 45km east from Moustiers to Castellane. For the best close-up views of the gorge, however, head south near the village of La Palud-sur-Verdon halfway along, and follow the **Route des Crêtes** to the lip of the abyss.

La Palud-sur-Verdon

LA PALUD-SUR-VERDON, the closest village to the gorge, is the best base for exploring the area. Though there's not much to the village itself, which all but closes down out of season, it does have a certain bleak appeal. The **Maison des Gorges du Verdon** (daily except Tues: mid-March to mid-June and mid-Sept to mid-Nov 10am–noon & 4–6pm; mid-June to mid-Sept 10am–1pm & 4–7pm; ⊕04.92.77.32.02, ⊛lapaludsurverdon.com; exhibition €4), in the château in the heart of town, is a centre for environmental tourism that includes the **tourist office** and an exhibition on the gorge, and also offers **internet** access.

Several **hotel-restaurants** are located in and around the village. *Le Provence* (⊕04.92.77.38.88, ⊛verdonprovencehotel.com; ❸; closed Nov–March), just below the village on route de la Maline, has the most stunning position, while *Les Gorges du Verdon* (⊕04.92.77.38.26, ⊛hotel-des-gorges-du-verdon.fr; ❼; closed late Oct to early April), 500m from the start of the route des Crêtes and a few minutes' walk from the trails down into the gorge, is beautifully isolated and considerably fancier. *Le Panoramic*, in spacious grounds just west of the centre on route de Moustiers (⊕04.92.77.35.07, ⊛hrpanoramic.com; ❹; closed Nov–March), may not have such good views, but it's agreeable enough, while the twelve-room *Auberge des Crêtes* is 1km east of La Palud (⊕04.92.77.38.47, ⊛www.provenceweb.fr/04/aubergedescretes; ❹; closed early Nov to late March).

Right in the village centre, the *Perroquet Vert* **B&B** (⊕04.92.77.33.39, ⊛leperroquetvert.com; ❸; two-night minimum stay; closed Nov–March) is a rendezvous for climbers and walkers, and also serves simple meals. The two-star municipal **campsite** is 800m east on the route de Castellane (⊕04.92.77.38.13, ⊛lapaludsurverdon.com; €10.20; closed Oct–March).

Conversation in La Palud's social hub, the **bar-café** *Lou Cafetie*, is always thick with stories of near-falls, near-drownings and near-death from exposure. Most visitors dine in the hotels, but there's also a pizzeria and a crêperie. The **market** is on Sunday.

The Route des Crêtes

While not quite as spectacular as the Corniche Sublime, the **Route des Crêtes**, a 23-kilometre loop trip off the D952 south of La Palud, offers a succession of stunning canyon viewpoints, with sheer 800-metre drops in places. As traffic along the mid-section of the route is one-way, westbound, to complete the whole circuit you have to start from its more scenic eastern end, 1km east of La Palud.

For walkers, the best trail down to the river itself starts at La Maline, halfway along. Hiking to the Verdon, then following it on the **Sentier Martel** footpath and climbing back up at **Point Sublime**, near Rougon on the D952, takes seven hours, and is best done as part of a guided group, with one of the operators listed on p.222.

Unaccompanied shorter excursions into the canyon include the relatively easy **Sentier du Lézard**, marked from **Point Sublime**. Alternative routes, ranging from 30 minutes to four hours, offer the chance to pass through the **Couloir Samson**, a 670-metre tunnel with occasional "windows", and a stairway down to the chaotic sculpture of the river banks.

Castellane

Huddled at the foot of a sheer 180-metre cliff, the grey and rather severe-looking town of **CASTELLANE** is these days primarily a gateway community for visitors to the **Gorges du Verdon**, 17km southwest. In summer, thanks to its wide range of restaurants, hotels and cafés, it enjoys an animation rare in these parts.

Houses in Castellane's old quarter, the Vieille Ville, are packed close together; some of the lanes are barely shoulder wide. At 34 rue Nationale, a house where Napoleon stopped to dine on March 3, 1815 is now the **Musée du Moyen Verdon** (May–Sept daily except Tues 10am–1pm & 3–6.30pm; €4), which holds temporary exhibitions of variable interest.

A footpath from behind the parish church at the head of place de l'Église winds its way up to the chapel of **Notre Dame du Roc** at the top of the cliff. Not as demanding as it might at first appear, it soon passes the machicolated **Tour Pentagonal**, standing uselessly on the lower slopes. Twenty to thirty minutes should see you at the top; you won't actually see the gorge, but there's a pretty good view of the river disappearing into it and the mountains circling the town.

Practicalities

Castellane's **tourist office** is at the top of rue Nationale (July & Aug Mon–Sat 9am–12.30pm & 1.30–7pm, Sun 10am–1pm; Sept–June Mon–Fri 9am–noon & 2–6pm; ☏04.92.83.61.14, ⓦcastellane.org). Several operators run **rafting** and **cycling** trips in the Gorges du Verdon; see p.222.

The finest local **hotel**, the comfortable and very central ⚑ *Commerce* on place de l'Église (☏04.92.83.61.00, ⓦhotel-fradet.com; ❹; closed Nov–Feb), serves wonderful **food** in its garden, with dinner menus at €25 and €30. Cheaper alternatives include the neighbouring *Roc*, 3 place de l'Église (☏04.92.83.62.65, ⓦhotelduroc04 .com; ❷; closed Mon & all Nov), and the *Bon Accueil*, also very central on place Marcel-Sauvaire (☏04.92.83.62.01, ⓦauberge-du-bon-accueil.com; ❶; closed Oct to mid-April), where menus start at €16. You can get pasta dishes for around €9 at *La Main à la Pâte*, which has outdoor seating on rue de la Fontaine, and there's a pleasant ice-cream bar at the end of the same street. Wednesday and Saturday are **market** days.

In the hamlet of **Chasteuil**, north of the D952 7km west of Castellane, and reached by a very steep minor road with eleven switchback bends, the beautiful ⚘ *Gite Chasteuil* (☎04.92.83.72.45, ⓦgitedechasteuil.com; ❹) is a five-room **B&B** with spectacular mountain views.

All the nearby **campsites** are jammed full in summer. Options include the riverside *Frédéric-Mistral*, just west of Castellane on the D952 (☎04.92.83.62.27, ⓦwww.camping-fredericmistral.com; €18; closed mid-Nov to Feb), and the leafy four-star *Domain du Verdon*, another 1.5km west (☎04.92.83.61.29, ⓦwww .camp-du-verdon.com; €33; closed mid-Sept to mid-May), which has several pools and a crazy golf course.

North from Castellane

Following the D955 north of Castellane brings you after 5km to the southern shore of the **Lac de Castillon**, created by another of the many hydroelectric projects that have progressively tamed the awesome power of the River Verdon.

With good train and road access, plenty of accommodation in the Alpine village of **St-André-des-Alpes** (as well as Castellane itself), and well-organized facilities for outdoor activities, particularly water and airborne sports, this is an easy corner of Haute Provence to explore. Traditional Provence is never far away, as the sight of sheep taking over the roads on their way to or from their summer pastures may well remind you.

Lac de Castillon

Slightly milky and an unearthly shade of aquamarine, the hundred-metre-deep **Lac de Castillon** is a popular bathing spot in high summer, with closely supervised **beaches**, **boats** for rent, and plenty of opportunities for **waterskiing**. At its southern tip, the D955 crosses the awe-inspiring **Barrage de Castillon**, where there's a small parking area if you want to stop for a closer look, though bathing is forbidden. The gleam of gold up in the hills on the opposite bank is the Buddhist centre of Mandarom.

The village of **ST-JULIEN-DU-VERDON**, 5km north of the dam, was a casualty of the creation of the lake. Today it's a tiny place, with nothing to suggest that this was once Sanctus Julienetus, on the Roman road from Nice to Digne. Still, it's a pleasant, quiet spot if you just want to laze about by calm water with a gorgeous backdrop of mountains, and has both a two-star **campsite**, *Camping du Lac* (☎04.92.89.07.93, ⓦcamping-rafting-verdon.com; €14; closed mid-Sept to mid-June), which also offers rafting, and a **hotel-restaurant**, *Le Pidanoux* (☎04.92.89.05.87, ⓦwww.verdon-provence.com /pidanoux.htm; ❶).

St-André-les-Alpes

Unlike so many tightly huddled Provençal villages, **ST-ANDRÉ-LES-ALPES**, 8km north of St-Julien, sprawls amid open meadows. Low-key but ever-increasing tourist development, with the construction of wooden chalets and villas to all sides, has given it a straggly feel, though its central streets and squares lie open to magnificent views of the surrounding mountains. Whether the lake itself is visible depends on current water levels; as a rule, it ends 1km or more south.

Beautiful **hiking** and **biking** trails radiate out from St-André; pick up a helpful free guide, in English, at the **tourist office** on place Marcel-Pastorelli (June to mid-Sept Mon–Sat 9am–12.30pm & 2.30–6pm, Sun 10am–12.30pm; mid-April to May & mid-Sept to mid-Oct Mon–Fri 9am–noon & 2–5.30pm, Sat 10am–noon & 4–6pm; mid-Oct to mid-April Mon–Fri 9am–noon & 2–5pm; ☏04.92.89.02.39, ⓦot-st-andre-les-alpes.fr). The **gare Chemin de Fer de Provence,** across the N202 northeast of the centre, is served by trains between Dignes and Nice.

Of the seven **hotels** in and around St-André, the *France* (☏04.92.83.56.29; ❶) offers budget rooms above a large brasserie on the central place Charles Bron, while the *Lac et Forêt* (☏04.92.89.07.38, ⓦlacforet.com; ❶), 1km south towards St-Julien, rents **bikes**. The two-star municipal **campsite**, *Les Iscles* (☏04.92.89.02.29, ⓦsaint-andre-les-alpes.fr; €11.50; closed Oct–April), by the confluence of the Verdon and the Issole nearby, has good facilities. Several hotels have their own **restaurants**, and *La Table de Marie*, place Charles Bron (☏04.92.89.16.10), serves pizzas and salads for around €10.

Paragliding and **hang-gliding** are popular here, around Mont Chalvet to the west of the village; both are very well organized and regulated by Aerogliss, south of the village (☏04.92.89.11.30, ⓦaerogliss.com). Short flights for the less experienced take place in the morning, and five-day beginners' courses start at €485. *Natur Elements* (☏04.92.89.13.26, ⓦnaturelements.com) organize **walks**, and **rafting**, **canyoning** and **canoeing** on the Lac de Castillon and Gorges du Verdon.

Massif les Monges and Seyne

North of Digne, the mountains that reach their highest peak at Les Monges (2115m) form an impassable barrier, as far as roads go, between the valleys running down to Sisteron and the Durance and those of the Bléone's tributaries. There are footpaths for serious **walkers**, and just one road loops south of Les Monges linking Digne and Sisteron across the **Col de Font-Belle**. Fantastic forested paths lead off past vertical rocks from the pass.

The D900a, which follows first the course of the Bléone, and then the Bès torrent, before joining the main D900 and continuing north to **Seyne-les-Alpes**, passes many of the protected sites of the **Réserve Naturelle Géologique de Haute Provence**, where shrubs, flowers and butterflies are now the sole visible wildlife. After heavy rain the waters tear through the **Clues de Barles and Verdaches** like a boiling soup of mud in which it's hard to imagine fish finding sustenance.

Making a livelihood from the land here is difficult. A lot of "*marginaux*" (hippies or anyone into alternative lifestyles) manage to survive, making goat's cheese and doing seasonal work; the indigenous *paysans* are more likely to be opening *gîtes* and servicing the city dwellers who come for **trekking** or **skiing** trips. But it's still very wild and deserted, with little accommodation other than *gîtes* and *chambres d'hôtes*; petrol stations are also few and far between.

Seyne-les-Alpes

SEYNE-LES-ALPES lies in a distinctly alpine landscape 40km north of Digne, its highest point topped by a Vauban fort. Quiet for most of the year, Seyne experiences its main influx in winter, when its three skiing stations, **St-Jean,**

Local **ski resorts** include Pra-Loup (☎04.92.84.10.04, ⓦpraloup.com); Ste-Anne/La Condamine (☎04.92.84.30.30, ⓦwww.sainte-anne.com); Jausiers (☎04.92.81.21.45, ⓦjausiers.com); and Le Sauze/Super-Sauze (☎04.92.81.05.61, ⓦsauze.com). During the skiing season a **free bus** does the rounds of the resorts from Barcelonnette. Pra-Loup's pistes link up with La Foux d'Allos (see p.231).

Chabanon and **Le Grand Puy**, are in operation. It also has the only surviving **horse fair** in southeast France – held on the second Saturday of October – and a mule breeder's competition at the start of August.

The **tourist office**, off the Grande Rue on place d'Armes (July & Aug Mon–Sat 9am–12.30pm & 2.30–6.30pm, Sun 9am–12.30pm; Sept–June Mon–Fri 9am–noon & 2.30–5pm; ☎04.92.35.11.00, ⓦvallee-de-la-blanche.com), provides information about **skiing**, **walking** and **horseriding**. For **accommodation**, there's *La Chaumière* hotel-restaurant, 33 Grande Rue (☎04.92.35.00.48, ⓦhotel-seyne.com; ❸), and *Au Vieux Tilleul* (☎04.92.35.00.04, ⓦvieux-tilleul.fr; ❷; closed first three weeks in Dec, lunch served Aug only), 1km from the town centre at Les Auches, with a happy combination of pool and skating rink, and a restaurant with dinner menus from €20. Below the town, on either side of the river, are two **campsites**, the three-star *Les Prairies* (☎04.92.35.10.21, ⓦcampinglesprairies .com; €19; closed mid-Sept to mid-April) and the two-star, year-round *Blanche* (☎04.92.35.02.55, ⓦwww.camping-de-la-blanche.net; €14.50). As well as a couple of **bars**, the Grande Rue also holds a pizzeria, *La Bugade* (☎04.92.35.10.90), with menus from €9.

Barçelonnette

From the northern border of Provence at the Lac de Serre-Ponçon, the D900 follows the River Ubaye to little **BARÇELONNETTE**, passing through a dramatic landscape of tiny, irregular fields backed by the jagged silhouettes of mountains that look like something out of a vampire movie. The town owes its Spanish-sounding name, "Little Barcelona", to its foundation in the thirteenth century by Raimond Béranger IV, count of Provence, whose family came from the Catalan city. Although snow falls here around Christmas and stays until Easter, and there are several **ski resorts** nearby, summer is the main tourist season.

Arrival, information and accommodation

Barcelonnette's **tourist office** is in a small courtyard just off place F-Mistral (July & Aug daily 9am–12.30pm & 1.30–7.30pm; Sept–June Mon–Sat 9am–noon & 2–6pm; ☎04.92.81.04.71, ⓦbarcelonnette.com). **Buses** from Marseille or Gap arrive on place Aimé-Gassier.

Bikes can be rented from Rando Passion/Maison de la Montagne, 31 rue Jules-Béraud (☎04.92.81.43.34, ⓦwww.rando-passion.com), who also provide guidance for **walks** and **VTT mountain biking** in summer and **snow-shoeing** and **igloo building** in winter. More than a dozen companies, including Alligator (☎04.92.81.06.06) and Aqua'Rider (☎06.32.42.50.15, ⓦaquarider.net), offer every conceivable white-water activity from **canyoning** and **canoeing** to **rafting**.

Almost all of Barcelonnette's attractive crop of well-priced **hotels**, and even some of its **campsites**, stay open year-round.

Hotels

L'Azteca 3 rue François-Arnaud
☎04.92.81.46.36, ⓦwww.azteca-hotel.fr.
Extremely pleasant hotel, in a nineteenth-century
Mexican-style villa, with superb views of the
mountains. ❹
Cheval Blanc 12 rue Grenette ☎04.92.81.00.19,
ⓦwww.chevalblancbarcelonnette.com. Inexpensive, central Logis de France, above an attractive
bar and restaurant. Closed Nov. ❸
Grand Hôtel 6 place Manuel ☎04.92.81.03.14,
ⓦgrandhotel-barcelonnette.fr. Comfortable
old-fashioned and very central hotel, with 21
wood-panelled bedrooms, some capable of
sleeping five guests. ❻

Grande Épervière 18 rue des Trois Frères Arnaud
☎04.92.81.00.70, ⓦhotelgrandeeperviere.com.
Imposing mansion turned upmarket hotel, set in its
own park. ❺

Campsites

Camping du Plan 52 av Émile-Aubert
☎04.92.81.08.11, ⓦcampingduplan.fr. This three-
star site is the closest to town, 500m southwest
along the D902 towards the Col de la Cayolle.
€13.45. Closed Oct to mid-May.
Le Tampico 70 av Émile-Aubert ☎04.92.81.02.55.
Year-round two-star riverside campsite, 1km
southwest of town. €13.50.

The Town

Barçelonnette is an immaculate little place, with sunny squares where old men
wearing berets play *pétanque*, backed by views of snowcapped mountains. All the
houses have tall gables and deep eaves, and a more ideal spot for doing nothing
would be hard to find. In the central square, place Manuel, a white clocktower
commemorates the centenary of the 1848 revolution.

The town has an unlikely link with **Mexico**: many local sheep farmers and wool
merchants emigrated to Latin America in the late nineteenth century to make their
fortunes, before returning home to build their dream houses. In one of these grand
villas, *La Sapinière* at 10 avenue de la Libération, the **Musée de la Vallée** (Jan–May
& Oct to mid-Nov Wed–Sat 2.30–6pm; June to early July & Sept Tues–Sat
2.30–6pm; early July to Aug daily 10am–noon & 3–7pm; €3.30) details the life
and times of the people of the Ubaye Valley, and the emigration to Mexico and
the travels of a nineteenth-century explorer from the town. In summer, the
ground floor becomes an information centre for the **Parc National du Mercantour** (mid-June to mid-Sept daily 10am–noon & 3–7pm; ☎04.92.81.21.31), a
national reserve stretching from the mountain passes south of Barçelonnette
almost to **Sospel**. Staff provide maps, advise on walks and mountain refuges, and
tell visitors about the fauna and flora.

Eating and drinking

In addition to the dining rooms in its hotels, Barçelonnette holds enough **restaurants** to feed the whole valley. At the Wednesday and Saturday **markets** on place
Aimé-Gassier and place St-Pierre, you'll find all manner of sweets, jams and
alcohol made from locally picked bilberries, pâtés made from local birds – thrush,
partridge, pheasant – and the local juniper liquor, *Génépi*. **Nightlife** is limited to
the *St Tropez* and *Chocas* bars on place Manuel.

Restaurants

Adelita rue Donnadieu ☎06.22.81.16.12. Cheap
and cheerful Mexican food in the heart of town.
La Plancha place Paul Raymond
☎06.22.81.12.97. Mountain specialities such as
tartiflette, potato *gratin*, and grilled-meat platters,
for around €15.

Villa Morelia Le Château, Jausiers
☎04.92.84.67.78, ⓦwww.villa-morelia.com. This
gastronomic restaurant, 9km east of Barçelonnette
in a neo-Mexican folly that also houses a plush spa
hotel, serves a delicious nouvelle cuisine menu for
€68. Closed March, April, Nov & Dec.

Moving on from Barçelonnette: the mountain valleys

Four routes from Barçelonnette cross the watershed of Mont Pelat, La Bonette, Chambeyron and their high gneiss and granite extensions. The Col d'Allos leads into the **Haut-Verdon** Valley; the Col de la Cayolle into the **Haut-Var** Valley; the road across the summit of La Bonette to the **Tinée** Valley; and the Col de Larche into Italy. All but the last are snowed up between November and April, and sometimes stay closed as late as June. Further east, the **Vésubie** rises just below the Italian border; like the Tinée and the Verdon it runs into the Var.

The Haut-Verdon Valley

The most westerly route from Barçelonnette crosses the **Col d'Allos** (closed Nov–May) at 2250m to join the River Verdon just a few kilometres from its source. A mountain refuge on the pass, *Col d'Allos* (☎04.92.83.85.14; open Aug only), marks the junction with the GR56, which leads west to the Ubaye Valley and Seyne-les-Alpes, and east to the Col de Larche and the Tinée Valley. In late June pale wild pansies and deep blue gentians flower between patches of ice. The panorama is magnificent, though once you start backstitching your way down the side of the pass to the Verdon, the hideous vast hotels of **La Foux d'Allos** come into view.

La Foux d'Allos

Scruffy **LA FOUX D'ALLOS** is probably the cheapest Provençal resort in which to **ski** or snowboard, and its fifty lifts and 180km of pistes are open from late December to mid-April. The area joins up with Pra-Loup to the north, and the resort is quite high (1800–2600m) with over 250 snow cannons, so melting shouldn't be a problem. A day pass is €29, and skis/snowboards can be rented in season at Lantelme Sports, Le Centre (☎04.92.83.80.09), who for the rest of the year rent out bikes.

La Foux d'Allos and its neighbours are also keen to promote themselves as summer resorts, with all kinds of activities on offer at the Parc de Loisirs in Allos, from trampolining to horseriding, archery, courses in wildlife photography and watersports. A handful of lifts operate in July and August to transport VTT bikers to well-marked trails around the mountain.

The **tourist office** is in the Maison de la Foux (July, Aug & late Dec to April daily 9am–noon & 2–6.30pm; ☎04.92.83.80.70, ⓦ valdallos.com). **Hotels** include *Le Sestrière* (☎04.92.83.81.70, ⓦ lesestriere.com; ❸; closed May, Oct & Nov) and *Le Toukal* (☎04.92.83.82.76, ⓦ www.hotel-letoukal.com; ❸; closed May to late June & mid-Sept to Nov).

Allos and its lake

The medieval village of **ALLOS**, 9km south of La Foux d'Allos, was all but destroyed by fire in the eighteenth century; one tower of the ramparts half-survived and was turned into the current clocktower. The old livelihoods of tending sheep and weaving woollen sheets were all but dying out when tourism began at the start of the twentieth century, with the discovery of the **Lac d'Allos**, 13km east and 800m above Allos. Once skiing became an established pastime the agricultural days of Allos were numbered. Even so, despite all its *résidences secondaires*, it's not a bad place to spend a day or two.

To walk the whole way to the lake from Allos, follow the path that starts by the church. Alternatively, an uneven, single-track road weaves up 46 bends in 6km through a dense forest of larch trees to a busy car park, from which a 45-minute walk brings you to what was once the head of a glacier. At 2228m, the round and impossibly blue surface reflects the high amphitheatre half-circling it. The lake nourishes trout and char in its pure cold waters and mouflon and chamois bound around its banks. Looking in the direction of the one-time glacier flow, you can just see the peak of **Mont Pelat**, the highest mountain in the Parc National du Mercantour.

Practicalities

Allos' **tourist office** is at the northern end of the old village (July, Aug & mid-Dec to mid-April Mon–Sat 8.30am–noon & 2–6.30pm, Sun 9am–noon & 3–6.30pm; Sept to mid-Dec and mid-April to June Mon–Sat 9am–noon & 2–5pm, Sun 9am–noon; ℡04.92.83.02.81, Ⓦvaldallos.com). The Parc National du Mercantour runs an information office in the same building (℡04.92.83.04.18, Ⓦmercantour.eu). **Skis** and **bikes** can be rented from Au Petit Allossard, rue du Pré de Foire (℡04.92.83.14.62, Ⓦwww.aupetitallossard.sport2000.fr).

Hotel-restaurants include the *Gentianes* on Grande Rue in the old village (℡04.92.83.03.50; ❸), which serves full meals and crêpes; and the more upmarket but characterless *Plein Soleil* (℡04.92.83.84.13, Ⓦwww.hotelpleinsoleil.com; ❸) on avenue des Mélèzes in Super-Allos, the modern extension northeast of the village, which has a restaurant specializing in fondue and *raclette*. There's a very comfortable **B&B**, *La Ferme Girerd-Potin*, 5km northwest on route de la Foux (℡04.92.83.04.76, Ⓦchambredhotes-valdallos.com; ❸), and a **gîte d'étape**, the *Chalet Auberge L'Autapie* (℡04.92.83.06.31, Ⓦlautapie.com; half board only, €32 per person). Walkers who book well in advance can also stay at the *Refuge du Lac d'Allos* beside the lake itself (℡04.92.83.00.24; ❶; closed mid-Sept to June).

Colmars-les-Alpes

The next town downstream from Allos, **COLMARS-LES-ALPES**, is an extraordinarily well-preserved stronghold, whose name comes from a temple to Mars built by the Romans high on the adjacent hill. Colmars' all-but-intact sixteenth-century ramparts, complete with arrow slits and small square towers, were constructed on the orders of François I of France to reinforce the defences that had existed since 1381, when Colmars became a border town between Provence and Savoy. When Savoy declared war on France, in 1690, Vauban was called in to make the town even more secure, and designed the **Fort de Savoie** and the **Fort de France** at either end. Their corresponding gateways, the Porte de France and Porte de Savoie, now form the town's two principal entrances, adorned with climbing roses.

Inside the walls, you find yourself in a quiet, atmospheric, somewhat rough-hewn old Provençal town, with cobbled streets and fountained squares. The Fort de Savoie is only open in summer (mid-June to mid-Sept daily 10am–2.30pm & 3–6.30pm, closed Tues & Fri mornings; €3; tickets from the tourist office), when exhibitions of local customs and costumes are set up beneath the magnificent larch-timbered ceilings. All in all, there's not a lot to do in Colmars except wander around and soak up the atmosphere, or take a twenty-minute walk east to the Lance waterfall.

Colmars lies at the junction of the Verdon Valley road with the D78, which climbs northeast between the Frema and Encombrette mountains and descends to the Var Valley at St-Martin-d'Entraunes. Six kilometres along the road, signed left, the **Ratery ski-station** (☎04.92.83.40.92, ⓦratery.com) rents **bikes** in summer. You can **trek** from here over the Encombrette to the Lac d'Allos or east across the Col des Champs (closed mid-Nov to mid-May) to the Var at Entraunes.

Practicalities

Colmars' **tourist office** is outside the walls by the Porte de la Lance (July & Aug daily 8am–7pm; Sept–June Tues–Sat 9am–12.15pm & 2–5.45pm; ☎04.92.83.41.92, ⓦcolmars-les-alpes.fr). The one **hotel**, *Le France* (☎04.92.83.42.93; ❸; closed Jan to late Feb), is nearby, just across the D908 opposite the walled town, and has a garden restaurant that serves pizza in summer. There's also a **gîte d'étape**, the *Gassendi* (☎04.92.83.42.25, ⓦgite-gassendi-colmars.fr; ❶), in a twelfth-century Templar hospice on rue St Joseph, which holds six dorms with ten or twelve beds each, and a couple of private single rooms. The very scenic *Bois Joly* **campsite** is ten minutes' walk away, beside the river (☎04.92.83.40.40; €11.10; closed Oct–April).

The *Lézard* **restaurant**, on the corner of Grande Rue and place Neuve (☎04.92.83.64.41; closed Oct–April), serves *raclette* and doubles as a *salon de thé*, while *Le Gaulois* (☎04.92.83.41.16), facing the church, offers inexpensive salads and pizzas.

Beauvezer

South of Colmars, the D908 sticks to the Verdon, a wide, dramatic torrent in winter or spring, a wide, messy track of scattered boulders and branches in summer. Five kilometres along, **BEAUVEZER** perches high above its right bank. A wonderful ancient village, it's rich with the smell of old timber, while its ancient stone wash basins bear witness to its linen-making past. Beside the beautiful ochre church on place de l'Église, *Le Bellevue* (☎04.92.83.51.60, ⓦwww.lebellevue.eu; ❸) is one of the prettiest **hotel-restaurants** in Haute Provence, and has some large family rooms.

The D908 continues south for 23km from Beauvezer to St-André-Les-Alpes (see p.227), while forking southeast after 7km onto the D908 will take you towards Annot instead (see p.234).

The Haut-Var Valley

The D902 from Barçelonnette to the **Haut-Var Valley** starts by heading south, climbing through a deep gorge cut by the **River Bachelard**. It then turns abruptly east, continuing beside the river as it squeezes between Mont Pelat to the south and the ridge of peaks to the north, whose shapes have given them the names Pain de Sucre (Sugarloaf), Chapeau de Gendarme (Gendarme's Hat) and Chevalier (Horseman). At the *Bayasse* refuge (☎04.92.81.07.31, ⓦrefuge.bayasse.free.fr; ❶), the D902 turns south towards the **Col de la Cayolle**, while a track and the GR56 continue east towards La Bonette and the Tinée Valley.

Having switchbacked down south from the Col de la Cayolle, the road becomes the D2202. The **Var** now makes its appearance, pouring southwards towards Guillaumes, and beyond that down through the **Gorges de Daluis** to Entrevaux (see p.235). Its banks are punctuated with chapels built before and after disasters of avalanches, floods, landslides and devastating storms. Many are superbly decorated, like the Renaissance Chapelle de St-Sébastien, just north of **Entraunes**, and the church at **St-Martin-d'Entraunes**, with its Bréa retable.

Guillaumes

Tucked beneath the ruined Château de la Reine Jeanne, **GUILLAUMES**, the valley's minor metropolis and a favourite with cyclists in summer, is a traditional resting place for sheep on their way between the Haut-Var summer pastures and Nice. Most flocks now travel by lorry, but the old **sheep fairs** on September 16 and the second Saturday of October are still held. Winter sees a migration in the opposite direction, as the residents of the Côte d'Azur flock to the ski resorts of Valberg and Beuil, to the east of Guillaumes, on the fabulous road that climbs over to the Tinée Valley.

Guillaumes holds a small **tourist office** (daily 10am–noon & 2–6pm; ☎04.93.05.57.76, ⓦpays-de-guillaumes.com), on the main road opposite the town hall, and a couple of **hotels**. The old-fashioned *Renaissance* (☎04.93.05.59.89, ⓦhotelrenaissance.fr; ❹), 100m up on the right, just past the bridge at 7 place Napoléon III, has simple, brightly coloured rooms and a restaurant serving menus at €14 and €20, with seating outdoors in summer; there's also the smaller *Chaudrons* (☎04.93.05.50.01; ❷) on the main road.

The Gorges de Daluis

About 5km south of Guillaumes, the Var enters the dramatic red-rocked **Gorges de Daluis**. Drivers heading upstream here (northwards) enjoy better views; the downstream carriageway is in tunnels much of the way. Walkers can take a closer look at the gorge by following the two-kilometre Sentier du Point Sublime from Pont de Berthèou on the D2202 to the Point Sublime itself. The Pont de la Mariée is a popular spot for **bungee-jumping** (mid-July to Aug daily 1–5pm; €60; ⓦwww.saut-elastique.com/bon-spot-pont-mariee.htm).

The Lower Var Valley

The main N202 climbs east of St-Julien-du-Verdon (see p.227) to meet the Var river after 24km. From there, as first the D4202 and then the D6202, it follows the **Lower Var Valley** for another 40km to its semi-subterranean confluence with the Tinée, and thus provides direct access to Nice along the spectacular gorge known as the **Défilé de Chaudan**. This riverside route is also followed by the Chemin de Fer de Provence, and by steam trains in summer. The major highlight along the way is the medieval fortified town of **Entrevaux**, but several lesser communities also make pleasant stops.

Annot

Surrounded by hills a couple of kilometres north of the N202, 17km east of St-Julien-de-Verdon, the town of **ANNOT** centres on a large open *cours*, lined by plane trees. This is bounded to one side by the river Vaire and to the other by a compact **Vieille Ville**, a flavourful tangle of pretty arcades, mysterious passage-ways, thick arches and gateways that nonetheless lacks any businesses or particular tourist attractions. While Annot is not in itself as lovely or picturesque as Entrevaux, it's a popular holiday centre, and makes an excellent base for walks, up past strange sandstone formations to rocky outcrops with names like *Chambre du Roi* (the King's Chamber) and *Dent du Diable* (the Devil's Tooth).

Practicalities

Annot's helpful **tourist office** on place du Germe just outside the old quarter (March–Oct Mon–Sat 9am–noon & 3–6pm, Sun 9am–noon; Nov–April Mon–Sat

9am–noon & 3–5pm; ☏04.92.83.23.03, ⓦannot.fr) organizes guided tours of the Vieille Ville (June–Sept Tues & Fri 10.30am; €3; extended walks April–June, Sept & Oct Sat 2.45pm & Sun 10am; July & Aug Wed 10am & Sun 10am; €6). The **gare Chemin de Fer de Provence** is not far southeast.

Well-priced **hotels** include the *Beau Séjour* (☏04.92.83.21.08, ⓦhotel-beausejour -annot.com; ❷), a Logis de France by the entrance to the Vieille Ville on place du Revelly, which serves good food both indoors and out, with menus at €15 and €21. *L'Avenue*, on avenue de la Gare (☏04.92.83.22.07, ⓦhotel-avenue.com; ❹; closed Nov–Feb), has small cosy rooms and another good **restaurant** (dinner nightly, lunch Sun only), with menus at €20 and €30. There's a very pleasant two-star **campsite**, *La Ribière*, just north of town on D908 towards Fugeret (☏04.92.83.21.44, ⓦla-ribiere.com; €12.70; closed late Oct to Feb).

Entrevaux

The absurdly photogenic village of **ENTREVAUX** stands on the north bank of the River Var 15km east of Annot, and 6km east of the southern end of the Gorges de Daluis (see opposite). Entrevaux was once a key border town between France and Savoy, and the only access to its old walled centre is via a single-arched drawbridge across the rushing river. The bridge was fortified by Vauban, whose linking of the town with a ruined **château** (access at any time; €3), perched atop a steep spur 135m above the river, gives the site a menacing character. Originally the château could only be reached by scrambling up the rock, but by the seventeenth century this had become unacceptable, and Vauban built the double-walled ramp, plus attendant bastions, that zigzags up the rock with ferocious determination.

The former **cathedral** (summer 9am–7pm; winter 9am–5pm), in the lower part of the old town, is well integrated into the military defences, with one wall forming part of the ramparts and its belfry a fortified tower. The interior, however, is all twirling Louis Quinze, with misericords, side altars and organ as over-decorated as they could possibly be. Just beyond the church, through the **Porte d'Italie**, you can escape from Baroque opulence and military might alike.

▲ Entrevaux

A bizarre labour of love, the **Musée Moto**, on rue Serpente in the heart of the village (May–Sept daily 10am–12.30pm & 2–6pm; free, but donations gratefully accepted), consists of a rather amazing collection of old motorcycles squeezed into a tiny house. Prize specimens include a gleaming Harley-Davidson from 1917, and a Narcisse tandem from 1951.

Practicalities

Entrevaux's **tourist office** (July & Aug daily 9am–7pm; March–June & Sept daily 9am–noon & 2–5pm; Oct–Feb Tues–Sat 10am–noon & 2–5pm; ☎04.93.05.46.73, ⓦentrevaux.info), in the left-hand tower of the drawbridge, organizes guided tours of the town (July & Aug; €3.80) in medieval costume. The **gare Chemin de Fer de Provence**, on the Nice–Dignes line and also served by the **steam-train** trips detailed on p.349, is just downstream on the south bank.

There are no **hotels** in the old town proper, but the *Vauban*, immediately across the river at 4 place Moreau (☎04.93.05.42.40, ⓦhotel-le-vauban.com; ❷; closed Sun pm & Mon, Sept to mid-July), offers reasonable rooms, not all en-suite, and has a restaurant specializing in trout, pasta and the local dry beef sausage (*secca de boeuf*), with menus from €17.

Of the handful of places to **eat** in the walled village, the *Planet* on place Panier (☎04.93.05.49.60) serves pasta specials and has a €21 menu. Otherwise, the *Bar au Pont-Levis* (☎04.93.05.40.12; closed Fri), near the *Vauban*, is a popular rendezvous for English-speaking visitors.

Puget-Théniers

East of Entrevaux, the broad Var Valley holds abundant pear, apple and cherry orchards. **PUGET-THÉNIERS**, 13km along, is a presentable but not especially attractive country town, though its **Vieille Ville**, on the right bank of the River Roudoule, is full of thirteenth-century houses, some with symbols of their original owners' trades on the lintels. The left bank is dominated by the great semicircular apse of the Romanesque **church**, outreaching even the ancient cedar alongside, and suggesting a fort or prison more than a place of worship.

On the *cours* below the old town, in front of the station, a statue of a naked woman with bound hands commemorates **Auguste Blanqui**, born here in 1805. A leader of the Paris Commune of 1871, Blanqui spent forty years in prison for – as the inscription states – "fidelity to the sacred cause of workers' emancipation". There are few French revolutionaries for whom the description "heroic defender of the proletariat" is so true, and none who came from a more isolated, unindustrialized region.

Practicalities

The **tourist office** (June–Aug Mon–Fri 9am–12.30pm & 2–6pm, Sat & Sun 9am–7pm; Sept–May Mon–Sat 9am–noon and 2–5.30pm; ☎04.93.05.05.05, ⓦwww.provence-val-dazur.com) is on the N202, alongside the gare Chemin de Fer de Provence. On summer Sundays, under the name of Le Train Aux Pignes, **steam-train excursions** along the valley connect Puget-Théniers with Touët-sur-Var to the east and Entrevaux to the west (mid-May to mid-Oct, departs Puget-Théniers Sun 10.25am, Entrevaux Sun 4.30pm; round-trip €17.50; reservations essential ☎04.97.03.80.80, ⓦtrainprovence.com).

Across the road from the station, the *Alizé* **hotel** (☎04.93.05.06.20; ❸) offers reasonable rooms and a pool, and there's a two-star municipal **campsite** by the river (☎04.93.05.10.53; €13; closed Oct–Feb).

On summer evenings the **cafés** and **restaurants** on place A-Conil in the Vieille Ville and down along the Roudoule towards the Var are livelier than you'd expect from a small *haut-pays* town. The best food of all, however, is at *Les Acacias* (☎04.93.05.05.25; closed Wed), 1km east on the main road, where *cuisine de terroir* using the local produce can be enjoyed on a €13.20 lunch menu, or for €30 in the evenings.

Touët-sur-Var and the Gorges du Cians

Eight kilometres east of Puget-Théniers, the River Cians joins the Var. The road along this tributary, the D28, leads to the ski resort of Beuil, passing first through the Gorges Inférieures du Cians, close to the confluence, and then the **Gorges du Cians** proper, an ominous chaos of water tumbling between looming red schist cliffs. Much of the route is tunnelled.

Crammed against a cliff not far beyond the confluence, **TOUËT-SUR-VAR** holds a remarkable church, built over a small torrent that's visible through a grille in the floor of the nave. The village's highest houses look as if they're falling apart, but in fact the gaps between the beams are open galleries where the midday sun can reach the rows of drying figs.

There's nowhere to stay in Touët, but it has a good **restaurant**, the *Auberge des Chasseurs*, on the main road (☎04.93.05.71.11; menus at €21 & €30; closed Tues), serving local specialities which involve game and wild mushrooms in autumn.

Clues de Haute Provence

West of the River Var, north of Vence and the Route Napoléon in the Pre-Alpes de Grasse, lies the area known as the **Clues de Haute Provence**, *clues* being the word for the gorges cut through the limestone mountain ranges by their torrential rivers. The seclusion of this arid, sparsely populated region is disturbed only by the winter influx of skiers heading to the 1777-metre summit of the **Montagne du Cheiron**.

Each claustrophobic and seemingly collapsible *clue* opens onto a wide and empty landscape of white and grey rocks with a tattered carpet of thick oak and pine forest. The horizons are always closed off by mountains, some erupting in a space of their own, others looking like coastal cliffs trailing the **Cheiron**, the **Charamel** or the 1664-metre-high **Montagne de Thorenc**. It's the sort of scenery that fantasy films take place in, with wizards throwing laser bolts from the mountains.

Not all the passes stay open in winter – roadside notices forewarn of closures. Routes that go through the *clues* rather than over passes are manageable for cyclists: this is gorgeous, clean-air, long-freewheeling and panoramic terrain. There are plenty of footpaths, with the **GR4** as the main through-route for walkers from Gréolières to Aiglun across the Cheiron.

Accommodation is scarce. What hotels there are tend to be very small, with a faithful clientele booking them up each year, while campsites, too, are thin on the ground. Even winter accommodation at **Gréolières** and **Gréolières-les-Neiges** is minimal, as visitors tend to come up for a day's skiing or have their own weekend places.

From Vence, you approach the *clues* via the Col de Vence, which brings you down to **Coursegoules**. Approaching from Grasse and the Loup Valley, the road north leads to Gréolières, 11km west of Coursegoules.

Coursegoules

The bare white rocks that surround **COURSEGOULES** are not the most hospitable of sites for a working village, so it's no surprise that many of the houses here have become second homes. The population has steadily declined to three hundred or so people who don't need to eke a living from the soil-scoured terrain. The **hotel** *L'Auberge de l'Escaou*, on the lovely place des Tilleuls in the old village (℡ 04.93.59.11.28, Ⓦ auberge-escaou.com; ❹), has a really nice **restaurant** on its terrace, serving a €25 dinner menu, and there's also a crêperie and small bistro nearby.

Gréolières and around

GRÉOLIÈRES, 11km west, seems an equally unpromising site for habitation. Originally a stopping point on the Roman road from Vence to Castellane, it's now surrounded by ruins, of Haut-Gréolières to the north and a fortress to the south. While the village is liveliest during the winter, it passes as a summer resort as well, and is a popular site for paragliding.

The **tourist office** is at 21 Grande Rue (Mon–Fri 9am–noon & 2–6pm; ℡ 04.93.59.97.94, Ⓦ greolieres.fr). There are no hotels in the village, but you can **eat** well and cheaply at *La Vieille Auberge*, on the central place Pierre-Merle (℡ 04.93.59.95.07), and the *Barricade* pizzeria, 14 place de la Barricade (℡ 04.93.59.98.68; closed Mon & Tues).

Heading west around the mountains from Gréolières brings you through the Clue de Gréolières, carved by a tributary of the Loup, to **GRÉOLIÈRES-LES-NEIGES**, 18km away by road. The closest ski resort to the Mediterranean, this is a centre for **cross–country skiing** (℡ 04.93.59.70.57, Ⓦ stations-greolieres -audibergue.com). Fourteen lifts ascend Mont Cheiron in winter, while a single chairlift operates in July and August for summer panoramas. Once again, there are no **hotels**, just some furnished apartments, but a handful of **cafés** and **restaurants** stay open year-round.

Thorenc and St-Auban

Thirteen kilometres west of Gréolières, off the D2, the paragliding and cross-country-skiing resort of **THORENC** was originally founded by English and Russians a century ago. The dense woods and style of the older buildings give it an almost Central European atmosphere. Lively in both winter and summer, it holds a very pleasant small **hotel-restaurant**, *Les Merisiers*, 24 avenue du Belvédère (℡ 04.93.60.00.23, Ⓦ aubergelesmerisiers.com; menus at €23 & €28; ❷; closed Tues, plus mid-March to mid-April).

To the north, the narrow and rough D5 crosses the Montagne de Thorenc by the Col de Bleine, then the D10 takes over for the ascent of Charamel, without a moment's pause in the twisting climb. The D10 leads to Aiglun while the D5 takes the easier westward route to tiny **ST-AUBAN** and its *clue*. With its back to the mountainside, St-Auban rises above the grassy valley, its wide southern views making up for the plainness of the village itself. The gash made by the River Esteron has left a jumble of rocks through which the water tumbles beneath overhanging cliffs riddled with caves and fissures. In summer, rock-climbing and canyoning are possible in the narrow *clue*.

St-Auban's only **hotel-restaurant** is *Le Tracastel* (℡ 04.93.60.43.06, Ⓦ hotel -restaurant-gite.letracastel.fr; ❸; closed Nov–Easter), but there's also a *gîte equestre* where guests can arrange horse rides (reservations through the *mairie*; ℡ 04.93.60.41.23 or 04.93.60.43.20; ❷).

Briançonnet

Downstream from St-Auban, **BRIANÇONNET** enjoys one of the most stunning positions in all inland Provence. From its cemetery, the views stretch southwards past the edge of the Montagne de Charamel across kilometres of uninhabited space. The Romans had a settlement here and the present houses are built with stones from the ancient ruins, with odd bits of Latin still decipherable in the walls. There's just one street with a boulangerie, a *tabac*, a small museum of local history, a church, and one tiny **hotel-restaurant**, *Le Chanan* (⊕04.93.60.46.75; ❷).

From here you can head north across the **Col de Buis** (usually closed Nov to mid-April) to Entrevaux or Annot, or east towards the Clue d'Aiglun and the Clue de Riolan.

The Route des Crêtes

Clinging to the steep southern slope of the Montagne de Charamel, the switchback **Route des Crêtes** (D10) requires concentration and nerve. For long stretches there are no distracting views, only thick forest matted with mistletoe. After the hamlet of Le Mas, which hangs on the edge of a precipitous spur below the road, trees can no longer get a root-hold in the near-vertical golden and silver cliffs; the narrowing road crosses high-arched bridges over cascading streams that fall to smoothly moulded pools of aquamarine.

Just before Aiglun you cross the Esteron as it shoots out from the high-pressure passage (too narrow for a road) that splits the Charamel and the Montagne St-Martin. The most formidable of all the *clues*, it's impossible to explore. You can, however, walk for roughly 3km south along the GR4 from the D10, 1.5km west of the *clue*, to the **Vegay waterfall**, halfway between Aiglun and Gréolières-les-Neiges, where water destined for the Esteron plummets down a vertical cliff face.

In the village of **AIGLUN**, the lovely six-room *Auberge de Calendal*, 1 rue Mont St-Martin (⊕04.93.05.82.32, ⓦauberge-aiglun.com; ❷; closed Wed Oct–March), has a nice restaurant. East from Aiglun, the campanile and silvery olive groves of the ancient fortified village of La Sigale flicker into view.

ROQUESTERON, 10km east of Aiglun, was divided for a hundred years by the France–Savoy border, which followed the course of the Esteron. It holds one **hotel**, the *Passeron* at 25 boulevard Salvago (⊕04.93.05.91.01; ❷). From Roquesteron you can either follow the D17 above the Esteron to the river's confluence with the Var, or take the tangled D1, through passages of rock seamed in thin vertical bands, to **BOUYON**, from where the D8 heads back to Coursegoules. Both routes lead through a succession of eagle's-nest villages. Bouyon is home to a great-value **hotel-restaurant**, the *Catounière*, 12 place de la Mairie (⊕04.93.59.07.15; ❶; closed Oct–Easter).

The Tinée Valley

The longest tributary of the Var, the **Tinée**, rises just below the 2800-metre summit of **La Bonette**, roughly 30km southeast of Barçelonnette (see p.229) by road. The mountains on its left bank – under whose shadow **St-Étienne** and **Auron** nestle – rise up to the Italian border, while the river heads south to cut a steep, narrow valley before joining the Var 30km from the sea.

Across La Bonette

Claiming to be the highest stretch of tarmac in Europe, the D64 across **La Bonette** gives a feast of high-altitude views. Though the actual summit of the mountain, a ten-minute scrabble up scree from the road, is not particularly exciting, and all the

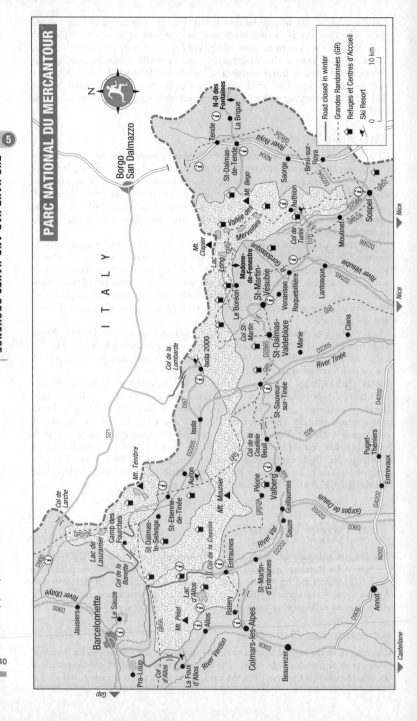

PARC NATIONAL DU MERCANTOUR

N

Road closed in winter
Grandes Randonnées (GR)
Refuges et Centres d'Accueil
Ski Resort

0   10 km

ITALY

Borgo
San Dalmazzo

N-D des
Fontaines

Tende
La Brigue

St-Dalmas-
de-Tende

Saorge

Breil-sur-
Roya

River Roya

N204

GR52A

D6566

GR52

Authion

Mt. Bego

Vallée des
Merveilles

Sospel

Nice

Mt. Clapier

Lac
Long

Col de Turini

D70

Moulinet

GR52

GR52A

Madone-
de-Fenestre

Gordolasque

Le Boréon

St-Martin-
Vésubie

Venanson

Lantosque

Roquebillière

River Vésubie

D2565

Nice

Isola 2000

Col St-
Martin

St-Dalmas-
Valdeblore

Marie

Clans

Col de la
Lombarde

D2205

River Tinée

D97

St-Sauveur-
sur-Tinée

Isola

D28

Mt. Ténibre

GR5

Col de la
Couillole

Puget-
Théniers

Entrevaux

Col de
Larche

Camp des
Fourches

Auron

Beuil

D28

D4202

GR5/56

St-Etienne-
de-Tinée

Mt. Mounier

Péone

Valberg

Sauze

Guillaumes

Gorges de Daluis

D2205

D902

Jausiers

Lac de
Lauzanier

St-Dalmas-
le-Selvage

Col de la
Cayolle

GR52

D202

N202

River Ubaye

D900

Col de la
Bonette

Entraunes

River Var

Annot

D908

Le Sauze

GR56

Mt. Pelat

Lac
d'Allos

St-Martin-
d'Entraunes

Barcelonnette

Ratery

Pra-Loup

Col
d'Allos

Allos

Colmars-les-Alpes

Beauvezer

La Foux
d'Allos

River Verdon

D908

Gap

Castellane

more ugly for its military training camp, the green and silent spaces of the approach, circled by barren peaks, are magical.

Before the hairpins begin for the southern descent, at **Camp des Fourches**, you can abandon your wheels and take the **GR5/56** north and parallel with the Italian border to the Col de Larche, then northwest towards **Larche**, where there's a *gîte* (T 04.92.84.30.80; ❷; closed Oct to mid-Jan & mid-May to June). While it's not exactly a stroll, once you've climbed to the Col de la Cavale (after 5km or so) it's more or less downhill all the way, with the Ubayette torrent as your guide, and the **Lac de Lauzanier**, 5km on from the Col de la Cavale, a spot you may never want to leave.

A short way down from the Camp des Fourches there's another *gîte*, the *Gîte de Bousiéyas* (T 04.93.02.42.20; ❶; closed mid-Sept to mid-June). About 5km on, a track on the left to the tiny hamlet of **Vens** leads to a footpath that follows the Vens torrent to the Lacs de Vens.

St-Étienne-de-Tinée and Auron

Continuing south as the D2205, with the Tinée alongside, the road descends to the small, isolated town of **ST-ÉTIENNE-DE-TINÉE**, which comes to life only during its sheep fairs, held twice every summer, and the Fête de la Transhumance at the end of June. On its western side, off boulevard d'Auron, a cable car then chairlift climb to the summit of **La Pinatelle** (€7.20), thereby linking the village to the **ski resort** of **AURON**, 7km south of St-Étienne, which is also accessible on a dead-end road. Its 21 lifts and 135km of pistes are used by skiers in winter (Dec–April; €28.50 per day), and a few remain open for hikers and mountain bikers in **summer** (July & Aug; €9 per day).

The **tourist office** at 1 rue des Communes-de-France (daily 9am–noon & 2–5pm; T 04.93.02.41.96, W www.auron.com) organizes tours (€3.50) of the town's chapels, the museums of milk-making and traditional crafts and of the old school. Just up from the Pont St-Antoine, at the northern end of the village, the **Maison du Parc National du Mercantour** has displays and information about the park (daily 2–5.30pm; T 04.93.02.42.27, W mercantour.eu). Georges Sports 2000 (T 04.93.23.00.28, W www.auronski.com), on the main square in Auron, **rents** bikes in summer and ski equipment in winter.

There are two **hotel-restaurants** in town – the *Regalivou*, 8 boulevard d'Auron (T 04.93.02.49.00, W leregalivou.free.fr; ❸), and *Des Amis*, 1 rue Val Gélé (T 04.93.02.40.30; ❷) – as well as a few alpine-style restaurants. The *Café Autheman*, on the corner of the main square, has a good selection of beers.

The next stretch downstream from St-Étienne holds nothing but white quartz and heather. Only the silvery sound of crickets competes with the water's roar until you reach **Isola**, an uneventful village at the bottom of the climb to the purpose-built ski resort of **ISOLA 2000** (W www.isola2000.com), a jumble of concrete apartment blocks high in the mountain, just below the tree line, built to accommodate the skiers who use its 22 lifts and 120km of piste (Dec–April; €28.50 per day).

St-Sauveur-sur-Tinée

Beyond Isola, road and river turn south through the Gorges de Valabre, and the drop in altitude is marked by sweet chestnut trees taking over from the pines. The pleasantly sleepy village of **ST-SAUVEUR-SUR-TINÉE** is dominated by its medieval needle belfry, which perches above the river in Mediterranean rather than Alpine fashion. The adornments of the Romanesque gargoyled church include a fine fifteenth-century retable, behind the bloodied crucifix, and a fifteenth-century statue of St Paul above the side door outside.

There's not a lot to do here, other than sit in the sun above the river or head off along the GR52A, but it's an attractive place to pause, perhaps in the small *Café du Village* on the main road. Two **hotels** stand nearby at the southern end of the village: the cosy *Auberge de la Gare*, 1 avenue des Blavets (℡04.93.02.00.67; ❶), and the *Relais d'Auron*, 18 avenue des Blavets (℡04.93.02.00.03; ❷). The two-star municipal **campsite** is in *quartier* Les Plans (℡04.93.02.03.20; €14.50; closed mid-Sept to mid-June).

From St-Sauveur, you can either head west along the D30 towards Valberg and the Haut-Var Valley, a dramatically precipitous climb, or follow the Tinée south, passing far below the charming perched villages of Marie, Clans and La Tour, all of which have medieval decorations in their churches.

The Vésubie Valley

Four kilometres south of St-Sauveur-sur-Tinée, the D2565 heads off east, to climb abruptly to the scattered **Commune of Valdeblore**, with its ancient village of **St-Dalmas**. It then descends to **St-Martin-Vésubie**, at the head of the **Vésubie Valley**. South from St-Martin, road and river head for the Var, passing **Roquebillière**, the perched village of **Lantosque**, and the approach to the pilgrimage chapel of **Madonne d'Utelle**. An alternative southern route from the valley crosses east to the **Col de Turini** and down the **River Bévéra** towards Sospel.

The Commune de Valdeblore and St-Dalmas

Straddling the Col St-Martin between the Tinée and Vésubie valleys, the **COMMUNE DE VALDEBLORE** consists of a series of villages strung along the D2565. The most interesting of these, **ST-DALMAS**, was built on the remains of a Roman outpost, and lies at the strategic crossroads between the most accessible southern route across the lower Alps, linking Piedmont with Provence, and a north–south route that connects Savoy with the sea. The former importance of this region is clear from the dimensions of the **Église Prieurale Bénédictine** (mid-June to mid-Sept afternoons only), parts of which date from the tenth century. A gruesome glazed tomb reveals a 900-year-old skeleton; more appealing are the fragments of fourteenth-century frescoes in the north chapel. The present structure is Romanesque, plain and fierce with its typically Alpine bell tower and rounded apsidal chapels.

Across the Col St-Martin, 3km east of St-Dalmas, chairlifts at the ski resort of **La Colmiane** provide stunning views from the **Pic de Colmiane** (daily: Christmas–March 10am–4.50pm; July & Aug 10am–6pm; ℡04.93.23.25.90, ⓦcolmiane.com; ski pass €17.50 daily, chairlift alone €4.50).

St-Martin-Vésubie

Eleven kilometres east of St-Dalmas, the lovely little town of **ST-MARTIN-VÉSUBIE** is at its busiest in July and August, though even at the height of the season, it's not jam-packed. In late spring and early autumn it makes a perfect base for exploring the surrounding mountains, while in winter you can go for wonderful walks in snowshoes, or tackle assorted cross-country skiing routes.

The main artery of the old quarter, the **rue du Docteur-Cagnoli**, is a single-file cobbled street of Gothic houses with overhanging roofs and balconies, with a channelled stream flowing through its centre. Halfway along on the left, the

Wildlife of the Mercantour

The least shy mammal in these mountains is the **marmot**, a cream-coloured, badger-sized creature often seen sitting on its haunches in the sun. Chamois, mouflon and ibex are similarly unwary of humans, even though they were hunted here not so long ago. The male **ibex** is a wonderful, big, solid beast with curving, ribbed horns that grow to 1m long; the species very nearly became extinct, but the population is now stable. Another species of goat, the **chamois**, is also on the increase; the male is recognizable by the shorter, grappling-hook horns and white beard. The **mouflon**, introduced to the Mercantour in the 1950s, is the ancestor of domestic sheep. Other animals you might see include **stoats**, rare species of **hare**, and **foxes**, the latter the most abundant predator since bears and lynxes became extinct in the region. The most problematic predator, however, is the **wolf**, formerly extinct, but now stalking the region again, having crossed the border from Italy. With eight hundred sheep killed by wolves in a single year, sheep farmers are not happy.

The Mercantour is a perfect habitat for **eagles**, which have any number of crags on which to build their nests, and plenty to eat – including marmots. Pairs of **golden eagles** are breeding, while a rare vulture, the **lammergeier**, has been successfully reintroduced. Other birds of prey – **kestrels**, **falcons** and **buzzards** – wing their way down from the scree to the Alpine lawn and its torrents to swoop on lizards, mice and snakes. The **great spotted woodpecker** and the black-and-orange **hoopoe** are the most colourful inhabitants of the park. **Ptarmigan**, which turn snowy-white in winter, can sometimes be seen in June parading to would-be mates on the higher slopes in the north. **Blackcocks**, known in French as *tétras-lyre* for their lyre-shaped white tails, burrow into the snow at night and fly out in a flurry of snowflakes when the sun rises.

The **flowers** of the Mercantour are an unmissable glory. Over two thousand species are represented, about forty of which are unique to the region. The moment the snow melts, the lawn between the rocky crags and the tree line begins to dot with golds, pinks and blues. Rare species of **lily** and **orchid** grow here, as do the elusive **edelweiss** and the wild ancestors of various cultivated flowers – pansies, geraniums, tulips and gentian violets. Rarest of all is the **multi-flowering saxifrage** (*saxifraga florulenta*), a big spiky flower that looks as if it must be cultivated, though it would hardly be popular in suburban gardens since it flowers just once every ten years. Wild strawberries, raspberries and bilberries tempt you into the woods.

Camping, lighting fires, picking flowers, playing loud music or doing anything else that might disturb the delicate environment is strictly outlawed.

Chapelle des Pénitents Blancs is decorated with eighteenth-century paintings, while St-Martin's **church** at the end holds works attributed to Louis Bréa. Southeast of the church you can look down at the Madone de Fenestre torrent from place de la Frairie. In the opposite direction a narrow lane leads to the junction of rue Kellerman and the main road, beyond which is the old wash house and **Le Vieux Moulin**, the town's one museum (July & Aug Tues–Sun 2.30–6.30pm; Sept Sat & Sun 3–5.30pm; €3), which illustrates the traditional way of life of the Vésubiens.

Practicalities

St-Martin's **tourist office**, on place Félix-Fauré (July & Aug daily 9am–noon & 2–7pm; Sept–June Mon–Sat 9am–noon & 2–6pm, Sun 9am–noon; ℡04.93.03.21.28, ⓦsaintmartinvesubie.fr), keeps lists of *gîtes* and mountain refuges, and walking guides for the region. The Guides du Mercantour, on place de Marché (℡04.93.03.31.32, ⓦguidescapade.com), can arrange **canoeing**, **climbing**, **horse rides**, **walks** and **skiing**. La Librairie de Mercantour, 56 rue Cagnoli, is an excellent source of **books and maps** on the national park.

Hotels include the *Châtaigneraie* (☎04.93.03.21.22, ⓦraiberti.com; ❹; closed Oct–May), set in lovely gardens on the allées de Verdun, which has comfortable rooms that can sleep up to five guests, and a good restaurant; and the cute little *Gélas*, 27 rue Cagnoli (☎04.93.03.21.81, ⓦhotel-gelas.com; ❹).

The closest **campsite**, the two-star *Ferme St-Joseph* (☎06.70.51.90.14, ⓦcamping -alafermestjoseph.com; €16.90; closed mid-Oct to late April), lies to the south, on the route de Nice by the lower bridge over La Madone. The two-star *Le Champouns*, southwest on the route de Venanson (☎04.93.03.23.72, ⓦchampouns.com; €13.50), also has dorm accommodation and rental apartments.

Away from the hotels, the nicest local **restaurant** is the unpretentious and inexpensive *Treille*, 68 rue Cagnoli (☎04.93.03.30.85), with its leafy terrace.

Le Boréon

At **LE BORÉON**, a small, scenic mountain retreat 8km north of St-Martin on the D89, just inside the Parc du Mercantour, the *Alpha* **wolf reserve** (May–Aug daily 10am–6pm, last admission 4.30pm; April, Sept & school hols daily 10am–5pm, last admission 4pm; otherwise hours irregular, closed most of March, Nov & Dec; €9; ⓦalpha-loup.com) is an interesting place to visit, despite its lack of information and signage in English. In spring you can see the new-born cubs from three observation points.

Two **hotel–restaurants** specialize in locally caught trout: *Le Boréon*, quartier du Cascade (☎04.93.03.20.35, ⓦhotel-boreon.com; ❹; closed mid-Nov to Dec), and *Le Cavalet*, Lac du Boréon (☎04.93.03.21.46; ❻, half-board only). In fishing season, mid-March to early September, the hotels sell licences that allow you to fish for trout yourself.

Roquebillière

The old village of **ROQUEBILLIÈRE**, on the left bank of the Vésubie 13km southeast of St-Martin, has been rebuilt six times since the Dark Ages following catastrophic landslides and floods. After the last major disaster, in 1926, when half the buildings disappeared under mud, a new village was created high above the right bank of the river. The wide, tree-lined avenues of the *nouveaux village* lie in stark contrast to the crumpling, leaning, medieval houses bearing down over narrow passageways in the dark and sad *vieux village*.

The Gordolasque Valley

The D171 along the **Gordolasque Valley** above old Roquebillière heads north for 16km with paths leading off eastwards towards the Vallée des Merveilles. Where it ends, hikers can continue upstream past waterfalls and high crags to Lac de la Fous, to meet the GR52 running west to Madone de Fenestre and east to the northern end of the Vallée des Merveilles (see p.248). This triangle between Mont Clapier on the Italian border (3045m), Mont Bego (2873m) to the east and Mont Neiglier (2785m) to the west is a fabulous area for walking, but not to be taken lightly. All the **mountain refuges** here belong to the Club Alpin Français (☎04.93.62.59.99, ⓦffcam.fr) and may well be unsympathetic if you turn up unannounced.

Lantosque

South of Roquebillière, the D70 leaves the Vésubie Valley to head east through the chic resort of La-Bollène-Vésubie to the Col de Turini (see opposite). Staying with the Vésubie, you reach **LANTOSQUE**, which, like Roquebillière, has had its share of earth tremors and was badly flooded in 1993; nonetheless, its pyramid of winding, stepped streets survives in picturesque form. A wonderful café-brasserie, the *Bar des Tilleuls* on the lower *place*, serves copious and delicious *plats du jour* for around €12; on the other side of the river in *quartier* Rivet, the *Hostellerie de L'Ancienne Gendarmerie* (☏04.93.03.00.65, ⓦwww.vesubian.com/sites/hotel _ancienne_gendarmerie.htm; ❺; closed mid-Nov to Feb) is a swish **hotel** that also holds an excellent restaurant.

Utelle

Just before the river starts to pick up speed through the gorge that leads to its confluence with the Var, 11km south of Lantosque, the switchbacking D32 climbs east of the D2565 to reach yet another far-flung **chapel**, dedicated to **La Madone d'Utelle**. Set on a plateau above the village of **UTELLE**, it's high enough to be visible from the sea at Nice. According to legend, two Portuguese sailors lost in a storm in the year 850 navigated safely into port by a light they saw gleaming from Utelle. They erected a chapel here to give thanks, though the current one dates from 1806. Pilgrimages still take place on Easter Monday, the Monday of Pentecost, August 15 and September 8, and conclude with a communal feast on the grassy summit. You'll find reasonable **food** in the village at *La Bellevue* on route de la Madone, which also holds five rental apartments (☏04.93.03.17.19; ❹; menus from €14).

The Col de Turini

Four roads and two tracks meet at the **Col de Turini**, 15km east of Roquebillière. All give access to the **Forêt de Turini**, which covers the area between the Vésubie and Bévéra valleys. Larches grow in the highest reaches of the forest, giving way further down to firs, spruce, beech, maples and sweet chestnuts.

The road north from the col through the small ski resort of **Camp d'Argent** to L'Authion gives a strong impression of limitless space, following the curved ridge between the two valleys and overlooking a hollow of pastures. There are plenty of walks hereabouts, but the sun, the flowers and the wild strawberries and raspberries are so pleasant you might just want to stop in a field and listen to the cowbells. The nicest place **to stay** is *Le Relais du Camp d'Argent*, Turini (☏04.93.91.57.58, ⓦestive-mercantour.fr; ❹), a large modern chalet that also offers €25 dorm beds, and serves decent **meals** from €20.

Sospel and the Roya Valley

From the Col de Turini, the D2566 follows the valley of the River Bévéra southeast to **Sospel**, which straddles the main road and rail links from the French coast to the **Roya Valley**. The most easterly valley of Provence, the Roya is also the most accessible, being served by train lines from Nice, via Sospel, and from Ventimiglia in Italy, which converge just south of **Breil-sur-Roya**. When Nice became part of France in 1860, the upper Roya Valley was kept by the new King Victor Emmanuel II of Italy to indulge his passion for hunting, despite a plebiscite in which only one person in Tende and La Brigue voted for the Italian option. Only in 1947 was the valley finally incorporated into France, but everyone speaks French, albeit with a distinctly Italian intonation.

Sospel

The ruggedness of the surrounding terrain only serves to emphasize the placid idyll of **SOSPEL**, a dreamy Italianate town spanning the gentle River Bévéra. Its main street, avenue Jean-Médecin, follows the river on its southern bank before crossing the most easterly of the three bridges to become boulevard de Verdun, heading for the Roya Valley. The central bridge, the impossibly picturesque, eleventh-century **Vieux Pont**, with its tower between the two spans for collecting tolls, is the architectural lynchpin of the townscape. The scene is made yet more alluring by the balconied houses along the north bank, which back on to the grimy rue de la République: the banks are lush with flowering shrubs and trees, and one house even has a trompe-l'oeil street facade. Viewed from the eastern end of avenue Jean-Médecin, with the hills to the west and the bridge tower reflected in the water, this scene would be hard to improve.

Yet another vista in town rivals the river scene. Head down the deeply shadowed and gloomy rue St-Pierre from the eastern place St-Pierre, and when it suddenly opens onto **place St-Michel** you're confronted by one of the most beautiful series of peaches-and-cream Baroque facades in all Provence. Straight ahead is the **Église St-Michel** with its separate austere Romanesque clocktower. To the left are the **Chapelle des Pénitents Gris** and the **Chapelle des Pénitents Rouges**, while to the right are the medieval arcades and trompe-l'oeil decoration of the **Palais Ricci**.

The road behind the church, rue de l'Abbaye, which you can reach via the steps between the two chapels, climbs to an ivy-covered **castle ruin** that offers good views of town. Further up, along chemin de St-Roch, an even better view can be had from the **Fort St-Roch**, part of the ignominious interwar Maginot line, which houses the **Musée de la Résistance** (April–June Sat & Sun 2–6pm; July–Sept Tues–Sun 2–6pm; €5), illustrating the courageous local Resistance movement during World War II. Although under Italian occupation after June 1940, the town hall continued to fly the French flag; when the Germans took over in 1943, however, life became much harsher, and only a few of the Jews who had taken refuge here managed to escape south to Monaco. After Menton was liberated in September 1944, the Allied force advanced north carrying out airborne attacks on Sospel, but stopped 5km short. Sospel, therefore, was left to the mercy of the Germans, but with Allied artillery attacks adding to the casualties. At the end of October the Germans were forced to retreat, but not far enough, and the battle for Sospel continued until April 1945.

Practicalities

Sospel's friendly **tourist office** is at 19 avenue Jean-Médecin (Mon–Sat 10am–4pm, Sun 10am–12.30pm; ☏04.93.04.15.80, ⓦsospel-tourisme.com). The **gare SNCF** is southeast of town on avenue A-Borriglione.

The two best-value **hotels** stand side by side on boulevard de Verdun, just across the eastern bridge: at no. 9, the cheaper *France* (☏04.93.04.00.01, ⓦwww .hoteldefrance-sospel.com; ❸; closed mid-Nov to mid-Dec) has comfortable, colourful rooms, while the smarter *Étrangers*, at no. 7 (☏04.93.04.00.09, ⓦsospel.net; ❺; closed Dec–Feb), has a pool and a good restaurant (closed Tues & Wed lunch), with menus at €25–55. Of the four local **campsites**, the closest is the two-star *Le Mas Fleuri*, 2km upstream along the D2566 in *quartier* La Vasta (☏04.93.04.14.94, ⓦcamping-mas-fleuri.com; €19.40; closed Oct–March), which has a pool.

Restaurants include the *Sout'a Laupia*, 13 rue St-Pierre (☏04.93.04.24.23), which serves delicious traditional local cuisine at good prices; and the *Relais du Sel*, 3 boulevard de Verdun (☏04.93.04.00.43; closed Fri in low season), where you dine on a terrace above the river, with excellent menus starting at €22. *Bar Modern*, 17 avenue Jean-Médecin (☏04.97.00.00.42), doubles as an **internet café** and is a pleasant early evening drinking spot next to the river.

Breil-sur-Roya

Eight kilometres short of the Italian border, the town of **BREIL-SUR-ROYA** sits in a deep, narrow valley 23km north of Sospel, over the Col de Brouis. Here, the River Roya has picked up enough volume to justify a barrage, behind which a placid and aquamarine lake is ideal for canoeing. A place of modest industries – leather, olives and dairy products – Breil spreads back from both banks, with the old town on the eastern edge. A Renaissance chapel, with a golden angel blowing a trumpet from its rooftop cross, faces place Biancheri, while the vast eighteenth-century **Église Santa-Maria-in-Albis**, by the pont Charabot, is topped by a belfry with shiny multicoloured tiles.

Several good **walks** are signed from the village. For a short stroll, follow the river downstream past the barrage and the wash houses, then fork upwards through an olive grove to a tiny chapel and an old Italian gatehouse. The path eventually leads up to the summit of the Arpette, which stands between Breil and the Italian border. Alternatively, if you want to do some whitewater **canoeing** or **rafting** up through the Gorges de Saorge, or simply paddle more gently through the village, Roya Evasion, 11 boulevard Rouvier (☎04.93.04.91.46, ⓦroyaevasion.com), rents equipment and organizes guided trips.

Practicalities

Of the **hotels**, the *Castel du Roy*, 146 route de l'Aigara, off the route de Tende (☎04.93.04.43.66, ⓦcastelduroy.com; ❺; closed early Oct to March), is the most luxurious and has a very good **restaurant** (menus from €27), though the pleasant *Roya* on place Biancheri (☎04.93.04.48.10; ❸; closed Oct & Nov) is more central. The municipal two-star **campsite** (☎04.93.04.46.66, ⓦcamping-azur-merveilles .com; €18; closed Oct–March) is by the river, just upstream from the village.

Saorge and Fontan

The pretty village of **SAORGE**, 7km north of Breil, consists of a clutter of houses in grey and mismatched shades of red tumbling across a hillside, a scene that's brightened by the church and chapel towers, shimmering with gold Niçois tiles. Almost nothing in the village is level. Vertical stairways turn into paths lined with bramble; there's just one near-horizontal main street, and even that goes up and down flights of steps and through arches formed by the houses. At the end of this street a path leads across the cultivated terraces to **La Madone del Poggio**, an eleventh-century chapel guarded by an impossibly high bell tower topped by an octagonal spire; the chapel is private property, however, and can't be visited. Back in the village, there's a seventeenth-century **Franciscan convent** (daily except Tues: May–Sept 10am–noon & 2–6pm; Feb, March, Oct & Nov 10am–noon & 2–5pm; €5) with rustic murals around its cloisters, while the **Église St-Sauveur** daily 9am–5pm) holds rich examples of ecclesiastical art.

The only **accommodation** option is a rental apartment, available for weekends or entire weeks, owned by the village pizzeria, *Lou Pountin*, 56 rue Revelli (☎04.93.04.54.90, ⓦloupountin.fr; ❸; restaurant closed Mon & Tues lunch & Wed eve).

FONTAN, 2km upstream and boasting another shining Niçois-tiled belfry, has one **hotel** to fall back on. The *Terminus* (☎04.93.04.34.00, ⓦwww.hoterminus .fr; ❷), overlooking the Roya at the north end of the village, was named after the large abandoned station opposite which was built by Mussolini to transport rock salt from the mountains. The hotel's restaurant serves decent menus from €20, and has a beautifully painted ceiling. Saorge and Fontan share a **gare SNCF**, in the valley between the two villages.

La Brigue and Notre-Dame-des-Fontaines

The very appealing village of **LA BRIGUE**, 8km northeast of Fontan, lies on an eastern tributary of the Roya, just south of Tende, surrounded by pastures and with the perennial snowcap of Mont Bego visible to the west. Its Romanesque church, the **Église St-Martin**, is full of medieval paintings, including several by Louis Bréa, mostly depicting hideous scenes of torture and death. But the church, and the octagonal seventeenth-century **Chapelle St-Michel** alongside it, pale into insignificance compared with the sanctuary of **Notre-Dame-des-Fontaines**, 4km east.

From the exterior this seems to be a plain, graceful place of retreat, but inside it's something more akin to a slasher movie. Painted in the fifteenth century by Jean Baleison (the ones above the altar) and Jean Canavesio (all the rest), the sequence of restored **frescoes** contains 38 episodes. Each one, from Christ's flagellation, through the torment on the Cross to devils claiming their victims and, ultimate gore, Judas's disembowelment, is full of violent movement and colour. The chapel is open in summer only (daily 9.30am–7pm; €2.50; €1.50 guided tours organized by the tourist office, see below).

Practicalities

La Brigue's **tourist office** (daily 9am–12.30pm & 2–5.30pm; ☎04.93.79.09.34, ⓦlabrigue.fr) is on Place St-Martin, beside the church and adjoining a small museum of regional farming history (same hours; €3).

Both the **hotels** on Place St-Martin – the *Auberge St-Martin* (☎04.93.04.62.17, ⓦauberge-st-martin.fr; ❸), and the *Fleurs des Alpes* (☎04.93.04.61.05, ⓔhotel .fleurdesalpes@tiscali.fr; ❸; closed Wed, plus Dec–Feb) – have **restaurants** serving very satisfying meals for less than €20. *Le Mirval* (☎04.93.04.63.71, ⓦlemirval.com; ❷; closed Nov–March), downstream at 3 rue Vincent-Ferrier, offers rooms overlooking the Levenza stream.

The Vallée des Merveilles

The **Vallée des Merveilles** lies between two lakes over 2000m up on the western flank of Mont Bego. The first person to record his experience of this high valley of lakes and bare rock, a fifteenth-century traveller who had lost his way, described it as "an infernal place with figures of the devil and thousands of demons scratched on the rocks". These were no delusions: the rocks of the valley are carved with thousands of images, of animals, tools, people working and mysterious symbols, dating from the second millennium BC. More are to be found in the **Vallée de Fontanable** on the northern flank of Mont Bego, and west from the Vallée des Merveilles across the southern slopes of Mont des Merveilles. Very little is known about them and the instruments that fashioned them have never been found.

Over the centuries other travellers, shepherds and eventually tourists have added their own engravings to the collection. As a result explorations of the Vallée de Fontanable, and the Mont des Merveilles area, are restricted to one path unless accompanied by an official Mercantour guide.

The easiest route to the Vallée des Merveilles is the ten-kilometre trek (6–8hr) that starts at *Les Mesches* refuge, 8km west of St-Dalmas-de-Tende on the D91. The first part of the climb is through woods full of wild raspberries, mushrooms and bilberries, not all of it steeply uphill. Eventually you rise above the tree line and **Lac Long** comes into view. A few pines still manage to grow around the lake, and in spring the grass is full of flowers, but encircling you is a mountain wilderness. From the *Refuge des Merveilles* by the lake, you continue up through a fearsome valley where the rocks turn from black to green according to the light. From here to just beyond the **Lac des**

Merveilles you can start searching for the engravings. For the Vallée de Fontanable the path starts 4.5km further up the D91 from *Les Mesches* refuge, just before the Casterino information point.

Venturing into the area alone, it's perfectly possible to miss the engravings altogether, while blue skies and sun can quickly turn into violent hailstorms and lightning; it's best to go with a group. **Guided walks** start from *Les Mesches* refuge in summer (June Sat & Sun, hours vary; July & Aug daily 8am, 11am, 1pm & 3pm; Sept Fri–Wed 8am & 1pm; €10; ℡04.93.04.73.71, or contact local tourist offices). Several companies organize trips from further afield, including the Guides du Mercantour in St-Martin-Vésubie (see p.242; ℡04.93.03.31.32, ⓦguidescapade .com), and Destination Merveilles in Villeneuve-Loubet (℡04.93.73.09.07, ⓦwww .destination-merveilles.com).

Tende

TENDE, the highest town on the Roya, guards the access to the Col de Tende, which connects Provence with Piedmont but is now bypassed by a road tunnel. Though not especially attractive, Tende is fairly busy, with plenty of cheap accommodation, places to eat, bars to lounge around in and shops to browse round.

The town's old and gloomy houses are built with green and purple schist, but blackened by fumes from the heavy trucks that cross to and from Italy. Above them rise the cherry-coloured belfry of the **collegiate church**, the peachy-orange towers and belfries of various **chapels**, and a twenty-metre needle of wall which is all that remains of a château destroyed in the seventeenth century.

The **Vieille Ville** is fun to wander through, looking at the symbols of old trades on the door lintels, the overhanging roofs and the balconies on every floor. On place de l'Église, the **Collégiale Notre-Dame de l'Assumption** is more a repository of the town's wealth than a place of contemplation, with Baroque excess throughout. At the other end of town near the station, the seventeenth-century **Église St-Michel**, on place du Grande Marché, was entirely remodelled in the 1960s, when its *chevet* was replaced by a wall of glass looking onto the trees and shrubs of the former convent gardens. It was decorated by a local artist, some of whose dream-inspired paintings of a semi-symbolist, semi-surrealist nature, are dreadful, while others strike an eerily appropriate note.

The **Musée des Merveilles**, on avenue du 16 Septembre 1947 (May, June & early Oct daily except Tues 10am–6.30pm; July–Sept daily 10am–6.30pm; mid-Oct to April daily except Tues 10am–5pm; free; ⓦwww.museedesmerveilles .com), details the geology, archeology and traditions of the areas where engravings have been found. Alongside dioramas depicting the daily lives of Copper- and Bronze-Age peoples, reproductions of the rock designs are displayed, with attempts to decipher the beliefs and myths that inspired them. Whether or not you go to the Vallée des Merveilles, it's an invaluable insight into an intriguing subject.

Practicalities

Tende's **tourist office**, also known as the Maison de Mercantour, is at 103 avenue du 16 Septembre 1947 (mid-June to Sept Mon–Sat 9am–noon & 2–5pm, Sun 9am–noon; ℡04.93.04.73.71, ⓦwww.tendemerveilles.com). The **gare SNCF** is set back from the top of this same main street.

Inexpensive **hotels** in Tende include the *Miramonti*, by the station at 5–7 avenue Vassalo (℡04.93.04.61.82; ❷; closed mid-Nov to mid-Dec), and the basic *Centre*, 12 place de la République (℡04.93.04.62.19, ⓔhotel.du.centre@hotmail.fr; ❶; closed Nov–March). The **gîte d'étape** *Les Carlines*, along chemin Ste-Catherine past the cathedral at the edge of the town (☎04.93.04.62.74; ❶; closed Oct to mid-April), has one private room and €20 dorm beds, and enjoys gorgeous views down the valley. The one-star municipal **campsite** *Saint Jacques* is 500m down a path to the left of the *gare SNCF* (☎04.93.04.76.08; €6; June–Aug only).

Restaurants line up along avenue du 16 Septembre and rue de France, but there's nothing very special. *La Margueria* is a popular pizzeria at 19 avenue du 16 Septembre (☎04.93.04.60.532; closed Tues), with beams strung with dried herbs and garlic, and stuffed foxes on the walls.

Travel details

Trains

Chemin de Fer de Provence (Nice–Digne)

Nice to: Annot (4–5 daily; 2hr); Barrême (4–5 daily; 1hr 45min); Digne (4–5 daily; 3hr 15min); Entrevaux (4–5 daily; 1hr 30min); Puget-Théniers (4–5 daily; 1hr 30min); St-André-des-Alpes (4–5 daily; 2hr 25min); Thorame-Gare (4–5 daily; 2hr 15min); Touët-sur-Var (4–5 daily; 1hr 10min).

From **Digne** a regular SNCF bus links the Chemin de Fer de Provence with the SNCF Marseille–Sisteron line at St-Auban–Château-Arnoux (30min).

SNCF line

Nice to: Breil-sur-Roya (5 daily; 55min); La Brigue (3 daily; 1hr 35min); St-Dalmas-de-Tende (3 daily; 1hr 50min); Saorge-Fontan (3 daily; 1hr 15min–1hr 40min); Sospel (4 daily; 50min); Tende (3 daily; 1hr 40min–2hr 30min).

Buses

Aups to: Aiguine (1 daily; 35min); Cotignac (3 daily; 25min).
Barçelonnette to: Digne (2 daily; 1hr 45min); Gap (3 daily; 1hr 20min); Marseille (2 daily; 3hr 50min).
Digne to: Aix (4 daily; 2hr); Aups (2 daily; 30–40min); Avignon (3 daily; 3hr 15min); Barçelonnette (2 daily; 1hr 30min); Castellane (1 daily; 1hr 10min); Grenoble (1 daily; 4hr 50min); Marseille (4 daily; 2hr–2hr 30min); Moustiers-Ste-Marie (1 daily; 1hr 20min); Nice (4 daily; 3hr 15min); Puget-Théniers (1 daily; 2hr); St-André-les-Alpes (2–3 daily; 1hr); Seyne-les-Alpes (1 daily; 40min); Sisteron (2–3 daily; 1hr).

Draguignan to: Aix (3 daily; 2hr 30min); Aups (1 daily; 1hr–1hr 20min); Bargemon (5 daily; 45min); Barjols (1 daily; 1hr 10min); Brignoles (3 daily; 1hr); Callas (3 daily; 40min); Entrecasteaux (2 weekly; 45min); Fayence (4 daily; 1hr 40min); Grasse (2 daily; 2hr 45min); Lorgues (4 daily; 20min); St-Raphaël (12 daily; 1hr 15min–1hr 30min); Salernes (3 daily; 1hr 15min–1hr 45min); Seillans (3 daily; 1hr 20min); Tourtour (1 daily; 50min);
Villecroze (2 weekly; 1hr).
Fayence to: Draguignan (Mon–Sat 3 daily; 1hr 30min); Grasse (Mon–Sat 3 daily; 1hr); St Raphaël (Mon–Sat 4 daily; 1hr 20min).
Gréolières to: Grasse (1–2 daily; 35–50min).
Puget-Théniers to: Annot (1 daily; 20min); Barrême (1 daily; 1hr 10min); Digne (1 daily; 2hr); Entrevaux (1 daily; 10min); St-André-les-Alpes (1 daily; 1hr).
Riez to: Barjols (1 daily; 45min); Digne (3 daily; 15min); Manosque (1 daily; 1hr); Marseille (1–2 daily; 2hr); Moustiers-Ste-Marie (2 daily; 20min); Quinson (1 daily; 35min).
St-André-les-Alpes to: Allos (1–3 daily in high season; 1hr); Barrême (1 daily; 10min); Digne (1 daily; 1hr); La Foux d'Allos (1–3 daily; 1hr 15min); Nice (1 daily; 2hr).
St-Étienne-de-Tinée to: Auron (1–5 daily; 15min); Isola (1–4 daily; 15min); Nice (1–4 daily; 2hr 30min); St-Sauveur-de-Tinée (1–4 daily; 45min).
St-Martin-Vésubie to: Lantosque (3 daily; 30min); Nice (3 daily; 1hr 45min); Roquebillière (3 daily; 15min).
Sospel to: Menton (9 daily; 35min–1hr).
Thorame-Gare to: Allos (3 daily; 45min); Beauvezer (3 daily; 20min); Colmars-les-Alpes (3 daily; 30min); La Foux d'Allos (3 daily; 1hr 10min).

6

Toulon and the
southern Var

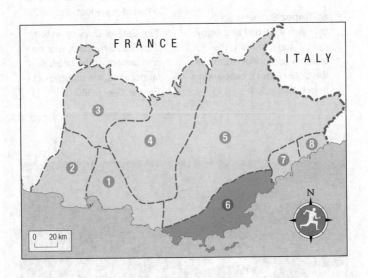

CHAPTER 6 # Highlights

✳ **Bandol Appellation Contrôlée** Sample the fine wines and explore the peaceful wine-growing country a little way inland from the bustle of the coast. See p.258

✳ **The island of Port-Cros** Take a glass-bottomed boat to explore the fascinating marine life off France's smallest national park. See p.272

✳ **St-Tropez** Suspend your cynicism for a day and enjoy the art, the absurdity, the glamour and sheer excess of the Côte d'Azur's best-known resort. See p.278

✳ **Massif des Maures** Escape the glitz and development of the coast to explore the sombre wooded hills, and the unspoilt country towns of Collobrières and La Garde-Freinet. See p.285 & p.288

✳ **Fréjus** Founded by Julius Caesar as a naval base, Fréjus has some of the best-preserved Roman remains along this coast, including a theatre, an amphitheatre and a ruined aqueduct. See p.293

✳ **The Esterel** Drive or walk in the most distinctive, rugged and ancient of the coast's landscapes, the craggy, red Esterel. See p.300

▲ Plage des Salins, St-Tropez

6

Toulon and the southern Var

he shoreline of the **Var** *département* represents a sizeable chunk of the Côte d'Azur and, thus, of the fabled allure of the south of France. Though much of the coast has been developed, the resorts are mostly small, and between the oversized marinas and dull apartment complexes, the characteristic landscape of pines, glimmering rocks and translucent sea still sometimes takes precedence – cheered in February by mimosa blossom and in autumn by the brilliance of the turning vines. Development notwithstanding, this is still a coastline that conjures up the visual magic that attracted Impressionists, Post-Impressionists and their 1950s cinematic successors. The nexus of the Côte's artistic fame and cinematic glamour – but also of vulgar display and hype – is the erstwhile fishing village of **St-Tropez**, possessed of charisma which none of its neighbours can match, though its prices and peak-season crowds trump all rhyme or reason just as emphatically.

Elsewhere, the pleasures are those of the seaside, which for the most part is neither conspicuously fashionable nor unduly dowdy. In the west, highlights include the excellent wines of the **Bandol** *appellation contrôlée* and the literary and historic associations of **Sanary-sur-Mer**. **Hyères** has attracted foreign visitors since the eighteenth century, while the crystal-clear waters and pristine ecosystems of the **Îles d'Hyères** lie just offshore. To the east, the **Corniche des Maures** is a long procession of small coastal villages turned resorts, and though it's hard to gauge quite where **Cavalière**, **Pramousquier** or **Le Trayas** start or stop, each is a little paradise of dense pinewoods and clean, sandy beaches, with the sublime garden at **Le Rayol** providing a standout diversion.

Behind this coast, the mournful **Massif des Maures** is more pristine still, its endless forests sheltering ancient monasteries and the timeless agricultural industries of cork oak and chestnut. The principal villages of **Collobrières** and **La Garde Freinet** still preserve (for now at least) some of their rural character in the face of the encroaching wealth of **St-Tropez**, its chic neighbours and beautiful peninsula. Facing St-Tropez across its bay is the middle-class resort of **Ste-Maxime**, beyond which the coast road follows the shoreline's twists and turns – without ever quite shaking off suburbia – all the way to **Fréjus**. This, the most ancient of the Var's coastal towns, is replete with monuments from its Roman and medieval heyday. The sun, sea and sand theme reasserts itself in Fréjus' twin town of **St-Raphaël**, before the coast turns wilder along the dramatically red, rocky corniche of the **Esterel**.

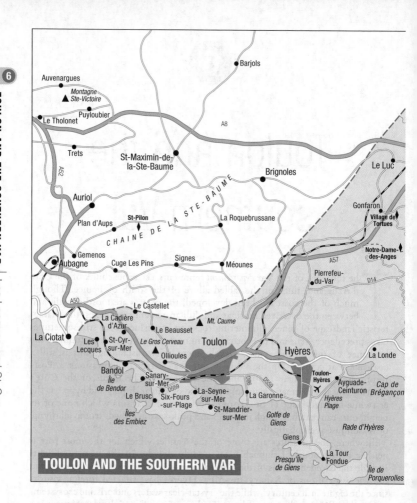

TOULON AND THE SOUTHERN VAR

The Var's one great urban agglomeration is the naval port (and departmental capital) of **Toulon**, blessed with a magnificent natural harbour, cursed by its reputation for racism and sleaze, and now slowly making good the political and aesthetic mistakes of its recent past. Though it lacks the obvious allure of the resorts, its importance as a transport hub means you're quite likely to pass through.

Les Lecques and St-Cyr

Wedged between the D559 coast road and the sea at the Var's western extremity, sedate **LES LECQUES** is a beach resort, pure and simple, strung along a sand-and-shingle beach that curves east from the town's marina to the pleasant little fishing port of La Madrague. From here, a wonderful twelve-kilometre coastal path meanders around Pointe Grenier to the *calanque* of Port d'Alon – where there's an informal bar/restaurant, *Chez Tonton Ju* (☎04.94.26.20.08; closed Nov to Easter)

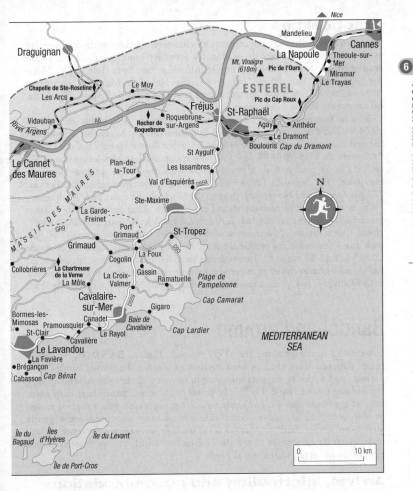

– before continuing to Bandol. Les Lecques itself claims to have been the Greek trading post of Tauroentum, site of a decisive naval battle between Caesar (the eventual victor) and Pompey for the control of Marseille. The remains of a **Roman villa**, now the **Musée de Tauroentum** (April & May Thurs–Sun 2–5pm; June–Sept Mon & Wed–Sun 3–7pm; Oct–March Sat & Sun 2–5pm; €3), on the route de la Madrague, date from the first century AD and boast three extant mosaics, patches of frescoes, a couple of interesting sarcophagi, numerous beautiful Greek and Roman vases and other household items.

Les Lecques merges with the village of **ST-CYR-SUR-MER** on the inland side of the D559, where the small **Centre d'Art Sébastien** on boulevard Jean-Jaurès (daily except Tues: June–Sept 9am–noon & 3–7pm; Oct–May 9am–noon & 2–6pm; €1) displays the paintings and tender terracotta statues of this Parisian-born artist (and friend of Picasso) in a beautifully restored former caper storehouse. On place de Portalis is a miniature, golden **Statue of Liberty**, sculpted by Bartholdi, the artist who created its better-known New York sister. Beyond these, St-Cyr's main attraction is its **vineyards**, which belong to the Bandol *appellation* (see box, p.258).

The **gare SNCF** serving both communities lies between them at the north end of avenue des Lecques; from the station it's a twenty-minute walk down to the **tourist office** (March–June & Sept–Oct Mon–Sat 9am–6pm; July & Aug Mon–Sat 9am–7pm, Sun 10am–1pm & 4–7pm; Nov–Feb Mon–Sat 9am–5pm; ℡04.94.26.73.73, ⓦwww.saintcyrsurmer.com), on place de l'Appel du 18 Juin, off avenue du Port in Les Lecques.

Of Les Lecques' **hotels**, *Beau Séjour Les Palmiers*, 34 avenue de la Mer (℡04.94.26.54.06, ⓦwww.beausejour-lespalmiers.fr; ⑤), has twelve individually themed rooms close to the sea, or there's the handsome *Grand Hôtel des Lecques*, 24 avenue du Port (℡04.94.26.23.01, ⓦwww.grand-hotel-les-lecques.com; ⑦), set in a large garden with a pool. Les Lecques also has a spacious three-star **campsite**, *Les Baumelles* (℡04.94.26.21.27, ⓦwww.campinglesbaumelles.net; €27 per tent; closed Nov–Mar), close to the beach on the route de la Madrague.

The widest choice of **restaurants** in Les Lecques is along the traffic-free seafront promenade near the marina, where *L'Abordage*, 2 quai Victor Gélu (℡04.94.26.45.09; closed Tues in winter) is the trendiest of the brasseries, with menus from €17.50. Just back from the beach on avenue du Port, the tiny, cluttered *Restaurant Samantha* (℡04.94.26.13.68; menu €15) offers simple bistro fare including a few Spanish dishes, and there's a smaller cluster of unpretentious eating places around the fishing harbour at La Madrague. St-Cyr has a **market** on Sunday at place G. Péri in the Vieille Ville.

Bandol and around

Continuing southeast along the D559 towards Toulon, **BANDOL** is a lively resort screened from the open sea by its vast marina. The town bustles with yachties and with day-trippers browsing in its many clothes shops, which range from cheap to chic. Bandol is rightly proud of its wines, which have their own distinct *appellation contrôlée*, and sampling and buying wine is much the best reason to stop over; the attractive countryside around town also holds some gentle attractions. Other than this, the sea is the main draw, whether for beach lazing, watersports or excursions to the **Île de Bendor**, which houses France's largest exposition of wines, spirits and alcohols.

Arrival, information and accommodation

From Bandol's **gare SNCF**, head down avenue de la Gare and avenue du 11 Novembre 1918 to reach the town centre and port. The **tourist office** is on allées Vivien by the quayside (Easter–June & Sept Mon–Sat 9am–noon & 2–6pm; July & Aug daily 9.30am–7pm; Oct–Easter Mon–Sat 9am–noon & 2–5pm; ℡04.94.29.41.35, ⓦwww.bandol.fr). You can rent **bikes**, motorized or not, at Holiday Bikes, 127 route de Marseille (℡04.94.32.21.89), west down avenue Loste on the other side of the rail lines from the station. There's **internet access** at the Espace Culturel Paul Ricard, place Lucien Grillon (Mon–Fri 9am–noon & 1.30–5.30pm).

One cheaper **hotel** worth considering is *L'Oasis*, 15 rue des Écoles (℡04.94.29.41.69, ⓦwww.oasisbandol.com; *demi-pension* only from mid-June to mid-Sept, otherwise ③; closed mid-Dec to mid-Jan), in a residential area between the town centre and Rènecros; there's also the very pleasant, good-value *Golf Hôtel*, right on Rènecros beach (℡04.94.29.45.83, ⓦwww.golfhotel.fr; ④). Bandol's top hotel, *Île Rousse*, 25 boulevard Louis Lumière (℡04.94.29.33.00, ⓦwww.ile-rousse.com; ⑨), has a direct access to Rènecros beach, vast, light rooms and a choice of restaurants. If you're **camping**, try the two-star *Vallongue* (☎04.94.29.49.55, ⓦwww.campingvar.com; closed Oct–Easter), 2.5km out of town on the D559.

The Town

Given **wine** is Bandol's main claim to fame, the obvious first port of call is the smart new **Oenothèque des Vins de Bandol** (Mon–Sat 10am–1pm & 3–7pm, Sun 10am–1pm; ⓦwww.maisondesvins-bandol.com) at the eastern end of the quai Charles-de-Gaulle opposite the casino. You can obtain information and maps of the various *domaines* here, but if you don't have the time for a self-guided tour of the local vineyards, this is also a good place to taste and buy, with helpful, friendly staff.

Bandol's most scenic sandy **beach** curves around **Anse de Rènecros**, an almost circular cove west of the port along boulevard Louis-Lumière. More secluded are the little coves and beaches along the coastal path to Les Lecques, which you reach from avenue du Maréchal-Foch on the western side of the Anse de Rènecros.

The Île de Bendor

If you're at all susceptible to the allure of islands, you may want to take the short boat trip (April–June & Sept 7am–midnight; July & Aug 7am–2am; Oct–March 7.45am–5pm; €10 April–Sept, €8 Oct–March) from Bandol's quay to the rocky **ÎLE DE BENDOR**. Uninhabited when it was bought by *pastis* tycoon **Paul Ricard** in the 1950s, it's nowadays more tourist honeypot than desert island, cluttered from end to end with attractions of various kinds, including a **museum** dedicated to Ricard advertising (summer only: daily 10.30am–12.30pm & 3–6pm; free), and the **Musée des Vins et des Spiritueux EUVS** (April–Sept Wed–Sun 10.40am–2pm & 4–7.30pm; open daily during July–Aug; free), which in addition to its vast display of wines, spirits and bottles also organizes cocktail nights and workshops. The man who created all this, Paul Ricard, died in 1997 and is buried at the highest point of the island.

For most of the year, outdoor activities on the island revolve around the **Club International de Plongée** (☎04.94.29.55.12, ⓦcipbendor.com), which offers diving training from beginner to instructor level, including classes for children from the age of eight upwards.

Eating and drinking

In the centre of Bandol, you'll find plenty of **restaurants** along rue de la République and allée Jean-Moulin, parallel to the port. The *Auberge du Port*, 7 allée Jean-Moulin (☎04.94.29.42.63; menu €38), has classic fish dishes, while the elegant restaurant *Les Oliviers* at the hotel *Île Rousse* (☎04.94.29.33.00; see opposite) is the place for rabbit roasted with rosemary, *girolles* and *garrigue* herbs, or rack of lamb with aubergine ravioli; menus start at €36. Arguably as good is *Le Clocher*, 1 rue de la Paroisse (☎04.94.32.47.65; menus from €20; closed Wed), with specialities including prawn and sardine *nems* and scallop *tartelette*. For picnic fare there's a Tuesday-morning **market** on the quayside.

Bandol's **bars** tend towards the sophisticated: *Le Bistro* at 6 avenue Jean-Moulin is chic and modern, with a long cocktail list and light meals from €14, while *Le 38 Caffe* and *L'Escale*, further along the port on quai Charles-de-Gaulle, are similarly fashionable.

Around Bandol

Despite creeping suburbanization, the countryside north of Bandol makes good **cycling** country: you could head for the perched medieval village of **La Cadière**

The wines of Bandol

Winemaking in these relatively infertile coastal hills dates back to the Phoenician colony that later became Roman Tauroentum. The quality of the wines – which is boosted by the unusually low yields – was acknowledged as early as the eighteenth century, when despite decrees promoting cereal production over wine, Bandol's vines were spared by official *dérogation*. The Bandol **appellation d'origine contrôlée** (or AOC) was established in 1941, making it one of France's oldest. *Domaines* were replanted with the region's traditional cinsault, grenache and **mourvèdre** grapes, the latter of Spanish origin and the dominant grape in the superb reds and sublime pale, dry rosés; the whites, though rare, are also worth trying. Bandol **reds** must contain a minimum of 50 percent mourvèdre, though some winemakers push this percentage far higher. The result is a rich, dark red wine that develops notes of leather, truffle and black fruits as it matures.

The Bandol AOC spreads in an arc along the A50 autoroute from **St-Cyr** in the west to **Ollioules** in the east, with the densest concentration of vineyards still focused on La Cadière. Most can be visited for tasting and buying; those with international reputations include the **Domaine Tempier** at Le Plan du Castellet (Mon–Fri 9am–noon & 2–5.30pm; ☏04.94.98.70.21, ⓦwww.domainetempier.com), **Château de Pibarnon** at La Cadière (Mon–Sat 9am–noon & 2–6pm; ☏04.94.90.12.73, ⓦwww .pibarnon.com) and the organic **Domaine de Terrebrune** at 724 chemin de la Tourelle, Ollioules (Mon–Sat 9am–12.30pm & 2–6pm; ☏04.94.74.01.30, ⓦwww .terrebrune.fr), which has an excellent *restaurant gastronomique*, *La Table du Vigneron* (☏04.94.88.36.19).

d'Azur (take the road above the station, left on the D559, then right), and then across the valley to the more touristy fortified hamlet of **Le Castellet**, with its vast car parks, perfumed boutiques and gloomy, crypt-like bastion of a twelfth-century church, plus wonderful panorama of the vineyards below.

Approximately 6km southeast of Le Castellet, south of Le Beausset, is **Le Vieux Beausset**, whose Romanesque **Chapelle Notre-Dame** (daily: July & Aug 3–7pm; April–June & Sept 2–6pm; Oct–March 2–5pm) rewards the long and winding approach with a superb panoramic view.

The Cap Sicié peninsula

The coastal approach to Toulon from the west takes you via the congested neck of the **Cap Sicié peninsula**. On the western side, **Six-Fours-les-Plages** sprawls between pretty **Sanary-sur-Mer** and **Le Brusc**, from where you can get boats to another of Ricard's islands, **Île des Embiez**. The eastern side of the peninsula merges with Toulon's former shipbuilding suburb of **La Seyne-sur-Mer**, while at the southern end a semi-wilderness of high cliffs and forest reigns.

Sanary-sur-Mer

"Next morning the sun came through the French window, the window gave onto a balcony, the balcony to a sea front; small boats bobbing at harbour. Pretty, my mother said."

Sybille Bedford, *Quicksands, a Memoir*

So the little harbour of **SANARY-SUR-MER**, 5km east of Bandol, seemed to the novelist and travel writer Sybille Bedford in the mid-1920s, when she saw it for the first time. And so it remains, with its pastel pink and yellow facades and comically dignified little *mairie*. The harbour preserves its fishing-port charm; the headland to the west its discreetly desirable villas.

Then as now, Sanary was not the most fashionable place in the south of France, but its lack of cachet made it affordable to writers and intellectuals in the interwar years. **Aldous Huxley** wrote *Eyeless in Gaza* and *Brave New World* at his Villa Huley on allée Thérèse in between dips at the Gorguette beach; later, after the Nazis came to power, many of Germany's cultural elite found temporary refuge here. **Thomas Mann** held court at his villa on chemin de la Colline, later torn down by the Nazis to make way for coastal defences; his near-neighbour was Alma Mahler, widow of the composer, while **Brecht** sang anti-Hitler songs in the cafés on the *quai*. A plaque on the tourist office wall commemorates Sanary's German connection; the office will supply you with information on landmarks associated with the exiles, many of which are now marked with plaques. Huxley's villa, now known as Les Flots, and Sybille Bedford's house in chemin du Diable are among those still standing

Literary fame aside, the pleasures of Sanary are those of the coast: café lounging on the port, swimming from La Gorguette or the coves of Portissol and Beaucours; and diving in the clear waters to the west of the town. The thirteenth-century **Tour Romane** by the port holds a small **diving museum** (July & Aug daily 10am–12.30pm & 4–7.30pm; free), based around the collection of one of the pioneers of the modern sport, Frédéric Dumas, who worked with Jacques Cousteau.

Practicalities

Hourly buses run from Bandol's quay to Sanary. The **gare SNCF**, which Sanary shares with neighbouring Ollioules, is 2.5km north of the centre; note that buses into town don't necessarily link up with train arrivals. The **tourist office** is by the port at 1 quai du Levant (July & Aug Mon–Sat 9am–7pm, Sun 9.30am–12.30pm; April–June, Sept & Oct Mon–Fri 9am–6pm, Sat 9am–1pm & 2–5pm; Nov–March Mon–Fri 9am–12.30pm & 2–5.30pm, Sat 9am–12.30pm & 2–5pm; ☎04.94.74.01.04, ⒲www.sanarysurmer.com).

Good **accommodation** options include the *Centre Azur* hostel (☎04.94.74.18.87, ⒲www.ymca-sanary.org; doubles ❶, dorms €25.90), at 149 avenue du Nid between Portissol and La Cride, a little west of the centre, or there's the attractive and historic *Hôtel de la Tour*, 24 quai Général-de-Gaulle (☎04.94.74.10.10, ⒲www .sanary-hoteldelatour.com; ❹), from which Sybille Bedford first glimpsed Sanary's port. There's also a three-star **campsite**, *Campasun Parc Mogador*, on chemin de Beaucours west of the town centre (☎04.94.74.53.16, ⒲www.campasun.com; €31 per tent; closed Nov to mid-March).

As to places to **eat**, the smart *Café de Lyon* at 2 quai Charles-de-Gaulle (☎04.94.74.00.38) does salads from €9.50 and fish dishes from €12; its neighbour ⚓ *Le Nautique* is a good place for a drink, and both are former haunts of Sanary's literary exiles. For more elaborate fare, *L'enK*, at 13 rue Louis-Blanc (☎04.94.74.66.57; menu €31), offers creative cuisine with a few Asian touches. Sanary's **market** day is Wednesday.

Six-Fours-les-Plages and Le Brusc

Sanary merges seamlessly along the D559 into **SIX-FOURS-LES-PLAGES**, which at first seems nothing but sprawling suburbs littered with hoardings. A small road off the D63, to the north, however, takes you up to the **Chapelle de Pépiole** (daily 3–6pm; free), a stunning sixth-century construction in the midst of pines, cypresses and olive trees. Six-Fours' well-kept sand-and-shingle beaches are also worth seeking out; the nicest is the **Plage du Cros**, just before the pleasant harbour of **LE BRUSC**, from which a **coastal footpath** winds its way along the wild headlands of Cap Sicié itself. The path offers heady views in every direction, but as it can get pretty windy up here, exploring the cliffs should be done with a certain amount of caution even on a calm day. The sturdy sentinel of **Notre-Dame-de-Mai** (Oct–April every first Sat of the month, plus May 9am–noon & 2.30–5.30pm for pilgrimages; free), once a primitive lighthouse, provides a suitable objective. Back in Le Brusc, you can reward yourself with a generous fish dinner at *Le St-Pierre*, 47 rue de la Citadelle (T04.94.34.02.52; closed Sun eve & Mon out of season), which has menus at €21.50, €26.50 and €35.50.

Île des Embiez

Larger than its sister island to the west, Paul Ricard's second island, the **Île des Embiez** (Wwww.les-embiez.com), offers more in the way of natural beauty, with a couple of pocket-handkerchief beaches and low cliffs that are a riot of flowers in spring; there's even a themed nature trail to follow. With its vast marina and miniature road train, tennis courts and football pitch, it's not exactly Robinson Crusoe country, however. The major attraction is the **Institut Océanographique Paul Ricard** (daily 10am–12.30pm & 1.30–5pm, closed Sat pm from Sept–June; €4.50; Wwww .institut-paul-ricard.org), with an aquarium and exhibitions on underwater matters.

There are frequent **ferry crossings** from Le Brusc (daily: April–June & Sept 7am–11.30pm; July & Aug 7am–12.30am; Oct–March 7am–7.40pm; journey time 10min; €12).

Toulon

Viewed from the heights of Mont Faron or Notre-Dame-du-Mai, it's clear why **TOULON** had to be a major port, for the city stands on a magnificent natural harbour. The heart-shaped bay of the Petite Rade gives over 15km of shoreline around Toulon and its suburb **La Seyne-sur-Mer** to the west. Facing the city, about 3km out to sea, is **St-Mandrier**, a virtual island connected to the Cap Sicié peninsula by the isthmus of Les Sablettes and protecting the Grande Rade both northwards and eastwards.

Toulon is home to the French Navy's Mediterranean Fleet, continuing a naval tradition that dates back to the 15th century. The city's strategic importance made wartime destruction almost inevitable; the entire fleet was scuttled here in November 1942 to avoid it falling into the hands of the Germans, while the waterfront was severely battered during the Allied landings of 1944. Postwar reconstruction did Toulon few aesthetic favours; its stock fell further in 1995 when local elections returned a racist *Front National* administration to the town hall with a policy of "preference for the French". Long since returned to the political mainstream, Toulon has slowly set about regenerating its historic core and rebuilding its tattered image.

Though the high apartment buildings and wide highways slicing through the centre don't make the approach to Toulon very alluring, a gentrification programme is slowly beautifying the Vieille Ville. A smart **gallery** of modern art attracts touring shows from Paris, and the port is increasingly a stopover for cruise liners. There are also no fewer than 25 **fountains** dotted around the city centre; a free walking map from the tourist office details the position and age of each one. Other compensations of a stay here include good markets and the superb views from **Mont Faron**; alternatively, there are fine sand-and-shingle **beaches** to the east of town and across the Petit Rade at La-Seyne-sur-Mer.

Arrival, information and accommodation

The **gare SNCF** and **gare routière** are on place Albert-1er. Walking straight out of the station down avenue Vauban will bring you to the place d'Armes. Crossing the square and following the busy avenue that runs east parallel to the coast, you'll reach avenue de la République, where the **tourist office** is at no. 334 (Mon & Wed–Sat 9am–6pm, Tues 10am–6pm, Sun 10am–noon, plus weekdays and Sat until 8pm July & Aug; ☎04.94.18.53.00, ⊛www.toulontourisme.com), which can supply you with a city **bus map**. To reach the seaside suburb of Le Mourillon, take bus #3 (direction "Mourillon") or #23 (direction "Quatre Saisons") from the centre. **Internet access** is available at ten cafés across the city, including Cyber Espace, 88 boulevard Georges-Clemenceau (☎04.94.22.93.11). Hotel **accommodation** in Toulon is affordable and of a good standard.

Hotels

Hôtel des Allées 18 allée Amiral Courbet ☎04.94.91.10.02, ⊛www.hoteljaures.fr. One of the cheapest in town, opposite the Base Navale, with soundproofed, a/c rooms including one that sleeps four. Reception is at its sister hotel, *Le Jaurès*, one block back at 50 rue Jean Jaurès. ❷

Best Western La Corniche 17 littoral Frédéric Mistral ☎04.94.41.35.12, ⊛www.bestwestern -hotelcorniche.com. Very pleasant hotel in the seaside suburb of La Mourillon, with a/c, soundproofed rooms, parking and free wi-fi. ❺

Little Palace 6 rue Berthelot ☎04.94.92.26.62, ⊛www.hotel-littlepalace.com. Smart and comfortable two-star hotel in the Vieille Ville, close to the Opéra and with attractive decor. ❸

Les Trois Dauphins 9 place des Trois Dauphins ☎04.94.92.65.79, ⊛www.hotel-littlepalace.com. Simple rooms on a small square in the heart of the Vieille Ville; sister hotel to the *Little Palace* opposite. ❶

The City

Vieux Toulon, crammed in between boulevard de Strasbourg and avenue de la République on the old port, has a fine scattering of fountains, a decent selection of shops (particularly clothing stores), and an excellent **market** (Tues–Sun) around rue Landrin and cours Lafayette. The nicest (and liveliest) parts of the old town are around the **Cathédrale Notre Dame de la Seds** and imposing nineteenth-century **Opéra**, with plenty of café terraces that offer people-watching opportunities. Big chunks of the eastern side of Vieux Toulon disappeared with the construction of the ugly but useful **Mayol** shopping centre; traffic-free quai Cronstadt fronting the **port** is more alluring, with plenty more sunny café terraces. Bear in mind, though, that avenue de la République (one block inland) and the quieter streets of the southern old town can still be a little seedy by night.

The vast expanse of the **Arsenal**, on place Monsenergue, marks the western end of the Vieille Ville, with its grandiose eighteenth-century gateway leading to the **Musée de la Marine** (Mon & Wed–Sun 10am–6pm; €5), where visitors are greeted by Pierre-Louis Ganne's depiction of the battle of Trafalgar. The museum displays figureheads, an extensive collection of model ships and an enormous fresco showing the old arsenal before it was burnt by the British (see p.264), as well as stark black-and-white photos that illustrate the aftereffects of the scuttling of the French fleet in 1942. To the north on Toulon's Haussmann-inspired main east–west artery, the grandiose **Musée d'Art** (Wed–Sun noon–6pm; free), at 113 boulevard Maréchal-Leclerc, has a small but eclectic collection spanning eighteenth- and nineteenth-century works by Toulon artists, paintings by Fragonard and Felix Ziem and more modern pieces by the likes of Niki de St Phalle and Yves Klein. It shares a building with the **Muséum**

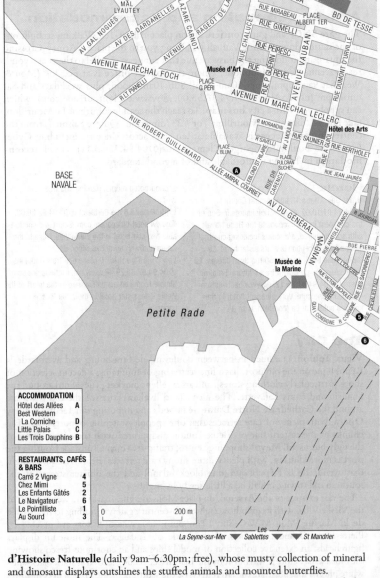

TOULON

RD PT
MAL
LYAUTEY

AV GAL NOGUÈS

AV DES DARDANELLES

AV LAZARE CARNOT

RAGEOT DE LA TOUCHÉ

AVENUE

AVENUE MARÉCHAL FOCH

R LT PIANELLI

RUE ROBERT GUILLEMARD

PLACE
G PÉRI

Gare SNCF

BD P TOESCA

RUE MIRABEAU

RUE GIMELLI

PLACE
ALBERT 1ER

BD DE TESSÉ

RUE CHALUCET

RUE PEIRESC

RUE GIMELLI

Musée d'Art

RUE P GUÉRIN

RUE REVEL

AVENUE VAUBAN

RUE DUMONT D'URVILLE

AVENUE DU MARÉCHAL LECLERC

R MORANDIN

R SAVELLI

PLACE
BLUM

ALLÉE AMIRAL COURBET

LIEU LUD ST HILAIRE

AV J MOULIN

RUE SAUNIER

PLACE
FULCRAN
SUCHET

RUE DR CARENCE

AV DU GÉNÉRAL

RUE A GUIOL

Hôtel des Arts

RUE BERTHOLET

RUE JEAN JAURÈS

R JOURDAN

RUE PIERRE

MAGNAN

RUE MATOLY FRANCE

RUE DE L'ÉQUERRE

RUE VICTOR MICHOLET

RUE EMILE CRESP

RUE CONSIGNE R CONSIGNE

RUE DES SAVONNIERES

RUE CHEVALIER PAUL

Musée de
la Marine

BASE
NAVALE

Petite Rade

ACCOMMODATION

Hôtel des Allées	A
Best Western La Corniche	D
Little Palais	C
Les Trois Dauphins	B

RESTAURANTS, CAFÉS & BARS

Carré 2 Vigne	4
Chez Mimi	5
Les Enfants Gâtés	2
Le Navigateur	6
Le Pointilliste	1
Au Sourd	3

0   200 m

Les
La Seyne-sur-Mer ▼   Sablettes ▼   ▼ St Mandrier

d'Histoire Naturelle (daily 9am–6.30pm; free), whose musty collection of mineral and dinosaur displays outshines the stuffed animals and mounted butterflies.

Further east, at 236 boulevard Maréchal-Leclerc, is the handsome **Hôtel des Arts** (Tues–Sun 10am–1pm & 3–7pm; free), housed in the Beaux Arts former Conseil General building and attracting big touring exhibitions from the major Parisian galleries. The most impressive public artworks in the city, however, are Pierre Puget's sculptures of **Atlantes**, holding up all that is left of the old town hall

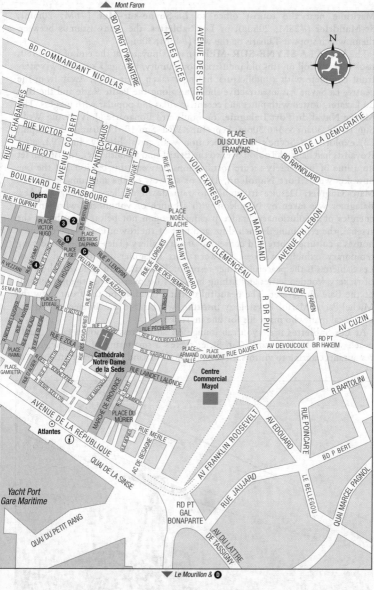

on quai Cronstadt. It's thought that Puget, working in 1657, modelled these immensely strong, tragic figures on galley slaves as allegories of might and fatigue.

Around the Petite Rade

Various companies offer **boat trips** around both the Grande and Petite Rade, but a cheaper option is to take one of the **ferries** that run regularly from Toulon's Gare

Maritime near the tourist office to **La-Seyne-sur-Mer** (#8M; 20min); **St-Mandrier** (#28M; 20min); or **Les Sablettes**, the sandy isthmus between them, which stops at Tamaris on the way (#18M; 30min).

The loss of **LA SEYNE-SUR-MER**'s naval shipyards at the end of the 1980s took a heavy toll on this old industrial community, though a smart new waterfront complete with a public park has now taken their place. Away from the centre, La Seyne has an attractive shoreline along the Petite Rade and the Baie du Lazaret, dotted with pines and eccentric villas and popular with joggers. The **Musée Naval du Fort Balaguier** on boulevard Bonaparte (July & Aug Wed–Sun 10–11.30am & 3–6.30pm; Sept–June Wed–Sun 10–11.30am & 2–5.30pm; €3) explores La Seyne's long association with naval history. In 1793, after Royalists had handed Toulon over to the British and Spanish fleet, the British set up a line of immensely secure fortifications between this bastion and the one now known as **Fort Napoleon**, 1km or so west of the museum on chemin Marc-Sangnier. Despite its ability to rain down artillery on any attacker, Balaguier was taken by Napoleon with a bunch of volunteers, who sent the enemies of revolutionary France packing, though not before they burnt the arsenal, the remaining French ships and part of the town. Fort Napoleon now houses a cultural centre and contemporary art gallery (Tues–Sat 2–6pm during temporary exhibitions; free). Between Fort Balaguier and the sand spit of Les Sablettes is the peaceful former resort of **Tamaris**, with its lovely shoreline of rickety wooden jetties and fishing huts on stilts overlooking the mussel beds of the Baie du Lazaret. The beautiful oriental building on the front, now the Michel Pacha Marine Physiology Institute, was built in the nineteenth century by a local man who made his fortune in Turkey.

At **Les Sablettes** itself you can lounge on an impressive, south-facing sandy beach with a view towards Cap Sicié; there's a smattering of bar-glaciers and restaurants catering to visitors. Beyond the neck of sand is the pretty little port of

▲ Mont Faron cable car

ST-MANDRIER-SUR-MER, with the security gates of a *terrain militaire* beyond it. The occasional juxtaposition of port-side cafés and rusty old frigates anchored offshore is delightfully odd.

Mont Faron

The best way to appreciate the magnificence of Toulon's harbour is to ascend the 542-metre **Mont Faron**. By road, avenue Emile-Fabre becomes route du Faron, snaking up to the top and descending again from the northeast, a journey of 18km in all. The road is a one-way slip of tarmac with few barriers on the hairpin bends, looping up and down through a pristine landscape of pine and rock. The fastest way to reach the summit, however, is to take bus #40 (direction "Super Toulon" or "Mas du Faron"; stop "Téléphérique") to boulevard Amiral-Vence, from where a **cable car** operates (open daily from 9.30am; closed Dec to early Feb and Mon out of season; last ascent varies according to season; ☎04.94.92.68.25; €6.60 return); it's a bit pricey but the views are a treat.

Mont Faron's summit is threaded with paths and dotted with picnic spots, and the views over Toulon are quite breathtaking. The peak area also holds a **memorial museum** (daily: May–Sept Tues–Sun 10am–noon & 2–6.30pm; Oct–April Tues–Sun 10am–noon & 2–5.30pm; €3.80), dedicated to the Allied landings in Provence that took place in August 1944, with gripping screenings of original newsreel footage. There's a restaurant, *Le Drap d'Or*, close to the museum and another further along the summit near the **zoo** (May–Sept daily 10am–6.30pm; Oct–April 2–5.30pm; €8.50), which specializes in big cats.

Eating, drinking and nightlife

There are plenty of **brasseries**, **cafés** and **restaurants** facing Toulon's port, though greater culinary ambition is to be found in the cluster of streets around the Opéra; there's plenty of choice, too, along the littoral Frédéric-Mistral in Le Mourillon, which is also a good spot to immerse yourself in Toulon's lively, student-orientated **nightlife** scene; pick up the free *Le Petit Bavard* **guide** from the tourist office for hints on where to go. Worthy after-dark options in La Mourillon include *Bar à Thym*, 32 boulevard Dr-Cuneo (☎04.94.41.90.10), a good place for an after-beach beer, with occasional live music, and *Côte Jardin*, 437 littoral Frédéric-Mistral, which has a live singer on Thursdays and a DJ on Fridays and Saturdays. Back in town, *Le Navigateur*, 128 avenue de la République (☎04.94.92.34.65), is a big bar facing the port with 150 different beers and a 6–8pm happy hour.

Restaurants

Carré 2 Vigne 14 rue de Pomet
☎04.94.92.98.21. Provençal and Italian influences blend on the menu of this delightful small restaurant close to the Opéra, with dishes like *socca galette* and cannelloni with *daube de boeuf*. *Plats* around €16. Closed Sun and Mon.

Chez Mimi 83 av de la République
☎04.94.24.97.42. Good couscous from around €12.50, in suitably Moorish blue-and-white tiled surroundings. Closed Mon.

Les Enfants Gâtés 7 rue Corneille
☎04.94.09.14.67. Charmingly informal place with a chalked-up menu of international dishes, from an *assiette* of fish to stir-fries; *plats* from around €12.50.

Le Pointilliste 43 rue Picot ☎04.94.71.06.01.
Restaurant *gastronomique* serving treats such as Mont Ventoux pork with wood mushroom gnocchi or crisp foie gras with hazelnuts; menus €20, €35 and €55. Closed Sun & lunch Sat & Mon.

Au Sourd 10 rue Molière ☎04.94.92.28.52.
Toulon's oldest restaurant serves wonderful fish dishes like monkfish *feuilleté* with basil cream or poached turbot with morels and green asparagus. Menus €27 and €35. Closed Sun and Mon.

East towards Cap Garonne

Neat artificial beaches stretch along the shoreline east from Le Mourillon; beyond them, Toulon merges with **Le Pradet**, from where the D86 winds south along the coast to **La Garonne**. The little resort has a sailing school, a pleasant west-facing shingle-and-sand beach, and a scattering of restaurants including one, *Le St Pierre* (T04.94.31.30.16), right on the beach, serving swordfish with *sauce vierge* for around €16. South of the port, a sideroad leads to the protected nature reserve of Cap Garonne and the **Musée de la Mine de Cap Garonne** (Wed, Sat, Sun & public holidays: July & Aug 2–6pm; Sept–June 2–5pm; guided tours every 45min from 2.30pm; €6.50), a treasure trove of semi-precious minerals, including malachite, azurite and cyanotrichite. There's also an exhibition on the history of the miners themselves. Back on the west side of the Cap, the little harbour of **Les Oursinières** holds a very pleasant small hotel, *L'Escapade* (T04.94.08.39.39, W www.hotel-escapade.com; ❼), with a pool, garden and a restaurant. **Bus #91** (direction "Oursinières") serves La Garonne and Les Oursinières from Toulon.

Hyères

HYÈRES is the oldest resort of the Côte d'Azur, listing among its pre-twentieth-century admirers Empress Joséphine, Queen Victoria, Tolstoy and Robert Louis Stevenson. It was particularly popular with the British, being closer, and more southerly, than its rival Nice. To winter at Hyères in style one needed one's own villa, hence the expansive gardened residences that spread seawards from the Vieille Ville, giving the town something of the atmosphere of a spa. By the early twentieth century, however, Nice and Cannes began to upstage Hyères, and when the foreign rich switched from winter convalescents to summer sunbathers, Hyères, with no central seafront, lost out.

Today it has the rare distinction on the Côte of not being totally dependent on the summer influx, with the export of flowers, exotic plants and trees important to the local economy. It's also a garrison town, home to the French army's 54th artillery regiment and to a naval air station. Hyères is consequently rather appealing: the Vieille Ville is neither a sanitized tourist trap nor a slum, and the locals aren't out to squeeze maximum profit from the minimum number of months.

Arrival and information

Hyères' **Vieille Ville** lies on the slopes of Casteou hill, 5km from the sea. Avenue des Îles d'Or and its continuation, avenue Général-de-Gaulle, mark the border with the **modern town**, of which avenue Gambetta is the main north–south axis. At the coast the peculiar **Presqu'île de Giens** is leashed to the mainland by an isthmus, known as **La Capte**, and a parallel sandbar enclosing the salt marshes. Hyères' **main port** is at **Hyères-Plages** at the top of La Capte, with the village-resorts of **Le Ceinturon**, **Ayguade** and **Les Salins d'Hyères** strung out along the coast to the northeast.

The **gare SNCF** is on place de l'Europe, 1.5km south of the town centre; frequent buses connect it with the more central **gare routière** on place Mal-Joffre. The modern Hyères-Toulon **airport** is between Hyères and Hyères-Plage, 3km from the centre with a regular shuttle to the centre.

The **tourist office** is in the Forum du Casino at 3 avenue Ambroise-Thomas (July & Aug daily 9am–7pm; Sept–June Mon–Fri 9am–6pm, Sat 10am–4pm; T04.94.01.84.50, W www.hyeres-tourisme.com). **Bikes** and mopeds can be rented

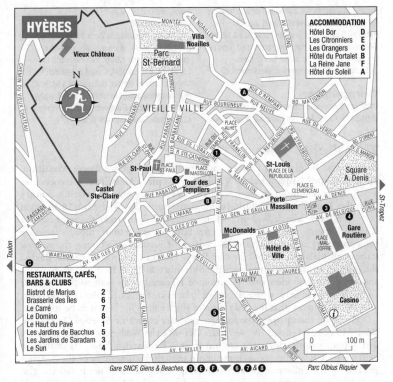

HYÈRES

Vieux Château

Villa Noailles

Parc St-Bernard

MONTÉE DE NOAILLES

AV. P. LONG

ACCOMMODATION
Hôtel Bor **D**
Les Citronniers **E**
Les Orangers **C**
Hôtel du Portalet **B**
La Reine Jane **F**
Hôtel du Soleil **A**

CHEMIN DU VIEUX CHÂTEAU

RUE BARRUC

RUE ST-BERNARD

VIEILLE VILLE

RUE BOURGNEUF

RUE D'ORIENT

RUE NEUVE

BD. MATIGNON

RUE DE VERDUN

PLACE ALHET

AV. G. MANGIN

RUE ST-CLAIR

RUE PARADIS

RUE BARBACANE

RUE DE L'ORATOIRE

RUE STE-CATHERINE

RUE DU FRANKLIN

RUE STE-CLAIRE

St-Paul

PLACE ST-PAUL

PLACE MASSILLON

R. MASSILLON

St-Louis
PLACE DE LA RÉPUBLIQUE

BD. STRASBOURG

Square A. Denis

Castel Ste-Claire

RUE RABATON

Tour des Templiers

PLACE G. CLEMENCEAU

AV. A. DENIS

RUE CURIE

PASSAGE A. SAMARIN

BD. V. BASCH

RUE DE LIMANS

AV. DU PORTALET

Porte Massillon

AV. GEN. DE GAULLE

AV. DE BELGIQUE

Gare Routière

BD. WARTHON

PLACE G. PERI

AV. DES ÎLES D'OR

AV. DR. P. PERON

McDonalds

AV. J. CLOTIS

PLACE MAL-JOFFRE

MOULIS

Hôtel de Ville

AV. DU MAL LYAUTEY

AV. DU M. FOCH

AV. J. JAURES

AV. A. THOMAS

AV. GALLIENI

AV. GAMBETTA

RUE DE BREST

Casino

AV. E. MILLET

AV. AICARD

RUE DE BREST

0   100 m

Toulon

St-Tropez

RESTAURANTS, CAFÉS, BARS & CLUBS
Bistrot de Marius **2**
Brasserie des Îles **6**
Le Carré **7**
Le Domino **8**
Le Haut du Pavé **1**
Les Jardins de Bacchus **5**
Les Jardins de Saradam **3**
Le Sun **4**

Gare SNCF, Giens & Beaches, **D**, **E**, **F**, ▼ **6**, **7** & **8**   Parc Olbius Riquier ▼

---

from Holiday Bikes on rue Jean-d'Agrève close to the port (☏04.94.38.79.45). For **internet** access the local *McDonald's* on avenue Gambetta offers free wi-fi.

Accommodation

With a few exceptions, **hotels** in Hyères are not that expensive, nor very memorable. There are only three in the Vieille Ville, but more in the modern town and along the coast from the east side of the Presqu'Île to L'Ayguade; there are also plenty of **campsites** on the coast, some housing hundreds of pitches. Places in central Hyères stay open all year, while those near the sea tend to close for the winter.

Hotels

Hôtel BOR 3 allée Emile-Gérard, Les Pesquiers ☏04.94.58.02.73, ⊛ www.hotel-bor.com. Smart, timber-clad designer hotel right on the beach, with an elegant but pricey restaurant. **7**

Les Citronniers 1134 bd du Front de Mer, L'Ayguade ☏04.94.66.41.81, ⊛ www.hotel citronnier.com. With just seven bright, modern rooms, the hotel is a labour of love for M. "Fredo" Pellegrino and his family who rescued it from ruin. **6**

Les Orangers 64 av des Îles d'Or ☏04.94.00.55.11, ⊛ www.orangers-hotel.com.

This pleasant small hotel is situated in a historic villa district, west of the modern centre, and has an attractive garden and terrace. **3**

Hôtel du Portalet 4 rue de Limans ☏04.94.65.39.40, ⊛ www.hyeres-hotel-portalet .com. In the lower (and busier) part of the old town, with tastefully designed rooms, double glazing and free wi-fi. Pets are accepted, for a charge. **5**

La Reine Jane le port de l'Ayguade ☏04.94.66.32.64, ⊛ www.reinejane.com. Overlooking the port at Ayguade, this is a friendly place with a restaurant, bar and terrace to make up for its out-of-town location. Closed Jan. ❹

Hôtel du Soleil rue d'Rempart ☎04.94.65.16.26, ⓦwww.hotheldusoleil.com. Well-positioned hotel in the Vieille Ville, high up at the foot of parc St-Bernard, with 22 simply furnished rooms. ❹

Campsites

Camping Bernard Le Ceinturon ☎04.94.66.30.54, ℻04.94.66.48.30. Two-star campsite close to the

beach, and one of the more modest-sized options. Closed Oct–Easter.

Le Capricorne route des Vieux Salins ☎04.94.66.40.94, ⓦwww.campingcapricorne .com. Two-star site 1.5km from the beach at Les Salins; €16 per tent. Closed Oct–March.

Clair de Lune av du Clair de Lune ☎04.94.58.20.19, ⓦwww.campingclairdelune.com. Family-friendly, shady three-star on Giens with a 10.30pm curfew. €25 per tent. Closed mid-Nov to Jan.

The Vieille Ville

To the west of place G. Clemenceau a medieval gatehouse, **Porte Massillon**, opens onto rue Massillon and the Vieille Ville. At **place Massillon**, you encounter a perfect Provençal square, with terraced cafés looking onto the twelfth-century **Tour des Templiers** (open during exhibitions: April–Oct Wed–Mon 10am–noon & 4–7pm; Nov–March Wed–Sun 10am–noon & 2–5pm; free), the remnant of a Knights Templar lodge. The tower now hosts art exhibitions, though these are sometimes less impressive than their dramatic setting: don't miss the narrow staircase that leads to the roof for a bird's-eye view of the medieval centre. Behind the tower, rue Ste-Catherine leads uphill to place St-Paul, from where you have another panoramic view over a section of medieval town wall to the Golfe de Giens. It's around here, where the crumbly lanes are festooned with bougainvillea, wisteria and yuccas, that the real charm of the Vieille Ville begins to be apparent.

Dominating the square is the former collegiate church of **St-Paul** (April–Sept Wed–Mon 10am–noon & 4–7pm; Oct–March Wed–Sun 10am–noon & 2–5.30pm), whose wide steps fan out from a Renaissance door. Its distinctive belfry is pure Romanesque, as is the choir, though the simplicity of the design is masked by the collection of votive offerings hung inside. The decoration also includes some splendid wrought-iron candelabras and a Christmas crib with over-life-size *santons*.

To the right of St-Paul's, a Renaissance house bridges rue St-Paul, its turret supported by a pillar rising beside the steps. Through this arch you can reach rue St-Claire which leads to the entrance of **parc Ste-Claire** (daily; summer 8am–7pm;

Semaine Olympique de Voiles

Thanks to its idyllic waters and consistently strong winds, the Hyères bay is one of the world's best-known sailing centres, bustling year-round with windsurfers, kite-surfers and sailors alike. Each April, for the last forty-odd years, the town has hosted the **Semaine Olympique de Voiles**, a major six-day regatta when some fifty national teams and more than a thousand ships descend on the bay in what amounts to a rehearsal for the Olympic Games, with many countries using the competition to select their future teams. With sponsors, support teams and around a thousand crew thronging the streets and bars, a festive atmosphere prevails in town, with flags of all nations hanging from balconies and windows; while down by the port, crowds brace the weather for glimpses of boats offshore. During the event hotels around the port are at a premium, and although those in the Vieille Ville are less in demand, it's still advisable to book at least three months in advance.

If watching the event inspires you to try out sailing yourself, the International Yacht Club de Hyères (IYCH), 61 avenue du Docteur-Robin (☎04.94.57.00.07, ⓦwww.iych .com), has a sailing school.

winter 8am–5pm; free), the exotic gardens around **Castel Ste-Clair**. Now housing the offices of the Parc National de Port Cros, the castle was originally owned by the French archeologist Olivier Voutier (who discovered the Venus de Milo), before becoming home to the American writer Edith Wharton.

Back at St-Paul's church, if you follow rue Paradis north, you'll reach the **Porte Barruc**, at the side of which you can ascend to **parc St-Bernard** (same hours as parc Ste-Claire; free), an enjoyable warren full of almost every Mediterranean flower known. At the top of the park, along montée des Noailles – which can be reached by car from cours de Strasbourg and avenue Long – is the **Villa Noailles** (during exhibitions only: Sept–June Wed–Sun 10am–12.30pm & 2–5.30pm; July & Aug Mon & Wed–Sun 10am–noon & 4–7.30pm), an angular Cubist mansion designed by Mallet-Stevens in the 1920s, with gardens enclosed by part of the old citadel walls. All the luminaries of Dada and Surrealism stayed here and left their mark, including Man Ray who used it as the setting for one of his most inarticulate films, *Le Mystère du Château de Dé*. To the west of the park and further up the hill you come to the remains of Hyères' **Vieux Château** (free access), whose keep and ivy-clad towers outreach the oak and lotus trees and give stunning views out to the Îles d'Hyères and east to the Massif des Maures.

The modern town

The switch from medieval to eighteenth- and nineteenth-century Hyères is particularly abrupt, with wide boulevards and open spaces, opulent villas, waving palm fronds and stuccoed walls marking the modern town. Most of the former aristocratic residences and grand hotels now have more prosaic functions, though the **casino** (daily 10am–4am), south of the *gare routière*, is still in use. Unfortunately its elegant Beaux Arts exterior and interior have lost much of their original character due to crude modernization, and the interior will disappoint all but the most hardened gamblers.

South of the casino, at the bottom of avenue Olbius-Riquier, is Hyères' botanic garden, the **Parc Olbius Riquier** (summer 7.30am–8pm; winter 7.30am–6pm; free), which opened in 1868. Pride of place is given to the palms, of which there are 28 varieties, plus yuccas, agaves and bamboos. There's a hothouse full of exotics including banana, strelitzia, hibiscus and orchids, and a small zoo and miniature train to keep children amused.

Down to the coast

Hyères' coastal suburbs offer plenty of opportunities for bathing, though mosquitoes can be a problem, so bring insect repellent. The eastern side of the isthmus of the **Presqu'Île de Giens** is a series of narrow sand-and-pebble beaches, with warm, shallow water, packed out in summer; plage de la Bergerie in the south is about the nicest. To the northeast, traffic fumes and proximity to the airport detract from the charms of the seaside between Hyères-Plage and Le Ceinturon, despite the pines and ubiquitous palms. It's more pleasant further up by the little fishing port of **Les Salins d'Hyères**. East of Les Salins, where the coastal road finally turns inland, you can follow a path between abandoned salt flats and the sea to a naturist beach.

Alternatively, there's the less sheltered **L'Almanarre** beach on the west side of Les Salins: the French sailing championships are sometimes held here, and it's a popular surfers' hangout. L'Almanarre is the site of the ancient Greek town of **Olbia** (contact Hyères tourist office for information on visits). Founded in the fourth century BC on a small knoll by the sea, Olbia was a maritime trading post, and excavations here have revealed Greek and Roman remains, including baths, temples and homes, plus parts of the medieval abbey of St-Pierre de L'Almanarre.

From L'Almanarre, the route du Sel (closed to cars Oct–April) leads down the sandbar on the western side of the Presqu'Île, giving you glimpses of the salt pans and flamingoes that lie between the sandbar and the beach resorts on the eastern side. At the south end of the sandbar sits the placid seaside community of **Giens**, with its **Tour Fondue**, built by Richelieu on the eastern side overlooking the port that serves the Îles d'Hyères.

Regular **buses** from Hyères' *gare routière* run to Giens, L'Almanarre, Hyères-Plage and Le Ceinturon.

Eating, drinking and markets

The best places to eat and drink in Hyères are the **restaurant terraces** on place Massillon. There's a food **market** on place de la République on Tuesday and Thursday mornings and along avenue Gambetta on Saturday morning, while organic produce is sold on place Vicomtesse-de-Noailles on Tuesday, Thursday and Saturday mornings. There's also a food market at the port on Sundays.

Hyères' **nightlife** is a rather scattered affair, with the port-side café terraces having the edge over the more sedate old town. The most popular disco is *Le Domino* at 85 avenue de l'Arrogane in La Capte (Thurs–Sun 8pm–dawn; ☎06.11.52.96.19).

Restaurants, cafés and bars

Bistrot de Marius 1 place Massillon ☎04.94.35.88.38. Upmarket little place serving an excellent *soupe de poisson*. Menus €19–32. Closed Mon in July & Aug.

Brasserie des Îles Port St Pierre ☎04.94.57.49.75. A swish brasserie at the port serving a big *plateau de fruits de mer*, and menus from €26 to €43.50. Closed Mon out of season.

Le Carré Port St Pierre ☎04.94.48.84.53. A popular pre-club bar down on the port with a huge, lively terrace.

Le Haut du Pavé 2 rue du Temple ☎04.94.35.20.98. Excellent Provençal and Mediterranean-style cooking. Menus €26 & €32. Closed Mon & Tues out of season.

Les Jardins de Bacchus 32 av Gambetta ☎04.94.65.77.63. Try novel concoctions such as duck and foie gras ravioli on menus from €29 to €53. Closed Sat lunch, Sun eve & Mon.

Les Jardins de Saradam 35 av de Belgique ☎04.94.65.97.53. A pretty North African restaurant serving reasonable *brik*, tagines and couscous opposite the *gare routière*. Closed Sun eve & Mon out of season.

Le Sun 20 av de Belgique ☎04.94.65.02.48. Clubby bar close to the *gare routière*, with karaoke and billiard tables. Open until 2am.

The Îles d'Hyères

A haven from tempests in ancient times, then the peaceful habitat of monks and farmers, in the Middle Ages the **Îles d'Hyères** (also known as the Îles d'Or) became a base for piracy and coastal attacks by a relentless succession of aggressors, against whom the few islanders were powerless. In 1550, Henri II tried to solve the problem by turning the islands into penal colonies, but the convicts themselves turned to piracy, even attempting to capture a ship of the royal fleet from Toulon. Forts were built all over the islands from the sixteenth century onwards, when François I started a trend of fort building that lasted into the twentieth century, when the German gun positions on Port-Cros and Levant were knocked out by the Americans. Some of the forts exist to this day, with a few having been rebuilt, others left half-destroyed or abandoned.

The military presence endures, and has at least spared the islands from the otherwise inevitable pressure for development. Today the Parc National de Port-Cros and the Conservatoire Botanique de **Porquerolles** protect and document the islands' rare species of wild flowers. **Port-Cros** and its small neighbour Bagaud are just about uninhabited, so the main problem there is controlling the flower-picking and litter-dropping habits of visitors. On **Levant**, the military rule all but a tiny morsel of the island.

The Îles d'Hyères are a very fragile environment, their wild, scented greenery and fine-sand beaches contrasting with the overpopulated, overdeveloped mainland. A host of measures protects them, and in hot, dry weather forest areas may well be out of bounds due to the fire risk. If you want to **stay**, bear in mind that hotels are scarce, popular and expensive; book ahead.

Getting to the islands

There are ferries to the Îles d'Hyères, from numerous ports along the Côte d'Azur, though some services only operate in summer. Departures are from **Cavalaire-sur-Mer** (summer only; ☎04.94.00.45.77) to Port-Cros (1hr) and Porquerolles (1hr 25min); **La Croix-Valmer** (summer only; ☎04.94.55.11.80) to Port-Cros (45min) and Porquerolles (1hr 45min); **La Londe**, Port de Miramar (summer only; ☎04.94.05.21.14) to Port-Cros (45min) and Porquerolles (30min); **Le Lavandou** *gare maritime* (☎04.94.71.01.02) to Île du Levant (35min–1hr), Port-Cros (35min–1hr) and Porquerolles (40min); **Port d'Hyères** (☎04.94.57.44.07) to Île du Levant (1hr 30min) and Port-Cros (1hr); and **La Tour Fondue** Presqu'Île de Giens (☎04.94.58.21.81; bus #67 from the Port d'Hyères) to Porquerolles (20min), plus 35-minute cruises in a glass-bottomed catamaran around La Tour Fondue (summer only: 4 daily except Sat; €12.50). Prices for parking at La Tour Fondue vary from €3 to €6, but there are plenty of spaces, though you may have a fair walk back down to the harbour.

Porquerolles

PORQUEROLLES is the most accessible of the islands, with a permanent village around the port, a few hotels and plenty of places to eat. In summer, the island's population expands dramatically, but there is some activity year-round. This is the

▲ Plage d'Argent, Porquerolles

only cultivated island and it has its own wine, with three Côte de Provence *domaines* which can be visited.

The **village** began life as a nineteenth-century military settlement, with its central square, the place d'Armes, being the old parade ground. It achieved notoriety of the non-military kind in the 1960s, when Jean-Luc Godard filmed the bewildering finale of his film *Pierrot le Fou* here, as well as at the calanque de la Treille, at the far end of the plage de Notre-Dame. Overlooking the village is the ancient **Fort Ste-Agathe**, whose origins are unknown, though evidence suggests it was already in existence by 1200, and was refortified in the sixteenth century by François I, who built a tower with five-metre-thick walls to resist cannon fire. The fort has a small **museum** (mid-May to Sept daily 10am–noon & 2–6pm; €4), which traces the history of the island and the work of the national park. The ticket also gives access to the Bonheur windmill behind the fort.

Five minutes south of the village, in Le Hameau, the **Maison du Parc** (daily except Sat: April–June & Sept–Oct 9.30am–12.30pm & 2–6pm; July & Aug 9.45am–12.30pm & 2.30–6.45pm; free) opens its gardens and orchards to the public to wander around. The orchards are particularly interesting, as the Conservatoire is concerned with preserving biodiversity through protecting traditional and local varieties of fruit trees. If you prefer a wilder environment, however, you're better off continuing south to the **lighthouse** and the **calanques** to its east, both of which make good destinations for an hour's walk. Be aware, though, that it's not safe to swim on this side of the island, as the southern shoreline is all cliffs. The best swimming is from the sandy **beaches** on either side of the village: the closest is the **plage d'Argent**, a 500-metre strip of white sand around a curving bay, backed by pine forests and a single restaurant; the longest and most beautiful beach is the **plage de Notre-Dame**, 3km northeast of the village, while the **plage de la Courtade** and the **plage d'Argent** are closer to the port.

Practicalities

There's a small **information centre** by the harbour (daily: April–Sept 9am–5.30pm; Oct–March 9am–12.30pm; ℡04.94.58.33.76, Ⓦwww.porquerolles.org), where you can pick up basic maps of the island; there's also a bank with an ATM nearby. Gravel tracks criss-cross the island, so it's worthwhile renting **bikes** from one of the nine outlets in the village. **Hotels** in Porquerolles cost upwards of €100 a night and need to be booked months in advance. The most luxurious is *Le Mas du Langoustier* (℡04.94.58.30.09, Ⓦwww.langoustier.com; closed Oct to mid-April) at the western end of the island, which insists on either full or half board, at €212 per person (full board). More reasonable, though still pricey, are *Les Medes* (℡04.94.12.41.24, Ⓦwww.hotel-les-medes.fr; ❽) on the edge of the village, and *Auberge l'Arché de Noé* (℡04.94.58.33.71; Ⓦwww.arche-de-noe.com; ❽) on place d'Armes. There is no **campsite** and *camping sauvage* is strictly forbidden.

Most of the **cafés** and **restaurants** in the village cater for wealthier tourists, who can snack on lobster at *Le Mas du Langoustier* (menus €55–105). Slightly more affordable is the grilled fish at the *Auberge des Glycines* on place d'Armes (℡04.94.58.30.36; menus from €19.90), while *La Plage d'Argent* (℡04.94.58.32.48; closed Oct–March), overlooking the beach, serves decent fish lunches for €15–24.

Port-Cros

The dense vegetation and hills of **PORT-CROS** make exploring considerably harder going than on Porquerolles, even though it is less than half the size. Aside from ruined forts and a handful of buildings around the port, the only intervention on the island's wildlife is the classification labels on some of the plants and the extensive network of paths. You are not supposed to stray from these, though given the thickness of the undergrowth, doing so would be difficult.

With just 35 permanent residents, the island is France's smallest national park and a protected zone – smoking is forbidden outside the port area, as is picking any flowers. It's the only one of the islands with natural springs, and boasts the richest **fauna and flora**: kestrels, eagles and sparrowhawks nest here; there are shrubs that flower and bear fruit at the same time, while more common species such as broom, lavender, rosemary and heather flourish in abundance. If you come armed with a botanical dictionary, and the leaflet provided by the **Maison du Parc** (T04.94.01.40.70) at the port, you'll have no problem spotting all the different species.

One kilometre northeast of the port is the nearest beach, the **plage de la Palud**, backed by dense vegetation. On the way to the beach, you'll find the **Fort de L'Estissac** (July–Sept 10am–6pm; free), housing an exhibition on the national park and the island's protected marine life. The best way to see some of this for yourself is to take a glass-bottomed boat-trip from La Tour Fondue (see p.271 for details), though more serious divers will want to head for the island's southern shore to explore the waters round the **Ilot de la Gabinière**. Walkers will enjoy the paths that cross the island from the port via the **Vallon de la Solitude** and **Vallon de la Fausse-Monnaie** to the cliff-bound south coast; alternatively, there's a signed ten-kilometre **circuit of the island**.

Staying on Port-Cros is not much of an option: *Le Manoir d'Hélène* (T04.94.05.90.52, W monsite.wanadoo.fr/hotelmanoirportcros; ❽; closed mid-Oct to mid-April) is prohibitively expensive, as are the five rooms at the *Hostellerie Provencale* (T04.94.05.90.43, W www.hostellerie-provencale.com; half-board only, €130 per person; closed Nov–Easter). The island's **restaurants** are not cheap either, though there are a few places where you can pick up a sandwich or a slice of pizza. Camping is forbidden.

Île du Levant

Ninety percent military reserve, the **ÎLE DU LEVANT** is almost always humid and sunny. Cultivated plant life grows wild with the result that giant geraniums and nasturtiums climb three-metre hedges, overhung by immense eucalyptus trees and yucca plants.

The tiny bit of the island spared by the military is dominated by the nudist colony of **Héliopolis**, founded in the early 1930s; nudity is also compulsory on the beaches of Bain de Diane and Les Grottes. About sixty people live here year-round, joined by thousands of summer visitors and many more day-trippers. The residents' preferred street dress is "*les plus petits costumes en Europe*", on sale as you get off the boat.

Visitors who come just for a few hours tend to be treated as voyeurs. If you stay, even for one night, you'll generally receive a much friendlier reception, but in summer without advance booking you'd be lucky to find a room or camping pitch. Among the cheaper places to **stay** is the eight-roomed *Chez Valéry* (T04.94.05.90.83, W www.chezvalery.fr; ❺; closed Nov–March), in a leafy setting a short walk from the village square. Slightly more upmarket is the small and very charming *La Brise Marine*, in the centre of the village (T04.94.05.91.15, W www.labrisemarine.net; ❻). For more luxury, try the very smart and equally central *Héliotel* (T04.94.00.44.88, W www.heliotel.info; ❽), with luxuriant gardens. In addition, there is a naturist **campsite**, *La Pinède* (T04.94.05.92.81; €25 per tent), set on a hillside and with sea views. Levant has a better choice of **places to eat** than the other islands, with the hotel restaurants being the best bet.

The Corniche des Maures

The Côte d'Azur really gets going to the east of Hyères in the resorts of the **Corniche des Maures**, a twenty-kilometre stretch of coast from Le Lavandou to the Baie de Cavalaire. Multi-million-dollar residences lurk in the hills, pricey yachts in the bays, and seafront prices start edging up, yet the attractions are primarily natural: beaches that shine silver from the mica crystals in the sand, shaded by tall dark pines, oaks and eucalyptus; glittering rocks of purple, green and reddish hue; and chestnut-forested hills keeping winds away. There are even unspoilt stretches where it's possible to imagine what all this coast looked like in bygone years, notably around **Cap de Brégançon**, at the **Domaine de Rayol gardens**, and between **Le Rayol** and the resort of **Cavalaire-sur-Mer**.

Transport around the Corniche is the biggest problem. The coast road is narrow and littered with hairpin bends: it's served by regular buses year-round, though they are very slow, as are the cars that follow. Cycling is strenuous, though a decent bridleway follows much of the coast. There are no trains.

Bormes-les-Mimosas

You can almost smell the money as you spiral uphill from the D559 into immaculate **BORMES-LES-MIMOSAS**, 20km east of Hyères. It's indisputably medieval, with a restored castle at the top, protected by spiralling lines of pantiled houses backing onto short-cut flights of steps. The castle is private, but there is a public terrace alongside it with attractive views. The winding alleys of the village are oddly named, with addresses such as "alleyway of lovers", "street of brigands", "gossipers' way", and "arse-breaker street". They're stuffed full of arts and crafts ateliers, and there's a small **Musée d'Art et d'Histoire** at 103 rue Carnot (Oct–May Tues 10am–noon & 2–5.30pm, Wed 2.30–5.30pm, Thurs–Sun 10am–noon; June–Sept Tues 10am–noon & 3–6.30pm, Wed 3–6.30pm, Thurs–Sun 10am–noon; free), displaying early twentieth-century regional painting.

Although it only dates from 1968, Bormes-les-Mimosas' name is apt, particularly in February when you'll see a spectacular display of the tiny yellow pom-poms. Despite their popularity along the whole of the Côte d'Azur, mimosa are no more indigenous to the region than Porsches, having been introduced from Mexico in the 1860s.

Bormes' bland pleasure port at **La Favière** is flanked by spot-the-spare-metre-of-sand beaches. To the south the tip of **Cap Bénat** can be reached on foot along a coastal path from La Favière's beach. From Cap Bénat westwards to the bland modern seaside extension of **La Londe**, vineyards and private woods will block your way, as well as the security arrangements around the château at **Cap de Brégançon**, which is the holiday home of the president of the Republic. In summer you will have to pay for parking if you want to use the public tracks down to the shore from the La Londe-Cabasson road (cars €8–9). However, once you've reached the water you can wander along the gorgeous beaches as far as you like, with no apartment buildings amongst the pine trees, not even villas, just the odd mansion in the distance surrounded by its vineyards.

Practicalities

Bormes-les-Mimosas is served by a **minibus** from La Favière (4–6 daily; 15min; free); otherwise, it's a two-kilometre walk uphill from Le-Pin-de-Bormes on the main Hyères–Le Lavandou road. Minibuses arrive at the top of the village, near place Gambetta, where you'll also find the **tourist office** (April–Sept daily 9.30am–12.30pm & 2.30–6.30pm; Oct–March Mon–Sat 9am–12.30pm & 1.30–5.30pm; ☏04.94.01.38.38, ⓦwww.bormeslesmimosas.com).

There are a few decent **hotels** and **campsites**, all of which need to be booked in advance in high season. This being the Côte proper, there's no shortage of interesting, if costly, **restaurants**. A reasonably priced and excellent quality option is *La Tonnelle de Gil. Renard* on place Gambetta (℡04.94.71.34.84), with menus from €27 to €42. The prettiest place in town is without doubt *Lou Portaou* (℡04.94.64.86.37; closed Tues & Sat lunch; menus from €24), tucked into a crumbling medieval gateway at cubert des Poètes. Run-of-the-mill meals including pizzas can be had at *La Pastourelle*, 41 rue Carnot (℡04.94.71.57.78), with menus from €19.

Hotels

Bellevue place Gambetta ℡04.94.71.15.15, ⓦwww.bellevuebormes.com. Simple but pleasant, this is the best-value option in old Bormes village. ❸

Hostellerie du Cigalou place Gambetta ℡04.94.41.51.27, ⓦwww.hostellerieducigalou .com. Plush, recently refurbished hotel-restaurant in Bormes village with just twenty individually styled rooms. ❽

Les Palmiers 240 chemin du Petit Fort, Cabasson ℡04.94.64.81.94, ⓦwww.hotellespalmiers.com. Very attractive and peaceful, with its own path to the beach. Half-board only in high season. Closed mid-Nov to mid-Jan. ❻

Campsites

Camp du Domaine route de Bénat, La Favière ℡04.94.71.03.12, ⓦwww.campdudomaine.com. Four-star site right by the sea. €32.50 per tent. Closed Nov–Feb.

Clau-Mar-Jo 895 chemin de Bénat ℡04.94.71.53.39, ⓦwww.camping-clau-mar-jo.fr. Four-star site between the D559 and the port, much smaller than *Camp du Domaine*. €28 per tent; closed mid-Oct to mid-March.

Les Cyprès route de Bénat ℡04.94.64.86.50. Two-star site close to the port in La Favière. €18 per tent Closed Oct–March.

Le Lavandou

Five kilometres from Bormes, **LE LAVANDOU** is an out-and-out seaside resort, with sandy beaches, a scattering of pastel-painted high-rise hotels and an unpretentious atmosphere. Its origins as a Mediterranean fishing village are betrayed by the dozen or so remaining fishing vessels, which are kept in business by the region's upmarket seafood restaurants. Merging with Bormes to the west and St-Clair to the east, Le Lavandou concentrates its charm in the tiny area between avenue du Général-de-Gaulle and quai Gabriel Péri, where café tables overlook the *boules* pitch and the traffic of the seafront road. Three narrow stairways lead back from here to rue Patron-Ravello, place Argaud and rue Abbé Helin, each lined with specialist shops and cafés.

However, it's the coast that is the real attraction, and there's no shortage of watersports and boat trips on offer: the Centre International de Plongée diving school offers initiation **dives** (℡04.94.71.54.57, ⓦwww.cip-lavandou.fr; €40) while Cap Sud on the port (℡04.94.71.59.33, ⓦwww.capsud83.net) rents jet skis and speedboats. For **beaches**, St-Clair, just to the east of town, is pleasant enough, but if you're after the area's fabled stretches of silver sand you need to carry on east to any of the string of villages between here and Cavalaire-sur-Mer.

Practicalities

Buses stop on the avenue de Provence a short walk west of the **tourist office** on quai Gabriel Péri (May–Sept daily 9am–12.30pm & 2.30–6.30pm; Oct–April Mon–Sat 9am–noon & 2–5.30pm; ℡04.94.00.40.50, ⓦwww.ot-lelavandou .com). **Ferries** to the Îles d'Hyères (daily) and St-Tropez (Tues April–Sept) leave from the *gare maritime* in front of the tourist office (see below). You can rent **bikes** from Holiday Bikes, avenue Vincent Auriol (℡04.94.15.19.99).

In summer your chances of finding a **hotel** room are pretty slim. Prices are similar to Bormes, but with rather less charm at the bottom end of the range. For **food**, *La Bouée* at 2 rue Charles Cazin (℡04.94.71.11.88) is quite reasonable, with seafood-based menus at €25–35, while *Le Pêcheur*, on quai des Pêcheurs (☎04.94.71.58.01; menus from €23; closed Thurs), offers fresh fish caught by the restaurant's owner. As for **café** lounging, you can take your pick along quai Gabriel-Péri: the *Brasserie du Centre* on place Ernest-Reyer is about the smartest.

Hotels

Auberge de la Calanque 62 av du Général-de-Gaulle ☎04.94.71.05.96, ⍟perso.orange.fr/aubergelacalanque. Upmarket and comfortable, if slightly faded, and close to the centre. Closed Nov–March. **⑧**

Hôtel l'Oustaou 20 av Général-de-Gaulle ☎04.94.71.12.18, ⍟www.lavandou-hotel-oustaou.com. One of the best budget options in the centre of town. **②**

Les Roches av des Trois Dauphins in Aiguebelle ☎04.94.71.05.07, ⍟www.hotelroches.com.

Luxury hotel on the water's edge, with stunning views from its restaurant (menus from €60) and an illustrious list of former guests that includes Churchill and Bogart. Rooms start at €240. **⑨**

Campsite

Camping de Pramousquier av Ducourneau, Pramousquier ☎04.94.05.83.95, ⍟www.campingpramousquier.com. Three-star site 400m from the beach. €17.50 per tent. Closed Oct to late April.

Cavalière to Cavalaire-sur-Mer

The D559 east from Le Lavandou curves its way through steep wooded hills that reach down to the sea. This, along with the St-Tropez peninsula it leads to, is the most beautiful part of the Côte d'Azur, boasting silvery beaches and sections of unspoiled tree-backed coastline.

West of St-Clair, the next **beaches** you come to are in the tiny, secluded *calanques* either side of **Pointe du Layet**, at Plage du Rossignol and the naturist Plage du Layet. The village of **CAVALIÈRE** has a long, wide beach and hilltops that outreach the houses, while a couple of kilometres further on at **PRAMOUSQUIER**, you can look up from the turquoise water to woods undisturbed by roads and buildings. A further 4km east, the villages of **LE CANADEL** and **LE RAYOL** have gradually merged and colonized the hills behind them. At Le Canadel, the sinuous D27 to La Môle leaves the coast road and spirals up past cork-oak woodland to the **Col du Canadel**, giving unbeatable views en route.

Le Rayol, however, is best known as home to the beautiful **Domaine du Rayol gardens** (daily: Jan–March & Nov–Dec 9.30am–5.30pm; April–June & Sept–Oct 9.30am–6.30pm; July & Aug 9.30am–7.30pm; €8; English audioguide €2.50), which extend down to the Figuier bay and headland. The land originally belonged to a banker who, before going bust at Monte Carlo in the 1930s, built the Art Nouveau mansion through which you enter the gardens; it's nowadays rather dilapidated, as is the beautifully situated Art Deco villa at the far side of the *domaine*. Areas of the garden are dedicated to plants from different parts of the world that share the climate of the Mediterranean: Chile, South Africa, China, California, Central America, Australia and New Zealand. Apart from the extraordinary diversity of the vegetation, the garden is memorable for the loveliness of its setting, with cooling breezes and views of its small sandy beach and crystal-clear turquoise waters (off-limits to visitors). In July and August, you can take a snorkelling tour of the "Jardin Marine" immediately offshore (book at least a week in advance; ☎04.98.04.44.00; €17). There are also various engaging themed tours of the garden given by professional gardeners.

East from Le Rayol, the corniche climbs away from the coast through 3km of open countryside, sadly scarred most years by fire, before ending with the sprawl of **CAVALAIRE-SUR-MER**. Here the tiny *calanques* give way to a

long stretch of sand and flat land that has been exploited for tl
rentable space. In its favour, Cavalaire is very much a family resort ↳
stuck on glamour.

Practicalities

In Le Rayol, the **tourist office** on place Michel-Goy (Mon–Sat 9.30am–12.3
& 3.30–6.30pm; ℡04.94.05.65.69, ⓦwww.lerayolcanadel.fr) has details эt
possible walks, including the Ex-Voie Férée, a former railway track. Cavalaire-sur-
Mer's tourist office (mid-June to mid-Sept daily 9am–7pm; mid-Sept to mid-June
Mon–Fri 9am–12.30pm & 2–6pm; Sat 9am–12.30pm; ℡04.94.01.92.10, ⓦwww
.cavalaire-sur-mer.fr) is prominently sited in the Maison de la Mer, where avenue
des Alliés meets promenade de la Mer, and has lists of hotels and campsites. **Bikes**
can be rented nearby at Holiday Bikes, les Régates du Port (℡04.94.64.18.17).

Finding **rooms** in this area outside July and August should not present a
problem. There are a number of hotels in Cavalaire-sur-Mer, with first choice
being the small, upmarket *La Calanque*, rue de la Calanque (℡04.94.01.95.00,
ⓦwww.residences-du-soleil.com/lacalanque; ❾; closed Jan–March), beautifully
perched on a low cliff overlooking the sea a little way out of town; rooms start at
€200. In Pramousquier, *Le Mas* (℡04.94.05.80.43, ⓦwww.hotel-lemas.com; ❹;
closed Nov–March), above the main road at 9 avenue Capitaine-Ducourneau, is a
good option with a pool and great views.

The place to **eat** and **drink** is *Le Maurin des Maures* on the main road at Le Rayol
(℡04.94.05.60.11; lunch menu €13.50 Mon–Sat, dinner €23.50), serving fresh
grilled fish, *bourride* and *aioli*. Facing the port in Cavalaire, *Le Rescator*
(℡04.94.15.42.10) is a *restaurant gastronomique* with lunch menus from €18.50 and
bouillabaisse for €49, while the neighbouring *Le Dan Rozel* (℡04.94.64.10.86;
closed Nov–March) serves decent crêpes. For **nightlife**, *Le Tropicana* **disco** on
Le Canadel's beach (mid-July to late Aug Thurs, Fri & Sat; ℡04.94.05.61.50) stays
open until the early hours.

La Croix-Valmer

At the eastern end of Cavalaire-sur-Mer's bay lies another exceptional stretch of
wooded coastline, the **Domaine de Cap Lardier**. This pristine coastal conservation area snakes around the southern tip of the St-Tropez peninsula, and is best
accessed from **LA CROIX-VALMER**, even though the village centre is some
2.5km from the sea. Being slightly inland, however, adds to its charm, since some
of the land down to the sea is taken up by vineyards that produce a decent wine.
Local legend maintains that Emperor Constantine stopped here with his troops on
his way to Rome and had his famous vision of the sun's rays forming a cross over
the sea, which converted him – and therefore ultimately all of Europe – to the new
religion; hence the "cross" in the name of the village, which only came into
existence in 1934.

To reach the best **beach** in the vicinity, Plage du Gigaro, and the start of the
paths to Cap Lardier, you need to take boulevard Georges-Selliez from place des
Palmiers (the D93), turn right into boulevard de Sylvabelle, then left along
boulevard Gigaro. It's a four-kilometre walk, so you may prefer to catch the
navette or **shuttle bus** (June–Sept; every 35min) from outside the tourist office
(see below).

Practicalities

La Croix-Valmer's **tourist office** (mid-June to mid-Sept Mon–Sat 9.15am–12.30pm
& 2.30–7pm, Sun 9am–1pm; mid-Sept to mid-June Mon–Fri 9.15am–noon &

...m, Sat & Sun 9.15am–noon; ℡04.94.55.12.12, Ⓦwww.lacroixvalmer.fr) is at Esplanade de la Gare, just up from the central junction, rond point du Brost. **Bikes** and scooters can be rented from Holiday Bikes (℡04.94.79.75.12) on boulevard Georges-Selliez, east of the village centre. One of the cheapest places **to stay** is the small, family-run *Hostellerie La Ricarde*, Plage du Débarquement (℡04.94.79.64.07, Ⓦwww.hotel-la-ricarde.com; ❸; closed Oct–March), which is near the beach. At the other end of the scale, *Le Château de Valmer* on the road to Gigaro (℡04.94.55.15.15, Ⓦwww.chateauvalmer.com; ❾; closed Oct–April) is a seriously luxurious old Provençal manor house within walking distance of the sea; rooms start at €300 in high season. There's one **campsite**, the pricey four-star *Sélection* (℡04.94.55.10.30, Ⓦwww.selectioncamping.com; €32.50 per tent; closed mid-Oct to mid-March), on boulevard de la Mer, just 400m from the sea and with excellent facilities.

There are some tempting **restaurants** along the beach, though none is particularly cheap; the best is *Souleias* (℡04.94.55.10.55; closed Oct–April), with menus from €54 to €92, while good (if pricey) pizzas are guaranteed at *Le Coin de l'Italien – Pepe le Pirate*, Plage de Gigaro (℡04.94.79.67.16), the last restaurant before the conservation area.

St-Tropez and around

The origins of **ST-TROPEZ** are not unusual for this stretch of coast: a fishing village that grew up around a port founded by the Greeks of Marseille, it was destroyed by the Saracens in 739 and finally fortified in the late Middle Ages. Its sole distinction was its inaccessibility, stuck out on a peninsula that never warranted real roads. St-Tropez could be reached easily only by boat as late as the 1880s, when the novelist **Guy de Maupassant** sailed his yacht into the port during his final high-living binge before the onset of syphilitic insanity.

Soon after Maupassant's visit, the Neo-Impressionist painter **Paul Signac** sailed down the coast in his boat, named after Manet's notorious painting *L'Olympia*. Bad weather forced him to moor in St-Tropez and, being rich and impulsive, he decided to have a house built there – *La Hune*, on what is now rue Paul-Signac, was designed by fellow painter Henri van de Velde. Signac opened his doors to impoverished friends who could benefit from the light, the beauty and the distance from the respectable convalescent world of Cannes and Nice. **Matisse** was one of the first to take up his offer; the locals were shocked again, this time by Madame Matisse modelling in a kimono. **Bonnard**, **Marquet**, **Dufy**, **Derain**, **Vlaminck**, **Seurat**, **Van Dongen** and others followed, and by the eve of World War I, St-Tropez was fairly well established as a hang-out for bohemians.

The 1930s saw a further artistic influx, this time of writers as much as painters: **Jean Cocteau** came here; **Colette** lived for fourteen years in a villa outside the village, describing her main concerns as "whether to go walking or swimming, whether to have rosé or white, whether to have a long day or a long night"; while **Anaïs Nin**'s journal records "girls riding bare-breasted on the back of open cars; an intensity of pleasure" and undressing between bamboo bushes that rustled with concealed lovers.

But it wasn't until after World War II that St-Tropez achieved international celebrity. In 1955, Roger Vadim arrived to film **Brigitte Bardot** in *Et Dieu Créa La Femme*, and the cult of Tropezian sun, sex and celebrities took off, creating a tourist boom which to this day sees the village groaning under the sheer weight of visitor numbers in high season. As the summer playground of Europe's youthful rich, St-Tropez remains undeniably glamorous, its oversized yachts and infamous champagne "spray" parties creating an air of hedonistic excess; on warm nights there's a delicious buzz of excitement around the port. Be warned, however, that if you don't have the holiday budget of a supermodel or Formula One racing driver, St-Tropez's sheer expense and occasional haughtiness towards visitors can make it feel like a party you're not invited to.

Arrival, information and accommodation

On entering St-Tropez from the west, the road from La Foux divides into two one-way avenues: the right (inward) fork passes the **gare routière** at place Blanqui; if you arrive by car, turn left here to reach the vast car park on the **Nouveau Port**. From here, avenue du 11-Novembre-1918 passes the **post office** to reach the **Vieux Port**, where the Vieille Ville rises above the eastern quay. The **tourist office** is on the Vieux Port at the start of quai Jean-Jaurès (April–June, Sept & Oct 9.30am–12.30pm & 2–7pm; July & Aug daily 9.30am–1.30pm & 3–8pm; Nov–March 9.30am–12.30pm & 2–6pm; ℡08.92.68.48.28, Ⓦwww.ot-saint-tropez .com). You can rent **bikes** from Location Mas, 3 rue Quaranta (℡04.94.97.00.60).

The tourist office can help with **hotel** reservations (hotline ℡04.94.55.22.00), although with ever more people wanting to pay homage to St-Tropez, accommodation is a problem, and if you have your own transport, you may be better off staying in La Croix-Valmer or even Cavalaire-sur-Mer (see p.276). Out of season you may be luckier, though in winter many hotels close. Staying in St-Tropez is an expensive business, with a bias towards the top end of the market; even the "budget" options are noticeably more expensive than their equivalents elsewhere on the coast.

Camping near St-Tropez can be just as difficult; the sites at the plage du Pamplonne rent well-equipped, expensive tiki huts, not emplacements for tents. In summer it's worth checking out the signs for **camping à la ferme** that you'll see along the D93, but make sure you know the charges first.

Hotels

B Lodge 23 rue de l'Aïoli ℡04.94.97.06.57, Ⓦwww.hotel-b-lodge.com. A comfortable hotel overlooking the citadel, and a bit quieter than those in the centre, with thirteen smart modern rooms but no lift, and only the suite is air conditioned. ❼

Kube rte de St-Tropez ℡04.94.97.20.00, Ⓦwww.muranoresort.com. Gorgeous white designer hotel on the road from La Foux, with an infinity pool facing the sea and an ice bar in the basement; there's a free chauffeur-driven shuttle to the Vieux Port. Rooms start at €390 in high season. ❾

Les Lauriers rue du Temple ℡04.94.97.04.88, Ⓔhotelleslauriers@wanadoo.fr. Small and very good value, with its own garden. Close to place des Lices. Closed Nov–April. ❺

Lou Cagnard 18 av Paul-Roussel ℡04.94.97.04.24, Ⓦwww.hotel-lou-cagnard.com. One of the best of the cheaper options: central, with a decent garden and quiet at night time. Closed Nov & Dec. ❹

La Ponche 3 rue des Remparts ℡04.94.97.02.53, Ⓦwww.laponche.com. An old block of fishermen's houses, luxuriously furnished and with a host of famous names in its guest book. Rooms start at €300 in high season. Closed Nov–March. ❾

Résidence de la Pinède plage de la Bouillabaisse ℡04.94.55.91.00, Ⓦwww.residencepinede.com. With a wonderful location on its own private beach and just 39 rooms, this luxurious hotel has spacious rooms tastefully decorated in pale colours, with marble-lined bathrooms; its restaurant is reckoned to be St-Tropez's best. Prices are eye-watering, with rooms from €705 in high season. Closed Oct–April. ❾

Campsites

La Croix du Sud rte des Plages ℡04.94.55.51.23, Ⓦwww.campeole.com. A four-star site 3km from Ramatuelle towards the Plage de Pampelonne (see p.284). €21.50 per tent. Closed Oct–March.

Les Tournels on rte de Camarat ℡04.94.55.90.90, Ⓦwww.tournels.com. Vast but well-situated four-star site, 1km from the sea. €48 per tent.

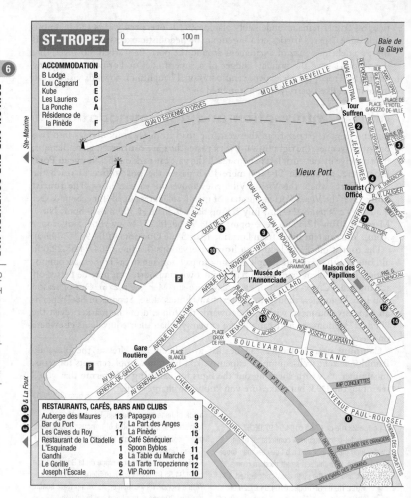

ST-TROPEZ

| 0 | 100 m |

ACCOMMODATION
B Lodge	B
Lou Cagnard	D
Kube	E
Les Lauriers	C
La Ponche	A
Résidence de la Pinède	F

Baie de la Glaye

MÔLE JEAN REVEILLE

QUAI D'ESTIENNE D'ORVES

Vieux Port

QUAI DE L'EPI

QUAI H. BOUCHARD

AVENUE DU 11-NOVEMBRE-1918

AVENUE DU 8-MAI-1945

Tour Suffren

QUAI JEAN-JAURÈS

QUAI SUFFREN

Tourist Office

Musée de l'Annonciade

PLACE GRAMMONT

RUE DE LA POSTE

RUE ALLARD

Maison des Papillons

RUE GEORGES CLEMENCEAU

RUE DES TISSERANDS

RUE ETIENNE BERNY

RUE DES CHARRONS

RUE BOUTIN

RUE JOSEPH QUARANTA

R.J. AICARD

BOULEVARD LOUIS BLANC

CHEMIN PRIVÉ

IMP. CONQUETTES

Gare Routière

PLACE BLANQUI

AV DU GENERAL-DE-GAULLE

AV GENERAL LECLERC

CHEMIN DES AMOUREUX

AVENUE PAUL-ROUSSEL

BOULEVARD DES ORANGERS

BOULEVARD DES JASMINS

RESTAURANTS, CAFÉS, BARS AND CLUBS
Auberge des Maures	13	Papagayo	9
Bar du Port	7	La Part des Anges	3
Les Caves du Roy	11	La Pinède	15
Restaurant de la Citadelle	5	Café Sénéquier	4
L'Esquinade	1	Spoon Byblos	11
Gandhi	8	La Table du Marché	14
Le Gorille	6	La Tarte Tropezienne	12
Joseph l'Éscale	2	VIP Room	10

The Town

Beware of coming to St-Tropez in high season, unless you arrive by yacht, helicopter or on the ferry from Ste-Maxime (4 hourly in high season; €6.60 single, €12 return; ℡04.94.49.29.39, ⓦwww.bateauxverts.com), for the traffic jams can be appalling and the crowds around the port oppressive. Nor are the beaches particularly clean, lacking the Blue Flag status of those at La Croix-Valmer and Ste-Maxime. Time your trip for a spring or autumn day, however, and you'll understand better why this place has charmed so many for so long.

The **Vieux Port**, rebuilt after its destruction in World War II, is where you get the classic St-Tropez experience: the quayside café clientele eyeing the Martinisippers on their gin-palace motor yachts, with the latest fashions parading in between, defining the French word *frimer* (derived from sham) which means exactly this – to stroll ostentatiously in places like St-Tropez. You may be surprised how entertaining the spectacle can be, though it's undeniably a little

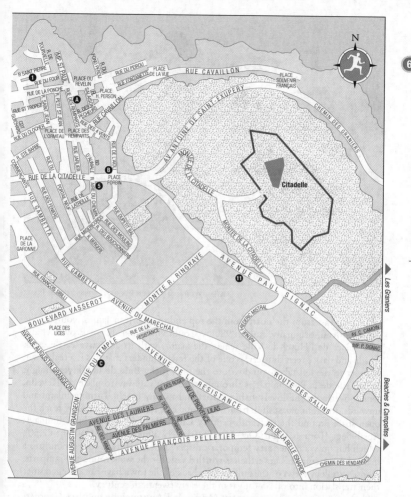

vulgar – a sort of human zoo in which the conspicuously rich are willing exhibits. The portside is at its most magical in late September and early October during **Les Voiles**, the regatta which sees the harbour swap ugly motor yachts for beautiful sailing vessels, and cruise liners dotting the Golfe de St-Tropez beyond.

The other pole of St-Trop's life is **place des Lices**, southeast of the Vieux Port, with its battered old plane trees, *pétanque* players and benches on which to sit and watch – a rather nicer option than the café-brasseries fringing the *place*, which are a bit too smugly Champs-Elysées in style. In the streets between here and the port – rue François Sibilli and rue Georges Clemenceau – and the smaller lanes in the heart of the old village you can window-shop or buy haute couture, antiques, *objets d'art* and classy trinkets to your heart's content. One of the narrowest lanes is rue Etienne Berny where, at no. 9, you'll find the **Maison des Papillons** (June–Sept Wed–Mon 10am–noon & 2–7pm; Sept–May Wed–Mon 10am–noon & 2–6pm; €3), a butterfly museum housing 4500 pinned specimens, including many rare and endangered species.

▲ Dining alfresco along the Plage de Pampelonne, St-Tropez

Heading east from the port, from the top end of quai Jean-Jaurès, you pass the **Tour Suffren**, originally built in 980 by Count Guillaume 1er of Provence, and enter place de l'Hôtel-de-Ville where the *mairie*, with its attractive earthy pink facade and dark green shutters, is one of the few reminders that this is a real town. A street to the left takes you down to the tiny, rocky **Baie de la Glaye**; straight ahead, rue de la Ponche passes through an ancient gateway to place du Revelin, which overlooks the lovely **fishing port** and its tiny beach. Turning inland and upwards, struggling past shop fronts, stalls and café tables, you can finally reach the open space around the sixteenth-century **Citadelle** (daily except bank holidays: April–Sept 10am–6.30pm; Oct–March 10am–12.30pm & 1.30–5.30pm; €2.50), which has only a rather arty temporary display pending future conversion into a maritime museum. It's nevertheless worth a visit for the walk round the ramparts, whose excellent views of the gulf and the back of the town have not changed since their translation into oil on canvas in the early twentieth century.

These paintings can be seen at the **Musée de l'Annonciade** on place Georges-Grammont just west of the port (July & Aug daily 10am–noon & 2–7pm; Sept & Dec–June Mon & Wed–Sun 10am–noon & 2–6pm; €5, or €6 during temporary exhibitions), reason in itself for a visit to St-Tropez. It was originally Signac's idea to have a permanent exhibition space for the Neo-Impressionists and Fauves who painted here, though it was not until 1955 that collections owned by various individuals were put together in this deconsecrated sixteenth-century chapel. The museum features representative works by Signac, Matisse and most of the other artists who painted in St-Tropez: grey, grim, northern scenes of Paris, Boulogne and Westminster, and then local, brilliantly sunlit landscapes by the same brush. Two winter scenes of the village by Dufy contrast with Camille Camoin's springtime *Place des Lices* and Bonnard's boilingly hot summer view. The museum is a real delight, both for its contents – unrivalled outside Paris for the 1890 to 1940 period – and for the fact that it is often the least crowded place on the port.

Eating and drinking

Eating in St-Tropez is notoriously expensive. The correlation between price and quality is weaker here than anywhere else on the Côte d'Azur, even at the top end of the market, where there are several very good restaurants but, arguably, no really great ones. As a rule of thumb, avoid the obvious hotspots of the Vieux Port or place des Lices, and instead browse the restaurant menus in the lanes that climb towards the church and Citadelle to find the best value. Prime **drinking** spots are along the port and on place des Lices.

Place aux Herbes has a daily fish **market**, and the main food market takes place on place des Lices on Tuesday and Saturday mornings.

Cafés and snacks

Bar du Port 7 quai Suffren. With its stylish, modern but vaguely retro-Sixties decor, this café-bar is the epitome of St-Tropez idling – and not as expensive as some.

Le Gorille quai Suffren. Straightforward quayside café, where you can get omelettes, salads and the like for around €12.50.

Café Sénéquier quai Jean-Jaurès. The top quayside café: it's horribly expensive, particularly for drinks, but sells sensational nougat (also available from the shop at the back).

La Tarte Tropezienne 36 rue G-Clemenceau. A celebrated patisserie which claims to have invented this eponymous sponge and custard cake; they also do sandwiches and quiches to take away at lunchtime.

Restaurants

Auberge des Maures 4 rue du Dr-Boutin ☎04.94.97.01.50. Specializes in chargrilled fish and meat, with a menu at €48. Evenings only; closed mid-Nov to late Feb.

Restaurant de la Citadelle 27 bis rue de la Citadelle ☎04.94.97.60.15. Traditional and rather charming, with plenty of Provençal specialities on its €15 and €25 menus.

Gandhi 3 quai de l'Épi ☎04.94.97.71.71. Curries and tandoori, with a good selection of fish and

shellfish, too. Lunch menu €16.50, otherwise *plats* from around €11.

Joseph l'Éscale 9 quai Jean-Jaurès ☎04.94.97.00.63. One of a number of restaurants in the burgeoning *Joseph* empire – this one specializes in fish and seafood. Menus from around €39.

La Part des Anges 6 rue de l'Église ☎04.94.97.60.15. A few tables on the narrow street outside, and a two-course *formule* at €15. *Plats du jour*, for around €14, include *onglet* with shallots. Closed mid-Nov to mid-Dec.

La Pinède plage de la Bouillabaisse ☎04.94.55.91.00. Arnaud Donckele presides over the kitchens at St-Tropez's most renowned restaurant, where you might feast on turbot *yuzu gremolata* with slipper lobster ravioli and marjoram-scented crab; menus €95 and €155. Closed Oct to late April.

Spoon Byblos av Paul Signac ☎04.94.56.68.00. Celebrity chef Alan Ducasse's celebrated mix-and-match approach to gastronomy, served in the glamorous surroundings of the *Byblos Hotel* and with a 300-bottle wine cellar. Menu €89.

La Table du Marché 38 rue G. Clemenceau ☎04.94.97.85.20. It's hard to get a table here, but its worth the wait for true bistro-style *gourmandise*; lunch menu €19.50, otherwise *plats* from around €21.

Nightlife

In season, St-Tropez stays up late, as you'd expect. The **pétanque games** on place des Lices continue till well after dusk, the port-side spectacle doesn't falter till the early hours, and even the shops stay open well after dinner. If you have pots of cash and want to sample the infamous St-Tropez **nightlife**, head for *Papagayo* (☎04.94.97.07.56) in the Résidence du Nouveau Port, with a piano bar and theme nights; the glitzy *VIP Room* (☎04.94.97.14.70) at the same location; or *Les Caves du Roy* (☎04.94.97.16.02) in the flashy *Hôtel Byblos* on rue Paul-Signac, which is the most expensive and probably the tackiest. Alternatively, there's the **gay** disco *L'Esquinade* (☎04.94.56.26.31), a long-standing St-Tropez institution that's popular with gays and straights alike. Clubs open every night in summer, and usually weekends only in winter; your chances of getting in will depend on who's on the door, and whether they think you look the part.

The beaches

The nearest beach to St-Tropez, within easy walking distance, is **Les Graniers**, below the citadel just beyond the Port des Pêcheurs along rue Cavaillon. From here a path follows the coast around the **Baie des Canebiers**, which has a small beach, to Cap St-Pierre, Cap St-Tropez, the very crowded **Salins** beach and right round to **Plage Tahiti**, 12.5km from St-Tropez. This eastern area of the peninsula is where the rich and famous have their vast villas, with helipads and artificial lakes in acres of heavily guarded grounds.

Plage Tahiti is at the top end of the almost straight five-kilometre north-south **Plage de Pampelonne**, the famous bronzing belt of St-Tropez and initiator of the topless bathing cult. The water is shallow for 50m or so and exposed to the wind, and it's sometimes scourged by dried sea vegetation, not to mention slicks of industrial pollutants. But spotless glitter comes from the rash of beach bars and restaurants built out over the coarse sand, all with patios and sofas, all serving cocktails and ice creams (as well as full-blown meals), and all renting out beach mattresses and matching parasols. Though you'll see people naked on all stretches of the beach, only some of the bars welcome visitors carrying wallets and nothing else. *Club 55* (April–Oct and Christmas; ℡04.94.55.55.55; à la carte from €60), named after the year when Vadim's film crew scrounged food from what was then a family beach hut, is *the* classic among them, though nowadays *Nikki Beach* is the hot celebrity haunt.

The beach ends with the headland of **Cap Camarat**, beyond which the private residential settlement of Villa Bergès grudgingly allows public access to the Plage de l'Escalet. Another coastal path leads to the next bay, the **Baie de la Briande**, where you'll find the least populated beach of the whole peninsula. You can continue to **Cap Lardier** with a choice of paths upwards and downwards and along the gorgeous shore all the way round to La Croix-Valmer.

To **get to the beaches** from St-Tropez, there's a frequent minibus service from place des Lices to Salins in summer. Alternatively, you could rent **bikes** in St-Tropez (see p.279) and cycle out. For **drivers**, if you want to avoid the high parking fees that all the beaches charge, you'll need to leave your car some distance from the sea and risk being prey to thieves.

The interior of the peninsula

In contrast to its crowded coastline, the **interior** of the St-Tropez peninsula is almost uninhabited, thanks to government intervention, complex ownerships and the value of some local wines. The best view of this richly green, wooded and flowering countryside is from the hilltop village of **Gassin**, its lower neighbour **Ramatuelle**, or the tiny road between them, the beautiful route des Moulins de Paillas where the ruined windmills once caught every wind.

Gassin

The highly chic village of **GASSIN** gives the impression of a small ship perched on a summit. Once a Moorish stronghold, it is perhaps best known today as the birthplace of French soccer idol David Ginola. It's a perfect place for a blow-out dinner, sitting outside by the village wall with a spectacular panorama east over the peninsula. Of the handful of restaurants, *Bello Visto*, place dei Barri (℡04.94.56.17.30, Ⓦwww.bellovisto.eu; ➌; restaurant closed Dec–Feb), serves decent Provençal specialities, with menus from €28, and also has nine good-value rooms.

Ramatuelle

RAMATUELLE is bigger than its neighbour, though just as old, and is surrounded by some of the best Côte de Provence vineyards – the top selection of wines can be tasted at Les Maîtres Vignerons de la Presqu'île de St-Tropez by the La Foux junction on the N98. The twisting and arcaded streets of Ramatuelle itself are inevitably full of arts and crafts shops selling works of dubious talent, but the village is very pleasant nonetheless. The central Romanesque **Église Notre-Dame** that formed part of the old defences has heavy gilded furnishings from the Chartreuse de la Verne (see p.286) and an impressive early seventeenth-century door carved out of serpentine. Gérard Philippe, perhaps the most beautiful French actor ever to have appeared on screen, is buried in Ramatuelle's cemetery.

Opposite the church, on place de l'Ormeau, the small **tourist office** (spring & autumn Mon–Sat 9am–1pm & 3–7pm; July & Aug daily 9am–1pm & 3–7.30pm; winter Mon–Fri 9am–12.30pm & 2–6pm; ℡04.98.12.64.00, @www.ramatuelle -tourisme.com) can supply a list of *campings à la ferme*. Of the few **hotels** in the village, try the fairly basic *Chez Tony*, 31 avenue Clemenceau (℡04.94.79.20.46; ❸), or *L'Ecurie du Castellas* (℡04.94.79.20.67, @www.lecurieducastellas.com; ❻), just outside the village on the road to Gassin, with panoramic views and an excellent **restaurant**; otherwise, a good place to eat is *Au Fil à la Pâte*, 7 rue Victor-Léon (℡04.94.79.16.40; closed Nov–Feb), which serves great dishes of fresh pasta as well as meat or fish specials from €16.

The Massif des Maures

The secret of the Côte d'Azur is that despite the crowds and traffic of the coast, Provence is still just behind – old, sparsely populated, village-oriented and dependent on the land for its produce, not its real-estate value. Between Marseille and Menton, the most bewitching hinterland is the sombre **Massif des Maures** that stretches from Hyères to Fréjus. Darkly forested, its name derives from the Provençal and Latin words for dark, *mauram* and *mauro*.

The highest point of these hills stops short of 800m, but the quick succession of ridges, the sudden drops and views, and the curling, looping roads are pervasively mountainous. Where the lie of the land gives a wide bowl of sunlit slopes, vines are grown. Elsewhere the hills are thickly forested, with Aleppo pines, holly, sweet chestnuts and gnarled cork oaks, their trunks scarred in great bands where their bark has been stripped.

Much of the massif is inaccessible even to **walkers**. However, the GR9 follows the most northern and highest ridge from Pignans on the N97 past Notre-Dame-des-Anges, La Sauvette, **La Garde-Freinet** and down to the head of the Golfe de St-Tropez. There are other paths and tracks, such as the one following the Vallon de Tamary from north of La Londe-des-Maures to join one of the roads snaking down from the Col de Babaou to Collobrières. Some of the smaller backroads don't go very far and many are closed to the public in summer for fear of forest fires, but when they are open, this makes exceptional countryside for exploring by mountain bike or on foot. Bear in mind, however, that at certain times of the year the entire Massif is thick with hunters.

For **cyclists**, the D14 that runs through the middle, parallel to the coast, from Pierrefeu-du-Var north of Hyères to **Cogolin** near St-Tropez, is manageable and stunning.

Collobrières and around

At the heart of the massif is the ancient village of **COLLOBRIÈRES**, reputed to have been the first place in France to adopt **cork-growing** from the Spanish. From the Middle Ages until recent times, cork production has been the major business of the village; however, the main industry now is *marrons glacés* and every other confection derived from sweet chestnuts.

The forests surrounding Collobrières seem endless, and much of the village itself seems lost in time. Yet on the other side of the river, the **Confiserie Azurienne** exudes efficiency and modern business skills. The factory itself can't be visited but there's a small exhibition (daily 9am–12.30pm & 2–6pm; free) of old machinery used for processing chestnuts, and a shop that sells the signature marrons glacés plus ice cream, jam, nougat and bonbons, all made with chestnuts, as well as a sunny terrace on which to enjoy the delicious chestnut-flavoured ice cream. For the fanatic, there's also the annual *Fête de la Châtaigne*, the **chestnut fair**, at the height of the harvest on the last three Sundays of October, with special dishes served in restaurants and roast chestnuts sold in the streets.

Practicalities

Parking can be a headache at Collobrières, with the main tourist car park some distance back from the welcoming **tourist office** on boulevard Charles-Caminat (Tues 10am–noon & 3–5pm, Thurs 3–5pm, Wed, Fri & Sat 9am–noon & 3–5pm; ☎04.94.48.08.00, ⓦwww.collobrieres-tourisme.com), which can supply details of various **walks** and **riding** trails through the massif and some excellent local *gîtes*.

There are two **hotels** in the village: the comfortable *Notre-Dame*, 15 avenue de la Libération (☎04.94.48.07.13, ⓔhotelnotredame@gmail.com; ❺), and the excellent-value *Auberge des Maures*, 19 boulevard Lazare-Carnot (☎04.94.48.07.10, Ⓕ04.94.48.02.73; ❶); both are small, so it's advisable to book in advance in summer. The small, one-star municipal **campsite**, the *St-Roch*, is open May to August (☎04.94.48.08.00). Given the fire risk, *camping sauvage* is forbidden.

For food other than chestnuts and the fare at the hotels, the **restaurant** *La Petite Fontaine*, 1 place de la République (☎04.94.48.00.12; closed Sun eve & Mon), is congenial and affordable (and books up fast), with menus from €25. South of the village, signed off the D41 to Bormes at the Col de Babaou, the *Ferme de Peïgros* (☎04.94.48.03.83; lunch only, plus dinner in July & Aug; menus from €15) is an isolated farmhouse in wonderful surroundings serving its own produce. If you want to buy some local **wines**, head for the Cave des Vignerons on avenue de la Libération; the **market** in place de la Libération is on Thursdays and Sundays.

Around Collobrières

Writing at the end of the nineteenth century, Maupassant declared that there was nowhere else in the world where his heart had felt such a pressing weight of melancholy as at the ruins of **La Chartreuse de la Verne** (June–Aug daily 11am–6pm; Sept–Dec & Feb–May 11am–5pm; closed during periods of high fire risk; €6). Since then a great deal of restoration work has been carried out on this Carthusian monastery, abandoned during the Revolution and hidden away in total isolation, 12km east of Collobrières on a winding but largely paved track off the D14 towards Grimaud. It remains a desolate spot, though; the buildings of this once vast twelfth-century complex, in the dark reddish-brown schist of the Maures, combined for decorative effect with local greenish serpentine, appear gaunt and inhospitable, but the atmosphere is indisputable.

Another religious settlement concealed in these hills is **Notre-Dame-des-Anges** (Mon–Sat 6.45am–8pm, Sun 8am–8pm), 11km north of Collobrières on the Gonfaron road and almost at the highest point of the Maures. As a place of worship it goes back to pagan times, but in its nineteenth-century remodelled form it lacks the atmosphere of La Verne. The main point of a visit for most people is to take in the expansive views stretching from the Alps to the sea.

About 20km north of Collobrières and 2km east of Gonfaron on the D75 to Les Mayons, **Le Village des Tortues** (daily: winter 9am–6pm; summer 9am–7pm; €7; Ⓦ www.villagetortues.com) is not just a tourist attraction but a serious conservation project to repopulate the native Hermann tortoise. A million years ago the tortoises populated a third of France, but now, due to the ever-increasing threat of urbanization, forest fires, theft of eggs and sale as pets, this rare creature only just survives in the Massif des Maures. The tortoises are cared for and protected here, and you can look round their large enclosures where you'll see the tiny babies, "juveniles" and those soon to be released back into the wild.

Cogolin

Just 8.5km from St-Tropez, **COGOLIN** is renowned for its craft industries, including reed-making for wind instruments, pipes for smoking, wrought-iron furniture, silk yarn and knotted wool carpets, all offering one-off, made-to-order, high-quality and high-cost goods for the Côte d'Azur market.

It's possible to visit some of the **craft factories**; the helpful tourist office (see below) can provide a *guide pratique*, and help with making appointments. Alternatively, you can just pop into the retail outlets. The production of **pipes** from briarwood is on show at Courrieu, 58 avenue Clemenceau (Mon–Sat 9am–noon & 2–6pm), while world-famous musicians drop in on Rigotti, on rue F. Arago, to replace the reeds of their oboes, bassoons and clarinets; unfortunately, they open their doors only to professionals. Typically pretty Provençal **faïence** is on sale at La Poterie de Cogolin, 24 rue Carnot (Mon–Sat 10am–12.30pm & 3.30–7pm).

On the way out of town, before joining the N98 heading west, the **Cave des Vignerons**, on rue Marceau (Ⓣ04.94.54.40.54), is worth a visit to sample some of the local wines, said to have impressed Julius Caesar.

Practicalities

From the **gare routière** on avenue Georges-Clemenceau, heading upwards to the central place de la République takes you to the **tourist office** (July & Aug Mon–Sat 9am–1pm & 2–6.30pm; March–June & Sept–Oct Mon–Fri 9am–12.30pm & 2–6.30pm, Sat 9.30am–12.30pm; Nov–Feb Mon–Fri 9am–12.30pm & 2–6pm, Sat 9.30am–12.30pm; Ⓣ04.94.55.22.02, Ⓦ www.cogolin-provence.com).

Hotels in Cogolin are reasonable and are a viable alternative to staying in congested St-Tropez: the best-value option is the comfortable and amiable *Le Coq* on place de la République (Ⓣ04.94.54.13.71, Ⓦ www.coqhotel.com; ❸), while next door, *Bliss* (Ⓣ04.94.54.15.17, Ⓦ www.bliss-hotel.com; ❻) is more upmarket, with a hint of St-Tropez trendiness. For **food**, try the very pretty, semi-*gastronomic* *La Petite Maison*, 34 boulevard de Lattre de Tassigny (Ⓣ04.94.54.58.49; closed Sun & Thurs out of season), with menus at €25 and €32, or *Lili Chez Allan*, along the road at no. 24 (Ⓣ04.94.54.47.70; closed Sun lunch & Mon), with regional delicacies like Sisteron lamb with rosemary; *plats* start at €23.50.

Grimaud and around

Four kilometres north of Cogolin, **GRIMAUD** is a film set of a *village perché*, where the cone of houses enclosing the twelfth-century church, culminating in the spectacular ruins of a medieval castle, appears as a single, perfectly unified entity, decorated by its trees and flowers. The most vaunted street in this ensemble is the narrow **rue des Templiers**, which leads up past the arcaded Gothic house of the Knights Templar to the pure Romanesque **Église St-Michel**. The views from the **château ruins** (free access) are superb, and the monumental, sharply cut serpentine window frames of the shattered edifice stand in mute testimony to its former glory.

These days Grimaud is an exclusive little village whose "corner shop" sells antiques and contemporary art. There's a small **tourist office** at 1 boulevard des Aliziers, just off the main road through the village (Mon–Sat: July & Aug 9am–12.30pm & 3–7pm; April–June & Sept 9am–noon & 2.30–6.15pm; Oct–March 9am–12.30pm & 2.15–5.30pm; ℡04.94.55.43.83, Ⓦwww.grimaud -provence.com). If you're on a budget and need a place to stay it's worth carrying on to La Garde-Freinet (see below), although *Le Coteau Fleuri* (℡04.94.43.20.17, Ⓦwww.coteaufleuri.fr; menu from €45; ❹), on place des Pénitents at the western edge of the village, offers a few reasonable **rooms** above its good restaurant. **Campers** should head for *Camping Charlemagne* (℡04.94.43.22.90, Ⓦwww .camping-charlemagne.com; €22 per tent), at le Pont de Bois, 2km outside the village on the road to Collobrières.

For **food**, you can get decent *plats du jour* at *L'Écurie de la Marquise*, 3 rue du Gacharel (℡04.94.43.27.26; menu from €16.50). For more serious fare, settle down on the vine-covered terrace of the *Café de France* on place Neuve (℡04.94.43.20.05; menu €25; closed Mon). On the lower side of place Neuve, the *Pâtisserie du Château* tearoom (closed Wed) sells wonderful cakes and fresh, nutty breads. The village **market** is held on Thursdays.

Port Grimaud

Avoiding the St-Tropez traffic chaos is tricky if you're visiting **PORT GRIMAUD**, the ultimate Côte d'Azur property development, half standing, half floating at the head of the Golfe de St-Tropez just north of La Foux. It was created in the 1960s by developer François Spoerry – whose tomb is in the village church – as a private pleasure lagoon with waterways for roads and yachts parked at every door. The houses are in exquisitely tasteful old Provençal style, and their owners, amongst them Joan Collins, are extremely well-heeled. Anyone can wander in for a gawp: the main visitors' entrance is 800m up the well-signed road off the N98, surrounded by vast (and distinctly unpicturesque) parking areas. You don't pay to get in, but you can't explore all the islands without renting a boat or taking a crowded boat tour (€5). Even access to the church tower costs €1. There are plenty of places to **eat** and **drink**, though they are clearly aimed at visitors rather than the residents.

La Garde-Freinet

The attractive village of **LA GARDE-FREINET**, 10km north of Grimaud, was founded in the late twelfth century by people from the nearby villages of St-Clément and Miremer. The original fortified settlement sat further up the hillside, and the foundations of its **fort** are visible above the present-day village. To explore it, you'll have to make the steep one-kilometre clamber along a path from the car park at place de la Planète; the tourist office can supply a simple map, or it's signposted from place de l'Hubac above the tourist office.

During the insurrectionary days of Louis Napoleon's coup d'état, La Garde-Freinet played a radical role. Not only did its cork workers form a successful cooperative in 1851, but in their struggle with the landowners women played as strong a role as men – so much so that the prosecuting magistrate of Aix wrote to the minister of justice warning him that La Garde-Freinet, with its new form of socialism in which women took part, would encourage other villagers to abandon public morals and descend into debauchery.

Although La Garde-Freinet is slowly adopting the chic airs of the nearby coast, it still retains an authentic, rural feel for now, with tempting food shops selling organic produce and good local wines. The **Conservatoire du Patrimoine de la**

Garde (Tues–Sat 10am–12.30pm & 2.30–5.30pm, free), next door to the tourist office, has displays on local natural and cultural interest. For hikers, the GR9 **route des Crêtes** to the west of the village passes along a tremendously scenic forested ridge, though if the fire risk is high the paths are likely to be closed.

Practicalities

The helpful **tourist office** operates from La Chapelle St-Jean on place de la Mairie (July & Aug 9.30am–1pm & 4–6.30pm; April, May, June & Sept Mon–Sat 9.30am–12.30pm & 3.30–5.30pm; Oct–March Tues–Sat 9.30am–12.30pm & 2–5pm; ℡04.94.43.67.41, ⓦwww.lagardefreinet.com), and provides information on all the Maures region, including suggested walks.

   Accommodation prospects are reasonable: both *La Claire Fontaine* on place Vieille (℡04.94.43.63.76; ❶) and *Le Fraxinois* on rue François-Pelletier (reception at the *Tabac-Presse*; ℡04.94.43.62.84, ⓦwww.hotelfraxinois.com; ❸) are incredibly good value for this part of the world. There's also a **campsite** close at hand: *La Ferme de Bérard* (℡04.94.43.21.23; €12.50 per tent; closed Nov–Feb), 5km along the D558 towards Grimaud, with its own pool and restaurant.

   In the evenings, *Le Carnotzet* **restaurant** and **bar** on the exquisite place du Marché is the place to be (℡04.94.43.62.73; *plats* €14), with regular jazz and blues concerts. More elaborate food is served up in the rampant garden of *La Faucado* (℡04.94.43.60.41; closed Tues out of season) on the main road to the south, with à la carte from €25; booking is essential. Pigeon fanciers, in the culinary sense, should try *La Colombe Joyeuse* on the place Vieille (℡04.94.43.65.24; menu €18; closed Tues in winter) for its game and pigeon in honey and red wine.

Ste-Maxime and around

STE-MAXIME, which faces St-Tropez across the gulf, is an archetypal Côte resort: palmed corniche and enormous pleasure-boat harbour, beaches crowded with confident, bronzed windsurfers and waterskiers, a local history museum in a defensive tower that no one goes to, and a proliferation of estate agents. It sprawls a little too far – most of the coast road to Fréjus is built up – but the magnetic appeal of the water's edge is hard to deny. Compared to its more famous neighbour, though, it's all rather lacking in atmosphere.

   Its sandy **beaches**, however, have the Blue Flags for cleanliness that St-Tropez's lack, and there's a string of fancy concessions along the east-facing **Plage de la Nartelle**, 2km from the centre round the Pointe des Sardinaux towards Les Issambres. The Plage de la Nartelle merges seamlessly into the **Plage des Eléphants**, named after the cartoons of Jean de Brunhoff, creator of Babar the elephant, who had a holiday home in Ste-Maxime.

   Ste-Maxime's rather pretty Vieille Ville is a good place for browsing through **markets**: there's a covered flower and food one on rue Fernand-Bessy (mid-June to Sept Mon–Sat 1.30am–1pm & 4.30–8pm, Sun 7.30am–1pm; Oct to mid-June Tues–Sun 8am–1pm); a Thursday-morning food market on and around place du Marché; bric-a-brac every Friday morning (9am–noon) on place Jean-Mermoz; and arts and crafts in the pedestrian streets each evening (mid-June to mid-Sept 5–11pm).

   Ten kilometres north of town on the road to Le Muy, the marvellous **Musée du Phonographe et de la Musique Mécanique** at parc St-Donat (Easter–June & Sept Wed–Sun 10am–noon; July & Aug 10am–noon & 4–6.30pm; €3) is the result of one woman's forty-year obsession with collecting audio equipment. The facade resembles Hansel and Gretel's fantastical biscuit house, but is actually modelled on an eighteenth-century Limonaire mechanical music machine. Inside, displays include one of Thomas Edison's "talking machines" of 1878, the first recording machines of the 1890s and an amplified lyre (1903). Almost half the exhibits still work, and you may find yourself listening to the magical, crackling sounds of an original wax cylinder recording from the 1880s played on the equipment it was made for.

Practicalities

Buses arrive in town along the seafront and stop in front of the **tourist office** on the promenade Simon Lorière (June–Sept daily 9am–1pm & 3–7pm; Oct–May Mon–Sat 9am–noon & 2–6pm; T 04.94.55.75.55, W www.ste-maxime.com). **Bikes** and **mopeds** can be rented at Quad N'Bike, 7 rue Gabriel Péri (T 04.94.43.24.32).

The tourist office can advise on **hotel** vacancies, which are rare in summer. There's plenty of choice for places **to eat**. The *Hostellerie de la Belle Aurore*, 5 boulevard Jean-Moulin (T 04.94.96.02.45; closed Mon lunch, Wed & mid-Oct to mid-March), serves gourmet dishes from around €35 on a sea-view terrace, while the less expensive *L'Hermitage*, 118 avenue Général-de-Gaulle (T 04.94.96.04.05; menu €30), specializes in fish dishes.

Hotels
Auberge Provençale 49 rue Aristide-Briand
T 04.94.55.76.90, F 04.94.55.76.91. Welcoming, good-value small hotel close to the centre of town, with a restaurant. ❸
Castellamar 21 av G-Pompidou
T 04.94.96.19.97. Small hotel on the west side of the river but close to the centre and the sea. Closed Oct–March. ❸
Hôtellerie de la Poste 11 bd Frédéric-Mistral
T 04.94.96.18.33, W www.hotelleriedusoleil.com.

Smart hotel right in the centre of town, with very appealing rooms. ❻

Campsites
Baumette rte du Plan de la Tour
T 04.94.96.14.35, W www.labeaumette.com.
Some 2km out of town, up in the hills off the D74. €21.44 per tent. Closed Nov–Feb.
Les Cigalons quartier de la Nartelle
T 04.94.96.05.51, W www.campingcigalon.com.
Decent two-star seaside site. €23 per tent. Closed mid-Oct to March.

Along the coast to St-Aygulf

Beyond Ste-Maxime, its suburb **Val d'Esquières** merges with **Les Issambres**, the seaside extension of Roquebrune, and **St-Aygulf**, belonging to the *commune* of Fréjus, along the fast and rather dangerous coast road. For all its relentless suburban sprawl, this stretch has its attractions, notably a shoreline of rocky coves and *calanques*, shaded by shapely pines and alternating with golden crescents of sand. If the seaside development gets too much, you can always head up and away into the empty eastern extremity of the Massif des Maures (see p.285).

Practicalities
Hotels worth trying include *La Quiétude*, set back from the corniche in Les Issambres (T 04.94.96.94.34, W www.hotel-laquietude.com; ❺; closed Nov–March), and *Le Catalogne*, on avenue de la Corniche d'Azur in St-Aygulf (T 04.94.81.01.44, W www.hotelcatalogne.com; ❻; closed Nov–March), with a pleasant, shaded garden. Renovated Citroën 2CVs can be rented from Escapa'deuche on chemin de la Rivière in Les Issambres (T 06.15.77.67.57). The Corniche des Issambres has a scattering of good places to **eat**, while in St Aygulf, *Le Pointu* on place de la Galiote dishes up a brilliant *moules marinières* for €10.20. St-Aygulf has a good **market**, too (Tues & Fri), and great *poulets rôtis* from a permanent stall overlooking the main square on boulevard Honoré-de-Balzac.

Inland: the Argens Valley

The **River Argens** meets the Mediterranean in unspectacular style between St-Aygulf and St-Raphaël. It's an important source of irrigation for orchards and vines, but as a waterway it has little appeal, being sluggish, full of breeding mosquitoes and on the whole inaccessible. The geographical feature that dominates the lower Argens Valley, and acts as an almost mystical pole of attraction, is the **Rocher de Roquebrune** between the village of **Roquebrune-sur-Argens** and the town of **Le Muy**.

Roquebrune-sur-Argens and around

The village of **ROQUEBRUNE-SUR-ARGENS** lies on the edge of the Massif des Maures, 12km from the sea, facing the flat valley of the Argens which opens to the northeast. Some of its sixteenth-century defensive towers and ramparts remain, and almost every house within them is four hundred years old or more, joined together by vaulted passageways and tiny cobbled streets. Two fountains face each other across picturesque rue des Portiques, where the houses are arcaded over the pavement; beyond it, ancient houses huddle around the imposing village church.

To sample some of the delicious local red and rosé **wines** (phone first), visit the Domaine de Marchandise, route de Marchandise (℡04.94.45.42.91), or the Domaine des Planes on the D7 to St-Aygulf (℡04.98.11.49.00). There's more wine – and other local food products – to taste and buy at the Maison du Terroir, 4 place Alfred Perrin. Delicious nougat and chocolate can be bought from Courreau, 2 montée St-Michel.

The **tourist office**, on avenue Gabriel-Péri (June & Sept Mon–Sat 9.30am–noon & 2–6pm; July & Aug Mon–Sat 9.30am–7pm, Sun 9.30am–1pm & 3–5.30pm; Oct–May Mon–Wed & Fri–Sat 9.30am–noon & 2–6pm, Thurs from 10.30am; ℡04.94.19.89.89, ⓦwww.roquebrunesurargens.fr), can provide information on walks and sports.

Accommodation options in the village are limited. The tourist office can supply a list of *chambres d'hôtes*, but otherwise it's a choice between budget chain hotels: *Formule 1* (℡08.91.70.52.52; ❶) on rond point des 4 Chemins next to the exit from the A8 autoroute, and the *B&B Hôtel*, at La Garillans on the D7 (℡04.94.45.45.00; ❸). Between the village and St-Aygulf the road is lined with mega **campsites**, but more pleasant pitches can be found on local farms; ask at the tourist office. Of the **restaurants**, *Le Gaspacho*, 21 avenue Général-de-Gaulle (℡04.94.45.49.59; closed mid-Dec to mid-Jan), serves Provençal specialities, with a menu at €11.

Rocher de Roquebrune

Three kilometres west of Roquebrune, the rust-red mass of the **Roquebrune rock** erupts unexpectedly out of nothing, as if to some purpose. Even the A8 autoroute thundering past its foot fails to bring it into line with the rest of the coastal scenery glimpsed from the fast lane. To reach it, coming from Roquebrune, take the left fork just after the village, signed to La Roquette; at the next fork you can go left or right depending on which side of the mountain you want to skirt. The right-hand route runs alongside the highway towards **Notre-Dame-de-la-Roquette**, an erstwhile place of pilgrimage (now closed to the public), while the left-hand fork takes you round the quieter, steeper southern side.

The tourist office in Roquebrune can sell you a map outlining four **hiking routes** which ascend the rock from the north, east and west. All but one are challenging in their latter stages, so wear appropriate walking boots.

Chapelle de Ste-Roseline

West of Roquebrune, the DN7 skirts around **Le Muy**, one of the first Var villages to be liberated in the landings of 1944, before intersecting with the D1555 to Draguignan. A little way north of the junction, the D91 leads left to the **Chapelle de Ste-Roseline** (Tues & Wed 2.30–6.30pm, Thurs–Sun 2.30–6pm; free). The old abbey buildings of which the chapel is part are a private residence belonging to a wine grower, and you can also visit the cellars and taste the *cru classé* named after the chapel (Mon–Fri at 2.30pm; €4).

The chapel's **interior** is really rather ghoulish. Saint Roseline was born in 1263 and spent her adolescence disobeying her father by giving food to the poor. On one occasion he caught her and demanded to see the contents of her basket; the food miraculously turned into rose petals. She became the prioress of the abbey and when she died her body refused to decay. It was paraded around Provence until it got lost. A blind man found it and it now, supposedly, lies in a glass case in the chapel, shrivelled and brown but not quite a skeleton. What's worse are her eyes – one lifeless, the other staring at you – displayed in a gaudy frame on a wall. Louis XIV is said to be responsible for the dead eye. On a pilgrimage here he reckoned the eyes smacked of sorcery so he had his surgeon pierce one. Life immediately left it. Horror objects apart, the chapel has a fabulous mosaic by **Chagall** showing angels laying a table for the saint; some beautifully carved seventeenth-century choir stalls; and an impressive Renaissance rood-loft in which peculiar things happen to the legs of the decorative figures.

Les Arcs-sur-Argens

Eight kilometres west of Le Muy, the picturesque medieval village of **LES ARCS-SUR-ARGENS** has been immaculately restored, with its skyline dominated by a Saracen lookout tower, the sole remnant of a thirteenth-century castle. Les Arcs is one of the centres for the Var wine industry, and at the **Maison des Vins** (June, Sept & Oct Mon–Sat 10am–7pm, Sun 10am–5pm; July & Aug daily 10am–8pm; Nov–May Mon–Sat 10am–6pm, Sun 10am–5pm) you can taste and buy wine and cheeses and pick up details of local *vignerons* to visit and *routes du vin* to follow: it's on the DN7 just west of the village towards Vidauban.

The **tourist office** on place Général-de-Gaulle (July & Aug Mon–Sat 9.15am–12.15pm & 2.15–6.30pm; Sept–June Mon–Thurs 9.15am–12.15pm & 1.45–6pm; Fri 9.15am–12.15pm & 2–6pm; ☎04.94.73.37.30, ⒲www.ville -lesarcs.com) has plenty of information on the surrounding area. The nicest place to **stay**, if your budget will stretch, is the exclusive hotel *Le Logis du Guetteur* on place du Château (☎04.94.99.51.10, ⒲www.logisduguetteur.com; ❽), which clusters at the base of the Saracen tower. Less expensive rooms are available at *L'Avenir* (☎04.94.73.30.58; ❷), on avenue de la Gare by the *gare SNCF*, halfway between the village and the DN7. The **restaurant** in *Le Logis* is good (menus €25–95), as is *La Vigne à Table* (☎04.94.47.48.47; menus from €25; closed Sun eve & Mon), the Maison des Vins' very beautiful restaurant, which also serves an eight-course menu *dégustation* with matched wines for €75. The best day to visit Les Arcs is Thursday when a busy **market** is held on the central square.

St-Raphaël and Fréjus

The urban agglomeration of **St-Raphaël** on the coast and **Fréjus**, centred 3km inland, has a history dating back to the Romans. Fréjus was established as a naval base under Julius Caesar and Augustus, St-Raphaël as a resort for its veterans. The ancient port at Fréjus, or Forum Julii, had 2km of quays and was connected by a walled canal to the sea, which was considerably closer back then. After the battle of Actium in 31 AD, the ships of Antony and Cleopatra's defeated fleet were brought here.

The area between Fréjus and the sea is now the suburb of **Fréjus-Plage** with a glitzy 1980s marina, **Port-Fréjus**. St-Raphaël merges with Fréjus and Fréjus-Plage, which in turn merge with **Boulouris** to the east. West of Fréjus a vast modern out-of-town shopping strip – amongst the largest in the South of France – spreads west as far as the A8 autoroute. Despite the obsession with facilities for the seaborne rich – there were already two pleasure ports at St-Raphaël before Port-Fréjus was built – this is no bad place for a stopover. There's a wide range of hotels and restaurants, some interesting sightseeing in Fréjus, and good transport links with inland Provence and the coast eastwards along the Corniche d'Esterel.

Fréjus

The population of **FRÉJUS**, remarkably, was greater in the first century BC than it is today – if you count only the residents of the town centre, which lies well within the Roman perimeter. But very little remains of the original Roman walls that once circled the city, and the harbour that made Fréjus an important Mediterranean port silted up early on and was finally filled in after the Revolution. It is instead the medieval centre, with its lively shopping and cafés and intimate, small-town side streets full of tiny houses, that evokes a feel for this ancient town.

Arrival, information and accommodation

Around nine trains a day from St-Raphaël stop at **Fréjus gare SNCF**, a journey of four minutes. Buses between the two towns are much more frequent and take around twenty minutes, arriving at the Fréjus **halte routière** on place Paul-Vernet on the east side of the town centre. The **tourist office** is nearby at Le Florus II, 249 rue Jean-Jaurès (April & May Mon–Sat 9.30am–6pm; July & Aug Mon–Sat

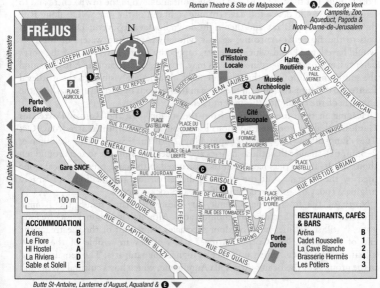

6

TOULON AND THE SOUTHERN VAR | St-Raphaël and Fréjus

www.roughguides.com

293

9am–7pm; Oct–March Mon–Sat 9.30am–noon & 2–6pm; plus Sun 9.30am–noon during school holidays; ℡04.94.51.83.83, Ⓦwww.frejus.fr). Here, you can buy the useful Fréjus Pass (see opposite) and pick up a helpful street map of the entire Fréjus–St Raphaël conurbation. **Bikes** can be rented from Decathlon, ZI La Palud (℡04.98.12.71.71).

Hotels are not as plentiful in Fréjus as in St-Raphaël, but it's generally a quieter place to stay. There's a **youth hostel** a couple of kilometres from the centre, and plenty of **campsites** along the route des Combattants d'Afrique du Nord west of the town. These are mostly on a vast scale, however – the largest has almost 800 pitches – and only a few are especially close to the sea.

Hotels

Aréna 145 rue Général-de-Gaulle ℡04.94.17.09.40, Ⓦwww.arena-hotel.com. Rather elegant, if a bit small, with pretty rooms in a converted bank in Fréjus centre. Roman columns surround the swimming pool. ❼

Le Flore 35 rue Grisolle ℡04.94.51.38.35, Ⓦwww.hotelleflore.com. Pleasant two-star hotel in the Vieille Ville, with just eleven rooms. Pets welcome. ❹

La Riviera 90 rue Grisolle ℡04.94.51.31.46, ℻04.94.17.18.34. Not very modern, but clean, central and perfectly acceptable, with one room that sleeps up to four people. ❶

Sable et Soleil 158 rue Paul-Arène, Fréjus-Plage ℡04.94.51.08.70, Ⓦwww.sableetsoleil.com. A pleasant, small, modern hotel, 300m from the sea. ❸

Hostel and campsites

HI Hostel Auberge de Jeunesse de Fréjus, chemin du Counillier ℡04.94.53.18.75, Ⓦwww.fuaj.org. Located in a small pine grove, 2km from Fréjus centre on bus #7 or #10 (stop "Auberge de Jeunesse"), with dorm beds for €13.20. Reception closed 11am–5.30pm.

Le Dattier rte des Combattants d'Afrique du Nord ℡04.94.40.88.93, Ⓦwww.camping-le-dattier.com. A four-star site 3.5km north of Fréjus. €27 per tent. Closed Oct–March.

Site de Gorge Vent quartier de Bellevue ℡04.94.52.90.37, Ⓦwww.camping-gorge-vent.com. A two-star site off the DN7 towards Cannes, 3km from the town centre. €28 per tent.

The Roman town

Taking a tour of the **Roman remains** gives you a good idea of the extent of Forum Julii, but they are scattered throughout and beyond the town centre and to see them all would take a full day. Turning right out of the *gare SNCF* along Rue du Capitaine René Blazy and then right down boulevard Séverin-Decuers brings you to the **Butte St-Antoine**, against whose east wall the waters of the port would have lapped, and which once was capped by a fort. It was one of the port's defences, and one of the ruined towers may have been a lighthouse. A path around the southern wall follows the quayside (odd stretches are visible) to the medieval **Lanterne d'Auguste**, built on the Roman foundations of a structure marking the entrance of the canal into the ancient harbour.

Heading in the other direction from the station, past the Roman **Porte des Gaules** and along rue Henri-Vadon, leads you to the **amphitheatre** (May–Oct Tues–Sun 9.30am–12.30pm & 2–6pm; Nov–April Tues–Sun 9.30am–12.30pm & 2–5pm; €2), smaller than those at Arles and Nîmes, but still able to seat around ten thousand. Its upper tiers have been reconstructed in the same greenish local stone used by the Romans, but the vaulted galleries on the ground floor are largely original. Today, it's still used for bullfights and rock concerts.

North of the town, along avenue du Théâtre-Romain, stands the Roman **theatre** (same hours and price as amphitheatre). Although its original seats are long gone, it still sometimes hosts outdoor spectacles. Northeast of the theatre, at the end of avenue du XV Corps-d'Armée, a few arches are visible of the forty-kilometre **aqueduct**, which was once as high as the ramparts. The remains stand in the grounds of the Beaux-Arts Villa Aurélienne, which hosts cultural events and

Le Fréjus Pass

Available from the tourist office, the Le Fréjus Pass, is valid for seven days and gives access to the amphitheatre, the Roman theatre, the Musée Archéologie, Notre-Dame-de-Jerusalem and the Musée d'Histoire Locale. It costs €4.60 for adults; concessions are €3.10, under 12s €2. To visit any one of the sights individually costs €2.

conferences. Closer to the centre in rue des Moulins are the arcades of the **Porte d'Orée**, positioned on the former harbour's edge, the only remaining monumental arch of what was probably a bath complex.

The medieval town

The **Cité Episcopale**, or cathedral close, takes up two sides of **place Formigé**, the marketplace and heart of both contemporary and medieval Fréjus. It comprises the cathedral, flanked by the fourteenth-century bishop's palace, now the Hôtel de Ville, the baptistry, chapterhouse, cloisters and archeological museum.

By far the most beautiful and engaging component of the ensemble is the **cloisters** (June–Sept daily 9am–6.30pm; Oct–May Tues–Sun 9am–noon & 2–5pm; €5). Slender marble columns, carved in the twelfth century, support a fourteenth-century ceiling of wooden panels painted with apocalyptic creatures. Out of the original 1200 pictures, 400 remain, each about the size of this page. The subjects include multiheaded monsters, mermaids, satyrs and scenes of bacchanalian debauchery. The oldest part of the complex is the **baptistry** (same ticket as cloisters, access by guided tour only), one of France's most ancient buildings, built in the fourth or fifth century and, as such, contemporary with the decline and fall of the city's Roman founders. Its two doorways are of different heights, signifying the enlarged spiritual stature of the baptized, and it was used in the days of early Christianity when adult baptism was still the norm. Parts of the early Gothic **cathedral** (same hours; free) may belong to a tenth-century church, but its best features, apart from the coloured diamond-shaped tiles on the spire, are Renaissance: the choir stalls, a wooden crucifix on the left of the entrance, and the intricately carved doors with scenes of a Saracen massacre. The **Musée Archéologie** (May–Oct Tues–Sun 9.30am–12.30pm & 2–6pm; Nov–April Tues–Sun 9.30am–12.30pm & 2–5pm; €2) on the upper storey of the cloisters has as its star pieces a complete Roman mosaic of a leopard and a copy of a renowned double-headed bust of Hermes. You can wander through the modern courtyard of the Hôtel de Ville, but you get a better view of the orange Esterel stone walls of the Episcopal Palace from rue de Beausset.

Close by, in an old bourgeois town house at 153 avenue Jean-Jaurès, is the small **Musée d'Histoire Locale** (same hours and price as Musée Archéologie), with reconstructions of past life including an old school classroom, plus displays on traditional local trades.

Around Fréjus

The environs of Fréjus hold several reminders of France's colonial past, a beautiful chapel decorated by Cocteau and evidence of a terrible disaster which befell Fréjus half a century ago. More light-hearted diversions are to be found in the town's zoo and water park.

About 2km north of the town centre at the junction of rue Henri-Giraud and the DN7 to Cannes, there's a Vietnamese pagoda, the **Pagode Hong Hien** (daily: June–Sept 9am–7pm; Oct–May 9am–5pm; €1.50), built by colonial troops and still maintained as a Buddhist temple. Alongside it stands the massive **memorial** (daily except Tues 10am–5.30pm) to the dead of the Indo-Chinese wars of the 1940s and 1950s. It is inscribed with the name of every fallen Frenchman; the sheer length of the lists suggests the years 1950–54 were the most bloody. It's reachable by bus #2 (direction Domaine du Capitou, stop "Mémorial d'Indochine") or #3 (direction St Raphaël, stop "Mémorial d'Indochine").

Just off the DN7 at La Tour de Mare is the last of Jean Cocteau's artistic landmarks, the chapel of **Notre-Dame-de-Jerusalem** (May–Oct Tues–Sun 9.30am–12.30pm & 2–6pm; Nov–April Tues–Sun 9.30am–12.30pm & 2–5pm; €2). Conceived as the church for a failed artistic community, the octagonal building was not completed until after Cocteau's death in 1963, and the interior was completed to Cocteau's plans by Edouard Dermit. The Last Supper scene inside includes a self-portrait of Cocteau; the building's exterior is covered in elegantly simple mosaics and its floors with vibrant blue tiles.

The bleakest day in Fréjus' recent history is recalled by the **site de Malpasset**, deep in the Forêt Communale de Fréjus and signposted off the rond-point du Gargalon on the D37. At 9.13pm on the rainy night of December 2 1959, the newly completed Malpasset dam across the Reyran valley collapsed, releasing 50 million cubic metres of water to create a forty-metre wave which swept along the narrow valley, obliterating everything in its path – including the construction workers' camp on the site of the new autoroute, just below the dam. As the wave neared the coast it fanned out, widening the trail of destruction; it was still 3m high when it raced through Fréjus twenty minutes later. Fifty farms were swamped and some 423 people killed; the death toll was never accurately established as many victims were swept out to sea. Afterwards, various theories were advanced as to why such a highly engineered structure should have failed so catastrophically. Eventually it was found that the geological survey had failed to pinpoint a fault line at the site, which subsequently allowed pressure to build up under the dam. Far from failing structurally, the entire left side of the dam was simply pivoted off its foundations by the force of the water.

How violent that force was is evident as you approach the site, for long before you reach Malpasset great chunks of steel-reinforced concrete litter the riverbed like outsized boulders. The road fords the river then passes under the autoroute to a car park, from which a path (free access 6am–9pm) climbs to a viewing point. The dam is left more or less as it was, its graceful but incomplete arc poignantly terminated a few metres from the valley side. Forest has long since re-colonized the valley floor behind it.

Fréjus' **zoo** is just north of the autoroute at Le Capitou, 5km north of the town (daily: March–May & Sept–Oct 10am–5pm; June–Aug 10am–6pm; Nov–Feb 10am–4.30pm; €14; ⓦwww.zoo-frejus.com; bus #2, direction Domaine du Capitou, stop "Zoo"). There's more family fun at the **Aqualand water park**, off the D559 to St-Aygulf (July & Aug daily 10am–7pm; second half June & Sept daily 10am–6pm; €24.50, children €18; bus #9, direction St-Aygulf, stop "Aqualand"), complete with Europe's biggest wave pool, plus paddle boats, galleons and other water-based attractions, and an 18-hole mini-golf course. Next door, the **Base Nature** (ⓣ04.94.51.91.10) offers a vast range of sporting activities including sand-yachting, skateboarding and rollerblading. Whilst in the area, you might want to take a look at the the **Mosquée Missiri de Djenné**, west of Le Capitou off the D4 to Bagnols, a strange, guava-coloured, fort-like building built by colonial troops in typical West African style. You can't enter it, but can just glimpse the murals inside from the perimeter fence.

The **Étangs de Villepey** wetland nature reserve (dawn–dusk; free), off the RN98 between Fréjus and St-Aygulf, offers walks and birdwatching.

Eating, drinking and nightlife

Fréjus is not a bad place for menu-browsing and café-lounging, with reasonably priced places to **eat** scattered throughout the Vieille Ville. There's a string of options to choose from at Fréjus-Plage, and more upmarket seafood outlets at Port-Fréjus. For **nightlife**, the port and beach are the places to aim for, with Fréjus' two discos, *L'Odysée* and *La Playa*, both on the seafront boulevard de la Libération.

Cafés and restaurants

Aréna 145 av Général-de-Gaulle
℡04.94.17.09.40. Attached to the hotel of the same name (see p.294), this decent restaurant serves excellent fish dishes; menus start at €26. Closed Sat lunch & all day Mon.

Brasserie Hermès place de la Mairie
℡04.94.17.26.02. Generous salads and *plats du jour* from €8.50, and an outdoor terrace right opposite the cathedral. Menu €17.

Cadet Rousselle place Agricola
℡04.94.53.36.92. Good-value crêperie with a €13 three-course menu, salads and pizza, and a huge range of sweet and savoury crêpes. Closed Mon & Thurs lunch.

La Cave Blanche place Calvini ℡04.94.51.25.40. Smart restaurant opposite the Musée Archéologie, with *duo* of rascasse and sea bass, lamb with tarragon or *tournedos rossini* with foie gras on its *carte*; menus €20–40.

Les Potiers 135 rue des Potiers ℡04.94.51.33.74. Charmingly located in a tiny backstreet, this is one of the best restaurants in Fréjus, serving dishes made with fresh seasonal ingredients. Menus from €25 to €36. Closed Tues & Wed lunch.

St-Raphaël

A large resort and now one of the richest towns on the Côte, **ST-RAPHAËL** became fashionable at the turn of the twentieth century. It lost many of its *belle époque* mansions and hotels in the bombardments of World War II; some, like the *Continental*, have been rebuilt virtually from scratch in a modern style, others have undergone more gradual restoration. Meanwhile, the tiny **old quarter** (*vieux quartier*) beyond place Carnot on the other side of the rail line is pleasantly low-key, no longer the town's major commercial focus but one of the better places to stroll and browse.

Arrival, information and accommodation

St-Raphaël's **gare SNCF**, on rue Waldeck-Rousseau in the centre of the town, is the main station on the Marseille–Ventigmilia line; the **gare routière** is just across the rail line from the *gare SNCF*, on place du Dr-Régis. The **tourist office** is at the port on quai Albert 1er (July & Aug daily 9am–7pm; Sept–June Mon–Sat 9am–12.30pm & 2–6.30pm, Sun hours vary; ℡04.94.19.52.52, ⓦwww.saint-raphael.com).

There are plenty of **hotels** in St-Raphaël, from seafront palaces to backstreet budget options. They can all get extremely busy in summer, however, so it's worth booking in advance. If you prefer **camping**, head east along the Esterel coast – the large three-star *International de L'Ile d'Or*, above the D559 at Boulouris (℡04.94.95.52.13; closed Nov to mid-March), is a good bet, with sea views.

Hotels

Beau Séjour promenade René-Coty
℡04.94.95.03.75, ⓦwww.hotelbeausejour.fr. One of the less expensive seafront hotels, with a pleasant terrace. Closed Dec–March. ❺

Bellevue 22 bd Félix-Martin
℡04.94.19.90.10, ⓦwww.hotelbellevue.150m.com. Excellent value for its central location, with simple but attractive and a/c rooms. Book well in advance. ❷

Continental promenade René-Coty
℡04.94.83.87.87, ⓦwww.hotels-continental.com. A modern seafront hotel rebuilt on the site of its illustrious predecessor in 1993, with a/c, private parking and light, spacious rooms.

Hôtel de France 25 place Galliéni ℡04.94.95.19.20, ⓦwww.hoteldefrance-saintraphael.com.

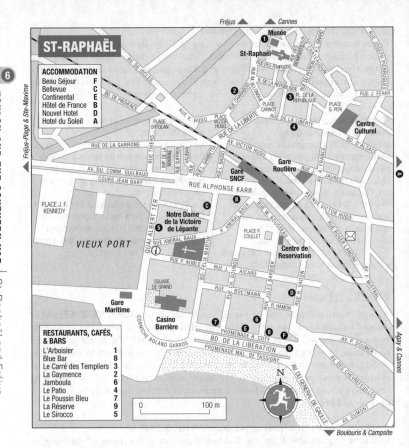

ST-RAPHAËL

Fréjus ▲ ▲ Cannes

ACCOMMODATION

Beau Séjour	F
Bellevue	C
Continental	E
Hôtel de France	B
Nouvel Hotel	D
Hotel du Soleil	A

RESTAURANTS, CAFÉS, & BARS

L'Arboisier	1
Blue Bar	8
Le Carré des Templiers	3
La Gaymence	2
Jamboula	6
Le Patio	4
Le Poussin Bleu	7
La Réserve	9
Le Sirocco	5

0   100 m

Boulouris & Campsite

A plain and simple option, in a potentially noisy location opposite the station. ④

Nouvel Hôtel 6 av Henri-Vadon ☎04.94.95.23.30, ⓦwww.nouvelhotel.net. A cheerful and reasonably smart tourist hotel, near the station. ④

Hôtel du Soleil 47 bd du Domaine de Soleil, off bd Christian-Lafon ☎04.94.83.10.00, ⓦwww.hotel-dusoleil.com. A small, pretty villa with its own garden to the east of the centre; studios are available to rent, too. ④

The Town

On rue des Templiers, to the north of the stations, in the courtyard of a crumbling fortified Romanesque church, you'll find fragments of the Roman aqueduct that brought water from Fréjus. Further along rue des Templiers, there's a local history and underwater archeology **museum** (Tues–Sat: June–Sept 10am–noon & 2–6pm; free), which contains Neolithic, Paleolithic and Bronze Age artefacts and a large collection of amphorae. To the east, on place Gabriel-Péri, stands the town's contemporary **Centre Culturel** (Tues–Sat 8.30am–7pm). Primarily a library, it also hosts interesting temporary art exhibitions.

Heading back towards the port, you'll pass St Raphaël's principal landmark, the towering, florid late nineteenth-century church of **Notre Dame de la Victoire de Lépante**, on boulevard Félix-Martin. Its interior houses a representation of St Raphaël, the symbol of the city. From here, it's a brief stroll to the broad promenade René-Coty, lined with grand hotels – look out for the opulent stucco flowers adorning La Rocquerousse apartment buildings, next to the *Hôtel Beau Séjour*. The promenade culminates with the grandiose Résidence La Méditerranée, built in 1914, at 1 avenue Paul-Doumer: continue along here, and you'll find a fine *fin-de-siècle* villa, Les Palmiers.

The sandy **beaches** stretch between the Vieux Port in the centre and the newer Port Santa Lucia, with opportunities for every kind of watersport. **Boats** leave from the *gare maritime* on the south side of the Vieux Port to St-Tropez, Port Grimaud, Port-Cros (July and August only) and the islands off Cannes as well as the much closer *calanques* of the Esterel coast. If you're tired of sea and sand and want to lose whatever money you have left on slot machines or blackjack, the **Casino Barrière** on square de Gand overlooking the Vieux Port (daily 10am–dawn) will be only too happy to oblige.

Eating

You'll find reasonable **brasseries**, pizzerias, crêperies and **restaurants** of varying quality around the port and along the promenades, with smaller and more individual (but not necessarily more expensive) places inland in the *vieux quartier*. **Food markets** are held daily (except Mon) on place Victor-Hugo and place de la République, with fish sold in the mornings at the Vieux Port.

L'Arboisier 6 av de Valescure ⓣ04.94.95.25.00. Inventive cuisine from chef Philippe Troncy, such as *onglet* with sherry and Szechuan pepper. €30 lunch menu. Closed Mon & Tues out of season.

Le Carré des Templiers 2 place de la République ⓣ04.94.83.64.07. Smart *vieux quartier* restaurant that develops a clubby edge on weekend nights. Lunch menu at €18, evening menus from €28.

Le Patio 54 rue de la Liberté ⓣ04.94.83.63.39. Creative Provençal cooking, with dishes like stuffed fillets of sole with lemon and coriander *confit*, with local wines to accompany the meal. €20 lunch menu, dinner from €21. Closed Sun eve & Mon.

Le Sirocco 35 quai Albert 1ᵉʳ ⓣ04.94 95 39.99. Smart but staid sea-view restaurant specializing in fish. The menus range from €20.50 to €39.50, but the wine is expensive.

Drinking, nightlife and entertainment

For **drinking**, *Blue Bar* on rue Jules-Barbier above Plage du Veillat has a decent selection of beers. *La Gaymence*, at 16 rue Charabois, is St Raphaël's only gay bar, with regular cabaret; *La Réserve*, on promenade René-Coty, is the stereotypical Côte d'Azur **disco** (open from 11pm), while *Jamboula*, at 133 rue Jules-Barbier, plays hip-hop and R&B.

If you're in St-Raphaël in early July, try to catch some of the bands playing in the international competition of New Orleans **jazz** bands: ask at the tourist office for details of venues.

Listings

Bike rental Atout Cycles, 330 bd Jean-Moulin ⓣ04.94.95.56.91.
Car rental Most are in or near the *gare SNCF*: Avis is on place Pierre Coullet ⓣ04.94.95.60.42; Budget is on av de la Gare ⓣ04.94.82.24.44; and Europcar at 54 place Pierre-Coullet ⓣ04.94.95.56.87.
Diving Club Sous l'Eau, at Port Santa Lucia to the east of the town centre (ⓣ04.94.95.90.33,

ⓦwww.clubsousleau.com), takes divers out to the numerous wartime wrecks and underwater archeological sites off the coast.
Emergency Hôpital Intercommunal Bonnet, av André-Léotard, Fréjus ⓣ04.94.40.21.21; SOS Médecins ⓣ04.94.95.15.25.
Police Commissariat, rue de la République ⓣ04.94.95.00.17.
Taxi ⓣ04.94.83.24.24.

The Esterel

The 32-kilometre **Corniche de l'Esterel**, the sole stretch of wild coast between St-Raphaël and the Italian border, remains untouched by property development – at least between **Anthéor** and **Le Trayas** – its backdrop a 250-million-year-old arc of brilliant red volcanic rock tumbling down to the sea from the harsh crags of the **Massif de l'Esterel**. From the two major routes between Fréjus and **La Napoule**, the coastal D559 and rail line, and the inland DN7, minor roads lead into this steeply contoured and once deeply wooded wild terrain. The **shoreline**, meanwhile, is a mass of little beaches – some sand, some shingle – cut by rocky promontories.

The inland route

The high, hairpin **inland route** is a dramatic drive, though this is by no means uninhabited wilderness any longer, as the lack of topsoil means it hasn't been exploited for agriculture. Prior to the twentieth-century creation of the corniche, the coastal communities here were linked only by sea. The inland route (DN7), however, is ancient, following in parts the Roman Via Aurelia.

Because of the fire risk many of the minor roads and paths are subject to closure during the summer months: call the information line on ☎04.98.10.55.41 to check the current situation. All fires, and even cigarettes, are banned all year round, and vehicle access is prohibited between 9pm and 6am. This makes **walking** even more enjoyable, though camping is strictly forbidden. The tourist office in St-Raphaël (see p.297) can provide details of paths and of the peaks that make the most obvious destinations. The highest point is **Mont Vinaigre**, which you can almost reach by road on the N7; a short, signposted footpath leads up to the summit. At 618m it's hardly a mountain, but the view from the top is spectacular.

The corniche

With half a dozen train stations and twelve buses a day between St-Raphaël and Agay, this is a very accessible coastal stretch for non-drivers. Boats also run along

▲ Cyclist on the Corniche de l'Esterel

the coast from St-Raphaël's *gare maritime*; hikers can follow the *sentier littoral* as far as Le Dramont, though the route is occasionally blocked by the campsites along the shoreline. Along the stretch between Anthéor and Le Trayas, each easily reached beach has its summer snack-van, and by clambering over rocks you can usually find a near-deserted cove.

Le Dramont, Agay and Anthéor
The merest snatch of clear hillside and brasserie-less beach distinguishes Boulouris from **LE DRAMONT**, 7km east of St-Raphaël, where the landing of the 36th American division in August 1944 is commemorated. The path around the lighthouse-topped **Cap du Dramont** gives fine views out to sea, though looking inland the most severe and recent encroachment on the Esterel is revealed – the "designer village" of **Cap Esterel**, squatting smugly on the ridge between Le Dramont and Agay.

In contrast, Le Dramont's close neighbour **AGAY** is one of the least pretentious resorts of the Côte d'Azur, beautifully situated around a deep horseshoe bay edged by sand beaches, red porphyry cliffs and pines. Both Agay and its eastern neighbour **ANTHÉOR** suffer a little from the creeping contagion of housing estates edging ever higher up their hills, but once you get above the concrete line, at the **Sommet du Rastel**, for example (signed up Agay's avenue du Bourg or boulevard du Rastel), you can begin to appreciate this wonderful terrain. Note, however, that many of the roads leading off the corniche are open to residents only.

There are plenty of **campsites** in this area: along the Valescure road near the River Agay you'll find the four-star *Les Rives de L'Agay* (℡04.94.82.02.74, ⓦwww.lesrivesdelagay.fr; €38 per tent; closed Nov–Feb), and the three-star *Agay-Soleil*, by the beach at 1152 boulevard de la Plage (℡04.94.82.00.79, ⓦwww.agay-soleil.com; €28.90 per tent; closed Nov–March) There's also no shortage of **hotels**: less expensive options include *Les Flots Bleus* on boulevard Eugène Brieux in Anthéor (℡04.94.44.80.21, ⓦwww.hotel-cote-azur.com; ❸; closed Nov to late March). Agay has a **waterski school**, Fun Ski School (℡06.07.08.17.17, ⓦwww.funskischool.com), which also offers banana boat trips, parascending and wakeboarding.

Le Trayas
LE TRAYAS is on the highest point of the corniche and its shoreline is the most ragged, with wonderful inlets to explore. You can also trek to the Pic de l'Ours from here (about 3hr; the path is signed from the *gare SNCF*).

The **hotel** *Relais des Calanques*, route des Escalles (℡04.94.44.14.06, ⓕ04.94.44.10.93; ❼), nestles above a cove, the water almost lapping at its terrace where good fish is served (menu €35).

Travel details

Trains	
Les Arcs-sur-Argens to: Fréjus (frequent; 15min); St-Raphaël (every 1–2hr; 15–20min); Toulon (approx hourly; 27min–1hr).	1–2hr; 3min); Cannes (every 20–40min; 20–40min); Les Arcs-Draguignan (1–2 hourly; 15–20min); Le Dramont (every 1–2hr; 10min);
Hyères to: Toulon (7 daily; 20min).	Le Trayas (9 daily; 20min); Marseille (1–2 hourly;
St-Raphaël to: Agay (every 1–2hr; 10–12min); Anthéor (every 1–2hr; 15min); Boulouris (every	1hr 40min); Nice (1–2 hourly; 50min–1hr 10min); Toulon (1–2 hourly; 45–55min).
	Toulon to: La Seyne-Six Fours (every 15min–1hr; 5min); Les Arcs (every 1–2hr;

35min–1hr); Marseille (every 15min at peak times; 40min–1hr); Ollioules–Sanary (every 15min–1hr; 10min).

Buses

Note that there are reduced services on Sundays and holidays.

Fréjus to: Cogolin (2 daily; 1hr); Les Issambres (9 daily; 15min); Nice Airport (4 daily: 1hr 5min); Roquebrune-sur-Argens (7 daily; 25min); Ste-Maxime (9 daily; 30min); St-Tropez (9 daily; 1hr).

Hyères to: Bormes (14 daily; 20min); La Croix-Valmer (8 daily; 1hr 10min); Le Lavandou (14 daily; 35min); Le Rayol (8 daily; 50min); St-Tropez (7 daily; 1hr 30min); Toulon (every 30min–1hr; 35min–1hr).

Le Lavandou to: Bormes (13 daily; 5min); Cavalaire-sur-Mer (8 daily; 30min); Hyères (13 daily; 40min); La Croix-Valmer (8 daily; 35min); Le Rayol (8 daily; 15min); St-Tropez (7 daily; 55min); Toulon (13 daily; 1hr 15min).

Ste-Maxime to: Cogolin (9 daily; 30min); La Foux (9 daily; 15min); Les Arcs (3 daily; 30min); Grimaud (7 daily; 20min); St-Tropez (9 daily; 30min).

St-Raphaël to: Cogolin (2 daily; 1hr 10min); Draguignan (8 daily; 1hr); La Foux (9 daily;

1hr 5min); Les Issambres (9 daily; 35min); Nice Airport (4 daily; 1hr 20min); Ste-Maxime (9 daily; 50min); St-Tropez (9 daily; 1hr 20min).

St-Tropez to: Bormes (6 daily; 1hr 5min); Cavalaire-sur-Mer (6 daily; 25min); Cogolin (5 daily; 20min); Gassin (4 daily; 25min); Grimaud (5 daily; 25min); Hyères (6 daily; 1hr 30min); La Croix-Valmer (6 daily; 20min); La Foux (10 daily; 15min); La Garde Freinet (2 daily; 40min); Le Lavandou (6 daily; 55min); Le Rayol (6 daily; 35min); Les Issambres (9 daily; 35min); Ramatuelle (4 daily; 35min); Ste-Maxime (10 daily; 30min); St-Raphaël (10 daily; 1hr 20min); Toulon (6 daily; 2hr 10min).

Toulon to: Aix (7 daily; 1hr 15min); Bandol (hourly; 35–50min); Brignoles (6 daily; 1hr 20min–1hr 35min); Draguignan (2 daily; 1hr 55min); Hyères (every 25–45min; 40min–1hr 10min); Le Lavandou (14 daily; 1hr 15min); St-Tropez (7 daily; 2hr 10min); Sanary (hourly; 40min); Six-Fours (hourly; 30min).

Ferries

Toulon to: Bastia Corsica (1–2 daily; 8hr 30min); Ajaccio (1–2 daily; 6hr 15min–8hr 30min).

Cannes and the western Riviera

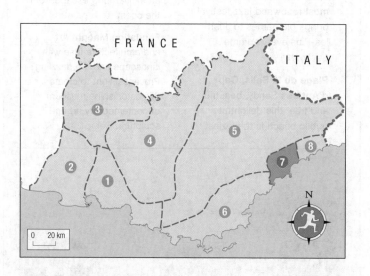

CHAPTER 7

Highlights

✳ **Promenade de la Croisette, Cannes** Pop on your shades, turn on your iPod and rollerblade along the Riviera's most glamorous seafront. See p.310

✳ **Îles des Lérins** Clean, pine-scented air, peaceful walks and shimmering rocks and water, just minutes from the centre of Cannes. See p.315

✳ **Jazz à Juan** The Riviera's most renowned jazz festival brings big names to Juan-les-Pins every summer. See p.321

✳ **Plage de la Salis, Cap d'Antibes** Sandy, beautiful and free, this delightful public beach is the laziest

way to enjoy the millionaires' cape. See p.326

✳ **Chapelle du Rosaire** Matisse's final masterpiece – the modern master oversaw every stunning detail of this profoundly moving convent chapel in Vence. See p.340

✳ **St-Paul-de-Vence** A favourite haunt of Riviera artists, this quintessential Provençal hill village makes an exhilarating escape from the coast. See p.342

✳ **Fondation Maeght** Art and architecture fuse with landscape and the dazzling Provençal light to create this astonishing museum of contemporary art and sculpture. See p.343

▲ Plage de la Salis, Cap d'Antibes

Cannes and the western Riviera

The stretch of coast between the Massif de l'Esterel and the River Var makes up the **western French Riviera**. As much legend as reality, the region has been a playground for the rich and famous for the better part of two centuries. Such names as Cannes, Juan les Pins and Antibes conjure up powerful images, of a fantasy land where the sparkling blue sea is speckled with boards, bikes and skis, and where extravagant yachts moor tantalizingly out of reach, disgorging their privileged cargo to fill the glamorous bars and restaurants or populate the latest event in the celebrity-studded calendar. To some extent, that's still true, even though it's long since lost any sense of exclusivity: this now ranks among the most developed and densely populated coastal strips in Europe.

Summer crowds and traffic can make travelling slow and unpleasant – speedy and inexpensive **train** connections offer a convenient alternative to driving – but once you're there, each individual resort has its own appeal. It's also possible simply to visit the coast on day-trips, and stay inland in historic towns like **Vence** and **Grasse**, or lovely villages such as **St-Paul-de-Vence** and **Tourrettes-sur-Loup**.

Though it shares much in common with the coast east of the Var, the western Riviera has a rather different **history**. Unlike the formerly Savoyard (and strongly Italianate) Nice and Menton, Cannes and Antibes were always Provençal, the latter almost a border town, just a few kilometres west of the frontier on the Var. The fishing village of **Cannes** itself was discovered in the 1830s by a retired British chancellor, Lord Brougham, who couldn't get to Nice because of a cholera epidemic. From the beginning, tourism here was more exclusive than in bustling, raffish Nice, with aristocrats and royals from across Europe and North America building opulent mansions in the years before World War I. During the 1920s, as Coco Chanel popularized the suntan and the glamorous *Eden Roc* on Cap d'Antibes stayed open year-round for the first time, the season switched from winter to summer. A new kind of elite took centre stage, notably film stars like Charlie Chaplin and Maurice Chevalier; the era was immortalized in F. Scott Fitzgerald's *Tender is the Night*. Then, in 1936, the socialist government of Léon Blum granted French workers their first paid holidays, and the democratization of the Riviera began.

War in 1939 interrupted everything – including Cannes' first film festival – but by the 1950s **mass tourism** took off in earnest and the real transformation began. Locals quickly realized that servicing the new influx of visitors was far more profitable than working on the land or at sea, and overenthusiastic property development

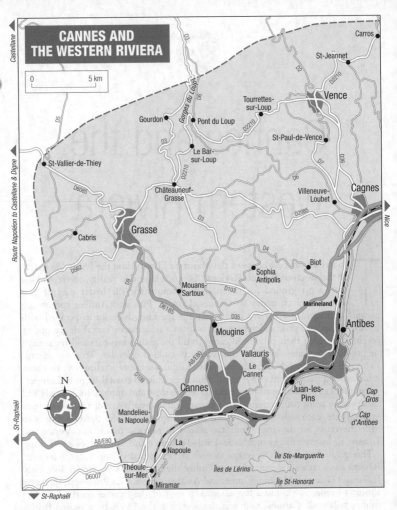

CANNES AND THE WESTERN RIVIERA

0   5 km

Castellane

Carros

St-Jeannet

Gourdon   Pont du Loup

Tourrettes-sur-Loup

Vence

St-Vallier-de-Thiey

Le Bar-sur-Loup

St-Paul-de-Vence

Châteauneuf-Grasse

Villeneuve-Loubet

Cagnes

Route Napoléon to Castellane & Digne

Cabris

Grasse

Nice

Biot

Sophia Antipolis

Mouans-Sartoux

Marineland

Mougins

Antibes

Vallauris

Le Cannet

Cannes

Juan-les-Pins

Cap Gros

St-Raphaël

Mandelieu-la Napoule

Cap d'Antibes

La Napoule

Île Ste-Marguerite

Théoule-sur-Mer

Îles de Lérins

Miramar

Île St-Honorat

St-Raphaël

and sheer pressure of numbers have been problems ever since. The coast is now built up for its entire length, while inland the hills between the villages are carpeted with disorientating, featureless suburbia.

The appeal of the coast, however, remains clear enough, most notably in the legacies of the **artists** who stayed here: Picasso in **Antibes** and **Vallauris**; Léger in **Biot**; Matisse in **Vence**; Renoir in **Cagnes-sur-Mer**; and all of them in **St-Paul-de-Vence** and **Haut-de-Cagnes**.

Cannes

With its immaculate seafront hotels and exclusive beaches, glamorous yachts and glitzy designer boutiques, **CANNES** is in many ways the definitive Riviera resort of popular fantasy. It's a place where appearances definitely count, especially during the **film festival**, when the orgy of self-promotion reaches its annual peak.

Although its urban sprawl stretches several kilometres east, west and inland, Cannes lacks the must-see sights and general sense of dynamism of a genuine city. At heart, it's just a beach resort, and while the central **Plage de la Croisette** remains the preserve of an opulent elite, it's actually possible to come here for a straightforward, unpretentious seaside holiday, with plenty of free sandy **beaches** west of the port, and hotels and restaurants to suit all pockets. In terms of sightseeing, the two most enjoyable attractions are the self-contained old-town quarter of **Le Suquet**, and the sublimely peaceful **Îles de Lérins**, just a short boat-ride out to sea.

Arrival, information and getting around

Cannes' main **tourist office** is at the Palais des Festivals (daily: July & Aug 9am–8pm; Sept–June 9am–7pm; ℡04.92.99.84.22, Ⓦcannes.travel), and there's another information office (Mon–Sat 9am–7pm) at the central **gare SNCF** on rue Jean-Jaurès. **Buses** from inland towns such as Grasse arrive at the *gare routière* next door (℡04.93.39.31.37), while buses that serve the city and the coast to either side – including line #210 to the airport at Nice (€14.20 one-way) – use the main *gare routière*, overlooking the Vieux Port on place B-Cornut Gentille (℡08.25.82.55.99, Ⓦbusazur.com).

Driving on Cannes' narrow, traffic-clogged streets is cramped and unpleasant. The various multistorey car parks in the centre charge around €3 per hour, or €19 overnight; there's free street parking east of the Parc de la Roseraie, beyond the eastern end of the Croisette.

Urban buses run from outside the Hôtel de Ville; you can buy individual tickets for €1, a *carnet* of ten for €9.50 and a weekly pass, the *Carte Palm'Hebdo*, for €11. A useful and enjoyable service is the open-top #8 bus along the seafront from the quai Laubeuf to Palm Beach Casino on Pointe Croisette, at the other end of the bay. **Bikes** can be rented from Mistral Location, near the old port at 4 rue Georges-Clemenceau (℡04.93.39.33.60, Ⓦmistral-location.com).

Accommodation

Cannes holds a wide range of **hotels** to suit all budgets, though it has to be said that €50 or €60 here doesn't get you nearly as nice a room as it might inland. Book well in advance for the cheaper options. Room rates in winter (Nov–March) tend to be less than half what's indicated below. The tourist office runs a **reservation website**, on Ⓦcannes-hotel-reservation.com. **Camping** opportunities are not good: the sites are well over capacity and far from central; pitching in Mandelieu, 7km west, is likely to be easier and cheaper.

Hotels

Alnea 20 rue Jean-de-Riouffe ℡04.93.68.77.77, Ⓦhotel-alnea.com. Small, inexpensive hotel, near both the sea and the old town, with cheerfully updated seaside decor, a/c, and the service and style that you'd expect from a pricier place. Bike rental available. ❹

Beau Séjour 5 rue des Fauvettes ℡04.93.39.63.00, Ⓦcannes-beausejour.com. Modern hotel, in a quiet location a short walk northwest of Le Suquet, with an extensive garden, a small pool, and an attractive terrace. All rooms have balconies. ❽

Best Western Hôtel Univers 2 rue Maréchal-Foch ℡04.93.06.30.00, Ⓦwww.bw-hotelunivers.com. Comfortable if rather conventional hotel in a well-soundproofed central location. A rooftop terrace offers views over the town. ❻

Canberra 120 rue d'Antibes ℡04.97.06.95.00, Ⓦhotel-cannes-canberra.com. With its heated pool and garden terrace, this classy and very tasteful boutique-style hotel, in the thick of Cannes' designer shopping district, makes a cool oasis in summer. ❾

Carlton Intercontinental 58 bd de la Croisette ℡04.93.06.40.06, Ⓦwww.intercontinental.com.

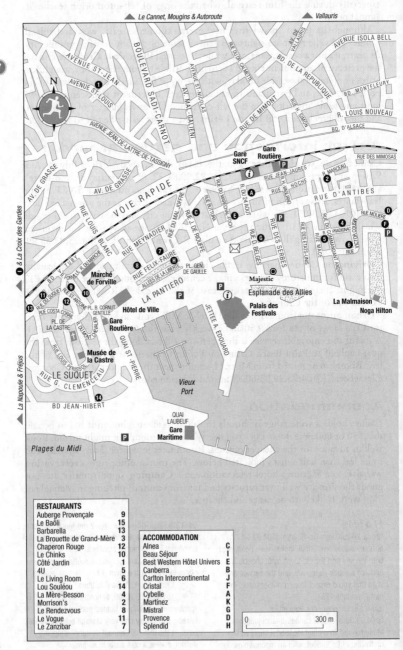

▲ Le Cannet, Mougins & Autoroute   ▲ Vallauris

RESTAURANTS

Auberge Provençale	9
Le Baôli	15
Barbarella	13
La Brouette de Grand-Mère	3
Chaperon Rouge	12
Le Chinks	10
Côté Jardin	1
4U	5
Le Living Room	6
Lou Souléou	14
La Mère-Besson	4
Morrison's	2
Le Rendezvous	8
Le Vogue	11
Le Zanzibar	7

ACCOMMODATION

Alnea	C
Beau Séjour	I
Best Western Hôtel Univers	E
Canberra	B
Carlton Intercontinental	J
Cristal	F
Cybelle	A
Martinez	K
Mistral	G
Provence	D
Splendid	H

0   300 m

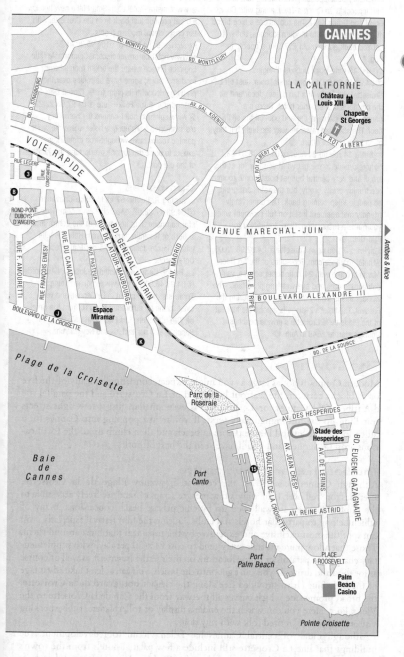

Legendary *belle époque* palace hotel that starred in Hitchcock's *To Catch a Thief*, along with Cary Grant and Grace Kelly. The rooms are a nice blend of grand tradition and modern touches, but will set you back a minimum €372 for a double in Aug. **❾**

Cristal 13 rond-point Duboys-d'Angers ☏04.92.59.29.29, ⓦhotel-cristal.com. Just off La Croisette with funky (if a tad dated) decor and all the comforts of a superior hotel. There's a panoramic restaurant, bar and pool on the sixth floor. The standard rates are way too high, but they often have special offers. **❾**

Cybelle 14 rue du 24 Août ☏04.93.38.31.33, ⓦhotelcybelle.fr. You get what you pay for at this small and very central budget hotel; some rooms are frankly pretty grotty, but the rates are great, so people keep coming back. The unnervingly friendly management insist on full payment when you make a reservation. Closed mid-Nov to mid-Dec. **❸**

Martinez 73 bd de la Croisette ☏04.92.98.73.00, ⓦhotel-martinez.com. Top suites at the Art Deco *Martinez* come with 24-hour butler service, vast outdoor terraces and eye-watering price tags – no wonder this is simply *the* place to stay during the Festival. The hotel's Z-plage is among the hippest of the Plage de la Croisette's private beaches. Doubles start at €549 in Aug. **❾**

Mistral 13 rue des Belges ☏04.93.39.91.46, ⓦwww.mistral-hotel.com. Smart little new hotel, in a great position just back from the Croisette, with ten crisp, clean, modern rooms. **❻**

Provence 9 rue Molière ☏04.93.38.44.35, ⓦwww.hotel-de-provence.com. Comfortable little Logis de France where the bright rooms have modern fittings; some have balconies over the pretty garden with its palm trees. Closed Dec. **❻**

Splendid 4–6 rue Félix-Fauré ☏04.97.06.22.22, ⓦwww.splendid-hotel-cannes.fr. Charmingly old-fashioned *belle époque* hotel where the white-painted rooms have wrought-iron trimmings; expect to pay extra for one overlooking the yachts of the old port. **❼**

Campsites

Camping Bellevue 67 av Maurice-Chevalier ☏04.93.47.28.97, ⓦparcbellevue.com. Three-star campsite 3km northwest of the centre in the suburb of Ranguin; bus #2 from Hôtel de Ville (stop "Sainte-Jeanne"). €25 per tent. Closed Oct–March.

Le Ranch Camping chemin St-Joseph, l'Aubarède ☏04.93.46.00.11, ⓦwww.leranchcamping.fr. Three-star site 2km out in Le Cannet, and very close to the A8 autoroute; bus #10 from the Hôtel de Ville (direction "Les Pins Parasols", stop "Le Ranch"). €23 per tent. Closed Nov–March.

The Town

Modern Cannes is not as large as you might expect, consisting basically of the five or so blocks between the seafront boulevard of **La Croisette** and the parallel rue d'Antibes. Old Cannes, or **Le Suquet**, is even smaller, just a few tight streets spiralling up the hill immediately west. If you're just popping into Cannes for a quick look, take a stroll beside the main beach and then climb up to the fortifications atop Le Suquet, and you'll have seen the best of both.

The beaches and town centre

Although Cannes' *raison d'être*, the celebrated, swanky **Plage de la Croisette**, stretches for well over 1km, only a few meagre scraps of sand are freely accessible to the public. The rest is swallowed up by chic private beach concessions, many of which belong to particular hotels and clubs. During the film festival especially, you can spot the most exclusive and expensive by the paparazzi that buzz around them. Those that allow mere mortals entry tend to cost €15–20 per day, with supplementary charges for parasols or prime locations on their jetties (*pontoons*), as well of course as for food and drink. If you can't get onto the beach, you can at least take advantage of the little blue chairs provided free along the elegant **boulevard de la Croisette**, the broad promenade which curves all the way from the Cap de la Croisette to the Vieux Port. Here you can watch the endless display of rollerbladers, rubbernecking visitors and genteel retired folk with tiny dogs.

Although much of central Cannes has fallen victim to redevelopment, the buildings that line La Croisette still include a few palatial hotels from the town's nineteenth-century golden age, notably the **Carlton Intercontinental**, whose cupolas were inspired by the breasts of a famous courtesan, and the Art Deco **Martinez**. Rather overshadowed by the seafront glitz, the beautiful **La Malmaison**, at no. 47, started life as the tearoom of the now-vanished *Grand Hotel*, built in 1863 and demolished a century later. It now stages temporary exhibitions of modern and contemporary art (Tues–Sun: April, May & Sept 10am–1pm & 2.30–6.30pm; June–Aug 10am–1pm & 3–7pm; Oct–March 10am–noon & 2.30–6pm; €3). Further east, the **Espace Miramar** (Tues–Sun: June–Sept 2–7pm; Oct–May 1–6pm; free) also hosts temporary exhibitions.

▲ Facade of the *Carlton Intercontinental* hotel, Cannes

Dominating the western end of La Croisette, the vast, ugly **Palais des Festivals** resembles a misplaced concrete missile silo. The main focus of the film festival, it also hosts a steady stream of conferences, tournaments and trade shows throughout the year. Outside, you can compare hand sizes with film stars from Sharon Stone to Mickey Mouse, whose imprints have been set, Hollywood-style, in tiles on the pavement. As the tradition pretty much stopped at the end of the 1980s, the stardust is wearing off the names and tiles alike.

West of the Palais, the **Vieux Port** fills up with extraordinarily sumptuous yachts in summer; tourists gather to watch white-frocked crews serve dinner to millionaires on their decks. Inland from here, the streets in between the western end of La Croisette and the rue d'Antibes form the South of France's most extensive luxury **shopping** district, stuffed with designer names such as Bulgari, Cartier, Chanel, Lacroix and Vuitton, and also hold the city's most stylish **nightclubs**. This part of town looks its best in the weeks leading up to Christmas, when the streets glitter with tasteful white lights and the crowds of summer are long forgotten.

Extensive and very sandy **free beaches** line the **boulevard du Midi**, which starts below Le Suquet and runs west from the port towards the suburb of La Bocca. Although the road is backed by a distinctly unglamorous railway line and the water isn't always the cleanest, the atmosphere is unpretentious and family-oriented, and kiosks sell simple snacks and ice creams.

Le Suquet

Back in the eleventh century, the hill known as **Le Suquet** became the property of the Îles de Lérins monks. It still holds a castle built by the *abbé* in 1088, with the white stone twelfth-century Romanesque **Chapelle de Ste-Anne** alongside. After several centuries in which a small town took root around the religious settlement, a dispute arose between the monks and the townsfolk who wanted their own parish and priest. Two hundred years after their initial demand in 1648, **Notre-Dame de l'Espérance** was finally built beside the Chapelle de Ste-Anne.

The castle and chapel are now home to the **Musée de la Castre** (Tues–Sun: April, May & Sept 10am–1pm & 2–6pm; June–Aug 10am–1pm & 3–7pm; Oct–March 10am–1pm & 2–5pm; €3), which as well as fascinating pictures and prints of old Cannes displays strong ethnology and archeology collections, with an

---

The Cannes Film Festival

Each May Cannes hosts the world's most famous movie festival, the **Festival International du Film** (Ⓦfestival-cannes.com). It was first conceived in 1939, as a rival to the Venice film festival, which had fallen under the influence of Mussolini; as only pro-fascist films had any chance of winning prizes there, an alternative competition was planned for Cannes. However, World War II intervened, and the first Cannes festival took place in 1946.

Even if winning Cannes' top prize, the **Palme d'Or**, can't compete with Oscars for box-office effect, within the movie world it is unrivalled. Some years it seems as if the big names are all too busy talking finance in LA to come to Cannes; the next they're all begging for the accolades. In contrast to all the attendant glitz and froth, the Festival has become renowned for rewarding politically committed (and/or controversial) film-makers,

The festival is strictly an event for film professionals and the associated media, and without proper accreditation you won't get into the Palais des Festivals. However, it is possible to gain entry to the open-air *Cinéma de la Plage*, which screens certain official selections to the public (tickets available at the tourist office).

emphasis on the south Pacific. Its highlight, however, is the brilliant collection of musical instruments from all over the world, including Congolese bell bracelets, an Ethiopian ten-string lyre, an Asian "lute" with a snakeskin box, and an extraordinary selection of drums. Climb the medieval tower in the museum courtyard for the best view of Le Suquet and the town below.

Although Le Suquet used to house the city's poorer residents, the streets leading to the summit have become gentrified, and the various places to **eat** and **drink** increasingly tourist-oriented and chic, if (for the most part) less overtly trendy than in the streets behind La Croisette.

La Croix des Gardes

The best place to get a sense of Cannes' largely lost nineteenth-century elegance is the leafy suburb of **La Croix des Gardes**, just a few hundred metres west of Le Suquet. From the outset, Cannes' aristocratic visitors preferred to build their own villas, many of which have survived. Thus Lord Brougham's elegant **Château Eléonore** still stands on avenue du Dr Raymond-Picaud on the plot he bought after his enforced sojourn in the then-unknown village of Cannes in 1834. Close by, across the road, the **Villa Victoria** was constructed in an unmistakeably English Victorian Gothic style in 1852 by Sir Thomas Woolfield, a developer who built and sold around 30 villas in the town. Neither is open to the public, but you can visit the opulent **Villa Maria Thérèse**, a Beaux-Arts mansion just around the corner at 1 avenue Jean-de-Noailles, built in 1881 for the Dowager Baroness Rothschild. Set in a lovely garden with winding paths and waterfalls, it now houses Cannes' **multimedia library** (Tues–Sat 9.30am–6pm), along with the city archive.

Le Cannet

Although nominally a town in its own right, **Le Cannet**, 4km northeast of the city centre along the busy boulevard Sadi-Carnot (**bus routes** #1A or #4 from the Hôtel de Ville), forms an indistinguishable part of Cannes' urban sprawl. It was originally built on land belonging to the Îles de Lérins monks to house 140 Ligurian families brought here to tend the orange trees, and its old part, along rue St-Sauveur, still preserves a certain villagey charm.

Le Cannet's current claim to fame is that **Pierre Bonnard** bought the Villa le Bosquet here in 1926, and lived here from 1939 until his death in 1947. Perhaps the most private of the Riviera's great artists, he is buried in the town's Notre Dame des Anges cemetery. Born in the suburbs of Paris in 1867, he found fame early as a member of the Nabis, followers of Gauguin, and subsequently created his own style, distinguished by intense colour and a highly domestic choice of subject matter. As part of a project to open a Bonnard museum, the **Espace Bonnard** (daily 2–7pm during exhibitions), in the Jardins de Tivoli, regularly attracts interesting temporary art shows.

Eating and drinking

Cannes holds hundreds of **restaurants**, covering the spectrum from €14 lunchtime menus to €100-plus blowouts, though quality across the board can be patchy. Many stay open very late, so getting a meal after midnight is no great problem. The best areas for inexpensive dining are **rue Meynadier**, Le Suquet and **quai St-Pierre** on the Vieux Port, which is lined with **brasseries** and **cafés**. Reserving a table is advisable at almost all the places listed below. Thanks to the vigour of the Forville **market**, two blocks north of the Vieux Port, local chefs have access to the finest and freshest ingredients.

Note that many Cannes visitors also make the pilgrimage to eat in the nearby village of **Mougins** (see p.317), renowned for its gourmet restaurants.

Restaurants

Auberge Provençale 10 rue St-Antoine
☎ 04.92.99.27.17, ⓦ www.auberge-provencale
.com. Generous portions of Provençal cooking in a rustic setting at Cannes' oldest restaurant, which opened in 1860 and offers a few outdoor tables. The one set menu, at €29, features *aioli* followed by steamed cod.

Barbarella 16 rue St-Dizier
☎ 04.92.99.17.33. Philippe Starck *Ghost* chairs and Japanese-influenced food contrast with the quiet location of this gay-friendly restaurant in Le Suquet. The sushi of fruits is a must. Menus from €40. Dinner only, closed Mon (daily during Festival).

La Brouette de Grand-Mère 9 bis rue d'Oran
☎ 04.93.39.12.10. Dinner-only restaurant, where the only menu (€38) includes an aperitif and wine, with filling dishes such as a *cuisse de lapin* or *pot au feu*. Fun and good value. Closed Sun, plus late June to mid-July.

Chaperon Rouge 17 rue St-Antoine
☎ 04.93.99.06.22. Friendly restaurant, with tables squeezed onto a terrace beside a steep alley leading up to Le Suquet; this is a very touristy district, but the hectic evening hurly-burly is fun and the food is actually pretty good, with a €27 menu that features gazpacho plus either a whole bream or salmon with ginger.

Côté Jardin 12 av St-Louis ☎ 04.93.38.60.28, ⓦ restaurant-cotejardin.com. Intimate family-run restaurant with a small garden and terrace. Changing daily menus at €30 and €38 on the blackboard feature Provençal classics and plenty of fish. Closed Sun & Mon.

Lou Souléou 16 bd Jean-Hibert ☎ 04.93.39.85.55. Cosy, relaxed fish specialist serving a good range of very reasonably priced seafood in view of the sea, down below Le Suquet. Menus from €23. Closed Mon & Wed evenings.

La Mère-Besson 13 rue des Frères-Pradignacs
☎ 04.93.39.59.24. Long-standing dinner-only local favourite, where each day sees a different speciality, such as cod and *aioli* on Fridays, *filet de rascasse*, or *lottes à la Provençale* (tiny fried monkfish). Menus at €27 and €32. Closed Sun and Christmas.

La Palme d'Or *Hôtel Martinez*, 73 La Croisette
☎ 04.92.98.74.14. A renowned temple of taste, where the stars celebrate their film-festival prizes with some of the most exquisite and original food this coast has to offer. Menus at €83 and €189 without drinks, à la carte will probably cost even more. Closed Sun & Mon (except during Festival), plus Tues in winter, and all Jan & Feb.

Le Rendezvous 35 rue Félix-Fauré
☎ 04.93.68.55.10. Large, bright, modern reinterpretation of an Art Deco bistro, one of a number facing the port where comfort levels are high and fish is to the fore. Menus from €22, with the €30 option including the likes of ravioli with cep mushrooms and fillet of daurade. Closed late Jan to mid-Feb.

Nightlife

As you might expect, Cannes abounds with exclusive **bars** and **clubs**, nowhere more so than in the tight little grid of streets bounded by rue Macé, rue V. Cousin, rue Dr Monod and rue des Frères-Pradignacs. As is so often the case in the South of France, the boundaries between restaurant, bar and club are somewhat blurred, so that you can frequently dine, drink and dance – at a price – in the same venue.

Cannes' **lesbian and gay** bar scene is smaller than that in Nice, but smart and a good deal more relaxed, and some venues attract hetero as well as gay visitors. If you are determined to lose money, choose from **casinos** at the Palais des Festivals, at the Palm Beach at the eastern end of La Croisette or in the *Noga Hilton* hotel. There's also a fairly lively year-round **theatre**, **dance** and **music** scene, centred on the Palais des Festivals, the Théâtre Palais Croisette in the *Noga Hilton*, and the Théâtre La Licorne in La Bocca. The **Stade des Hespérides** in the district of La Croisette is the venue for occasional concerts as well as major sporting events.

Bars and clubs

Le Baôli Port Pierre Canto, bd de la Croisette
☎ 04.93.43.03.43, ⓦ www.lebaoli.com. Spectacular luxury restaurant/disco with Asian food, an "exotic" outdoor setting with palms and tented pavilions, and no shortage of VIP visitors, from Paris Hilton to Ivana Trump. Nightly 8pm–5am. Closed Nov–April.

Le Chinks 88 rue Meynadier. Trendy lounge & cocktail bar close to the Vieux Port and Le Suquet, playing jazz, swing and salsa and serving overpriced Thai food.

4U 6 rue des Frères-Pradignac ⓣ04.93.39.71.21, ⓦbar4u.com. Locals and visitors alike crowd round the central counter in this bar, a popular early-evening rendezvous with DJs later on. The name's pronounced in English, not French, incidentally. Nightly 6pm–2.30am.

Le Living Room 17 rue Dr Monod ⓣ06.26.17.25.82. DJ bar-restaurant with a jazz and soul soundtrack and simple, slick modern decor. Thurs–Sat 6.30pm–2.30am.

Morrison's 10 rue Teisseire ⓣ04.92.98.16.17, ⓦmorrisonspub.com. The inevitable Irish pub, a few blocks back from the seafront, and also featuring an upscale lounge. Nightly until 2am.

Le Vogue 20 rue du Suquet ⓣ04.93.39.99.18. Smart, rather pricey Le Suquet bar where the champagne is always on ice and the atmosphere usually chilled. Mixed gay and hetero crowd. Tues–Sun 7.30pm–2.30am.

Le Zanzibar 85 rue Félix-Fauré ⓣ04.93.39.30.75, ⓦlezanzibar.com. Dance music meets matelot chic at this long-established gay bar. Daily 6pm–4am.

Listings

Airport Cannes-Mandelieu, 6km southwest of the centre ⓣ04.93.90.40.40, ⓦwww.cannes .aeroport.fr.

Bookshop Cannes English Bookshop, 11 rue Bivouac-Napoleon ⓣ04.93.99.40.08, ⓦcannesenglishbookshop.com.

Emergencies SOS médecins ⓣ08.25.00.50.04; Hôpital de Cannes, av des Broussailles ⓣ04.93.69.71.50.

Lost property 1 av St Louis ⓣ04.97.06.40.00.

Pharmacy Call ⓣ04.93.06.22.22 for address of emergency pharmacy after 7.30pm.

Police Commissariat Central de Police, 1 av de Grasse ⓣ04.93.06.22.22.

Post office 22 rue Bivouac-Napoleon.

Taxis Cannes Allo Taxi ⓣ08.90.71.22.27.

Îles de Lérins

The **Îles de Lérins** would be lovely anywhere, but at just a fifteen-minute ferry ride from Cannes, they make an idyllic escape from the modern city. Known as Lerina, or Lero, in ancient times, the two islands, Ste-Marguerite and St-Honorat, have a long historical pedigree and today offer the gentle pace and tranquillity the Riviera so often lacks.

Getting to the islands

Boats for both islands leave from the quai des Îles at the seaward end of Cannes' quai Laubeuf. Drivers should park elsewhere if possible; parking at the terminal is very expensive.

Trans Côte d'Azur offer up to sixteen daily services to **Ste-Marguerite** (ⓣ04.92.98.71.30, ⓦtrans-cote-azur.com; round-trip €11). The first boat leaves Cannes at 7.30am and the last at 5.30pm in July & Aug, 4.30pm otherwise; the last boat back to Cannes leaves Ste-Marguerite at 7pm in July & Aug, 6pm otherwise. The same company also offer day-trips to the island from **Nice** in summer (ⓣ04.92.00.42.30; departs quai Lunel at 9am; July to mid-Sept daily; June & late Sept Tues, Thurs, Sat & Sun; €32).

Planaria send between seven and ten ferries daily to **St-Honorat** (ⓣ04.92.98.71.38, ⓦwww.cannes-ilesdelerins.com; round-trip €11), with the first sailing at 9am (8am on Sun), and the last boat back departing at 6pm (May–Sept) or 5pm (Oct–April).

Ste-Marguerite

Of the two islands, **STE-MARGUERITE** is the more animated, with plenty of day-trippers and a working boatyard, though it still has clear water and beautiful scenery, and is large enough to find seclusion if you're prepared to leave the crowded port and follow paths through the thick woods of Aleppo pines and evergreen oaks.

A very obvious path leads up from the ferry dock, past the boatyard, to the imposing **Fort Ste-Marguerite** (April & May Tues–Sun 10.30am–1.15pm & 2.15–5.45pm; June–Sept daily 10.30am–5.45pm; Oct–March Tues–Sun 10.30am–1.15pm & 2.15–4.45pm; €3.20), a Richelieu commission that failed to prevent the Spanish occupying both Lérins islands between 1635 and 1637; the fortifications were later completed by Vauban. A cell within is renowned for having held the **Man in the Iron Mask** for eleven years of his long captivity, between 1687 and 1698; a quasi-mythical character who died in the Bastille in 1703, and whose true identity has never been proved, his legend was popularized by novelist Alexandre Dumas. Other prisoners held here included Huguenots imprisoned for refusing to submit to Louis XIV's vicious suppression of Protestantism. A series of murals created in the 1990s covers the cell walls, and depicts painter Jean le Gac as a prisoner. As well as three Roman **cisterns** – Ste-Marguerite has no natural springs, so water supply has always been a problem – the fort also holds a barracks-style hostel used by school and youth groups, and the **Musée de la Mer**, displaying artefacts discovered by underwater archeologists, such as amphorae from a Roman shipwreck and ceramics from a tenth-century Arab vessel.

The quickest route to the island's peaceful southern shore, the **allée des Eucalyptus**, heads south from roughly halfway around the fort; follow the outer perimeter of the walls, and keep going straight on when you come to a sign pointing left towards *La Guérite* (see below). A pleasant fifteen-minute stroll ends abruptly at the seashore, looking across the lovely turquoise channel that separates Ste-Marguerite from St-Honorat. Stone-built picnic tables are scattered at the water's edge, and many visitors swim here, though the shore is lined not by beaches so much as compacted masses of dried vegetation. The most enjoyable way to get back to the ferry is to follow the coastal **Chemin de la Ceinture**, which offers great views back to Cannes once you round the headland at either end.

Ste-Marguerite is an expensive place to **eat and drink**, and options are limited, so at the very least it's worth bringing plenty of water. Close to the ferry dock, a couple of summer-only snack stalls sell *pan bagnats*, and the **restaurant** *l'Escale* (℡04.93.43.49.25) serves a €22 lunch menu. If you walk all the way around the inland side of the fort and drop back down to sea level via the steep stairway on the far side, you'll come to the absurd but very welcome beachfront *La Guérite* (℡04.93.43.49.30), a Club Med-style place divided between a very expensive à la carte restaurant where lunch costs at least €40, and a shaded terrace snack bar serving sandwiches for €8–10 or a delicious salad Niçoise for €16.

St-Honorat

ST-HONORAT, the smaller southern island, has belonged to monks almost continuously since Honoratus, a former Roman noble seeking peace and isolation, founded a monastery here in 410 AD. Visitors soon began to arrive, and a monastic order was established to structure the growing community. By the end of Honoratus' life, the Lérins monks had monasteries all over France, held bishoprics in Arles and Lyon, and were renowned throughout the Catholic world for their contributions to theology. **St Patrick** trained here for seven years before setting out for Ireland.

Most of the present **abbey** buildings date from the nineteenth century, though vestiges of medieval and earlier construction survive in the church and cloisters. You can visit the austere church, but not the residential areas, where 25 Cistercian monks live and work, tending an apiary and a vineyard that produces a sought-after white wine, sold in the abbey's shop. Behind this complex, on the sea's edge, stands an eleventh-century **fortress**, a monastic bolthole connected to the original abbey by a tunnel, and used to guard against invaders, especially the Saracens. Of all the protective forts along this coast, only this one looks as if it could still serve its original function.

The other buildings on St-Honorat are the churches and chapels that served as retreats. **St-Pierre**, beside the modern monastery, **La Trinité**, to the east, and **St-Sauveur**, west of the harbour, remain more or less unchanged. By **St-Cabrais**, on the eastern shore, a furnace with a chute for making cannonballs shows that the monks were not without worldly defensive skills.

Today, the main attraction of the island is its tranquillity. There are no cars or hotels, and just one small **restaurant** by the landing stage, *La Tonelle* (☎04.92.99.18.07; closed Nov–March), serving menus from €17 or a magnificent *bouillabaisse* for €90. Beyond lie the cultivated vines, lavender, herbs and olive trees mingled with wild poppies and daisies; and the pine and eucalyptus trees, shading the paths beside the white rock shore and mixing their scent with rosemary, thyme and wild honeysuckle.

Around Cannes

A couple of small towns in the hills immediately inland from Cannes are worth visiting before you head further afield. The pretty but somewhat sanitized hilltop village of **Mougins** is renowned as home to some of the finest restaurants in Provence, while the pottery town of **Vallauris**, a short distance west, was where Pablo Picasso made his remarkable postwar experiments with ceramics.

Mougins

If **MOUGINS**, 8km north of Cannes, is the first Provençal village you visit, you may well be charmed by its hilltop site, exquisitely preserved lanes and associations with Man Ray and with Picasso, who had his last studio here and who died here in 1973. If, however, you arrive with images of such villages as Cotignac, Simiane la Rotonde or even St-Paul de Vence fresh in mind, Mougins may strike you as rather over-praised, a pretty bauble lost in a sea of bland suburbia and lacking any genuine character of its own.

Mougins today is effectively a **culinary** theme park. It was at the **Moulin de Mougins**, across the Cannes-Grasse highway from the old village on avenue Notre Dame de Vie, that legendary, now-retired chef Roger Vergé perfected his *Cuisine of the Sun*, a modern reworking of Provençal cooking that won him (and Mougins) international acclaim in the 1970s. The *Moulin* and the village alike remain pilgrimage destinations for fans of contemporary cuisine – especially the moguls and mega-stars who attend the Cannes Film Festival – with an astonishing number of high-class restaurants crammed into the gorgeous medieval centre. In September each year, the community hosts the **Festival International de Gastronomie Mougins** (ⓦlesetoilesdemougins.com).

In the village itself, the winding lanes are thick with ateliers and small galleries. An excellent **photography museum** (July–Sept daily 10am–8pm; Sept, Oct & Dec–June Mon–Fri 10am–6pm, Sat & Sun 11am–6pm; free), just beyond the Porte Sarrazine, hosts changing exhibitions and has its own small collection that includes portraits of Jacques Lartigue and Picasso. At the top end of the village, the old wash house, **Le Lavoir**, on avenue J.C.-Mallet (March–Oct daily 11am–7pm;

free), forms another exhibition space for the visual arts, its wide basin of water playing reflecting games with the images and the light.

The **Musée de l'Automobiliste** (June–Sept daily 10am–6pm; Dec–May Tues–Sun 10am–1pm & 2–6pm; €7), alongside the A8 autoroute to Nice 3km southeast, will delight even those who don't share the passion for its subject. No expense has been spared on this indulgent dedication to the motorcar and its two-wheeled relations. Sculptures made of shiny, tangled exhaust pipes line the pathway to the hangar-like museum space, where exhibits include glamorous vintage cars such as a 1933 Hispano-Suiza, as well as German army vehicles, record-breaking racing cars and a large collection of miniature motors.

Practicalities

The local **tourist office** is just below the village centre, at 18 boulevard G-Courteline (July & Aug daily 9am–7pm; Sept–June Mon–Fri 9am–5.30pm, Sat 9.30am–5pm; ☏04.93.75.87.67, ⓦwww.mougins-coteazur.org). **Drivers** reach the nearby car park by spiralling up the hillside from the main D6285, twice tunnelling beneath major roads. The village is also on the frequent #600 **bus** service between Cannes and Grasse.

Central **hotels** (☏04.92.28.43.43, ⓦwww.lemascandille.com; ⓽) tend to be very expensive: tastefully decorated rooms at *Le Mas Candille*, a deluxe spa amid olive groves and cypresses on boulevard Clément-Rebuffel, start at €400 a night, while the simple but handsome accommodation in the *Moulin de Mougins* itself costs half that (☏04.93.75.78.24, ⓦmoulindemougins.com; ⓾). *Les Liserons de Mougins*, well beyond walking distance 2km north towards Mouans-Sartoux, at 608 avenue St-Martin (☏04.93.75.50.31, ⓦwww.hotel-liserons-mougins.com; ❸), makes a good-value alternative; it's a pretty old country house, with sun-splashed rooms, climbing flowers, a pleasant breakfast terrace and a pool.

Although none of Mougins' fine array of **restaurants** is particularly cheap, you don't have to spend a fortune unless you want to. Dinner menus at the *Moulin de Mougins* (see above; closed Mon & Tues) cost €90 and €160, but its attractive former cooking school, *L'Amandier*, close to the main car park on place des Patriotes (☏04.93.90.00.91), has a lunch menu at €25, and dinner from €34. The main village square, place du Vieux Village, holds several less grand but still appealing and dependable options: the *Rendez-Vous de Mougins* (☏04.93.75.87.47, ⓦwww.aurendezvous-mougins.com) serves excellent Provençal dinner menus at €19.80 and €25, while prices and quality at the *Restaurant de la Méditerranée* (☏04.93.90.03.47) are similar.

Vallauris

The small town of **VALLAURIS**, 6km east of Cannes above Golfe-Juan, is remarkable only for its long-standing tradition of making **pottery**, and its more recent association with **Picasso**. Despite being set on sloping hills, it's not a hill village in the usual sense; it's just an ordinary and not particularly attractive little town. That said, the very fact that it feels genuinely lived-in, and the backstreets close to the centre are bustling with day-to-day activity, make it a refreshing change from so many prettified Riviera communities.

Ceramics became established here early in the sixteenth century, when the bishop of Grasse rebuilt Vallauris after its population had been decimated by plague, and settled Genoese potters here to exploit the clay soil and abundant timber. By the end of World War II, however, aluminium had become a much more popular material for pots and plates. It took the intervention of Picasso to reverse Vallauris' decline. In 1946, while installed in the castle at Antibes, the artist met some of the town's few remaining potters, and was invited to Vallauris by the owner of a ceramics studio, Georges Ramié. Hooked on clay, Picasso spent the next two years working at Ramié's **Madoura workshop**. Today the main street, avenue Georges-Clemenceau, is almost entirely given over to pottery shops, while the Madoura workshop (Mon–Fri 10am–12.30pm & 3–6pm; closed Nov), just off to the left halfway up, is now a gallery with exclusive rights to reproduce – and sell – Picasso's designs. Other classy commercial galleries include **Sassi-Milici**, 65 bis avenue Georges-Clemenceau (daily: July & Aug 10.30am–7pm; Sept–June 10.30am–1pm & 2–6.30pm)

A gift from Picasso to the town, the bronze **Man with a Sheep**, stands in the main square, place Paul-Isnard, beside the church and neat little castle. The municipality had some misgivings about the sculpture but decided that the possible affront to their conservative tastes was outweighed by the benefits to tourism of Picasso's international reputation. They needn't have worried; the statue looks quite simply like a shepherd boy and sheep.

The local authorities then offered Picasso the task of decorating the early medieval deconsecrated **chapel** in the castle courtyard (daily except Tues: mid-June to mid-Sept 10am–12.15pm & 2–6pm; mid-Sept to mid-June 10am–12.15pm & 2–5pm; €3.30), which he finally did in 1952. The space is tiny and, with the painted panels covering the vault, has the architectural simplicity of an air-raid shelter, which indeed it was during the war. Picasso's subject is *War and Peace*. At first glance it's easy to be unimpressed (as many critics still are) – it looks mucky and slapdash, with paint runs on the unyielding plywood surfaces. Stay a while, however, and the passion of this violently drawn pacifism slowly emerges. On the *War* panel a music score is trampled by hooves and about to be engulfed in flames; the figure of "valiant resistance" tenuously holds the scales of justice; a shield bears the outline of a dove; and skeletons unleash creepy-crawlies and pestilence from a deathly chariot. *Peace* is represented by symbols of creativity and fecundity, including Pegasus; people dancing and suckling babies; trees bearing fruit; owls; books; and general innocent mischief.

The ticket for the chapel also gives admission to the castle's **Musée de la Céramique/Musée Magnelli** (same hours), which exhibits many of the ceramics Picasso made at the Madoura, ranging from plates and more complicated vessels to carved woodblocks, as well as paintings by Alberto Magnelli.

Practicalities

Vallauris' **tourist office** (July & Aug daily 9am–7pm; Sept–June Mon–Sat 9am–12.15pm & 1.45–5pm; ☎04.93.63.82.58, ⓦwww.vallauris-golfe-juan.fr) and main car park is on place du 8 Mai 1945, at the foot of avenue Georges-Clemenceau. **Buses** from Cannes and the *gare SNCF* at Golfe-Juan arrive behind the castle.

Vallauris is a place to visit for an afternoon, rather than to spend a night. Avenue Georges-Clemenceau is lined with workaday **restaurants**, cafés and bars; the pick of the bunch is *l'Escalier Gourmand* at no. 47 (☎04.93.00.08.74), where lunch specials served on the upstairs terrace cost around €12.

West of Cannes

Immediately **west of Cannes**, the western end of the Riviera holds a handful of little resorts, such as **La Napoule** and **Théoule-sur-Mer**. While they're not worth going out of your way to see, the coastal D6908 makes an enjoyable route west towards St-Raphaël (see p.297), running beyond La Napoule along the dramatic **Corniche de l'Esterel**.

La Napoule

The small former fishing port of **LA NAPOULE** stands 8km west of Cannes, beyond the city's small airport. The fantasy **castle** (early Feb to early Nov gardens daily 10am–6pm, castle tours 11.30am, 2.30pm, 3.30pm & 4.30pm; early Nov to early Feb gardens Mon–Fri 2–5pm, Sat & Sun 10am–5pm, castle tours Mon–Fri 2.30pm & 3.30pm, Sat & Sun 11.30am, 2.30pm & 3.30pm; gardens €3.50, castle tour €6; Ⓦchateau-lanapoule.com) that dominates the waterfront was erected atop the three towers and gateway of a fourteenth-century fort by American sculptor Henry Clews and his wife. A classic pre-World War I folly, it features lovely gardens, and holds a collection of Clews' odd and gloomy works, represented on the outside by the grotesques on the gateway.

La Napoule is technically just the seaside portion of the larger community of **Mandelieu-La Napoule**. Mandelieu, up the hill away from the sea, is a character-less golfing resort with minimal appeal to casual visitors.

Practicalities

La Napoule's seasonal **tourist office** is opposite the port on avenue Henri-Clews (April–June & Sept–Oct Mon–Fri 9.30am–12.30pm & 2–6pm; July–Aug daily 10am–12.30pm & 2.30–7pm; ℡04.92.97.99.27, Ⓦot-mandelieu.fr). Not far away, across from the beach, *La Calanque*, 404 avenue Henri-Clews (℡04.93.49.95.11; ❹), is a nice **hotel** where rooms offer views of the castle and the sea, and a pretty **restaurant** serves fine Provençal fish dishes. The cheaper *Villa Parisiana*, a few blocks inland on rue de l'Argentière, is more peaceful (℡04.93.49.93.02, Ⓦvillaparisiana.com; ❸).

Théoule-sur-Mer and Miramar

The ruggedly picturesque **Corniche de l'Esterel** extends for 20km westwards from **THÉOULE-SUR-MER**, 2.5km down the coast from La Napoule, all the way to St-Raphaël. Théoule itself is a quiet, rather low-key place with a sandy beach, large marina, and a small castle that can't be visited. Beyond it the coast runs south, becoming wilder and more dramatic around the Pointe de l'Esquillon as it approaches the little village of **MIRAMAR**.

Théoule has its own **tourist office**, at 1 corniche d'Or (Mon–Sat 9am–7pm, Sun 9am–2pm; ℡04.93.49.28.28, Ⓦwww.theoule-sur-mer.org), but the best place to **stay** hereabouts is the splendid pink *Tour de l'Esquillon*, high up on the corniche in Miramar (℡04.93.75.41.51, Ⓦesquillon.com; ❽), which has breathtaking views, plus its own beach and a fine restaurant.

Juan-les-Pins

JUAN-LES-PINS, just 9km east of Cannes, is another luminous Côte d'Azur name. Though perhaps not as glamorous as it once was, it's still an appealing resort, with sandy beaches, haunting reminders of its former Art Deco glory, plenty of nightlife and a renowned **jazz festival**, **Jazz à Juan**.

Arrival, information and accommodation

The **tourist office** is at 51 boulevard Guillaumont on the seafront at the western end of town (Mon–Sat 9am–noon & 2–6pm, Sun in school hols only 10am–12.30pm & 2.30–5pm; ℡04.97.23.11.10, Ⓦantibesjuanlespins.com). The **gare SNCF** is just a couple of hundred metres inland from here, on avenue de l'Esterel, while the most central local bus stops are "Pin Doré" and "Rond Point Joffre".

Juan-les-Pins holds an abundant crop of **hotels**, clustered especially around avenue Gallet, between avenue de l'Esterel and the seafront, and avenue Alexandre III which crosses it.

Hotels

Belles Rives 33 bd Edouard-Baudoin ⓣ04.93.61.02.79, ⓦbellesrives.com. This gorgeous Art Deco hotel preserves Juan-les-Pins' most authentic aura of 1930s glamour, but even the cheapest inland-facing rooms start at €245 in high season. ⑨

Mimosas rue Pauline ⓣ04.93.61.04.16, ⓦhotelmimosas.com. Grand but very welcoming white villa, in lush gardens ten minutes' walk up from the sea, with rooms of varying sizes – the cheapest are rather small – and a lovely pool. Free parking. Closed Oct–April. ⑤

Pinède 7 av Georges-Gallice ⓣ04.93.61.03.95. Very central, inexpensive hotel only just back from the seafront, with some family-sized rooms. ③

Pré Catelan 27 av des Palmiers ⓣ04.93.61.05.11, ⓦprecatelan.fr. Peaceful and very comfortable hotel, in attractive gardens on the corner of av Lauriers, near the sea and the station, with large spacious rooms, some sleeping four. ⑥

The Town

Unlike St-Tropez, Juan-les-Pins was never a fishing village, just a pine grove by the sea, and although its casino was built in 1908, it wasn't until the late 1920s that it really took off as the original summer resort of the Côte d'Azur. In the 1930s, when the likes of Charlie Chaplin and Maurice Chevalier were regular visitors, revealing swimsuits were reputedly first worn here and waterskiing was invented. Juan-les-Pins' trail-blazing style continued to attract aristocrats, royals, writers, dancers and screen stars throughout the 1950s and 1960s.

For more than thirty years after it closed in 1976, the town's central landmark, the eerily beautiful Art Deco **Hotel Provençal**, slipped gradually into utter dereliction, and seemed to symbolize the decline in local fortunes. Built by the American railroad magnate Frank Jay Gould, who was also responsible for the Palais de la Méditerranée in Nice, it has now finally been converted into apartments, just in time for a more global economic downturn to threaten its future once again. Gould's own home, the 1912 **Villa Vigie**, stands behind high walls across the road from the hotel.

Compared to the *Provençal*, the modern *Meridien* hotel and casino is merely a blandly oversized blot on the seafront. Nevertheless, as a **beach** resort Juan has considerable appeal, with 2km of sheltered sand, much of it almost entirely obscured by private beach and restaurant concessions, and half a dozen waterskiing outfits if you fancy emulating those 1930s pioneers.

Another wonderful, peeling remnant from Juan's heyday stands at the western end of the seafront. Complete with minaret, cupolas and domes, the **Villa El**

Jazz à Juan

The best jazz event on the Côte d'Azur, Juan-les-Pins' open-air **Festival International de Jazz** (known simply as Jazz à Juan), takes place during the **middle two weeks of July**. The main venue is La Pinède Gould, just above the beach by the casino. Juan-les-Pins is twinned with New Orleans, so there's always a strong contingent of performers from the Crescent City. The music is always chosen with serious concern for every kind of jazz, both contemporary and traditional, rather than commercial popularity. For full details of tickets and schedules, contact the tourist offices in Antibes and Juan-les-Pins.

Djezair, 1 boulevard Charles-Guillaumont, was built in exuberant neo-Moorish style by Antibes architect Ernest Truch in 1922. An ancient, beautiful pine grove near the eastern end of the promenade, **Jardin de la Pinède** (known simply as La Pinède), plays host to the **jazz festival**, and boasts a Hollywood-style **celebrity walk** with the handprints of Sydney Bechet, B.B. King, Stéphane Grappelli, Dave Sanborn and others.

Eating and drinking

The sublime *La Passagère* excepted, Juan-les-Pins is not blessed with particularly memorable **restaurants**; take your pick from the countless menus along the boulevards around La Pinède. Many stay open until midnight.

Café de la Plage 1 bd Edouard-Baudouin ⓣ04.93.61.37.61. This pleasant seafront spot offers everything from seafood to cocktails and ice cream, with lunchtime *plats* for €13.
Helios Plage promenade du Soleil ⓣ04.93.61.85.77. The smartest of the beach concessions, with *plats* from around €22. Closed Oct to mid-April.

La Passagère *Hôtel Belles Rives*, 33 bd Edouard-Baudoin ⓣ04.93.61.02.79. Modern Mediterranean delights served in lovely, restored Art Deco surroundings; the terrace has wonderful views over the bay. Lunch menu €48, dinner menus €80–150. Closed Mon & Tues in low season.

Nightlife

The fads and reputations of Juan-les-Pins' various **clubs** may change, but in general opening hours are midnight to dawn. Count on searching appraisal of your attire, and paying around €20 for entrance plus your first drink. Hotspots include *Whisky a Gogo*, 5 rue Jacques Leonetti (ⓣ04.93.61.26.40), *Le Milk*, avenue G-Gallice (ⓣ04.93.67.22.74, ⓦmilk-discotheque.com), and *Minimal*, avenue Guy-de-Maupassant (ⓣ06.16.24.45.27, ⓦminimal-club.com). The perennially popular **live music** venue *Le Pam-Pam*, 137 boulevard Wilson (ⓣ04.93.61.11.05, ⓦpampam.fr), often has Brazilian bands; arrive early to grab a seat.

The Route Napoléon

The pines and silver sand between Juan-les-Pins and Cannes, now **Golfe-Juan**, witnessed Napoleon's return from exile in 1815. Having been in command of the Mediterranean defences as a general in 1794, with Antibes' Fort Carré as his base, the emperor knew the bay well. This time, however, his emissaries to Cannes and Antibes were taken prisoner upon landing, though the local men in charge decided not to capture him. The lack of enthusiasm for his return was enough to persuade the ever-brilliant tactician to head north, bypassing Grasse, and take the most isolated snowbound mule paths up to Sisteron and onwards – the path commemorated by the modern **Route Napoléon**. By March 6 he was in Dauphiné; on March 19 he was back in Paris' Tuileries Palace. One hundred days later he lost the battle of Waterloo and was finally and absolutely incarcerated on St Helena.

It's said that on the day he landed at Golfe-Juan, Napoleon's men accidentally held up the prince of Monaco's coach travelling east along the coast. The Revolution incorporated Monaco into France but the restored Louis XVIII had just granted back the principality. When the prince told the former emperor that he was off to reclaim his throne, Napoleon replied that they were in the same business and waved him on his way.

For **other sections of the Route Napoléon**, see 'Grasse' on p.332, 'Sisteron' on p.180, and 'Castellane' on p.226.

Antibes

Centring on its walled old town, almost abutting against the waves 1.5km east of Juan-les-Pins, **ANTIBES** is a delightful resort that has largely escaped the overdevelopment that blights so many of its neighbours. Graham Greene, who lived here for over twenty years, considered it the only place on the Riviera to have preserved its soul, and it remains a bustling little place, its animated streets full of bars and restaurants, swarming with Anglophones and yachting types, and hosting one of the finest **markets** along the coast. In addition, its castle holds a superb **Picasso collection**, while the views from the town's ramparts towards the Alps are wonderful.

Immediately south, the peninsula known as the **Cap d'Antibes** is dominated by the world's super-rich, many of whom live – or at least maintain homes – here, though the southern Cap still retains pinewoods that hide the exclusive mansions. As well as offering intermittent access to the wonderful rocky shore, the Cap holds a couple of beautiful gardens, the **Jardin Thuret** and the **Villa Eilenroc**.

Arrival and information

Antibes' helpful **tourist office**, on the northwest edge of the old town at 11 place du Général-de-Gaulle (Mon–Fri 9am–12.30pm & 1.30–6pm, Sat 9am–noon & 2–6pm, Sun 10am–12.30pm & 2.30–5pm; ℡04.97.23.11.11, Ⓦantibesjuanlespins.com), is a couple of hundred metres south of the **gare SNCF**. The **gare routière**, another 100m east on place Guynemer (℡04.93.34.37.60, Ⓦenvibus.fr), has frequent buses to the *gare SNCF* and nearby towns. **Bikes** can be rented from Midi Location Service, Galerie du Port, rue Lacan (℡04.93.34.48.00).

Hotels

Though really inexpensive **hotels** are thin on the ground, Antibes holds a reasonable selection of moderately priced two- and three-star **hotels**, and there's a **youth hostel** on the Cap. The nearest **campsites** are a few kilometres north of the city in the *quartier* de la Brague (bus #10 or one train stop to Gare de Biot).

Hotels

Beau Site 141 bd Kennedy ℡04.93.61.53.43, Ⓦhotelbeausite.net. This white-painted inn, set in a lovely garden amid some of Antibes' most exclusive villas, offers plain, tiled rooms that represent great value, plus a welcome pool. Closed early Nov to Feb. ⑤

Cap Eden Roc bd Kennedy ℡04.93.61.39.01, Ⓦedenroc-hotel.fr. A celebrity haunt since F. Scott Fitzgerald used it as the setting for *Tender is the Night*, this luxury hotel has a prime position in 25 acres on Cap d'Antibes. With all the usual comforts you'd expect at this price, it even has its own landing stage. Closed mid-Oct to mid-April. ⑨

Étoile 2 av Gambetta ℡04.93.34.26.30, Ⓦhoteletoile.com. Good-value, comfortable if slightly characterless modern two-star between the *gare SNCF* and town centre, with a/c and wi-fi. ③

Jabotte 13 av Max Maurey ℡04.93.61.45.89, Ⓦjabotte.com. Tranquil and very relaxing hotel, 50m from the beach in Cap d'Antibes, and twenty minutes' walk from town. Ten cosy, individually styled rooms, and evening cocktails in the delightful courtyard garden. ⑥

Mas Djoliba 29 av de Provence ℡04.93.34.02.48, Ⓦwww.hotel-djoliba.com. Fine old Provençal farmhouse, between the Vieille Ville and the main beach, with a large garden and pool; very pleasant. Closed mid-Nov to mid-March. ⑦

Modern 1 rue Formilière ℡04.92.90.59.05, Ⓦmodernhotel06.com. Welcoming and inexpensive little hotel, tucked away in a pedestrian lane in the heart of the old town, though the very plain modern rooms are duller than the cute exterior might suggest. ⑤

Ponteil 11 impasse Jean-Mensier ℡04.93.34.67.92, Ⓦleponteil.com. Friendly, pretty Logis de France hotel with the feel of a B&B, in a quiet location at the end of a cul-de-sac near the sea, and surrounded by luxuriant vegetation. Free

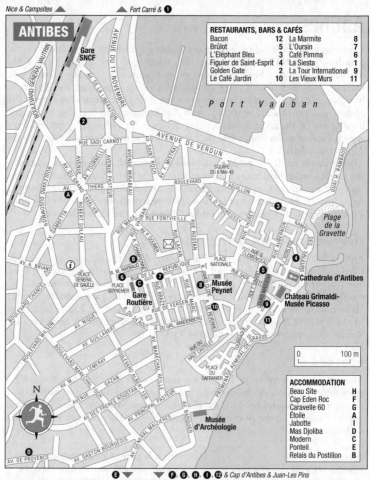

Map labels:

Nice & Campsites ▲ ▲ Fort Carré & ❶

ANTIBES

Gare SNCF

AVENUE DU 11 NOVEMBRE

BOULEVARD GÉNÉRAL VAUTRIN

AVENUE DE LA LIBÉRATION

RUE SADI CARNOT

AV. DE GRAND CAVALIER

AV. THIERS

ROBERT SOLEAU

AV. GAMBETTA

AV. DUGOMMIER

AVENUE PASTEUR

AV. TOURNELLY

AVENUE MIRABEAU

AVENUE DU 8 MAI

RUE SAINT ROCH

AV. MISTRAL

RUE MACÉ

RUE VAUBAN

RUE FONTVIEILLE

RUE DE LA RÉPUBLIQUE

RUE THURET

RUE AUBERNON

RUE LACAN

RUE ROSTAN

R. CHAMPIONNET

R. M. RAYBAUD

RUE DE L'ORME

RUE SADE

RUE DE L'HORLOGE

RUE ARAZY

RUE DE MARC

R. DU GÉNÉRAL VANDENBERG

RUE DE FERSEN

PLACE NATIONALE

Port Vauban

AVENUE DE VERDUN

SQUARE DU 8 MAI 45

BOULEVARD

D'AGUILLON

GAL. D'ANDREOSSY

RAMPE DES SALUTS

QUAI H. RAMBAUD

Plage de la Gravette

RUE G. CLEMENCEAU

RUE SAINTE

COURS MASSÉNA

Cathédrale d'Antibes

Château Grimaldi-Musée Picasso

Musée Peynet

Gare Routière

PLACE GÉNÉRALE DE GAULLE

PLACE GUYNEMER

AV. À. BRIAND

BOULEVARD CHANCEL

BOULEVARD WILSON

AV. NIQUET

AV. GUILLABERT

BOULEVARD MARÉCHAL FOCH

AV. LEMERAY

RUE DU 24 AOÛT

BOULEVARD MARÉCHAL JUIN

AV. MARÉCHAL REILLE

BOULEVARD ALBERT 1ER

AV. GAZAN

AV. DES FRÈRES ROUSTAN

AV. PRINCIPAL PASTEUR

AV. GÉNÉRAL MAZIÈRES

AV. GASTON BOURGEOIS

AV. DE PROVENCE

RUE DU HAUT CASTELET

PLACE DU SAFRANIER

PROMENADE AMIRAL DE GRASSE

TRAVERSE DU GRASSE

AV. BARQUIER

Musée d'Archéologie

N

0   100 m

RESTAURANTS, BARS & CAFÉS

Bacon	12	La Marmite	8
Brûlot	5	L'Oursin	7
L'Eléphant Bleu	3	Café Pimms	6
Figuier de Saint-Esprit	4	La Siesta	1
Golden Gate	2	La Tour International	9
Le Café Jardin	10	Les Vieux Murs	11

ACCOMMODATION

Beau Site	H
Cap Eden Roc	F
Caravelle 60	G
Étoile	A
Jabotte	I
Mas Djoliba	D
Modern	C
Ponteil	E
Relais du Postillon	B

❷ ❸ ❹ ❺ ❻ ❼ ❽ ❾ ❿ ⓫

ⓔ ▼ ▼ ⓕ, ⓖ, ⓗ, ⓘ, ⓬ & Cap d'Antibes & Juan-Les Pins

---

parking, small plain rooms. Half board only in high season. Closed mid-Nov to Jan. ❻

🏃 **Relais du Postillon** 8 rue Championnet ☎ 04.93.34.20.77, ⓦ relaisdupostillon.com. Charming, gay-friendly and very central little hotel, with a wide range of comfortable, individually decorated rooms above a high-quality restaurant and bar. ❸

Hostel and campsites

Camping Antipolis av du Pylone, La Brague ☎ 04.93.33.93.99, ⓦ camping-antipolis.com. Four-star campsite, 3km north of Antibes and 800m from the sea. €29.50 per tent in high season. Closed mid-Sept to early April.

Camping Les Embruns 63 rte de Biot, La Brague ☎ 06.48.11.17.39, ⓦ campingembruns-antibes.com.

Three-star site, near the beach just north of the gare de Biot – which is actually closer to Antibes than it is to Biot itself. €24 per tent. Closed mid-Oct to late May.

Camping Logis de la Brague 1221 rte de Nice, La Brague ☎ 04.93.33.54.72, ⓦ camping -logisbrague.com. Three-star campsite, 3km north of Antibes around 1km back from the sea. €18.50 per tent in high season. Closed Oct–April.

Caravelle 60 272 bd de la Garoupe, Cap d'Antibes ☎ 04.93.61.34.40, ⓦ clajsud.fr. Youth hostel by the sea that needs booking well in advance; meals are taken outdoors under the pine trees. Take bus #2 from *gare routière* (stop "Auberge de Jeunesse"). €18 per night including breakfast. Closed Oct–April.

The Town

Very little remains of the medieval centre of Antibes, thanks to border squabbles from the fifteenth century until the Revolution, when Antibes belonged to France and Nice to Savoy. The finest surviving stretch of **walls** line the seafront near the little crescent of the old port, with a tiny little beach in front.

Lording it over the ramparts, the **Château Grimaldi**, rebuilt in the sixteenth century but still with its twelfth-century Romanesque tower, is a beautifully cool, light space with hexagonal terracotta floor tiles. In 1946, Picasso was offered this dusty old building – by then already a museum – as a studio. Several extremely prolific months followed before he moved to Vallauris, leaving all his Antibes output to what is now the **Musée Picasso** (late June and early Sept daily 10am–6pm; July & Aug Mon, Tues, Thurs, Sat & Sun 10am–6pm, Wed & Fri 10am–8pm; mid-Sept to mid-June daily 10am–noon & 2–6pm; €6). Although he donated other works later on, the bulk of the collection belongs to this one period, when he was involved in one of his better relationships; Matisse was just up the road in Vence; the war was over; and the 1950s had not yet changed the Côte d'Azur forever. There's an uncomplicated exuberance in the numerous still lifes of sea urchins, the goats and fauns in Cubist non-disguise, and the wonderful *Ulysses and the Sirens*, a great round head against a mast around which the ship, sea and sirens swirl. The materials reveal postwar shortages – odd bits of wood and board instead of canvas, and boat paint rather than oils. Picasso also makes a subject here for other painters and photographers, including André Villers, Brassaï, Man Ray and Bill Brandt.

Picasso's old studio, on the second floor, holds several anguished works by Nicolas de Staël, who lived in Antibes for the last few months of his life, painting the sea, gulls and boats with great washes of grey, before he committed suicide in 1955. A wonderful terrace overlooking the sea is adorned by Germaine Richier sculptures along with works by Miró, César and others.

Alongside the castle, the **cathedral** was built on the site of an ancient temple. The choir and apse survive from the Romanesque building that served the city in the Middle Ages, while the nave and stunning ochre facade are Baroque. Inside, in the south transept, a sumptuous altarpiece by Louis Bréa is surrounded by immaculate panels of tiny detailed scenes.

One block inland, on cours Masséna, which marked the limit of the original Greek settlement, the **covered market** (daily 6am–1pm; closed Mon Sept–May) overflows with Provençal goodies including delicious olives, and a profusion of cut **flowers**, a long-standing Antibes speciality. In the afternoons, a **craft market** (Easter–Sept Thurs–Sun; Oct–Easter Thurs–Sat) takes over from about 3pm (4.30pm on Sat), and when the stalls pack up, café tables take their place.

A couple of other museums may take your fancy. On the ramparts along promenade Amiral-de-Grasse, the Bastion St-André houses the **Musée d'Archéologie** (late June and early Sept Tues–Sun 10am–noon & 2–6pm; July & Aug Tues, Thurs, Sat & Sun 10am–noon & 2–6pm, Wed & Fri 10am–noon & 2–8pm; mid-Sept to mid-June Tues–Sun 10am–noon & 2–6pm; €6), which gathers together the Greek, Roman, medieval and later finds of the region. The **Musée Peynet** on place Nationale (July & Aug Mon, Tues, Thurs, Sat & Sun 10am–noon & 2–6pm, Wed & Fri 10am–noon & 2–8pm; Sept–June Tues–Sun 10am–noon & 2–6pm; €3) pays homage to the Antibes cartoonist Raymond Peynet, whose most famous creation was the 1940s series of *The Lovers*, a truly old-fashioned conception of romance which, if you're not careful, may even induce nostalgia. It also displays work by other humourists.

Luxury yachts and humble fishing boats jostle amicably for space in Antibes' harbour, stretching north from the old port. The headland at its northern end is topped by the splendidly situated **Fort Carré** (Tues–Sun: mid-June to mid-Sept 10am–5.30pm; mid-Sept to mid-June 10am–4pm; €3), transformed by Vauban in the seventeenth century into an impregnable fortress.

Cap d'Antibes

Antibes' longest beach, the sandy and utterly irresistible **Plage de la Salis**, which runs along the eastern neck of the **Cap d'Antibes** south of town, is a rarity along the Riviera. Access to it is free, with no big hotels blocking the way – the success of Juan-les-Pins spared this side of the Cap from unchecked development in the days before planning laws were tightened. Above the southern end of the beach, at the top of chemin du Calvaire, stands the **Chapelle de la Garoupe** (daily 10am–noon & 2.30–7pm), full of ex-votos for deliverances from accidents, ranging from battles with the Saracens to collisions with speeding Citroëns. Much the best reason to make the trail up here, however, is for the stunning panoramic **views** across Cap d'Antibes towards both Juan-les-Pins and Antibes; you can see as far as the Esterel and to Nice and beyond. Next to the church is a powerful lighthouse whose beam is visible 70km out to sea.

A second public beach, **Plage de la Garoupe**, stretches along boulevard de la Garoupe before the promontory of Cap Gros. From here, a footpath follows the shore to join the chemin des Douaniers, which continues to the southern end of the Cap d'Antibes. At the southern end of the Cap d'Antibes, on avenue Mrs L.D. Beaumont, stands the grandiose **Villa Eilenroc** (Sept–June: gardens Tues & Wed 9am–5pm; villa Wed 9am–noon & 1.30–5pm; closed July & Aug; free), designed by Charles Garnier, architect of the casino at Monte Carlo, and surrounded by 28 acres of lush gardens. Its equally magnificent neighbour, the Château de la Croé, was home, after the 1936 abdication, to the Duke and Duchess of Windsor.

Much of the southern tip of the Cap d'Antibes is a warren of private roads with no-entry signs barring all but residents. To see the fabled "bay of million-aires", east of **Point de l'Ilette**, it's simpler to take a **boat trip** from Juan-les-Pins (departures every 1hr 30min in summer from Ponton Courbet; T 04.93.67.02.11, W visiobulle.com; €12). West of the *Hôtel du Cap Eden Roc*, however, the shore is accessible once again at the Batterie du Graillon, where you'll find the **Musée Napoléonien** (Tues–Sat: mid-June to mid-Sept 10am–6pm; mid-Sept to mid-June 10am–4.30pm; €3), which documents the general's return from Elba with the usual paraphernalia of hats, cockades, model ships and signed commands. There are lovely views from the slightly grubby public beach adjacent to the fort. Walking or cycling up the western side of the Cap from here is a joy; you pass the tiny **Port de l'Olivette**, full of small, unflashy boats, as well as rocks, jetties, tiny sandy beaches, and grand villas hiding behind high walls.

Dominating the middle of the Cap, on boulevard du Cap, the **Jardin Thuret** (Mon–Fri: summer 8am–6pm, winter 8.30am–5.30pm; free; W jardin-thuret .antibes.inra.fr) was established in the nineteenth century by botanist Gustav Thuret. It now tests and acclimatizes subtropical trees and shrubs in order to diversify the Mediterranean plants of France.

Eating and drinking

Old Antibes holds places to eat at every turn: Place Nationale and cours Masséna are lined with **cafés**; rue James-Close has nothing but **restaurants**, and rue Thuret and its side streets also offer numerous menus to browse through. Places to **drink** are especially thick on the ground by the port.

Restaurants

![icon] **Restaurant de Bacon** bd de Bacon, Cap d'Antibes ☎04.93.61.50.02, ⓦrestaurantdebacon.com. Among the very finest fish restaurants along the coast, overlooking Vieux Antibes and serving fabulous fish soups and stews, including a magnificent *bouillabaisse* at €99 per person. Lunch menu €49, dinner €79. Closed Mon, Tues lunch & Nov–Feb.

Brûlot 3 rue Frédéric-Isnard ☎04.93.34.17.76. This veteran local institution serves up fine Provençal favourites from its wood-fired oven, like *socca* chick-pea pancakes or baked fish. Lunch menu at €14 on weekdays, dinner menus from €25. Their dinner-only sister restaurant next door, *Brûlot Pasta*, is equally recommended. Closed Sun eve & Mon in low season, plus first 3 weeks of Aug, and late Dec to mid-Jan.

L'Eléphant Bleu 28 bd de l'Aguillon ☎04.93.34.28.80. Reasonably authentic Thai specialities, served as hot as you like, plus good Chinese, Vietnamese and vegetarian dishes and sushi, in smart surroundings on the port. Menus at €19 & €23; veggie menu €18. Closed Sun.

Figuier de Saint-Esprit 14 rue St-Esprit ☎04.93.34.50.12, ⓦchristianmorisset.fr. Superb albeit expensive restaurant, hidden away in a pretty lane near the Picasso museum, and serving classic Provençal meat and fish dishes both indoors and in a fig-shaded courtyard. Dinner menus at €55 & €75. Closed lunch Mon & Wed, & all Tues.

Le Café Jardin 23 rue des Bains ☎04.93.34.42.66, ⓦlecafejardin.fr. Friendly little brasserie/café in a very peaceful spot in the back lanes of the old town, with a couple of tables out on the street, a nice bar, and a courtyard filled with twee ceramic frogs. Breakfast is €6, a plate of three cheeses with wine and salad €6, and lunch menus start at €13.50. Daily 8am–7.30pm.

La Marmite 20 rue James-Close ☎04.93.34.56.79. One of several good restaurants along this street, with *cassoulet de moules* or *terrine de poisson* on the €28 fish menu, plus cheaper menus at €15.50 and €23. Closed Tues lunch & all Mon.

L'Oursin 16 rue de la République ☎04.93.34.13.46, ⓦrestaurant-loursin.fr. High-class fish and traditional seafood, with menus starting at €12 lunch, €25 dinner, and offering sushi on the first weekend of the month. Closed Mon Oct–May.

Café Pimms corner of rue de la République and place Guynemer ☎04.93.34.13.46, ⓦpimmscafe.ifrance.com. Daytime brasserie, with carousel decor and a friendly atmosphere. Whether you order salad, pasta, or a daily *plat*, it will cost in the range of €9–12. Daily 7am–8pm.

Les Vieux Murs 26 promenade Amiral-de-Grasse ☎04.93.34.06.73, ⓦlesvieuxmurs.com. In a perfect setting near the castle on the ramparts, this restaurant serves very classy food, such as king crab with Niçois ratatouille or scallops with orange butter. Lunch menu €34, otherwise €44 or €60. Closed Tues lunch in season, all Mon mid-Sept to mid-April.

Nightlife

Many **cafés** and **bars** stay open late, with boulevard d'Aguillon next to the port being the liveliest spot for a drink. Antibes' most popular **nightclub** is the refurbished *La Siesta* (☎04.93.33.31.31), between Antibes and La Brague on the route du Bord-de-la-Mer, with gaming rooms, a disco, restaurant and bar. Serious dancers, however, will have more choice in neighbouring Juan-les-Pins (see p.320). Antibes has a couple of decent **jazz** clubs – *La Tour International* (☎04.93.34.17.70; closed Mon), 6 cours Masséna, Vieille Antibes, and *Bar en Biais* (☎04.93.74.10.98, ⓦbarenbiais-jazzclub.com), 600 Première avenue, Nova Antipolis – as well as one **gay club**, the *Golden Gate* (☎04.93.74.24.74) at 4 rue Honoré-Ferrare.

Biot

The pretty *village perché* of **BIOT**, 4km up from the coast and a total of 5km northwest of Antibes, is famous for its rich **arts and crafts** tradition. Long a centre of pottery production and now home to several glassworks, Biot is usually packed out in high season, as visitors drawn by the excellent **Fernand Léger museum** nearby stay on to browse the village's wide array of shops, studios and galleries.

Arrival, information and accommodation

Biot's **tourist office** (July & Aug Mon–Fri 10am–7pm, Sat & Sun 2.30–7pm; Sept–June Mon–Fri 10am–1pm & 2–6pm, Sat & Sun 1–5pm; ℡04.93.65.78.00, ⓦbiot.fr) is on the main village street, at 46 rue St-Sébastien. Although Biot does officially have a **gare SNCF**, it's not near the village itself, but down by the sea at La Brague, 4km south, along a road that's much too dangerous and unpleasant to walk. Regular **buses** between the village and Antibes do however call at the station, while in summer regular free shuttle buses also connect the village with **car parks** around its perimeter.

There's very little **accommodation** in Biot, so it's worth booking well in advance to stay at the simple, inexpensive *Galerie des Arcades*, 16 place des Arcades (℡04.93.65.01.04; ❸), on a lovely little square in the medieval centre of the village, and which has a good restaurant (see below). If you don't mind staying outside town, the *Domaine du Jas*, 1km southeast at 625 route de la Mer (℡04.93.65.50.50, ⓦdomainedujas.com; ❻), is a fancier alternative with a pool.

Good **campsites** in the vicinity include the one-star *Mistral*, 800m up from the sea at 1780 route de la Mer (℡04.93.65.61.48, ⓦcampinglemistral.com; €18.10; closed early Oct to late March), and the three-star *L'Eden*, 243 chemin du Val-de-Pôme (℡04.93.65.63.70, ⓦcamping-eden.fr; €18.10; closed Nov–March), a couple of hundred metres from the Léger museum.

The village

The artist **Fernand Léger**, who lived in Biot for a few years at the end of his life, was first attracted to the village by its **potteries**; one of his old pupils had set up shop here to produce ceramics of his master's designs. Today, the former Chapelle des Pénitents Blancs, just along from the tourist office at 9 rue St-Sébastien, houses a small **Musée d'Histoire et de Céramique Biotoises** (Wed–Sun: July–Sept 10am–6pm; Oct–June 2–6pm; €2), which underlines the importance of the potteries to the historical development of the village.

Several local **glass-makers** encourage visitors to admire, and ideally buy, the famous and beautiful hand-blown bubble glass (*verre bullé*). You can watch glass-blowers at work at the **Verrerie de Biot** – established in 1956, a year after Léger's death – on chemin des Combes just north of the centre (mid-June to mid-Sept Mon–Sat 10am–8pm, Sun 10.30am–1.30pm & 2.30–7.30pm; mid-Sept to mid-June Mon–Sat 10am–6pm, Sun 10.30am–1.30pm & 2.30–6.30pm; free; ⓦverreriebiot.com), and also learn more by visiting the on-site **Eco-musée du Verre** (guided tours only Mon–Fri 11.30am & 4.30pm; €6).

Musée Fernand Léger

A stunning, life-affirming collection of paintings by Fernand Léger is displayed at the **Musée Fernand Léger** (daily except Tues: June–Oct 10am–6pm; Nov–May 10am–5pm; €5.50, under-26s free; ⓦwww.musee-fernandleger.fr), 1km southeast of the village on the chemin du Val-de-Pôme. Even the museum building is a pleasure: with its giant mosaic murals, it transcends its mundane suburban setting.

Léger was turned off from the abstraction of Parisian painters by his experiences of fighting alongside ordinary working people in World War I. Not that he favoured realism, but he wanted his paintings to have popular appeal. Understanding that in the modern world, art competes with images generated by advertising, cinema and public spectacle, he set about producing work with a similar visual power.

Without any realism in the form or facial expressions, the people in such paintings as *Four Bicycle Riders* or the various *Construction Workers* are forcefully present as they engage in their work or leisure, and are visually on an equal footing with the objects. Almost all the collection here is displayed in two very spacious white galleries upstairs; while it's not scrupulously chronological, Léger's earlier, Cubist works come first.

Theme parks

Several large-scale attractions for **children** line up along the main coast road, well away from the village. These include the performing dolphins of **Marineland** on the N7 (daily 10am–6.30pm, later in high season; closed Jan; adult €35, under-13 €27; Ⓦmarineland.fr), which is also home to the water toboggans, chutes and slides of **Aquasplash** (mid-June to Aug daily 10am–7pm; first fortnight of June & Sept Sat & Sun 10am–7pm; adult €24, child €19).

The **Antibesland** funfair is almost opposite Marineland (April to mid-June Sat, Sun & public hols 2–7pm; second fortnight of June Mon–Fri 8.30pm–1am, Sat 4pm–1am, Sun 3pm–1am; July & Aug Mon–Sat 5pm–2am, Sun 3pm–2am; Sept Sat & Sun 4pm–2am; free entry, rides €1.50–4; Ⓦazurpark.com).

Eating and drinking

Brasseries, pizzerias and all kinds of **restaurants** jostle for space in Biot village. The finest of the pack is *Le Jarrier*, 30 passage de la Bourgade (Ⓣ04.93.65.11.68; closed Mon & Tues), where dinner menus range from €21 to €95. The *Galerie des Arcades* (see above; closed Sun eve & Mon) is an appealing combination of café, art gallery and restaurant, serving traditional Provençal dishes at tables under the arcades; *plats du jour* cost around €16. There's a weekly **market** in the village on Tuesdays.

Villeneuve-Loubet

The Riviera shore reaches its trashy nadir at **Villeneuve-Loubet-Plage**, 6km straight up the coast from Antibes, where the giant **Baie des Anges** marina dominates the waterfront. Built in the 1970s to a design by André Minangoy, the petrified sails of its colossal residential blocks are visible all the way from Cap d'Antibes to Cap Ferrat. By the time the French government began to be concerned at the despoliation of the Côte d'Azur, the marina's luxury apartments were worth far too much for it to be demolished. So there it stands, a clever, well-maintained but hugely intrusive piece of modernism. The commercial squalor that surrounds it is even harder to stomach – an unsightly mess of drive-in restaurants, petrol stations and out-of-town retail sheds wedged between the autoroute and the sea.

Across the autoroute, the quieter and altogether more attractive village of **VILLENEUVE-LOUBET**, on the River Loup, clusters around an undamaged twelfth-century castle (closed to the public), which was once home to François I. Villeneuve's riverside park and pastures are a stopover point for migrating birds, but its main claim to fame is the **Musée de l'Art Culinaire**, 3 rue Escoffier (July & Aug Mon, Tues, Thurs & Sun 2–7pm, Wed & Fri 10am–noon & 2–7pm; Sept, Oct & Dec–June daily except Sat 2–6pm; €5; Ⓦfondation-escoffier.org), in the house where **Auguste Escoffier** was born in 1846. The son of a blacksmith, he began his restaurant career at thirteen, skivvying for his uncle in Nice, and was by the end of the century known as "the king of chefs and the chef of kings". In London he was the *Savoy's* first head chef, then the *Carlton's*, and he fed almost every European head of state. *Pêche melba* was his most famous creation, but his significance for the history of *haute cuisine* was in breaking the tradition of health-hazard richness and quantity. He was also a technical innovator, who invented dried potato and a breadcrumb maker.

As well as items related to Escoffier's own life, the museum tells the history of French cuisine, and includes a re-creation of an eighteenth-century Provençal kitchen. It was the invention of the stove or *potager* that revolutionized French cooking: by making it possible to cook dishes simultaneously at a wide range of temperatures, it paved the way for the development of elaborate menus.

Practicalities

A couple of simple, inexpensive **hotels** stand close to the heart of the village: the *Parc*, 1 avenue de la Libération (℡04.93.20.88.13, ⓦhotelduparcvilleneuve .com; ❸; closed Christmas–April), and the *Hostellerie du Loup*, a little further south at 194 avenue des Plans (℡04.92.02.97.87; ❷). Good local **restaurants** in the pedestrianized centre include *Le Chat Plume*, just down the hill from the museum at 5 rue des Mesures (℡04.93.73.40.91, ⓦchatplume.com; closed Mon, Sun, & Tues lunch), which serves hearty *cuisine de terroir* in cheerfully quirky surroundings, with dishes such as *cuisse de lapin* on marinated artichokes on menus that start at €16 for lunch, €28 for dinner. *L'Auberge Fleurie*, nearby at 11–13 rue des Mesures (℡04.93.73.90.92; closed Wed, plus Thurs in low season), offers the likes of salmon escalope with saffron or carpaccio of beef with truffle oil, at very similar prices but in a more formal setting.

Cagnes

Slashed through by three major roads and with an awe-inspiring traffic problem, the various parts of the **CAGNES** agglomeration are rather confusing. The narrow coastal strip, known as **Cros-de-Cagnes**, consists of a small, pleasant old quarter, with fishing boats pulled up on its broad, pebbly beach. Scruffy, modern **Cagnes-sur-Mer**, which constitutes the town centre, is inland above the autoroute, a bustling but rather characterless place notable only for **Renoir's house**. The original medieval village, **Haut-de-Cagnes**, overlooks both town and coast from the northwest heights, and holds a stunning **castle** containing the fabulous **Donation Suzy Solidor**.

Arrival and information

Each component of Cagnes has its own **tourist office**. In **Cagnes-sur-Mer**, it's at 6 boulevard Maréchal-Juin (July & Aug Mon–Fri 9am–12.30pm & 2–6pm, Sat 9am–12.30pm; Sept–June Mon–Fri 9am–noon & 2–6pm, Sat 9am–noon; ℡04.93.20.61.64, ⓦcagnes-tourisme.com); in **Cros-de-Cagnes**, it's at 99 boulevard de la Plage (July & Aug daily 9am–7pm; June & Sept Mon–Sat 9am–noon & 2–6pm; Oct–May Mon–Fri 9am–noon & 2–6pm; ℡04.93.07.67.08); and up in **Haut-de-Cagnes**, it's place du Dr-Morel (July & Aug daily 10am–1pm & 3–7pm; June & Sept Wed–Sun 10am–1pm & 3–7pm; Oct–May Wed–Sun 2–6pm; ℡04.92.02.85.05).

Both Cagnes-sur-Mer and Cros-de-Cagnes have their own **gares SNCF**, while local **bus** routes centre on place M. Bourdet in Cagnes-sur-Mer. From there, bus #41 runs to Cros-de-Cagnes and the seafront; bus #49 to the Renoir museum; and #44 up to Haut-de-Cagnes.

Driving is phenomenally challenging, and nowhere more so than up in the narrow lanes of Haut-de-Cagnes. The extraordinary **car park** up in the hilltop village is well worth experiencing, however; you leave your vehicle in what looks like a car wash, from which it's whisked away and filed in some subterranean cavern until you return.

Accommodation

Although the largest choice of **hotels** is down in Cros-de-Cagnes, assuming you don't mind not being by the sea it's much nicer to stay up in the peace of Haut-de-Cagnes. There are also plenty of **campsites** around, most of them in wooded locations inland.

Hotels

Beaurivage 39 bd de la Plage, Cros-de-Cagnes ℡04.93.20.16.09, ⓦbeaurivage.biz. Neat little hotel, straight across from the beach; some rooms have sea-view balconies, but the ones at the back are much quieter. ❹

Le Cagnard 45 rue Sous Barri, Haut-de-Cagnes ℡04.93.20.73.21, ⓦcagnard.free.fr. Very comfortable rooms, some with sea views, tucked into the ancient castle guardroom up in the medieval hilltop village, with a good restaurant (see p.332). Closed mid-Nov to mid-Dec. ❼

Le Grimaldi 6 place du Château, Haut-de-Cagnes ℡04.93.20.60.24, ⓦhotelgrimaldi.com. Charming old village house, with five cosy modernized rooms, set behind a large terrace restaurant on the square, and adjoining the *Black Cat* jazz club. ❼

Les Terrasses du Soleil place Notre Dame de la Protection, Haut-de-Cagnes ℡04.93.73.26.56, ⓦwww.terrassesdusoleil.com. Attractive *chambre*

d'hôte in the former village home of songwriter Georges Ulmer, with two B&B rooms and two suites. ❻

Turf 13 rue des Capucines, Cros-de-Cagnes ℡04.93.20.64.00. Simple but perfectly adequate rooms, in a motel-like building set back slightly from the seafront. ❸

Campsites

Todos 159 chemin Vallon des Vaux ℡04.93.31.20.05, ⓦwww.homair.com. Three-star site 4km north of Cros-de-Cagnes, with a large heated pool, bar and restaurant. €24 per tent. Closed mid-Sept to early May.

Val de Fleuri 139 chemin Vallon des Vaux ℡04.93.31.21.74, ⓦcampingvalfleuri.fr. Well-equipped two-star site, adjacent to *Le Todos* 4km from the sea, with a pool and children's playground. €19.50 per tent. Closed Nov to mid-Feb.

Renoir's house

Surrounded by olive and rare orange groves on the chemin des Collettes, around 1km east of Cagnes-sur-Mer up avenue Renoir, **Les Collettes**, the house that **Renoir** had built in 1907 and where he spent the last twelve years of his life, is now the **Musée Renoir** (daily except Tues: May–Oct 10am–noon & 2–6pm; Nov–April 10am–noon & 2–5pm; closed first week Dec; €4, or €6 with Château-Musée Grimaldi). Renoir was captivated by the olive trees and by the difficulties of rendering "a tree full of colours". One of the two studios in the house, north-facing to catch the late afternoon light, is arranged as though Renoir had just popped out. Despite the rheumatoid arthritis that had forced him to seek a warmer climate than Paris, he painted every day at Les Collettes, strapping the brush to his hand when moving his fingers became too painful.

Portraits of Renoir here by his closest friends, displayed in the house, include Albert André's *À Renoir Peignant*, showing the ageing artist hunching over his canvas; a bust by Aristide Maillol; a crayon sketch by Richard Guido; and Dufy's *Homage to Renoir*. Renoir's work is represented by several sculptures including two bronzes – *La Maternité* and a medallion of his son Coco – some beautiful, tiny watercolours in the studio, and ten paintings from his Cagnes period (the greatest, the final version of *Les Grandes Baigneuses*, hangs in the Louvre).

Haut-de-Cagnes

For many years the haunt of successful artists, **HAUT-DE-CAGNES**, an easy walk up from Cagnes-sur-Mer and also accessible on bus #44, is as perfect a hilltop village as you'll find on the Riviera. No architectural excrescences spoil the tiers of tiny streets, and even the flowers spilling over terracotta pots or climbing soft stone walls appear perfect.

The ancient village backs up to the crenellated **château**, which once belonged to the Grimaldis of Monaco and now houses the **Château-Musée Grimaldi** (daily except Tues: May–Oct 10am–noon & 2–6pm; Nov–April 10am–noon & 2–5pm; €4, or €6 with Renoir's house), comprising the **Musée de l'Olivier**, the **Donation Solidor** and exhibition space for **contemporary art**. The castle's Renaissance interior is itself a masterpiece, with tiers of arcaded galleries, vast frescoed ceilings, stuccoed historical reliefs and gorgeously ornamented chambers and chapels. The Donation Solidor consists of wonderfully diverse portraits of cabaret star Suzy Solidor, by the likes of Dufy, Cocteau, Laurençin, Lempicka, Van Dongen and Kisling. Solidor's career spanned the 1920s to the 1970s, and she spent her last 25 years in Cagnes. She was quite a character: extremely talented, independent and sexy, she declared herself a lesbian years before the word, let alone the preference, was remotely acceptable, and was the inspiration for the British music-hall song "*If you knew Suzy, like I know Suzy*". Each canvas clearly reveals the qualities that most endeared her to each artist, or the fantasies she provoked, giving a fascinating insight into the art of portraiture as well as a multi-faceted image of the woman.

Eating, drinking and nightlife

Haut-de-Cagnes and Cros-de-Cagnes hold the finest local **restaurants**, while for café lounging, the squares to either side of the castle in Haut-de-Cagnes are the obvious spots. In July and August, the place du Château here hosts open-air jazz concerts, and it holds a year-round jazz club, *Le Black Cat*, at no. 4 (Wed–Sun 7pm–2am; ℡04.92.08.04.69, ⊛leblackcat.fr), which usually has live music on Fridays and Saturdays from 9pm.

Restaurants

Le Cagnard 45 rue Sous Barri, Haut-de-Cagnes ℡04.93.20.73.21, ⊛cagnard.free.fr. Exceptionally smart and expensive restaurant in the medieval village, serving delicious, refined menus that start at €58 lunch, €76 dinner. Closed mid-Nov to mid-Dec.

Fleur de Sel 85 montée de la Bourgade, Haut-de-Cagnes ℡04.92.20.33.33, ⊛www.restaurant -fleurdesel.com. Delicious Provençal cuisine, such as slow-roasted bream with ratatouille or octopus salad, served in a lovely old hilltop house. Menus range €33–56. Closed Wed & Thurs lunch, plus two weeks in Jan.

Josy-Jo 2 rue du Planastel, Haut-de-Cagnes ℡04.93.20.68.76. Provençal delicacies dished up in the space that served as Soutine's workshop in the interwar years, on menus at €30 and €42. Closed Sat lunch, Sun & mid-Nov to late Dec.

Le Neptune 3 bd de la Plage, Cros-de-Cagnes ℡04.93.20.10.59, ⊛leneptunerestaurantplage .com. Attractive beachfront restaurant, with parasol-shaded tables and fine seafood. Lunch menus from €14, dinner from €20.

Grasse

GRASSE, which enjoys stunning uninterrupted views over the Côte d'Azur from its hillside location 16km inland from Cannes, has been capital of the **perfume industry** for almost three hundred years. While still home to several leading *parfumiers*, and assiduously promoting its image as a sweet-smelling tourist destination, it's

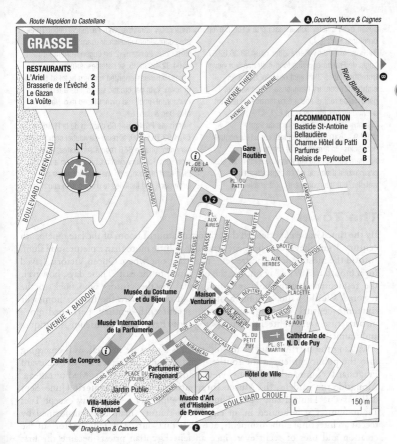

GRASSE

RESTAURANTS

L'Ariel	2
Brasserie de l'Évêché	3
Le Gazan	4
La Voûte	1

ACCOMMODATION

Bastide St-Antoine	E
Bellaudière	A
Charme Hôtel du Patti	D
Parfums	C
Relais de Peyloubet	B

Draguignan & Cannes

a far cry now from the medieval town depicted in Patrick Süskind's novel *Perfume*. If you're at all interested in the scent business, the various museums and factories make Grasse worthy of a day-trip, and for that matter it has a gritty sense of being a genuine lived-in community that many of its neighbours lack, but it's not really a place to plan a long stay.

Arrival, information and accommodation

Grasse's former casino, on cours Honoré-Cresp on the uphill side of the central gardens, houses the main **tourist office** (July to mid-Sept Mon–Sat 9am–7pm, Sun 9am–1pm & 2–6pm; mid-Sept to June Mon–Sat 9am–12.30pm & 2–6pm; ☎04.93.36.66.66, ⓦgrasse-riviera.com). There's no train station, but the **gare routière** is on the north side of the Vieille Ville at the Notre-Dames-des-Fleurs car park, with an annexe of the tourist office nearby on avenue Thiers (same hours).

Not only does the centre of Grasse holds surprisingly few **hotels**, but some of the few there are – like the prominent *Panorama* – are best avoided. You may well prefer to stay in more rural locations nearby.

Hotels

Bastide St-Antoine 48 av Henri-Dunant
☎04.93.70.94.94, ⓦjacques-chibois.com.

Gorgeous and extremely luxurious country-house hotel, 1km south of the centre, that's best known for its restaurant (see p.336). Its nine rooms and seven even fancier suites cost up to €1000; even breakfast is €29. ❾

Bellaudière 78 av Pierre Ziller ☎04.93.36.02.57. Logis de France enjoying long-distance sea views from the slopes 3km east of town. Set in an eighteenth-century farmhouse, it has simple, good-value rooms and a nice terrace restaurant, serving dinner menus from €21. ❹

Charme Hôtel du Patti place du Patti ☎04.93.36.01.00, ⓦhotelpatti.com. This central hotel, close to a multistorey car park on the northern edge of the old town, is much more like a chain motel than you might expect from its website, but the rooms are comfortable and

reasonably attractive, with Provençal decor. Three are adapted for wheelchair users. ❺

Hôtel des Parfums 2 bd Eugène-Charabot ☎04.92.42.35.35, ⓦhoteldesparfums.com. Large, business-oriented modern hotel at the top of town, with panoramic views plus a terrace restaurant, pool and gym. Closed mid-Nov to mid-Dec & Jan. ❻

Relais de Peyloubet 65 chemin de la Plâtrière ☎04.93.70.69.90, ⓦrelais-peyloubet.com.fr. Five very comfortable B&B rooms and suites, in an eighteenth-century *bastide*, perched on a hillside 2km east of town, with magnificent views and a large pool, and facilities to barbecue in summer. ❻

The Town

By the time Grasse experienced the aristocratic tourist boom of the late nineteenth century, its medieval core has degenerated into little more than a picturesque slum. Instead the most desirable addresses – including one where Queen Victoria stayed for a month in 1891 – lay outside the old town, to the east. These days, however, the residential suburbs hold minimal appeal for the visitors who flock to the restored **Vieille Ville**, a hubbub of life and noise where the former homes of sixteenth-century tanning merchants, seventeenth-century perfumed-glove manufacturers and eighteenth-century *parfumiers* have become museums, boutiques and municipal offices.

Walking the narrow lanes of the old town is a pleasure in itself, as is emerging into the public gardens at the southern end, where the terrace above Boulevard Fragonard commands fabulous views down to the distant Mediterranean. Alongside the gardens, the **Musée International de la Parfumerie** (June–Sept daily except Thurs 10am–7pm, Thurs 10am–9pm; Oct–May daily except Tues 11am–6pm; €3) is housed in an eighteenth-century mansion, transformed by recent architectural embellishments, at 8 place du Cours. This tells the story of the creation and uses of scent ever since ancient Egyptian priests became the first *parfumiers*, along with a fascinating parallel account of how perfumes have been marketed and sold – often using Egyptian or other "exotic" iconography – and a general history of the beauty and make-up industries. Prize exhibits include a travelling case that belonged to Marie Antoinette; there's also a greenhouse filled with gently scented herbs and flowers, and visits culminate with an account of the role Grasse has played in industrializing the whole process.

Just around the corner, the small, Fragonard-owned **Musée Provençal du Costume et du Bijou**, 2 rue Jean-Ossola (daily 10am–1pm & 2–6.30pm; free), does exactly what it claims. Besides a room filled with jewels, several more hold mannequins dressed in various traditional regional costumes, dimly lit to preserve their vivid colours.

Nearby at 2 rue Mirabeau, a luxurious town house commissioned by Mirabeau's sister now serves as the **Musée d'Art et d'Histoire de Provence** (June–Sept daily 10am–6.30pm; Oct & Dec–May daily except Tues 10am–12.30pm & 2–5.30pm; €3). As well as retaining many of its gorgeous fittings and original eighteenth-century kitchen, it displays a historical collection that includes wonderful eighteenth- to nineteenth-century faïence from Apt and Le Castellet, Mirabeau's death mask, a tin bidet, six prehistoric bronze leg bracelets, *santons* and oil presses.

At the opposite end of the gardens, the delightful **Villa-Musée Fragonard** (same hours and fee as **Musée d'Art et d'Histoire**), 23 boulevard Fragonard, celebrates

Rococo painter Jean-Honoré Fragonard. The son of an early and not very successful Grassois perfumed-glove maker, he returned to live in this villa when his work fell out of favour after the Revolution. The staircase features impressive wall paintings by his son Alexandre-Evariste, while the salon is graced by copies of the panels depicting *Love's Progress in the Heart of a Young Girl*, which Jean-Honoré painted for Louis XV's mistress, Madame du Barry.

Cradled in the alleyways at the south end of the old town, the former **Bishop's Palace** – now the Hôtel de Ville – and the cathedral (daily: July–Sept 9.30–11.30am & 3–6.30pm, Oct–June 9.30–11.30am & 3–5.30pm) were built in the twelfth century, replacing a two-hundred-year-old fortress. Despite endless alterations, the cathedral still has its high gaunt nave, in which the starkly unadorned ribbed vaulting is supported from the side walls. Its astonishing, weighty columns and the walls surrounding the altar were fractured in a fierce fire after the Revolution, giving the masonry an incredible, organic cave-like feel.

Scents and Sensibility: the parfumeries of Grasse

Making perfume is usually presented as a mysterious process, an alchemy, turning the soul of the flower into a liquid of luxury and desire. The reality, including traditional methods of *macération* – mixing the blossoms with heated animal fat – and *enfleuration* – placing the flowers on cold fat, then washing the result with alcohol and finally distilling it into the ultimately refined essence – is distinctly less romantic, but every bit as intriguing.

Around thirty major **parfumeries** are located in and around Grasse, most of them producing the different essences-plus-formulas that are then sold to Dior, Lancôme, Estée Lauder and the like, for use in their own brand-name perfumes. Although synthetic ingredients have long formed an essential part of their repertoire, they still use copious amounts of locally grown lavender, jasmine and roses. To extract 1kg of essence of lavender takes 200kg of lavender; for 1kg of cabbage rose essence, over 3000kg of roses are needed. Perfume contains twenty percent essence (eau de toilette contains ten percent; eau de Cologne five or six percent) and the bottles are extremely small. The major cost to this multi-billion-pound business is marketing. On strictly cost-accounting grounds, the clothes created by the grand Parisian couturiers serve simply to promote their latest fragrances.

For a fairly close-up look at production, visit the **Parfumerie Fragonard** (Feb–Oct daily 9am–6pm; Nov–Jan Mon–Sat 9am–12.30pm & 2–6.30pm; free), which is spread over two venues. The first, the **Usine Historique** at 20 boulevard Fragonard, shows traditional methods of extracting essence and has a collection of antique cosmetics bottles and bejewelled flagons. The second, the **Fabrique des Fleurs** at Les Quatre Chemins outside town, 3km towards Cannes, is more informative, and at least admits to modernization of the processes. A world map shows the origins of various strange ingredients: resins, roots, moss, beans, civet (extract of a wild cat's genitals), ambergris (whale intestines), bits of beaver, and musk from Tibetan goats all help to produce the array of scents that the "nose" – as the creator of the perfume's formula is known – has to play with. A professional "nose" (of whom there are fewer than fifty) can recognize five or six thousand different scents.

Other *parfumeries* offering free tours in French and English include **Galimard** at 73 route de Cannes (guided visits daily: summer 9am–6.30pm; winter 9am–12.30pm & 2–6pm; free) and at 5 route de Pégomas (two-hour workshops by appointment at 10am, 2pm & 4pm; €45; you create your own fragrance under the guidance of a master *parfumeur*; ☎04.93.09.20.00, ⊛galimard.com); **Molinard** at 60 boulevard Victor-Hugo (March–Sept daily 9am–6.30pm; Oct–Feb Mon–Sat 9am–12.30pm & 2–6pm; free; ⊛molinard.com); and **Fleuron de Grasse**, 190 route de Pégomas (July & Aug Mon–Sat 8.30am–noon & 1.30–7pm; Sept–June Mon–Fri 8.30–11.45am & 1.30–5pm; free).

Place aux Aires, further north, hosts a daily **flower and vegetable market** (mornings only). Ringed by arcades of different heights, it was at one time the exclusive preserve of the tanning industry.

Eating and drinking

Old Grasse is disappointingly short of good **restaurants**, though one or two hidden gems are tucked away on the lanes. As for **bars**, place aux Aires offers the best chance to meet the locals; *L'Ariel* is a good place to start. If you want to make your own picnic, *Maison Venturini*, 1 rue Marcel-Journet (closed Sun & Mon), sells fabulous sweet *fougassettes*, flavoured with the Grasse speciality of orange blossom.

Restaurants

Bastide St-Antoine 48 av Henri-Dunant ⊕04.93.70.94.94, ⊛jacques-chibois.com. Grasse's finest restaurant is at the bougainvillea-bedecked hotel of the same name on the south side of town (see p.333); owner Jacques Chibois is a former Gault Millau chef of the year. Lunch menus at €59, or €145 on Sunday; dinner is €190.

Brasserie de l'Évêché 9 place de l'Évêché ⊕04.93.36.40.12. This friendly informal brasserie, facing the fountains in a pretty square below the

cathedral, serves decent lunch menus from €15.

Le Gazan 3 rue Gazan ⊕04.93.36.22.88. Friendly and very traditional little place, in the heart of the old town, with a small terrace and intimate dining room. Menus from €20 lunch, €27 dinner. Closed Fri eve, Sat eve & all Sun in winter.

La Voûte 3 rue du Thouron ⊕04.93.36.11.43. Popular local restaurant in the old town, serving up pizzas as well as Provençal specialities from its wood-fired oven, with dinner menus at €22 and €26, and open-air seating in summer.

Around Grasse

The main highlight of the countryside immediately surrounding Grasse is the attractive village of **Cabris**, but two routes out of the area offer wonderful scenic views. The **Route Napoléon** heads northwest through the mountains towards Castellane, while to the northeast the gorges of the **Loup River** pass the cliff-hanging stronghold of **Gourdon**, and **Le-Bar-sur-Loup**'s reminders of mortality. East of the river, the hillside road towards Vence holds one final treat, the delightful village of **Tourrettes-sur-Loup**.

Cabris

CABRIS, just 6km southwest of Grasse, has all the trappings of a picture-postcard village: a ruined château providing panoramas from the Lac de St-Cassien to the Îles de Lérins, sometimes even Corsica; arty residents who decamped here from Grasse; and no shortage of *immobiliers* trading on fat local property prices. The best place to **stay** is the lovely *Auberge du Vieux Château* on place Mirabeau (⊕04.93.60.50.12, ⊛aubergeduvieuxchateau.com; ❹), with wonderful views, though dinner menus in its high-class dining room (closed Mon & Tues Sept–June) start at €45. Delicacies at the warm and welcoming *Petit Prince* **restaurant**, overlooking a park lined with chestnut trees at 15 rue Frédéric-Mistral (⊕04.93.60.63.14, ⊛lepetitprince-cabris.com; closed Wed, plus Tues Sept–June), include a *parmentier* of *boudin noir* with apples and a cider sauce. Menus cost €23–33.

The Route Napoléon: St-Vallier-de-Thiey

Built in the 1930s to commemorate the path taken by the emperor in March 1815 after his escape from Elba, the D6085 north from Grasse is known as the **Route Napoléon**. The road doesn't follow the imperial boot-tracks precisely, going far off course in places, but it serves a useful purpose. After several kilometres of zigzagging bends you get fantastic views back to Grasse, its basin and the coast.

The first village you come to – **ST-VALLIER-DE-THIEY**, 12km from Grasse – holds some prehistoric dolmens and tumuli. The **tourist office** at 10 place du Tour (March–Oct Mon–Sat 9am–noon & 3–6pm; Nov–Feb 9am–noon & 3–5pm; ℡04.93.42.78.00, ⓦsaintvallier.ifrance.com) can provide a walking map of how to find them. *Le Préjoly*, a presentable little **hotel** on place Rougière at the entrance to the village (℡04.93.60.03.20, ⓦleprejoly.com; ❹; closed Jan), adjoins a restaurant with the same name but different management (℡04.93.42.60.86, menus €18–37, closed Sun eve, Tues eve & Wed in low season). There's also a **campsite** nearby, the three-star *Parc des Arboins* on the Route Napoléon (℡04.93.42.63.89).

Beyond St-Vallier, the Route Napoléon heads, almost uninterrupted by settlements, towards Castellane (see p.226). Wayside stalls sell honey and perfume; each little hamlet has a petrol station and hotel-restaurant; and every so often you see a commemorative plaque carved with Napoleon's winged eagle.

Along the Gorges de Loup

Of the two alternative routes that follow the stunning Gorges de Loup, the lower, along the east bank of the Loup, is the more compelling. Both leave the main D2085 at **Châteauneuf-Grasse**, 6km east from Grasse.

Le-Bar-sur-Loup

The lower road, the D2210, passes through **LE-BAR-SUR-LOUP** after just 3.5km. The little **Église de St-Jacques** here contains an altarpiece attributed to the Niçois painter, Louis Bréa, and a tiny but detailed fifteenth-century *Danse Macabre*, painted on a wooden panel. This latter shows courtly dancers being picked off by Death's arrows, and their souls being thrown by devils into the toothed and tongued mouth of hell. Alongside, a Provençal poem warns of the heavy risk involved in committing such grievous sins as dancing.

From here, you can follow the **gorges road** itself, the D6, through dark, narrow twists of rock beneath cliffs that look as if they might tumble at any minute, through the sounds of furiously churning water, to corners that appear to have no way out.

Gourdon

The higher of the two roads from **Châteauneuf-Grasse**, the D3, climbs 8km along the northern balcony of the gorges to tiny **GOURDON**, a *village perché* teetering on the very brink of the abyss. Though the village itself is swamped in souvenir shops, the view from place Victoria at the top is extraordinary.

Gourdon also holds a redoubtable immaculately restored, privately owned **château**, which contains **museums** of history (June–Sept daily 11am–1pm & 2–7pm; Oct–May daily except Tues 2–6pm; €5; ⓦchateau-gourdon.com), and **decorative and modern arts** (guided tours only: July & Aug noon, 3pm & 5pm; Sept–June by appointment; €10).

Gourdon's best **restaurant**, *Le Nid d'Aigle*, at the top of the village on place Victoria (℡04.93.77.52.02, ⓦnid-daigle.fr; closed Mon eve & Fri), enjoys breathtaking views, and serves brasserie menus from €22 for lunch, €37 for dinner.

Tourrettes-sur-Loup

At the southern end of the Gorges du Loup, 3km north of Le-Bar-sur-Loup, the D6 on the east bank meets the D2210, which climbs away east from the river towards Vence. Eight kilometres along, and just 6km west of Vence,

TOURRETTES-SUR-LOUP is an artisans' paradise, preserving just the right balance between crumbly attractiveness and modern comforts. The three towers from which the village derives its name – and the rose-stone houses that cling to the high escarpment – almost all date from the fifteenth century; the best views can be had from the curious rock shelf known as Les Loves, just above the town.

The oldest and most charming part of the village is accessed via two gateways that lead south from the main place de la Libération, which adjoins the D2210. Beyond the fine portals, the Grande Rue loops between the two, lined with expensive ateliers selling clothes, sculpture, jewellery, leather, fine art and the like. A viewing platform at the southern end commands a majestic prospect all the way to the Mediterranean.

During Tourrettes' famous **violet festival**, on the first or second Sunday in March, floats are decorated with thousands of blooms. Violets, which thrive in the mild microclimate, are grown here in vast quantities for the perfume trade as well as for subsidiary cottage industries such as old-fashioned candied violets.

Practicalities

Unlike so many hill villages, Tourrettes is readily accessible by **car**. There's usually room to park in the main place de la Libération, alongside the D2210, where the local **tourist office** is at no. 2 (July & Aug daily 10am–1pm & 2.30–6.30pm; Sept–June Mon–Sat 10am–1pm & 2–5.30pm; ☏04.93.24.18.93, ⓦwww .tourrettessurloup.com).

Tourrettes' classiest **accommodation** option is the ⚑ *L'Auberge de Tourrettes*, on the edge of the village at 11 route de Grasse (☏04.93.59.30.05, ⓦwww.auberge detourrettes.fr; ⑥), where most of the tasteful and very comfortable bedrooms enjoy great views. Three-star local **campsites** include the *Camassade*, 523 route de Pie-Lombard (☏04.93.59.31.54, ⓦcamassade.com; €23.50), 3km west towards Pont du Loup and, further west, the fancier *Rives du Loup*, 2666b route de la Colle (☏04.93.24.15.65, ⓦrivesduloup.com; tents €25.50, rooms ④; closed Oct– March), which also offers hotel-style rooms.

Good **restaurants** dotted around the historic core include the *Médiéval*, 6 Grand Rue (☏04.93.59.31.63; menus at €25 and €35; closed Wed & Thurs); the upscale *Bacchanales*, 21 Grand Rue (☏04.93.58.87.04; menus €30–48; closed Mon & Tues); and the quirky *Lou Coucoun*, in a cellar at 1 rue du Château (☏04.93.24.16.12; closed Sun pm & Mon), which serves *socca* pancakes for €10 or a *plat du jour* for €11.50. Be sure to try the local violet-flavoured **ice cream** while you're in Tourrettes, too.

Vence

Sheltered by the Pre-Alpes that rise to its rear, the delightful hill town of **VENCE**, 10km up from the sea, is unusual in having an appealing modern quarter that for once complements rather than simply engulfs its ravishing, walled historic core, **Vieux Vence**. It helps, of course, that **Henri Matisse** chose the new town as the site of his magnificent **Chapelle du Rosaire**, but more generally the bustle of the boulevards outside the walls, and particularly the lively cafés of the main place du Grand-Jardin, make a welcome contrast to the tranquil ancient lanes of the old town.

Vence was originally founded by a Ligurian tribe, the Nerusii. They put up stiff opposition to Augustus Caesar, but to no avail; Roman funeral inscriptions and votive offerings remain embedded in the fabric of its cathedral. During the Dark Ages, the local bishop, **Saint Véran**, organized the city's defence; after his death in 481 he was canonized by popular request. The Saracens, however, subsequently razed both the town and St-Véran's cathedral to the ground. Thereafter, Vence was plagued until the Revolution by rivalry between its barons and its bishops.

In the 1920s Vence became a haven for painters and writers, including André Gide, Paul Valéry, Soutine, Dufy and D.H. Lawrence, who died here in 1930. Matisse moved here near the end of World War II, to escape the Allied bombing of the coast.

Arrival, information and accommodation

The main square of the new town, place du Grand-Jardin beside the western gateway of Vieux Vence, holds the **tourist office** (July & Aug Mon–Sat 9am–7pm, Sun 10am–6pm; March–June & Sept–Oct Mon–Sat 9am–6pm; Nov–Feb Mon–Sat 9am–5pm; ℡04.93.58.06.38, Ⓦvence.fr), the **gare routière**, and a large underground **car park**. You can hire **bikes** from Vence Motos on avenue Henri Isnard (℡04.93.58.56.00).

As well as attracting visitors in its own right, Vence is very popular as a peaceful base for trips not just in the surrounding hills but down to the coast, and holds an excellent range of well-priced **hotels**.

Hotels

Closerie des Genêts 4 impasse Maurel ℡04.93.58.35.18. Peaceful, slightly old-fashioned and very welcoming ten-room hotel on the southern edge of Vieux Vence, with an attractive garden and sea views from some rooms. The good-value restaurant is closed Sun & Mon. ❸

Diana 79 av des Poilus ℡04.93.58.28.56, Ⓦhotel-diana.fr. Modern building in a quiet and convenient location just 200m from the centre, and enjoying lovely views. Comfortable rooms, some with balconies and half with kitchenettes, and an open-air jacuzzi. ❺

Provence 9 av Marcellin-Maurel ℡04.93.58.04.21, Ⓦhotelleprovence.com. Quirky, arty little hotel, just across from the old town but hidden from the main road behind a bougainvillea-, fuschia- and rose-choked garden. The rooms may need a little refreshing, but they're stylish in a shabby Provençal-chic sort of way, and throwing up the shutters to see the garden in the morning – let alone enjoying breakfast down there – is priceless. ❸

Auberge des Seigneurs place du Frêne ℡04.93.58.04.24, Ⓦauberge-seigneurs.com.

Lovely, very friendly old inn, just within Vieux Vence, with six rooms named after the painters who lodged there; the food is excellent. Closed Nov to mid-March. ❺

Victoire 4 place du Grand-Jardin ℡04.93.24.15.54, Ⓦhotel-victoire.com. Sound-proofed, very central hotel beside the tourist office on the main new-town square, and offering spruced-up rooms at reasonable prices. ❹

Villa Roseraie 14 av H-Giraud ℡04.93.58.02.20, Ⓦwww.villaroseraie.com. Classic, rich Provençal nineteenth-century inn on the road to the Col de Vence northwest of town, with ancient cedars and magnolias overhanging the terrace. Charming reception, tasteful rooms, and a lovely garden pool. Closed Nov to mid-Dec, Jan 7 to mid-Feb. ❻

Campsite

Domaine de la Bergerie rte de la Sine ℡04.93.58.09.36, Ⓦcamping-domainedela bergerie.com. Three-star site in the woods 2km west off the road to Tourrettes-sur-Loup, with a summer-only pool and restaurant. Closed mid-Oct to late March. €22 per tent.

The Town

Any visit to Vence should be timed to ensure that you get to see **Matisse's chapel** in the new town, which is only open for limited hours. Killing some time in the diminutive old town of **Vieux Vence** is hardly a chore, however – with its ancient houses, gateways, fountains and chapels, it's absolutely exquisite. While holding its fair share of chic boutiques and arty restaurants, it also has an everyday feel with ordinary people going about their business, seeking out the best market deals, and stopping for a chat and a *petit verre* at little cafés.

Vieux Vence

Vence's castle, the **Château de Villeneuve Fondation Emile Hugues** (summer Tues–Sun 10am–6pm; winter Tues–Sun 10am–12.30pm & 2–6pm; €5), was built just outside the city walls during a calm period of fifteenth-century expansion. Rebuilt in the seventeenth century, it was renovated in 1992 to become a beautiful temporary exhibition space for works by artists like Matisse, Dufy, Dubuffet and Chagall – all associated with the town – along with other modern and contemporary art. Out in front, **place du Frêne** is named for its 450-year-old ash tree.

The **Porte du Peyra**, and the tower that surmounts it, which have remained more or less untouched since the twelfth century, provide the best entry into Vieux Vence. **Place du Peyra**, within the medieval walls, has the town's oldest fountain. The narrow, cobbled **rue du Marché** off to the right is a busy street of tiny and delectable food shops, all with stalls (and all closed Mon). Behind it, **place Clemenceau**, centring on the cathedral, hosts a Tuesday and Friday clothes **market**.

St-Véran Cathedral is a tenth- and eleventh-century replacement for the church over which St-Véran presided in the fifth century, which had in turn been built on the ruins of a Roman temple to Mars and Cybele. Like so many of the oldest Provençal churches, it's basically square in shape, with an austere exterior. Although centuries of subsequent alterations have left none of the clear lines of Romanesque architecture, fragments of its Merovingian and Carolingian predecessors, and of Roman Vence, still remain. In the chapel beneath the belfry, two reliefs from the old church show birds, grapes and an eagle, while more stone birds, flowers, swirls of leaves and interlocking lines are embedded in the walls and pillars throughout the church. The purported **tomb of St-Véran**, in the southern chapel nearest the altar, is a pre-Christian sarcophagus. Later adornments include some superb, irreverent Gothic carved **choir stalls**, housed alongside powerfully human, if crude, polychrome wooden statues of the Calvary, up above the western end of the nave. In the baptistry, a Chagall **mosaic** depicts the infant Moses being saved from the Nile by the Pharaoh's daughter.

East of the cathedral, **place Godeau** is almost totally medieval save for the column in the fountain, presented to the city, along with its twin on place du Grand-Jardin, by the Republic of Marseille during the third century. Follow rue St-Lambert and rue de l'Hôtel-de-Ville down from here to reach the original eastern gate, the **Porte du Signadour**, outside which another fifteenth-century fountain on place Antony-Mars celebrates the town's expansion.

Matisse's Chapelle du Rosaire

It's worth travelling a very long way indeed to see the ravishing and profoundly moving Chapelle du Rosaire (Mon, Wed & Sat 2–5.30pm, Tues & Thurs 10–11.30am & 2–5.30pm, Sunday Mass 10am; usually also open Fri 2–5.30pm during school hols, check with the tourist office; closed mid-Nov to mid-Dec; €2.60), which Henri Matisse spent four of the final years of his life designing in every meticulous detail. Matisse was too ill to attend its dedication in 1951, but in a statement read out at the ceremony he said "in spite of all its imperfections, I consider it as my masterpiece". Inconspicuous but for its blue-and-white tiled roof, topped by a wrought-iron cross, the simple modern structure stands beside the D2210 to St-Jeannet, 1km east of old Vence, at 466 avenue Henri-Matisse.

In 1941, while convalescing from an operation for cancer, Matisse advertised for a "young and pretty nurse". Having developed a strong rapport with successful applicant Monique Bourgeois, who also posed for him, he bought a home in Vence after she joined the Dominican convent here, in 1943, as sister Jacques-Marie.

Although he did not consider himself a Christian, Matisse agreed to help the young nun with the new convent chapel; as he later put it "my only religion is the love of the work to be created, the love of creation, and great sincerity".

The artist moved back to his huge rooms in Nice in 1949, to work on the designs using the same scale as the chapel. A photograph shows him in bed, drawing studies for the figure of St-Dominic on the wall with a paintbrush tied to a long bamboo stick. It's not clear how much this bamboo technique was a practical solution to his frailty, and how much a solution to an artistic problem. Some critics suggest Matisse wanted to pare down his art to the basic essentials of human communication, and thus needed to remove his own stylistic signature from the lines.

The **murals** on the chapel walls – faceless black outlines on white tiles – so thoroughly achieve this goal that some visitors are disappointed, not finding the "Matisse" they expect. The east wall is the most shocking; it shows the *Stations of the Cross*, each one numbered and scrawled as if it were an angry doodle on a pad. The full-length windows in the west and south walls are the aspect of the chapel most likely to live up to expectations. They provide the only source of colour, which changes with the day's light through opaque yellow, transparent green and watery blue, playing across the black-and-white murals, floor and ceiling.

Despite the prominent signs requesting silence, the chapel repeatedly fills with excited, chattering tour groups. A nun is usually on hand to calm things down, and point out the symbolism of every aspect of Matisse's vision: the overall configuration of the chapel; the stone of the east-facing altar, chosen for its resemblance to bread; the raw anguish of the figures; the door of the confessional, alluding to the artist's trips to Morocco; and the chasubles, crucifix and candelabra. Matisse was even responsible for the various resplendently colourful silk **vestments**, matching different moments in the liturgical calendar; ideally you'd see them worn by the priest at Sunday Mass, but during the week they're displayed in the gallery beyond, which also holds a gift shop.

Eating, drinking and nightlife

The squares and lanes of Vieux Vence abound in **restaurants**, **bars** and **cafés** in all price ranges, and there are also several appealing alternatives in the newer streets beyond.

Between early July and early August, in **Les Nuits du Sud** (@nuitsdusud.com), big-name Latin and World musicians perform open-air concerts on the place du Grand-Jardin, mostly on Friday and Saturday evenings.

Restaurants

Les Agnes 4 place Clemenceau ☎04.93.58.50.64. Lively old-town restaurant, close to the cathedral, serving Provençal dishes like roast salmon with sun-dried tomato risotto on dinner menus at €23 and €29. Closed Sun & Mon.

La Farigoule 15 av Henri-Isnard ☎04.93.58.01.27, @lafarigoule-vence.fr. Formal restaurant, just outside the old town behind the tourist office, where you can eat indoors or in a smart little courtyard. Dinner menus at €29.50 and €39.50 offer small, precise portions of exquisitely flavoured dishes such as roast cod, and excellent desserts. Closed Tues.

La Litote 5 rue l'Évêché ☎04.93.24.27.82, @lalitote.com. The outdoor tables of this lovely, secluded old-town restaurant fill the delightful little place de l'Évêché, beneath its single spreading tree. Changing daily menus of Provençal specialities, including *bouillabaisse*, start at €15.50 for lunch, €25 for dinner. Closed Sun eve & all Mon, plus Tues mid-Nov to mid-Dec, and second half of Jan.

Pêcheur du Soleil 1 place Godeau ☎04.93.58.32.56. An astounding choice of pizzas from €8.50, in a pretty location close to the cathedral. Closed Mon.

St-Paul-de-Vence

The beautiful fortified village of **ST-PAUL-DE-VENCE** squeezes onto a hilltop just 3km south of Vence towards Cagnes, although the combination of twisting roads and undulating hills can make it unexpectedly hard to find. While the village itself is a delight, and is usually crammed with visitors throughout the summer, its popularity owes as much to the **Fondation Maeght**, a wonderful museum of modern art and sculpture tucked into the woods nearby, as it does to its medieval core.

The village

St-Paul stands on its own separate eminence alongside the D7. You can't miss its most famous landmark, right outside the walls on the only approach road – the **Colombe d'Or**, a hotel-restaurant (see opposite) that's celebrated not so much for its food as for the art on its walls, donated in lieu of payment for meals by the then-impoverished Braque, Picasso, Matisse and Bonnard in the lean years following World War I.

Beyond that, you pass through the ramparts to find a miniature jewel of a village, where the old stone cottages that line the winding lanes hold around seventy contemporary art galleries and ateliers. Most of those are concentrated along the central rue Grande, so it's normally possible to escape the crowds simply by exploring any alleyway that catches your eye, or heading for the walls. At the far end of the village, a little **cemetery** (daily: summer 7.30am–8pm; winter 8am–5pm) outside the ramparts, perched above the fields, holds the simple grave

▲ *Boules* players, St-Paul-de-Vence

of **Marc Chagall**. There's also a peculiar little local history **museum** on place de l'Église (daily: April–Oct 10am–noon & 3–6pm; Dec–March 2–5pm; €3), with historical dioramas to tempt anyone weary of shopping.

Fondation Maeght

The remarkable **Fondation Maeght**, which opened in 1964 ten minutes' walk west of the village (daily: July–Sept 10am–7pm; Oct–June 10am–6pm; Ⓦwww .fondation-maeght.com; €11), is the artistic centre that most fully represents the link between the Côte d'Azur and modern European art. It was established by art collectors Aimé and Marguerite Maeght, who knew all the great artists who worked in Provence. Spanish architect José Luis Sert was commissioned to design the building, and assorted painters, sculptors, potters and designers to decorate it. Both structure and ornamentation were conceived as a single project, with the aim of creating a museum in which the concepts of entrance, exit and *sense de la visite* would not apply.

Once through the gates, any idea of dutifully checking off a catalogue of priceless museum pieces crumbles. Giacometti's *Cat* is sometimes stalking along the edge of the grass, Miró's *Egg* smiles above a pond, and his totemed *Fork* is outlined against the sky. It's hard not to be bewitched by the Calder mobile swinging over watery tiles, by Léger's flowers, birds and a bench on a sunlit rough stone wall, by Zadkine's and Arp's metallic forms hovering between the pine trunks, or by the clanking tubular fountain by Pol Bury. And all this is just a portion of the garden.

The **building** itself is superb: multi-levelled and flooded with daylight, with galleries opening on to terraces and courtyards, blurring the boundaries between inside and outside. It houses an impressive collection, including sculpture, ceramics, paintings and graphic art by Braque, Miró, Chagall, Léger, Kandinsky, Dubuffet, Bonnard, Dérain and Matisse, along with more recent artists. Not all the works are exhibited at any one time, however, and in summer, when the main annual exhibition is mounted, only those that make up the decoration of the building are on show.

Practicalities

St-Paul's **tourist office** is where you first come into the walled village, at 2 rue Grande (June–Sept Mon–Fri 10am–7pm, Sat & Sun 10am–1pm & 2–7pm; Oct–May Mon–Fri 10am–6pm, Sat & Sun 10am–1pm & 2–6pm; ☏04.93.32.86.95, Ⓦsaint-pauldevence.com). The village is on **bus** route #400 between Nice and Vence, via Cagnes.

As most visitors just come for the day, St-Paul is a very quiet place to spend a night. **Accommodation** at the *Colombe d'Or*, described above (☏04.93.32.80.02, Ⓦwww.la-colombe-dor.com; ❾; closed late Oct to late Dec & first half of Jan), consists of comfortable wood-beamed rooms in a sixteenth-century house, with a pool alongside; the restaurant is all à la carte, with a lunchtime *plat du jour* at €25. The least expensive central option is the *Hostellerie Les Remparts de St-Paul*, in the heart of the village at 72 rue Grande (☏04.93.32.09.88, Ⓔhostellerie -lesremparts@orange.fr; ❹), where the en-suite rooms are pretty but far from luxurious, and a good-value restaurant (closed Sun pm & Mon) occupies a terrace with views out over the hills.

Eating in St-Paul seldom comes cheap, but a few reasonably priced options are scattered through the village, such as *La Sierra*, beside the western ramparts just below rue Grande (☏04.93.32.82.89), which has another lovely garden terrace and serves anything from an *assiette Provençal* for €15 or a *plat du jour* at €12 to pizzas and crêpes.

Travel details

Trains

Cannes to: Nice (approx every 20min peak time; 40min), via Juan-les-Pins (10min), Antibes (15min), Biot (18min), Villeneuve-Loubet-Plage (22min), Cagnes-sur-Mer (25min) and Cros-de-Cagnes (30min); Marseille (approx every 30min–1hr; 2hr); St-Raphaël (every 30min–1hr; 35min–1hr 5min).

Buses

Antibes to: Aéroport Nice-Côte-d'Azur (every 20min; 20–45min); Biot (hourly; 35–40min); Cannes (every 20min; 30–35min); Juan-les-Pins (every 20–30min; 8min); Nice (every 20min; 45min–1hr 10min); Vallauris (hourly; 25min).
Cannes to: Aéroport Nice-Côte-d'Azur (every 20min; 1hr 5min–1hr 15min); Antibes (every

20min; 25–35min); Cagnes *Gare SNCF* (every 20min; 50min–1hr); Le Cannet (every 15–30min; 20–25min); Golfe-Juan (every 20min; 15–20min); Grasse (every 20min; 40–50min); Mougins (every 20min; 20min); La Napoule (every 15–45min; 40min); Nice (every 20min; 1hr 20min–1hr 35min); Vallauris (every 30min; 15min).
Grasse to: Le-Bar-sur-Loup (11 daily; 15min); Cagnes (every 30–50min; 50min); Cannes (every 15–45min; 40min–1hr); Digne (1 daily; 2hr 25min); Mougins (every 15–45min; 20–30min); Nice (every 30–50min; 1hr 25min); St-Vallier (7 daily; 20–30min); Tourrettes-sur-Loup (3 daily; 30–45min); Vence (3 daily; 50–55min).
Vence to: Nice (approx every 30min; 50min), via St-Paul-de-Vence (5–10min) and Cagnes (25min).

8

Nice and the eastern Riviera

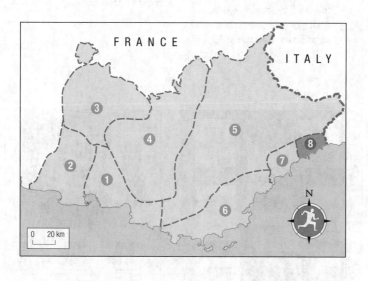

FRANCE

ITALY

8

N

0   20 km

CHAPTER 8

Highlights

✳ **Vieux Nice** From the flower market at dawn to bar-hopping in the early hours, Nice's mellow, Mediterranean heart buzzes with street life.
See p.354

✳ **Niçois villages** Explore craggy Peillon and unspoilt Lucéram, the *villages perchés* of Nice's wild and underpopulated hinterland, where villagers still live off the land, producing olives, goat's cheese, herbs and vegetables. See p.363 & p.365

✳ **Villa Ephrussi de Rothschild** Visit this handsome mansion and its exquisite gardens to find out how the other half used to live.
See p.369

✳ **Plage Mala** Relax on this secluded, idyllic Riviera beach just minutes from Monaco.
See p.371

✳ **The Casino at Monte Carlo** Break the bank at the world's most famous casino.
See p.378

▲ Vieux Nice facades

Nice and the eastern Riviera

E ast of the River Var, the Riviera is subtly different. For much of its history the coastline between Nice and the Italian border was part of the Kingdom of Savoy, only becoming securely French in 1860. Even today a certain Italian influence lingers, in the cooking of Nice and in the architecture of Vieux Nice, Villefranche and Menton. The landscape changes, too: east of Nice the Alpes-Maritimes come crashing down to the sea and the coastline is often thrillingly scenic.

The Riviera's largest city, **Nice** became fashionable as a winter resort in the eighteenth century, as aristocratic visitors – many of them invalids – made the journey south to escape the brutal northern winters. Right up to World War I they built their villas here or sojourned in the opulent palace hotels, most of which have long since been converted to apartments, though their architecture remains and often lends the city an appealing, eccentric face. Gradually, other resorts grew to rival Nice, each with its own speciality: **Menton** for tuberculosis sufferers, **Monte Carlo** in the comic-opera principality of Monaco with its casino.

After World War I many of the old aristocratic visitors never returned: they were dead, impoverished or scattered by revolution and war. In their place came artists and intellectuals: **Matisse** and **Dufy** made Nice their home, **Isadora Duncan** met her end there; **Cocteau** favoured Villefranche, and **Somerset Maugham** Cap Ferrat. The introduction of *congés payés* in 1936 brought thousands of ordinary French men and women to a coast that had hitherto been an elite retreat for wealthy foreigners.

www.roughguides.com

French Riviera Pass

The **French Riviera Pass** allows unlimited access to almost fifty of the most important art and history museums, monuments and gardens on the Riviera and in Monaco; it also allows reduced-price entry to water parks and reductions in shops, restaurants and craft ateliers. A one-day pass costs €24, a two-day pass €36 and a three-day pass €54, and they're available online at ⓦ www.frenchrivierapass.com and at Nice's tourist offices. Before you buy, it's worth noting that admission to Nice's municipally controlled museums is free anyway, so if you're visiting Nice alone, the pass is probably not worth bothering with.

The democratization continued after the war, and though the marriage in 1956 of film star Grace Kelly to Prince Rainier of Monaco set the seal on the Riviera's glamour image, the reality was increasingly different. The bucolic Mediterranean coast of Smollett's day is nowadays a thing of distant memory.

Nevertheless, there's much to enjoy: the food, vivacious street life and superb culture of **Nice**, and the unspoilt villages in the city's hinterland, which guard superb artworks from the medieval School of Nice in their churches and chapels. There are the thrills of the **corniches** along the mountainous coast between Nice and Menton, and the vicarious pleasures of the independent principality of **Monaco**.

Speedy and inexpensive **bus** and **train connections** make it easy to visit the coastal towns on a day-trip from Nice; transport links inland are rather more sparse.

Nice

The capital of the Riviera and fifth-largest town in France, **NICE** lives off a glittering reputation, its former glamour now gently faded. First popularized by English aristocrats in the eighteenth century, Nice reached its zenith in the *belle époque* of the late nineteenth century, an era that left the city with several extraordinary architectural flights of fancy. Today, more than a quarter of Nice's residents are over 60, their pensions and investments contributing to the high ratio of per capita income to economic activity. Among visitors Italians dominate, especially on summer weekends.

Far too large to be considered simply a resort, Nice has all the advantages and disadvantages of a major Mediterranean city: superb cultural facilities, wonderful street life and excellent shopping, eating and drinking, but also a high crime rate, graffiti blight and horrendous traffic. Yet for all that, the sun shines, the sea sparkles and a thousand sprinklers keep the lawns and flowerbeds lush. On summer nights the old town buzzes with contented crowds, and it's hard not to be utterly seduced by the place.

Nice's charm has long been at odds with its reactionary **politics**. For decades municipal power was the monopoly of a dynasty whose corruption was finally exposed in 1990, when Mayor Jacques Médecin fled to Uruguay, only to be extradited and jailed. Médecin was succeeded by Jacques Peyrat, a former Front National member and friend of Jean-Marie Le Pen. Nice politics took a slight turn towards the political centre in 2008 with the election of Christian Estrosi – a protégé of Nicolas Sarkozy – as the city's mayor.

Nice has retained its historical styles almost intact: the medieval labyrinth of **Vieux Nice**, the Italianate facades of **modern Nice** and the rich exuberance of *fin-de-siècle* residences dating from when the city was Europe's most fashionable winter retreat. It also preserves mementoes from the **Roman** period, when the region was ruled from here, and from the era of its Greek founders. Of late, Nice has smartened up its act with extensive **refurbishment** of its public spaces and the construction of a new **tramway**; conservative it may be, but this is not a city that rests on its laurels. Nice's many **museums**, meanwhile, are a treat for art lovers: within France the city is second only to Paris for the sheer range on offer.

Arrival, information and city transport

From terminals 1 and 2 at the **airport**, fast bus services connect with the city: #99 goes to the *gare SNCF* on avenue Thiers, just west of the top end of avenue Jean-Médecin (every 30min; €4), and #98 to the *gare routière* (every 20min; €4), which is close to Vieux Nice. The regular bus #23 (30min; €1) also serves the *gare SNCF* from Terminal 1. **Taxis** are plentiful at the airport and will cost €22–32 into the city centre.

The helpful but busy main **tourist office** is beside the **gare SNCF** on avenue Thiers (June–Sept Mon–Sat 8am–8pm, Sun 9am–7pm; Oct–May Mon–Sat 8am–7pm, Sun 10am–5pm; ℡08.92.70.74.07, ⊚www.nicetourisme.com). There are also annexes at 5 promenade des Anglais (June–Sept Mon–Sat 8am–8pm, Sun 9am–7pm; Oct–May Mon–Sat 9am–6pm; ℡08.92.70.74.07), and at terminal 1 of the airport (June–Sept daily 8am–9pm; Oct–May Mon–Sat 8am–9pm; ℡08.92.70.74.07).

Buses are frequent and run until early evening (roughly 8–9pm, after which five Noctambus night buses serve most areas from Station J.C. Bermond on the north

---

Chemin de Fer de Provence

The Chemin de Fer de Provence (⊚www.trainprovence.com) runs one of France's most scenic and fun railway routes from the Gare de Provence on Nice's rue Alfred-Binet (4 daily; 3hr 25min). The line runs up the Var valley into the hinterland of Nice, and climbs through some spectacular scenery, past places such as the tremendous fortified town of **Entrevaux** (see p.235), before terminating at **Digne-les-Bains** (see p.214). Note that at present, the first trains of the day in each direction run only half-way, after which passengers switch onto buses.

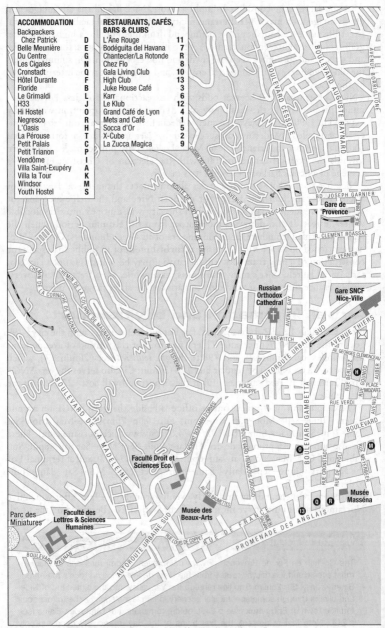

ACCOMMODATION		RESTAURANTS, CAFÉS, BARS & CLUBS	
Backpackers Chez Patrick	D	L'Âne Rouge	11
Belle Meunière	E	Bodéguita del Havana	7
Du Centre	G	Chantecler/La Rotonde	R
Les Cigales	N	Chez Flo	8
Cronstadt	Q	Gala Living Club	10
Hôtel Durante	F	High Club	13
Floride	B	Juke House Café	3
Le Grimaldi	L	Karr	6
H33	J	Le Klub	12
Hi Hostel	O	Grand Café de Lyon	4
Negresco	R	Mets and Café	1
L'Oasis	H	Socca d'Or	5
La Pérouse	T	X-Cube	2
Petit Palais	C	La Zucca Magica	9
Petit Trianon	P		
Vendôme	I		
Villa Saint-Exupéry	A		
Villa la Tour	K		
Windsor	M		
Youth Hostel	S		

▼ Musée d'Art Naïf, Phoenix Parc & Nice-Côte d'Azur Airport & Camping Terry

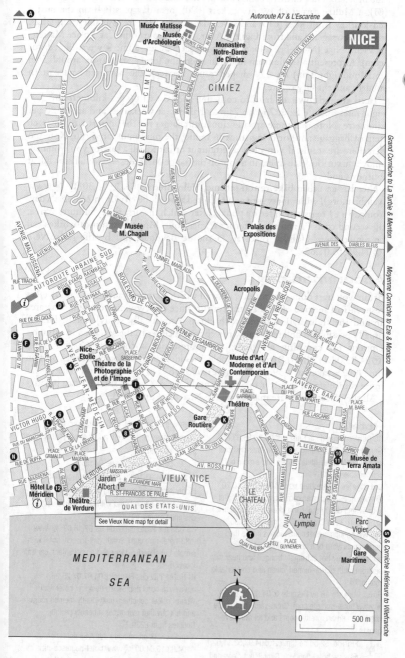

NICE

CIMIEZ

Musée Matisse
Musée d'Archéologie
Monastère Notre-Dame de Cimiez

Musée M. Chagall

Palais des Expositions

AVENUE DES DIABLES BLEUS

TUNNEL MARLAUX

Acropolis

AUTOROUTE URBAINE SUD

Nice-Etoile

Théâtre de la Photographie et de l'Image

Musée d'Art Moderne et d'Art Contemporain

Théâtre

Gare Routière

VICTOR HUGO

VIEUX NICE

Jardin Albert 1er

Hôtel Le Méridien

Théâtre de Verdure

QUAI DES ETATS-UNIS

See Vieux Nice map for detail

LE CHATEAU

Port Lympia

Parc Vigier

Musée de Terra Amata

Gare Maritime

MEDITERRANEAN SEA

N

0   500 m

8

NICE AND THE EASTERN RIVIERA

Grand Corniche to La Turbie & Menton ▶

Moyenne Corniche to Eze & Monaco ▶

S & Corniche Inférieure to Villefranche ▶

www.roughguides.com

351

side of Vieux Nice until 1.10am. Fares are flat-rate and you can buy a single ticket (€1), a Multi+ carnet of twenty tickets (€20), or a day pass (€4) on the bus; a ten-journey Multi pass (€10) and seven-day passes (€15) are available from *tabacs*, kiosks, newsagents and from Ligne d'Azur, the transport office, at 3 place Masséna in Vieux Nice (Mon–Fri 7.45am–6.30pm, Sat 8.30am–6pm; Ⓦwww.lignedazur .com). At present a single **tram** line is in operation (every 5min from around 5am until midnight/1am) on a V-shaped route between the northern and eastern suburbs and the city centre.

Taxis around town are hard to come by, and cost €1.66 per kilometre by day; night rates operate from 7pm to 7am and all day at weekends, and are €2.20 per kilometre. Note that there are additional surcharges for the airport run, for each item of baggage and for being stuck in traffic; the minimum fare is €6. Note too that there are scams: if you allow a restaurant or bar to call a cab for you, you may enjoy a luxurious ride home in a top-of-the-range Mercedes – with a hefty bill at journey's end.

Nice has an urban **bike rental** scheme, **Vélo Bleu** (Ⓣ04.30.00.30.01, Ⓦwww .velobleu.org), with ninety hire points dotted around the city open 24 hours a day. You pay a €1 registration fee by phone, after which the first thirty minutes is free, the second costs €1 and thereafter it's €2 per hour. **Mopeds** and **motorbikes** can be rented from Holiday Bikes at 23 rue de Belgique, just by the *gare SNCF* (Ⓣ04.93.16.01.62).

Accommodation

Before you start doing the rounds, it's well worth taking advantage of the NiceRes **reservation service** offered by the tourist office (Ⓦwww.niceres.com). The area around the train station teems with cheap (occasionally seedy) hotels, but it's usually possible to find reasonably priced rooms closer to the sea, even in summer. Options for **camping** are poor: the nearest site is the tiny *Camping Terry* (Ⓣ04.93.08.11.58), 768 rte de Grenoble St-Isodore, 6.5km north of the airport on the N202 – take bus #59 from the *gare routière* to "Les Combes" stop. There is far more choice across the river in St Laurent du Var or Cagnes-sur-Mer (see p.330).

All the places below are marked on the Nice map, pp.350–351.

Hotels

Du Centre 2 rue de la Suisse Ⓣ04.93.88.83.85, Ⓦwww.nice-hotel-centre.com. Gay-friendly hotel with funky Matisse-style murals and simple but comfortable rooms. ④

Les Cigales 16 rue Dalpozzo Ⓣ04.97.03.10.70, Ⓦwww.hotel-lescigales.com. Stylish tourist hotel with simple decor; quiet and close to the beach. ⑦

Cronstadt 3 rue Cronstadt Ⓣ04.93.82.00.30, Ⓦwww.hotelcronstadt.com. Hidden inside the garden courtyard of a large residential block, slightly gloomy but extremely tranquil and near the seafront, with old-fashioned, clean and comfortable rooms. ⑥

Hôtel Durante 16 av Durante Ⓣ04.93.88.84.40, Ⓦwww.hotel-durante.com. Great-value mid-range hotel, with smart, pretty rooms and an attractive garden.

Floride 52 bd de Cimiez Ⓣ04.93.53.11.02, Ⓦwww.hotel-floride.fr. Simple but clean and charming budget hotel in Cimiez, close to the Chagall museum and with a few single rooms. Free private parking. ③

Le Grimaldi 15 rue Grimaldi Ⓣ04.93.16.00.24, Ⓦwww.le-grimaldi.com. Highly successful reworking of a *belle époque* hotel: smart, central, and with chic, individually designed rooms. ⑦

H33 33 rue Pastorelli Ⓣ04.93.62.18.82, Ⓦwww .h33-hotel-nice.com. Small, gay-friendly hotel with simple but cheerful decor and a convenient, central location. ④

Hi Hotel 3 av des Fleurs Ⓣ04.97.07.26.26, Ⓦwww.hi-hotel.net. Swish designer hotel with vibrant colour schemes, individually themed rooms and a lobby that resembles a beauty parlour. Doubles from €239. ⑨

Negresco 37 promenade des Anglais Ⓣ04.93.16.64.00, Ⓦwww.hotel-negresco-nice .com. This legendary seafront palace hotel is a genuine one-off, with its own private beach, masses of art and a few wacky touches, including the occasionally garish colour schemes. Doubles from €360 in high season. **9**

🏃 **L'Oasis** 23 rue Gounod ☎04.93.88.12.29, ⓦwww.hoteloasis-nice.com. In a delightfully quiet and leafy setting for central Nice, with small, simple but comfortable rooms and good prices for the standard of accommodation offered. In summer breakfast is served in the garden. **5**

La Pérouse 11 quai Rauba-Capeu ☎04.93.62.34.63, ⓦwww.hotel-la-perouse.com. Quite simply the best-situated hotel in central Nice, at the foot of Le Château, and wonderfully peaceful for such a central location. From €260 in high season. **9**

Petit Palais 17 av Émile-Bieckert ☎04.93.62.19.11, ⓦwww.petitpalaisnice.com. Set in hilly Cimiez, this attractive, quiet and comfortable *belle époque* mansion was the former home of writer and actor Sacha Guitry. **6**

Petit Trianon 11 rue Paradis ☎04.93.87.50.46, ⓦwww.lepetittrianon.fr. Prettily renovated, soundproofed rooms on a single floor of an apartment building close to the beach. No lift. **4**

Vendôme 26 rue Pastorelli ☎04.93.62.00.77, ⓦwww.vendome-hotel-nice.com. Traditional hotel with high ceilings, chandeliers, friendly staff and smart, comfortable rooms. **7**

Villa la Tour 4 rue de la Tour ☎04.93.80.08.15, ⓦwww.villa-la-tour.com. A good (if potentially noisy) location in Vieux Nice, with a roof terrace and individually designed rooms; the cheaper ones are small and basic. **3**

Windsor 11 rue Dalpozzo ☎04.93.88.59.35, ⓦwww.hotelwindsornice.com. Fashionable, modern boutique-style hotel, with rooms designed by artists, a relaxation suite on the top floor and a swimming pool in the verdant courtyard at the back. **5**

Hostels

Backpackers Chez Patrick first floor, 32 rue Pertinax ☎04.93.80.30.72, ⓦwww.backpackers chezpatrick.com. Cheerful hostel close to the station, with kitchen and no curfew. €24 per dorm bed.

Belle Meunière 21 av Durante ☎04.93.88.66.15, ⓦwww.bellemeuniere.com. Efficiently run backpacker hotel in a lovely old bourgeois house, with the bonus of a garden. Top-floor rooms get rather hot. Dorm beds from €17; rooms **2**

🏃 **Villa Saint-Exupery** 22 av Gravier ☎04.93.84.42.83, ⓦwww.vsaint.com. Impressive modern hostel, some way out of central Nice but well run and well equipped, with wi-fi, kitchens and laundry facilities. Take the tram (direction "Las Planas", stop "Compte de Falicon"); ring ahead and they'll pick you up from the tram stop. €30 per dorm bed.

Youth Hostel rte Forestière du Mont-Alban ☎04.93.89.23.64, ⓦwww.fuaj.org. Four kilometres out of town and not a lot cheaper than sharing a hotel room. Take bus #14 from place Masséna (direction "place du Mont-Boron", stop "L'Auberge"); the last bus from the centre leaves at 7.30pm. €17.90 per dorm bed. Reception 6.30am–noon & 5pm–midnight. Closed Oct–April.

The City

It doesn't take long to get a feel for the layout of **Nice**. Shadowed by mountains that curve down to the Mediterranean east of its port, it still breaks up more or less into old and new. Vieux Nice groups beneath the hilltop park of **Le Château**, its limits signalled by boulevard Jean-Jaurès, built along the course of the **River Paillon**. Along the seafront, the celebrated **promenade des Anglais** runs for 5km until forced to curve inland by the runways of the airport. The central square, **place Masséna**, is at the bottom of the modern city's main street, **avenue Jean-Médecin**, while off to the north is the exclusive hillside suburb of **Cimiez**.

Le Château

For initial orientation, with brilliant sea and city views, fresh air and a cooling waterfall, head for the park of **Le Château** (daily: April, May & Sept 8am–7pm; June–Aug 8am–8pm; Oct–March 8am–6pm). There's no fortress here today; it was destroyed by the French in the early eighteenth century when Nice belonged to Savoy. This is, however, where Nice began as the ancient Greek city of Nikea – hence the mosaics and stone vases in mock Grecian style. Excavations have revealed Greek and Roman levels beneath the foundations of the city's first,

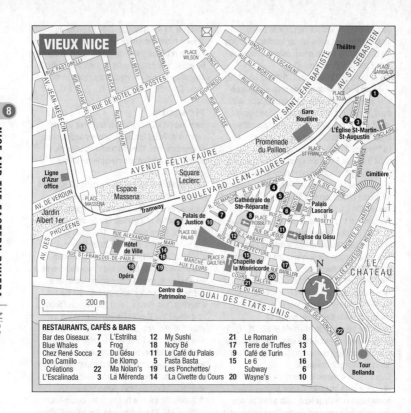

VIEUX NICE

RESTAURANTS, CAFÉS & BARS

Bar des Oiseaux	7	L'Estrilha	12	My Sushi	21	Le Romarin	8
Blue Whales	4	Frog	18	Nocy Bé	17	Terre de Truffes	13
Chez René Socca	2	Du Gésu	11	Le Café du Palais	9	Café de Turin	1
Don Camillo		De Klomp	5	Pasta Basta	15	Le 6	16
Créations	22	Ma Nolan's	19	Les Ponchettes/		Subway	6
L'Escalinada	3	La Mérenda	14	La Civette du Cours	20	Wayne's	10

eleventh-century cathedral on the eastern side of the summit. Rather than ruin-spotting, however, the real pleasure here lies in looking down on the scrambled rooftops and gleaming mosaic tiles of Vieux Nice, the yachts and fishing boats in the port on the eastern side and along the sweep of the promenade des Anglais. In the **cemetery** to the north of the park are buried the two great Niçois revolutionaries, Giuseppe Garibaldi and Léon Gambetta, though casual visitors aren't particularly welcome. A moving Jewish war memorial includes an urn of ashes from the crematoria of Auschwitz.

To reach the park, you can either take the lift (€0.90) by the **Tour Bellanda**, at the eastern end of quai des États-Unis, or climb the steps.

Vieux Nice

Most of Nice's wonderful street life – and a fair amount of its street crime – is concentrated in the dense warren of medieval streets that make up **Vieux Nice**. Once considered little more than a slum, it has changed markedly over the years, yet despite decades of gradual gentrification, the teeming *quartier* is still very far from sanitized. It's an intriguing and often charming place, full of contradictions: churches of the most opulent Italianate Baroque rub shoulders with mean, scruffy alleyways where washing hangs high overhead, while the flipside of the elegant restaurant terraces and colourful markets is a dodgy undercurrent, particularly at night. Vieux Nice is, without doubt, the repository of Nice's Mediterranean soul, but though it has an almost Neapolitan vibrancy and chaos in high summer, it can seem eerie and deserted in winter once the tourists have departed.

The streets are too narrow for buses and much of it is effectively car- (though not necessarily scooter-) free. It's an area made for walking. The central square is **place Rossetti**, where the soft-coloured Baroque **Cathédrale de Ste-Réparate** (daily 9am–noon & 2–6pm) just manages to be visible from the eight narrow streets which meet here. There are cafés to relax in, with the choice of sun or shade, and a magical ice-cream parlour, *Fenocchio*, with an extraordinary choice of flavours.

The real magnet of Vieux Nice, however, is the **cours Saleya**, with its splendidly Baroque **Chapelle de la Miséricorde** (Tues 2.30–5.30pm), and its adjacent places Pierre-Gautier and Charles-Félix. These wide-open, sunlit spaces, lined with grandiloquent municipal buildings and Italianate chapels, are the site of the city's main **market** (Tues–Sun 6am–1.30pm), where there are gorgeous displays of fruit, vegetables, cheeses and sausages – along with cut and potted flowers and scented plants. On Monday the stalls sell bric-a-brac and secondhand clothes (7am–6pm), while summer nights see café and restaurant tables filling the **cours Saleya** to create the Riviera's most animated free show. Leading west off the *cours*, rue St-François-de-Paule is home to the suitably grand *belle époque* **Opéra**, opened in 1885, with its plush red and gold interior.

Heading north past the **place du Palais de Justice** with its Saturday market of old paintings, books and postcards, the narrow **rue du Marché** and its continuations – rue de la Boucherie, rue du Collet, rue St-François-de-Paule and rue Pairolière – have the atmosphere of a covered market, lined with food stores and invitingly laid-out clothes, with special offers and sales year-round. The diminutive **fish market** is in place St-François (Tues–Sun 6am–1pm), its odours persisting till late at night when all the old streets are hosed down with enough water to go paddling. A short detour north from here will bring you to the Baroque **L'Église St-Martin-St-Augustin** on place St-Augustin (Tues–Sun 8am–noon & 2–6pm), which contains a fine *Pietà* by Louis Bréa.

Heading back south along rue Droite, you'll pass the **Palais Lascaris** at no. 15 (daily except Tues; 10am–6pm; free), an extravagantly decorated seventeenth-century palace built by a family whose arms, engraved on the ceiling of the entrance hall, bear the motto "Not even lightning strikes us". It's all very noble, with frescoes, tapestries and chandeliers, along with a collection of porcelain vases from an eighteenth-century pharmacy. The Palais Lascaris is soon to provide a home for a new Museum of Music. Further down the road, more Baroque splendours can be seen at the seventeenth-century **Église du Gésu** (Tues 3–7pm).

A worthwhile detour onto the quai des États-Unis brings you to the **Centre du Patrimoine** (Mon–Fri 8.30am–5pm; free), a mine of information (in French) on Nice's rich artistic, architectural and historic heritage. The Centre also organizes numerous themed **walking tours** of the city.

The galleries of Vieux Nice

Vieux Nice has several small art galleries worth seeking out. **Galerie des Ponchettes**, 77 quai des États-Unis (Tues–Sun 10am–6pm; free), and the neighbouring **Galerie de la Marine**, 59 quai des États-Unis (same hours; free), both host temporary exhibitions displaying the work of promising young artists. **Espace Sainte Réparate**, 4 rue St-Réparate (same hours; free), is a municipal gallery that loans out works to schools and institutions. Also worth tracking down are **Galerie Renoir**, 8 rue de la Loge on the corner of rue Droite (Tues–Sat 10am–noon & 2–6pm; free) and, diagonally opposite at 14 rue Droite, the **Galerie du Château** (same hours; free).

The stately, red-ochre **place Masséna** is the hub of the new town, built in 1835 across the path of the River Paillon and now crossed by the city's gleaming modern tramway. Renovated in 2007, the square is graced by seven human figures by Spanish artist Jaume Plensa; they're suspended high above the ground and are most beautiful by night, when they're illuminated. Steps lead up from Vieux Nice to the south side of the square; the new town lies to the north. To the west, the **Jardins Albert-1er** lead down to the promenade des Anglais; to the east, the **Espace Masséna** provides cooling fountains and a focus for the city's Christmas festivities.

The course of the Paillon is the site of some of Nice's bigger prestige projects, creating an unfortunate physical barrier between Vieux Nice and the modern city. The giant, unsubtle concrete **Acropolis** conference centre, up beyond traverse Barla, is the most banal. Far more impressive is the vast, futuristic **Musée d'Art Moderne et d'Art Contemporain** (MAMAC; Tues–Sun 10am–6pm; free), composed of four marble-clad towers linked by steel and glass bridges, with the giant **Tête Carrée** sculpture terminating the view to the northeast. It's undeniably a bold and confident work of architecture, though the building hasn't aged well; the base of the towers is fenced off due to crumbling cladding panels, while the piazza outside is a favourite gathering place for Nice's drunks. Nevertheless, MAMAC is one of the cultural highlights of Nice and not to be missed. It has a rotating exhibition of its collection of the avant-garde French and American movements of the 1960s to the present. **Pop Art** highlights include Lichtenstein cartoons and Warhol's Campbell's soup tin, while more contemporary exhibits include works by Anish Kapoor and Antony Gormley. Pride of place goes to Nice's own **Yves Klein**, who has a room devoted to him, his celebrated 1960s happenings and his uniquely vibrant shade of blue; there's also a room given over to the colourful work of the Franco-American sculptor, painter and *Vogue* fashion model **Niki de Saint Phalle**, who died in 2002 having donated 170 works to the museum. Don't miss the roof terrace, which offers wonderful views over Vieux Nice.

The modern city centre

Running north from place Masséna, **avenue Jean-Médecin** is the city's rather dull main **shopping** street. The late nineteenth-century architecture and trees make it indistinguishable from any other big French city, as do the usual chain stores – including FNAC, Galeries Lafayette and Virgin – though the extensive refurbishment work on the Centre Nice Etoile mall and the opening of the tramway have cheered things up a little. More inviting shopping, including Nice's densest knot of **couturier shops**, is concentrated west of place Masséna on rue du Paradis and rue Alphonse-Karr. Both intersect with the pedestrianized **rue Masséna**, a tourist haunt full of bars, *glaciers* and fast-food outlets. A side turning off avenue Jean-Médecin brings you to the **Théâtre de la Photographie et de l'Image** at 27 boulevard Dubouchage (Tues–Sun 10am–6pm; free): a photographic museum which displays the fascinating works of Charles Nègre, who shot local views of Nice between 1863 and 1866, just after the city and surrounding area had been ceded to France. There are also regular temporary exhibitions on photographic themes.

The chief interest of the modern town, however, is its architecture: eighteenth- and nineteenth-century Italian Baroque and Neoclassical, florid *belle époque*, the occasional slice of Art Deco, and unclassifiable exotic aristo-fantasy. The most gilded, elaborate edifice is the early twentieth-century **Russian Orthodox Cathedral**, beyond the train station, at the end of avenue Nicholas II, off boulevard Tsaréwitch (Mon–Sat: May–Sept 9am–noon & 2.30–6pm; Oct 9.15am–noon &

▲ Russian Orthodox Cathedral, Nice

2.30–5.30pm; Nov to mid-Feb 9.30am–noon & 2.30–5pm; mid-Feb to April 9.15am–noon & 2.30–5pm; €3), reached by bus #64, #71, #75 or #175 (stop "Tzaréwitch").

The promenade des Anglais

The point where the Paillon flows into the sea marks the start of the famous palm-fringed **promenade des Anglais**, which began as a coastal path created by nineteenth-century English residents for their afternoon stroll. It was here that the dancer **Isadora Duncan** met a dramatic death one September evening in 1927, throttled by her own scarf as it caught in the wheel of the open car in which she was travelling. Today, the promenade itself is slowly being throttled by the pounding traffic that crawls past some of the most fanciful architecture on the Côte d'Azur.

Past the first building, the glittery Casino Ruhl, is the 1930s Art Deco facade of the **Palais de la Méditerranée**, all that remains of the original municipal casino, closed due to intrigue and corruption, and finally demolished; a new casino and hotel have subsequently been inserted behind the original facade. Nearby, at 2 rue du Congrès, **Galerie Ferrero** is something of an institution in the art world, with a collection including works by Yves Klein. Further along, with its entrance at 65 rue de France, is the **Musée Masséna** (daily except Tues 10am–6pm; free), the city's art and history museum, which charts Nice's development from Napoleonic times up to the 1930s. The fascinating pictures of old Nice aside, it's worth a visit to see the sumptuous proportions of a grand old Niçois villa.

The most celebrated of all the promenade buildings is the opulent **Negresco Hôtel** at no. 37, filling up the block between rues de Rivoli and Cronstadt. Built in 1912, it's one of the great surviving European palace-hotels, still independently owned and run, though you'll have to stay or eat there if you want to see anything of its palatial (and occasionally downright odd) interior, as they nowadays actively discourage non-residents. For all its swank, the *Negresco's* exterior seems permanently in need of a lick of paint – and the plastic chairs on its terrace simply don't cut it in a hotel of this class.

A kilometre or so west and a couple of blocks inland, at 33 avenue des Baumettes, is the **Musée des Beaux-Arts** (Tues–Sun 10am–6pm; free), housed in a mansion built by a Ukrainian princess in 1878. Highlights include 28 works by Raoul Dufy, the result of a bequest to the city from Mme Dufy. There are also whimsical canvases by Jules Chéret, who died in Nice in 1932, a room dedicated to Vanloo, a tiny bust of Victor Hugo by Rodin and some very amusing Van Dongens. In addition, works by Monet, Sisley, Degas and Ziem grace the walls. The museum is reached by bus #38 (stop "Chéret").

Further west still, the **Musée International d'Art Naïf Anatole Jakovsky** is behind the promenade and the expressway at avenue de Fabron (daily except Tues 10am–6pm; free; bus #9, #10 or #12 to stop "Fabron"). Housed in the Château Ste-Hélène, former home of the parfumier Coty, the museum displays six hundred examples of *art naïf* from the eighteenth century to the present day, including works by Vivin, Rimbert, Bauchant and the Yugoslavian masters Yvan, Generaliã and Laakoviã.

Right out by the airport, the **Phoenix Parc Floral de Nice**, 405 promenade des Anglais (daily: April–Sept 9.30am–7.30pm; Oct–March 9.30am–6pm; €2; exit St-Augustin from the highway or bus #9, #10 or #23 from Nice), is a cross between botanical gardens, bird-and-insect zoo, and theme park: a curious jumble of automated dinosaurs and mock Mayan temples, alpine streams, ginkgo trees and cockatoos. The greenhouse full of fluttering butterflies is the star attraction. The park is also home to the **Musée Départmental des Arts Asiatiques**, beside the lake (daily except Tues: May to mid-Oct 10am–6pm; mid-Oct to April 10am–5pm; free). Housed in a beautiful building designed by Japanese architect Kenzo Tange, the museum displays artworks from India, China, Japan and Cambodia, as well as hosting touring exhibitions: there are also regular afternoon tea ceremonies.

The beaches and the port

Although the water is reasonably clean, Nice's beach is painfully pebbly, and the stretch west of Le Château is broken up by fourteen private beach concessions that, from April to October, charge steep fees to enter. East of the port a string of rocky coves includes the **Plage de la Réserve** opposite Parc Vigier (bus #20 or #30), and Coco Beach, popular with the local gay community.

The **port**, flanked by gorgeous red-ochre eighteenth-century buildings and headed by the Neoclassical Notre-Dame du Port, is full of bulbous yachts but has little quayside life despite the restaurants along quai Lunel, though a new programme of improvement aims to tame the ferocious traffic. There is a **flea market** at place Robilante (Tues–Sat 10am–6pm). Just to the east of the port at 25 boulevard Carnot is the **Musée de Terra Amata** (Tues–Sun 10am–6pm; free; bus #81 or #100, stop "Gustavin"), a museum of human paleontology on the site of an early human settlement dating back 400,000 years – a time when the sea level was much higher than it is today and much of the site of present-day Nice was submerged. The site was the camp of a tribe of hunters, located on a pebbly beach.

Cimiez

Nice's northern suburb, **Cimiez**, has always been posh. The approach up boulevard de Cimiez is punctuated by vast *belle époque* piles, many of them former hotels; at the foot of the hill stands the gargantuan *Majestic*, while the summit is dominated by the equally vast *Hôtel Régina*, built for a visit by Queen Victoria. The heights of Cimiez were the social centre of the town's elite some 1700 years ago, when the city was

Cemenelum, capital of the Roman province of Alpes-Maritimes. Part of a small amphitheatre still stands, and excavations of the Roman baths have revealed enough detail to distinguish the sumptuous facilities for the top tax official and his cronies from the plainer public and women's baths. The **archeological site** is overlooked by the impressive, modern **Musée d'Archéologie**, 160 avenue des Arènes (daily except Tues 10am–6pm; free), which displays all the finds and illustrates the city's history up to the Middle Ages; take bus #15, #17 or #22 (stop "Les Arènes").

Close by is the **Musée Matisse**, 164 avenue des Arènes (daily except Tues 10am–6pm; free), housed in a seventeenth-century villa painted with trompe l'oeil. Matisse wintered in Nice from 1916 onwards, staying in hotels on the promenade – from where he painted *Storm over Nice* – and then, from 1921 to 1938, renting an apartment overlooking place Charles-Félix. It was in Nice that he painted his most sensual, colour-flooded canvases featuring models as oriental odalisques posed against exotic draperies. In 1942, when he was installed in the *Régina*, he said that if he had gone on painting in the north "there would have been cloudiness, greys, colours shading off into the distance". As well as the Mediterranean light, Matisse loved the cosmopolitan life of Nice and the presence of fellow artists Renoir, Bonnard and Picasso in neighbouring towns. He returned to the *Régina* from Vence in 1949, having developed his solution to the problem of "drawing in colour" by cutting out shapes and putting them together as collages or stencils. He died in Cimiez in November 1954, aged 85.

The museum's collection has work from every period, including an almost complete set of his bronze sculptures. There are sketches for one of the *Dance* murals; models for the Vence chapel plus the priests' robes he designed; book illustrations including those for a 1935 edition of Joyce's *Ulysses*; and excellent examples of his cut-out technique, of which the most delightful are *The Bees* and *The Creole Dancer*.

The Roman remains and the Musée Matisse back onto an old **olive grove**, one of the best open spaces in Nice and venue for the July **jazz festival** (see p.362). At its eastern end on place du Monastère is the **Monastère Notre-Dame de Cimiez** (Mon–Sat 9am–6pm; free), with a flamboyant pink Gothic facade of nineteenth-century origin topping a much older and plainer porch. Inside there's more gaudiness, reflecting the rich benefactors the Franciscan order had access to, but also three masterpieces of medieval art: a *Pietà* and *Crucifixion* by Louis Bréa and a *Deposition* by Antoine Bréa. Adjoining the monastery is the **Musée Franciscain** (Mon–Sat 10am–noon & 3–5.30pm; free), which paints a picture of the mendicant friars and relates the gruesome fate that befell some early martyrs. You can also look into the first cloister of the sixteenth-century **monastic buildings**, and visit the peaceful **gardens**. To the north of the monastery is the **cemetery** where Matisse and Raoul Dufy are buried.

At the foot of Cimiez hill, just off boulevard Cimiez on avenue du Docteur-Menard, the **Musée Chagall** (daily except Tues: May–Oct 10am–6pm; Nov–April 10am–5pm; €7.50, or €9.50 during temporary exhibitions), custom-built to house the artist's Biblical Message paintings, was opened by him in 1972. The rooms are light, white and cool, with windows allowing you to see the greenery of the garden beyond the pinky red shades of the *Song of Songs* canvases. The seventeen paintings are all based on the Old Testament and are complemented by etchings and engravings. To the building itself, Chagall contributed a mosaic, the painted harpsichord and the *Creation of the World* stained-glass windows in the auditorium. To get there, take bus #15 or #22 (stop "Musée Chagall").

Eating and drinking

Nice is a great place for **food**, whether you're picnicking on market fare, snacking on **Niçois specialities** like *pan bagnat* (a bun stuffed with tuna, salad and olive oil), *salade Niçoise*, *pissaladière* (onion tart with anchovies) or *socca* (a chickpea flour pancake), or dining in the palace hotels. The **Italian** influence is strong, with pasta on every menu; **seafood** and **fish** are also staples, with good *bourride* (fish soup), *estocaficada* (stockfish and tomato stew), and all manner of sea fish grilled with fennel or Provençal herbs. The local Bellet wines from the hills behind the city provide the perfect light accompaniment. For **snacks**, many of the cafés sell sandwiches with typically Provençal fillings such as fresh basil, olive oil, goat's cheese and *mesclun*, the green-salad mix of the region.

Despite the usual fast-food chains and tourist traps dotted around, most areas of Nice have plenty of reasonable **restaurants**. Vieux Nice has a dozen on every street catering for a wide variety of budgets, while the port quaysides have excellent, though pricey, fish restaurants. From June till September it's wise to **reserve** tables, or turn up before 8pm, especially in Vieux Nice – and though browsing menus is half the fun it's best not to leave your selection too long, as not all Niçois kitchens stay open particularly late.

Vieux Nice restaurants

The restaurants below are all marked on the Vieux Nice map on p.354.

Chez René Socca 2 rue Miralhéti, off rue Pairolière ☎04.93.92.05.73. The cheapest meal in town: you can buy helpings of *socca*, *pissaladière*, stuffed peppers, pasta or calamari at the counter and eat with your fingers on stools ranged haphazardly across the street; the bar opposite serves the drinks. Closed Mon and Jan.

Don Camillo Créations 5 rue des Ponchettes ☎04.93.85.67.95. Elegantly modern restaurant with contemporary Niçois/Italian dishes like calamari and artichoke risotto with bacon foam; €24 lunch menu; dinner menus €42–75. Closed Sun & Mon.

L'Escalinada 22 rue Pairolière ☎04.93.62.11.71. Good Niçois specialities on a €24 menu – *pissaladière* to start, then you help yourself to chickpea salad from a huge pot. The location is pretty, at the foot of a stepped side street.

L'Estrilha 13 rue de l'Abbaye ☎04.93.62.62.00. Reservations essential in summer for this popular restaurant that serves *bourride*, *civet de lapin* and *daube Niçoise*. Closed Mon out of season.

Frog 3 rue Milton Robbins ☎04.93.85.85.65. Creative reworking of Provençal classics such as *daube de boeuf* with chocolate and orange using organic produce, plus hilarious (perhaps deliberate) mis-translations on the English menu. *Plats du jour* around €15. Open until midnight.

Du Gesú 1 place du Jésus ☎04.93.62.26.46. Extremely popular restaurant with a great atmosphere, set in an attractive church square in the heart of Vieux Nice and serving no-nonsense Niçois/Provençal food, including good *daube* and pizzas. Pizzas from €7.50, main courses around €12. Closed Sun.

La Mérenda 4 rue Raoul Bosio. Courgette fritters, *tripe à la Niçois* and the like from Dominic le Stanc, former chef at *Chantecler*. À la carte only, around €25. No phone, no smoking, no credit cards. Closed Sat, Sun, & two weeks in Aug.

My Sushi 18 cours Saleya ☎04.93.62.16.32. Chic and reasonably priced sushi bar, with menus from €18. Open daily until 11pm.

Pasta Basta 18 rue de la Préfecture ☎04.93.80.03.57. Excellent fresh pasta from €4.50, plus a bewildering variety of sauces from €2.40 – and they hand you the block of parmesan to grate yourself. Try the *merda de can*.

Le Romarin 2/4 place de la Halle aux Herbes ☎04.93.85.65.20. A plum Vieux Nice position on a small square, with generous portions of Niçois specialities served to a mixed crowd of tourists and locals. Menus from €16.30. Closed Jan & Mon & Tues lunch off season.

Terres de Truffes 11 rue St-François-de-Paule ☎04.93.62.07.68. Fashionable but intimate and tasteful restaurant with dishes based on a wide variety of fresh truffles. Menu *dégustation* €49.

Café de Turin 5 place Garibaldi ☎04.93.62.29.52. Queues around the block for the spectacular seafood, including *plateaux de fruits de mer*, at this restaurant on the edge of Vieux Nice. There are seafood stalls in the street outside if you get tired of waiting.

Greater Nice restaurants

The restaurants below are all marked on the Nice map on pp.350–351.

L'Âne Rouge 7 quai des Deux-Emmanuel ☎04.93.89.49.63. Lobster is the speciality of this port-side gourmet's palace. Classic and very expensive. Lunch menu €23, dinner menus from €35. Closed all day Wed, Thurs lunch & most of Feb.

Chantecler and La Rotonde *Hôtel Negresco*, 37 promenade des Anglais ☎04.93.16.64.00. The *Chantecler* is the grandest restaurant in Nice, and is seriously expensive if you order à la carte, but chef Jean-Denis Rieubland's €60 lunch menu, with wine and coffee, provides a good idea of how sublime Niçois food is at its best. At *La Rotonde* you can taste simpler dishes on a €31.50 menu; its carousel-themed decor is, however, the stuff of nightmares. Closed Mon, Tues & early Jan to early Feb.

Chez Flo 4 rue Sacha-Guitry ☎04.93.13.38.38. Wonderful big brasserie in the grand, Parisian manner, serving *choucroute*, *confit de canard*, seafood and great *crème brûlée* in the Art Deco surroundings of a theatre where Mistinguett and Piaf performed. Two courses €20.28; three courses with wine €29.98. Last orders at midnight on Fri & Sat.

Karr 10 rue Alphonse Karr ☎04.93.82.18.31. Elegantly modern restaurant that's a popular pit stop for the designer shopping crowd, serving an international menu of grilled fish, chicken and steak. Lunchtime *formule* €14. Closed Sun.

Mets and Café 28 rue Assalit ☎04.93.80.30.85. Good-value, busy budget brasserie close to many of the backpacker hostels, with a €10.50 menu and no shortage of custom. Closed Sun.

Socca d'Or 45 rue Bonaparte ☎04.93.56.52.93. Extremely cheap *socca* and pizza a few blocks back from the port. Closed Wed & Sun.

La Zucca Magica 4 bis quai Papacino ☎04.93.56.25.27. Long-established, homely Italian vegetarian restaurant on the port, with a sound reputation but a tendency to overdo the cheese. Around €25, no credit cards. Closed Sun & Mon.

Cafés

The bars and cafés below are all marked on the Vieux Nice map on p.354, except *Grand Café de Lyon*, which is marked on the Nice map on pp.350–351.

Grand Café de Lyon 33 av Jean-Médecin. One of the more attractive big *terrasse* cafés on the main street.

Nocy-Bé 6 rue Jule-Gilly. Diminutive Vieux Nice tea bar, with tapas and a huge selection of teas. Open daily until 12.30am.

Le Café du Palais place du Palais. A prime alfresco lounging spot on the handsome square by the Palais de Justice.

Les Ponchettes and La Civette du Cours cours Saleya. At the Le Château end of the market-place, these neighbouring cafés have cane seats fanning out a good 50m from the doors. Open late in summer.

Nightlife

Vieux Nice's British- and Irish-style **pubs** have long been very popular with young expat travellers – in fact, you're more likely to hear English than French spoken in some of them. Along with their encyclopedic range of beers or whiskies they often feature live **bands**, though the music tends not to be very original. For the older, more affluent generation, the luxury **hotel bars** with their jazzy singers and piano accompaniment have held sway for decades. As for the **clubs**, bouncers judging your wallet or exclusive membership lists are the rule.

Nice's **lesbian and gay scene** has broadened in recent years, with a wider selection of venues and a more relaxed attitude: the annual Pink Parade takes place in July.

Vieux Nice bars and clubs

The places below are all marked on the Vieux Nice map on p.354.

Blue Whales 1 rue Mascoïnat. Intimate venue with a friendly atmosphere and live music on Fridays. Open daily till 4.30am.

De Klomp 6 rue Mascoïnat. Dutch-style brown café with a big selection of draught beers and whiskies, plus regular live music. Mon–Sat 5.30–2.30am.

Ma Nolan's 2 rue St-François-de-Paule. Vast, slick Irish pub with regular live music, televised Irish and British sport plus Guinness on draught and pies to

eat. You might as well not be in France, but it's popular with a younger crowd. There's a second branch on the port.

Bar des Oiseaux 5 rue St-Vincent. Eccentric cabaret bar and theatre with live jazz, bossa nova, *chanson* and flamenco. Open lunchtime Mon–Fri & Thurs–Sat eves until 11pm.

Le 6 6 rue Raoul Bosio. Smart lesbian and gay music bar, with regular live entertainment including drag, *rai* (Algerian funk/rap music) and karaoke. Tues–Sun from 10pm.

Subway 19 rue Droite. Reasonably priced disco, specializing in reggae, soul and rock. Wed–Sat until 5am; beers €6, cocktails €8.

Wayne's 15 rue de la Préfecture. Big, popular rock bar on the edge of Vieux Nice, still the lynchpin of the area's nightlife despite its vaguely Neanderthal sexual politics. Regular live British bands plus live sport on TV. Open until 2am daily.

Greater Nice bars and clubs

The places below are all marked on the Nice map on pp.350–351.

Bodéguita del Havana 14 rue Chauvain. Wildly popular Cuban salsa bar with DJs and live music. Smart dress required. Open Tues–Sun until 2am.

Gala Living Club 5 quai des Deux-Emmanuel. Slick port-side club with a VIP area, cigar cellar and hideously expensive drinks. Open Wed–Sat midnight–5am.

High Club 45 Promenade des Anglais. Big seafront disco spinning mainstream house and disco sounds. Popular with a younger clientele; €10 entry. Open Fri & Sat 11.30pm–5am.

Juke House Café 6 rue Defly. Tiny American-style cocktail bar where the focus is on the eponymous jukebox; very popular with a young, local crowd. Tues–Sat until midnight.

Le Klub 6 rue Halevy. Nice's largest and best gay club attracts a young, stylish crowd including women and some heteros. Wed–Sun 11.30pm–5am.

La Perle 26 quai Lunel. Bar, lounge and Asian restaurant. Open Tues–Sun until 2.30am.

X-Cube 13 av Maréchal-Foch. Slick, stylish minimalist gay men's lounge bar attached to a sex shop and cruising club. Daily until 2.30am.

Entertainment, sport and festivals

Of Nice's many festivals – which begin with the celebrated Mardi Gras **Carnival** and associated flower processions in February – probably the most interesting is the **Festival de Jazz**, staged in late July in the amphitheatre and gardens of Cimiez (for details, check ⓦ www.nicejazzfestival.fr). The city's biggest sporting event is the **Triathlon de Nice** in June when competitors from all round the world swim 3.8km in the Baie des Anges, cycle 180km in the hills behind the city and run 42km ending up along the promenade des Anglais.

Nice's **opera**, Opéra de Nice, 9 rue St-François-de-Paule (ⓣ04.92.17.40.00), and **theatre**, Théâtre National de Nice, promenade des Arts (ⓣ04.93.13.90.90), are the city's twin temples to high culture, with classical music and ballet also finding a home at the opera house. Some of the smaller independent theatres, such as Théâtre de la Cité, 3 rue Paganini (ⓣ04.93.16.82.69), stage the most exciting shows. The best **cinemas** are Cinéma Mercury, 16 place Garibaldi (ⓣ08.36.68.81.06), and the art-house Cinémathèque de Nice, 3 esplanade Kennedy (ⓣ04.92.04.06.66), which show subtitled films in the original language, as does the more mainstream UGC Rialto, 4 rue de Rivoli (ⓣ08.92.68.00.41). The major touring **rock concerts** are usually held at the Palais Nikaïa, 163 route de Grenoble (ⓣ04.92.29.31.29).

The best place for up-to-date **listings** for concerts, plays, films and sporting events is FNAC at 44–46 avenue Jean-Médecin, where you can also buy **tickets** for most events.

Shopping

Food and wine are among the most tempting souvenirs to take home from Nice; the very pretty **Alziari**, 4 rue St François de Paule, is famous for its olive oils, while **Lou Canice**, 7 rue Mascoïnat, sells all manner of edible delights, from sweet and savoury biscuits to flavoured oils and local wines. **Cave Bianchi**, 7 rue de la Terrasse, is a good place to sample wines from Nice's own *appellation contrôlée*, Bellet. **Patisserie Lac**, 18 rue Barla, sells classy chocolate, macaroons and chocolate-coated ginger.

Listings

Airlines Aer Lingus ⓣ08.21.23.02.67; Air France ⓣ36.54; Air Transat ⓣ08.25.12.02.48; British Airways ⓣ08.25.82.54.00; British Midland ⓣ01.41.91.87.04; Delta ⓣ08.11.64.00.05; EasyJet ⓣ08.26.10.33.20.

Airport information ⓣ08.20.42.33.33.

Boat trips Trans Côte d'Azur, quai Lunel
(℡04.92.00.42.30, ⓦwww.trans-cote-azur.com)
runs summer trips to Îles de Lérins, Monaco and
St-Tropez.
Bookshop English-language books are available
from The Cat's Whiskers, 30 rue Lamartine
℡04.93.80.02.66.
Car parks Acropolis; promenade du Paillon;
promenade des Arts; *gare SNCF*; place Masséna;
cours Saleya.
Car rental Major firms have offices at the airport
and/or at the *gare SNCF*, on av Thiers. Try also:
Europcar, 3 av Gustave V ℡08.25.82.76.74; or
Hertz, 9 av Gustav V ℡04.93.87.11.87.
Consulate Canada, 10 rue Lamartine
℡04.93.92.93.22; UK, 22 av Notre Dame
℡04.93.62.94.95.
Disabled access Transport for people with
reduced mobility ℡04.97.11.40.53.
Emergencies SAMU ℡15; SOS Médecins
℡08.10.85.01.01; Riviera Medical Services
(English-speaking doctors) ℡04.93.26.12.70;
Hôpital St-Roch, 5 rue Pierre-Dévoluy
℡04.92.03.33.33; SOS Dentaire ℡04.93.76.53.53.

Ferries to Corsica *SNCM gare maritime*, quai du
Commerce ℡04.93.13.66.99, ⓦwww.sncm.fr;
Corsica Ferries, quai Amiral Infernet
℡08.25.09.50.95.
Internet Internet Café, 30 rue Pertinax; Taxi Phone
Internet, 10 rue de Belgique.
Laundry Best One, 16 rue Pertinax; Lavomatique,
corner of rue Lamartine & Pertinax.
Lost property 1 rue Raoul-Bosio
℡04.97.13.44.10.
Money exchange American Express, Nice Côte
d'Azur airport; Change Méditerranée 17 av
Médecin; Travelex, 13 av Thiers.
Pharmacy 7 rue Masséna ℡04.93.87.78.94; 66
av Jean-Médecin ℡04.93.62.54.44.
Police Commissariat Central de Police, 1 av
Maréchal-Foch ℡04.92.17.22.22.
Post office 21 av Thiers.
Taxis ℡04.93.13.78.78.
Trains General information and reservations
℡36.35; for information on the Chemin de Fer de
Provence, go to 4 bis rue Alfred-Binet
℡04.97.03.80.80.

Niçois villages

The **foothills of the Alps** come down to the northern outskirts of Nice, and right down to the sea on the eastern side of the city: a majestic barrier, with the highest peaks snowcapped for much of the year. From the sea, the wide course of the Var to the west appears to be the only passage northwards. But the hidden river of Nice, the **Paillon**, also cuts its way to the sea through the mountains past small, fortified medieval settlements. The **Nice–Turin railway line** follows the Paillon for part of its way – one of the many spectacular train journeys of this region. If you have your own transport you'll find this is serious, hairpin-bend country where the views are a major distraction. **Buses** from Nice to its villages are infrequent.

With their proximity to the metropolis, the *villages perchés* of **Peillon**, **Peille**, **Lucéram**, **L'Escarène**, **Coaraze** and **Contes** are no longer entirely peasant communities, though the social make-up remains a mix. You may well hear Provençal spoken here and the **traditional festivals** are still communal affairs, even when the participants include the well-off Niçois escaping from the coastal heat. The links between the city and its hinterland are strong: the villagers still live off the land and sell their olives and olive oil, goat's cheese or vegetables and herbs in the city's markets; many city dwellers' parents or grandparents still have homes within the mountains, and for every Niçois this wild and underpopulated countryside is the natural remedy for city stress.

Peillon

For the first 10km or so along the River Paillon, after you leave the last of Nice, the valley is marred by quarries that supply the city's constant demand for building materials. However, once you reach Peillon's nearest *gare SNCF* at Ste-Thècle, the road begins to climb, looping for 5km through olive groves, pine forest and brilliant pink and yellow broom before you reach the gates of **PEILLON**'s medieval enclave. By bus #360 from Nice, the closest you can get is the "Les Moulins" stop, from where it is a 3.5-kilometre uphill walk.

Peillon is beautifully maintained, right up to the lovely place de l'Église at the top. There is very little commerce and very little life during the week – most of the residents commute to their jobs in Nice. Just outside the village stands the **Chapelle des Pénitents Blancs**, decorated with violent fifteenth-century frescoes similar to those by Jean Canavesio at La Brigue (see p.248). You can peer through the grille across the chapel door; depositing a twenty cent coin illuminates the interior. From the chapel a path heads off across the hills northwards to Peille. It's a two-hour walk along what was once a Roman road, and a more direct route than going via the valley.

Peillon has an extremely attractive **hotel–restaurant**, *Auberge de la Madone* (☎04.93.79.91.17, Ⓦwww.chateauxhotels.com/madone; ❻; closed early Nov to mid-Dec & three weeks in Jan), with balconies overlooking the valley; booking is essential. If you're on a tighter budget, try *Le Pourtail*, under the same management, across the street (❷). The **restaurant** at the *Auberge de la Madone* (closed Wed) is excellent, offering a €30 lunch menu.

Peille

PEILLE lies at the end of a long climb from the valley below, the journey up from the *gare SNCF* replete with hairpin bends. The atmosphere here is very different to that in Peillon. The village was excommunicated several times for refusing to pay its bishop's tithes, and its republicanism was later manifested by the domed thirteenth-century Chapelle de St-Sébastien being turned into the **Hôtel de Ville**, and the Chapelle des Pénitents Noirs into a communal **oil press**. Peille claims to be the birthplace of the Roman emperor Pertinax, who was assassinated within thirteen weeks of his election on account of his egalitarian and democratic tendencies.

The main square, **place de la Colle**, is graced with a Gothic fountain and two half-arches supporting a Romanesque pillar. It's also home to the medieval **court house** bearing a plaque recalling Peille's transfer of its rights over Monaco to Genoa. On nearby rue St-Sébastien the former salt tax office, the **Hôtel de la Gabelle**, still stands. Peille's small **Musée du Terroir** on place de l'Armée (Mon–Sat 10am–1pm & 3–6pm, Sun 3–6pm; free) is fascinating, not so much for the exhibits but because the captions are written in the village's own dialect, Peilhasc. The only thing detracting from the beauty of the village is the view to the southwest, marred by the cement-quarrying around La Grave, its suburb down in the valley by the rail line. You can, however, take labyrinthine winding routes to La Turbie, Ste-Agnès or L'Escarène from the village, on which precipitous panoramas – and slow progress – are assured. More adventurous visitors to Peille make the circuit of its **Via Ferrata**, which includes a rope bridge and rockface; there's a €3 charge to make the circuit and you need to book in advance; you can hire the necessary equipment locally. For more information enquire at the *Bar l'Absinthe* (☎04.93.79.95.75).

Three **buses** (#116) a day make the connection between Nice and Peille from Monday to Saturday, but there's no Sunday service; the **gare SNCF** is at La Grave, 7km from the village. It's worth timing your visit for lunchtime so that you can **eat** at the superb ⚜ *Restaurant Cauvin/Chez Nana* on place Carnot (☎04.93.79.90.41; menu €25; closed Tues & Wed), which does a great blow-out Sunday lunch with real Provençal cooking and a generous choice of hors d'oeuvres; or you can snack at *La Voute* (crêpes from €4) or drink at *L'Absinthe*

– both at the end of rue Centrale. If you want to **stay** there are various *gîtes*, bookable through the Gîtes de France website.

L'Escarène

At **L'ESCARÈNE** the rail line leaves the Paillon and heads northeast to Sospel (see p.245). In the days before rail travel, this was an important staging post on the road from Nice to Turin, when drivers would harness up new horses to take on the thousand-metre Braus pass, which the rail line now tunnels under. There's not a great deal to see, other than the great Baroque church of **St Pierre-es-Liens**, with its wonderful eighteenth-century church organ inside; directly opposite, *Café de l'Union* is a pleasant lunch stop.

Lucéram

Following the Paillon upstream for 6km from L'Escarène, you pass the outwardly unobtrusive fifteenth-century **Chapelle de St-Grat**, with gorgeous frescoes by Jean Beleison, a colleague of Louis Bréa. Just 1km further on, clinging to the side of the valley, the village of **LUCÉRAM** has the friendliness of a peasant community, full of thin cats and mangy dogs. Its communal oil press remains in service and at the start of the olive season in October the villagers dip their traditional *brissaudo* – toasted garlic bread – in the virgin oil. At Christmas the shepherds bring their flocks into church and after Mass make their offerings of dried figs and bread.

Lucéram is well-known locally for its annual **Circuit des Crèches**, which brings around 50,000 visitors to the village in the weeks before Christmas. During this period more than 400 nativity scenes are displayed in the streets of Lucéram and the neighbouring community of Peïra-Cava; at other times of year there's a smaller selection at the **Musée de la Crèche** (access via the tourist office; €2). The museum is en route to the church of **Ste-Marguerite**, whose belfry rises proudly above the village houses, its Baroque cupola glittering with polychrome Niçois tiles. Inside are some of the best late-medieval artworks in the Comté de Nice, though several have been removed and taken to Nice's Musée Masséna (see p.357). All these works belong to the School of Nice, and both the Retable de Ste-Marguerite, framed by a tasteless Baroque baldaquin, and the painting of Saints Peter and Paul, with its cliff-hanging castle in the distance, are attributed to Louis Bréa. Another of Lucéram's chapels, the nearby **Chapelle St-Jean**, has a pretty painted Baroque bell tower and houses a collection of old agricultural and hunting tools, the **Musée des Vieux Outils**.

There are more examples of work by Jean Beleison on the walls and ceilings of the **Chapelle de Notre-Dame de Bon Coeur**, 2km northwest of the village off the road to the St-Roch pass. Although you can't go inside, you can view the paintings from outside.

Lucéram has a small **tourist office** on place Adrien-Barralis (Tues–Sat 9am–noon & 2–6pm, Sun 2–6pm; ☎04.93.79.46.50), which you'll need to visit to gain entry to the museums or church, which are otherwise locked; it's a good idea to phone in advance. There's a small cluster of eating places around the *mairie*, including the pizzeria *Bocca Fina*, with a €15 lunch menu.

Coaraze

COARAZE overlooks the valley of the Paillon de Contes, a tributary running west of the main Paillon. From Lucéram the D2566 ascends to the pass of St-Roch, from which the D15 hangs over near-vertical descents, turning corners onto thrilling vistas of these beautiful but inhospitable mountains.

Coaraze is one of the more chic Niçois villages, with many an artist and designer in residence, and it doesn't pander to the tourist trade in the slightest. The facades of the post office and *mairie*, and place Félix-Giordan near the top of the village, are decorated with **sundials** signed by various artists including Cocteau and Ponce de Léon. The latter decorated the **Chapelle Notre-Dame du Gressier** northwest of the village in 1962, known now as the Chapelle Bleue for the single colour he used in the frescoes. Place Félix-Giordan also has a **lizard mosaic** and a Provençal poem engraved in stone. The church, destroyed and rebuilt three times, is famous for the number of angels in its interior decoration, 118 in all.

Coaraze has a volunteer-run **tourist office** on place Ste-Catherine below the village (℡04.93.79.37.47), which has the key to the church and chapel, but as it isn't always staffed, it's best to phone ahead.

Châteauneuf-de-Contes

Across the river from Contes, 9km downstream from Coaraze, a road winds up the mountainside to **CHÂTEAUNEUF-DE-CONTES**, a hilltop gathering of houses around an eleventh-century Romanesque church. About 2km further on, a path to the left leads to a more recent **ruined village**, the Bourg Mediéval (also called Châteauneuf-de-Contes), which was last inhabited before World War I. That this village was abandoned gradually is evident from the varying degrees of decay. Ivy-clad towers and crumbling walls rise up among once-cultivated fig trees and rose bushes, while insects buzz in the silence and butterflies flit about the wild flowers that have replaced the gardens. The views over Contes, Coaraze and the surrounding rugged landscape are superb. A boom across the track leading to the site supposedly closes to vehicular traffic at 8pm nightly, but there's otherwise nothing to stop you wandering around at will.

The corniches

Three **corniche roads** run east from Nice to the independent principality of Monaco and on to Menton, the last town of the French Riviera. Napoleon built the **Grande Corniche** on the route of the Romans' Via Julia Augusta. The **Moyenne Corniche** dates from the first quarter of the twentieth century, when aristocratic tourism on the Riviera was already causing congestion on the coastal road, the **Corniche Inférieure**. The upper two are popular for shooting car commercials and action films, but they're dangerous roads: Grace Kelly, princess of Monaco, who was filmed driving the corniches in *To Catch a Thief*, died more than 25 years later when she took a bend too fast as she descended from La Turbie to the Moyenne Corniche.

Buses serve all three routes; the **train** follows the lower corniche; and all three are superb means of seeing the most mountainous stretch of the Côte d'Azur. For long-distance panoramas you follow the Grande Corniche; for precipitous views the Moyenne Corniche; and for close-up encounters with the architectural riot of the continuous coastal resort, take the Corniche Inférieure. If you want to **stay**, the biggest choice is along the Corniche Inférieure or in the chic (and expensive) *village perché* of Èze.

The Corniche Inférieure and Cap Ferrat

The characteristic **Côte d'Azur mansions** that represent the unrestrained fantasies of the original owners parade along the **Corniche Inférieure**, a series of

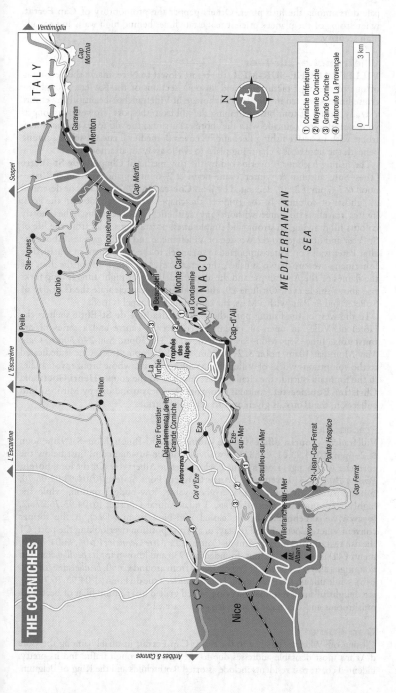

THE CORNICHES

Ventimiglia

ITALY

Cap
Mortola

Garavan

Menton

Cap Martin

Sospel

Roquebrune

Ste-Agnes

Gorbio

Beausoleil

Monte Carlo

La Condamine

MONACO

Cap-d'Ail

Peille

L'Escarène

L'Escarène

L'Escarène

Peillon

La
Turbie

Trophée
des
Alpes

Parc Forestier
Départemental de la
Grande Corniche

Astrorama

Èze

Col d'Èze

Èze-
sur-Mer

Beaulieu-sur-Mer

St-Jean-Cap-Ferrat

Pointe Hospice

Cap Ferrat

Villefranche-sur-Mer

Mt
Alban

Mt Boron

Nice

MEDITERRANEAN
SEA

N

0   3 km

① Corniche Inférieure
② Moyenne Corniche
③ Grande Corniche
④ Autoroute La Provençale

Antibes & Cannes

pale dots among the lush pines. Others pepper the promontory of **Cap Ferrat**, where some of the planet's priciest real estate hides behind high walls and equally high security.

Villefranche-sur-Mer

VILLEFRANCHE-SUR-MER, the resort closest to Nice, marks the beginning of one of the most picturesque and unspoilt sections of the Riviera, though the cruise liners attracted by the deep anchorage in Villefranche's beautiful bay ensure a steady stream of tour buses climbing the hill from the port. However, as long as your visit doesn't coincide with the shore excursions, the old town on the waterfront, with its active fishing fleet and its covered, medieval **rue Obscure** running beneath the houses, is a charming place to while away an afternoon.

The fishing harbour is overlooked by the tiny medieval **Chapelle de St-Pierre** (Tues–Sun: autumn & winter 10am–noon & 2–6pm; spring & summer 10am–noon & 3–7pm; €2.50), decorated by **Jean Cocteau** in 1957 in shades he described as "ghosts of colours". In the guide to the chapel written by Cocteau, the artist invites travellers to enter without any aesthetic preconceptions. The ghostly colours fill drawings in strong and simple lines, portraying scenes from the life of St Peter and homages to the women of Villefranche and to the gypsies. Above the altar Peter walks on water supported by an angel, to the amusement of Christ. The fishermen's eyes are drawn as fishes; the ceramic eyes on either side of the door are the flames of the Apocalypse and the altar candelabras of night-time fishing forks rise above single eyes. On June 29, the local fishermen celebrate the feast day of St Peter and St Paul with a Mass, the only time the chapel is used.

To the west of the fishing port, the massive **Citadelle de St-Elme** shelters the Hôtel de Ville, an open-air cinema, a conference centre and a series of **art museums** (June–Sept Mon–Sat 12am–noon & 3–6.30pm, Sun 2–6.30pm; Oct–May Mon–Sat 10am–noon & 2–5.30pm, Sun 1.30–6pm; free). One is dedicated to the voluptuous works of Villefranche sculptor **Volti**, whose bronze woman lies in the fountain outside the citadel gates; another, to the couple **Henri Goetz** and **Christine Boumeester**, contains two works by Picasso and one by Miró. A third collection, the **Roux**, is given over to ceramic figurines.

Practicalities

Villefranche's **tourist office** is in the Jardins François-Binon (Mon–Sat 9am–noon & 2–6pm; ☎04.93.01.73.68, ⓦwww.villefranche-sur-mer.com), just below the corniche as it changes from avenue Foch to avenue Albert-1er. Of the local **hotels**, *Pension Patricia*, 310 avenue de l'Ange Gardien, Pont St-Jean (☎04.93.01.06.70, ⓦhotel-patricia.riviera.fr; ❸), is a good-value, low-budget option, while the highly recommended *Hôtel Welcome*, 3 quai Amiral-Courbet (☎04.93.76.27.62, ⓦwww.welcomehotel.com; ❽; closed mid-Nov to mid-Dec), is the former convent where Cocteau used to stay, in a prime position overlooking the port. Of the fish **restaurants** on quai Amiral-Courbet, *La Mère Germaine* (☎04.93.01.71.39; menu €41) is the most famous, founded in 1938 and known for its *bouillabaisse*, but you might also try *La Fille du Pecheur* (tapas from around €3.50, *bouillabaisse* for two €45), while inland, the welcoming *La Grignotière*, 3 rue du Poilu (☎04.93.76.79.83), is a delightful small restaurant serving mixed grilled fish or mini fillet of beef with mushrooms and Béarnaise sauce; *plats du jour* are €18.

Cap Ferrat

Closing off Villefranche's bay to the east is **Cap Ferrat**, justifiably among the Côte d'Azur's most desirable addresses due to the lack of through traffic and its pretty, indented coast; past residents include assorted Rothschilds and the King of Belgium, but also the actor David Niven and writer Somerset Maugham. The one town, **ST-JEAN-CAP-FERRAT**, is a typical Riviera hideout for the wealthy: old houses overlooking modern yachts in a fishing port turned millionaires' resort. The #81 **bus** service from Nice and Villefranche serves the port, but beyond that there's no public transport.

The St-Jean **tourist office** is close to the Villa Ephrussi at 59 avenue Dénis-Séméria (June–Sept Mon–Fri 9am–5pm, Sat 9am–4pm; Oct–May Mon–Fri 9am–4pm; ℡04.93.76.08.90, ⓦwww.ville-saint-jean-cap-ferrat.fr). Cheaper **hotel** options are thin on the ground, with *La Frégate*, 11 avenue Dénis-Séméria (℡04.93.76.04.51, ℻04.93.76.14.93; ➋–➍), being the best bet. For deeper pockets, *Brise Marine*, 58 avenue J-Mermoz (℡04.93.76.04.36, ⓦwww.hotel-brisemarine.com; ➑; closed Nov–Jan), has spacious rooms 100m from the sea. If you really want to blow your savings, the *Grand Hôtel du Cap Ferrat*, 71 boulevard du Général-de-Gaulle (℡04.93.76.50.50, ⓦwww.grand-hotel-cap-ferrat.com; ➒), is a classic Riviera palace in a stunning site near the southern tip of the Cap, with opulent rooms and prices to match: expect to pay upwards of €560 for a double in high season.

The Cap's palace hotels have suitably opulent **restaurants**: otherwise, the best places to eat are on or close to the pleasure port: *Le Sloop* (℡04.93.01.48.63; menu €30; closed Wed lunch in summer, and all day Wed out of season) serves fresh fish cooked in delicate and original ways; while *La Voile d'Or* (℡04.93.01.13.13; around €90; closed Oct to mid-April), in the boutique hotel of the same name overlooking the port, provides very sophisticated and imaginative Mediterranean cuisine. Cheaper options on the port include *Le Pirate* (℡04.93.76.12.97), with a three-course menu for €20.

East of St-Jean's pleasure port you can follow avenue Jean-Mermoz then a **coastal path** out along the little peninsula, past the Plage Paloma to **Pointe Hospice**, where a nineteenth-century chapel cowers behind a twelve-metre-high turn-of-the-twentieth-century metal *Virgin and Child*. Back in St-Jean, another coastal path runs from avenue Claude-Vignon right round to chemin du Roy on the opposite side of the peninsula.

The one exception to the Cap's formidable privacy is the **Villa Ephrussi** (Feb–June & Sept to early Nov daily 10am–6pm; July & Aug daily 10am–7pm; late Nov–Jan Mon–Fri 2–6pm, Sat & Sun 10am–6pm; €10, €3 extra to visit first-floor collections; €15 combined ticket with Villa Kérylos), which was built in 1912 for Baroness Ephrussi, née Rothschild, a woman of unlimited wealth and eclectic tastes. The result is a wonderful profusion of decorative art, paintings and sculpture from the fourteenth to the nineteenth century of European to Far Eastern origin. Highlights include a fifteenth-century d'Enghien tapestry of hunting scenes; paintings by Carpaccio and other works of the Venetian Renaissance; Sèvres and Vincennes porcelain; Ming vases; Mandarin robes; and canvases by Fragonard, Monet, Sisley and Renoir. The baroness had a particular love of the eighteenth century, and would receive guests dressed as Marie Antoinette. Visits to the ground floor of the villa and its gardens are unguided, allowing you to explore at your own pace. In order to make the beautiful **gardens**, the baroness had a hill removed to level out the space in front, and then had tons of earth brought back in order that her formal French design could grow above the rock. One part of the park, the eastern slope, remained wild, because funds eventually ran out. Today, the highlights include the **musical fountains**, which perform every twenty minutes, and – when in bloom – the stunning **rose garden**, which offers wonderful views over the bay of Villefranche. In 1916 the baron died; when the baroness herself died in 1934 she bequeathed the house and 5000 works of art to the Académie des Beaux-Arts de l'Institut de France with the aim of creating a museum with an intimate feel, comparable to London's Wallace Collection.

Beaulieu-sur-Mer

To the eastern side of the Cap Ferrat peninsula, overlooking the pretty Baie des Fourmis and accessible by foot from St-Jean along the promenade Maurice-Rouvier, is **BEAULIEU-SUR-MER**, sheltered by a ring of craggy hills that ensures its temperatures are amongst the highest on the Côte, and that the town itself is one of its less developed spots. It's an appealing place, more tranquil than the bigger resorts and with a working harbour where you can buy freshly caught fish from the quayside, and it retains a couple of fine examples of *belle époque* architecture – most notably La Rotonde on avenue Fernand-Dunan, an opulent former hotel. Undoubtedly its most interesting attraction, however, is the **Villa Kérylos** (mid-Feb to early Nov & Jan 1–4 10am–6pm; July & Aug 10am–7pm; late Nov to mid-Feb Mon–Fri 2–6pm, Sat & Sun 10am–6pm; €8.50, or €15 combined ticket with Villa Ephrussi), a near-perfect reproduction of an ancient Greek villa, just east of the casino on avenue Gustave-Eiffel. The only concessions made by Théodore Reinach, the archeologist who had it built, were glass in the windows, a concealed piano, and a minimum of early twentieth-century conveniences. He lived here for twenty years, eating, dressing and behaving as an Athenian citizen, taking baths with his male friends and assigning separate suites to women. However perverse the concept, it's visually stunning, with faithfully reproduced frescoes, ivory and bronze copies of mosaics and vases, authentic antiquities and lavish use of marble and alabaster. Not the least of its attractions is the fabulous waterside location with views across to St-Jean-Cap-Ferrat.

Practicalities

The **tourist office** on place Georges-Clemenceau (July & Aug Mon–Sat 9am–12.30pm & 2–7pm, Sun 9am–12.30pm; Sept–June Mon–Fri 9am–12.15pm & 2–6pm, plus Sat until 5pm; T04.93.01.02.21, Wwww.otbeaulieusurmer.fr) is next to the **gare SNCF**, five minutes' walk from Villa Kérylos. A couple of economical **accommodation** options include the family-run *Hôtel Riviera* (T04.93.01.04.92, Wwww.hotel-riviera.fr; ❸), right in the centre near the sea at 6 rue Paul-Doumer, and *Select*, 1 rue André Cane (T04.93.01.05.42, Wwww.hotelselect-beaulieu.com; ❹), which is basic but clean and comfortable, and

▲ Villa Kérylos, Beaulieu-sur-Mer

excellent value for this part of the coast. For those on a bigger budget, *Quality Hôtel Carlton*, 7 avenue Edith Cavell (T04.93.01.44.70, Wwww.carlton-beaulieu .com; ©), has pretty rooms with balconies, a short walk from the sea.

The best **restaurant** in town is at *La Réserve*, 5 boulevard du Général-Leclerc (T04.93.01.00.01; closed Nov to mid-Dec; menus €90–145), which features refined Mediterranean cuisine in suitably opulent palace hotel surroundings. If you prefer something a little more low-key, *Le Petit Darkoum*, 18 boulevard Maréchal-Leclerc (T04.93.01.48.59), is an atmospheric Moroccan restaurant with menus from €23; while *Le Berlugan*, 48 boulevard Maréchal-Leclerc (T04.93.01.02.97; closed Tues and Wed), is an amiable, relaxed brasserie serving up pizza from €8.50 and pasta from €10.50. *Le Beaulieu*, 45 boulevard Marinoni, is a good bet for **drinks** and coffee in smart surroundings.

Èze-sur-Mer and Cap d'Ail

The next stop on the train is **ÈZE-SUR-MER**, the little seaside extension of **Èze** village on the Moyenne Corniche (see below), with a narrow shingle beach and fewer pretensions than its western neighbours – though that doesn't stop Bono from U2 from owning a villa here. There's a small **tourist office** (May–Oct Mon–Sat 10am–1pm & 2–6pm; T04.93.01.52.00) by the train station and a shuttle bus up to Èze village every hour or so (€1). Reasonable **accommodation** is available at *Panta Rei* (T04.93.01.51.46, Wwww.pantarei-eze.com; ©) on avenue de la Liberté, right on the seafront.

CAP D'AIL feels equally informal, though it suffers from the noise and congestion of the lower and middle corniches running closely parallel. As you descend to the sea from the main road, however, the noise is quickly left behind. Cap d'Ail's tiny eastern promontory has for years maintained one of the few open public spaces left on the Riviera, around the little **bar-restaurant** *Le Cabanon* on Point des Douaniers, which serves its faithful customers who come down here to fish, play *boules* or just look out to sea. A coastal path leads east from here to **Monaco** and also – rather more temptingly – winds west around the headland to the pretty little **Plage Mala**, one of the most secluded and attractive beaches on the eastern Riviera. The way there is dotted with imposing old villas; in places the path is a bit of a scramble, and it can get slippery if the sea is rough. If you're tempted to **stay**, the *Thalassa Relais International de la Jeunesse*, 2 avenue R-Gramaglia (T04.93.81.27.63, Wwww.clajsud.fr; €18 dorm; open April–Oct), is right on the coastal path near the **gare SNCF**. The *Hôtel de Monaco*, 1 avenue Pierre-Weck (T04.92.41.31.00, Wwww.hoteldemonaco.com; ©), offers rather more luxurious accommodation close to Plage Mala and has a private bar and secluded garden. You can **eat** seafood in idyllic surroundings at *La Pinède*, 10 boulevard de la Mer (T04.93.78.37.10; menus from €30; closed Wed and Nov–Feb), in a pine grove just above the coastal path.

The Moyenne Corniche

The first views from the **Moyenne Corniche** are back over Nice as you grind up Mont Alban, which, with its seaward extension, Mont Boron, separates Nice from Villefranche. Two forts command these heights: **Fort Boron** which is due to be transformed into an architectural institute by the star architect Jean Nouvel, and **Fort Alban**, as endearing a piece of military architecture as is possible to imagine – though now overgrown, it still remains in one piece, with its four tiny turrets glimmering in glazed Niçois tiles. The fort was continually taken by the enemies of Villefranche, who could then make St-Elme surrender in seconds. You can wander freely around the fort and see why Villefranche's citadel, so unassailable from the sea, was so vulnerable from above. To reach it you turn sharp right off the corniche along route Forestière before you reach the Ville-franche pass. The #14 bus from Nice stops at Chemin du Fort from which the fort is signed.

Once through the pass, the cliff-hanging car-chase stretch of the Moyenne Corniche begins, with great views, sudden tunnels and little habitation.

Èze

ÈZE is unmistakeable long before you arrive, its streets wound around a cone of rock below the corniche, whose summit is 470m above the sea. From a distance the village has the monumental medieval unity of Mont St-Michel and is a dramatic sight to behold, but seen up close, its secular nature exerts itself. Of the *villages perchés* in Provence, only St-Paul-de-Vence can compete with Èze for catering so single-mindedly to tourists, and it takes a mental feat to recall that the labyrinth of tiny vaulted passages and stairways was designed not for charm but from fear of attack.

The ultimate defence, the castle, no longer exists, but the **Jardin Exotique** (March 9.30am–5.30pm; April 9am–6pm; May & Oct 9am–6.30pm; June & Sept 9am–7pm; July & Aug 9am–8pm; Nov–Feb 9.30am–5pm; €5) which replaces it offers fantastic views from the ruins and a respite from the commerce below. Also worth visiting for atmosphere alone is the **Chapelle des Pénitents Blancs** on place du Planet, where the crucifix, of thirteenth-century Catalan origin, has Christ smiling down from the Cross.

From place du Centenaire, just outside the old village, you can reach the shore through open countryside via the **sentier Frédéric-Nietzsche**. The philosopher Nietzsche is said to have conceived part of *Thus Spoke Zarathustra* on this path. You arrive at the Corniche Inférieure at the eastern limit of Èze-sur-Mer.

Practicalities

Èze's **tourist office**, on place du Général-de-Gaulle just above the main car park (April–June & Sept 9am–6pm; July & Aug daily 9am–7pm; Oct–March Mon–Sat 9am–5pm; ☎04.93.41.26.00, ⓦwww.eze-riviera.com), can supply a map of the many footpaths through the hills linking the three corniches.

Of places to stay, *Le Golf Hôtel*, at place de la Colette on the Moyenne Corniche (☎04.93.41.18.50, ⓕ04.93.41.26.58; ❸; closed two weeks in Dec & all of Jan), is the most reasonable option. Alternatively, if you want to splash out, there are two four-star luxury **hotels**, both with top-quality **restaurants**: *Château Eza* (☎04.93.41.12.24, ⓦwww.chateza.com; ❾), where you can feast on €39 or €49 menus featuring caviar and blinis followed by pear *millefeuille* with poached dates; rooms in high season start at €395. At the *Château de la Chèvre d'Or*, rue de Barri (☎04.92.10.66.66, ⓦwww.chevredor.com; ❾; closed Nov–early March), rooms start at €290 in high season, and the cheapest menu is €65. Far more affordable meals can be found at *Le Nid d'Aigle*, at the very top of the village (☎04.93.41.19.08; closed evenings and all Wed Nov–Easter, and Tues, Wed & Thurs evenings rest of the year), which serves simple Provençal fare of salads and the like from around €10; and the *Auberge du Cheval Blanc* as you enter the village (☎04.93.41.03.17; lunch menu €13.50), which serves hearty Provençal dishes washed down with pitchers of *vin de pays*.

The Grande Corniche

At every other turn on the **Grande Corniche** you're tempted to park your car and enjoy the distant views, which uniquely extend both seaward and inland, but there are frustratingly few truly safe places to do so. At certain points, such as **Col d'Èze**, you can turn off upwards for even higher views.

Col d'Èze

The upper part of Èze is backed by the **Parc Forestier de la Grande Corniche**, a wonderful oak forest covering the high slopes and plateaux of this coastal range. Paths are well signed, and there are picnic and games areas and orientation tables – in fact it's rather over-managed, but at least it isn't built on. If you take a left (coming from Nice) to cross the col and keep following route de la Revère, you come, after 1.5km or so, to an observatory, **Astrorama** (March–June & Sept–Oct Fri & Sat 7–11pm; July & Aug Tues–Sat 7–11pm; €9), where you can admire the evening and night sky through telescopes.

If you want **to stay**, the *Hôtel L'Hermitage*, on the corniche (℡ 04.93.41.00.68, Ⓦ www.ezehermitage.com; ⑤), has magnificent views, and a **restaurant** serving reasonable meals (menus from €25).

La Turbie

After eighteen stunning kilometres from Nice, you reach **LA TURBIE** and the **Trophée des Alpes**, a sixth-century monument to the power of Rome and the total subjugation of the local peoples. Originally a statue of Augustus Caesar stood on the 45-metre plinth, which was inscribed with the names of 45 vanquished tribes and an equally long list of the emperor's virtues. In the fifth century the descendants of the suppressed were worshipping the monument – to the horror of St Honorat, who did his best to have the graven image destroyed. However, it took several centuries of barbarian invasions, quarrying and incorporation into military structures before the trophy was finally reduced to rubble in the early eighteenth century by Louis XIV's engineers, who blew the fortress up to prevent it being used by the king's enemies. Its painstaking reconstruction was undertaken in the 1930s, and it now stands, stateless, at 35m.

Viewed from a distance along the Grande Corniche, however, the *Trophée* can still hold its own as an imperial monument. If you want to take a closer look and see a model of the original, you'll have to buy a ticket for the fenced-off plinth and its little **museum** (Tues–Sun: mid-May to mid-Sept 9.30am–1pm & 2.30–6.30pm; mid-Sept to mid-May 10am–1.30pm & 2.30–5pm; €5). You can climb up to the viewing platform and enjoy the spectacular view, extending to the Esterel in the west and Italy in the east.

In La Turbie itself, just west of the *Trophée*, the eighteenth-century **Église de St-Michel-Archange** is a Baroque concoction of marble, onyx, agate and oil paint, with pink the overriding colour, and, among the paintings, a superb *St Mark writing the Gospel* attributed to Veronese. The rest of the town is less colourful, with rough-hewn stone houses, most of them medieval, lining rue Comte-de-Cessole, the main street which was part of the Via Julia leading to the *Trophée*.

For those thinking of **staying**, there's plenty of style and atmosphere at the thirteenth-century 🄰 *Hostellerie Jérôme*, 20 Comte-de-Cessole (℡ 04.92.41.51.51, Ⓦ www.hostelleriejerome.com; ⑤), on the Via Julia in the heart of the old village and with a beautiful *restaurant gastronomique* (menus €65 & €120). The same team owns the smart but much more affordable *Café de la Fontaine* on the main road through the village (℡ 04.93.28.52.79; *plats du jour* from around €13).

Roquebrune-Cap Martin

As the corniche descends towards Cap Martin, it passes the eleventh-century castle of **ROQUEBRUNE** and its fifteenth-century village nestling round the base of the rock. The **castle** (daily: Jan, Nov & Dec 10am–12.30pm & 2–5pm; Feb,

March & Oct 10am–12.30pm & 2–6pm; April–June & Sept 10am–12.30pm & 2–6.30pm; July & Aug 10am–12.30pm & 3–7.30pm; €3.70) might well have become yet another Côte-side architectural aberration, thanks to its English owner in the 1920s. He was prevented from continuing his "restorations" after a press campaign brought public attention to the mock-medieval tower by the gateway, now known as the *tour Anglaise*. The local authority has since made great efforts to kit the castle out in medieval fashion, and one of the best, if perhaps not most authentic, ideas has been to create an **open-air theatre** for the concerts and dance performances held here in July and August, with a spectacular natural backdrop down the precipitous slopes to Monaco and the coast.

Roquebrune itself is a real maze of passages and stairways that eventually lead either to one of the six castle gates or to dead ends. If you find yourself on rue de la Fontaine you can leave the village by the Porte de Menton and see, on the hillside about 200m beyond the gate, an incredible spreading **olive tree** that was perhaps one hundred years old when the count of Ventimiglia first built a fortress on Roquebrune's spur in 870 AD.

Southeast of the old village, just below the joined middle and lower corniches and the station, is the peninsula of **Cap Martin**, with a **coastal path** giving access to a wonderful shoreline of white rocks and wind-bent pines. The path is named after **Le Corbusier**, who spent several summers in Roquebrune and drowned tragically off Cap Martin in 1965. His grave – a work of art designed by himself – is in the cemetery (square J near the flagpole), high above the old village on promenade 1er DFL, and his beach house, the **Cabanon Le Corbusier** (guided visits Tues and Fri booked in advance through the tourist office; €8) is on the shore just east of the pretty **Plage du Buse**, the beach just below the station. It's a restful, low-key spot, with a simple café right on the beach. Further west, the **Plage du Golfe Bleu** is similar. East of Plage du Buse, a coastal path threads its way right round the tip of Cap Martin, linking up with avenue Winston Churchill on the eastern side to bring you to Roquebrune-Cap Martin's main **beach**, the Plage de Carnolès. It's a spacious enough stretch of shingle, though much less restful than the beaches west of the Cap. At the junction of the Via Aurelian and Via Julia is a remnant from the Roman station. Known as the **Tombeau de Lumone**, it comprises three arches of a first-century BC mausoleum, with traces of frescoes still visible under the vaulting.

Practicalities

There's limited **parking** at the entrance to Roquebrune's *Vieux Village*. If you come by train, it's a steep walk uphill from the **gare SNCF**: turn right out of the station, ascending to avenue de la Côte d'Azur by the steps at the end of sentier de la Gare; at the top, a second flight of steps (the sentier Saft) ascends to the Grande Corniche, from where a third set will bring you to the village. Down in the modern town centre and just up from the beach, you'll find the **tourist office** at 218 avenue Aristide-Briand (June & Sept Mon–Sat 9am–12.30pm & 2–6.30pm; July & Aug Mon–Sat 9am–7pm, Sun 10am–5pm; Oct–May Mon–Sat 9am–12.30pm & 2–6pm; ☎04.93.35.62.87, ⊛www.roquebrune-cap-martin.com).

Hotels to try include *Reine d'Azur*, 29 promenade du Cap (☎04.93.35.76.84, ⊛www.hotelreinedazur.com; ❻), overlooking the Plage de Carnolès on the coast, or, in the old village, 🍴 *Les Deux Frères*, place des Deux-Frères (☎04.93.28.99.00, ⊛www.lesdeuxfreres.com; ❻), where rooms #1 and #2 have awesome views and are worth booking well in advance.

There's no shortage of **restaurants** in Roquebrune village: try the atmospheric *Au Grand Inquisiteur*, 18 rue du Château (☎04.93.35.05.37; menus at €23 & €29; closed Mon & Tues, & lunch Fri), or the restaurant at *Les Deux Frères* (see above; lunch menu €28, dinner €48; closed Sun eve, all day Mon, & Tues lunch). For a real gourmet treat, try the panoramic **restaurant** *Le Vistaero* in the *Vista Palace Hotel* on the Grande Corniche (☎04.92.10.40.00), with menus at €58 and €85.

Monaco

Viewed from a distance, there's no mistaking the thick cluster of towers that is **MONACO**. Though rampant property development rescued the principality from postwar decline, much of its former Italianate prettiness was elbowed aside in the process, leaving it looking like nowhere else on the Riviera. Not for nothing was **Prince Rainier**, who died in 2005, known as the Prince Bâtisseur.

It may have lost its looks, but this tiny state – no bigger than London's Hyde Park – retains its comic opera independence. It has been in the Grimaldi family's hands since the fourteenth century (save for the two decades following the French Revolution) and, in theory, Monaco would again become part of France were the royal line to die out. For the last hundred years the principality has lived off gambling, tourism and its status as a tax haven.

Along with the Pope and the house of Liechtenstein, **Prince Albert II** is one of Europe's few remaining constitutionally autocratic rulers, with right of refusal over any changes to the constitution – though since the late Prince Rainier's constitutional 1962 reforms, the monarch's power is no longer absolute. Monaco has a 24-member parliament of limited power, elected by universal suffrage and (since 2003) with competing parties, but the prince has the power to dissolve it. The only other authority is the Société des Bains de Mer (SBM), which owns the casino, the opera house and some of the grandest hotels.

Along with its reputation for great wealth, Monaco latterly acquired an unwelcome reputation for wheeler-dealer **sleaze**. On his accession in July 2005, the US-educated Albert declared he no longer wished to be known – in the words of Somerset Maugham – as "a sunny place for shady people". He signalled that the principality would be more discriminating in granting residence, and in 2005 Sir Mark Thatcher, the son of former British Prime Minister Margaret Thatcher, was declared *persona non grata*. Albert then set about complying with EU banking regulations and trying to get Monaco off an OECD list of uncooperative tax havens – a policy which finally came to fruition in 2009. The principality now levies a withholding tax on the interest income of EU citizens resident here, which it rebates to the resident's country of origin. Even so, Monaco remains home to 6000 non-French expats out of a total population of 32,000, many of them British – including Roger Moore and Shirley Bassey. Hopes that Monaco under Albert might take a more sensitive line on **development** were dashed in 2009, when plans for the 49-storey Tour Odéon skyscraper hard against the French border were approved despite protests from residents in Beausoleil, who feared the tower would blot out their views and cast them into perpetual shade.

One time to avoid Monaco – unless you're a motor-racing fan – is the end of May, when racing cars burn around the port and casino for the **Formula 1 Monaco Grand Prix**. Every space in sight of the circuit is inaccessible without a ticket, making casual sightseeing – or sneaky free views of the race – out of the question.

Arrival and information

The three-kilometre-long state consists of several distinct quarters. The pretty old town of **Monaco-Ville** around the palace stands on the high promontory, with

Phone codes in Monaco

When **phoning** Monaco from France you must use the international dialling code
☎00377 (instead of the ☎04 French area prefix); calls to France from Monaco begin
☎0033, dropping the first zero of the local code.

the densely built suburb and marina of **Fontvieille** in its western shadow. **La
Condamine** is the old port quarter on the other side of the rock; **Larvotto**, the
rather ugly bathing resort with artificial beaches of imported sand, reaches to the
eastern border; and **Monte Carlo** is in the middle. French **Beausoleil**, uphill to
the north, is merely an extension of the conurbation – the border is often
unmarked and always easily crossed on foot.

The **gare SNCF** is on avenue Prince-Pierre in La Condamine, a short walk from
place d'Armes, at which **buses** from Nice, La Turbie and Menton stop, though
they also generally stop in Monte Carlo. There's an annexe of the **tourist office**
at the gare SNCF (Tues–Sat 9am–5pm), but the main office is at 2a boulevard des
Moulins near the casino (Mon–Sat 9am–7pm, Sun 11am–1pm; ☎92.16.61.16,
ⓦ www.visitmonaco.com); local bus #4 from the train station stops here
("Casino-Tourisme" stop).

Buses in Monaco run from 7am to 9pm or shortly thereafter, with flat-rate
tickets (€1). A single *bus de soirée* does the rounds of the principality every thirty

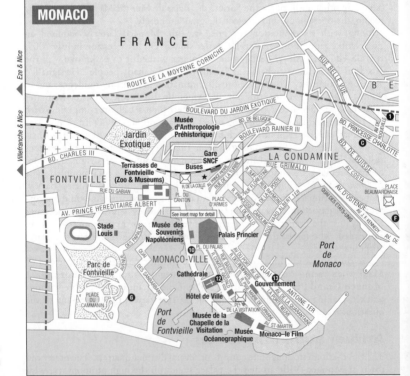

minutes until just after midnight, with an hourly night bus from 1–4am on Saturdays and Sundays. Unusually for the region, **car parking** in Monaco is plentiful, if expensive. **Bikes** can be rented from Monte-Carlo-Rent, quai des Etats-Unis (☎99.99.97.79), on the port. Two very useful public services are the incredibly clean and efficient free **lifts** linking lower and higher streets (marked on the tourist office's map), and the solar-powered **water bus** that crosses the harbour (every 20min, 8am–7.40pm; €1), which will save your legs if you're walking from Monte Carlo to the old town.

As for the practicalities of statehood, there are no **border formalities** and the euro is valid **currency**. Note, however, that wearing just bathing costumes, or displaying bare feet or chests, is illegal once you step off the beach.

Accommodation

Monaco has relatively few **hotels**, and most are pitched firmly at the top end of the market. **La Condamine** has a scattering of less expensive places, though most don't represent particularly good value – there are cheaper options across the invisible border in **Beausoleil**. The most prestigious hotels cluster around the casino in **Monte Carlo**.

Monaco has no **campsite**, and **caravans** are illegal in the state. Camping vehicles must be parked at the Parking des Écoles in Fontvieille, but can't stay overnight.

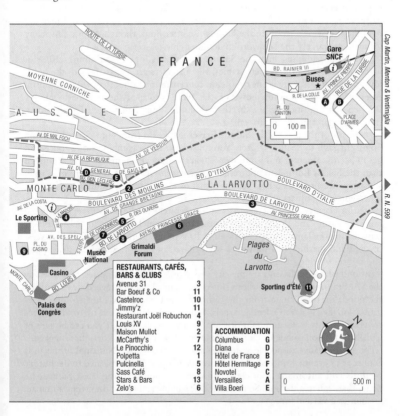

Hotels

Villa Boeri 29 bd du Général-Leclerc, Beausoleil, France ☎04.93.78.38.10, ⊛www.hotelboeri.com. A cheapish option with reasonably sized rooms, some with sea views, and only a couple of minutes' walk from Monte Carlo centre. Don't be put off by the scruffy exterior – it's rather better inside. **❹**

Columbus 23 av des Papalins ☎92.05.90.00, ⊛www.columbusmonaco.com. Luxurious boutique hotel in Fontvieille, with crisp modern decor, sea views and prices a little lower than the palace hotels. Doubles from €285. **❾**

Diana 17 bd du Général-Leclerc, Beausoleil, France ☎04.93.78.47.58, ⊛www.monte-carlo.mc /hotel-diana-beausoleil. Cheap and fairly comfortable, if somehow rather glum, but very close to Monte Carlo centre. **❷**

Hôtel de France 6 rue de la Turbie ☎93.30.24.64, ⊛www.monte-carlo.mc/france.

Good value for the principality, with bright rooms and plenty of inexpensive eating options nearby. **❺**

Hôtel Hermitage Square Beaumarchais ☎98.06.40.00, ⊛www.montecarloresort.com /hotelhermitage. One of two opulent *belle époque* palace hotels owned by the Societé des Bains de Mer, the *Hermitage* boasts a glass dome by Gustav Eiffel and fabulous views over the harbour. Doubles in high season from €475. **❾**

Novotel 16 bd Princesse Charlotte ☎99.99.83.00, ⊛www.novotel.com. One of the principality's better mid-priced options, with modern, comfortable rooms plus a pool, gym and sauna. **❼**

Versailles 4 av Prince Pierre ☎93.50.79.34, ⊛www.monte-carlo.mc/versailles. A/c two-star hotel, with just fifteen en-suite rooms above a pizzeria in La Condamine. **❼**

Monte Carlo

The heart of **MONTE CARLO** is its **casino**, the one place not to be missed on a trip to Monaco. Entrance is restricted to those over 18 and you have to show your passport or ID card. There is a dress code: *tenue correcte* is required and men are requested to wear a jacket in the *salons privés* after 8pm, though despite this many visitors are scarcely the last word in designer chic.

In the first gambling hall, the **Salons Européens** (open from 2pm; €10), slot machines surround the roulette tables, the managers are Vegas-trained, the lights low and the atmosphere is one of solemn concentration rather than wild hedonism. Above this slice of Nevada, however, the decor is turn-of-the-twentieth-century Rococo extravagance, while in the adjoining Pink Salon Bar, female nudes smoking cigarettes adorn the ceiling.

The heart of the place is the **Salons Privés** (Mon–Fri from 4pm, Sat & Sun from 3pm), through the Salles Touzet. You must look like a gambler, not a tourist, to get in (so no cameras), and hand over €20 at the door. Even more richly decorated than the Salons Européens and rather more extensive, the atmosphere in here in the early afternoon or out of season is that of a cathedral: no clinking coins, just quiet-voiced croupiers and sliding chips.

Charles Garnier, the nineteenth-century architect of the Paris Opera, designed both the casino and the adjacent **Opera House**, which is open to ticket holders only during the January to March season. Its typically Baroque interior is an excess of gold and marble with statues of pretty Grecian boys, frescoed classical scenes and figures waving palm leaves.

Around **place du Casino** are the city's *hôtels-palais* and grands cafés, all owned by the SBM monopoly. Luxury shops cluster here and along **boulevard des Moulins**; the goods on offer range from the cashmere booties at Baby Dior to some very grown-up jewels at Van Cleef & Arpels. People here really do live up to their stereotypes: you may not catch sight of Caroline and Stéphanie, but you can be sure of a brilliant fashion parade of clothes and jewels, luxury cars and designer luggage.

For an alternative to people-watching, head for the **Musée National** in the Villa Sauber at 17 avenue Princesse-Grace (daily 10am–6pm; €6). Dedicated to the history of **dolls** and **automata** from eighteenth-century models to the latest Barbies, it's better than you might think. Some of the doll's-house scenes and the creepy automata are quite surreal and fun.

▲ Changing of the Guard, Palais Princier

Monaco-Ville

Though rather over-restored and lifeless, **MONACO-VILLE** is the one part of the principality where the developers have been reined in, and it retains a certain toy-town charm despite the surfeit of shops selling Grimaldi mugs and assorted junk. It is also home to the **Palais Princier**, whose state apartments and throne room can be visited on a self-guided tour (April–Oct 10am–6.15pm; €8), with Prince Albert's voice on the audioguide. Despite the palace's modest size and military origins as a thirteenth-century Genoese fortress, the part you see certainly feels suitably palatial, thanks in part to major embellishment by the Grimaldis during the latter half of the sixteenth century. The palace courtyard conceals a massive sixteenth-century cistern designed to ensure a water supply in time of siege. These days, the main group besieging it is camera-clicking tourists; if you're outside the palace at 11.55am, you'll catch the daily changing of the immaculate, white-uniformed guard.

There are also a number of small museums and attractions in Monaco-Ville more or less connected to the Grimaldis: you can look at Napoleonic relics and items from the palace's historical archives at the **Musée des Souvenirs Napoléoniens et Collection des Archives Historiques du Palais**, place du Palais (Jan–March & Dec Tues–Sun 10.30am–5pm; April–Oct daily 10am–6.15pm; €4); see the tombs of Prince Rainier and Princess Grace in the rather dull nineteenth-century **Cathédrale** (daily 8am–7pm summer, until 6pm winter) on rue Colonel; and even watch Monaco the movie at **Monaco – le Film**, parking des Pecheurs (Jan–June & Sept–Oct 2–5pm; July & Aug 2–6pm; €7).

If you've had your fill of Grimaldis, check out the **Musée de la Chapelle de la Visitation**, place de la Visitation (Tues–Sun 10am–4pm; €3), which displays part of the religious art collection of Barbara Piasecka Johnson (an heir to the Johnson & Johnson fortune). This small but exquisite collection includes works by Zurbarán, Rivera, Rubens, and a rare, early religious work by Vermeer, *St Praxedis*.

One of Monaco's best, though pricey, sites is the **aquarium** in the basement of the **Musée Océanographique**, avenue St-Martin (April–June & Sept

9.30am–7pm; July & Aug 9.30am–7.30pm; Oct–March 10am–6pm; €13), where delicate leafy sea dragons, living nautiluses and hideous angler fish are just some of the bizarre and colourful inhabitants. This is also an institute for serious scientific research, and claims to be the only place in the world that has succeeded in keeping living corals in its aquariums. Films by the famous underwater explorer Jacques Cousteau, who for many years was the director of the institute, are screened in the museum's conference hall.

Bus #1 or #2 will take you from place d'Armes to Monaco-Ville; **by car** head for the Parking du Chemin des Pêcheurs from where there's a lift up to avenue St-Martin by the Musée Océanographique. Motor vehicle access to Monaco-Ville itself is restricted to residents of Monaco and the adjacent French *département* of Alpes-Maritimes.

Fontvieille, the Jardin Exotique and La Condamine

Below the rock of Monaco-Ville, by the Port de Fontvieille, a modern complex, the **Terrasses de Fontvieille** (bus #5 or #6), houses yet more museums. The **Collection de Voitures Anciennes de SAS le Prince de Monaco** (daily 10am–6pm; €6) is an enjoyable miscellany of old and not so old cars, both prestigious and humble – there's everything from a 1928 Hispano-Suiza worthy of Cruella de Ville to Princess Grace's elegant 1959 Renault Florida Coupé; hardened petrol heads will doubtless gravitate to Nigel Mansell's 1989 Formula 1 Ferrari, but gentler souls might prefer the cute little Autobianchi 110 FB5 convertible or the lovely 1963 Facel Vega. The **Musée Naval** (daily 10am–6pm; €4) contains 250 model ships; the **zoo** (June–Sept 9am–noon & 2–7pm; Oct–Feb 10am–noon & 2–5pm; March–May 10am–noon & 2–6pm; €4) has exotic birds, hippopotamuses and monkeys; and the museum of stamps and coins, the **Musée des Timbres et des Monnaies** (July & Aug daily 9.30am–6pm; Sept–June 9.30am–5pm; €3), has rare stamps, money and commemorative medals dating back as far as 1640.

Monaco's parks and gardens are uniformly immaculate. High above Fontvieille on boulevard du Jardin Exotique is Monaco's prime garden, the **Jardin Exotique** (mid-May to mid-Sept 9am–7pm; mid-Sept to mid-May 9am–6pm or dusk; €7; bus #2), full of bizarre cacti emerging from the hillside. Admission also includes entry to the **Musée d'Anthropologie Préhistorique**, tracing the history of the human race from Neanderthal man to Grimaldi prince, and the **Grotte de l'Observatoire**, prehistoric caves with illuminated stalagmites and stalactites.

The yachts in the **Port de Monaco** in **La Condamine** are, as you might expect, gigantic. Also on the port at quai Albert-1er is a fabulous public Olympic-size, saltwater **swimming pool** with high-dive boards (May to mid-Oct 9am–6pm, except during the Grand Prix; €7).

Eating

La Condamine and Monaco-Ville are replete with **restaurants**, **brasseries** and **cafés**, and there's a scattering of mid-priced options along Larvotto beach and the port, but good food and reasonable prices don't always coincide on Monaco: the best-value cuisine is usually Italian. It's really not worth going upmarket here unless you're prepared to contemplate €90 or more a head, in which case there are a few worthy contenders for your money. The best daily food **market** is in rue du Marché in Beausoleil.

Cafés and restaurants

Avenue 31 31 av Princesse Grace ☎97.70.31.31. Stylish, modern Michelin-listed brasserie in Larvotto, with lunchtime *formules* from around €15, a €39 evening menu and plenty of fish and salads on its informal *carte*.

Bar Boeuf & Co 26 av Princesse Grace ☎98.06.71.71. Set in the Sporting d'Été in Larvotto, this is the funkier of the two Alain Ducasse operations in Monaco, with a trendy fusion dinner menu (around €90) based on sea bass (*bar*) and beef. Closed Oct–April.

Castelroc place du Palais ☎93.30.36.68. Long-established and nowadays pretty smart, with a strategic location opposite the Palais Princier. It serves fish dishes and Monégasque specialities, with *plats du jour* from €20 and a menu at €40. Closed Sat.

Restaurant Joël Robuchon *Hôtel Métropole*, 4 av de la Madone ☎93.15.15.10. Luxurious surroundings and superlative cooking under the aegis of one of France's most respected chefs. Lunch – with menus at €29–76 – is a relative steal; the evening *découverte* menu costs €180.

Louis XV *Hôtel de Paris*, place du Casino ☎98.06.88.64. Alain Ducasse's Monaco flagship, in the *belle époque* splendour of one of the grandest palace hotels and making plentiful use of excellent local produce. Around €195. Closed Tues, Wed & Dec.

Maison Mullot 19 bd des Moulins ☎97.98.15.60. Clean, bright patisserie and *chocolatier* on Monte Carlo's main strip, with a good selection of ice creams.

Le Pinocchio 30 rue Comte F-Gastaldi ☎93.30.96.20. Dependable Italian joint in Monaco-Ville, strategically located for sightseeing and with a pretty outdoor terrace. Hearty home-made pasta dishes, with *plats* from €13.

Polpetta 2 rue Paradis ☎93.50.67.84. A pleasant Monte Carlo restaurant with attractive terrace and vaulted dining hall, serving Provençal and Italian food; €30–50. Closed Fri & Sat lunch, & late June.

Pulcinella 17 rue du Portier ☎93.30.73.61. Traditional Italian cooking in Monte Carlo, with a 150-bottle wine list; around €38.

Nightlife, entertainment and festivals

There are better places for **nightlife** than Monaco, and the top discotheques like *Jimmy'z*, in the Sporting d'Été in Larvotto, are not going to let you in unless you're decked out in designer finery. The alternatives include traditional piano bars like *Sass Café* in avenue Princesse Grace, slick restaurant-bars like *Zelo's* in the Grimaldi Forum, or American- or British-style **bars** and pubs like the large, informal *Stars 'N' Bars* on the quai Antoine-1er, or the ubiquitous Irish joint, *McCarthy's*, 7 rue du Portier, for Guinness and occasional live music.

By contrast, the **opera season** (Nov–April) is pretty exceptional, the SBM being able to book up star companies and performers before Milan, Paris or New York gets hold of them. The programme of **theatre**, **ballet** and **concerts** throughout the year is also impressive, with the **Printemps des Arts** festival (March & April) seeing performances by famous classical and contemporary dance troupes from all over the world. The main booking office for ballet, opera and concerts is the casino foyer, place du Casino, Monte Carlo (Tues–Sun 10am–5.30pm; ☎98.06.28.28); for theatre, book at the Théâtre Princesse Grace, 12 avenue de l'Ostende, Monte Carlo (Tues–Fri 10am–1pm & 2–5pm; ☎93.25.32.27).

Monaco's **festivals** are spectacular, particularly the **International Fireworks** in July and August, which can be seen from as far away as Cap d'Ail or Cap Martin. Mid- to late January sees vast trailers entering Monaco for the **International Circus Festival** at the Espace Fontvieille, a rare chance to witness the world's best in this underrated performance art (details on ☎92.05.23.45). **Holidays** in Monaco are similar to those in France, with the addition of January 27 (Fête de Ste-Dévote) and November 19 (Fête Nationale Monégasque), and without Bastille (July 14), VE (May 8) or Armistice (Nov 11) days.

The **Monte-Carlo Automobile Rally** takes place at the end of January and the **Formula 1 Grand Prix** at the end of May. Every space in sight of the circuit, which runs round the port and the casino, is inaccessible without a ticket (☎93.15.26.00). Monaco also has a first-division **football team**, AS Monaco, whose home ground is the enormous Stade Louis II in Fontvieille, 3 avenue des Castelans (☎92.05.37.54, ⓦwww.asm-fc.com).

Listings

Banks Most banks have a branch in Monaco around bd des Moulins, av de Monte-Carlo and av de la Costa; hours are Mon–Fri 9am–noon & 2–4.30pm.

Consulates Britain, 20 bd Princesse-Charlotte (☎93.50.99.54); Canada, 1 av Henry-Dunant (☎97.70.62.42); Ireland, 5 av des Citronniers (☎93.15.70.00); South Africa, 30 bd Princesse-Charlotte ☎93.25.24.26.

Emergencies ☎18 or 93.30.19.45; Centre Hospitalier Princesse Grace, av Pasteur (☎97.98.97.69).

Money exchange Cie Monégasque de Change, parking du Chemin des Pêcheurs; Monafinances, 17 av des Spélugues.

Pharmacy Call ☎141 or 93.25.33.25 from public phones.

Police and lost property ☎17 (emergency) or 3 rue Louis-Notari (☎93.15.30.18).

Post office PTT Palais de la Scala, av Henri Dunant (Mon–Fri 8am–7pm & Sat 8am–noon).

Taxis ☎08.20.20.98.98.

Menton and around

Of all the Riviera resorts, **MENTON**, the warmest and the most Italianate, is the one that most retains an atmosphere of genteel, aristocratic tourism. It got its first boost as a resort in 1861 when a British doctor, James Henry Bennet, published a treatise on the benefits of Menton's mild winter climate to tuberculosis sufferers, and soon thousands of well-heeled invalids were flocking to the town in the vain hope of a cure. Today it is even more of a rich retirement haven than Nice, and it's precisely that genteel, slow promenading pace of the town that makes it easy to imagine the presence of arch duchesses, grand dukes, tsars and other autocrats, as well as sick artists such as Guy de Maupassant and Katherine Mansfield. It's also a classic border town, and in summer the streets and beaches are thronged with relaxed Italian day-trippers munching ice cream. Menton does not go in for the ostentatious wealth of Monaco nor the creative cachet of Cannes or some of the hilltop towns. What it chiefly glories in is its climate and its all-year-round lemon crops. Ringed by protective mountains, hardly a whisper of wind disturbs the suntrap of the city. Winter is when you notice the difference most, with Menton several vital degrees warmer than St-Tropez or St-Raphaël.

Perched in the hills around Menton, the stunning little unspoilt village of **Ste-Agnes** is known for its arts and crafts studios and stunning views, while its near-neighbour **Gorbio** is just as scenic, but more sleepy and traditional.

Arrival, information and accommodation

Roquebrune and Cap Martin merge into Menton along the three-kilometre shore of the **Baie du Soleil**. The modern town is arranged around three main streets parallel to the promenade du Soleil. The **gare SNCF** is on the top one, rue Albert-1er, from where it's a short walk northeast to the **gare routière** on avenue de Sospel. The **tourist office** is at 8 avenue Boyer (June to mid-Sept daily 9am–7pm; mid-Sept to May Mon–Sat 8.30am–12.30pm & 2–6.30pm, Sun 9am–12.30pm; ☎04.92.41.76.76, ⓦwww.tourisme-menton.fr), inside the Palais de l'Europe; it's not the most helpful on the Riviera, but it can supply information on visits to Menton's various gardens. The Vieille Ville lies further east, above the old port and the start of the Baie de Garavan. The district of Garavan, further east again, is the most exclusive residential area and overlooks the modern marina.

Accommodation, though good value, is difficult to find. Menton is as popular as the other major resorts, so in summer you should definitely book ahead, either directly or through the tourist office website. One delightful alternative to hotel accommodation is offered by M. Gazzano's pair of holiday apartments at 151 route de Castellar (☎04.93.57.39.73; €500 per week in high season), 2km from Menton and with a pool looking down over the wooded slopes to the sea.

Hotels

L'Aiglon 7 av de la Madone ☎04.93.57.55.55, ⓦwww.hotelaiglon.net. One of Menton's more characterful options, with a variety of room types in the elegant setting of a nineteenth-century residence, complete with lush gardens and a heated pool. **7**

Auberge Provençale 11 rue Trenca ☎04.93.35.77.29, ⓕ04.93.28.88.88. Centrally located above a restaurant, with reasonably priced, soundproofed rooms and a garden. **4**

Beauregard 10 rue Albert-1er ☎04.93.28.63.63, ⓔbeauregard.menton@wanadoo.fr. Not fancy, but with a relaxed atmosphere, wi-fi and a pretty terrace. **2**

Chambord 6 av Boyer ☎04.93.35.94.19, ⓦwww.hotel-chambord.com. Slightly swisher sister hotel to the *Moderne*, with large, modern en-suite rooms, many with balconies. Close to the tourist office, the sea and the town centre. **7**

Moderne 1 cours George-V ☎04.93.57.20.02, ⓦwww.hotel-moderne-menton.com. One of the best of the more central options, this is a good-value modern, a/c hotel, where many rooms have balconies. **5**

Napoléon 29 porte de France ☎04.93.35.89.50, ⓦwww.napoleon-menton.com. Elegantly modern seafront hotel in Garavan, with a pool and garden, and mountain or sea views from the rooms. **7**

Hostel and campsite

HI youth hostel plateau St-Michel ☎04.93.35.93.14, ⓦwww.fuaj.org. This well-run hostel is up a gruelling flight of steps (signposted Camping St-Michel) from the northern side of the railway to the east of the station, or take bus #6 from the *gare routière* (direction "Ciappes de Castellar", stop "Camping St-Michel"). Good food and views. €17.10 per dorm bed. Reception 8am–noon & 5–11pm. Closed mid-Oct to April.

Camping St-Michel rte des Ciappes ☎04.93.35.81.23, ⓕ04.93.57.12.35. Reasonably priced campsite in the hills above the town, adjacent to the HI youth hostel. Closed mid-Oct to March except for Fête du Citron.

The Town

Menton's history, like that of Monaco, almost took an independent path. In the revolutionary days of 1848, Menton and Roquebrune, both at the time under Monaco's jurisdiction, declared themselves an **independent republic** under the protection of Sardinia. When the Prince of Monaco came to Menton in the hope that his regal figure would sway the people, he had to be rescued by the police from a furious crowd and locked up overnight for his own protection. Eventually, following an 1860 vote by Roquebrune and Menton to remain in France, Grimaldi agreed to the sale of the towns to the French state for four million francs. Shortly afterwards, sick travellers from the north began to arrive in numbers.

Today, the town's greatest attraction is not the health-giving properties of its winter climate but the fabulous **Vieille Ville** around the parvis St-Michel. Other highlights include the works of **Jean Cocteau** – in particular his decoration of the registry office – and the **gardens** in Garavan. Menton's beaches may be stony but they're popular, and in summer the gritty plage des Sablettes on the harbour has a fashionable edge.

The modern town

The **Salle des Mariages**, or registry office, in the Hôtel de Ville on place Ardoino, was decorated in inimitable style by **Jean Cocteau** (1889–1963) and can be visited by asking the receptionist by the main door (Mon–Fri 8.30am–noon & 2–5pm; €1.50). On the wall above the official's desk a couple face each other, with strange topological connections between the sun, her headdress and

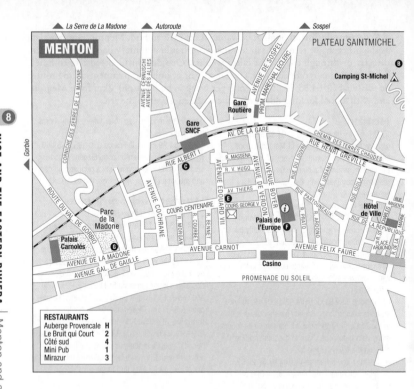

his fisherman's cap. The *Saracen Wedding Party* on the right-hand wall reveals a disapproving mother of the bride, spurned girlfriend of the groom and her armed vengeful brother amongst the cheerful guests. On the left wall is the story of *Orpheus and Eurydice* at the doomed moment when Orpheus has just looked back. Meanwhile, on the ceiling are *Poetry rides Pegasus*, tattered *Science juggles with the Planets*, and *Love*, open-eyed, waiting with bow and arrow at the ready.

The **Musée de Préhistoire Régionale**, at the top of rue Lorédan-Larchey close to the Hôtel de Ville (Mon & Wed–Sun 10am–noon & 2–6pm; free), is one of the best on the subject. There are good videos to watch, life-size re-created scenes of early human life, and the famous 27,000-year-old skull of "Menton Man" found in a cave near the town, encrusted with shells and teeth from his headgear.

Close to the museum are the pretty **market halls** off quai de Monléon, where food and flowers are sold every morning. Behind place du Marché is the attractive place aux Herbes with a bric-a-brac market every Friday morning, and the pedestrianized rue St-Michel, lined with cafés and restaurants and citrus trees, linking the old and modern towns.

There are other works by Cocteau in the **Musée Jean Cocteau** (Mon & Wed–Sun 10am–noon & 2–6pm; €3), which he set up himself in the most diverting building on the front, a seventeenth-century bastion with tiled turrets on quai Bonaparte below the Vieille Ville. The building is decorated with pebble mosaics conceived by Cocteau and contains more Mentonaise lovers in the *Inamorati* series, a collection of delightful *Animaux Fantastiques* and the powerful tapestry of *Judith and Holopherne*, simultaneously telling the sequence of seduction, assassination and

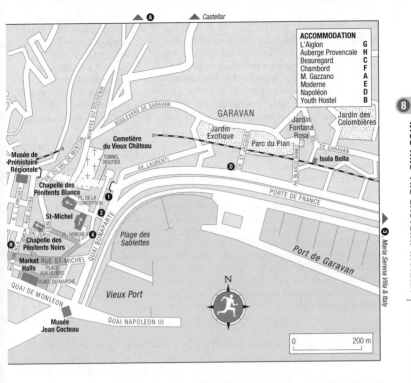

escape. The walls are also hung with photographs, poems, a portrait by his friend Picasso and ceramics.

At the far western end of the modern town, on avenue de la Madone, an impressive collection of paintings from the Middle Ages to the twentieth century can be seen in the sumptuous **Palais Carnolès** (Mon & Wed–Sun 10am–noon & 2–6pm; free; bus #7 from the *gare routière*, stop "Madone Parc"), the old summer residence of the princes of Monaco. Of the early works, the *Madonna and Child with St Francis* by Louis Bréa is exceptional; there are excellent Dutch and Venetian portraits; and an anonymous sixteenth-century École Français canvas of a woman holding a scale. The small modern and contemporary collection includes a wonderful Suzanne Valadon and works by Graham Sutherland, who spent some of his last years in Menton. The downstairs of the building is given over to temporary exhibitions, and there's a **jardin des sculptures** in the adjoining lime, lemon and orange grove. Due north of here, at 74 route du Val de Gorbio, is **La Serre de la Madone** (April–Oct Tues–Sun 10am–6pm; Dec–March Tues–Sun 10am–5pm; €8), a botanical garden of great tranquillity created in the interwar years by an American, Lawrence Johnston, who had already created a celebrated garden at Hidcote Manor in England.

The Vieille Ville

Where the *quai* bends round the western end of the Baie de Garavan from the Cocteau museum, a long flight of black-and-white pebbled steps leads to the **parvis St-Michel** and the perfect pink and yellow proportions of the **Église St-Michel** (Mon–Fri 10am–noon & 3–5.15pm). The interior of the church is a stupendous Italian Baroque riot of decoration, with an impressive vast organ casing, a sixteenth-century altarpiece in the choir by Antonio Manchello, and a host of paintings, sculptures, gilded columns, stucco and frescoes.

From the church, take a few more steps up to another square and the apricot-and-white marbled **Chapelle des Pénitents Blancs** (Sat 3–5pm), home to a collection of processional lanterns and with a fine trompe l'oeil over the altar. All this, as well as the pastel campaniles and disappearing stairways between long-lived-in houses, is a sure sign that you've arrived at the most Italianate and beautiful of the Riviera's *Vieilles Villes*.

From here, head north, or uphill. At the top you'll reach the bewitchingly beautiful and hauntingly sad **Cimetière du Vieux Château**, with its cream-coloured mid-nineteenth-century sculpted gravestones bearing diverse foreign names from Russian princes to William Webb-Ellis, credited, in public schools throughout England, with the invention of rugby; his grave is signposted. Many of Menton's young, consumptive visitors were buried here, and the grief etched in the gravestones is palpable, from the grave of 24-year-old Englishman James MacEwan – "gentle in spirit, patient in suffering" – to the Liverpool-born Arthur Edward Foster, who died aged 23 in 1887 – "God's finger touched him, and he slept" and the achingly romantic tribute (in German) from a widowed husband to the "unforgettable" Henriette van der Aue of Prague, who died at 33. If all this untimely death is a tad gloomy, there can at least be few lovelier final resting places, with sweeping views along the coast into Italy. The cemetery is in rather crumbly condition, and parts are undergoing restoration.

Garavan

If it's cool enough to be walking outside, the public **parks** up in the hills and the **gardens** of **Garavan**'s once-elegant villas make a change from shingle beaches. From the Vieux Cimetière you can walk or take bus #8 along boulevard de Garavan past houses hidden in their large, exuberant gardens.

The first public garden you come to from the cemetery along the boulevard de Garavan is the **Jardin Exotique** (daily except Tues: April–Sept 10am–12.30pm & 3.30–6.30pm; Oct–March 10am–12.30pm & 2–5pm; €5), which surrounds the Villa Val Rahmeh. Though there's a good variety of plants, it's not brilliantly maintained and you can get the same views for free from the **Parc du Pian**, an olive grove reached from the boulevard just past the Jardin Botanique. Further on, down avenue Blasco-Ibañez, is the garden of **Fontana Rosa** (guided visits Mon & Fri at 10am; €5), surrounding the former home of the Spanish author Vincente Blasco-Ibañez, bright with ceramic decoration and currently undergoing restoration. North up rue Webb-Ellis and chemin Wallaya behind the Garavan *gare SNCF* is the villa **Isola Bella**, the former home of author Katherine Mansfield, with a couple of plaques to identify it, though sadly it is not open to the public. Back on the seafront, the very last house before the Italian border is the **Maria Serena Villa** (guided tours on Tues at 10am; €5), designed by Charles Garnier for the family of Ferdinand de Lesseps.

Eating, drinking and entertainment

Menton has few exceptional **restaurants**, so most people usually cross into Italy for a blowout meal. The pedestrianized rue St-Michel is promising ground for cheap eats, with plenty of snack stops and an excellent Italian *gelato* stand. Many of Menton's **bars** are on the seafront and port, including *Mini Pub*, 51 quai Bonaparte. In summer, the Plage des Sablettes between the Vieux Port and the Port de Garavan is lined with beach bars, some of them quite stylish.

In August the pebbled mosaic of the Grimaldi arms on the parvis St-Michel is covered by chairs, music stands, pianos and harps for the **Festival de Musique de Menton**. The nightly concerts are superb and can be listened to from the quaysides without buying a ticket. If you want a proper seat, make a reservation at the tourist office.

More bizarrely, the town's **lemons** are celebrated in a citrus fruit festival every February and March, which is much the biggest event of the year in Menton.

Restaurants

Auberge Provencale 11 rue Trenca ☏04.93.35.77.29. The unpretentious restaurant of the eponymous hotel dishes up Provençal staples on a €14.30 three-course menu.
Le Bruit qui Court 31 quai Bonaparte ☏04.93.35.94.64. One of the more interesting options in the centre of town, specializing in foie gras and grilled fish, with a menu at €37.

Côté Sud 19 quai Bonaparte ☏04.92.84.27.86. Big, rather slick restaurant just up from the plage des Sablettes and pandering unashamedly to Italian visitors, with affordable pizza from €5.50 and pasta from €7.50.
Mirazur 30 av Aristide Briande ☏04.92.41.86.86, ⒲www.mirazur.fr. Menton's classiest restaurant, serving up ambitious *cuisine gastronomique* close to the Italian border in Garavan, with a €35 lunch menu and a blowout evening menu *dégustation* for €80.

Ste-Agnes

Ten kilometres northwest of Menton and 800m above sea level, **STE-AGNES** claims to be the highest coastal village in Europe – something you'll readily believe after completing the tortuous journey up and getting a glimpse of the breathtaking views over Menton. Though packed with crystal engravers, painters, herbalists, jewellers and leather workers, it's still a peaceful spot. Perched at the foot of a cliff, the village commands breathtaking views, especially from the ancient Saracen fortress at the top of the crag above. The Saracens had an impeccable eye for choosing defensive positions: such is the site's commanding vantage point that another important **fort** (June–Sept daily 10.30am–noon & 3–7pm; Oct–May Sat & Sun 2.30–5.30pm; daily during Fête du Citron; €4) was built into the mountain top a millennium later, this time as part of the Maginot defences of the 1930s.

Ste-Agnes is also an excellent starting point for **walks**; ask for information at the *syndicat d'initiative*, in the Espace de Culture et Traditions at the entrance to the village, or download some of the route descriptions and maps from the *département*'s website, ⒲www.cg06.fr. One popular route, offering the best chance of glimpsing Corsica, is up the **Pic Cime de Baudon** (1264m).

A hospitable place to stay in the village is the **hotel-restaurant** *Saint Yves* (☏04.93.35.91.45, ❶), some of whose rooms have good views. The best-quality **food** is served in *Le Logis Sarrasin* (☏04.93.35.86.89; menus €16–23), while *Le Righi*, beyond the Maginot fort (☏04.92.10.90.88; menus from €15), has the best views. Three **buses** (#10) make the 30-minute trek up to the village from the *gare routière* in Menton.

Gorbio

GORBIO, to the southwest of Ste-Agnes, is an exquisite hilltop village with very few arts and crafts boutiques or other tourist fodder, lending it a tranquil atmosphere that's rare for so scenic a place. Though the two villages are only 2km apart as the crow flies, the roads between them meet approximately 8km away, below the autoroute. Walkers can take a more direct route (a 45min walk): the road from Ste-Agnes drops downhill, and then crosses the path to Gorbio at L'Auribel bus stop, on a sharp hairpin bend after about 2km. You can also get to the village directly from Menton; bus #7 makes the climb six times daily from the *gare routière* in thirty minutes.

On the Thursday after Corpus Christi in June, the annual rite of the **Procession des Limaces** takes place, when the streets are illuminated by tiny lamps of snail shells filled with olive oil – a custom dating back to medieval times and occurring in villages throughout this area (check with the tourist office in Menton for exact dates).

Travel details

Trains

Nice to: Beaulieu (every 10–30min; 8min); Breil-sur-Roya (12 daily; 1hr–1hr 50min); Cannes (every 10–30min; 25–40min); Cap d'Ail (every 10–30min; 17min); Digne (4 daily; 3hr 25min); Entrevaux (4 daily; 1hr 30min); L'Escarène (6 daily; 40min); Èze-sur-Mer (every 30min; 13min); Marseille (every 30min–1hr; 2hr 30min–3hr 30min); Menton (every 10–30min; 30–35min); Monaco (every 10–30min; 16–21min); Peille (6 daily; 30min); Roquebrune-Cap Martin (every 10min–30min; 27–37min); Peillon (6 daily; 25min); St-Raphaël (every 30min–1hr; 50min–1hr 10min); Sospel (6 daily; 45min); Tende (3 daily; 1hr 40min); Villefranche (every 30min; 6min).

Buses

Menton to: Monaco (every 15min; 42min); Nice (every 15min; 1hr 25min); Nice airport (hourly; 1hr 5min).
Monaco to: Menton (every 15min; 42min); Nice (every 15min; 43min); Nice Airport (every 30min; 30–35min); La Turbie (6 daily; 30min).
Nice to: Aix (3–5 daily; 2hr 35min–3hr 45min); Cagnes-sur-Mer (every 15–20min; 25–45min);

Cannes (every 15–20min; 1hr 25min–1hr 40min); Coaraze (1 daily; 1hr); Contes (8 daily; 45min–1hr 5min); L'Escarène (9 daily; 45–50min); Èze (7 daily; 20min); Grasse (every 30–45min; 1hr 20min–1hr 30min); Lucéram (9 daily; 1hr); Marseille (3–5 daily; 3hr–4hr 15min); Menton (every 15min; 1hr 25min); Monaco (every 15min; 45min); Peille (3 daily; 1hr); St-Paul (every 30–45min; 50min); La Turbie (5 daily; 40min); Vence (every 20–35min; 55min–1hr 10min).

Ferries

Nice to: Corsica (summer 3–7 daily; winter 8 weekly; 3hr–8hr 15min).

Flights

Nice to: Birmingham (6 weekly; 2hr 15min); Bristol (3 weekly; 2hr 35min); Dublin (4 weekly; 2hr 35min); Liverpool (4 weekly, 2hr 20min); London City (4 weekly; 2hr 4min); London Gatwick (2 daily; 2hr 5min); London Heathrow (4–5 daily; 2hr 10min); London Stansted (3 weekly; 2hr 5min); Luton (1 daily; 2hr 10min); Montreal (1 weekly; 8hr 20min); New York (1 daily; 9hr); Paris (1–2 per hr; 1hr 30min).

Contexts

Contexts

History

From the Stone Age to the Celto-Ligurians

Although it can safely be assumed that Provence and southeastern France held substantial populations during the Stone Age – including in large areas that now lie beneath the sea – all the great discoveries from that era have been made in the southwest of the country. A few Paleolithic traces have been found at Nice and in Menton, but there's nothing to compare with the cave drawings of Lascaux.

The development of farming, characterizing the **Neolithic Era**, began in Provence around 6500 BC with the domestication of wild sheep. Around 3000 BC the **Ligurians** arrived from the east, settling throughout southern France and cultivating the land for the first time. It is to these people that the carvings in the Vallée des Merveilles, the few megalithic standing stones, and the earliest *bories* belonged. Certain Provençal word endings, such as *-osc*, *-asc*, *-auni* and *-inc*, which endure in place names, derive from Ligurian dialects passed down through Greek and Latin.

At some later point the **Celts** from the north moved into western Provence, bringing with them bronze technology. The first known fortified hilltop retreats, the *oppidi* (of which traces remain in the Maures, the Luberon, the upper Durance and the hills in the Rhône Valley), are attributed to this new ethnic mix, the **Celto-Ligurians**.

The Greeks discover Provence

As the Celto-Ligurian civilization developed, so did its trading links with other Mediterranean peoples. The River Rhône may have been named by traders from the Greek island of Rhodes (in French the name can be made into an adjective, *Rhodien*). Etruscans, Phoenicians, Corinthians and Ionians all had links with Provence. The eventual **Greek colonies** set up along the coast, starting with **Massalia** (Marseille) around 600 BC, were the result not of military conquest but of gradual economic integration. While Massalia was a republic with great influence over its hinterland, it was not a base for wiping out the indigenous peoples. Prestige and wealth came from its port and the city prided itself on its independence, which was to last well into the Middle Ages.

The Greeks introduced olives, figs, cherries, walnuts, cultivated vines and money. In the succeeding two centuries, further **colonies** were set up in La Ciotat, Almanarre (near Hyères), Bréganson, Cavalaire, St-Tropez (known as Athenopolis), Antibes, Nice and Monaco, while Mastrabala at St-Blaize and Glanum by St-Rémy-de-Provence developed within Massalia's sphere of influence. The **Rhône** was the corridor for commercial expeditions, including journeys as far north as Cornwall to acquire tin. Away from the coast and the river, however, the Celto-Ligurian lifestyle was barely affected.

Roman conquest

Unlike the Greeks, the **Romans** were true imperialists, imposing their organization, language and laws by military subjugation on every corner of their empire. During the third century BC Roman expansion focused on Spain, the Carthaginian power base from which Hannibal had set off with his elephants to cross first the Rhône, somewhere above Orange, and then the Alps, before attacking the Romans in upper Italy. Massalia's good diplomatic relations with Rome at this time served the city well when Spain was conquered, and the Romans set about securing the land routes to Iberia.

This they achieved remarkably quickly. Between 125 and 118 BC, **Provincia** (the origin of the name Provence) became part of the Roman Empire. Encompassing the whole of the south of France from the Alps to the Pyrenees, it stretched as far north as Vienne and Geneva, with Narbonne as its capital.

While Massalia and other areas remained neutral or collaborated with the invaders, many Ligurian tribes fought to the death. Thus the Oppidum d'Entremont of the Salyens was demolished, and a victorious new city, Aquae Sextiae (Aix), built at its foot in 122 BC. Pax Romana was still a long way off, however. **Germanic Celts** moving down from the Baltic managed to decimate several Roman legions at Orange in 105 BC, only to be defeated by a major campaign designed to prevent the barbarians from closing in on Italy. Massalia exploited every situation to gain more territories and privileges, while the rest of Provence grudgingly submitted. Finally, from 58 to 51 BC all of Gaul was conquered by **Julius Caesar**.

It was then that Massalia finally blew its hitherto successful diplomatic strategy by supporting Pompey in the Civil War. Caesar laid siege, defeated the city and confiscated all its territories, from the Rhône to Monaco. Unlike earlier emperors, Julius Caesar implanted his own people in Provence – St-Raphaël was founded for his veterans – and so too did his successor Octavian. While the coastal areas duly Latinized themselves, the **Ligurians** in the mountains, from Sisteron to the Roya Valley, refused to give up their identity without a fight. They kept Roman troops busy for ten years until their eventual defeat in 14 BC, which the Trophie des Alpes at La Turbie gloats over to this day.

This monument to Augustus Caesar was erected on the newly built **Via Aurelia**, which linked Rome with Arles, by way of Cimiez, Antibes, Fréjus and Aix (more or less along the route of the present-day N7). The **Via Agrippa** went north from Arles, through Avignon and Orange. Only the rebellious mountainous area was heavily garrisoned. Western Provence, with Arles as its main town, dutifully served the imperial interests, providing oil, grain and, most importantly, ships for the superpower that ruled western Europe and the borders of the Mediterranean for five centuries.

Christianity appeared in Provence during the third century and spread rapidly, becoming the official religion of the Roman Empire in the fourth. The **Lérins Monastery** was founded around 410 AD and the **Abbey of St-Victor** in Marseille six years later.

Rome falls: more invasions

For a while in the early fifth century, as the Roman Empire began to split apart, Germanic invaders bypassed Provence. By the time the Western Roman Empire finally collapsed in 476 AD, Provence was dominated by both the **Visigoths**, who had captured Arles and were terrorizing the lower Rhône valley, and the **Burgundians**, who had moved in from the east. The new rulers confiscated land, took slaves and generally made life for the locals even more miserable than usual.

Over the next two centuries, **Goths** and **Franks** fought over and partitioned Provence: famine, disease and bloodshed diminished the population, lands that had been drained returned to swamp, and intellectual life declined. Under the eighth-century **Merovingian dynasty** Provence was, in theory, part of the **Frankish empire**. But a newly emergent world power – **Islam** – had spread from the Middle East into North Africa and most of Spain. In 732 a Muslim army reached as far as Tours before being defeated by the Franks at Poitiers. At this point the local ruler of Provence rebelled against the central authority, and called on the **Saracens** (Muslims) to assist. Armies of Franks, Saracens, Lombards and locals rampaged through Provence, putting the Franks back in control.

Though the ports had trouble carrying on their lucrative trade while the Mediterranean was controlled by Saracens, agriculture developed under the Frankish **Carolingian dynasty**, particularly during the relatively peaceful reign of **Charlemagne**. When Charlemagne's sons and then grandsons squabbled over the inheritance, during the ninth century, Provence once again became easy prey.

Normans took over the lower Rhône, and the **Saracens** returned, pillaging Marseille and destroying its abbey in 838, sacking Arles in 842, and attacking Marseille again in 848. From a base at Fraxinetum (La Garde-Freinet), they controlled the whole Massif des Maures for a century.

The **hilltop villages** along the coast are commonly explained as the frightened response to the Saracens, even if little of what's now to be seen dates back this far. Well inland, people similarly retreated to whatever defensive positions were available. In the cities this would be the strongest building (the Roman theatre at Orange, for example). The Rhône Valley villagers took refuge in the Luberon and the Massif de la Ste-Baume.

Despite the terrors and bloodshed, the period also saw progress. The Saracens introduced basic medicine, the use of cork bark, resin extraction from pines, flat roof-tiles, and the most traditional Provençal musical instrument, the tambourine.

The counts of Provence

Guillaume Le Libérateur, count of Arles, expelled the Saracens for good at the end of the tenth century, and claimed Provence as his own feudal estate. A period of relative stability ensued. Forestry, fishing, irrigation, land reclamation, vine cultivation, beekeeping, salt-panning, river transport and renewed learning began to pull Provence out of the Dark Ages.

Politically, Guillaume and his successors retained considerable independence from their overlords (first the kingdom of Burgundy then the Holy Roman Empire). In turn they tended to confine their influence to the area around Arles and Avignon, while local lords held sway in rural areas and the cities developed their own autonomy. Although the Rhône officially formed the border between France and the Holy Roman Empire, the old economic, cultural and linguistic links between the two sides of the river endured.

In the **twelfth century**, Provence passed to the counts of Toulouse and was then divided with the counts of Barcelona, while various fiefdoms – amongst them Forcalquier, Les Baux and Beuil on the eastern side of the Var – refused integration. Power shifted repeatedly but, sporadic armed conflicts apart, the titleholder to Provence hardly affected the ordinary people, who were bound in serfdom to their immediate *seigneur*.

Thanks to the Crusades, **maritime commerce** flourished once again, as did trade along the Rhône, giving prominence to Avignon, Orange, Arles and, most of all, Marseille. In Nice, then under the control of the Genoese Republic, a new commercial town developed below the castle rock. The cities took on the organizational form of the Italian consulates, increasingly separating themselves from feudal power.

Troubadour poetry made its appearance in the *langue d'oc* language that was spoken from the Alps to the Pyrenees (and from which the **Provençal dialect** developed). Church construction looked back to the Romans for inspiration, producing the great Romanesque edifices of Montmajour, Sénanque, Silvacane, Thoronet and St-Trophime in Arles.

Raymond Béranger V, Catalan count of Provence in the early thirteenth century, took the unprecedented step of spending time in his domains. While fighting off the count of Toulouse and the Holy Roman Emperor, he made Aix his capital, founded Barçelonnette and travelled throughout the Alps and the coastal regions. For the first time since the Romans, Provence became an organized mini-state with a more or less **unified feudal system** of law and administration.

The Angevins

After Béranger's death, Provence turned towards France, and fell under the control of the **house of Anjou** until the end of the fifteenth century. The borders changed: Nice, Barçelonnette and Puget-Théniers passed to Savoy in 1388 and remained separate from Provence until 1860. Extraneous powers claimed or bought territories – the **popes at Avignon** (see p.119) and in the **Comtat Venaissin**; the Prince of Nassau in Orange. Though armed conflicts, revolts and even civil war in 1388 chequered its medieval history, Provence was at least spared the devastations of the Hundred Years' War, which never touched the region.

By the end of this period the trading routes from the Orient to Genoa and Marseille, and from Marseille to Flanders and London, were forming the basis of **early capitalism**, and spreading new techniques and learning. Though Marseille was not a great financial centre like Antwerp or Florence, its population became ever more cosmopolitan. Away from the coast and the Rhône, however, feudal villages continued in isolation. For a shepherd or forester in the mountains, life in Marseille or in the extravagant papal city of Avignon would have appeared to belong to another planet.

Provençal Jews exercised equal rights with Christians, owning land and practising assorted professions in addition to finance and commerce. Though concentrated in the western towns, they were not always ghettoized. But the moment disaster struck, such as the Black Death in the mid-fourteenth century, latent hostility became violently manifest. **The Plague** itself made no distinctions: half the population died in the recurring epidemics.

In **cultural and intellectual life** the dominant centres were the **papal court at Avignon**, and later **King René of Anjou's court at Aix**. However, Angevin rulers and foreign trade, art and architecture remained surprisingly unmarked by the major movements of the time. The popes tended to employ foreign artists and only in the mid-fifteenth century did native art develop around the **Avignon School**. At the same time the **School of Nice** emerged, more directly under Italian influence. Avignon acquired great **Gothic architecture** – the Palais des Papes and many of the churches – but elsewhere the only major examples of the new style were Tarascon's castle and the basilica of St-Maximin-de-la-Ste-Baume.

Around this time, the popes founded a **university in Avignon** (1303) which became famous for jurisprudence; Aix university was established a century later and in the mid-fourteenth century the first paper mills were in use. By King René's time, French was the official language of the court.

Union with France

The short-lived Charles III of Provence, René's heir, bequeathed all his lands to **Louis XI of France**, a transfer of power that the *parlement* of Aix glossed over and approved in 1482. Within twelve months every top Provençal official had been sacked and replaced by a Frenchman; the castles at Toulon and Les Baux were razed to the ground; and garrisons were placed in five major towns.

After Louis XI's death a more careful approach was taken to this crucial border province. The **Act of Union**, ratified by *parlement* in 1486, declared Provence to be a separate entity within France, enshrining the rights to its own law courts, customs and privileges. In reality, the ever-centralizing power of the French state was systematically to erode these rights.

The **Jewish population** provided a convenient diversion for Provençal frustrations. Encouraged, if not instigated, by the Crown, there were massacres, expulsions and assaults in Marseille, Arles and Manosque at the end of the fifteenth century. The royal directive was convert or leave – some, such as the parents of **Nostradamus**, converted, many fled to the Comtat, where Jews lost their papal protection in turn in 1570.

Meanwhile Charles VIII, Louis XII and François I involved Provence in their **Italian Wars**. **Marseille** became a **military port** in 1488, and in 1496 **Toulon** was fortified and its first **shipyards** opened. While the rest of the province suffered troop movements and requisitions, Marseille and Toulon benefited from extra funds and unchecked piracy against the enemies of France. Genoese, Venetian and Spanish vessels were regularly towed into Marseille's port.

The war took a more serious turn in the 1520s after the French conquest of Milan. **Charles V**, the new Holy Roman Emperor, retaliated by sending a large army across the Var and into Aix. The French concern was to protect Marseille at all costs. After the imperial forces had failed to take Marseille and retreated, the city was rewarded with the pomp and carnival of a royal wedding between François' second son, the future Henri II, and **Catherine de Médicis**. The Château d'If was built to protect the roadstead.

Another round in the war soon commenced. Charles V took back Milan, the French invaded Savoy and occupied Nice. In 1536 an even bigger **imperial army invaded**, and again the French abandoned inland Provence to protect Marseille and the Rhône Valley. The people of **Le Muy** stopped the emperor for one day with fifty local heroes, who were subsequently hanged for their pains. **Marseille** and **Arles** held out; French troops finally moved south down the Durance; dysentery and lack of sure supply lines weakened the imperial army. Twenty thousand Savoyards were dead or imprisoned by the time the imperial troops safely re-crossed the Var.

One effect of the Italian Wars was that Provence finally now identified itself with France, making it easier for the Crown to diminish the power of the *États*, impose greater numbers of French administrators, and, in 1539, decree that all administrative laws were to be translated from Latin into French, not Provençal.

Life in the early sixteenth century

Sixteenth-century Provence was ruled by two royal appointees – a governor and grand *sénéchal* (the chief administrator) – but the **feudal hierarchy** failed to achieve much control over the structure of society. Those few nobles who lived on their estates were often poorer than the merchants and financiers of the major cities. In remoter areas people cultivated their absent *seigneur*'s land as if it were their own; in other areas towns bought land off the feudal owners, and nearly half the population had their own holdings. Advances in irrigation, such as **Craponne's canal through the Crau**, were carried out independently from the aristocracy.

While not self-sufficient in grain, Provence exported surpluses of wine, fish and vermilion from the Camargue; textiles, tanneries, soap and paper all thrived; and new foods, such as oranges, pepper, palm dates and sugar cane, were imported. Olives provided the basic oil for food, commercial orchards appeared, and most families kept pigs and sheep: only vegetables were rare luxuries. People lived on their land, with the **old fortified villages** populated only in times of insecurity. Epidemics of the plague continued, however, and sanitation left a lot to be desired – a contemporary noted that even in Aix it "rained shit as often as it did in Arles or Marseille".

Certain larger towns set up **free schools**, while Aix, Marseille, Arles and Avignon established secondary colleges. **Nostradamus** (1503–66) achieved renown throughout France, although his books had to be printed in Lyon – there was as yet no market for printers in Provence.

Châteaux such as La Tour d'Aigue, Gordes and Lourmarin, with comfort playing an equal part to defence, were built, as were rich Marseille town houses like the Maison Diamentée and the Hôtel Cabre. The facade of St-Pierre in Avignon shows the Renaissance finally triumphing over Provence's artistic backwardness.

The Wars of Religion

The Italian Wars disrupted social and productive advances, but they were nothing compared with the **Wars of Religion** that put all France in a state of **civil war** during the second half of the sixteenth century. The clash between the reforming ideas of Luther and Calvin and the old Roman Catholic order was particularly violent in Provence. Avignon, as papal domain, was inevitably a rigid centre of Catholicism, while neighbouring Orange allowed Huguenots to practise freely. Haute Provence and the Luberon became centres for the new religion due to the influx of Dauphinois and Piedmontais settlers.

Incidents began to build up in the 1540s, culminating in the massacre of Luberon Protestants and the destruction of Mérindol (see p.174). In Avignon heretics were displayed in iron cages; in Haute Provence churches were smashed by the reformers; and in Orange Protestants pillaged the cathedral and seized control of the city. The regent Catherine de Médicis' **Edict of Tolerance** in 1562 only made matters worse. Marseille demanded and received an exemption; Aix promptly dispatched a Catholic contingent to massacre the Protestants of Tourves; Catherine's envoys prompted a massacre of Catholics at Barjols. The *parlement* chose to resign rather than ratify a new edict of tolerance in 1563, even though by now Orange had been won back to the established Church, the garrison of Sisteron had been massacred for protecting the Protestants and the last armed group of reformers had fled north.

When Catherine de Médicis and her son Charles XIV toured Provence in 1564, all seemed well. But within a few years fighting again broke out, with Sisteron once more under siege. In the mid-1570s trouble took a new turn, with the rivalry between Henri III's governor and *sénéchal* adding to the hostile camps. This state of civil war was only terminated by another major outbreak of **plague** in **1580**.

With the Protestant **Henri de Navarre** (the future Henri IV) becoming heir to the throne in 1584, the *Guerres de Religion* hotted up even more. The pope excommunicated Henri; and the leaders of the French Catholics (the de Guises) formed the **European Catholic League**, seized Paris and drove out the king, Henri III. Provence found itself with two governors – the king's and the League's appointees; two capitals – Aix and Pertuis; and a split *parlement*. After Henri III's assassination, Catholic Aix called in the duke of Savoy, whose troops trounced Henri de Navarre's supporters at Riez. At this point the main issue for the Provençaux was loyalty to the French Crown against invaders, rather than religion. Even the Aix *parlement* stopped short of giving Savoy the title to Provence, and after Marseille again withstood a siege, the duke gave up and went back home to Nice in 1592. For another year battles continued between the Leaguers and the Royalists. Finally Henri IV said his Mass; troops entered Marseille; and Provence reverted, war-damaged and impoverished, to **royal control**.

Louis XIII and Louis XIV

The **consolidation of the French state** initiated by Louis XIII's minister, **Richelieu**, saw the whittling away of Provençal institutions and ideas of independence, coupled with ever-increasing tax demands and enforced "free gifts" to the king.

As the power and prestige of the *États* and *parlement* dwindled, political power switched from feudal governors and *sénéchals* to *intendants*, servants of the state with powers over every aspect of provincial life, including the military. Having refused to provide the royal purse with funds in 1629, the *États* were not convoked again. The *noblesse d'épée* (the real aristos) were left disgruntled but impotent, while the clergy (the First Estate) also lost a measure of their former power.

It was a time of **plague**, **famine**, and yet more **religious strife and conflict**. The **war with Spain**, for which Toulon's fortifications were upgraded and forts added to Giens and the Îles d'Hyères, increased taxation, decimated trade and cost lives. When Marseille attempted to preserve its ancient independence by setting up a rebel council in 1658, the royal response was swift. Troops were sent in, rebels were condemned to the rack or the galleys, a permanent garrison was established and the foundations laid for the Fort St-Nicolas to keep an eye on "*ce peuple violent et libertin*".

While the various upheavals and ever-multiplying tax burden caused untold misery, progress in production (including the faïence industry), education and social provision carried on apace. The town houses of Aix, Marseille and Avignon, the Hospice de la Charité in Marseille, the Baroque additions to churches and chapels, all show wealth accumulating – gained, as ever, by maritime commerce.

As the reign of **Louis XIV**, the **Sun King**, became more grandiose and more aggressive, Provence, like all of France outside Versailles and Paris, was eclipsed. The **war with Holland** saw Orange and the valley of Barçelonnette annexed; Avignon and the papal Comtat swung steadily into the French orbit; attempts were made again to capture Nice. Wars that involved the English navy blockading the ports were as unwelcome to the local bourgeois as they were to those who had to fight.

As the *ancien régime* slowly dug its own grave the rest of the country stagnated. The pattern for Provence of wars, invasions and trade blockades became entrenched. To add to the gloom, another outbreak of **plague** killed half the population of Marseille in **1720**. The extravagance of Louis XV's court, where the Grassois painter Fragonard found his patrons, had few echoes in Provence. Aix had its grandiose town planning, Avignon its mansions, and Grasse its perfume industry, but elsewhere there was complete stagnation.

The Revolution

Conditions were ripe for revolution in Provence. The region had suffered a disastrous silk harvest and a sharp fall in the price of wine in 1787, and the severe winter of 1788–89 killed off olive trees. Unemployment and starvation were rife and the soaring cost of bread provoked riots in the spring of 1789.

In **July 1789**, while the Bastille was stormed in Paris, Provençal peasants pillaged their local châteaux and urban workers rioted against the mayors, egged on by the middle classes. There was only one casualty, at Aups. The following year **Marseillaise revolutionaries** seized the forts of St-Jean and St-Nicolas, with again just one dose of violence when the crowd lynched St-Jean's commander. **Toulon** was equally fervent in its support for the new order, and at **Aix** a counter-revolutionary lawyer and two aristocrats were strung up on lampposts. In the **papal lands**, where the crucial issue was reunion with France, Rome's representative was sent packing, and a revolutionary municipality installed.

Counter-revolutionaries regrouped in Carpentras, where bloody incidents included the ice-house massacre. However, 1792 saw Marseille's staunchly Jacobin National Guard, the **Féderés**, demolish counter-revolutionary forces in the Comtat and aristocratic Arles. Marseille's authorities declared that kingship was contrary to the principles of equality and national sovereignty. When the Legislative Assembly summoned all the Féderés to Paris to defend the capital and celebrate the third anniversary of the Bastille, five hundred Marseillais marched north singing Rouget de Lisle's **Hymn to the Army of the Rhine**. Written for the troops in that April's war with Germany and Austria, it was a major hit with the Parisian *sans-culottes*, and as the **Marseillaise** it became France's national anthem – especially after the attack on the Tuileries Palace was swiftly followed by the dethronement of the king. According to the Swedish ambassador, "Marseille's Féderés were the moving force behind everything in August 1792."

Provence had by now incorporated the papal states and was divided into **four départements**. Peasants were once again on the pillage, and still starving, while royalists and republicans fought it out in the towns. In 1793 the Var military commander was ordered to take Nice, a hotbed of émigré intrigue. Twenty thousand people fled the city but no resistance was encountered. The Alpes-Maritimes *département* came into existence.

That summer, political divisions between the factions of the Convention and the growing fear of a dictatorship by the Parisian *sans-culottes* provoked the **provincial Federalist revolt**. Fed up with conscription to wars on every frontier, the populace hankered after their former Provençal autonomy. Revolutionary cities found themselves fighting against government forces – a situation speedily exploited by the real **counter-revolutionaries**. In Toulon the entire fleet and the city's fortifications were handed over to the English. (The government eventually regained control of the city thanks to the young Napoleon.) Reprisals, in addition to the almost daily executions of the Terror, cost thousands of lives.

Much of Provence, however, had remained Jacobin, and so fell victim to the **White Terror of 1795** that followed the execution of Robespierre. The prisons of Marseille, Aix, Arles and Tarascon overflowed with people picked up on the street with no charge. Cannons were fired into the cells at point-blank range and sulphur or lighted rags thrown through the bars. The Revolution abandoned all hope of being revolutionary, and **anarchy reigned**. Provence was crawling with returned émigrés who readily attracted violent followers motivated by frustration, exhaustion and famine.

Napoleon and restoration

Provence's experience of **Napoleon** differed little from that of the rest of France, despite the emperor's close connection with the region (childhood at Nice; military career at Antibes and Toulon; then the escape from Elba). Order was restored and power became even more centralized, with *préfets* enlarging on the role of Louis XIV's *intendants*. Although the **concordat with the pope** re-establishing Catholicism as the state religion was widely welcomed, secular power reverted to the old *seigneurs* in many places – the new mayor of Marseille, for example, was a marquise.

It was the **Napoleonic wars** that lost the emperor his Provençal support. Marseille's port was again blockaded; conscription and taxes for military campaigns were as detested as ever; the Alpes-Maritimes *département* became a theatre of war and in 1814 was handed over (with Savoy) to Sardinia. Monaco followed suit the following year, though with the Grimaldi dynasty reinstalled in their palace.

The **restoration of the Bourbons** after Waterloo unleashed another White Terror. Provence was again bitterly divided between royalists and republicans, but there was no major resistance to the **1830 revolution** that put Louis-Philippe, the "Citizen King", on the throne. The new regime represented liberalism – well tinged with anti-clericalism and a dislike of democracy – and was welcomed by the Provençal bourgeoisie. Despite the ardent Catholicism of the *paysans*, and the large numbers of returning émigrés, the attempt by the duchess of Berry to bring back the "legitimate" royalty failed totally here.

1848 and 1851

The first half of the nineteenth century saw the first major **industrialization** of France, and, overseas, the conquest of Algeria. In Provence, Marseille was linked by rail with Paris and expanded its port to take steam ships; iron bridges over the Rhône and new roads were built; many towns demolished their ramparts to extend their main streets into the suburbs. By the 1840s the arsenal at Toulon employed over three thousand workers.

This emerging proletariat was highly receptive when socialist and feminist **Flora Tristan** did the rounds of France in 1844. A year later all the arsenal's different trades went on strike. Throughout industrialized Provence workers overturned their traditional *compagnons* (guilds) to form radical trade unions. Things hardly changed inland, however, as protectionist policies hampered the exchange of foodstuffs, and the new industries' demand for fuel eroded forestry rights. By 1847 the country (and most of Europe) was in severe economic crisis.

When news of the **1848 revolution** arrived from Paris, town halls, common lands and forests were instantly and peacefully reclaimed by the populace. The ensuing elections returned very moderate republicans, albeit including three manual workers in Marseille, Toulon and Avignon. Two months later, however, the economic situation was deteriorating again, and newly won improvements in working hours and wages were being clawed back by the employers. A demonstration in Marseille turned nasty and the **barricades** went up.

Elsewhere, the most militant action was in Menton and Roquebrune, both under the rule of **Monaco**, where the people refused to pay the prince's high taxes on oil and fruit. Sardinian military assistance failed to quell the revolt and the two towns declared themselves independent. His main source of income gone, the Grimaldi prince turned the focus of his state shrewdly towards **tourism** – already well established in Nice and Hyères – and opened the casino at Monte Carlo.

The 1848 revolution turned sour with the election of **Louis-Napoleon** as president in 1850. A law was introduced which in effect annulled the 1830 universal male suffrage by imposing a residency requirement. Laws against "secret societies" and "conspiracies" followed. Ordinary *paysans* discussing prices over a bottle of wine could be arrested; militants from Digne and Avignon were deported to Polynesia for belonging to a democratic party. Newly formed cooperatives were seen as hotbeds of sedition. All this inevitably accelerated politicization of the *paysans*.

When Louis-Napoleon made himself emperor in the **coup d'état of 1851**, Provence, as many other regions of France, turned again to revolt. Initially there were insufficient forces in the small towns and villages to prevent the rebels taking control. In order to take the *préfectures*, villagers and townspeople, both male and female, organized themselves into "*colonnes*" that marched beneath the red flag. Digne was the only *préfecture* they held, though, and then for only two days. Reprisals were bloody – another White Terror in effect, with thousands of rebels caught as they tried to flee. Of all the insurgents shot, imprisoned or deported, one in five were from Provence.

The Second Empire

The **Second Empire** saw huge changes in everyday life. **Marseille** became the premier port of France, with trade enormously expanded by the colonization of North and West Africa, Vietnam and parts of China. The ever-increasing depopulation of inland Provence suddenly became a deluge of migration to the coast and Rhône Valley. While the railway was extended along the coast, communications inland were ignored.

At the end of the **war for Italian unification** in 1860, **Napoléon III** regained the Alpes-Maritimes as payment for supporting Italy against Austria. A plebiscite in Nice gave majority support for **reunion with France**. To the north, Tende and La Brigue voted almost unanimously for France but the result was ignored: the new king of Italy wished to keep his favourite game-hunting grounds. Menton and Roquebrune also voted for France. While making noises about rigged elections, Charles of Monaco agreed to sell the two towns – despite their independence – to France. The sum was considerably more than the fledgling gambling and tourism industry was as yet bringing in and saved the principality from bankruptcy. **Monaco's independence**, free from any foreign protector, was finally established.

One casualty of this dispersal of traditional Provence was the Provençal language. This prompted the formation of the **Félibrige** in 1854, by a group of poets including **Frédéric Mistral** – a nostalgic, backward-looking and intellectual movement in defence of literary Provençal. There were other, more popularist, Provençal writers at the time, but they too were conservative, railing against gas lighting and any other innovation. The attempt to associate the language with some past golden age of ultra-Catholic primitivism only encouraged the association of progress with the French tongue – particularly for the Left.

By the end of the 1860s the **socialism** of the First International was gaining ground in the industrial cities, and in Marseille most of all. In the plebiscite of 1870, in which the country as a whole gave Napoleon III their support, the Bouches-du-Rhône *département* was second only to Paris in the number of "nons". It was not surprising therefore that Marseille had its own commune (see p.62) when the Parisians took up arms.

Honoré Daumier, the Marseillais caricaturist and fervent republican, was the great illustrator of both the 1851 and the 1871 events. In the middle of the century the **Marseille school of painting** developed under the influence of foreign travel and Orientalism, attracting to the city such artists as Puvis de Chavannes and Félix Ziem. Provence's greatest native artist, **Cézanne**, though living in Paris from the 1860s to the 1880s, spent a few months of every year in his home town of Aix, or in Marseille and L'Estaque. He was sometimes accompanied by his childhood friend **Zola**, and by **Renoir**, whom he introduced to this coast.

Third Republic: 1890–1914

Under the **Third Republic**, the division between inland Provence and the coast and Rhône Valley accentuated. Port activity at Marseille quadrupled with the opening of new trade routes along the Suez Canal and further colonial acquisitions in the Far East. Manufacturing began to play an equal role with commerce. The Rhône Valley orchards were planted on a massive scale, and light industries producing clothes, foodstuffs and paper developed in Aix and elsewhere to export to the North African colonies. Chemical works in Avignon produced the synthetics that spelt the rapid decline of the traditional industries of the small towns and villages of the interior – tanning, dyeing, silk and glass. Wine production, meanwhile, was devastated by phylloxera.

The one area of brilliance connected with the climate but not with commerce was **art** – painting in particular. Following on from Cézanne and Renoir, a younger generation of artists discovered the Côte d'Azur. The Post-Impressionists and Fauves flocked to St-Tropez in the wake of the ever-hospitable Paul Signac. Matisse, Dufy, Seurat, Dérain, Van Dongen, Bonnard, Braque, Friesz, Marquet, Manguin, Camion, Vlaminck and Vuillard were all intoxicated by the Mediterranean light, the climate and the ease of living. The escape from the rigours of Paris released a massive creative energy and resulted in works that, in addition to their radical innovations, have more *joie de vivre* than any other period in French art. Renoir retired to Cagnes for health reasons in 1907; for Matisse, Dufy and Bonnard the Côte d'Azur became their permanent home; and Van Gogh, always a man apart, had a spell in Arles.

Meanwhile, the **winter tourist season** on the coast was taking off. **Hyères** and **Cannes** had been "discovered" in the first half of the nineteenth century (and Nice even earlier). But increased ease of travel and the temporary restraint of simmering international tensions encouraged aristocratic mobility. The population of **Nice** trebled between 1861 and 1911; luxury trains ran from St Petersburg, Vienna and London; *belle époque* mansions and grand hotels rose along the Riviera seafronts; and gambling, particularly at Monte Carlo, won the patronage of the Prince of Wales, the Emperor Franz Josef and scores of Russian grand-dukes.

The native working class, meanwhile, were forming the first French Socialist Party, which had its opening congress in Marseille in 1879. Support came not just from the city but from towns and villages that had fought in 1851. In 1881 Marseille elected the first socialist *député*. By 1892 the municipal councils of Marseille, Toulon, La Ciotat and other industrial towns were in socialist hands. In Aix, however, the old legitimist royalists (those favouring the return of the Bourbons) still held sway.

World War I and the interwar years

The battlefields of **World War I** may have seemed far away in northern France and Belgium, but conscription brought the people of Provence into the war. The socialists divided between pacifists and patriots, but when, in 1919, France took part in the attack on the Soviet Union, soldiers, sailors and workers joined forces in Toulon and Marseille to support mutinies on French warships in the Black Sea. The struggle to have the mutineers freed continued well into 1920, the year in which the **French Communist Party** (PCF) was born.

War casualties led to severe depopulation in the already dwindling villages of inland Provence. **Land use** also changed dramatically, from mixed agriculture to a monocrop of vines, to provide the army ration of one litre of wine per soldier per day. Quantity, thanks to the Provençal climate, rather than quality was the aim, leaving acre upon acre of totally unviable vineyards after demobilization. With the growth in tourism, it was easiest to sell the land for construction.

The **tourist industry** recovered fairly quickly from the war. The *Front Populaire* of 1936 introduced paid holidays, encouraging native visitors to the still unspoiled coast. International literati – Somerset Maugham, Katherine Mansfield, Scott and Zelda Fitzgerald, Colette, Anaïs Nin, Gertrude Stein – and a new wave of artists, Picasso and Cocteau amongst them, replaced the defunct grand-dukes.

Marseille during the interwar years saw the evolution of characteristics that have yet to be obliterated. The activities of the fascist *Action Française* led to deaths during a left-wing counter-demonstration in 1925. Modern-style **corruption** snaked its way through the town hall and gangsters on the Chicago model moved in on the vice industries. Elections were rigged; revolvers were used at the ballot box.

The increasing popularity of the Communist Party in the city was due to its anti-corruption platform. After the failure of the *Front Populaire* (which the great majority of Provençaux had voted for, electing several Communist *députés*), Marseille saw constant pitched battles between the Left and Right.

World War II

France and Britain declared **war on Germany** together on September 3, 1939. The French Maginot line, however, swiftly collapsed, and by June 1940 the Germans controlled Paris and all of northern France. On June 22, Marshall Pétain signed the **armistice with Hitler**, which divided France between the Occupied

Zone – the Atlantic coast and north of the Loire – and "unoccupied" Vichy France in the south. Menton and Sospel were occupied by the Italians, to whom the adjoining Roya Valley still belonged.

With the start of the British counteroffensive in 1942, **Vichy France** joined itself with the Allies and was immediately occupied by the Germans. The port of Toulon was overrun in November, with the French navy scuppering its fleet rather than letting it fall into German hands.

Resistance fighters and passive citizens suffered executions, deportations and the wholesale destruction of Le Panier quarter in Marseille (see p.60). The **Allied bombings** of 1944 caused high civilian casualties and considerable material damage, particularly to Avignon, Marseille and Toulon. The **liberation** of the two great port cities was aided by armed popular revolt, but it was in the Italian sector – in Sospel and its neighbouring villages – that the fighting by the local populace was the most heroic.

Modern Provence

Before the Germans surrendered **Marseille** they made sure that the harbours were blown to bits. In the immediate **postwar years** the task of repairing the damage was compounded by a slump in international trade and passenger traffic. The nationalization of the Suez Canal also hit the city, spelling an end to its prime position on world trading routes. Company after company decamped to Paris, leaving growing unemployment.

Marseille's solution was to orient its **port** and industry towards the Atlantic and the inland route of the Rhône. The **oil industries** that had developed in the 1920s around the Étang de Berre and Fos were extended. The mouth of the Rhône and the Golfe de Fos became a massive tanker terminal. **Iron and steel works** filled the spaces behind the new Port de Marseille that stretched for 50km beyond the Vieux Port. In the process, the city's population boomed. The urgent demand for housing was met by badly designed, low-cost, high-rise estates proliferating north and east from the congested city centre.

While never halted, the depopulation of **inland Provence** was slowed by massive **irrigation and hydroelectric schemes**. The isolated *mas* or farmhouses, positioned wherever there happened to be a spring, were left to ruin or linked to the mains. Orchards, lavender fields and olive groves became larger, competition for early fruit and vegetables fiercer, and the market for luxury foods greater. The rich **Rhône Valley** continued to export fruit, wine and vegetables, while the river was exploited for irrigation and power, both nuclear and hydroelectric, and made navigable for sizeable ships.

After Algeria won back its independence in 1962, hundreds of thousands of French settlers, the **pieds noirs**, returned, bringing with them a virulent hatred of Arabic-speaking people. At the same time, the government encouraged immigration from its former colonies, North Africa in particular, with the (unkept) promise of well-paid jobs, civil rights and social security. The resulting tensions, not just in Marseille but all along the coast, made perfect fodder for the **parties of the Right**. From being a bastion of socialism at the end of World War II, Provence gradually turned towards intolerance and reaction.

Crime, corruption and politics

The hidden ties between the Provençal mafia – known as the **milieu** – and the region's town halls date back to the 1920s, but it wasn't until the shocking assassination of Hyères' *député*, **Yann Piat**, in 1994 that the demand for a "clean hands" campaign began in earnest.

Drug trafficking became a major problem in Marseille in the early 1970s as the notorious **French Connection** routed heroin from Turkey to the United States through the city's port, which at the time was controlled by Corsican mobsters. At the same time, regional politics were ripe for exploitation. As elsewhere in France, **municipal fiefdoms** evolved, offering opportunities for patronage, nepotism and corruption, along with the financial muscle that, until very recently, ensured incumbents a more-or-less permanent position.

Nice's police and judiciary were accused by Graham Greene in 1982 of protecting organized crime. Greene claimed he slept with a gun under his pillow after he detailed the corruption in *J'Accuse* (which was banned in France). The late **Jacques Médecin**, who succeeded his father as mayor of Nice in 1966, controlled public life in the city until his downfall in 1990 for political fraud and tax evasion; only when he fled to Uruguay were his mafioso connections finally discussed. Despite this, most Niçois gladly supported his sister Génevieve Assemat-Médecin as his successor; and those who didn't backed his daughter, Martine Cantinchi-Médecin, a Le Pen supporter. Finally extradited in 1994, Médecin served a short prison term and used his popularity to back the successful candidate in the 1995 municipal elections – **Jacques Peyrat**, a close friend of Le Pen and former member of the *Front National*. Re-elected in 2001, Peyrat made no secret of his desire to have the new public prosecutor, **Eric de Montgolfier** – who made his reputation fighting white-collar crime (notably Bernard Tapie) and political corruption – removed from his post, before his investigations into the Riviera underworld put yet another city magistrate into prison. More constructively, Peyrat was instrumental in creating CANCA, the Communauté d'Agglomération de Nice-Côte d'Azur, a loose grouping of communities in the Greater Nice area that aims to improve regional coordination on a range of topics, including parking, transport and the environment. Peyrat finally lost the 2008 municipal elections to **Christian Estrosi**, a member of the centre-right UMP party and protégé of Nicolas Sarkozy.

Toulon was another classic fiefdom, run for four decades by **Maurice Arreckx** and his clique of friends with their underworld connections, until he was put away when financial scandals finally came to light. His successor, and former director of finances, tried in vain to win back the voters but merely ran up more debts and lost to the *Front National* in 1995. Arreckx was sentenced to prison on two separate occasions (in 1997 and 2000), before dying of cancer in 2001. Prior to his death, investigators had found several Swiss bank accounts, where some of the money paid to Arreckx's campaign fund in return for a major construction contract was secreted.

François Léotard, the right-wing mayor of Fréjus, who held cabinet office (under Chirac in the late 1980s) and a seat in the *Assemblée Nationale*, was investigated for financial irregularities, but the case eventually ran out of time and the charges were dropped. **Cannes' mayor**, **Michel Mouillot**, was debarred from public office for five years and given a fifteen-month suspended sentence in 1989, then won his appeal and returned to the town hall only to be given an eighteen-month suspended sentence in 1996. **Pierre Rinaldi**, mayor of **Digne**, was investigated for fraud, **Jean-Pierre Lafond**, mayor of **La Ciotat**, for unwarranted interference, two successive mayors of **La Seyne** for corruption and abuse of patronage…and so the list went on.

Meanwhile, though the French Connection was ultimately smashed, **organized crime** continued to flourish, controlled both by the Italian mafia and – increasingly – by eastern European gangs; though the faces and nationalities change, the criminals of the Côte d'Azur preserve their well-deserved reputation for resourcefulness. The activities of the newer arrivals have included boat-jacking: yachts stolen to order from the coast's many marinas, and often used for drug trafficking and the smuggling of illegal immigrants before being resold in the ports of the Black Sea.

Ethnic tensions and the rise of the Front National

The corruption, waste and incompetence in the region's town halls was one element in the 1995 electoral breakthrough of **Jean-Marie Le Pen's neo-fascist Front National** (FN) party, which took control in Orange, Marignane and Toulon in that year's municipal elections. The significance of military bases to the region's economy also played its part (while the national government cut defence spending, Le Pen trumpeted his support for the military), but the most important factor was fear, born of a toxic brew of racism, unemployment and high crime rates.

The main electoral promise was "Priority for the French", by which the FN meant the "ethnically pure" French. Giving priority to white citizens over non-white is illegal, but there were nevertheless instances in Toulon of people of Algerian origin being overtaken in the housing queue.

In 1998 **internal feuding** split the party into two camps. Le Pen's deputy, **Bruno Mégret**, attempted to seize leadership, only to be expelled by Le Pen along with several Mégret supporters – including one of Le Pen's daughters. The ousted members immediately formed a new extreme-right breakaway party, the *Mouvement National Républicain* (MNR), headed by Mégret.

With the **municipal elections** of 2001, it looked as if the FN was splintering for good. Six years of misrule in Toulon convinced voters to back Hubert Falco of the *Démocratie Libérale* (DL) party, and Jacques Bompard of Orange was the only *Front National* mayor to be re-elected. It therefore came as a major shock when Le Pen returned in full force for the 2002 **presidential elections**, with first-round victories in five out of six *départements* in the PACA (Provence, Alpes, Côtes d'Azur) region, soundly defeating both Chirac and Jospin. But Le Pen was unable to build on this success; his candidature for the 2004 PACA presidential elections, the equivalent of a regional governor, was rejected on the grounds of non-residence in the region.

At about the same time as the presidential elections, **ethnic tensions** of other kinds began to manifest themselves, notably among France's Arab and Jewish communities – both the largest of their kind in Europe. In 2002, pro-Palestinian groups firebombed French synagogues, including one in Marseille; the attacks led to an outcry about "French anti-Semitism" across Europe and the US. The **civic unrest** across France during 2005, which saw youths – many, though not all, from deprived ethnic minority backgrounds – clash with police and hundreds of cars torched, was focused on Paris, rather than the south and, perhaps surprisingly, Marseille was relatively unaffected. However, an ugly echo of the 2005 events came to the city in October 2006, when teenagers threw a firebomb into a bus, burning several passengers, the most grievously injured of whom was a woman of French-Senegalese origin. Sharpening his tough-guy law-and-order credentials, the then-Interior Minister Nicolas Sarkozy responded by sending in riot police.

Of late, the far-right tide seems to be receding, partly as a result of splits within its own ranks. The region's sole surviving FN mayor, Jacques Bompard of Orange, joined the rival *Mouvement pour la France* (MPF) in 2005; in 2007, the FN trailed a distant fourth in the presidential elections, with just eleven percent of the national vote, and its financial problems parallel its decline in the polls. In the municipal elections of 2008 the Front was trounced, winning just two percent of the vote in its former stronghold of Toulon; the centre-right UMP was dominant in the east of Provence, with the left doing well in Bouches du Rhône and the Alpes de Haute Provence.

Mass tourism and the environment

A crucial factor in Provence's postwar history has been the rise of **mass tourism**. Since the 1960s, the number of visitors to the Côte d'Azur has grown beyond what – in any sane sense – could be considered manageable proportions. By the mid-1970s the coast had become a nearly uninterrupted wall of concrete, hosting eight million visitors a year. Agricultural land, save for a few profitable vineyards, was transformed into campsites, hotels and holiday housing. **Property speculation** and construction became the dominant economic activities, while the flaunting of planning laws and the ever-increasing threat to the **environment** – the area's prime asset – were ignored.

When **Brigitte Bardot** complained that her beloved **St-Tropez** was becoming a mire of human detritus, the media saw it as a sexy summer story. Then **ecologists** began to warn that the main oxygenating seaweed in the Mediterranean was disappearing because of yacht anchors damaging the sea bed, new jetties and marinas modifying the currents, and dust from building sites clouding the water. The loss of *Posidonia oceanica* is now affecting fish, and since the 1980s a non-native toxic algae, *Caulerpa taxifolia*, has spread from the Côte d'Azur around the Mediterranean, obliterating sea grasses and replacing them with largely sterile algal beds.

Urban expansion on the coast

If sun-worshipping set the region's tone for the first three postwar decades, the 1980s saw different forces at work. While the encouragement of summer tourism exacted its toll, a new type of visitor and resident was being encouraged: the expense-account delegate to **business conferences** and the well-paid employee of **multinational firms**. Towns like Nice and Cannes led the way in attracting the former, while the business park of **Sophia-Antipolis** north of Antibes showed how easy it was to persuade firms to relocate their information technology operations to the beautiful Côte d'Azur hinterland. The result is a further erosion of Provençal identity and greater pressure on the environment. Rather than countering the seasonal imbalance of tourism, business visitors have made consumption and congestion a year-round factor.

The money from business services and industry on the Riviera now outstrips income from tourism, and while in the big cities the distinctive Marseillais and Niçois identities have endured, elsewhere along the coast, continuities with the past have become ever harder to detect.

Inland Provence

Inland Provence has undergone a parallel transformation – more social than physical, with relatively little property development but a great deal of property price inflation, as high-salaried professionals from all over northern Europe buy their place in the sun. The Luberon, particularly, has become highly chic.

Some villages were rescued from extinction by the influx, though many are now lifeless out of season. In the Alpine valleys, the growth of ski resorts reversed centuries-old population decline, and the resultant damage to trees, soil and habitats has in part been offset by the creation of the **Parc National du Mercantour**, which has saved several Alpine animal and plant species.

Meanwhile, the *paysans* keeping goats and bees, a few vines and a vegetable plot are all of pensionable age. The cheeses and honey, the vegetables, olive oil and wine (unless it's AOC) must compete with Spanish, Italian and Greek produce, from land that doesn't have the ludicrously high values of Provence. The emergence in recent years of successful international companies such as l'Occitane en Provence and Oliviers & Co, however, offers one pointer to a viable economic future, trading on the magic of a Provençal image to target upmarket consumers, with prices to match.

Transport mania

Fast access to the Côte d'Azur has long obsessed planners in Paris. The **TGV** was extended to Marseille in 2001, and in 2009 the French government opted for the coastal route via Toulon for the TGV extension to Nice, though the precise course of the track has yet to be decided. But increasing Provence's accessibility merely exacerbates existing transport problems within the region. An attenuated but densely populated linear conurbation without a proper regional mass transportation system, the Riviera is particularly badly affected. Heavy traffic, gridlocks and stop-go jams are the norm on the roads, with the temptation to drive everywhere promoted by the suburban and commercial sprawl that has long since eliminated any clear distinction between the individual coastal towns. One rather dubious "solution" – a second autoroute along the Riviera parallel to the A8 – was rejected in the early 1990s. More obviously constructive was the 2005 reopening of the Cannes–Grasse **railway** to passengers. Meanwhile, within Provence's two major cities, Marseille and Nice, things have improved somewhat of late with the opening of new **tramways** and the debut of **public bike hire** schemes.

Books

B
esides their seminal role in French history and the cultural and artistic life of Europe, Provence and the Côte d'Azur have inspired many twentieth-century English, American and French writers, indulging in the high life like F. Scott Fitzgerald, slumming it with the bohemians like Anaïs Nin, or trying to regain their health like Katherine Mansfield. The two best-known Provençal writers of the twentieth century, Jean Giono and Marcel Pagnol, chronicled peasant life in inland Provence; many of their works have been turned into films.

Titles marked with the 🏃 symbol are particularly recommended.

History, society and politics

John Ardagh *France in the New Century: Portrait of a Changing Society*. A detailed journalistic survey of modern France which tries to provide a comprehensive overlook, but gets rather too drawn into party politics and statistics.

Mary Blume *Côte d'Azur: Inventing the French Riviera*. This attempt to analyse the myth only reconfirms it, mainly because the people Blume has interviewed all have a stake in maintaining the image of the Côte as a cultured millionaires' dreamland. Great black-and-white photos, however.

Robin Briggs *Early Modern France, 1560–1715*. Readable account of the period in which the French state started to assert control over the whole country. Strong perspectives on the provinces, including coverage of the Marseille rebellion of 1658.

James Bromwich *The Roman Remains of Southern France*. A comprehensive guide to the subject: detailed, well illustrated and approachable. In addition to accounts of well-known sites, it will lead you off the map to all sorts of discoveries.

Alfred Cobban *A History of Modern France*. Very complete, three-volume political, social and economic history from Louis XIV to de Gaulle.

Margaret Crosland *Sade's Wife*. An expert on Provence's most notorious resident examines how Renée-Pélagie de Montreuil coped with being married to the Marquis de Sade.

FX Emmanuelli *Histoire de la Provence*. Huge, well-illustrated tome by a group of French academics, which covers the province in as much detail as anyone could conceivably want.

Lawrence Durrell *Caesar's Vast Ghost*. Durrell long promised to write a huge and all-encompassing book about Provence; this much slimmer volume, published just before his death, is probably an easier read, with entertaining essays on, for example, bulls and Arles.

🏃 **John Noone** *The Man Behind the Iron Mask*. Fascinating enquiry into the mythical or otherwise prisoner of Ste-Marguerite fort on the Îles de Lérins, immortalized by Alexander Dumas.

Jim Ring *Riviera: The Rise and Fall of the Côte d'Azur*. Highly readable social history of the French Riviera and of the many nationalities who have shaped the region's history, culture and architecture.

Graham Robb *The Discovery of France*. Captivating study of the evolution and "civilization" of France since the Revolution, which makes a superb antidote to conventional narratives of kings and state affairs.

Simon Schama *Citizens*. A fascinating, accessible treatment of the history of the Revolution, with a

Provence and the Côte d'Azur in literature

Sybille Bedford *Jigsaw: an Unsentimental Education*. Bedford's own precarious childhood on the Côte d'Azur provides rich source material for her evocative novel, which roams between Germany, France and London and depicts the bohemian life of 1930s Sanary-sur-Mer in delicious detail. Sanary also features in Bedford's autobiographical memoir *Quicksands*.

Alexandre Dumas *The Count of Monte Cristo*. A runaway success when initially serialized during the 1840s, Dumas' long, engrossing tale of the prisoner of the Île d'If, who plots escape and revenge on those who wronged him, has never lost its grip on the public imagination.

Lawrence Durrell *The Avignon Quintet*. Five interlinked novels that offer a creative and romantic vision of a fast-disappearing way of life, both rural and urban, in Provence .

F. Scott Fitzgerald *Tender is the Night*. Glitter is interwoven with darkness in this dense but beautifully written tale of mental illness among the millionaire smart set, played out against the glamorous backdrop of the Riviera in the interwar years.

Jean Giono *The Horseman on the Roof*. This gripping and extraordinary novel of one man's odyssey through a Provence ravaged by a nineteenth-century cholera epidemic has a very contemporary, post-apocalyptic feel. Giono's other works, such as *To The Slaughterhouse*, *Two Riders of the Storm*, *Blue Boy*, and *The Man Who Planted Trees* are also recommended.

Sébastien Japrisot *One Deadly Summer*. Suspenseful modern novel of a girl's revenge; noir to the n-th degree.

Marcel Pagnol *The Water of the Hills: Jean de Florette and Manon of the Springs*. This rich evocation of hardship, intrigue and family vengeance in rural Provence in the early twentieth century has a humour, warmth and depth lacking from Claude Berri's admittedly ravishing 1986 film version.

Patrick Süskind *Perfume*. Hugely successful story of an orphan born with no smell, who gravitates to Grasse and becomes both a master *parfumier* and a mass murderer.

Émile Zola *The Masterpiece*. Born in Aix-en-Provence, Zola draws on his own life and that of his boyhood friend Paul Cézanne to tell the contrasting stories of a successful novelist and an artist obsessed with the creation of one great canvas. The novel offended Cézanne and ended their friendship.

fast-moving narrative and a reappraisal of the customary view of a stagnant, unchanging nobility in the years preceding the uprising.

Laurence Wylie *Village in the Vaucluse*. Sociological study of Roussillon, full of interesting insights into Provençal village life in the postwar years.

Theodore Zeldin *France 1845–1945*. Five thematic volumes on French history.

Travel

Carol Drinkwater *The Olive Farm*. Soft-focus memoir of the joys of expatriate life in rural Provence, written by a well-known British actress.

MFK Fisher *Two Towns in Provence*. Evocative memoirs of life in Aix-en-Provence and Marseille during the 1950s and 1960s.

John Flower and Charles Waite *Provence*. Waite's gorgeous photographs encompass landscapes, architectural details, markets and images obscure and familiar. Flower's text draws on over thirty years of residence and visits.

William Fotheringham *Put Me Back on My Bike: In Search of Tom Simpson*. An in-depth study of Simpson's life as a cyclist, leading up to his tragic death on Mont Ventoux.

Peter Mayle *A Year in Provence*. Though it's often blamed for contributing to the

Anglicization of rural Provence, there's really nothing to dislike about this best-selling memoir. A month-by-month account of the charms and frustrations of moving into an old Provençal farmhouse, it entertainingly covers everything from tips for wooing fickle French contractors to handicapping goat races.

Art and artists

Martin Bailey (ed) *Van Gogh: Letters from Provence*. Attractively produced in full colour – very dippable and very good value.

Martin Gayford *The Yellow House*. A tense and absorbing account of the nine extraordinary weeks in 1888 when Vincent van Gogh and Paul Gauguin shared a tiny house in Arles.

Françoise Gilot *Matisse & Picasso: A Friendship in Art*. A fascinating subject – two more different men in life and art would be hard to find.

D. and M. Johnson *The Age of Illusion*. Links French art and politics in the

interwar years, featuring Provençal works by Le Corbusier, Chagall and Picasso.

Jacques Henri Lartigue *Diary of a Century*. Book of pictures by a great photographer from the day he was given a camera in 1901 through to the 1970s. Contains wonderful scenes of aristocratic leisure and Côte d'Azur beaches.

Sarah Whitfield *Fauvism*. Good introduction to a movement that encompassed Côte d'Azur and Riviera artists Matisse, Dufy and Van Dongen.

Food and drink

Alain Ducasse *Flavours of France*. Celebrity cookbook that follows Ducasse from the kitchens of the *Louis XV* restaurant in Monte Carlo to *la Bastide de Moustiers*.

Hubrecht Duijker *Touring in Wine Country: Provence*. Guide to the top vineyards and wine cellars of Provence.

Kenneth James *Escoffier: the King of Chefs*. Biography of the famous chef who started his career on the Côte d'Azur.

Richard Olney *Lulu's Provençal Table*. Classic Provençal recipes and interesting commentary from Lulu Peyraud, proprietor of the Domaine Tempier vineyard in Bandol. Great black-and-white photos.

Roger Vergé *Cuisine of the Sun*. The classic cookbook of modern Provençal cuisine, from the legendary chef of the *Moulin de Mougins*.

Patricia Wells *The Provence Cookbook*. More than 200 recipes rooted in the *terroir*, plus vignettes on suppliers and markets, and wine-pairing suggestions.

Botany

W. Lippert *Fleurs de Haute Montagne*. Palm-sized colour guide to flowers,

available from French bookshops in the trekking areas.

Language

Language

French

F rench can be a deceptively familiar language because of the number of words and structures it shares with English. Despite this, it's far from easy, though the bare essentials are not difficult to master and can make all the difference. Even just saying "*Bonjour, Madame/Monsieur*" and then gesticulating will usually get you a smile and helpful service. People working in tourist offices, campsites, hotels and so on almost always speak English and tend to use it if you're struggling to speak French – be grateful, not insulted.

On the Côte d'Azur you can get by without knowing a word of French, with menus printed in at least four languages, and half the people you meet fellow foreigners. In Nice, Sisteron and the Roya Valley a knowledge of Italian would provide a common language with many of the natives. But if you can hold your own in French – however imperfectly – speak away and your audience will warm to you.

Provençal and accents

The one language you don't have to learn – unless you want to understand the meaning of the names of streets, restaurants or cafés – is **Provençal**. Itself a dialect of the *langue d'oc* (Occitan), it evolved into different dialects in Provence, so that the languages spoken in Nice, in the Alps, on the coast and in the Rhône Valley, though mutually comprehensible, were not precisely the same. In the mid-nineteenth century the *Félibrige* movement established a standard literary form in an attempt to revive the language. But by the time Frédéric Mistral won the Nobel Prize in 1904 for his poem *Mirèio*, Provençal had already been superseded by French in ordinary life.

Two hundred years ago everybody spoke Provençal, whether they were counts, shipyard workers or peasants. Today you might (if you're lucky) hear it spoken by the older generation in some of the remoter villages. It just survives as a literary language: it can be studied at school and university and there are columns in Provençal in some newspapers. But unlike Breton or Occitan proper, it has never been the fuel of a separatist movement.

The French that people speak in Provence has, however, a very marked **accent**. It's much less nasal than northern French, words are not run together to quite the same extent, and there's a distinctive sound for the endings – *in*, *-en*, and for *vin*, and so on, that is more like *ung*.

Pronunciation

One easy rule to remember is that **consonants** at the ends of words are usually silent. *Pas plus tard* (not later) is thus pronounced "pa-plu-tarr". But when the following word begins with a vowel, you run the two together: *pas après* (not after) becomes "pazaprey".

Vowels are the hardest sounds to get right. Roughly:

a	as in h**a**t	i	as in mach**i**ne
e	as in g**e**t	o	as in h**o**t
é	between g**e**t and g**a**te	o, au	as in **o**ver
è	between g**e**t and g**u**t	ou	as in f**oo**d
eu	like the **u** in h**u**rt	u	as in a pursed-lip version of **u**se

More awkward are the **combinations** *in/im*, *en/em*, *an/am*, *on/om*, *un/um* at the ends of words, or followed by consonants other than n or m. Again, roughly:

in/im	like the **an** in **an**xious	on/om	like the **don** in **Don**caster said by someone with a heavy cold
an/am, en/em	like the **don** in **Don**caster when said with a nasal accent	un/um	like the **u** in **u**nderstand

Consonants are much as in English, except that: "*ch*" is always sh, "*c*" is s, "*h*" is silent, "*th*" is the same as t, "*ll*" is like the y in "yes", "*w*" is v, and "*r*" is growled (or rolled).

Learning materials

French Dictionary Phrasebook (Rough Guides). Mini dictionary-style phrasebook with both English–French and French–English sections, along with cultural tips for tricky situations and a menu reader.

Get By In French (BBC Publications). Phrasebook and cassette. A good stepping stone before tackling a complete course.

Mini French Dictionary (Harrap/Larousse). French–English and English–French, plus a brief grammar and pronunciation guide.

Breakthrough French (Palgrave/McGraw Hill; book and two cassettes). An excellent teach-yourself course.

Pardon My French! Pocket French Slang Dictionary (UK Harrap). The key to understanding everyday French.

A Comprehensive French Grammar (Blackwell). Easy-to-follow reference grammar.

À Vous La France; France Extra; France-Parler (BBC Publications; EMC Paradigm). Comprising a book and two cassettes, these BBC radio courses run from beginner's to fairly advanced French.

French words and phrases

Basics

French nouns are divided into masculine and feminine. This causes difficulties with adjectives, whose endings have to change to suit the gender of the nouns they qualify. If you know some grammar, you will know what to do. If not, stick to the masculine form, which is the simplest – it's what we have done in this glossary.

today	aujourd'hui	that one	cela
yesterday	hier	open	ouvert
tomorrow	demain	closed	fermé
in the morning	le matin	big	grand
in the afternoon	l'après-midi	small	petit
in the evening	le soir	more	plus
now	maintenant	less	moins
later	plus tard	a little	un peu
at one o'clock	à une heure	a lot	beaucoup
at three o'clock	à trois heures	cheap	bon marché
at ten-thirty	à dix heures et demie	expensive	cher
at midday	à midi	good	bon
man	un homme	bad	mauvais
woman	une femme	hot	chaud
here	ici	cold	froid
there	là	with	avec
this one	ceci	without	sans

Talking to people

When addressing people you should always use *Monsieur* for a man, *Madame* for a woman, *Mademoiselle* for a girl. Plain *bonjour* by itself is not enough. This isn't as formal as it seems, and it has its uses when you've forgotten someone's name or want to attract someone's attention.

Excuse me	Pardon	please	s'il vous plaît
Do you speak English?	Vous parlez anglais?	thank you	merci
		hello	bonjour
How do you say it in French?	Comment ça se dit en français?	goodbye	au revoir
What's your name?	Comment vous appelez-vous?	good morning/ afternoon	bonjour
My name is…	Je m'appelle…	good evening	bonsoir
I'm English/ Irish/ Scottish/ Welsh/ American/ Australian/ Canadian/ a New Zealander	Je suis anglais[e]/ irlandais[e]/ écossais[e]/ gallois[e]/ américain[e]/ australien[ne]/ canadien[ne]/ néo-zélandais[e]	good night	bonne nuit
		How are you?	Comment allez-vous?/ Ça va?
		Fine, thanks	Très bien, merci
		I don't know	Je ne sais pas
		Let's go	Allons-y
		See you tomorrow	À demain
		See you soon	À bientôt
yes	oui	Sorry	Pardon, Madame/ Excusez-moi
no	non		
I understand	Je comprends		
I don't understand	Je ne comprends pas	Leave me alone! (aggressive)	Fichez-moi la paix!
Can you speak slower?	S'il vous plaît, parlez moins vite	Please help me	Aidez-moi, s'il vous plaît
OK/agreed	d'accord		

Finding the way

bus	autobus/bus/car		on foot	à pied
bus station	gare routière		Where are you going?	Vous allez où?
bus stop	arrêt		I'm going to...	Je vais à...
car	voiture		I want to get off at...	Je voudrais descendre à...
train/taxi/ferry	train/taxi/ferry		the road to...	la route pour...
boat	bateau		near	près/pas loin
plane	avion		far	loin
train station	gare (SNCF)		left	à gauche
platform	quai		right	à droite
What time does it leave?	Il part à quelle heure?		straight on	tout droit
What time does it arrive?	Il arrive à quelle heure?		on the other side of	à l'autre côté de
a ticket to...	un billet pour...		on the corner of	à l'angle de
single ticket	aller simple		next to	à côté de
return ticket	aller retour		behind	derrière
validate your ticket	compostez votre billet		in front of	devant
valid for	valable pour		before	avant
ticket office	vente de billets		after	après
how many kilometres?	combien de kilomètres?		under	sous
how many hours?	combien d'heures?		to cross	traverser
hitchhiking	autostop		bridge	pont

Questions and requests

The simplest way of asking a question is to start with *s'il vous plaît* (please), then name the thing you want in an interrogative tone of voice.

For example:

Where is there a bakery?	S'il vous plaît, la boulangerie?		Which way is it to the Eiffel Tower?	S'il vous plaît, la route pour la tour Eiffel?

Similarly with requests:

We'd like a room for two.	S'il vous plaît, une chambre pour deux.		Can I have a kilo of oranges?	S'il vous plaît, un kilo d'oranges?

Question words

where?	où?		when?	quand?
how?	comment?		why?	pourquoi?
how many/ how much?	combien?		at what time?	à quelle heure?
			what is/which is?	quel est?

Accommodation

a room for one/ two people	une chambre pour un/deux personnes
a double bed	un lit double
a room with a shower	une chambre avec douche
a room with a bath	une chambre avec salle de bain
for one/two/three nights	pour un/deux/trois nuits
Can I see it?	Je peux la voir?
a room on the courtyard	une chambre sur la cour
a room over the street	une chambre sur la rue
first floor	premier étage
second floor	deuxième étage
with a view	avec vue
key	clef
to iron	repasser
do laundry	faire la lessive
sheets	draps
blankets	couvertures
quiet	calme
noisy	bruyant
hot water	eau chaude
cold water	eau froide
Is breakfast included?	Est-ce que le petit déjeuner est compris?
I would like breakfast	Je voudrais prendre le petit déjeuner
I don't want breakfast	Je ne veux pas de petit déjeuner
Can we camp here?	On peut camper ici?
campsite	un camping/terrain de camping
tent	une tente
tent space	un emplacement
youth hostel	auberge de jeunesse

Driving

service station	garage
service	service
to park the car	garer la voiture
car park	un parking
no parking	défense de stationner/ stationnement interdit
gas station	station essence/station service
fuel	essence
(to) fill it up	faire le plein
oil	huile
air line	ligne à air
put air in the tyres	gonfler les pneus
battery	batterie
the battery is dead	la batterie est morte
plugs	bougies
to break down	tomber en panne
gas can	bidon
insurance	assurance
green card	carte verte
traffic lights	feux
red light	feu rouge
green light	feu vert

Health matters

doctor	médecin
I don't feel well	Je ne me sens pas bien
medicines	médicaments
prescription	ordonnance
I feel sick	Je suis malade
I have a headache	J'ai mal à la tête
stomach ache	mal à l'estomac
period	règles
pain	douleur
it hurts	ça fait mal
chemist	pharmacie
hospital	hôpital

Other needs

bakery	boulangerie	bank	banque
food shop	alimentation	money	argent
supermarket	supermarché	toilets	toilettes
to eat	manger	police	police
to drink	boire	telephone	téléphone
camping gas	camping gaz	cinema	cinéma
tobacconist	tabac	theatre	théâtre
stamps	timbres	to reserve/book	réserver

Numbers

1	un	21	vingt-et-un
2	deux	22	vingt-deux
3	trois	30	trente
4	quatre	40	quarante
5	cinq	50	cinquante
6	six	60	soixante
7	sept	70	soixante-dix
8	huit	75	soixante-quinze
9	neuf	80	quatre-vingts
10	dix	90	quatre-vingt-dix
11	onze	95	quatre-vingt-quinze
12	douze	100	cent
13	treize	101	cent-et-un
14	quatorze	200	deux cents
15	quinze	300	trois cents
16	seize	500	cinq cents
17	dix-sept	1000	mille
18	dix-huit	2000	deux milles
19	dix-neuf	5000	cinq milles
20	vingt	1,000,000	un million

Days and dates

January	janvier	Monday	lundi
February	février	Tuesday	mardi
March	mars	Wednesday	mercredi
April	avril	Thursday	jeudi
May	mai	Friday	vendredi
June	juin	Saturday	samedi
July	juillet	August 1	le premier août
August	août	March 2	le deux mars
September	septembre	July 14	le quatorze juillet
October	octobre	November 23	le vingt-trois novembre
November	novembre	1999	dix-neuf-cent-quatre-vingt-dix-neuf
December	décembre	2010	deux-mille-dix
Sunday	dimanche		

Food and drink terms

Basic terms

Pain	Bread	Cuillère	Spoon
Beurre	Butter	Cure-dent	Toothpick
Céréales	Cereal	Table	Table
Lait	Milk	L'addition	Bill
Huile	Oil	Offert/Gratuit	Free
Confiture	Jam	(Re)chauffé	(Re)heated
Poivre	Pepper	Cuit	Cooked
Sel	Salt	Cru	Raw
Sucre	Sugar	Emballé	Wrapped
Vinaigre	Vinegar	Sur place ou à emporter?	Eat in or take away?
Moutarde	Mustard		
Bouteille	Bottle	À emporter	Takeaway
Verre	Glass	Fumé	Smoked
Fourchette	Fork	Salé	Salted/spicy
Couteau	Knife	Sucré	Sweet

Snacks (*Casse-croûte*)

Un sandwich/ une baguette	A sandwich	nature/aux fines herbes	plain/with herbs
...au jambon/ fromage	...with ham/cheese	au fromage	with cheese
...au jambon beurre	...with ham & butter	Croque-monsieur	Grilled cheese and ham sandwich
...fromage beurre	...cheese & butter	Croque-madame	Grilled cheese, ham or bacon and fried egg sandwich
...au pâté (de campagne)	...with pâté (country-style)		
Oeufs...	Eggs...	Pan bagnat	Bread roll with egg, olives, salad, tuna, anchovies and olive oil
au plat(s)	Fried eggs		
à la coque	Boiled eggs		
durs	Hard-boiled eggs		
brouillés	Scrambled eggs	Tartine	Buttered bread or open sandwich
poché	Poached eggs		
Omelette...	Omelette...		

Soups (*soupes*) and starters (*hors d'œuvres*)

Bisque	Shellfish soup	Bourride	Thick fish soup with garlic, onions and tomatoes
Baudroie	Fish soup with vegetables, garlic and herbs		
		Consommé	Clear soup
Bouillabaisse	Soup with five fish and other bits to dip	Pistou	Parmesan, basil and garlic paste or cream added to soup
Bouillon	Broth or stock		

Potage	Thick vegetable soup	Assiette anglaise	Plate of cold meats
Rouille	Red pepper, garlic and saffron mayonnaise served with fish soup	Crudités	Raw vegetables with dressings
		Hors d'œuvres variés	Combination of the above plus smoked or marinated fish
Velouté	Thick soup, usually fish or poultry		

Pasta (*pâtes*), pancakes (*crêpes*) and flans (*tartes*)

Pâtes fraîches	Fresh pasta	Socca	Thin chickpea flour pancake
Nouilles	Noodles		
Raviolis	Pasta parcels of meat or chard, a Provençal, not Italian, invention	Panisse	Thick chickpea flour pancake
		Pissaladière	Tart of fried onions with anchovies and black olives
Crêpe au sucre /aux œufs	Pancake with sugar /eggs		

Fish (*poisson*), seafood (*fruits de mer*) and shellfish (*crustaces* or *coquillages*)

Aiglefin	Small haddock or fresh cod	Crevettes roses	Prawns
		Daurade	Sea bream
Anchois	Anchovies	Écrevisse	Freshwater crayfish
Amande de mer	Small sweet-tasting shellfish	Éperlan	Smelt or whitebait
		Escargots	Snails
Anguilles	Eels	Favou(ille)	Tiny crab
Araignée de mer	Spider fish	Flétan	Halibut
Baudroie	Monkfish or anglerfish	Friture	Assorted fried fish
		Gambas	King prawns
Barbue	Brill	Girelle	Type of crab
Bigourneau	Periwinkle	Grenouilles (cuisses de)	Frogs' (legs)
Brème	Bream		
Bulot	Whelk	Grondin	Red gurnard
Cabillaud	Cod	Hareng	Herring
Calmar	Squid	Homard	Lobster
Carrelet	Plaice	Huîtres	Oysters
Chapon de mer	Mediterranean fish (related to Scorpion fish)	Langouste	Spiny lobster
		Langoustines	Saltwater crayfish (scampi)
Claire	Type of oyster	Limande	Lemon sole
Colin	Hake	Lotte de mer	Monkfish
Congre	Conger eel	Loup de mer	Sea bass
Coques	Cockles	Maquereau	Mackerel
Coquilles St-Jacques	Scallops	Merlan	Whiting
		Morue	Salt cod
Crabe	Crab	Moules (marinière)	Mussels (with shallots in white wine sauce)
Crevettes grises	Shrimp		

Oursin	Sea urchin	Rouget	Red mullet
Pageot	Sea bream	Rouquier	Mediterranean eel
Palourdes	Clams	St-Pierre	John Dory
Poissons de roche	Fish from shoreline rocks	Saumon	Salmon
		Sole	Sole
Poulpe	Octopus	Telline	Tiny clam
Poutine	Small river fish	Thon	Tuna
Praires	Small clams	Truite	Trout
Raie	Skate	Turbot	Turbot
Rascasse	Scorpion fish	Violet	Sea squirt

...and fish terms

Aïoli	Garlic mayonnaise/ or the dish when served with salt cod and vegetables	Darne	Fillet or steak
		En papillote	Cooked in foil
		Estocaficada	Stockfish stew with tomatoes, olives, peppers, garlic and onions
Anchoïade	Anchovy paste or sauce		
Arête	Fish bone		
Assiette de pêcheur	Assorted fish	La douzaine	A dozen
Béarnaise	Sauce of egg yolks, white wine, shallots and vinegar	Frit	Fried
		Friture	Deep-fried small fish
		Fumé	Smoked
Beignets	Fritters	Fumet	Fish stock
Bonne femme	With mushroom, parsley, potato and shallots	Gelée	Aspic
		Gigot de mer	Baked fish pieces, usually monkfish
Brandade	Crushed cod with olive oil	Goujon	Several types of small fish, also deep-fried pieces of larger fish coated in breadcrumbs
Colbert	Fried in egg with breadcrumbs		
Croûtons	Toasted bread, often rubbed with garlic, to dip or drop in fish soups		

Meat (*viande*) and poultry (*volaille*)

Agneau (de pré-salé)	Lamb (grazed on salt marshes)	Cervelle	Brains
		Châteaubriand	Porterhouse steak
Andouille, andouillette	Tripe sausage	Cheval	Horse meat
		Contrefilet	Sirloin roast
Bœuf	Beef	Coquelet	Cockerel
Bifteck	Steak	Dinde, dindon, dindonneau	Turkey of different ages and genders
Boudin blanc	Sausage of white meats		
Boudin noir	Black pudding	Entrecôte	Ribsteak
Caille	Quail	Faux filet	Sirloin steak
Canard	Duck	Fricadelles	Meatballs
Caneton	Duckling	Foie	Liver

Foie gras	Fattened (duck/goose) liver	Porc, pieds de porc	Pork, pig's trotters
Gésier	Gizzard	Poulet	Chicken
Magret de canard	Duck breast	Poussin	Baby chicken
Gibier	Game	Ris	Sweetbreads
Graisse	Fat	Rognons	Kidneys
Jambon	Ham	Rognons blancs	Testicles
Langue	Tongue	Sanglier	Wild boar
Lapin, lapereau	Rabbit, young rabbit	Saucisson	Dried sausage
Lard, lardons	Bacon, diced bacon	Steack	Steak
Lièvre	Hare	Taureau/Toro	Bull meat
Merguez	Spicy, red sausage	Tête de veau	Calf's head (in jelly)
Mouton	Mutton	Tournedos	Thick slices of fillet
Museau de veau	Calf's muzzle	Travers de porc	Spare ribs
Oie	Goose	Tripes	Tripe
Os	Bone	Veau	Veal
Pintade	Guinea fowl	Venaison	Venison

Meat and poultry dishes

Aïado	Roast shoulder of lamb, stuffed with garlic and other ingredients		sausages, bacon and salami
Bœuf à la gardane	Beef or bull meat stew with carrots, celery, onions, garlic and black olives, served with rice	Coq au vin	Chicken cooked until it falls off the bone with wine, onions, and mushrooms
		Gigot (d'agneau)	Leg (of lamb)
		Grillade	Grilled meat
Canard à l'orange	Roast duck with an orange-and-wine sauce	Hâchis	Chopped meat or mince hamburger
Canard périgourdin	Roast duck with prunes, pâté de foie gras and truffles	Pieds et paquets	Mutton or pork tripe and trotters
Cassoulet	A casserole of beans and meat	Steak au poivre (vert/rouge)	Steak in a black (green/red) pepper-corn sauce
Choucroute	Pickled cabbage with peppercorns,	Steak tartare	Raw chopped beef, topped with a raw egg yolk

Meat and poultry terms

Blanquette, civet, daube, estouffade, hochepôt, navarin and ragoût	All are types of stew	Carré	Best end of neck, chop or cutlet
		Civit	Game stew
		Confit	Meat preserve
Aile	Wing	Côte	Chop, cutlet or rib
Blanc	Breast or white meat	Cou	Neck
Broche	Spit-roasted	Cuisse	Thigh or leg
Brochette	Kebab	Épaule	Shoulder

Mariné	Marinated	Garni	With vegetables
Médaillon	Round piece	Grillé	Grilled
Pavé	Thick slice	Marmite	Casserole
En croûte	In pastry	Mijoté	Stewed
Farci	Stuffed	Rôti	Roast
Au feu de bois	Cooked over wood fire	Sauté	Lightly cooked in butter
Au four	Baked		

For steaks:

Bleu	Almost raw	Bien cuit	Well done
Saignant	Rare	Très bien cuit	Very well cooked
À point	Medium		

Garnishes and sauces:

Américaine	White wine, Cognac and tomato	Chasseur	White wine, mushrooms and shallots
Arlésienne	With tomatoes, onions, aubergines, potatoes and rice	Chatêlaine	With artichoke hearts and chestnut purée
Au porto	In port	Diable	Strong mustard seasoning
Auvergnat	With cabbage, sausage and bacon	Forestière	With bacon and mushroom
Beurre blanc	Sauce of white wine and shallots, with butter	Fricassée	Rich, creamy sauce
		Galantine	Cold dish of meat in aspic
Bonne femme	With mushroom, bacon, potato and onions	Mornay	Cheese sauce
		Pays d'Auge	Cream and cider
Bordelaise	In a red wine, shallots and bone-marrow sauce	Piquante	Gherkins or capers, vinegar and shallots
Boulangère	Baked with potatoes and onions	Provençale	Tomatoes, garlic, olive oil and herbs
Bourgeoise	With carrots, onions, bacon, celery and braised lettuce	Véronique	Grapes, wine and cream

Vegetables (*légumes*), herbs (*herbes*) and spices (*épices*), etc

Ail	Garlic	Blette/bette	Swiss chard
Anis	Aniseed	Cannelle	Cinnamon
Artichaut	Artichoke	Câpre	Caper
Asperges	Asparagus	Cardon	Cardoon, a beet related to artichoke
Avocat	Avocado		
Basilic	Basil	Carotte	Carrot
Betterave	Beetroot	Céleri	Celery

Champignons: cèpes, chanterelles, girolles, morilles	Mushrooms of various kinds
Chou (rouge)	(Red) cabbage
Chou-fleur	Cauliflower
Ciboulettes	Chives
Concombre	Cucumber
Cornichon	Gherkin
Échalotes	Shallots
Endive	Chicory
Épinard	Spinach
Épis de maïs	Corn on the cob
Estragon	Tarragon
Fenouil	Fennel
Férigoule	Thyme (in Provençal)
Fèves	Broad beans
Flageolets	White beans
Fleur de courgette	Courgette flower
Genièvre	Juniper
Gingembre	Ginger
Haricots verts	String (French) beans
…rouges	…kidney beans
…beurres	…butter beans
…blancs	…white beans
Laitue	Lettuce
Laurier	Bay leaf
Lentilles	Lentils

Maïs	Corn
Marjoline	Marjoram
Menthe	Mint
Navet	Turnip
Oignon	Onion
Panais	Parsnip
Pélandron	Type of string bean
Persil	Parsley
Petits pois	Peas
Piment	Pimento
Pois chiches	Chickpeas
Pois mange-tout	Snow peas
Pignons	Pine nuts
Poireau	Leek
Poivron (vert, rouge)	Sweet pepper (green, red)
Pommes de terre	Potatoes
Radis	Radishes
Raifort	Horseradish
Riz	Rice
Romarin	Rosemary
Safran	Saffron
Sarrasin	Buckwheat
Sauge	Sage
Serpolet	Wild thyme
Thym	Thyme
Tomate	Tomato
Truffes	Truffles

Dishes and terms

Beignet	Fritter
Farci	Stuffed
Gratiné	Browned with cheese or butter
Jardinière	With mixed diced vegetables
À la parisienne	Sautéed in butter (potatoes); with white wine sauce and shallots
À l'anglaise	Boiled
À la grecque	Cooked in oil and lemon
Râpé(e)s	Grated or shredded
Pistou	Ground basil, olive oil, garlic and parmesan

Primeurs	Spring vegetables
Salade verte	Lettuce with vinaigrette
Gratin dauphinois	Potatoes baked in cream and garlic
Mesclum	Salad combining several different leaves
Pommes château, fondantes	Quartered potatoes sautéed in butter
Pommes lyonnaise	Fried onions and potatoes
Ratatouille	Mixture of aubergine, courgette, tomatoes and garlic
Rémoulade	Mustard mayonnaise, sometimes with

	anchovies and gherkins, also salad of grated celeriac with mayonnaise
Parmentier	With potatoes
Sauté	Lightly fried in butter
À la vapeur	Steamed
Je suis végétarien(ne). Il y a des plats sans viande?	I'm a vegetarian. Are there any non-meat dishes?
Biologique	Organic
Raclette	Toasted cheese served with potatoes, gherkins and onions
Salad Niçoise	Salad of tomatoes, radishes, cucumber, hard-boiled eggs, anchovies, onion,

	artichokes, green peppers, beans, basil and garlic (rarely as comprehensive, even in Nice)
Duxelles	Fried mushrooms and shallots with cream
Fines herbes	Mixture of tarragon, parsley and chives
Frisé(e)	Curly
Gousse d'ail	Clove of garlic
Herbes de Provence	Mixture of bay leaf, thyme, rosemary and savory
Petits farcis	Stuffed tomatoes, aubergines, courgettes, peppers
Tapenade	Olive and caper paste
Tomates à la provençale	Tomatoes baked with breadcrumbs, garlic and parsley

Fruits (*fruits*), nuts (*noix*) and honey (*miel*)

Abricot	Apricot	Marrons	Chestnuts
Amandes	Almonds	Melon	Melon
Ananas	Pineapple	Miel de lavande	Lavender honey
Banane	Banana	Mirabelles	Small yellow plums
Brugnon, nectarine	Nectarine	Myrtilles	Bilberries
		Noisette	Hazelnut
Cacahouète	Peanut	Noix	Nuts
Cassis	Blackcurrants	Noix	Walnut
Cerises	Cherries	Noix de cajou	Cashew nut
Châtaignes	Chestnuts	Orange	Orange
Citron	Lemon	Pamplemousse	Grapefruit
Citron vert	Lime	Pastèque	Watermelon
Dattes	Dates	Pêche (blanche)	(White) peach
Figues	Figs	Pistache	Pistachio
Fraises (de bois)	Strawberries (wild)	Poire	Pear
Framboises	Raspberries	Pomme	Apple
Fruit de la passion	Passion fruit	Prune	Plum
Grenade	Pomegranate	Pruneau	Prune
Groseilles	Redcurrants	Raisins	Grapes
Mangue	Mango	Reine-Claude	Greengage

...and terms

Agrumes	Citrus fruits	Flambé	Set aflame in alcohol
Beignet	Fritter	Fougasse	Bread flavoured with orange flower water or almonds, can also be savoury
Compôte	Stewed fruit		
Coulis	Sauce of puréed fruit		
Crème de marrons	Chestnut purée	Frappé	Iced

Desserts (*desserts* or *entremets*), pastries (*patisseries*) and confectionery (*confiserie*)

Bombe	A moulded ice-cream dessert	Macarons	Macaroons
		Madeleine	Small sponge cake
Brioche	Sweet, high-yeast breakfast roll	Marrons	Chestnut purée and cream on a Mont Blanc rum-soaked sponge cake
Calissons	Almond sweets		
Charlotte	Custard and fruit in lining of almond fingers		
		Mousse au chocolat	chocolate mousse
Chichis	Doughnuts shaped in sticks	Nougat	Nougat
		Palmiers	Caramelized puff pastries
Clafoutis	Heavy custard and fruit tart		
Crème Chantilly	Vanilla-flavoured and sweetened whipped cream	Parfait	Frozen mousse, sometimes ice cream
		Petit Suisse	A smooth mixture of cream and curds
Crème fraîche	Sour cream	Petits fours	Bite-sized cakes /pastries
Crème pâtissière	Thick eggy pastry-filling		
Crêpes suzettes	Thin pancakes with orange juice and liqueur	Poires Belle Hélène	Pears and ice cream in chocolate sauce
		Tarte Tropezienne	Sponge cake filled with custard cream topped with nuts
Fromage blanc	Cream cheese		
Gaufre	Waffle		
Glace	Ice cream	Tiramisu	Layered pudding of mascarpone cheese, alcohol and coffee
Île flottante/ œufs à la neige	Soft meringues floating on custard		
		Truffes	Truffles
		Yaourt, yogourt	Yoghurt

Terms

Barquette	Small, boat-shaped flan	Chocolat amer	Unsweetened chocolate
Bavarois	Refers to the mould, could be a mousse or custard		
		Coupe	A serving of ice cream
		Crêpes	Pancakes
Biscuit	A kind of cake	En feuilletage	In puff pastry
Chausson	Pastry turnover	Fondant	Melting

Galettes	Buckwheat pancakes	Savarin	A filled, ring-shaped cake
Gênoise	Rich sponge cake		
Pâte	Pastry or dough	Tarte	Tart
Sablé	Shortbread biscuit	Tartelette	Small tart

Cheese (*fromage*)

The cheeses produced in Provence are all either *chèvre* (made from goat's milk) or *brebis* (made from sheep's milk). The most renowned are the *chèvres*, which include Banon, Picodon, Lou Pevre, Pelardon and Poivre d'Ain.

Le plateau de fromages is the cheeseboard, and bread (but not butter) is served with it. Some useful phrases: *une petite tranche de celui-ci* (a small piece of this one); *je peux le goûter?* (may I taste it?).

And one final note: when in a restaurant or café always call the waiter or waitress Monsieur or Madame (Mademoiselle if a young woman). **Never** use garçon, no matter what you've been taught at school.

Glossary

French terms

These are either terms you'll come across in the Guide, or come up against on signs, maps, etc while travelling around.

ABBAYE abbey

ARRONDISSEMENT district of a city

ASSEMBLÉE NATIONALE the French parliament

AJ (*Auberge de Jeunesse*) youth hostel

BASTIDE medieval military settlement, constructed on a grid plan

BEAUX-ARTS fine arts museum (and school)

BORIE dry-stone wall, or building made with same

CALANQUE steep-sided inlet on coast, similar to Norwegian fjord, but not glacially formed

CAR bus

CFDT Socialist trade union

CGT Communist trade union

CHAMBRE D'HÔTE room for rent in private house

CHASSE, CHASSE GARDÉE hunting grounds

CHÂTEAU mansion, country house or castle

CHÂTEAU FORT castle

CHEMIN path

CIJ (*Centre d'Informations Jeunesse*) youth information centre

CODENE French CND

COL mountain pass

CONSIGNE luggage store

CÔTE coast

COURS combination of main square and main street

COUVENT convent, monastery

DEFENSE DE... It is forbidden to...

DÉGUSTATION tasting (wine or food)

DÉPARTEMENT county – more or less

DL (*Démocratie Libérale*) free-market party led by Alain Madelin

DONJON castle keep

ÉGLISE church

EN PANNE out of order

ENTRÉE entrance

FAUBOURG suburb, often abbreviated to fbg in street names

FERME farm

FERMETURE closing period

FN (*Front National*) fascist party led by Jean-Marie Le Pen

FO Catholic trade union

FOUILLES archeological excavations

GARE station; **ROUTIÈRE** – bus station; **SNCF** – train station

GÎTE D'ÉTAPE basic hostel accommodation primarily for walkers

GOBELINS famous tapestry manufacturers, based in Paris; its most renowned period was in the reign of Louis XIV (seventeenth century)

GR (*grande randonée*) long-distance footpath

HALLES covered market

HLM public housing development

HÔTEL a hotel, but also an aristocratic town house or mansion

HÔTEL DE VILLE town hall

JOURS FÉRIÉS public holidays

MAIRIE town hall

MARCHÉ market

MNR (*Mouvement National Républicain*) extreme-right party led by Bruno Mégret

PCF Communist Party of France

PLACE square

PORTE gateway

PRESQU'ÎLE peninsula

PS Socialist party

PUY peak or summit

QUARTIER district of a town

RELAIS ROUTIERS truckstop café-restaurants

RC (*Rez-de-Chaussée*) ground floor

RN (*Route Nationale*) main road

RPR Gaullist party led by Jacques Chirac

SANTON ornamental figure used especially in Christmas cribs

SI (*Syndicat d'Initiative*) tourist information office; also known as OT, OTSI and maison du tourisme

SNCF French railways

SORTIE exit

TABAC bar or shop selling stamps, cigarettes, etc

TABLE D'HÔTE meal served in lodging at the family table

TOUR tower

TRANSHUMANCE routes followed by shepherds for taking livestock to and from suitable grazing grounds

UDF (*Union pour la Démocratie Française*) centre-right party headed by François Bayrou

UMP right-wing coalition consisting of the RPR, UDF and DL parties; formed in 2002

VAUBAN seventeenth-century military architect – his fortresses still stand all over France

VIEILLE VILLE old quarter of town

VIEUX PORT old port

VILLAGE PERCHÉ hilltop village

ZONE BLEUE restricted parking zone

ZONE PIETONNÉ pedestrian precinct

Architectural terms

AMBULATORY covered passage around the outer edge of a choir of a church

APSE semicircular termination at the east end of a church

BAROQUE High Renaissance period of art and architecture, distinguished by extreme ornateness

CAROLINGIAN dynasty (and art, sculpture, etc) founded by Charlemagne, late eighth to early tenth century

CHEVET east end of church, consisting of apse and ambulatory, with or without radiating chapels

CLASSICAL architectural style incorporating Greek and Roman elements – pillars, domes, colonnades, etc – at its height in France in the seventeenth century and revived in the nineteenth century as NEOCLASSICAL

CLERESTORY upper storey of a church, incorporating the windows

FLAMBOYANT florid form of Gothic

FRESCO wall painting – durable through application to wet plaster

GALLO-ROMAN period of Roman occupation of Gaul (first to fourth century AD)

GOTHIC architectural style prevalent from the twelfth century to the sixteenth century, characterized by pointed arches and ribbed vaulting

MEROVINGIAN dynasty (and art, etc) ruling France and parts of Germany from the sixth to mid-eighth century

NARTHEX entrance hall of church

NAVE main body of a church

RENAISSANCE art-architectural style developed in fifteenth-century Italy and imported to France in the early sixteenth century by François I

RETABLE altarpiece

ROMANESQUE early medieval architecture distinguished by squat, rounded forms and naive sculpture

STUCCO plaster used to embellish ceilings, etc

TRANSEPT cross arms of a church

TYMPANUM sculpted panel above a church door

VOUSSOIR sculpted rings in arch over church door

Visit us online
www.roughguides.com
Information on over 25,000 destinations around the world

- **Read** Rough Guides' trusted travel info
- **Access** exclusive articles from Rough Guides authors
- **Update** yourself on new books, maps, CDs and other products
- **Enter** our competitions and win travel prizes
- **Share** ideas, journals, photos & travel advice with other users
- **Earn** points every time you contribute to the Rough Guide community and get rewards

BROADEN YOUR HORIZONS

Small print and Index

A Rough Guide to Rough Guides

Published in 1982, the first Rough Guide – to Greece – was a student scheme that became a publishing phenomenon. Mark Ellingham, a recent graduate in English from Bristol University, had been travelling in Greece the previous summer and couldn't find the right guidebook. With a small group of friends he wrote his own guide, combining a highly contemporary, journalistic style with a thoroughly practical approach to travellers' needs.

The immediate success of the book spawned a series that rapidly covered dozens of destinations. And, in addition to impecunious backpackers, Rough Guides soon acquired a much broader and older readership that relished the guides' wit and inquisitiveness as much as their enthusiastic, critical approach and value-for-money ethos.

These days, Rough Guides include recommendations from shoestring to luxury and cover more than 200 destinations around the globe, including almost every country in the Americas and Europe, more than half of Africa and most of Asia and Australasia. Our ever-growing team of authors and photographers is spread all over the world, particularly in Europe, the US and Australia.

In the early 1990s, Rough Guides branched out of travel, with the publication of Rough Guides to World Music, Classical Music and the Internet. All three have become benchmark titles in their fields, spearheading the publication of a wide range of books under the Rough Guide name.

Including the travel series, Rough Guides now number more than 350 titles, covering: phrasebooks, waterproof maps, music guides from Opera to Heavy Metal, reference works as diverse as Conspiracy Theories and Shakespeare, and popular culture books from iPods to Poker. Rough Guides also produce a series of more than 120 World Music CDs in partnership with World Music Network.

Visit www.roughguides.com to see our latest publications.

Rough Guide credits

Text editor: Polly Thomas
Layout: Sachin Tanwar
Cartography: Rajesh Chhibber and Rajesh Mishra
Picture editor: Nicole Newman
Production: Rebecca Short
Proofreader: Janet McCann
Cover design: Dan May and Chloë Roberts
Photographer: Michelle Grant
Editorial: **London** Andy Turner, Keith Drew,
Edward Aves, Alice Park, Lucy White, Jo Kirby,
James Smart, Natasha Foges, Róisín Cameron,
James Rice, Emma Traynor, Emma Gibbs,
Kathryn Lane, Monica Woods, Mani Ramaswamy,
Harry Wilson, Lucy Cowie, Lara Kavanagh, Alison
Roberts, Joe Staines, Peter Buckley, Matthew
Milton, Tracy Hopkins, Ruth Tidball; **Delhi**
Madhavi Singh, Karen D'Souza, Lubna Shaheen
Design & Pictures: **London** Scott Stickland,
Dan May, Diana Jarvis, Mark Thomas, Sarah
Cummins, Emily Taylor; **Delhi** Umesh Aggarwal,
Ajay Verma, Jessica Subramanian, Ankur Guha,
Pradeep Thapliyal, Anita Singh, Nikhil Agarwal,
Sachin Gupta.

Production: Liz Cherry
Cartography: **London** Ed Wright, Katie Lloyd-
Jones; **Delhi** Ashutosh Bharti, Animesh Pathak,
Jasbir Sandhu, Karobi Gogoi, Alakananda Roy,
Swati Handoo, Deshpal Dabas
Online: **London** Faye Hellon, Jeanette Angell,
Fergus Day, Justine Bright, Clare Bryson, Aine
Fearon, Adrian Low, Ezgi Celebi; **Delhi** Amit
Verma, Rahul Kumar, Narender Kumar, Ravi
Yadav, Debojit Borah, Rakesh Kumar, Ganesh
Sharma, Shisir Basumatari
Marketing & Publicity: **London** Liz Statham,
Jess Carter, Vivienne Watton, Anna Paynton,
Rachel Sprackett, Laura Vipond; **New York** Katy
Ball, Judi Powers; **Delhi** Ragini Govind
Reference Director: Andrew Lockett
Operations Assistant: Becky Doyle
Operations Manager: Helen Atkinson
Publishing Director (Travel): Clare Currie
Commercial Manager: Gino Magnotta
Managing Director: John Duhigg

SMALL PRINT

Publishing information

This seventh edition published June 2010 by
Rough Guides Ltd,
80 Strand, London WC2R 0RL
14 Local Shopping Centre, Panchsheel Park,
New Delhi 110017, India
Distributed by the Penguin Group
Penguin Books Ltd,
80 Strand, London WC2R 0RL
Penguin Group (USA)
375 Hudson Street, NY 10014, USA
Penguin Group (Australia)
250 Camberwell Road, Camberwell,
Victoria 3124, Australia
Penguin Group (Canada)
195 Harry Walker Parkway N, Newmarket, ON,
L3Y 7B3 Canada
Penguin Group (NZ)
67 Apollo Drive, Mairangi Bay, Auckland 1310,
New Zealand
Cover concept by Peter Dyer.

Typeset in Bembo and Helvetica to an original
design by Henry Iles.
Printed in Singapore
© Rough Guides 2010
Maps © Rough Guides

No part of this book may be reproduced in any
form without permission from the publisher except
for the quotation of brief passages in reviews.

444pp includes index

A catalogue record for this book is available from
the British Library

ISBN: 978-1-84836-502-5

The publishers and authors have done their
best to ensure the accuracy and currency of
all the information in **The Rough Guide to
Provence & the Côte d'Azur**, however, they
can accept no responsibility for any loss, injury,
or inconvenience sustained by any traveller as a
result of information or advice contained in the
guide.

1   3   5   7   9   8   6   4   2

Help us update

We've gone to a lot of effort to ensure that
the seventh edition of **The Rough Guide to
Provence & the Côte d'Azur** is accurate and
up-to-date. However, things change – places
get "discovered", opening hours are notoriously
fickle, restaurants and rooms raise prices or lower
standards. If you feel we've got it wrong or left
something out, we'd like to know, and if you can
remember the address, the price, the hours, the
phone number, so much the better.

Please send your comments with the subject
line "**Rough Guide Provence & the Côte d'Azur
Update**" to ©mail@roughguides.com. We'll credit
all contributions and send a copy of the next
edition (or any other Rough Guide if you prefer)
for the very best emails.

Have your questions answered and tell others
about your trip at ® www.roughguides.com

Acknowledgements

Greg Thanks and love above all to my wife Sam, for everything; everything else; and sharing such a fabulous time in Provence. Thanks also to everyone at Rough Guides; it was a real pleasure to work again with super-thorough editor Polly Thomas. Many thanks also to those readers who sent in updates via e-mail or letters.

Neville Thanks to Isabel at Travel Intelligence; to the staff at Hotel Floride in Nice; and for the professionalism of the many local tourist offices who helped with the production of this book, with a particular thank you to the team at La Ciotat. Thanks too to Greg Ward for being a congenial co-author; and to my editor, Polly Thomas, for her patience and good humour.

Readers' letters

Thanks to the readers who have taken the time to write in with comments and suggestions (and apologies if we've inadvertently omitted or misspelt anyone's name):

Bronwen and Arun Holden, E.A. Stuart.

Photo credits

All photos © Rough Guides except the following:

Intro
Spring in the Luberon © Hemis/Axiom
People on the beach, Nice © Rooney/Axiom
Traditional food market, Provence © Carlos Sanchez Pereyra/Axiom
Night view of Monte Carlo, Monaco © Gavin Hellier/photolibrary
Nice Carnival © Hemis/Axiom
Restaurants in Aix-en-Provence © D. Shaw/Axiom
Parc National du Mercantour © Phototravel/corbis
Route des Crêtes, Cap Canaille, Cassis © Gilles Rigoulet/Hemis/corbis

Things not to miss
01 Les Calanques, Cassis © Bruno Morandi/photolibrary
02 View to St-Jean-Cap-Ferrat © Justin Foulkes/photolibrary
03 Julius Caesar statue, Théâtre Antique, Orange © Peter Horree/Alamy
04 Stained-glass window, Musée Chagall © Visions Llc/photolibrary
06 Château at Les Baux-de-Provence © Greg Ward
07 Camargue horses © Aguilar Patrice/Alamy
08 Lavender field at Abbaye de Sénanque © Brian Jannsen/Alamy
09 Pilgrimage for Saint Sarah © Cristian Baitg Reportage/Alamy

11 Restaurant, Vieux Nice © Hughes Herve/corbis
12 Marseille harbour © Art Kowalsky/Alamy
13 Night view of Monte Carlo, Monaco © Gavin Hellier/photolibrary
14 Grand Canyon du Verdon © Claudio Beduschi/photolibrary
15 Palais des Papes, Avignon © Kordcom Kordcom/photolibrary
16 Fondation Maeght © Ken Welsh/photolibrary
17 Mont Ste-Victoire © Philadelphia Museum of Art/corbis
18 Antibes, French Riviera © Kevin Galvin/photolibrary
19 Park National du Mercantour © G. Bowater/Corbis

A taste of Provence colour section
Bouillabaisse © Tim Hill/Alamy
Calissons, Aix-en-Provence © Hemis/Alamy
Nougat in the market, Tarascon © Greg Ward
Socca restaurant, Nice © travelstock44/Alamy
Tapenade at a market, Vaucluse © Hemis/Alamy
Pistou © Bon Appetit/Alamy

Black and whites
p.86 Les Arènes, Arles © istock
p.109 Flamingos in the Camargue © istock

Index

Map entries are in colour.

Map symbols

maps are listed in the full index using coloured text

▪▪▪▪	National border	☀	Lighthouse
▪▪▪	Chapter division boundary	▲	Mountain peak
▬▬▬	Motorway	⚶	Skiing
═══	Road	◆	Point of interest
───	Minor road	◉	Accommodation
───	Unpaved road	▣	Restaurant
───	Pedestrianized street	✈	Airport
⊞⊞⊞	Steps	★	Bus stop
------	Path	Ⓜ	Métro station
▬▬	Railway	🅿	Parking
▬▪▬	TGV line	@	Internet
·——	Ferry route	ⓘ	Tourist office
───	River	✉	Post office
───	Wall	⛫	Chateau
☀	Viewpoint	▮	Building
⚠	Campsite	⊞	Church
⬠	Lodge	⊡	Cemetery
☈	Cliffs	▦	Park
☈	Waterfall	▨	Beach
∴	Archeological site		

www.roughguides.com

So now we've told you about the things not to miss, the best places to stay, the top restaurants, the liveliest bars and the most spectacular sights, it only seems fair to tell you about the best travel insurance around

WorldNomads.com
keep travelling safely